Fiscal Space

Fiscal Space

Policy Options for Financing Human Development

Edited by Rathin Roy and Antoine Heuty

publishing for a sustainable future

London • Sterling, VA

First published by Earthscan in the UK and USA in 2009

ISBN: 978-1-84407-587-4

Typeset by MapSet Ltd, Gateshead, UK
Cover design by Susanne Harris

For a full list of publications please contact:

Earthscan
Dunstan House
14a St Cross St
London EC1N 8XA, UK
Tel: +44 (0)20 7841 1930
Fax: +44 (0)20 7242 1474
Email: earthinfo@earthscan.co.uk
Web: **www.earthscan.co.uk**

22883 Quicksilver Drive, Sterling, VA 20166-2012, USA

Earthscan publishes in association with the International Institute for Environment and
Development

A catalogue record for this book is available from the British Library

Library of Congress Cataloging-in-Publication Data

Fiscal space : policy options for financing human development / edited by Rathin Roy and
Antoine Heuty.
      p. cm.
Includes bibliographical references and index.
ISBN 978-1-84407-587-4 (pbk.)
  1. Economic assistance—Developing countries. 2. Economic development—Developing
countries—Finance. I. Roy, Rathin, 1966- II. Heuty, Antoine.
HC60.F4934 2009
338.9009172′4—dc22

2008041806

FSC
Mixed Sources
Product group from well-managed
forests and other controlled sources
Cert no. SGS-COC-2953
www.fsc.org
© 1996 Forest Stewardship Council

Contents

List of Boxes, Figures and Tables

BOXES

FIGURES

TABLES

List of Contributors

Jean-François Brun, Senior Lecturer, CERDI, University of Auvergne, Clermont-Ferrand, France

Gérard Chambas, Researcher, CERDI, University of Auvergne, Clermont-Ferrand, France

Adama Diaw, Professor, Gaston Berger University, Saint-Louis, Senegal

Samuel Guérineau, Senior Lecturer, CERDI, University of Auvergne, Clermont-Ferrand, France

Sylviane Guillaumont Jeanneney, Professor, CERDI, University of Auvergne, Clermont-Ferrand, France

Antoine Heuty, Senior Economist, Revenue Watch Institute, New York, USA

Karel Jansen, Associate Professor, Institute of Social Studies, The Hague, The Netherlands

Choedchai Khannabha, Inspector-General, Ministry of Finance, Bangkok, Thailand

Emmanuel Letouzé, Policy Specialist, Post-conflict Economic Recovery, Bureau for Crisis Prevention and Recovery, UNDP, New York, USA

María Antonia Moreno, Associate Professor, Central University of Venezuela, Caracas, Venezuela

Fouzi Mourji, Professor, Hassan II University, Casablanca, Morocco

Indira Rajaraman, Emeritus Professor at the National Institute of Public Finance and Policy, New Delhi and Member, Thirteenth Finance Commission of India, New Delhi, India

Sanjay G. Reddy, Associate Professor, Barnard College, Columbia University, New York, USA

Francisco Rodríguez, Assistant Professor, Wesleyan University, Middletown, CT, USA

Rathin Roy, Economic Advisor to the Thirteenth Finance Commission of India, on leave from UNDP where he serves as Public Finance Advisor, Bureau for Development Policy, UNDP, New York, USA

List of Acronyms and Abbreviations

ABMI	Asian Bond Market Initiative
AD	Acción Democrática (Venezuela)
ADM	Municipal Development Agency (Senegal)
ADS	Social Development Agency (Morocco)
AFD	French Development Agency
AMPPE	Association for Mountain Parks Protection and Enjoyment
BAAC	Bank of Agriculture and Agricultural Cooperatives (Thailand)
BAJ	barnamaj al awaliyat al ijtima`iya (Social Priorities Programme) (Morocco)
BCEAO	Central Bank of West African States
BCI	Consolidated Investment Budget (Senegal)
BIBF	Bangkok International Banking Facility (Thailand)
BoI	Board of Investment (Thailand)
BRS	Regional Solidarity Bank (Senegal)
BTS	Bangkok Mass Transit System (Thailand)
BWI	Bretton Woods Institutions
CADL	local development support centre (Senegal)
CAR	capital asset ratio
CAS	Country Assessment Strategy
CCA-UNDAF	Common Country Assessment-United Nations Development Assistance Framework (Senegal)
CDG	Deposit and Management Fund (Morocco)
CDMT	Medium Term Expenditure Framework (Senegal)
CED	Oversight of Commitments and Expenses (Morocco)
CERP	Multipurpose Rural Development Centre (Senegal)
CF	cash in circulation
CFAA–CPAR	Country Financial Accountability Assessment – Country Procurement Assessment Report
CG	consultative group
CGE	Computable General Equilibrium
CGEM	General Confederation of Moroccan Enterprises (Morocco)

CGI	General Tax Code (Morocco)
CMR	Moroccan Pension Fund
CMS	Crédit Mutuel du Sénégal
COPEI	Comité de Organización Política Electoral Independiente(Venezuela)
COSEF	Commission Spéciale Education-Formation (Morocco)
CPIA	Country Policy and Institutional Assessment
CPS	consolidated public sector
DAC	Development Assistance Committee
DEPF	Directorate of Financial Studies and Forecasts (Morocco)
DGCL	Directorate General of Local Governments (Morocco)
DGDDI	Directorate General of Customs and Excise (Morocco)
DGI	Directorate General of Taxes (Morocco)
DHS	Demographic and Health Survey (Senegal)
DTA	double taxation agreement
DTP	diphtheria-tetanus-pertussis
ECLAC	United Nations Economic Commission for Latin America and the Caribbean
EFF	Extended Fund Facility
EPA	economic partnership agreement
ERP	European Recovery Program
EU	European Union
FDD	Decentralization Allocation Fund (Senegal)
FDI	foreign direct investment
FDL	Local Development Fund (Senegal)
FEC	Municipal Infrastructure Fund (Morocco)
FECL	Local Government Capital Development Fund (Senegal)
FIDES	Intergovernmental Decentralization Fund (Venezuela)
FIDF	Financial Institutions Development Fund
ESAM	Senegalese Household Survey
GATT	General Agreement on Tariffs and Trade
GDP	gross domestic product
GPBM	Moroccan Banks Professional Group
GSB	Government Savings Bank (Thailand)
HCF	Haut Commissariat au Plan (Morocco)
HCP	Department of Planning (Morocco)
HDI	Human Development Index
HIPC	heavily indebted poor country
ICOR	incremental capital output ratio
IDA	international development assistance
IEO	Independent Evaluation Office
IFI	international financial institution

IGAT	Inspectorate General of Territorial Administration (Morocco)
IGF	Inspectorate General of Finance (Morocco)
ILDH	Local Human Development Initiative (Morocco)
IMF	International Monetary Fund
INDH	National Human Development Initiative (Morocco)
INE	National Institute of Statistics (Venezuela)
ISI	import substitution industrialization
IVSS	Venezuelan Social Security Institute
IVT	Treasury Securities Intermediaries (Morocco)
LAC	Latin American and the Caribbean
LDC	least developed country
LIBOR	London Inter-Bank Offered Rate
LOAF	Financial Administration Organic Law for the Public Sector
LOI	Letter of Intent
MDG	Millennium Development Goal
MDRI	Multilateral Debt Relief Initiative
MEN	Ministry of Education (Morocco)
MENA	Middle East and North Africa
MIC	middle income country
MTEF	Medium-Term Expenditure Framework
NEPAD	New Partnership for Africa's Development
NESDB	National Economic and Social Development Board (Thailand)
NFPE	non-financial public enterprises
NPV	net present value
NTB	non-tariff barrier
ODA	overseas development assistance
OECD	Organization for Economic Cooperation and Development
OEEC	Organization for European Economic Cooperation
O&M	operations and maintenance
ONE	National Electricity Board (Morocco)
ONEP	National Water Board (Morocco)
OPCVM	Mutual Fund (Morocco)
OPCVM	Collective Investment Scheme (Senegal)
OPEC	Oil Producing and Exporting Countries
PAC	Commune Support Programme (Senegal)
PAGER	Programme for Connected Supply of Drinking Water to Rural Populations (Morocco)
PAMC	Land Survey Modernization Support Project (Senegal)
PAO	Provincial Administration Organization (Thailand)
PDEF	Education and Training Programme
PDVSA	Petróleos de Venezuela, Sociedad Anónima

PERG	Rural Electricity Programme (Morocco)
PNCRR	National Programme for Construction of Rural Roads (Morocco)
PNDS	National Health Improvement Plan
PNIR	National Rural Infrastructure Programme (Senegal)
PPP	purchasing power parity
PRECOL	Programme for the Strengthening and Equipment of Local Governments
PRGF	Poverty Reduction and Growth Facility
PRSP	Poverty Reduction Strategy Paper
RCCE	recurrent consequences of capital expenditure
R&D	research and development
RON	Research Octane Number
RT	roundtable
RTC	roundtable conference
SAP	structural adjustment programme
SARS	Severe Acute Respiratory Syndrome
SBA	Stand-By Arrangement
SCA	Strategy for accelerated growth (Senegal)
SGP	Stability and Growth Pact
SIGECOF	Integrated System of Financial Management and Control of Public Finance (Venezuela)
SODEA	Agricultural Development Corporation (Morocco)
SOGETA	Agricultural Land Management Corporation (Morocco)
SSF	stability and social facility
TFP	total factor productivity
TOFE	Tableau des Opérations Financières de l'Etat (table of government's financial operations, Senegal)
UNCDF	United Nations Capital Development Fund
UNDP	United Nations Development Programme
UNESCO	United Nations Educational, Scientific and Cultural Organization
VAT	value added tax
VSB	Cities Without Slums (Morocco)
WAEMU	West African Economic and Monetary Union
WAMU	West African Monetary Union
WHO	World Health Organization

Acknowledgements

The Associate Administrator of UNDP, Ad Melkert, has provided quiet institutional support and encouragement to this project without in any way seeking to manage the details and findings. We would like to place on record our appreciation of this. We would like to thank colleagues at the Bureau for Development Policy UNDP for their support and encouragement; in particular, Jan Vandemoortele and Terry McKinley for early support. Furthermore, Darryl McCleod, Patricia Caraballo, Sarah Renner, Selim Jahan, Olav Kjorven, Khalid Abu-Ismail and Paul Ladd have provided inputs and invaluable advice. Participants at the G-20 and G-24 conferences have also provided helpful feedback. From outside the UN, Ariel Buira, Nora Lustig, Anwar Shaikh, Paolo de Renzio and Jomo Sundaram have all been extremely helpful with ideas and advice, as have Sanjjiv Gupta and Elliot Harris at the International Monetary Fund. UNDP country offices in Senegal, Thailand and Morocco have provided important support and we would like to thank all our colleagues there.

Claudia Vinay has been instrumental in making this book happen. She joined the team at UNDP when only the really hard work – of converting unedited manuscript into final text – remained. She has shouldered this entire burden as the editors moved on to new responsibilities.

Ram Iyer has managed the operational requirements with his usual flair and aplomb. Marina Blinova has taken tasks off Rathin's shoulders and enabled him to devote 'space' to this project which would not otherwise have been there. To both, a big 'thank you'.

It is fair to say that every single colleague in the regional bureaus, regional service centres and country offices of the UNDP with whom we have interacted during the course of this project have been unstinting with their encouragement, enthusiasm and support. We can only thank them collectively, for making UNDP such a special place to work on 'ideas changing minds'.

We would like to dedicate this book to all those who dare to be different and to make a difference.

Introduction

Rathin Roy, Antoine Heuty and Francisco Rodríguez

On 8 September 2000, representatives from 191 nations gathered in the United Nations General Assembly to discuss the joint actions that could be taken on a global scale to address some of the world's most pressing problems. The economic conditions seemed to be in place for a major attack on poverty and economic deprivation. As a whole, the world economy was growing at an annual rate of 4.7 per cent, the highest it had seen since the 1970s (IMF, 2008). East Asia was recovering robustly from its 1997 financial crisis, while India and China seemed to be embarking on development processes capable of bringing billions of people into modern economic prosperity. While some signs of trouble were present – most notably a deepening economic crisis in Argentina, a country that had long been seen as one of the most successful implementers of market reforms in the developing world – these appeared to be exceptions to a generalized trend of growing prosperity.

What emerged from this meeting was an unprecedented commitment, embodied in the General Assembly's *Millennium Declaration*, to direct the energies of the international community towards the reduction or elimination of extreme poverty, disease and environmental degradation. What made this document different from the abundant stock of existing resolutions of international organizations was that it set out well-defined and verifiable goals for achievements that could be used to measure progress in its mission. The Millennium Declaration did not just promise to fight against poverty, it set out the goal of halving the proportion of people living on less than a dollar a day. It did not stop at a vague commitment to promote gender equality, sustainable development and improvements in access to education and health, it resolved to reduce maternal mortality by three quarters, to halt and begin to reverse the spread of HIV/AIDS, to halve the number of people without access to drinking water and sanitation and to ensure full access to primary education and gender equality in access to all levels of education. The full set of commitments, which quickly became known as the Millennium Development Goals (MDGs), is presented below:

1   Eradicate extreme poverty and hunger
2   Achieve universal primary education
3   Promote gender equality and empower women
4   Reduce child mortality
5   Improve maternal health
6   Combat HIV/AIDS, malaria and other diseases
7   Ensure environmental sustainability
8   Develop a global partnership for development

In putting forward this set of ambitious yet concrete goals, the leaders of the world also chose the yardstick by which their actions would be evaluated 15 years hence. From the outset, it was evident to those participating in the discussion that achieving these goals would be impossible without an impressive mobilization of efforts and resources. A first, basic precondition would be the maintenance of a robust rate of economic expansion. There is ample theoretical and empirical evidence that it is extremely difficult, if not impossible, to sustainably reduce poverty without economic growth (Dollar and Kraay, 2002). But there is also considerable variation in the rate at which countries are able to convert economic growth into poverty reduction (Ravaillon and Chen, 1997; Bourguignon, 2005; Rodríguez, 2008a), making it clear that growth alone cannot be counted on to achieve the MDGs. Whether these goals were to be achieved would thus depend not just on economic prosperity, but also on the extent to which the world could direct financial, administrative and political resources towards their achievement.

Evidently, a substantial amount of these resources would have to come from rich countries. This much was recognized less than two years later, when an international conference on financing for development ended in an unprecedented commitment to increase overseas development assistance (ODA) by developed nations to 0.7 per cent of gross domestic product (GDP). Such an increase would more than triple prevailing levels. As Jeffrey Sachs (2005, p290) has pointed out, this transfer of funds would, in itself, be enough to raise all 1.1 billion of the world's extreme poor to the basic needs level of US$1.08 a day.

By now, it is clear that this substantial expansion of foreign aid is unlikely to materialize. The latest estimates of ODA from developed countries puts it at 0.3 per cent of gross national income, slightly higher than the 2002 level of 0.2 per cent, but considerably below the target set in the Monterrey Consensus. Indeed, according to the Organization for Economic Cooperation and Development (OECD, 2007), development aid from OECD countries actually *declined* by 5.1 per cent in 2006. At the same time, there is a vibrant academic debate on the *merits* of increased foreign aid, with many economists contending that the evidence on the effectiveness of foreign aid in generating economic growth and promoting poverty alleviation is very weak.[1]

This book is concerned with understanding the means by which countries seeking to fulfil the commitments embodied in the MDGs can mobilize domestic resources for the fight against poverty. If the idea that it is neither expected nor desirable for foreign aid to completely cover the shortfall in resources necessary for achieving these goals is taken seriously, then it is necessary to undertake an exhaustive examination of the possibilities that states have for reorienting internal resources towards the objectives of poverty reduction. The search for these resources is, in a nutshell, what is called the search for 'fiscal space'.

UNDERSTANDING FISCAL SPACE

How should people think about domestic resource mobilization in this context and how is the concept of fiscal space understood? Peter Heller of the International Monetary Fund (IMF) has proposed that fiscal space be defined as 'the availability of budgetary room that allows a government to provide resources for a desired purpose without any prejudice to the sustainability of a government's financial position' (Heller, 2005, p3). A report to the Development Committee of the joint World Bank-IMF Board defined fiscal space in broadly similar terms as 'the gap between the current level of expenditure and the maximum level of expenditures that a government can undertake without impairing its solvency' (Development Committee, 2006, p14). These definitions embody the basic trade-off that is at the root of the discussion about obtaining resources for reducing poverty. How is it possible to ensure that governments spend enough to meet their poverty alleviation goals without, at the same time, allowing these increased spending levels to produce macroeconomic instability and thus destroy the conditions that are necessary for sustainable growth (which, as has been seen, is a precondition for poverty reduction)?

In this sense, the fiscal space discussion is far from new. The recognition of a conflict between the desire to use the state to lift people out of poverty and the need for prudent economic management to generate a prosperous economy has been present in economic theory since the writings of the classical economists. More recently, it was also at the root of the discussions between advocates of developmental import substitution strategies and orthodox monetarists during the 1960s and 1970s.[2] In some respects, the debate in recent years on how to create fiscal space has the quality of old wine in a new bottle. Finance ministries have always been concerned with how best to mobilize and utilize fiscal resources for desirable public policy purposes. This fact has led some economists to question the insightfulness of the term 'fiscal space'. Perotti (2007, pp16–19), for example, argues that the use of the term is confusing because attempts at a definition are mostly restatements of the policy decisions that governments have faced all along. It is known that in order to increase some government expenditures, it is necessary to reduce other current or future expenditures, increase current or future revenues, or inflate away the value of the nominal debt. It is also known that if one type of spending has a larger social marginal value than the other, then more should be spent on the more socially beneficial option and less spent on the other option. The concept of fiscal space, it is argued by some, appears to be too loosely defined to add anything to this discussion.

We recognize that some of the issues brought forward in the fiscal space debate are far from new. However, we believe that this discussion is useful and novel because it attempts to develop a framework for studying the interrelatedness of the different components of a government's decision to address its fiscal problems. For example, ODA flows are often related – implicitly or explicitly – to domestic resource mobilization efforts. Governments' abilities to collect taxes and spend effectively are important – albeit not unique – determinants of the aid allocation behaviours of donors. Similarly, expenditure efficiency is likely to play a role in the willingness of citizens to pay taxes, which ultimately influences tax performance. Looking at the different pillars of fiscal space independently would miss the interdependency between different financing instruments.

THE RELEVANCE OF DEVELOPMENT

We therefore suggest that one should not stop at identifying the restrictions implicit in the inter-temporal budget constraint and the multiple possible combinations of expenditure, revenue and debt policies necessary to address them. Instead, we propose that it is necessary to look at the country's development model and to understand the way in which it addresses the role of fiscal constraints and the need to mobilize resources for economic growth. We believe that the set of fiscal decisions facing a developing country may differ radically, depending on the type of expenditure or revenue generating strategy that the country is prioritizing as part of its development agenda. The study of fiscal space can be seen as the study of the endogenous determination of the components of fiscal policy as a result of alternative development strategies. In this sense the fiscal space debate brings to the table a new object of study, rather than just a new definition.

Our proposal to study the coherence between a nation's development strategy and its fiscal policy is related to, but distinct from, the existing literature on the relationship between fiscal policies and economic growth (see, for example, Barro, 1990; Easterly and Rebelo, 1994; Engen and Skinner, 1996). This literature – which has by and large not found robust effects of fiscal policy on growth – has been framed within the context of the linear cross-country regression framework initiated by the seminal work of Barro (1990).[3] One of the limitations of such an approach is that it is not adequately designed to capture the underlying nature of growth dynamics when multiple interactions exist between different potential determinants of economic growth (Rodríguez, 2007a, 2007b). This might be the case if, as we suggest here, the effectiveness of particular policies depends crucially on the type of development strategy being pursued by the government.

As an example, a substantial part of the discussion underlying the achievement of the MDGs has centred on understanding whether it is appropriate to conceive of countries as having fallen into a 'poverty trap'.[4] Believers in the poverty trap hypothesis argue that a scaling up of social investments is necessary to move the economy into equilibrium with sustainably high living standards. Conventional fiscal sustainability analysis would tend to view such a scaling up of expenditures as reckless because it appears to violate a society's inter-temporal solvency condition. But this analysis would be altered by the recognition that an economy's stream of future revenues will depend on whether it remains mired in the poverty trap or it jumps to a new equilibrium. Therefore, fiscal plans that appear unsustainable become sustainable once the links between fiscal policy and development are explicitly modelled.

The broader problem with the conventional approach is that, unless the links between fiscal policy and development are considered explicitly (for example, by taking into account the fact that certain types of expenditure may permanently raise an economy's steady-state level of income), an analysis of fiscal sustainability will only be able to capture the fiduciary (as opposed to the developmental) implications of increasing fiscal space in order to achieve a specific set of long-term development objectives. For this reason, existing assessment frameworks tend to underestimate the long-term payback to fiscal sustainability from implementing a transformational development strategy that a sound MDG-based national development strategy should embody.

It is no coincidence that almost every intergovernmental body concerned with public finance issues, from the Development Committee of the joint IMF-World Bank board to the G-24 group of developing countries, has placed fiscal space on the agenda of their annual meetings since 2006. In 2007 the G-20 group of finance ministers also devoted an entire session to this topic and commissioned interventions from current and former staff of the United Nations Development Programme (UNDP), the World Bank and the IMF on the subject. Of course, the present search for fiscal space may arise for several quite different reasons and these differences are important in understanding the fiscal space issues that preoccupy the G-20 countries. For many low-income countries, achieving the MDGs requires an expansion in public investments and, transitively, a significant permanent increase in the ratio of government expenditure to GDP. This requires finding sustainable finance, not at the margin, but in substantial measure. Aid can temporarily serve the purpose – though whether the aid delivered can be absorbed and spent is, in itself, an important macroeconomic issue. In addition, all countries face new challenges that require a fiscal response that is large in magnitude – for instance, in adaptation to, and mitigation of, the effects of climate change.

TOWARDS A NEW DEFINITION OF FISCAL SPACE

In order to fully bring these issues into consideration, it is important to go beyond the conceptual frameworks that have, until now, been used to think of fiscal space. Both the Heller (2005) and the Development Committee (2006) definitions cited above are, in effect, restatements of the inter-temporal budget constraint definition in which the interaction between fiscal policy and growth is not addressed. Such definitions, there-fore, end up conceptualizing fiscal space in residual terms ('room' or 'gap') and are fully open to the criticism put forward by Perotti (2007). In contrast, Roy and Heuty (2005, p170) define fiscal space as 'concrete policy actions for enhancing domestic resource mobilization, and the reforms necessary to secure the enabling governance, institutional and economic environment for these policy actions to be effective'. The focus on domestic resource mobilization in this definition underscores the fact that, ultimately, the sustainability and solvency of an economy depends on (a) the extent to which domestic financing mechanisms are able to support public expenditures, and (b) the fact that the mobilization of fiscal space in a sustainable manner is a function of the political economy context within which fiscal space is secured. Hence, the emphasis is on the set of feasible policy actions on the one hand and the prevailing political and economic environment on the other. In the same paper, Roy and Heuty provide an important example of this endogeny – 'savings realization failures' – that is, the macroeconomic, social and political factors inhibiting the channelling of savings into private and public investment. These political economy factors – and the argument that, ultimately, domestic resources must pay for public expenditures even if these are, temporarily, financed by grants or foreign concessional finance – are both most relevant in the long term rather than the short term. In other words, while the Heller (2005) and Development Committee (2006) definitions are primarily concerned with the short-term consequences (and mainly the potential adverse effects) of an increase in public expenditure, Roy and Heuty (2005) seek to evaluate how concrete policy actions may support trend-changes in the potential for domestic resource mobilization for pro-poor public investment.

The difference in emphasis thus arises because policy concerns differ. The Development Committee (2006) definition of fiscal space is concerned with raising incremental resources for development. Clearly this is not an adequate basis on which to assess the availability of fiscal space for low- and middle-income countries engaged in major development transformations aimed at securing long-term human develop-ment and economic growth. This latter focus is at the heart of the Monterrey Consensus and the MDG financing debate. In this context, giving overriding impor-tance to short-term fiscal stability (measured through annual fiscal balance) and solvency (measured through the ratio of debt to GDP) tends to underestimate the long-term real impact of spending on these development objectives. As Goldsborough (2007) points out, in IMF programmes 'the longer-term supply-side effects of higher public spending are, with some commendable recent exceptions, largely ignored in many macroeconomic frameworks'. This concern motivated the Development Committee to give the IMF and the World Bank the task of producing a paper on fiscal policy. In their report, they recognized the central role of fiscal policy in financing the provision of the public goods needed to achieve the MDGs within a longer time horizon and declared that their intent was to focus on 'how fiscal policy could be adapted to strengthen its role with respect to growth and the achievement of the MDGs' (Development Committee, 2006, pi). However, the definition they used was, in our opinion, inadequate for the purpose, causing the analysis to fall short of providing a way forward on the financing problem central to the Monterrey Consensus.

CONCEPTUAL APPROACHES

This volume starts out with three conceptual chapters that discuss in detail the concept of fiscal space, its relationship with the MDGs and its relevance for thinking about development strategies. These chapters lay out the context for the discussion in the policy arena, present the key theoretical debates and consider the most important conceptual issues that arise in its application.

Chapter 1, by Rathin Roy and Antoine Heuty, lays out the principal policy discussion that forms the context for the analysis of fiscal space: the commitment by the international community to achieve rapid and concrete improvements in the living standards of the world's most disadvantaged groups, as set out in the Millennium Declaration. Roy and Heuty argue that it is vital to understand how the plan for achieving these goals interacts with changes in the *regime of accumulation* if the process of mobilizing resources for achieving the MDGs is to be understood. For them, this *regime of accumulation* is the mode of distribution and reallocation of economic inputs into socio-economic outputs that is sustainable in light of changes in the production and consumption pattern over long periods. While concessional assistance can complement domestic resources for development, Roy and Heuty argue it can never substitute for them. It should be used to help create an enabling environment for non-concessional domestic mechanisms for supporting human development, and not as a direct financing instrument.

What such a new framework would look like is the subject of Chapter 2, authored by Rathin Roy, Antoine Heuty and Emmanuel Letouzé. The central premise of this chapter is that the sustainability of policies to create fiscal space is a function of *what* the fiscal space is used for. This, in turn, depends on the central economic policy challenges and the attendant interventions that need to be financed to secure these challenges. The balance of emphasis placed on the stabilization, allocation and distribution and growth functions of fiscal policy – as well as the indicators used to assess fiscal solvency and sustainability – would differ according to the timeframe of the analytical framework and the political economy context within which the interventions are made operational. The indicators used to assess fiscal solvency and sustainability will be very different if the assessment is carried out over a long-term, as opposed to a short-term, analytical context.

At the heart of the framework set out by Roy et al is the idea that there is a fundamental inconsistency between the desire to evaluate a fiscal policy according to its developmental implications and the strict fiduciary approach followed by most international financial institutions (IFIs). This idea is put forward in what the authors call the *fiscal space conjecture* – the proposition that the greater the public good characteristics of public sector investment projects, the lower the precision and the predictability of their fiduciary payback calculations, but the higher the precision and predictability of their development payback calculation. If this conjecture is correct, it establishes an inherent tension between the conventional mode of evaluation of fiscal programmes by IFIs, based on purely fiduciary calculations, and the desire to formulate fiscal policies that are deeply embedded in strategies for long-run development.

The same authors provide a concrete example of how these tensions play out in the formulation of specific public investment strategies in Chapter 3. There is a growing accumulation of evidence that the decline in the ratios of public investment – and particularly of public infrastructure investment – to GDP observed since the 1980s has been due to the inappropriateness of existing evaluation criteria used by IFIs to assess fiscal strategies and, in particular, to the emphasis on meeting strict fiscal targets that made no distinction between current and capital expenditures. The application of these criteria led countries to undertake illusory fiscal adjustments, in which a fiscal target was met by drawing down stocks of existing assets (public infrastructure).

While there exist a number of proposals to treat public investment differently from current expenditures in the setting of fiscal targets – such as the 'golden rule' imposed by UK governments since 1997 – the authors argue that these rules are self-limiting if their argument is based on a purely fiduciary as opposed to a human development calculation. The reason for this can be traced back to the fiscal space conjecture. Unless it is recognized that investments in human development may have an uncertain fiduciary payback, despite having a certain development payback, and a public finance framework that prioritizes long-run development objectives is adopted, then fiscal policy will suffer from a built-in bias against human development.

How much weight should be placed on the fiscal space conjecture? Are there solid reasons why it would be expected to be true? The next two chapters, by Sanjay Reddy and Francisco Rodríguez, respectively, attempt to answer this question theoretically and empirically. Reddy's article (Chapter 4) tackles the theoretical basis for the fiscal space conjecture by determining the exact conditions under which it would hold true. He concludes that, as long as the variance of the financial payback expected from an investment with high public good characteristics is greater than the variance of the financial payback expected from a comparable investment with low public good characteristics, and the variance of the non-financial payback of an investment with high public good characteristics is lower than the variance of the non-financial payback of a comparable investment with low public good characteristics, then the conjecture will hold. As these intuitively plausible claims are empirically unverified, Reddy notes, it is correct to call it a conjecture. Reddy warns that adopting a superficially rational 'risk-averse' public investment policy may have considerable developmental costs, as it may place too much emphasis on the low predictability of a project's financial payback, when this should be only one part of the overall risk assessment of a public investment project.

In Chapter 5, Francisco Rodríguez tackles this issue by studying the sustainability of fiscal expansions and their relationship with the composition of government spending. Rather than examining whether the assumptions of the fiscal space conjecture hold true, Rodríguez explores whether some of its implications are borne out in reality. Rodríguez's approach centres on understanding whether it is possible to enact large scaling up of public expenditures similar to those that appear to be necessary for achieving the MDGs. Using an econometric framework based on duration analysis, Rodríguez finds that the duration of expansions is positively related to the level of democracy and negatively related to increases in defence spending. This strengthens the evidence that indicates that the type of spending and the nature of the regime of accumulation matter for the sustainability of a fiscal strategy. These findings suggest that, given appropriate social and economic conditions, a scaling up of spending to achieve the MDGs need not generate unsustainable fiscal outcomes.

GOING TO THE COUNTRY LEVEL

Does the idea of fiscal space make sense at the country level? Can it help in understanding particular country and development experiences? Does it help in the design of coherent fiscal frameworks that will be useful in devising sustainable and human development oriented fiscal plans? These questions are answered by exploring the issues raised by the fiscal space debate in four very distinct economies: Morocco, Senegal, Thailand and Venezuela.

The country studies section of the book opens with an overview of the commonalities and differences between the four country cases written by Indira Rajaraman (Chapter 6). These countries differ in their progress towards meeting the MDGs. While Thailand has surpassed its MDG target for poverty and Morocco has made substantial progress, Venezuela and Senegal do not show major improvements.[5] As the author shows, there are also striking differences between the incremental capital output ratios (ICOR) displayed by countries. High ICORs in some countries suggest that the efficiency of investment, rather than the level of investment, might be the binding constraint. The study goes on to carry out a detailed comparative analysis of the performances of the four countries under review on the fiscal space dimensions of own revenue, public borrowing and external financing. Rajaraman highlights the need to evaluate the MDG targets in the context of an analysis of the efficiency of incremental capital formation and the need to develop multidimensional indicators of MDG progress. She also highlights three more needs: to emphasize own tax and non-tax revenues in the fiscal strategy, to understand the critical role of real growth, and to look for new sources of external financing, such as remittances.

The Moroccan case study, written by Jean-François Brun, Gerard Chambas and Fouzi Mourji, provides an interesting example. Cross-country regression analysis shows that Morocco has pretty much the level of domestic revenues that would be expected given its level of development, trade integration and structural characteristics. Thus there are no obvious inefficiencies in its revenue generating process – or, at least, no more inefficiencies than can be found in other countries of similar characteristics. However, through a detailed analysis of the different sources of government finance, the authors argue that it is possible to find additional 'room to manoeuvre' in external savings, virtuous seignorage and the expected effects of tax transition.

Senegal, as noted in Chapter 8 by Adama Diaw, Samuel Guérineau and Sylviane Guillaumont Jeanneney, is in an altogether different situation, as it requires a significant increase either in its growth rate or in the effectiveness of that growth in translating into poverty reduction so as to be able to achieve the MDGs. Having recently carried out a comprehensive national tax reform in 2004, there is probably little additional gain in this dimension – except perhaps in the area of local tax administration. Given Senegal's membership in the West African Economic and Monetary Union, seignorage cannot play a major role in increasing the level of resources available to the state. There is a dimension for enhanced fiscal space in regional market borrowing coming from Senegal's good handling of its public finances and the liquidity in the Senegalese economy or, more generally, in the Union.

The other two countries in the study are useful not just in themselves but because of the contrast that they provide. Thailand is a country that has already achieved the poverty MDG. Thus the vital question that a study of this country can help answer, as argued by Karel Jansen and Choedchai Khannabha in Chapter 9, is how it did it. Thailand was first of all a very rapidly growing economy during the past 50 years, so that the Thai experi-ence serves to buttress the argument that economic growth plays a vital role in generating not only poverty reduction through its direct effect on revenues, but also in increasing the availability of resources to direct in the fight against poverty. At first blush, Thailand's fiscal policy seems to make the case for a relative laissez-faire approach. Its emphasis on macroeconomic stability, its repression of labour organizations to keep wages low, and its relatively small size of overall government appear to support the hypothesis that it was the lack of government intervention that helped Thailand grow. However, deeper analysis shows that even though the overall size of government is small, spending on crucial items, such as infrastructure and social services, was actually quite high. Most importantly, Thailand's fiscal policy formed a part of a coherent – if conservative – development strategy that was based on a vision of a small yet powerful state that would support the private capitalist class in the process of accumulation.

Venezuela, by contrast, is a country with an embarrassment of riches at its disposal. According to the study by Francisco Rodríguez and María Antonia Moreno (Chapter 10), there are a set of concrete policy measures and institutional reforms that would allow Venezuela to increase fiscal revenues by ten percentage points of GDP. What is striking about Venezuela, however, is that it has decided to ignore this opportunity. While other Latin American economies achieve a much higher effective tax rate (as compared to Venezuela's non-oil taxation), Venezuela appears to have decided to use the additional resources derived from oil to provide its citizens with lower taxes, even if that means relatively high poverty rates for its level of development. This may be a reflection of the fact that Venezuela's rentier state political economy leads it to display a relatively low level of efficiency in its public expenditures, as illustrated by the poor results found in evaluations of the recent increase in social spending carried out by the Chávez administration.

THE WAY FORWARD

The basic idea behind this book is that fiscal strategies that complement social and economic policies to secure a development transformation require a departure from conventional approaches to fiscal planning. Economic theory and empirical evidence suggest that consideration should not only be given to how much the government spends and whether there are enough resources to pay for those expenditures. Rather, one must also consider what the government is spending resources on and how the composition and quality of spending, as well as the broader institutional context in which it occurs, can affect long-term fiscal viability.

The ideas that are put forward should not be interpreted as an endorsement of an 'anything goes' approach to fiscal policy. Prudent macroeconomic policymaking is believed to be a vital component of any strategy with the potential to achieve sustainable poverty reduction. We do believe, however, that the markers used to measure prudent action have to be re-evaluated in the context of a broader development discussion. Some investments might have extremely high social rates of return, even if they have an unpredictable effect on public finances. Whether a society is able to finance a fiscal expansion or not will depend on structural and institutional factors, including the capacity of its political system to distribute costs in ways that are perceived to be acceptable by different groups. Our proposal is that this fuller framework be incorporated in thinking about the financing of poverty reduction.

Meeting the MDGs is unlikely to be easy. Significant progress in poverty reduction has already been achieved: the proportion of people living on less than a dollar a day declined from nearly one-third to less than one-fifth of the world's population between

1990 and 2004. However, the recent increases in food prices, as well as the possibility of a worldwide recession, require serious thought about the prospects for continuing the fight against worldwide poverty in the midst of less favourable global conditions. The capacity that countries can use to mobilize domestic resources to continue their efforts to reduce poverty, as well as to protect the gains that have been made to this point, will be a crucial determinant of whether the historic commitment assumed at the turn of the millennium will be remembered as a turning point in the history of humankind, rather than as one more addition to a long list of unfulfilled promises.

NOTES

1   For two opposing views of this debate, see Rajan and Subramanian (2005) and Reddy and Minoiu (2006).
2   See, for example, the debates on the causes of inflation in Latin America captured in Baer and Kerstenetsky (1964).
3   Economic growth in a cross section of countries.
4   See Sachs et al (2004). For a critical evaluation of this hypothesis, see Easterly (2006).
5   More recent data, not available when the Venezuela country study was written, suggest a rapid decline in poverty during 2006 and 2007. However, preliminary data also suggest that Venezuela may have entered into a recession in the first quarter of 2008, a possibility that is likely to undo recent progress (Rodríguez, 2008b).

REFERENCES

Baer, W. and Kerstenetsky, I. (eds) (1964) *Inflation and Growth in Latin America*, Richard D. Irwin, Homewood, IL
Barro, R. (1990) 'Government spending in a simple model of endogenous growth', *Journal of Political Economy*, vol 98 (October), pp103–26
Bourguignon, F. (2005) 'The growth elasticity of poverty reduction: Explaining heterogeneity across countries and time periods', in T. Eicher and S. Turnovsky (eds) *Growth and Inequality*, MIT Press, Cambridge, MA, pp3–26
Development Committee (2006) 'Fiscal policy for growth and development: An interim report', background paper for the Development Committee Meeting, Washington DC
Dollar, D. and Kraay, A. (2002) 'Growth is good for the poor', *Journal of Economic Growth*, vol 7, no 3 (September), pp195–225
Easterly, W. (2006) 'Reliving the 50s: The big push, poverty traps, and takeoffs in economic development', *Journal of Economic Growth*, vol 11, no 2, pp289–318
Easterly, W. and Rebelo, S. (1994) 'Fiscal policy and economic growth: An empirical investigation', *Journal of Monetary Economics*, vol 32, no 3, pp417–458
Engen, E. and Skinner, J. (1996) 'Taxation and economic growth', *National Tax Journal*, vol 49 (December), pp617–42
Goldsborough, D. (2007) *The IMF and Constraints on Spending Aid*, UNDP International Poverty Centre, One pager no 35, UNDP, New York
Heller, P. (2005) *Understanding Fiscal Space*, IMF Policy Discussion Paper PDP/05/4, International Monetary Fund, Washington DC
IMF (International Monetary Fund) (2008) *World Economic Outlook Database*, International Monetary Fund, Washington DC

OECD (Organization for Economic Cooperation and Development) (2007) 'Development aid from OECD countries fell 5.1% in 2006', www.olis.oecd.org/olis/2007doc.nsf/ENGDAT CORPLOOK/NT00000E3A/$FILE/JT03225046.PDF

Perotti, R. (2007) *Fiscal Policy in Developing Countries: A Framework and Some Questions*, Policy Research Working Paper 4365, World Bank, Washington DC

Rajan, R. G. and Subramanian, A. (2005) *Aid and Growth: What does the Cross-Country Evidence Really Show?*, IMF Working Paper WP/05/127, International Monetary Fund, Washington DC

Ravallion, M. and Chen, S. (1997) 'What can new survey data tell us about recent changes in distribution and poverty?', *The World Bank Economic Review*, vol 5 pp57–82

Reddy, S. and Minoiu, C. (2006) *Development Aid and Economic Growth: A Positive Long-Run Relation*, Working Paper 29, United Nations, Department of Economics and Social Affairs, New York

Rodríguez, F. (2007a) *Cleaning Up the Kitchen Sink: Growth Empirics When the World is Not Simple*, Wesleyan Economics Working Paper no 2006-004, Department of Economics, Wesleyan University, Middletown, CT

Rodríguez, F. (2007b) *Policymakers Beware: The Use and Misuse of Regressions in Explaining Economic Growth*, Policy Research Brief no 5, UNDP International Poverty Centre, Brasilia, Brazil

Rodríguez, F. (2008a) 'What makes growth shared? On the political economy of inclusive development', paper presented at the 2008 World Bank Annual Conference on Development Economics, Cape Town, June 2008

Rodríguez, F. (2008b) 'Venezuela's revolution in decline: Beware the wounded tiger', *World Policy Journal*, vol 25, no 1, pp45–58

Roy, R. and Heuty, A. (2005) 'Investing in development: The MDGs, aid and sustainable capital accumulation', *Columbia Journal of International Affairs*, vol 58, no 2, www.undp.org/poverty

Sachs, J. (2005) *The End of Poverty*, The Penguin Press, New York

Sachs, J., McArthur, J., Schmidt-Traub, G., Kruk, M., Bahadur, C., Faye, M. and McCord, G. (2004) 'Ending Africa's poverty trap', *Brookings Papers on Economic Activity no 2*, Brookings Institution, Washington DC, pp117–216

1

Investing in Development: The Millennium Development Goals, Aid and Sustainable Capital Accumulation

Rathin Roy and Antoine Heuty[1]

INTRODUCTION

The only complaint I have against the system is that a considerable sum of money must be paid to the first fire engine that arrives, a smaller to the second, and so on, thus… if all their efforts prove ineffectual, the sufferer, who is already ruined by the destruction of his property… doubles his loss and adds to anguish of his mind. Notwithstanding the assistance of these machines there is scarcely a day when fires do not happen and cause much mischief; but no pains are taken to make the people build their houses on a better or more secure plan. (Abu Taleb Khan, 1814, vol II, pp169–170)

The MDGs are the world's time-bound quantified targets for addressing the multifaceted dimensions of a decent human existence, as pledged in the United Nations Millennium Declaration (2000). While the MDGs have become the fulcrum of international development, the formulation of a strategy to achieve the goals has given rise to heated debates on the responsibility of developed countries to deliver more and better aid and the need for developing countries to make adequate policy reforms to achieve the MDGs. This controversy highlights our limited knowledge of the complex linkages between aid, policies and long-term development outcomes.

In this chapter we argue that MDG financing should be designed to foster the sustainable, national, capital accumulation processes that are needed to underpin a successful MDG strategy. We argue that the success of any strategy, or 'business plan', to achieve the MDGs requires key changes in the current practices of policy design and implementation, and of the institutions that implement such business plans at national and global levels. We indicate two areas where such changes would enhance the sustainability of a chosen strategy or plan to achieve the MDGs.

The chapter is divided into five main sections, the first of which reviews the role of ODA approaches to development within the context of the creation of a sustainable capital accumulation process. The following section draws out the main sustainability challenges associated with an ODA-led investment 'big push' for creating long-term sustainable growth, with particular reference to the capital accumulation process. The third section highlights the policy implications of the discussion in the previous section, focusing on the links between the processes of capital accumulation and sustainable growth and poverty reduction. The importance of widening the 'fiscal space' available to developing countries to foster appropriate domestic regimes of accumulation is emphasized in the fourth section. Finally, we propose the development of a peer and partner mechanism to better locate the ownership of policy frameworks for achieving the MDGs within the context of the countries that have to implement MDG business plans.

THE MDGS AND THE PROCESS OF CAPITAL ACCUMULATION

The recent report to the UN Secretary General from the Millennium Project (headed by Professor Jeffrey Sachs), which is entitled *Investing in Development: A Practical Plan to Achieve the Millennium Development Goals* (UN Millennium Project, 2005; henceforth also referred to as the Millennium Project Report), sets out a practical plan to achieve the MDGs. In order to reach the MDGs at the country level, the report calls for a major increase in ODA from 0.25 per cent of donor GNP in 2003 to 0.54 per cent in 2015 (UN Millennium Project, 2005, pvii). While the report also emphasizes the need for domestic resource mobilization, debt relief and trade, it focuses mainly on the role of ODA in breaking the poverty trap and financing a major scaling up of public investment in developing countries to achieve the goals.

The report defines the challenge of achieving these goals in a novel and useful way:

> *The Goals are ends in themselves... [they] are also 'capital inputs' – the means to a productive life, to economic growth and to further development... So, many of the goals are part of capital accumulation defined broadly as well as objectives in their own right.*
> (UN Millennium Project, 2005, p28)

The novelty of this definition lies not in the identification of 'capital' as the principal input needed to achieve these goals, though this is important in its own right, and the report goes on to make a powerful case for resource transfers targeted at securing such capital. Rather, it is the identification of capital *accumulation* as the key economic *process* by which the goals are to be achieved that is innovative.

There is considerable dissonance within the economics profession on precisely how the capital accumulation process affects the achievement of desired development outcomes. Robert Solow's simplest model contends that the accumulation of capital hinges on the ability of a nation to give up current consumption (Solow, 1956, 2000). Deferring consumption depends on the ability of that nation to first meet the basic needs of its citizens with existing production technology and resource availability. A country that exists on the frontier of subsistence could make resources available for the creation of capital only at the expense of feeding a given proportion of its population. In this case, capital accumulation comes with the price of starvation. The case for aid then rests on the premise that relatively small transfers of resources from rich countries to countries on the frontier of subsistence avoid this trade-off, *ceteris paribus*.

More sophisticated models elaborate on this basic conclusion. An example is a paper (Lucas, 1988) in which three models are considered and compared to the evidence: a model emphasizing physical capital accumulation and technological change, a model emphasizing human capital accumulation through schooling, and a model emphasizing specialized human capital accumulation through learning by doing. The paper shows how a more elaborate definition of capital accumulation can be specified. However, this definition does not detract from the central premise that investment in either physical or human capital accumulation is a prerequisite for achieving desired development outcomes such as the MDGs.

Thus, ODA-led approaches to development, such as that encapsulated in the discourse on MDGs, can be interpreted as identifying the absence of an adequate (whether in magnitude or content) capital *accumulation process* as a binding constraint to securing the MDGs. It then follows that ODA relaxes this binding constraint.

The most sophisticated elaboration of this argument is contained in a paper (Sachs et al, 2004) which introduces the notion of a 'poverty trap'. The poverty trap is defined by the following conditions:

- Extreme poverty;
- Low savings rates because most households use all their income to meet basic needs and therefore have little discretionary income;
- A low 'threshold' level of infrastructure capital;
- High rates of population growth.

A combination of the above factors results in a situation where relatively small increases in public resources have little or no growth impact and transitively no effect on poverty and human development. The simultaneous existence of all these factors causes the poverty trap, which, in turn, is self reinforcing. The existence of such a poverty trap is at the crux of the Millennium Project Report, and the solution recommended, therefore, is to use ODA for a 'big push' large enough to break this self-reinforcing cycle. Such a drive would consist of a simultaneous deployment of resources to enhance infrastructure capital and provide for basic needs, so that the threshold level of infrastructure capital increases to a point where incremental applications of capital are able to make a real difference to growth. This would, in turn, enable savings rates to increase with discretionary income, once basic needs have been met, thus starting a virtuous cycle of growth and private savings that creates conditions for sustainable human development.

THE 'BIG PUSH' IN CONTEXT

It can be argued that the empirical evidence used to justify the poverty trap model in Kremer's commentary (Kremer, 2004) on 'Ending Africa's Poverty Trap' is consistent with the established argument that Sachs et al (2004) seek to refute – that poor government quality and inappropriate government policies are the main causes of low levels of income growth and human development in the developing world. Kremer cites a range of historical evidence of African countries with high levels of GDP that have seen falls in human development over the years. Furthermore, he points out that 'many people with money in Africa move it to Europe or elsewhere, rather than take advantage of the potentially huge returns available under poverty trap models to people who can reach a certain scale of investment' (Kremer, 2004, p218). The argument here is that the organization of the process of capital accumulation is one that inhibits the realization of domestic surpluses for growth and development enhancing investments, irrespective of the existent potential for such investments. In such a circumstance, a low savings rate is endogenous to the process of capital accumulation and not an exogenous variable. A big push might then create transformational conditions that may allow for the *poor* to increase their savings. It is silent on why the existing *non-poor* do not presently deploy their savings in the domestic arena and how (and whether) this could be changed. An attendant danger is that the savings of the non-poor (post the 'big push') may go the same way unless the process of capital accumulation is one that is able to sustainably deploy domestic savings to serve the needs of the development process. Enhanced domestic resource mobilization can either translate into increased resources for human capital and physical infrastructure, or the maintenance of a domestically financed enhanced stock of development assets.

Azam et al (1999) present another argument relevant to the organization of the process of capital accumulation. They argue that donor activities tend to 'crowd out' the institutional 'learning by doing' that is critical to improved governance, leading to a 'high aid-low institutional capacity' equilibrium. This supplements the above critique by hinting at the fact that there is no unchallenged *technocratic approach* to using the MDGs to create a plan to achieve sustainable development in Africa, or anywhere else, unless the process of achieving the goals is one that simultaneously fosters the conditions for its own sustainability.

In other words, is the achievement of the MDGs at the country level both a *necessary and a sufficient* condition for sustainable growth and human development? Even if Ethiopia, for example, receives sufficient levels of ODA and makes appropriate policy reforms to achieve the MDGs by 2015, will it graduate from the ranks of the least developed countries (LDCs) to sustain what has been created by the big push?

A negative answer to this question, implying the continuation of dependency on aid, would critically undermine the economic rationale and the political legitimacy of the goals, as defined by the Millennium Declaration. As world leaders gathered in September 2008 to review progress towards the MDGs, the questions were not only *whether* and *how* the quantitative goals will be reached, but, more importantly, whether achieving the targets will fulfil the vision articulated by the Millennium Declaration. In order to avoid or minimize the likelihood of a major political and economic failure for both developing and developed countries, it is critical to understand how to secure the achievement of the MDGs while building developing countries' policy and institutional environments to generate sustainable growth. This requires, in our view, a fuller understanding of the central importance of the capital accumulation *process*.

Before trying to understand the extent and implications of an ODA-financed public investment strategy for long-term sustainable growth, a clear definition of 'capital accumulation' is required. Drawing on the seminal works of Lipietz (1998) and Jessop (1991), in the context of developing countries, a *regime of accumulation* can be defined as a mode of distribution and reallocation of economic inputs (capital and labour, as well as domestic and external inputs) into socio-economic outputs that is sustainable in light of changes in the production and consumption pattern over a long period.[2] It should be distinguished from a *mode of regulation* that refers to the governance and institutional system that adjusts an accumulation regime over time.

A regime of accumulation framework describes the rather complex, often quantitative link between interventions at the macroeconomic and sector level and the development regime, which both determines and is determined by these interventions. An example of a schematic connection between interventions and the impacting *and* resultant development regime is outlined in Figure 1.1 below.[3]

In this example, 'institutional forms' at the macroeconomic level affect sectoral institutional arrangements and vice versa. The accumulation regime, embodying the principal variables defined in the 'poverty trap' argument, in turn affects and is affected by the nature of the existing development regime. The constituents of the accumulation and development regimes and macroeconomic system and sector variables may change depending on the context. But this form of schematization provides a frame of

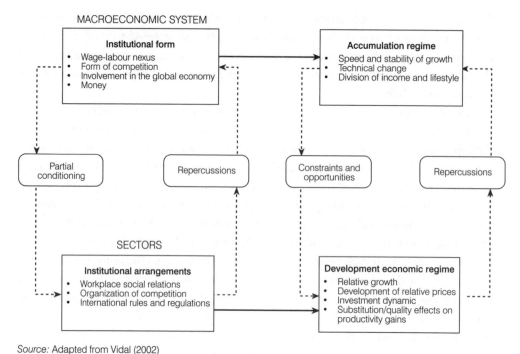

Source: Adapted from Vidal (2002)

Figure 1.1 *Regime of accumulation and development outcomes*

reference for the broader context on which, in the ultimate instance, depends the sustainability of development interventions, such as the 'big push'.

There is an ample accumulating body of evidence, sadly underused in the policy field, which links economic development processes to the regime of accumulation. A key finding in all these studies is that regimes of accumulation that sustain a virtuous cycle of economic development are diverse but tangible.[4] Mistral (1986) provides an empirical argument to show how the effectiveness of macroeconomic policy can be limited if the growth process is constrained by global economic trends and the extant international division of labour. A long-term study in Mexico (Aboites, 1995) found that export led industrialization, which provided the 'big push' in national economic development strategy, was inhibited by long-term institutional arrangements that did not allow the benefits of technical change and productivity gain opportunities that the export sector push provided. This in turn acted as a barrier to endogenous increases in the long-term competitiveness of the export sector. In Brazil, the inequality of income distribution plays a determining role in defining the regime of accumulation (Cartier-Bresson and Kopp, 1981; Juillard, 2002).

POLICY IMPLICATIONS

It is important to acknowledge the political and operational importance of the detailed business plan presented in the Millennium Project Report. The benefits of the strategy presented in the report for human development are evident and represent a vital first step towards securing fundamental economic and social human rights for the least advantaged. However, the Report is not, and does not claim to be, sufficient to achieve this lofty ideal that is central to the Millennium Declaration and the concerns of the developing world. The linkages between ODA-financed capital accumulation and long-term sustainable growth are tenuous and uncertain unless the capital accumulation process underlying the 'big push' is specified and the process embeds the necessary conditions for long-term sustainable growth.

Understanding the pursuit of the MDGs, as a process of generating sustainable regimes of accumulation, underscores the challenge to the international community to cope with the ambition of the Millennium Declaration beyond the specific quantitative targets set for each goal. The first challenge is to foster a regime of accumulation at the national level so as to free developing countries from reliance on external concessional financing for the provision of public goods and their full integration into the world economy. The second challenge is to promote country-specific modes of regulation that sustain and perpetuate an enabling accumulation regime. Under which circumstances are ODA inflows likely to favour the development of country regimes of accumulation? What are the conditions for these regimes of accumulation to be sustainable?

Thus, while foreign concessional assistance plays a fundamental role in fulfilling the vision defined in the Millennium Declaration, the real question is whether an 'ODA-led' approach to development is likely to generate long-term sustainable growth? Beyond the quantitative targets, an emerging concern is whether the mere realization of the baseline agenda for poverty reduction set by the goals will be sufficient to create the conditions for self-sustaining growth, ultimately necessary for human development to endure. The success of development strategies developed by Chile, Korea, Malaysia, Singapore and Thailand has not been contingent on significant foreign assistance, though such assistance did play an enabling role in many ways.

Though aid can be effective for providing basic public goods and higher living standards to the poor over a limited period of time, foreign assistance alone appears unlikely to generate sustainable regimes of accumulation. The lack of human and physical capital is undoubtedly a major reason for underdevelopment, but policies, institutions and the high degree of vulnerability to shocks in developing countries are as important for the success of their poverty reduction strategies and the establishment of long-term sustainable growth.

A recent UNDP report on development effectiveness stresses that while a good policy environment is important for development results, no single policy set can guarantee desired development outcomes (UNDP, 2003). Initial factor endowments as well as policy and institutional settings differ in each country and should guide national strategies for poverty reduction and sustainable growth. Thus, a small landlocked country with limited natural resources and capital, such as Laos, cannot follow the development model of a copper-rich country with maritime access, such as Chile. Similarly, accounting for country-specific governance and institutional factors is critical in explaining the diverging performances on both growth and poverty reduction in Africa. In short, while the theoretical conclusions of the poverty trap models demonstrate how capital scarcity can lead to underdevelopment, there needs to be complementary work on how the domestic capital accumulation process can be designed to sustain successful and sustainable poverty reduction strategies.

Thus, even if ODA-financed interventions to achieve the MDGs eventually lead to poverty reduction and foster capital accumulation – which may not be the case for the reasons advanced above – the sustainability of these virtuous outcomes is not automatically certain. In other words, the absence of adequate *modes of regulation* may undermine the persistence of accumulation regimes. The external and volatile nature of aid can undermine country ownership and increase vulnerability to shocks, which hinders the sustainability of regimes of accumulation. Substantial dependence on aid as the main financing source for the provision of public goods to achieve the MDGs will impact significantly on domestic patterns of consumption and production. An adequate mode of regulation needs to be in place to build an adequate productive and economic base that can sustain these achievements. There is evidence that, in Mexico, for example, disparities in the wage–labour nexus and an economy prone to external shocks fostered extreme international dependence with domestic productive capacities weak or even absent in a number of critical areas of the economy, becoming a major impediment for building self-supporting growth regimes (Talha, 2002). In Mexico and Venezuela, the external financial constraints of the 1980s led to the complete destabilization of the regulation mode, with consequent slippages in development results (Aboites et al, 2002).

The limits of ODA-led approaches to developing sustainable regimes of accumulation do not diminish the value or the usefulness of aid. On the contrary, they emphasize the need for more stable foreign assistance and for better coordination and harmonization among donors. They accentuate the need to define a more comprehensive strategy centred on country ownership to enhance human development and stimulate sustainable growth, supported by a reform of the international system.

The Millennium Project Report suggests the main elements for the reorganization of the international system to support 'MDG based poverty reduction strategies' (UN Millennium Project, 2005, pp193–236). In our view the Africa 'poverty trap' exemplifies the collective consequence of the failure of the international system to develop adequate *global* modes of regulation that allow developing countries to develop sustainable regimes of accumulation. In a period of increasing economic interconnectedness, the situation of poor countries can be analysed as a partial or a total disconnection from the global system.

Current volumes of foreign assistance are currently well below the global ODA target of 0.7 per cent of a country's gross national income for all OECD countries, set by the Monterrey Consensus. Even if this target were to be immediately met (and there is no possibility of this happening), it does not represent a significant transfer of resources likely to produce a new system of capital accumulation at the *global* level, though it can be a considerable inflow at the country level, for specific countries. However, global trade and financial regimes are critical determinants of developing countries' abilities to participate in the global economy and constitute sustainable accumulation regimes (Vidal, 2002). Yet the failure of the Bretton Woods monetary regime in the 1970s, the Asian Crisis in the 1990s and the current stalemate of the Doha trade round illustrate persistent failure on this score. Though the imbalances of the international regime paradoxically matter little to countries in the poverty trap, they begin to be critical factors in determining whether, and to what extent, they stay *out* of the trap when the ODA-financed 'big push' has worked.

FISCAL SPACE

The diagnosis encapsulated in the 'poverty trap' model provides a powerful description and a robust technical understanding of the challenges developing countries face in achieving the MDGs. However, we have been arguing that the emphasis on enhanced ODA does not address the political economy constraints that bind development efforts in low-income countries, and will not be sufficient for generating long-term sustainable growth.[5] Poor governance, absorptive capacity constraints and poverty traps are symptoms of a wider problem, which is highly context specific. It is the absence of a sustainable *domestic* capital accumulation *process* that is a fundamental obstacle to development, and of which the above factors are important symptoms. If the causes underlying this constraint are not addressed in country-specific terms, enhanced ODA may hinder, rather than facilitate, the development of an appropriate long-term regime of capital accumulation.

This is not an argument against enhanced ODA. Concessional external assistance can participate in the creation of a domestic regime of accumulation if it contributes to increasing the 'fiscal space' available to governments to enhance domestic resource mobilization. But developing countries will be locked into dependency if foreign assistance does not have a positive and significant impact on domestic resource mobilization.

Domestic public resources can be mobilized by:

- enhancing tax revenues so as to increase public savings (the surplus of current revenues over current expenditures);

- public sector access to savings from households and firms for investment in public expenditures focused on MDG attainment;
- increasing the efficiency of public expenditures by lowering the unit cost of providing public services without reducing the quality and quantity of these services.

Most policy research on fiscal reform has focused on efficiency issues, including tax administration, enhancing tax collection and debt sustainability. Relatively little attention has been paid to the question of *'fiscal space'* – identifying concrete policy actions for enhancing domestic resource mobilization, and the reforms necessary to secure the enabling governance, institutional and economic environments for these policy actions to be effective.

UNDP policy research at the country and regional levels reveals that the scope exists to enhance the 'fiscal space' available to governments to improve domestic resource mobilization, using both the above channels.[6] However, it is important to identify and design modes of resource mobilization that are pro-poor in nature, meaning that the instruments chosen are such that the net incidence of incremental domestic resource mobilization on the disposable income of the poor is minimized. This involves not only designing a progressive tax system, but also devising ways to access resources from the relatively well-off parts of the population through recourse to non-tax instruments, including public borrowing. Equity is therefore central to the design of a pro-poor resource mobilization strategy.

It has historically been the case that domestic borrowing for public investment has been an important source of resource mobilization for growth and development in many developing and, indeed, industrial countries. While domestic borrowing to finance government consumption is widely recognized as undesirable, domestic borrowing for appropriate public investments with demonstrable returns, in terms of socio-economic and human development, are regarded as perfectly acceptable in most developed countries. The 'rules' for fiscal deficits advocated by the previous British Chancellor, Gordon Brown, allow for borrowing for critical public investments.[7] It is imperative that long-term strategic thinking on such issues be encouraged and a policy platform be found to encourage such thinking in macroeconomic documents – such as Poverty Reduction Strategy Papers (PRSPs) – so that an important potential source of development finance is not overlooked by exclusively relying on short-term doctrinal evaluations of a country's domestic fiscal 'sustainability'.

Using foreign assistance to develop countries' capacities to widen fiscal space and enhance domestic resource mobilization is critical to fostering sustainable regimes of accumulation. Concessional assistance can complement domestic resources for development; it can never substitute for it or even act as the principal source of development assistance in the long term. ODA is thus more important in creating an enabling environment for non-concessional domestic mechanisms for supporting human development than a direct financing instrument *per se*. In our view, this is a critical factor, endogenous to the policy framework for implementing the MDGs, to which much more attention needs to be paid than is presently the case.

GOING BEYOND THE MONEY

Finally we turn to the governance framework within which MDG strategies are to be implemented in the coming decade. The Millennium Project 2005 provides a methodology to undertake MDG needs assessments, which is an important first step towards making the 'business case' for deploying additional resources to meet the MDGs. However, this 'business case' requires countries to make national and sectoral policy choices over the longer term. To what extent can such choices be universalized? Donor agencies and multilateral institutions tend to view this as a 'technical fix' and consider it possible to pre-specify a set of 'good policies' that all countries, with some customization, can and should be able to implement. Without such an *ex ante* judgement on good policies it would be impossible to prescribe policy conditionalities devoid of accusations of normative bias. Policy conditionalities are, and continue to be, the bread and butter of development assistance. A tool such as the World Bank's Country Policy and Institutional Assessment (CPIA), used to 'score' countries in terms of their existing policy and institutional environments, would be meaningless without some *ex ante* definition of 'good policies' and 'good institutions'.[8] Further, the political economy that underpins a capital accumulation process and that can be specified in a regime of accumulation, as we have done above, cannot be addressed by using a purely quantitative approach. A flexible approach is needed, based on the principle of adaptability and learning because it cannot be known in advance with any degree of certainty or precision how exactly the MDGs will be achieved and how much they will cost (Vandemoortele and Roy, 2004). Of course, MDG needs assessments are an essential prerequisite for promoting evidence-based policy reforms and public investment plans for the MDGs. Their implementation requires explicit, flexible and transparent alignment of a country's medium-term development strategy with the MDGs, to base the effort more firmly on learning, adaptability and a stronger sense of national ownership as we move towards 2015 (Reddy and Heuty, 2004).

Most policy frameworks are still not aligned with the MDGs, especially in low-income countries. In these countries, medium-term frameworks, such as PRSPs, are expected to simultaneously serve as an instrument for conditionality compliance and a development vision, with the disappointing result that the former variable determines the macroeconomic framework with gestural lip service paid to the latter (World Bank, 2004). Financially straitjacketed national governments have no choice but to collaborate in this charade. In such frameworks poverty reduction is seen as an automatic by-product of economic growth and macroeconomic stability. Governments and their external partners find it difficult to translate the concept of 'pro-poor policies' into practice. Equity remains the big absentee in most anti-poverty strategies. The majority of PRSPs pursue a rather conventional and unimaginative approach to poverty reduction. It is a tragedy, for instance, that countries with a high HIV prevalence rate have a macroeconomic framework that is not dissimilar from that of countries without HIV/AIDS. Such uniformity and orthodoxy is unlikely to lead us towards the MDGs by 2015.

A lot will have to be done to change the architecture of international development cooperation if this is to change. Here we can only propose a first step. The main intent of MDG costing is to enhance the synergy between the MDGs and national planning and budgeting, a process that can be facilitated by external partners. The periodic consultations between a developing country and its external partners, either in the form of a consultative group (CG) or a roundtable (RT) meeting,[9] provide an opportunity for substantive discussions about the main elements of the national strategy for poverty reduction. However, the emphasis of these meetings is often about compliance with rules and conditionalities associated with 'money changing hands', while the dimension of 'ideas changing minds' is frequently overshadowed. A 'Peer & Partner Review' can enhance the importance of the latter by building on CG/RT processes and be based on documents such as the PRSP.[10]

The 'Peer & Partner Review' is meant to make the periodic consultations with external partners less asymmetric, hence empowering national actors. The current mode, whereby a developing country faces a large number of bilateral donors and multilateral institutions, is not always conducive to an equal exchange and a frank debate. The 'Peer & Partner Review' would involve peer countries and a more select group of partners to review the anti-poverty strategy, programmes and financing plans. When Lesotho, for instance, meets with its external partners, the meeting could include representatives from Mozambique, South Africa, Zambia and, perhaps, from other land-locked countries such as Bolivia and Nepal. On the donor side, the number could be limited to keep the discussion manageable and to strike a better balance between developing and developed countries. A person of distinction could join the consultative process. The 'Peer & Partner Review' would help deepen the sense of national ownership and advance the case for home-grown poverty reduction strategies.

To turn the 'Peer & Partner Review' into a practical proposition, a number of steps will need to be taken. These include the following seven steps:

1   Initiate the process by national policymakers on a voluntary basis.
2   Choose the participating peers and partners.
3   Explore ways to link the review to similar initiatives by the New Economic Partnership for Africa's Development (NEPAD, 2002) and OECD Development Assistance Committee (DAC) (Fabrizio, 2002).
4   Build on existing mechanisms and documents, especially the PRSP and CG/RT consultations.

5   Keep the process light and flexible.
6   Consider a small functional secretariat to service the new mechanism, possibly composed of the World Bank, DAC and UNDP.
7   Share review reports widely and make them publicly available for MDG campaigning.

The Millennium Project Report has provided us with a business plan to achieve the MDGs. We feel that for this business plan to work, we will need to make significant changes in the way we go about the business of human development in the coming decade.

NOTES

1   The views and interpretations in this chapter are those of the authors and do not represent the views and policies of the United Nations Development Programme.
2   According to Lipietz (1988, p23]):
    The regime of accumulation is a mode of systematic distribution and reallocation of the social product which, over a prolonged period of time, is able to coordinate transformations in the conditions of production (volume of capital invested and its distribution among the branches and norms of production) with transformations in the conditions of final consumption (consumption norms of wage-earners and other social classes, collective spending, and so on).
    It is also stated in Jessop (1991, ppxxvii–xxviii) that:
    An accumulation regime is a complementary pattern of production and consumption that is reproducible over a long period. Accumulation regimes are sometimes analysed abstractly in terms of their typical reproduction requirements; but, specified as modes of growth, they can be related to the international division of labour. This concept is broadly macroeconomic. A mode of regulation is an emergent ensemble of norms, institutions, organizational forms, social networks and patterns of conduct that can stabilize an accumulation regime.
3   Systems dynamics based modelling approaches provide tools to quantify macro-assessment models that can incorporate such issues. A good example of such a model is the Threshold 21 model designed by the Millennium Institute (available at www.millenniuminstitute.net/national/model.html).
4   There is a complementary discourse on the impact of accumulation regimes (defined variously) on development processes that we do not discuss at length here. See, for example, Khan (1989), Roy (1999, 1994) and Taylor and Bacha (1976).
5   Or even necessary in some regions, like the Indian subcontinent, which contains a sizeable proportion of the world's poor.
6   McKinley (2003) and Roy and Weeks (2004) provide a conceptual argument for measures to enhance fiscal space within the context of pro-poor fiscal policy formulation; Beresford et al (2004) provide an empirical illustration in the Cambodian context.
7   Gordon Brown's 'golden rule' states that, over the cycle, spending of a current (as opposed to capital) nature should be balanced by revenues, and borrowing should only be countenanced to cover capital expenditure.
8   The CPIA index groups 20 indicators into 4 broad categories: economic management; structural policies; policies for social inclusion and equity; and public sector management and institutions. Countries are rated on their current status in each of these performance criteria, with scores from 1 (lowest) to 6 (highest). This index is updated annually (http://web.worldbank.org/WBSITE/EXTERNAL/TOPICS/EXTDEBTDEPT/0,,contentMDK:20268582~menuPK:576555~pagePK:64166689~piPK:64166646~theSitePK:469043,00.html).

9   RTs and CGs are the most visible forms of aid coordination. Most tend to be organized with a country focus. Typically, a CG is a two-day meeting held at the request of the finance minister of an aid-receiving country. The World Bank is responsible for convening, preparing background materials and serving as a chair for CGs. The pattern at CGs is for the IMF to report on monetary and fiscal policy and developments, the Bank to make a presentation on investment trends and, more recently, for the UNDP to discuss technical cooperation issues. This is followed by presentations by bilateral donors. An RT conference (RTC) is a formal meeting between the highest officials of the government and the principal donors to review the country's overall development performance, future strategy and financing requirements. The position of each donor with respect to the government's development strategy and its willingness to finance priority requirements is made clear. These conferences take place every two to four years and are limited in participation.

10   This proposal is detailed in Reddy and Heuty (2004).

REFERENCES

Aboites, J. (1985) 'Industrialisation et développement agricole au Mexique: Un analyse du régime d'accumulation de long terme, 1939–85', CEPREMAP 8727, Paris

Aboites, J., Miotti, L. and Quenan, C. (2002) 'Regulationist approaches and accumulation in Latin America', in R. Boyer and Y. Saillard (eds) *Regulation Theory – The State of the Art*, Edition la Découverte, Paris, Routledge, London, pp280–287

Abu Taleb Khan, M. (1814) *Travels of Mirza Abu Taleb Khan in Asia and Europe during the Years 1799, 1800, 1801, 1802, and 1803*, in the Persian language, 2 vols, C. Stewart, trans., Longman, Hurst, Rees and Orme, London

Azam, J-P., Devarajan, S. and O'Connell, S. A. (1999) *Aid Dependence Reconsidered*, Policy Research Working Paper No. 2144, World Bank, Washington DC

Beresford, M., Namazie, C., Roy, R., Sisovanna, S. and Sokha, N. (2004) *The Macroeconomics of Poverty Reduction in Cambodia*, UNDP, New York, Phnom Penh and Kathmandu

Cartier-Bresson, J. and Kopp, P. (1981) 'L'analyse sectionelle: Approche du système productif en Amérique Latine', Université de Picardie, France

Fabrizio, P. (2002) 'Peer review: A tool for co-operation and change. An analysis of an OECD working method', OECD Directorate for Legal Affairs, Paris

Jessop, B. (ed) (1991) *The Parisian Regulation School Regulation Theory and the Crisis of Capitalism*, 1, Edward Elgar, London, preface xxvii and xxviii

Juillard, Y. (2002) 'Accumulation regimes', in R. Boyer and Y. Saillard (eds) *Regulation Theory – The State of the Art*, Edition la Découverte, Paris, Routledge, London, pp153–160

Khan, M. (1989) 'Clientelism, corruption and capitalist development', unpublished PhD thesis, University of Cambridge, Cambridge

Kremer, M. (2004) 'Comment on Sachs et al., "Ending Africa's Poverty Trap"', in W. C. Brainard and G. L. Perry (eds) *Brookings Papers on Economic Activity*, vol 1, Brookings Institution Press, Washington DC, pp217–222

Lipietz, A. (1998) 'Accumulation, crises, and ways out: Some methodological reflections on the concept of "Regulation"', *International Journal of Political Economy*, vol 18, no 2, pp10–43

Lucas, R. (1988) 'On the mechanics of economic development', *Journal of Monetary Economics*, vol 22, pp3–42

McKinley, T. (2003) *The Macroeconomics of Poverty Reduction. Initial Findings of UNDP Asia-Pacific Regional Programme*, UNDP, Bureau for Development Policy, New York (mimeograph)

Mistral, J. (1986) 'Régime international et trajectoires nationales', in R. Boyer (ed) *Capitalisme fin de siècle*, Presse Universitaire de France (PUF), Paris

NEPAD (New Partnership for Africa's Development) (2002) 'The African Peer Review Mechanism', 10 June, NEPAD, Johannesburg, South Africa

Reddy, S. and Heuty, A. (2004) 'Achieving the Millennium Development Goals: A critique and a strategy', unpublished, available at www.millenniumdevelopmentgoals.org

Roy, R. (1994) 'The politics of fiscal policy', unpublished PhD thesis, Faculty of Economics and Politics, University of Cambridge, Cambridge

Roy, R. (1999) 'Economic theories of decentralisation: Towards an alternative political-economy approach', in M. Macintosh and R. Roy (eds) *Economic Decentralisation and Public Management Reform*, Edward Elgar, Cheltenham

Roy, R. and Weeks, J. (2004) 'Making fiscal policy work for the poor', paper presented at the G-24 Annual Meeting, 27–28 September 2004, Washington DC

Sachs, J., McArthur, J. W., Schmidt-Traub, G., Kruk, M., Bahadur, C., Faye, M. and McCord, G. (2004) 'Ending Africa's poverty trap', in W. C. Brainard and G. L. Perry (eds) *Brookings Paper on Economic Activity*, *vol I*, Brookings Institution Press, Washington DC, pp117–240

Solow, R. (1956) 'A contribution to the theory of economic growth,' *Quarterly Journal of Economics*, vol 70, pp65–92

Solow, R. (2000) *Growth Theory: An Exposition*, Oxford University Press, New York

Talha, L..(2002) 'Théorie de la régulation et développement', in R. Boyer and Y. Saillard (eds) *Regulation Theory – The State of the Art*, Edition la Découverte, Paris, Routledge, London, pp456–458

Taylor, L. and Bacha, E. (1976) 'An unequalising spiral: A first growth model for Belindia', *Quarterly Journal of Economics*, vol 90, pp197–218

United Nations (2000) 'A/RES/55/2 United Nations Millennium Declaration', United Nations, New York

UN Millennium Project (2005) *Investing in Development: A Practical Plan to Achieve the Millennium Development Goals*, Earthscan, New York

UNDP (United Nations Development Programme) (2003) *Development Effectiveness Report: Partnership for Results*, Evaluation Office, UNDP, New York

Vandemoortele, J. and Roy, R. (2004) *Making Sense of MDG Costing,* UNDP, Bureau for Development Policy New York, available at www.undp.org/poverty/docs/prm/MakingsenseofMDGcosting-August.pdf.

Vidal, J-F. (2002) 'International regimes', in R. Boyer and Y. Saillard (eds) *Regulation Theory – The State of the Art*, Edition La Découverte, Paris, Routledge, London, pp108–114

World Bank (2004) *The Poverty Reduction Strategy Initiative. An Independent Evaluation of the World Bank's Support Through 2003*, The World Bank Operations Evaluation Department, World Bank, Washington DC

2

Fiscal Space for What?
Analytical Issues from a Human
Development Perspective[1]

Rathin Roy, Antoine Heuty and Emmanuel Letouzé[2]

INTRODUCTION

This chapter proposes an analytical framework and policy instruments to secure fiscal space for financing a national development strategy. Our central premise is that the sustainability of policies to create fiscal space is a function of *what* the fiscal space is used for. This, in turn, depends on the central economic policy challenges and the attendant interventions that need to be financed to secure these challenges. The balance of emphasis placed on the stabilization, allocation, distribution and growth functions of fiscal policy would differ according to the timeframe of the analytical framework and the political economy context within which the interventions are operationalized. Finally the indicators used to assess fiscal solvency and sustainability will be very different if the assessment is carried out on a long-term, as opposed to short-term, analytical context.

The following section of the chapter provides an analytical framework for assessing fiscal space at the national level. It introduces the fiscal space diamond as a diagnostic tool for mapping the different fiscal instruments to secure fiscal space for the MDGs. The chapter then goes on to argue that the role of fiscal policy and the instruments for enhancing fiscal space depend on country specific challenges to achieve sustainable human development. It distinguishes between countries where managing the adverse effects of shocks and fostering more inclusive growth is the central policy challenge, from countries where a significant scaling up of public expenditures involving a significant and permanent increase in the ratio of government spending to GDP is required. In the subsequent section, we argue that expenditure switching, efficiency enhancing policy reforms, and the development of countercyclical mechanisms represent the most effective instruments for addressing the challenges of financing development in many middle-income countries. Finally, the chapter presents the main fiscal challenges for ensuring the sustainability of a scaling up of public investment and provides recommendations for designing a long-term exit strategy from aid.

A FRAMEWORK FOR ASSESSING FISCAL SPACE

Definitions and uses of fiscal space

Existing models estimating the cost of achieving the MDGs stress the magnitude of the financial gap to attaining the goals. This has given rise to concerns over the most appropriate instruments for enhancing 'fiscal space' for the MDGs. The term 'fiscal space' is still in definitional evolution, and there are different definitions that give emphasis to different aspects of resource mobilization policy. The 2006 Interim Report on *Fiscal Policy for Growth and Development* to the Development Committee of the joint World Bank/IMF Board (henceforth the Development Committee) defined fiscal space as 'The gap between the current level of expenditure and the maximum level of expenditures a government can undertake without impairing its solvency' (Development Committee, 2006, p14). Peter Heller, the then Deputy Director of the IMF Fiscal Affairs Department, defined fiscal space as 'The availability of budgetary room that allows a government to provide resources for a desired purpose without any prejudice to the sustainability of a government's financial position' (Heller, 2005, p3).

Both definitions conceptualize fiscal space in residual terms ('room' or 'gap'). In contrast, Roy and Heuty (2005, p170) define fiscal space as 'concrete policy actions for enhancing domestic resource mobilization, and the reforms necessary to secure the enabling governance, institutional, and economic environments for these policy actions to be effective'. The focus on domestic resource mobilization in this definition underscores the fact that, ultimately, the sustainability and solvency of an economy depends on (a) the extent to which domestic financing mechanisms are able to support public expenditures, and (b) the fact that the mobilization of fiscal space in a sustainable manner is a function of the political economy context within which fiscal space is secured. Hence, the emphasis is on the set of feasible policy actions on the one hand and the prevailing political and economic environment on the other.[3] These political economy factors, and the argument that ultimately domestic resources must pay for public expenditures even if these are, temporarily, financed by grants or foreign concessional finance, are both most relevant in the long term[4] rather than the short term. In other words, while the Heller (2005) and Development Committee (2006) definitions are primarily concerned with the short-term consequences and mainly the potential adverse effects of an increase in public expenditure, Roy and Heuty (2005) seek to evaluate how concrete policy actions may support trend changes in the potential for domestic resource mobilization for pro-poor public investment.

This difference in emphasis thus arises because policy concerns differ. The Development Committee definition of fiscal space is concerned with raising incremental resources for development. Clearly this is not an adequate basis on which to assess the availability of fiscal space for low- and middle-income countries engaged in major development transformations aimed at securing long-term human development and economic growth. This latter focus is at the heart of the Monterrey Consensus and the MDG financing debate. In this context, giving overriding importance to short-term fiscal stability, measured through annual fiscal balances, and solvency, as measured through the ratio of debt to GDP, tends to underestimate the long-term, real impact of spending on these development objectives. As Goldsbrough (2007) points out, with IMF programmes 'the longer term supply side effects of higher public spending are, with some commendable recent exceptions, largely ignored in many macroeconomic frameworks'. This concern motivated the Development Committee (2006) to task the staffs of the IMF and World Bank to produce a paper on fiscal policy in the first place. The staffs in their report recognized the central role of fiscal policy in financing the provision of public goods needed to achieve the MDGs within a longer time horizon and declared that their intent was to focus 'on how fiscal policy could be adapted to strengthen its role with respect to growth and the achievement of the MDGs' (Development Committee, 2006, pi). But the definition they used was, in our judgement, inadequate for the purpose, causing the analysis to fall short of providing a way forward on the financing problem central to the Monterrey Consensus.

A more generic definition that we use for this chapter is therefore:

> *Fiscal space is the financing that is available to government as a result of concrete policy actions for enhancing resource mobilization, and the reforms necessary to secure the enabling governance, institutional and economic environments for these policy actions to be effective, for a specified set of development objectives.*

In what follows, we argue that the analytical frameworks currently used to assess the sustainability and solvency of a fiscal expansion are of limited relevance to measure the developmental, as opposed to fiduciary,[5] implications of increasing fiscal space for a specific set of development objectives, such as the MDGs, that require governments to find fiscal space in the first place. For example, in the Development Committee report, an expansion of public expenditures is only desirable when it does not compromise 'macroeconomic stability', which is further referred to as 'short-term macroeconomic stability' (Development Committee, 2006 p19). Thus, the short term continues to act as a binding constraint on the long term. This framework allows for fiscal expansion only in situations where solvency is improved *and* macroeconomic stability is sustained. Even if fiscal space exists, that is, public expenditure improves solvency, the report deems fiscal expansion undesirable if it compromises short-term macroeconomic stability. The positive endogenous effects of the *outcomes* of additional public investment on solvency and stability are ignored. For instance, using fiscal space for increasing military spending will have a significantly different impact from investing in rural roads in the long run, but the standard analytical framework cannot distinguish between the fiduciary outcomes, not to mention developmental outcomes, of these very different spending decisions.

If fiscal policy should better incorporate long-term growth objectives, it is hard to see why the short-term macroeconomic impact of public expenditures is the major determining factor and thus a binding constraint in deciding on their appropriateness. Recent research establishes that the long-run macro-stability implications of a scaling up in public spending are rather different from those that emerge in a short-run analysis (Bruno and Easterly, 1998; Gupta et al, 2006).

A dynamic approach to fiscal space requires a better understanding of the long-term effects of fiscal expansion on economic growth and human development. The debate on the scaling up of public investment focuses on whether investment in infrastructure (IMF, 2004; Suescún, 2005) has a significant positive impact on growth. Further, does the magnitude (inter-temporally) of the impact allow for debt-financed investments in infrastructure greater than those admissible under fiscal rules that impose an overall ceiling on the fiscal deficit and debt/GDP ratios? On this count, the debate is inconclusive. The IMF (2004) reviews over 40 studies on the subject, spanning a variety of methodologies and country groups. The review highlights the fact that there is inconclusive evidence of a significant, positive, causal link between public investment levels and rates of economic growth over time and across countries. This inconclusiveness is largely explained by technical limitations, such as data constraints, especially in the sub-Saharan African context, methodological challenges and econometric limitations. For instance, there is a well-known concern that the right-hand-side variables of models designed to capture the impact of a set of factors, including the ratio of infrastructure investment to GDP, on growth are not independent or exogenous (Klitgaard, 2004).

This inconclusivity notwithstanding, the renewed interest in public investment within the development community and on the part of developing country governments has stemmed from the growing importance of the MDG agenda. In this respect, the IMF itself acknowledges that MDG-related investment gaps 'may adversely affect the growth potential of the affected countries, and limit targeted improvements in social indicators' (IMF, 2004, p3). There is a consensus in the literature and among development practitioners on the positive effect of infrastructure investment on productivity and output in different regional and sectoral settings (Leipziger et al, 2003; Estache, 2006). One of the most interesting features of the recent research has indeed been the refinement of the analysis of the channels through which, and conditions under which, output is most responsive to such investments, or to the lack thereof.

The 'poverty trap' (Sachs et al, 2004) and 'bottlenecks' (Willoughby, 2004) theories support the idea that investments in infrastructure yield substantial returns respectively in low-income (especially those slowly starting to move out of stagnation) and middle-income (in particular those that had been growing fast) countries (Willoughby, 2004). Additionally, there is strong evidence of the positive impact of investment in transportation and communication (and of rural roads in particular) and agricultural research and development (R&D), as well as in electricity (Fan et al, 2002; Klitgaard, 2004; Willoughby, 2004). The key message here is that the *types* of investments, and the channels and magnitude of their impact on output, are highly setting specific. The policy decision-making process must, therefore, be embedded in the local context, strengthening participation, ownership and, ultimately, the adequacy of the means to the end.

This is not a simplistic argument for privileging social spending over growth objectives. There is often a false dichotomy created between programmes that secure economic growth versus human development enhancing public investment programmes. The implicit assumption underlying this artificial dichotomy is that investment in economic infrastructure is growth enhancing and therefore sustainable, while social programmes would not offer economic returns that justify their existence. However, research in the context of the MDG agenda points to the positive impact of *public investments that secure tangible developmental outcomes*, such as those measured by the MDG indicators on long-term growth (Anderson et al, 2006). While, again, the relationships and interactions at play are not yet fully understood, there is solid and growing empirical evidence that better access to water, sanitation, health facilities and transportation can play a significant and direct role in lowering child mortality rates and the prevalence of malnutrition, as well as in promoting schooling and gender equality (UNDP and JICA, 2005). Further, there is evidence of complementarities, through reciprocal positive externalities, between policies and expenditures geared toward different developmental goals, such as health and schooling or access to water and health (Agenor and Neanidis, 2006). The report of the Commission for Africa (2005, p234) emphasizes the 'failure to appreciate the important complementarities between investment in infrastructure and social sectors [which] have also contributed to the fall in spending on infrastructure and a lack of emphasis on it in many national poverty reduction strategies'.

It is obvious and well known that, *ceteris paribus*, improving a child's health improves its class attendance and ability to learn, and that better access to water decreases infant mortality figures. A study (Leipziger et al, 2003, p10) surveying 20 developing countries concludes that 'increasing the poorest quintile's access to piped water from its dismally low 3 per cent level to the level of the richest quintile at 55 per cent would eliminate more than one-quarter of the difference in infant mortality between these two groups, and more than one-third of the difference in child mortality'. In Morocco, road improvements resulted in a rise in primary school enrolment from 28 to 68 per cent (World Bank, 1996). Similarly, investment in electricity increased the number of Colombian children reading books in the evening from 43 to 72 per cent (Ndulu et al, 2005).

The existence of such complementarities makes a strong case for a scaling up of multisectoral public expenditure programmes, given that the payback from an integrated package focusing on several developmental goals is higher than the sum of the paybacks of its components taken separately.

A key conclusion is that a strong case exists for a wide array of setting-specific public interventions that can positively impact growth and human development through several channels. This can stimulate growth, both directly through the provision of physical capital, and indirectly through its impact on human capital (through developmental outcomes). It can also foster human development, both directly and through the 'trickle down' effect.

What, then, would be the desirable features of a fiscal framework that supports a human development oriented public expenditure strategy, whose results can be measured in terms of progress towards quantifiable long-term development goals, such as the MDGs?

An analytical framework for assessing fiscal space

In the above section, we made the analytical case for a long-term fiscal framework that would better suit the needs of the Monterrey Consensus and the critical policy question in the fiscal area for the MDGs: the availability of sustainable and adequate resources to finance public expenditures for the MDGs. Following the IMF, we would view a sustainable fiscal policy as one that (a) does not undermine fiscal sustainability in the long term, and (b) that is not charity based or relying on exogenous, and as has been frequently pointed out, highly volatile sources of external finance, such as bilateral aid and concessional and non-concessional foreign borrowing. Such a policy requires:

- an analytical framework that specifies the main features of a long-term resource mobilization framework (see Box 2.1 for an example of such a framework);
- specific indicators to assess fiscal sustainability and, if possible, suggest fiscal *rules* that could be deployed to secure the long-term sustainability of such a framework.

There are two major differences in designing an analytical framework for long-term fiscal policy as opposed to one for the short term. The first is that of *long-term endogeneity*. In the short run, the different instruments used to create fiscal space do not depend on the *object of their* spending to assess whether they are sustainable. This is apparent in the case of efficiency gains and aid. Misspent aid will not make a fiscal strategy less sustainable in the short run, and the potential Dutch Disease associated effects with an expansion in

BOX 2.1 THE FISCAL SPACE DIAMOND

This representation of fiscal space builds on the fiscal space diamond presented by the Development Committee (2006). The objective of the diamond is to address the questions that arise when policymakers wish to know, 'What are the macro-fiscal possibilities to raise fiscal space to achieve intended policy goals?'. Such a diagnostic of fiscal space needs to be highly country specific to have operational relevance.

The fiscal space diamond has four 'pillars' that collectively constitute the universe of avenues to secure fiscal space. The diamond is created by putting the four pillars together in Cartesian space, with the area of the diamond representing the aggregate fiscal space available in the country. The diamond does not include seignorage, which is not commonly considered to be a desirable option. Governments can create fiscal space through the following types of fiscal instruments:

- ODA through aid and debt relief;
- Domestic revenue mobilization through improved tax administration or tax policy reforms;
- Deficit financing through domestic and external borrowing;
- Reprioritization and raising efficiency of expenditures.

The diamond is constructed by (a) mapping the four pillars, one on each axis, with the total resources available under each head representing a point on the axis; and (b) joining the points. It is, of course, possible to design different variations of this generic diamond. For example, if one were to calculate the grant element of a concessional loan then that part of the loan could be put under the aid pillar with the balance under the loan pillar. The diamond can be constructed in incremental or absolute terms.

There are many different situations in which the diamond can be used as an operational tool, depending on the policy assumptions. In the short run, for example, expenditure switching policies and tax *policy* measures to increase revenue would be of limited value compared to measures that make public expenditures more Pareto-efficient (for example, productivity gains) and tax *administration* reform measures. Conversely in the long term the latter measures are unlikely to have as great a size significance compared with the former.

It is therefore essential to define precisely the policy assumptions underlying the diamond, the timeframe within which the different measures take effect and whether the policy actions that could be taken to tap into a source of fiscal space are endogenous or exogenous to *domestic* policy-making. In Annex 2.1 (page 61), we present a detailed example of such a diagnostic. In summary, there are five steps to its construction:

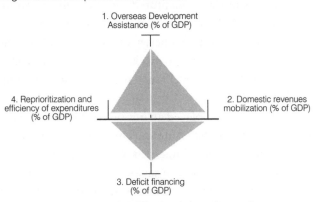

Figure 2.1 *The fiscal space diamond*

1 Identify macroeconomic context and human development issues.
2 Identify short- and long-term fiscal challenges.
3 Identify whether challenges are exogenous or endogenous in the short term.
4 Build the diamond.
5 Present the overall analytical framework.

ODA will not be radically tempered or enhanced depending on whether the aid is spent on guns or butter.[6] In particular, the case for domestic borrowing becomes more or less persuasive in the long term the greater the development payback from such borrowing. Similarly, long-term sustainability would ultimately require reduced reliance on the main exogenous source of fiscal space, foreign aid. For this reason UNDP and IMF work on this issue (Roy and Heuty, 2005; Gupta et al, 2006; Roy et al, 2006) has highlighted the value of developing a strategy for *exit* from aid, for reasons of assessing fiscal sustainability, if not for deeper political economy reasons, as a complement to strategies that propose achieving the MDGs through scaling up public investments.

A second important difference arises when one asks the following questions. Will Brazil and Ethiopia be spending on the same things to secure the MDGs? Will the same fiscal instruments be used? Different development situations will require different kinds of spending, in fact, with different weights placed on the functions of public finance, to secure the MDGs.

For both these reasons, it is *operationally* important to ask the question, 'Fiscal space for *what?*'

FISCAL SPACE FOR WHAT?

The capital accumulation process generated by the Marshall Plan, officially known as the European Recovery Program (ERP) offers a compelling example of the importance of the dynamics between external assistance and domestic resource mobilization. The Marshall Plan dispensed over US$13 billion between 1948 and 1952 to Western European countries constituted as the Organization for European Economic Cooperation (OEEC). Over 80 per cent of this aid was in the form of grants. France was the second largest beneficiary of Marshall Aid and the largest recipient, if indirect aid in the form of drawing rights is included (Lynch, 1997). Marshall Aid made its most important contribution to French reconstruction by supporting modernization of the French steel industry.

Aid from the US played an important role in increasing Europe's supply of funds for investment. Marshall Aid supplemented domestic sources of investment finance, as European incomes and domestic savings collapsed following the war. Table 2.1 underscores the progressive rise in savings in France and the UK that gradually replaced aid financing received during the first years of the Marshall Plan.

In France, the savings rate grew from 19 per cent between 1948 and 1951 to 27 per cent between 1952 and 1960. The scaling up in public investment for infrastructure was financed through short-term mortgages and loans on promissory notes, to provide credit for industries. Eichengreen (1995) emphasizes the catalytic role of the Marshall Plan in rebuilding and modernizing European economies and fostering capital accumulation.

Table 2.1 *Savings in France and the UK, 1946–1960*

	1946–1951	1948–1951	1952–1960
France	n.a.	19	27
UK	9	13	16

Note: Savings are calculated as the sum of investment and the current account surplus
Source: Eichengreen (1995)

The history of economic reconstruction in Europe after World War II raises critical issues for financing development in poor countries to achieve the MDGs. The present international context does not realistically allow for the possibility of replicating a Marshall Plan for developing countries. However, the successful transition from reliance on aid to domestic resource mobilization underscores the fundamental importance of generating and mobilizing savings over the long term to achieve sustainable development. European countries' experience also underscores the importance of the *instruments* and the *use* of fiscal space that are critical to successful capital accumulation in developing countries. Thailand offers a more recent example of successful development transformation (see Box 2.2).

It is important in this context to distinguish between the *purposes* for which fiscal space is generated in different socio-economic situations.

The challenges for achieving sustainable development across different income groups of developing countries differ significantly (see Table 2.2). There are large contrasts between low-income countries and middle-income countries (MICs) in terms of poverty incidence (the proportion of people below the poverty line in low-income countries is nearly three times as much as in MICs), health (infant mortality is twice as high in low-income countries) and education (the literacy rate is about 90 per cent in MICs as against 58 per cent in low-income countries). These contrasts have major

Table 2.2 *Socio-economic indicators by income group*

Variable	Year	Income levels				
		Low	Middle	Lower middle	Upper middle	High
Growth rate of GDP (%)	1990–2003	2.5	2.3	2.7	2.5	2.7
Growth volatility	1980–2003	3.0	2.0	2.3	1.8	0.8
Infant mortality ratio (per 1000 live births)	2003	79.8	29.8	31.4	17.8	-
Adult literacy rate (%)	2002	58.0	89.9	89.8	91.5	-
Population with access to safe drinking water (%)	2002	75.7	83.0	82.2	90.5	99.4
Gini coefficient	2003	35.7	43.7	43.1	48.7	34.1
Poverty incidence (US$1 a day)	2003	35.5	13.1	13.9	6.8	2.0

Source: World Development Indicators Online Database; UNDP (2005)

BOX 2.2 THE CASE OF THAILAND'S DEVELOPMENTAL
TRANSFORMATION

Thailand offers a more recent example of how fiscal policy contributed to a sustained process of capital accumulation that has enabled the country to achieve an upper middle-income status in a few decades.

Thailand's development progress has been remarkable. Between 1950 and 2000, GDP per capita increased sevenfold, while the incidence of poverty was reduced by four-fifths, down to 11 per cent of the population. This was achieved through high growth rates ranging between 7 and 8.5 per cent on average between 1960 and the 1997 crisis,[7] supported by a savings/investment nexus that grew steadily stronger until the crisis. Growth rates peaked in the early 1990s when savings and investment reached respectively 34 per cent and 40 per cent of GDP, up from 11.5 per cent and 13.6 per cent in the 1950s. As a result, Thailand has achieved most of its MDGs, or is close to doing so.

This process has been largely domestically driven and financed, with little contribution and influence from ODA sources.[8] Chapter 9 provides interesting insights on how fiscal policy contributed to, and was impacted by, the socio-economic development of Thailand. The main lesson is that Thailand's transformation was supported by a cautious yet indisputable and well-targeted fiscal expansion. Between 1955 and 1985, the share of government expenditures over GDP rose from 11.5 per cent to 18.5 per cent, stabilizing at around 16 to 17 per cent today.

The increase is even more pronounced than the figures suggest. 'Per capita government expenditure at constant (1988) prices increased from around Bt2200 in 1970 to around Bt9500 in 2003' (Chapter 9, p363). Further, an increasing share of this incremental spending was dedicated to capital and social services expenditures, 'areas which support the private sector accumulation process and which promote human development'. Private investment benefited from crowding in (rather than crowding out) effects. The resulting growth provided incremental private income that stimulated consumption and savings, whose rapid financialization was subsequently beneficial to domestic investment, while inflation was kept at low single-digit figures.

Thus, well-targeted public investment and human development-related spending have been the main drivers of the fiscal expansion. In the long term, the government was able to implement policies that secured fiscal sustainability while supporting a significant permanent increase in per capita public spending.

---

implications for the magnitude of the fiscal space required to achieve sustainable development in countries of differing income groups. It is also important to stress the heterogeneity of the MIC group: the upper middle-income countries exhibit indicators that are close to those of high-income countries, but the lower middle-income countries still face significant chronic poverty (13.1 per cent of their population is below the US$1 a day poverty line).

Middle-income countries include 10 of the 20 countries with the highest levels of inequality in the World. Latin America is the most unequal region in the world, with Africa a close second (Bouillon and Buvinic, 2003). Ferranti et al (2004) and Easterly (2002) show that inequality has a negative impact on long-term economic growth. Bruno et al (1998) also show that lower initial inequality raises the likelihood that growth will reduce poverty. Reducing inequality is critical to the attack on poverty because an inclusive growth process benefits the poor in the short run. The dynamic effect of a decrease in inequality improves the distribution in each period, that is, it improves 'initial conditions', which stimulate growth over the long run. In the absence of inclusive growth, middle-income countries may experience sharp recessions and fall back to low-income status because of social exclusion and inequality (Rodrik, 1999).

The incidence of poverty and the degree of inequality confront developing countries with significantly different challenges in the design of their national development strategies. The role of fiscal policy and the instruments for enhancing fiscal space need to respond to these two different socio-economic situations. The first situation (which we refer to as 'Scenario 1' in the rest of this chapter), prevalent in most developed countries and in many upper middle-income countries, is one in which the achievement of internationally agreed development goals involves two objectives for fiscal policy:

1   Managing the downsides caused by structural shocks;
2   Addressing poverty and other development objectives that enhance economic welfare principally by fostering the inclusivity of the development process by increasing access of the relatively poorer sections of the population to key public goods.

In this situation, it is the *stabilization* and *allocation* roles of fiscal policy (Musgrave, 1959) that are at the cutting edge of pro-development policy formulation. With respect to the first objective, the focus is on designing appropriate countercyclical fiscal policies to avoid anticipated shocks and to mitigate the impact of unanticipated adverse structural shocks (Dervis and Birdsall, 2006; Vos et al, 2007). The second objective focuses on securing fiscal space for *income transfers*, such as conditional cash transfers, and/or expanding the availability of public goods at the margin so as to improve the quality of and access to public goods, reducing waiting lists for medical procedures in hospitals, reducing class sizes in poorer areas and so on. This would typically require the development of expenditure switching policies that would reorient the focus of government expenditures towards increasing access to public goods. Fiscal space can thus be secured in this case through a combination of redistributive revenue and expenditure policies that:

•   increase the availability of targeted public services and income-generating opportunities for the relatively poorer sections of the population to purchase public goods;
•   increase the availability and quality of public goods, with possibly some marginal increases in public spending if there is a strong case for doing so.

When fiscal policy is focused on the stabilization, allocation and redistribution functions of public finance then there is unlikely to be a substantial permanent increase in the size of the government in the economy (G/GDP ratio). Equally, on the revenue side, there is unlikely to be a significant permanent increase in the public sector borrowing requirement. Hence, the issue is to find adequate fiscal space to secure the above objectives without typically requiring structural changes in the pattern of resource mobilization[9] or a permanent increase in the size of the public sector.

The second situation (which we refer to as 'Scenario 2'), prevalent in most low-income countries, is one in which the objective of fiscal policy is to finance a sustained and permanent increase in public investment of sufficient magnitude to support economic growth and deliver the basic necessities to secure a development transformation. The time horizon to achieve this transformation is 10 to 20 years. In this context, the *growth* and *allocation* functions of fiscal policy are at the cutting edge of pro-development policy formulation. This typically implies a permanent increase in government spending in the economy (G/GDP ratio) over the long term. The expansion of government spending is consistent with 'Wagner's law' (Wagner, 1911), which states that government activity increases as economies grow. The literature (Murthy, 1993; Lin, 1995; Bohl, 1996; Payne and Ewing, 1996; Chang, 2002) confirms the positive relationship between government spending and economic growth. Yet recent research (Akitoby et al, 2004) shows that this correlation does not necessarily imply causality.

Where such development transformations are initially financed through scaling up aid, it is clear that in the second scenario the magnitude of permanent fiscal space that needs to be found to sustain the achievements secured by an aid-financed scaling up is of a higher order than that required in the first scenario.

Countries at different stages of development typically face different policy challenges that require specific fiscal instruments for enhancing fiscal space. However, this typology does not imply that expenditure switching policies are not pertinent in low-income countries or that MICs ought not to use public sector borrowing if there are major infrastructure gaps that cannot be addressed by the private sector or public–private partnerships. The objective of the distinction between poor countries, requiring a scaling up of investment to address chronic poverty, and MICs, where inequality and shocks constitute the main constraints to sustainable development, is to establish a *hierarchy of instruments* to enhance fiscal space in specific development contexts. While aid, tax policy, borrowing and expenditure policies play a critical role in enhancing fiscal space in all countries, socio-economic disparities and the differential magnitude of the effort to achieve internationally agreed development goals across countries require a substantial rethinking of the purposes of fiscal policy. The second section of Chapter 3 explains the rationale for a scaling up of public investment.

FISCAL SPACE FOR INCLUSIVE GROWTH AND RISK MITIGATION

Fiscal space for inclusive growth

The main structural challenges to achieving long-term economic growth and sustainable human development in upper MICs are inequality and social exclusion. As poverty levels in typical (upper) MICs reflect unequal distribution of income and assets rather than low levels of GDP, the domestic resource mobilization policy can play a major role in the implementation of social policies and the redistribution mechanisms necessary to achieve sustainable human development, including the MDGs.

In this context, aid is unlikely to represent a significant source of fiscal space for inclusive growth. According to OECD figures (Randel et al, 2004), upper MICs received just 4 per cent of total bilateral aid between 2000 and 2004. Though aid flows to upper MICs represent 40 per cent of total ODA,[10] aid volatility and concerns about its effectiveness undermine the case for ODA-financed national development strategies in these countries (UNDESA, 2007). Typically, international capital flows represent a more significant source of financing for development than ODA.

A government can enhance fiscal space for human development through more effective tax and expenditure policies. Public revenues as a proportion of GDP averaged nearly 43 per cent in developed countries, but only 28 per cent in MICs and 23 per cent in low-income countries in 2000. The differences across income groups are due to the disparities in tax revenues, which reach 38 per cent of GDP in high-income countries, 25 per cent in MICs and 19 per cent in low-income countries (UNDESA, 2007). Tax policy reform to enhance fiscal space for human development needs to weigh the benefits of incremental financing for transfers and public goods provision against the economic distortions of the tax. Tax policies and systems vary greatly from country to country, reflecting different socio-political histories and tax collection capacities. The heterogeneity of tax systems and their performances among upper middle-income and developed countries require detailed assessments at the country level. The level of development, trade openness and other structural factors determine the tax base, that is, the tax potential a government can expect to collect.[11]

The structure of the tax system also plays a role in determining the progressivity of tax and transfer policies. Progressive taxation can foster inclusive growth through redistribution. However, the literature suggests that it is the expenditure side of the budget, not tax policy, which should be a primary redistributive tool (Tanzi, 1998). Some studies argue that taxation is a limited tool for reducing inequalities in income distribution because of tax evasion. Alesina (1998) finds that the tax systems in Latin America did not contribute to better distribution outcomes. A review of existing studies on tax incidence in 36 countries (Chu et al, 2000) suggests that the redistributive effects of the taxes are not as large in developing countries as they are in industrialized countries. The ineffectiveness of tax policy to achieve better distribution outcomes has two policy implications. First, tax policy does not represent a major instrument for fostering inclusive growth, and second, a detailed analysis of the incidence of taxation is critical to minimize the burden of incremental taxation on the poor and improve the progressivity of the tax system over the long run.

There is considerable scope to enhance the fiscal space available to governments in middle-income countries through pro-poor expenditure switching. Yet this is not to argue that governments should simplistically earmark some percentage of their budgets to basic social services. It is difficult to specify *ex ante* the size of the potential gains from expenditure reallocation and the sectors where efficiency can be improved. Gupta et al (2001) demonstrate that the marginal benefits of education and health spending decrease rapidly. This implies that governments should exercise caution before expanding government expenditure on education and health when the initial level of spending is already high.

Increasing expenditure *efficiency* is often suggested as the main instrument enhancing fiscal space for human development. Efficiency gains need to be weighed against distributive concerns. In other words, the *benefit incidence*, who receives the benefit of government services, and *expenditure incidence*, how government spending affects private incomes, are important considerations when addressing the policy challenges for achieving sustainable human development in (upper) middle-income and industrialized countries. An efficient allocation of resources implies that public spending optimizes the level of desired welfare, that is, it is impossible to allocate more funds to one sector without decreasing the welfare outcomes secured in another sector. A study of the health sector in Egypt found that many local hospitals have occupancy rates below 50 per cent (Gericke, 2004). Similarly, post-Communist countries have excess capacity in health care facilities and personnel that undermines the effectiveness of the health care systems (Langenbrunner, 2005).

Expenditure switching and efficiency enhancing reforms can therefore create fiscal space through a reallocation of resources from lower priority to higher priority sectors/sub-sectors or through productive efficiency gains. It is essential to carefully measure the incidence of public spending on desired development outcomes. This assessment is critical to guide the allocation of expenditures and the budget-making process.

Inequality is a major constraint to securing human development outcomes, such as the MDGs, and to fostering inclusive growth (Gottschalk, 2000). This can be done through redistributive income transfers or by more effective targeting to improve the access of poor and vulnerable groups to public goods. The objective of this section is not to discuss the different mechanisms for targeting public spending. Gottret and Schieber (2006) suggest, for instance, that well-designed conditional cash transfers have the potential to improve human capital and health outcomes and reduce poverty in middle-income countries. Sen (1995) points out that the development of an effective targeting system is undermined by (a) asymmetric information between potential beneficiaries, (b) moral hazard, (c) administrative costs of the programmes, (d) stigmatization of beneficiaries, and (e) concerns regarding the sustainability of the programmes, as potential beneficiaries are politically weak. These difficulties decrease as income levels rise because the poor represent a smaller portion of the population and the state has a greater capacity to manage programmes effectively. Hence targeting is an attractive policy option for enhancing fiscal space in MICs.

Expenditure switching policies and efficiency gains represent powerful instruments to enhance fiscal space. The potential for additional fiscal space is correlated to the development of the country for three related reasons. First, the scope for expenditure switching is determined by the size of the public sector, which is correlated to the output of the country (Wagner's Law). Second, productive inefficiency can be addressed through long-term capacity development programmes that limit low-income countries' abilities to secure fiscal space through active expenditure switching policies over the short run. Third, addressing political economy constraints to reforms is critical to improve income distribution that often represents a binding constraint to sustainable development in MICs. In addition, detailed country assessments of tax performance and incidence will need to identify policy reforms that will enhance government revenue.

Countercyclical fiscal policy

Contributing to macroeconomic stability is one of the three objectives assigned to fiscal policy (Musgrave, 1959). It is undisputed that macroeconomic stability has a central influence on the long-term growth performance of the economy. However, fiscal interventions to secure macroeconomic stability have been narrowly focused on price stability and fiscal solvency. A broader definition is needed as macroeconomic stability 'is also about avoiding large swings in the economy and employment' in countries vulnerable to shocks (Vos et al, 2007, p4).

The stabilization function of fiscal policy plays a more critical role in developing countries, which tend to be more vulnerable to exogenous shocks, than in high-income countries. A typical developing country is more prone to be hit by shocks, often put in greater danger if shocks occur, and is less equipped to mitigate their consequences than high-income countries (Braun and di Gresia, 2003; Williamson, 2005). The typical economic structure, geographic location and patterns of integration in the international trade and financial systems are the most common risk factors faced by developing countries. Over the past two decades, such risks have caused sharp variations in revenues, balance of payment shocks due to capital volatility, and natural disasters, to mention a few. When such shocks do occur, developing countries are also put in great danger as they potentially face severe and long-lasting consequences. Developing the countries' abilities to respond and mitigate these potentially disastrous effects is also limited by lower technical and institutional capacities, including the absence or underdevelopment of public insurance schemes and fiscal transfer systems.

Fiscal policy plays a central role in risk prevention and shock mitigation by smoothing economic activity over time and reducing uncertainty. The objective of this section is not to engage in a theoretical debate on the effectiveness of countercyclical fiscal policy for stabilization but to discuss its relevance and instruments in different development contexts. Developing countries do not constitute a homogenous group but display differences, particularly between countries belonging to different income groups. The relevance of countercyclical policies to maintain and/or restore stability in case of shock is not merely a positive function of a country's overall fragility. Countercyclical, fiscal policy usefulness also depends on the severity of the shock[12] and the government's capacity to respond to such events.

Many middle-income countries have enjoyed phases of accelerated growth in the past, but these have rarely been stable and growth has proved to be highly volatile (Gavin and Perotti, 1997; Braun and di Gresia, 2003; Loser, 2006). Between 1990 and 2004 the standard deviation of output growth in (selected) developing countries, as a whole was, 1.10, while it was 1.79 and 1.73 for the subsets of Latin American and the Caribbean (LAC) and Middle Eastern countries (cited in Loser, 2006), where almost half of the middle-income countries are concentrated. The integration of MICs into financial markets has contributed to a combination of high and volatile rates of growth. However, capital account liberalization also exposed them to balance of payment shocks that eventually led to major financial crises in the 1990s. During a period of economic slowdown, capital market volatility can result in overcorrection that will increase the severity and duration of the recession. 'Hence the importance of giving these countries some room for manoeuvre in designing and implementing countercyclical, macroeconomic policies' (UNDESA, 2007, p26).

The pro-cyclical nature of macroeconomic policies, and social spending, in Latin America is a key challenge for the development of the region. According to Braun and di Gresia (2003, p3), 'political constraints and weak institutions make saving during good times difficult', while 'limited creditworthiness makes borrowing during recessions close to impossible'. As a result, governments tend to increase pro-poor spending during expansions, and to contract it during recessions, which exacerbates the effect of an economic downturn on the vulnerable segments of the population. The weakness of automatic stabilizers, such as unemployment insurance schemes, results in pro-cyclical discretionary responses (Braun and di Gresia, 2003). According to a study by Ferranti et al (2000), pro-cyclical fiscal policy accounts for 15 per cent more of the excess volatility of growth in Latin America as compared to East Asia.

Changes in the terms of trade and export conditions constitute another significant source of volatility and shocks. Middle-income countries have made significant efforts in the last two decades to open their economies to international trade.[13] Yet, 'the concentration of their exports (by markets and by products),[14] and the instability of their average prices mean that revenues from international sales fluctuate sharply' (UNDESA, 2007). This, in turn, affects the ability of fiscal policy to play its countercyclical role.

The absence of well-functioning countercyclical mechanisms is particularly problematic in MICs in an MDG achievement perspective. Middle-income countries, and significant segments of their populations, face the danger of downward mobility, *precisely* because they are not among the poorest. Among developing countries, during the period 1978 to 2003, it is the MIC group that demonstrates the greatest mobility, while low-income countries and high-income countries were less likely to change income categories. More interestingly, within these movements, 'there have been more cases of countries going down than in the other direction', indicating that social and economic progress can be reversed dramatically in MICs (World Bank, 2007, p6). The relative size of the private sector in the economy, which grows as income levels rise, also calls for stability to attract and retain foreign direct investment (FDI).

A large range of instruments exist, or have been proposed, to reduce the variability of key macroeconomic aggregates, most of these are more adapted to MICs than to low-income countries. These measures include proposals, such as safety nets, insurance schemes, social transfers (notably conditional cash transfer programmes) and employer-of-last-resort plans (Wray, 1997; Kregel, 2006). Macro-financial instruments can also be deployed to insure greater stability: debt management instruments, commodity stabilization funds, such as in Chile and Colombia, a stability and social investment facility for high debt emerging countries (Dervis and Birdsall, 2006), and other facilities including a countercyclical, financing mechanism (Loser, 2006). While vulnerability to shocks is a common characteristic of developing countries, technical, financial, institutional and political capacity constraints often undermine the ability of lower middle-income and low-income countries to design and implement countercyclical fiscal policies effectively.

FISCAL SPACE FOR SCALING UP

We now turn to Scenario 2, which has been the focus of much of the current debate on scaling up. While this debate has many dimensions we focus on the question, 'What would be the major factors that would inform the design of a fiscal policy for a development transformation that requires a scaling up in public investments?'. We acknowledge that there are several issues to do with the sustainability of such a scaling up. In this chapter our focus is specifically on the fiscal dimensions of scaling up (see Gupta et al, 2006; Heller et al, 2006).

The starting point for our analysis is the medium- to long-term fiscal framework. Typically this should reflect a government's policy perspective on how to achieve growth and, ideally, a costed plan that specifies a set of interventions that would need to be publicly financed to achieve the MDGs.

In the short run, countries embarking on such a development transformation will immediately face a number of challenges. Chief among these is the volatility and unpredictability of future aid flows. Macroeconomic stability considerations may, in the face of such volatility, tempt the authorities to pose stringent limits on the amount of aid that they are willing to programme into the fiscal framework for spending. In addition, short-term financial programming will need to take account of the related 'absorption-spending'[15] issues that arise when governments seek to coordinate fiscal, monetary and exchange rate policies when seeking to implement a strategy based on scaled up aid financing.

The short-term macroeconomic challenges of scaling of aid are central issues at the heart of the present policy debate on financing for development (Gupta et al, 2006). The focus in this chapter is more on the long-term implications of scaling up investment to achieve the MDGs. In this context, there are two important issues:

1   The above short-term considerations point to the fact that no financing strategy that envisions financing MDG-related interventions, based on scaled up aid flows *in perpetuity*, is sustainable.
2   In the long term, fiscal sustainability will, therefore, depend critically on the extent to which a country's macroeconomic condition will allow it to define a credible 'exit' strategy from aid-financed fiscal spending on the development transition. This implies that a fiscal strategy that defines the path for such an exit is a necessary condition for the fiscal sustainability of a long-term financing strategy to secure a development transformation.

A recent report by the Independent Evaluation Office (IEO) of the IMF (IMF, 2007) makes the case for a rather different policy approach to the short-term sustainability challenges than has hitherto been the case.[16] It suggests that some IMF programmes with low-income countries may be unduly restricting the spending of additional aid. But the results vary a lot from country to country. According to the IEO, at the margin, an IMF programme targets only 27 cents of each additional dollar of aid for use towards higher public expenditures, that is, a fiscal expansion. The rest is supposed to go to building up external reserves or paying down domestic debt.

The findings of the IEO report are even more striking when this overall result is disaggregated according to countries' initial conditions. It turns out that what the IMF recommends for the use of additional aid depends critically on a country's initial conditions:

•   If external reserves are low (less than 2.5 months of imports), virtually all aid is programmed to be saved in the form of higher reserves.
•   If reserves are above this level, but domestic macro conditions fail a very high test of stability, which the IEO proxies by a low inflation rate, the vast bulk of extra aid (85 cents of each dollar) is channelled to reducing domestic debt.
•   Only if reserves are high and domestic macro conditions are highly 'stable' is most additional aid programmed for higher fiscal spending.

Goldsbrough (2007) argues that the share allocated to reserves should depend on how long the higher aid flows are expected to last. He also points out that the exact linkages between domestic debt reduction and macro-objectives, such as economic growth, are opaque and highly country dependent. It is impossible to say what the appropriate trade-off is without some analysis of how effective additional public spending would be, which in most cases has not been done. In other words, short-term targeting of prudential indicators, such as domestic debt/GDP ratios, to restrain government spending tends to result in underutilization of aid resources. This underestimates the real returns from additional public spending.

The case for analysing the impact of additional public spending on outcome variables (growth and human development) is of course all the more compelling in the long term. When a country embarks on a development transformation that is marked by (a) clearly identifiable development outcomes, such as those embodied by the MDGs, (b) an agreed set of interventions that collectively can assure the achievement of these outcomes, if adequately financed, and (c) a widespread acknowledgement that aid financed public expenditures would be required to secure the development transformation, then what would be the desirable features of a fiscal framework that supports such a development transformation?

The fiscal space conjecture

An important difference in the long run is, of course, that the impact of public expenditures on desired outputs, such as growth and capital accumulation, is endogenous. If this endogenous impact is positive then, *ceteris paribus*, short-term negative impacts on indicators of macroeconomic stability will need to be *managed* rather than *avoided* as long as indicators show that the long-run impact of such an expansion is positive. In other words, the desirability of the fiscal expansion must be assessed by weighing the cost of short-run instability against the expected long-term benefits.

Why is this not done, typically, and what is the reason that, as pointed out by Goldsbrough (2007) and others, current fiscal frameworks tend to underestimate the returns from well-targeted publicly financed interventions to secure tangible development outcomes, such as the MDGs, despite there being considerable evidence to the contrary? In a separate paper (Roy et al, 2006) we have shown that an important reason for this is what we term the 'fiscal space conjecture'.

This problem can be defined as follows: the outputs from a given set of public investments are *public goods*. Different public goods vary in the intensity to which they display *public good characteristics*.

The public finance literature identifies the *characteristics* of a public good[17] as:

- non rival consumption,
- non-excludability,
- jointness in supply.

Our conjecture then is:

For any public investment programme,[18] the more the public good characteristics of the public investment outputs, the less the precision[19] and predictability[20] of the *fiduciary* payback calculation. The less the public good characteristics, the more the precision and predictability of the *fiduciary* payback calculation.

And:

For any public investment programme the more the public good characteristics of the public investment outputs, the more the precision and predictability of the *development* payback calculation. The less the public good characteristics, the less the precision and predictability of the *development* payback calculation.

The existence and magnitude of public good characteristics affect the two paybacks differently for three principal reasons:

1 Jointness in supply and non-rivalry in consumption make it difficult to assign unit costs and benefits to individual agent recipients. As a result proxies have to be used to calculate prices and returns.
2 Non-excludability makes individual price calculation or market-based revenue earmarking problematic.
3 The fiduciary returns from public investments with strong public good characteristics are dependent on the second order impacts on revenue and expenditure.

The above jointly reduce the precision and predictability of calculations of the expected direct fiduciary return of a public investment with strong public good characteristics. They do not, however, affect the precision and predictability of the calculation of the expected development payback. Conversely, the impact of public investments with weak public good characteristics on developmental outcomes tends to be second order in nature, reducing the precision and predictability of the calculation of the expected development payback.

The following example will illustrate the difference between *fiduciary payback* and *development payback*. Consider two public investment programmes:

1 a programme of public investments to increase the capacity of the country's airports;
2 a programme of public investments to reduce infant mortality.

Both programmes have quantifiable indicators. In the first case, the *fiduciary payback* from successful completion of the public investment programme is clearly calculable.

The returns from the capacity expansion are determinable, over time, by projecting demand and supply estimates and the marginal returns based on the impact of the enhanced capacity expansion (given projected demand) on price. In fiduciary terms the public sector returns have a clear impact on the fiscal deficit by enhancing revenue.

The development payback is not so clear. The same problems that render the empirical investigations into the relation between public investment and growth inconclusive (discussed under 'Definitions and uses of fiscal space', above) make forecasts of the positive impact of the public investment on development variables, growth, employment and so on, problematic (for simplicity we are ignoring negative externalities in all cases). In this circumstance one can be more confident of the predictability and precision of the fiduciary calculus than of the development calculus.

In the case of the infant mortality programme, the story is reversed. Medical and public health expertise can identify which interventions would be necessary (schools, hospitals, doctors, drugs and teachers) to ensure that a given public investment programme would reduce infant mortality. 'Needs assessments' (Millennium Project, 2005) exercises and MDG-based simulation models, like the World Bank's 'Maquette for MDG simulation' (Lofgren and Diaz-Bonilla, 2006) can specify the sequencing and timeframe for such exercises.[21] As long as the exercises are credible and comprehensive one can be reasonably confident of the development payback, that is, a reduction in infant mortality within a specified timeframe.

The fiduciary payback is more difficult to calculate. There is no stream of direct financial returns flowing from this programme. Any returns would come through positive impacts on revenue and GDP and would affect the fiscal deficit through those channels. Perhaps a more healthy population in the long run will also generate expenditure savings on the health budget. But it is clear that the predictability and precision of fiduciary payback forecasts will be poorer than those for the development payback in this case.[22]

This simple example illustrates and explains our fiscal space conjecture. It also explains why, despite the political acknowledgement of the human development agenda and the specification of quantifiable development goals, there continues to be a tension between the need to secure fiduciary and developmental outcomes. Typically, policymakers resolve the issue by making one payback (development) contingent upon satisfactory achievement of the other (fiduciary), with the outcome that, as pointed out by Goldsbrough (2007) and others, the real returns from public investments tend to be underestimated. Conversely, proposals for long-term MDG-based national development strategies that provide a clear rationale for achieving the developmental outcomes, quantified by the MDG indicators, are faulted for being vague and imprecise on exactly how such ambitious scaled up plans could be implemented without adversely affecting the sustainability and solvency of the fiscal system. It is difficult to offer a ready made solution in the face of this diagnosis. What we shall attempt to do below is set out a 'roadmap' of the principal issues on which attention needs to be focused to bring about a satisfactory resolution.

First, it should be noted that the fiscal space conjecture does not deny the possibility that a harmonious solution exists in which fiscal paybacks and development paybacks are simultaneously secured. Indeed the contemporary history of successful development is precisely about simultaneously securing such paybacks. The fiduciary returns to improved economic development for China, Vietnam, Malaysia and South Korea can, in hindsight, be judged to have been perfectly compatible with the impressive strides in poverty reduction made by these countries. UNDP-commissioned research also demonstrates how the fiscal space conjecture was managed (if not entirely resolved) in Thailand (Chapter 9).

Second, it should be clear that as far as technical work on fiscal affairs goes, there have been very few systematic attempts to calculate the development payback of a scaled up public investment programme. This is so not because such a payback is difficult to calculate; rather, we feel it is due to a paradigmatic dogmatism regarding the role of public finance, which keeps it confined to a policy arena where the fiscal function is viewed as being essentially prudential in nature.[23] The caricature of the development-oriented health minister or the dynamic energy of an infrastructure minister pitted against the conservative prudential finance bureaucracy captures this almost cultural dogmatism among and about 'people of the fiscal system'. This will clearly have to change if progress is to be made.

It is in the above context that the argument that exit from aid is, in fact, a *necessary* condition to define a sustainable fiscal strategy becomes relevant. Sachs et al (2004) argue that the returns from investments in basic human capabilities (as embodied by the MDGs) are sufficiently high to justify very large increases in flows of development assistance. However the implicit assumption behind this argument is that multiple fiscal equilibria[24] exist, one in which the economy can be in a low-revenue/low-investment setting, and another in which the economy can be in a high-revenue/high-investment setting. Foreign aid helps the economy transition between these two equilibria, but the new situation can only be sustained through access to alternative sources of finance, in other words, through an increase in the other three quadrants of the diamond (see Figure 2.2).

For this reason, this chapter argues with Gupta et al (2006), that a strategy of exit from aid, or a strategy that plans for significantly diminished reliance on aid, is a *necessary operational condition* to defining a sustainable fiscal path for an aid-financed development transformation, underpinned by a long-term MDG-based national development strategy.

The above should not be interpreted simplistically to mean that aid-financed strategies need to be replaced by revenue-financed strategies. In a paper elsewhere (Roy and Heuty, 2005) we argue that, while the theoretical conclusions of poverty trap models demonstrate how capital scarcity can lead to underdevelopment, it is ultimately the impact of an ODA-led strategy on the domestic capital accumulation process that will determine the success of MDG-based national development strategies. We argue that ultimately there will need to be a transition to reliance on domestic resources to finance

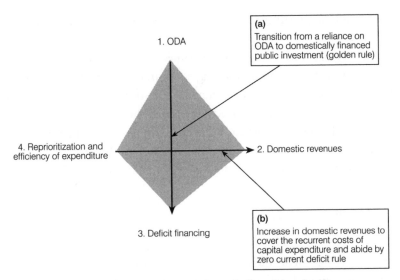

Figure 2.2 *'Scenario 2 country' – exit from aid and scaling up*

sustained expenditure on the interventions needed to *maintain* the development transformation secured by the initial ODA-financed rise in G/GDP ratios. We are *not*
arguing that such a transition will happen within the same time horizon as that in which
the development transformation is sought to be secured. Many countries that make
significant progress towards the MDGs by 2015 will continue to require ODA to
finance both capital and current expenditures to sustain their achievements. However,
fiscal stability would require a quantification of the extent to which, and the timeframe
in which, consumption expenditures would be increasingly financed through domestic
revenues, while investment needs would be increasingly met through a combination of
(mainly) domestic and (some) international borrowing.

Fiscal rules and indicators for the long term

Having, therefore, identified the broad dimensions of a long-term fiscal framework
within which to underpin a development transformation, such as that implied by an
MDG-based national development strategy, we proceed in this section to outline possible rules and indicators that would help operationalize such a long-term fiscal
framework.

Economic theory establishes that, *ex post*, investment (I) equals savings (S):

$$I \equiv S$$

In the context of economic development, the investment savings identity has traditionally been interpreted as an important constraint for securing development finance. This
has often resulted in an emphasis on short-term macroeconomic stability at the expense

of investment and long-term economic growth (Development Committee 2006, 2007; Roy et al, 2006).

A dynamic approach to savings and investment provides a powerful understanding of the accumulation process underpinning economic growth and has major implications for economic policymaking in low-income countries. An inter-temporal approach to the investment/savings dynamic needs to address the following analytical challenge to explain *how* equilibrium is achieved. What channels link investment to human development outcomes, including (a) economic growth, and (b) the MDGs?

The inter-temporal investment-savings entity can be written as:

$$\sum I_t \equiv \sum S_t, \forall\, t = 0, 1, 2, \ldots t - 1, t$$

This allows for savings/investment imbalances to exist temporarily, but for closure to occur over the time period t. Alternatively this can be expressed as d(S) = d(I) for all t, such that the above holds.

Let S = (Y − C) +A. That is, there are no foreign capital inflows, but there is foreign aid (A). C is total consumption (of domestic and foreign goods and services) and Y is the GDP.

Now consider an expansion in foreign aid, entirely in grant form each year commencing in year 1 of an amount dA for (t−1) years. Assume the aid is absorbed and spent. In such a case d(S) = dA = d(I) for each time period 1, 2, …, t−1 (assuming Y and C are constant). At time t there is no aid. In such a case, clearly either d(I) must adjust downwards or something must happen to d(S).

Given our assumption of no foreign capital inflows, that is d(A) = 0 at time period t, in order to sustain positive investment levels, d(S) must be the result of an increase in d(Y−C) – that is, there must be either GDP growth or reduced consumption.

This is intuitively the case for saying that an important determinant of the fiscal sustainability of an aid-financed strategy is the savings rate when there is exit from aid. And if reduced consumption is not desirable, then there needs to be growth in GDP (dY > 0) to an extent that if, *inter alia*, generates an increase in savings that is sufficient to substitute for the aid financing. The net result of higher levels of production *and* consumption, as well as higher rates of saving *and* investment relative to GDP, collectively constitutes a higher order *process* of capital accumulation at time t than was the case at time period 0. The alternative scenario is simply a reversion to the capital accumulation *process* that existed at time 0.

Allowing for foreign capital inflows merely broadens the argument, but does not change it from a macro-*fiscal* perspective (there are important implications from a balance of payments perspective, consideration of which is outside the scope of this chapter). It should be clear from the above that at time period t capital inflows would need to be higher, *ceteris paribus*, than domestic inflows to substitute for the increase in aid at time t. This would have the same end-result, a higher order capital accumulation process if the policy to attract capital succeeded and the reverse if it failed.

From the fiscal perspective the preceding is of direct interest especially when the 'I' referred to above is public investment. Assuming a fiscal rule that requires that the current deficit be zero, and, as a simplifying assumption, zero government saving, the aid-financed scaling up in public investment would need to be replaced over time through recourse to either domestic or foreign borrowing[25]. The decision on which path to take would be country specific, but domestic borrowing at reasonable interest rates has the great merit of not detracting from a country's GDP, though there are important implications for the *distribution* of GDP (Lerner, 1948). The point above is that, if for this or some other reason, the policy choice is to finance the exit from aid domestically, then it is a requirement that d(S) increase to allow this to happen at time t. For this to occur without negative effects on consumption, a higher order capital accumulation process would be required.

The examples of the Marshall Plan in France and the UK, and Thailand's recent experience, discussed above, empirically show the role of capital accumulation in the development process.

For all these reasons, therefore, the projected savings/GDP ratio is an important *indicator* of the sustainability of an aid financed development strategy. It is important to emphasize here that this ratio would serve as an *indicator* and *not* as an *objective* of fiscal policy. There is a vast body of theoretical and empirical research on the savings–growth relationship, and the position that policymakers wish to adopt on that debate would determine whether or not an increased savings rate is a desirable policy objective. The point we are making here is, simply, that the future projected rate of savings would provide an indicator as to the extent to which aid-financed capital expenditures could, in the future, be financed to scale using domestic resources. Such an indicator would allow us to asses the feasibility of using a 'golden rule' for a long-term fiscal framework, that is, that domestic borrowing be used exclusively to finance capital investments.

Second, *what* these investments are matters critically for fiscal sustainability. It is also important to specify further norms or rules on *which* investments should be financed. As we argued above, existing indicators ignore or lead to fiscal strategies that underestimate (Goldsbrough, 2007) the positive endogenous outcomes of public spending. But for this to be so, we must first be satisfied that the objects of government spending are those that are likely to lead to such positive, endogenous outcomes as the development transformation begins to take place. The most obvious case for being so convinced is when a credible plan exists to achieve a set of quantifiable development outcomes (such as the MDGs), and is operationalized by identifying a critical set of interventions that collectively would secure such outcomes, and make it both necessary and fiscally prudent to adequately calculate the development (as opposed to fiduciary) payback from enhanced fiscal space in the long term.

Chapter 5 of this book (by Rodríguez) finds, in this context, that the sustainability of fiscal expansions depends on the *types* of expenditures. If the development payback is sufficiently high, then deficit-financed public investments are compatible with fiscal sustainability and an expanded G/GDP ratio. In this context the authors find that (a) democracy and (b) education expenditures tend to have more sustainable fiscal expansions, with defence spending having a *negative* effect on sustainability. Clearly, therefore, the sustainability of a fiscal expansion is critically dependent on the *purposes* for which the expansion is undertaken. It is critical from the perspective of fiscal sustainability (not just welfare maximization) whether such investments happen in defence spending or education, for instance.

A corollary to the above argument is that norms and/or rules within the long-term fiscal framework that specified the type of financing would not encourage privileging infrastructure investments over other investments by excluding them from any fiscal sustainability calculus (see pages 32–38 for a detailed discussion). Instead we would argue that the case for a fiscal expansion would depend on the total package of investments in interventions that can be demonstrated to bring development payback (precisely and predictably, as defined earlier) measured by assessing the quantitative progress made as a result of such interventions to secure a set of development outcomes, such as the MDGs.

While these rules and indicators provide guidelines for fiscal space for securing the capital spending required for a development transformation, what about current (recurrent) spending?[26]

Most budgets classify current and capital expenditures separately. However the fiscal deficit does not make this distinction, being defined as the difference between current revenues and current *and* capital expenditures.[27] A fiscal rule that recognizes the distinction between current and capital expenditure line items in the budget will ensure that fiscal restraint does not discourage growth in the aggregate public capital *stock* (the corresponding on-budget *flow* variable being gross public sector capital formation). On this count, the current budget deficit/surplus would be a logical indicator to choose.

We, therefore, argue that a zero current deficit rule is an important long-term policy target for fiscal responsibility in a long-term fiscal framework. While some allowances may be made for current deficits during a development transformation, with external grant financing making up the shortfall, the long-term fiscal framework must plan for all such expenditures to be financed entirely out of current revenues. This is a non-negotiable requirement for a prudent long-term fiscal policy. It is salutary to note the importance that has been attached to securing this fiscal target by, for example, the finance minister of India, even in a situation where high growth and booming current account surpluses afford that country room to manoeuvre and where historic and present-day current deficits do not immediately threaten fiscal solvency.

In this context we would argue that it is important to follow strictly the present definition of what items are treated as current (or recurrent) expenditures in the economic classification of public expenditures. Again it is necessary to emphasize this point because of the confusion between the definition of current expenditure as used in the economic classification and the argument that public expenditures are outputs 'constructed by the public sector that provide longer-term benefits to society over time' (Mintz and Smart, 2006), and should be treated as capital expenditures. For example, health services use labour, doctors and nurses, and buildings, hospitals and dispensaries to produce health services. The joint output, health services, yields returns in the future through higher income paid to a healthier workforce. Why then should public expenditures on teachers or nurses' salaries not be treated as capital expenditures, given that they yield returns in the future?

There are two reasons for not doing this:

1 **The exhaustion principle** – the services provided by teachers and health workers are 'exhausted' or fully delivered when their job is done (teaching children, treating patients).
2 **The recurrent financing need principle** – the services do not, on their own, create future human capital, which is created through a combination of capital inputs (such as hospitals) to which we apply current inputs (such as doctors and nurses) on a continuous and recurrent basis, which is why current expenditures are sometimes referred to as recurrent expenditures.

Jointly, when these principles are applied, then, it means that those inputs that would require current (or recurrent) financing to produce the same output (health services) should be treated as current expenditures. It is for this reason that depreciation is also treated as a recurrent expenditure. There are accounting alternatives to secure predictable funding for such expenditures that can be implemented if that is the wish of policymakers. For example, a trust fund whose income would pay teachers' salaries could be created, whereby the income from the fund would pay the salaries even while the corpus of the fund could, in principle, be accounted for as capital spending; however, this would not allow expenditure items that are classified as current expenditures to be excluded from such classification.

Such a rule has the added merit of acting as an automatic stabilizer on domestic borrowing, when supplemented by rigorous procedures that require the recurrent consequences of capital expenditure (RCCE) to be calculated and accounted for in budget estimates as a prior condition for clearing capital expenditure proposals.[28]

Thus, the above rules and indicators would provide the long-term complement to short-term assessments of fiscal solvency and sustainability. Replacing the fiscal deficit as the summary indicator of fiscal prudence with a more stringent zero current deficit rule liberates space for exit from aid to a degree consistent with the availability of future domestic resources, as signalled by the forecasted savings/GDP ratio. The macroeconomic analysis that informed the design of such a fiscal framework would therefore need to specify the future impact of the development transformation on the revenue base and the savings rate to enable fiscal policymakers to assess the extent to which scaling up plans were sustainable in the long term. In the long term, the sustainability would be contingent on the availability of *domestic* fiscal space to finance government's current and capital expenditures and would be operationalized using fiscal rules that would be very different from those used to assess short-term sustainability and solvency. They would not contradict the short-term rules; in the short run it would remain important whether short-term government fiscal solvency, Dutch Disease effects, absorption spending issues and so on were being managed or not. However, it would remove a major policy impediment to assessing the sustainability of scaling up from a long-term perspective, the use of short-term rules and analytical frameworks to assess the long-term availability of fiscal space with the consequent underestimation of the real economic payback from a well-designed and implemented strategy to secure development transformations, such as those implied by the MDGs.

CONCLUSION

The Millennium Declaration posed a challenge to the development policy community, to change the lives of the world's poor and vulnerable through a global partnership that would collectively implement a development transformation necessary for this purpose. The MDGs presented a concrete set of time-bound development targets to secure this transformation, with the Monterrey Consensus reaffirming the global commitment to securing and deploying resources for this purpose. In this chapter we have argued that securing such a development transformation while assuring fiscal sustainability provides the answer to the question of, 'Fiscal space for *what*?', which is also necessary to address the question, 'Is fiscal space sustainable?'. For this reason, in this chapter we have moved away from an accounting and incremental definition of fiscal space towards a policy-oriented definition.

Following the IMF, we view a sustainable fiscal policy as one that (a) does not undermine fiscal sustainability in the long-term by jeopardizing the long-term fiduciary sustainability of the fiscal system, and (b) that is not charity based or relying on exogenous highly volatile sources of external finance. We illustrate the endogeneity of the question, 'Fiscal space for what?' by illustrating the different implications in two quite common development scenarios. Both scenarios have a common development objective, to secure financing for interventions that are targeted to secure *a specific set of development objectives*, such as the MDGs. The first scenario is one in which the achievement of internationally agreed development goals involves a strategy for inclusive growth. Here the focus is on reducing income inequalities and increasing the access of the poor and vulnerable to public goods through a combination of efficiency improvements and expenditure switching policies, and protecting the development process from structural shocks through active countercyclical fiscal policies. In this situation, it is the *stabilization* and *allocation* roles of fiscal policy that are at the cutting-edge of pro-development policy formulation. The second scenario is one in which the objective of fiscal policy is to finance a permanent increase in public investment to secure the same internationally agreed development goals. In this context the *growth* and *allocation* functions of fiscal policy are at the cutting edge of pro-development policy formulation.

In the short run, countries embarking on development transformations of the type implied in Scenario 2 face a number of challenges, including aid volatility, Dutch Disease effects, and fiscal, monetary and exchange rate policy coordination to manage 'absorption spending' issues. However, the negative consequences of these effects on short-term stability need to be *managed* to mitigate their impact on public financing of interventions to secure the development transformation, rather than considered as binding constraints on securing the financing available for such transformations. In other words, the desirability of the fiscal expansion must be assessed by weighing the costs of short-run instability against the expected long-term benefits. Further, in countries where the scaling up is initially financed by ODA, a strategy to exit from aid becomes operationally necessary to secure long-term fiscal sustainability.

Existing analytical frameworks are of limited use in this context and there continues to be a tension between the need to secure fiduciary and developmental outcomes. Typically, policymakers resolve the issue by making one payback (development) contingent upon satisfactory achievement of the other (fiduciary), with the outcome that the real returns from public investments tend to be underestimated. It is therefore necessary to define better long-term indicators and in this context we propose three types of indicators:

1   The future projected rate of savings would serve as an indicator (but not necessarily a policy objective) of the extent to which aid-financed capital expenditures could, in the future, be financed using domestic resources. Such an indicator would allow us to assess the feasibility of using a 'golden rule' for a long-term fiscal framework.
2   It is also important to specify further norms or rules on *which* investments should be financed. A 'needs assessment' exercise helps specify such investments.
3   A fiscal rule that recognizes the distinction between current and capital expenditure line items in the budget will ensure that fiscal restraint does not discourage growth in the aggregate public capital *stock* (the corresponding on-budget *flow* variable being gross public sector capital formation). For a long-term fiscal framework we argue that a zero current deficit rule is an important long-term policy target for fiscal responsibility. On this count, the current budget deficit/surplus would be a logical indicator to choose. Targeting a zero current deficit would also act as an automatic stabilizer on borrowing for investment thereby reinforcing the golden rule. Allowances would need to be made for temporary deviations from this rule. However, a non-negotiable requirement for a prudent long-term fiscal policy is that

such a rule should be enforced across the time horizon of policymaking, so that the trend is towards a zero fiscal deficit over the time horizon of a development strategy, with domestic revenues replacing ODA budget support.

Our proposals are not, by any means, less fiscally disciplinary than those currently in use. They are of course very different and more suited to long-term fiscal targeting for a development transformation. A hard current budget deficit rule imposes real limits on runaway government spending and a savings indicator imposes a stringent policy requirement: that either the economy grows sufficiently fast in the long term to allow the development payback to replace aid-financed scaling up, or the economy reverses course with lower levels of private absorption to pay for the scaling up in public good provisioning, substituting for aid. There are two alternatives we do not name here. The first, a reversal on the Millennium Declaration and a world in which human development in many countries does not rise to meet the expectations expressed at the Millennium Summit. The second is continued reliance on volatile, unpredictable and exogenous international charity to finance development outcomes into the foreseeable future.

A long-term fiscal framework is meant to complement, not replace, existing fiduciary assessments focused on short-term fiscal solvency and sustainability. Indeed the latter are essential prerequisite inputs for the former. However, the absence of such instruments does not mean that an exercise, where such short-term instruments are used for want of anything better, is either appropriate or desirable. Institutionally the mandate and expertise of the chief dispenser of technical advice on fiscal affairs, the IMF, is focused on short-term fiscal analysis and on sound public financial management. To operationalize the long-term perspective required to meet the development financing challenge posed by the MDGs, and to respond to the Monterrey Consensus, it would be important to devise an institutional arrangement in which long-term development payback assessments conducted by UN development agencies inform IMF technical and surveillance work, particularly Article IV activities, on a mandatory basis. A collaborative effort using IMF expertise on fiduciary instruments and the UN system expertise in demonstrating the long-term human development payback from well-designed public investment programmes, in equal partnerships with other development partners and developing country groupings, is therefore a matter of pressing urgency.

ANNEX 2.1 — THE FISCAL SPACE DIAMOND
AS A DIAGNOSTIC TOOL: THE CASE OF SIERRA LEONE

The fiscal space diamond is used as a diagnostic tool to widen a government's policy options. It provides a snapshot of the country's key macro-fiscal issues through an assessment of the structuring elements and key challenges of each of the diamond's four pillars (ODA, domestic revenues, deficit financing and reprioritization, and efficiency of expenditures). It also helps identify the endogenous or exogenous nature of the various options and to draw policy conclusions. The criteria for determining whether an option is endogenous or exogenous, short-term or long-term, are not generic to a specific policy option. The judgement is based on the country's context.

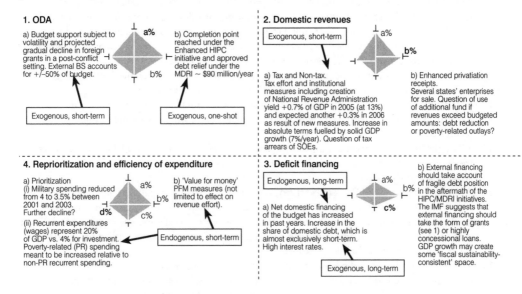

Figure 2.A1 *The fiscal space diamond: Sierra Leone*

NOTES

1   This chapter was peer reviewed by Paul Ladd, Policy Advisor, UNDP and Anuradha Seth, Policy Advisor, UNDP. We would also like to acknowledge the research assistance of Patricia Caraballo.

2   Rathin Roy is a Public Finance Advisor, Antoine Heuty a Public Finance Economist, and Emmanuel Letouzé a Research Analyst with the Poverty Group, Bureau for Development Policy, UNDP, New York. The views and interpretations in this chapter are those of the authors and do not represent the views and policies of UNDP.

3   The same paper provides an important example of this endogeneity, 'savings realization failures'. That is, macroeconomic, social and political factors inhibiting the channelling of savings for private and public investment.

4   The short term refers to the budget cycle and existing two- to three-year development frameworks, such as PRSPs. The long term refers to the period within which a development

transformation (embedded in a set of development targets) can occur. While the development transformation can take place over a defined time horizon (typically 10 to 20 years) the long-term fiscal framework goes beyond the timeframe required for such change to happen.

5   These terms are defined in the section 'Fiscal space for scaling up'.

6   Though it would if spent on tradable versus non-tradable goods; but that is not immediately pertinent in this context. Dutch Disease is a common term in fiscal policy that tries to explain the apparent relationship between the exploitation of natural resources and a decline in the manufacturing sector, combined with moral fallout. The theory is that an increase in revenues from natural resources will de-industrialize a nation's economy by raising the exchange rate, which makes the manufacturing sector less competitive and public services entangled with business interests. The term is related to deindustrialization in The Netherlands after the discovery of natural gas reserves.

7   Causing GDP to double every 8 to 10 years for almost 40 years.

8   ODA represented 0.8 per cent of gross national income between 1960 and 2004, on average.

9   This does not preclude structural changes in tax policy that impact the relative incidence of taxation. In fact, such changes may complement other pro-development policies if they improve distributional equity, though this is not a requirement for a pro-development fiscal policy.

10 Many countries in this category are heavily indebted and have yet to receive debt relief, which would provide a significant, albeit one time, increase in fiscal space.

11 The tax effort of a government can be assessed by looking at the difference between the expected and the actual ratio of tax to GDP (Chambas et al, 2006).

12 For instance, an electricity shutdown due to a shortfall of fuel imports is potentially more harmful in a major industrial city than in a rural village employing traditional farming techniques.

13 '67 of the 84 middle-income countries for which the necessary data is available are members of the World Trade Organization, and 14... are at different stages in the accession process' (UNDESA, 2007, p32).

14 According to the World Bank (UNDESA, 2007, p32), 'their export patterns are concentrated in two ways, (i) by markets; at least 29 countries ship more than 50 per cent of their exports to a single market, and (ii) by products; for 46 per cent of upper-middle-income countries and 37 per cent of lower-middle-income countries, the weighting of their first three export products exceeds 50 per cent of their total exports'.

15 The distinction between the 'absorption and spending' of aid refers to the use of the foreign exchange received and its utilization in the real economy. When official aid is transferred to an economy, the foreign exchange accrues in the first instance to central bank reserves, while the recipient government is credited with the counterpart value in domestic currency. Gupta et al (2006) define absorption and spending as follows:
   • Absorption is defined as a widening of the current account deficit (excluding aid), with increased imports financed by more aid, or possibly reduced exports as a result of higher domestic demand. Absorption depends on both domestic demand management and exchange rate policy.
   • Spending is defined as a widening of the fiscal deficit (excluding aid) due to additional aid, as a result of higher government expenditures or lowered taxation.

16 We are only quoting this report to illustrate the problem, not to argue that the IMF restrictions are the only (or even the principle) factor causing volatility and unpredictability.

17 Here we define public goods following Atkinson and Stiglitz (1987), who define the characteristics more broadly than the original (Samuelson, 1954) definition. We are trying here to avoid using terminology, such as 'pure' and 'impure' public goods, 'quasi' public goods and so on, since no universally accepted technical lexicon exists. For our purposes, 'public good characteristics' suffices. We make the simplifying assumption that the characteristics are additively separable. We also assume that all goods can be rank ordered as possessing higher or lower observable public good characteristics.

18 A note of caution is in order here. There are some public goods where the desired outcomes cannot be quantified. The conjecture would not hold for these. Examples include an improved security environment, better foreign relations and greater religious freedom. Such outcomes would need to be proxied by specific quantifiable indicators (lower crime, fewer violent conflicts because of religion and so on.).

19 By *precision* we mean the degree of expected error in *ex ante* calculations of payback.

20 By *predictability* we mean the degree of observed error in *ex post* payback outcomes.

21 A 'needs assessment' compares a country's current situation with the MDG targets and identifies the combination of public investments that would enable the country to achieve the MDGs by 2015. This needs assessment should identify the particular barriers that prevent faster economic development and greater progress towards poverty reduction, and establish a set of specific interventions that address and remove these obstacles. A needs assessment thus provides a methodology for identifying key interventions that require a significant scaling up through 2015 to achieve the MDGs. See Millennium Project (2005, p51 and Chapter 13). The Millennium Project has applied its approach in Bangladesh, Cambodia, Dominican Republic, Ghana, Kenya, Tajikistan, Tanzania, Uganda and Yemen. The World Bank 'maquette' has been applied in Ethiopia, Nicaragua and Peru.

22 Note that both cases are *ceteris paribus*. Poor implementation, absorptive capacity constraints and so on, would have negative impacts on predictability and precision, but there is no reason to believe that such negative impacts would be dependent upon the public good characteristics of the public investment output.

23 We recognize that development is a risky business with potentially serious prudential and fiduciary consequences when things go wrong, as they all too often do. The fact that it is possible to achieve the MDGs by 2015, should donors make good on their ODA commitments, is, in itself, not a cause for celebration. Structural shocks, volatile financing for a scaled up public investment programme, and even natural disasters and political conflicts can detract from expected results. These risks and uncertainties have direct and tangible fiduciary impacts that can be of a magnitude that would threaten or even reverse achievements on the MDG front. Such shocks and volatilities, more generally, a combination of random events due to uncertainty that, collectively, have a negative structural impact on macro-fiscal fundamentals, such as the debt stock, can, over time, seriously reduce the capacity of a country to engage in structural transformation to achieve development results of the type called for by the MDGs. It is therefore important not to assume these away but to devise instruments to mitigate their impact.

24 The alternative assumption is, of course, that aid will be required in perpetuity to allow countries to stay permanently above a single permanent equilibrium. An assumption we reject as too unrealistically imperial to hold water.

25 There are, of course, important balance of payments implications of foreign (including concessional) borrowing that impact on debt sustainability. We acknowledge this constraint but treat it as exogenous within the scope of this chapter.

26 Current spending is defined per the economic classification as all government consumption expenditure.

27 There is, of course, the issue of which expenditures fall under each category, a point we take up later in this section.

28 It is important to make annual revisions of the RCCE that are subject to significant changes over time.

REFERENCES

Agenor, P-R. and Neanidis, K. C. (2006) 'The allocation of public expenditure and economic growth', Discussion Paper Series, Centre for Growth and Business Cycle Research, Manchester

Akitoby, B., Clements, B., Gupta, S. and Inchauste, G. (2004) 'The cyclical and long-term behavior of government expenditures in developing countries', IMF Working Papers 04/202, International Monetary Fund, Washington DC

Alesina, A. (1998) 'The political economy of macroeconomic stabilizations and income inequality: Myths and reality', in V. Tanzi and K. Chu (eds) *Income Distribution and High-Quality Growth*, MIT Press, Cambridge, MA, pp299–326

Anderson, E., de Renzio, P. and Levy, S. (2006) 'The role of public investment in poverty reduction: theories, evidence and method', UNDP and Overseas Development Institute Working Paper 263, ODI, London

Atkinson, A. and Stiglitz, J. (1987) *Lectures on Public Economics*, McGraw-Hill, New York

Bohl, M. T. (1996) 'Some international evidence on Wagner's Law', *Public Finance*, vol 51, pp185–200

Bouillon, C. and Buvinic, M. (2003) 'Inequality, exclusion and poverty in Latin America and the Caribbean: Implications for development', Inter-American Development Bank document presented at the Seminar on Social Cohesion in Latin America, Brussels, 5–June 2003

Braun, M. and di Gresia, L. (2003) 'Towards effective social insurance in Latin America: the importance of countercyclical fiscal policy', Inter-American Development Bank Research Department Working Paper 487, presented at the seminar 'Dealing with Risk: Implementing Employment Policies Under Fiscal Constraints', Milan, 23 March 2003

Bruno, M. and Easterly, W. (1998) 'Inflation crises and long-run growth', *Journal of Monetary Economics*, vol 41, pp3–26

Bruno, M., Ravallion, M. and Squire, L. (1998) 'Equity and growth in developing countries: old and new perspectives on the policy issues', in V. Tanzi and K. Chu (eds) *Income Distribution and High-Quality Growth*, MIT Press, Cambridge, MA, pp117–146

Chambas, G., Brun, J-F., Combes, J. L., Dulbecco, P., Gastambide, A., Guérineau, S., Guillaumont, S. and Rota Graziosi, G., (2006) 'Assessing fiscal space in developing countries', Concept Paper commissioned by UNDP, CERDI, Clermont-Ferrand, www.undp.org/poverty/prmgmt.htm

Chang, T. (2002) 'An econometric test of Wagner's Law for six countries based on cointegration and error-correction modeling techniques', *Applied Economics*, vol 34, pp1157–1169

Chu, K-Y., Davoodi, H. and Gupta, S. (2000) 'Income distribution and tax, and government social spending policies in developing countries', in G. A. Cornia (ed) *Inequality Growth and Poverty in an Era of Liberalization and Globalization*, Oxford University Press, Oxford

Commission for Africa (2005) *Our Common Interest*, Commission for Africa, London, www.commissionforafrica.org/english/report/introduction.html

Dervis, K. and Birdsall, N. (2006) 'A stability and social investment facility for high debt countries', Working Paper 77, Center for Global Development, Washington DC

Development Committee (2006) 'Fiscal policy for growth and development – an interim report', paper presented at the Development Committee Meeting, Washington DC

Development Committee (2007) 'Fiscal policy for growth and development – further analysis and lessons from country case studies', paper presented at the Development Committee Meeting, Washington DC

Easterly, W. (2002) 'Inequality does cause underdevelopment: new evidence', Working Paper 1, Center for Global Development, Washington DC

Eichengreen, B. (1995) *Europe's Post War Recovery*, Cambridge University Press, Cambridge

Estache, A. (2006) 'Infrastructure: A survey of recent and upcoming issues', World Bank Working Paper Version 2.0, World Bank, Washington DC

Fan, S., Zhang, L. and Zhang, X. (2002) 'Growth, inequality, and poverty in rural China: The role of public investments', Research Report 125, International Food Policy Research Institute (IFPRI), Washington DC

Ferranti, D. de, Perry, G., Gill, I. and Servén, L. (2000) *Securing Our Future in a Global Economy*, World Bank, Washington DC

Ferranti, D. de, Perry, G., Ferreira, F. and Walton, M. L. (2004) *Inequality in Latin America: Breaking with History?*, World Bank, Washington DC

Gavin, M. and Perotti, R. (1997) 'Fiscal policy in Latin America', in B. S. Bernanke and J. Rotemberg (eds) *NBER Macroeconomics Annual 1997*, MIT Press, Cambridge, MA

Gericke, C. (2004) 'Financing health care in Egypt: Current issues and options for reform', paper presented at the Global Medical Forum Middle East Summit, Beirut, 11–13 May

Goldsbrough, D. (2007) 'The IMF and constraints on spending aid', One Pager No. 34, UNDP International Poverty Centre, Brasília

Gottret, P. and Schieber, G. (2006) *Health Financing Revisited. A Practitioner's Guide*, World Bank, Washington DC

Gottschalk, R. (2000) 'Growth and poverty reduction in developing countries: How much external financing will be needed in the new century', paper prepared for Multilateral Development Banks project commissioned by the Ministry of Foreign Affairs, Sweden

Gupta, S., Powell, R. and Yang, Y. (2006) *Macroeconomic Challenges of Scaling Up Aid to Africa. A Checklist for Practitioners*, International Monetary Fund, Washington DC

Heller, P. S. (2005) 'Understanding fiscal space', IMF Policy Discussion Paper, International Monetary Fund, Washington DC

Heller, P. S., Katz, M., Debrun, X., Thomas, T., Koranchelian, T. and Adenauer, I. (2006) 'Making fiscal space happen! Managing fiscal policy in a world of scaled-up aid', WIDER Research Paper No. 2006/125, UNU-WIDER, Helsinki, Finland

IMF (International Monetary Fund) (2004) *Public Investment and Fiscal Policy*, IMF, Washington DC

IMF (2007) *An Evaluation of the IMF and Aid to Sub-Saharan Africa*, IMF Independent Evaluation Office, Washington DC

Klitgaard, R. (2004) 'On infrastructure and development', paper prepared for the Planning Workshop for Infrastructure in East Asia: The Way Forward, Manila, 15–16 January

Kregel, J. A. (2006) 'ELR as an alternative development strategy', speech at the Levy Economics Institute for the Conference on Employment Guarantee Policies: Theory and Practice, New York, 13–14 October

Langenbrunner, J. C. (2005) *Health Care Financing and Purchasing in ECA: An Overview of Issues and Reforms*, World Bank, Washington DC

Leipziger, D., Fay, M., Wodon, Q. and Yepes, T. (2003) 'Achieving the MDGs – the role of infrastructure', Policy Research Working Paper 3163, World Bank, Washington DC

Lerner, A. (1948) 'The burden of the national debt', in *Income, Employment, and Public Policy: Essays in Honor of Alvin H. Hansen. Annals of the American Academy of Political and Social Science*, vol. 260, *Postwar Reconstruction in Western Germany (Nov.)*, pp230–231

Lin, C-A. (1995) 'More evidence on Wagner's Law for Mexico', *Public Finance*, vol 2, pp267–277

Lofgren, H. and Diaz-Bonilla, C. (2006) 'MAMS: A framework for analyzing MDGs and poverty reduction strategies', DECPG, World Bank, paper presented during the 5th PEP Research Network General Meeting, 18–22 June 2006, Addis Ababa

Loser, C. (2006) 'A countercyclical financing mechanism for developing countries: Wishful thinking or policy requirement?', paper prepared for the G-24 Meeting in Singapore, September, G-24, Washington DC

Lynch, F. (1997) *France and the International Economy*, Routledge, London

Millennium Project, (2005) *Investing in Development: A Practical Plan to Achieve the MDGs*, Report to the UN Secretary General, Earthscan, New York

Mintz, J. M. and Smart, M. (2006) 'Incentives for public investment under fiscal rules', Policy Research Working Paper 3860, World Bank, Washington DC

Murthy, N. R. V. (1993) 'Further evidence on Wagner's Law for Mexico: An application of cointegration analysis', *Public Finance*, vol 48, pp77–85

Musgrave, R. A. (1959) *Theory of Public Finance: A Study in Public Economy*, McGraw-Hill, New York

Ndulu, B., van Niekerk, L. K. and Reinikka, R. (2005) 'Infrastructure, regional integration and growth in sub-Saharan Africa', in J. J. Teunissen and A. Akkerman (eds) *Africa in the World Economy: The National, Regional and International Challenges*, FONDAD, The Hague

Payne, J. and Ewing, B. (1996) 'International evidence on Wagner's hypothesis: A cointegration analysis', *Public Finance*, vol 51, no 2, pp258–74

Randel, J., German, T. and Ewing, D. (eds) (2004) *The Reality of Aid*, Zed Books, London

Rodrik, D. (1999) 'Where did all the growth go? External shocks, social conflict and growth collapse', *Journal of Economic Growth*, vol 4, no 4, pp385–412

Roy, R. and Heuty, A. (2005) 'Investing in development: The MDGs, aid and the sustainable capital accumulation', *Columbia School of International and Public Affairs Journal*, vol 58, no 2, pp161–176, available at www.undp.org/poverty

Roy, R., Heuty, A. and Letouzé, E. (2006) 'Fiscal space for public investment: towards a human development approach,' paper prepared for the G-24 Meeting in Singapore, September 2006, UNDP, New York, available at www.g24.org/rroy0906.pdf

Sachs, J., McArthur, J., Schmidt-Traub, G., Kruk, M., Bahadur, C., Faye, M. and McCord, G. (2004) 'Ending Africa's poverty trap', *Brookings Paper on Economic Activity*, no 1, pp117-240

Samuelson, P. (1954) 'The pure theory of public expenditure', *The Review of Economics and Statistics*, MIT Press, Cambridge, MA, pp387–389

Sen, A. (1995) 'The political economy of targeting', in D. Van de Walle and K. Neat (eds) *Public Spending and the Poor*, John Hopkins University Press, Baltimore, MD pp11–24

Suescún, R. (2005) 'Fiscal space for investment in infrastructure in Colombia', Policy Research Working Paper Series 3629, World Bank, Washington DC

Tanzi, V. (1998) 'Fundamental determinants of inequality and the role of government', IMF Working Paper 178, IMF, Washington DC

UNDESA (2007) 'Development cooperation with middle-income countries', chapter 1 of the Background Paper to the Special Conference on Development Cooperation with Middle-Income Countries, Madrid, 1–2 March 2007, United Nations, New York

UNDP (2005) *Human Development Report 2005*, UNDP, New York

UNDP and JICA (2005) *Making Infrastructure Work for the Poor*, UNDP, New York

Vos, R., Sánchez, M. V., and Inoue, K. (2007) 'Constraints to achieving the MDGs through domestic resource mobilization', DESA Working Paper 36, United Nations, New York

Wagner, A. (1911) 'Staat in nationalokonomischer hinsicht', in J. Conrad, L. Elster, W. Lexis and E. Loening (eds) *Handworterbuch der Staatswissenschaften*, 3rd edn, Book VII, pp743–745

Williamson, J. (2005) 'Policies to reduce the vulnerability of low-income countries' in J. Joost Teunissen and A. Akkerman (eds) *Protecting the Poor: Global Financial Institutions and the Vulnerability of Low-Income Countries*, FONDAD, The Hague, pp14–34

Willoughby, C. (2004) *How Important is Infrastructure for Pro-Poor Growth?*, OECD, Paris

World Bank (1996) *Morocco - Socio-economic Influence of Rural Roads: Fourth Highway Project*, World Bank, Washington DC

Wray, L. R. (1997) 'Government as employer of last resort,' Working Paper 213, The Levy Institute, Annandale-on-Hudson, NY

3

Fiscal Space for Public Investment: Towards a Human Development Approach[1]

Rathin Roy, Antoine Heuty and Emmanuel Letouzé

INTRODUCTION

A development transformation requires a sustained period of increased investment spending to support economic growth and deliver the basic services necessary to achieve human development. While both public and private investments have a key role to play in this context, the state, and therefore public investment, has a key role to play in kickstarting growth, reducing poverty and providing the capital goods and investments needed to secure human development objectives. In short, a development transformation requires a major scaling up in public investment.

Yet the current fiscal rules used to assess fiscal solvency and sustainability limit the scope for such a scaling up. This has important human development implications. This chapter examines the basis for this argument and explores the analytical and policy possibilities that can be used to create a fiscal framework that enables countries to engage in development transformations that require public investment-led scaling up.

This issue is of first importance with international agreement on a set of quantified, time-bound indicators, the MDGs, that were agreed as key international development objectives (United Nations, 2000). The international community reemphasized its commitment to the MDGs at the 2005 Global Summit that called for developing countries 'to adopt, by 2006, and implement comprehensive national development strategies to achieve the internationally agreed development goals and objectives, including the Millennium Development Goals' (United Nations, 2005, paragraph 22a).

The next section presents a summary of the evidence that restrictive fiscal targets used in fiscal reform programmes, chiefly the fiscal deficit and the debt/GDP ratio, are an important reason for the observed decline in public investment/GDP ratios (and in particular, infrastructure/GDP ratios) globally. The following section examines the analytical reasoning underlying the causal link between restrictive fiscal targets and reduced infrastructure spending, and the consequent case for advocating alternative fiscal rules that exclude public investments on infrastructure from deficit calculations. Then we present and assess arguments put forth by scholars and policymakers that the standard fiscal framework used by the Bretton Woods Institutions approach is unsuitable for an assessment of the long term development needs of a typical developing country. The subsequent section provides a review of the Bretton Woods Institutions' response to the new development challenge raised by the MDGs. The final section provides policy recommendations for the design of a fiscal framework that supports a human development-oriented, public investment strategy.

TRENDS IN PUBLIC INVESTMENT SPENDING AND THE DEVELOPMENT CHALLENGE

Public investment spending has been declining since the 1980s

The fact that public investment, and especially public infrastructure investment spending, has been declining as a share of GDP in the developing world over the past two decades, and during the 1980s in particular, has been well documented. The phenomenon has affected certain countries or regions and specific sectors more than others, but a general trend is clearly observable, with pronounced declines in public investment spending occurring during the 1980s in particular (see Figure 3.1).

These declines are particularly pronounced in low-income countries embarking on the development process that have a historically low stock of public and infrastructure assets. A particular example highlights the magnitude of the problem from a development perspective, even in a context where public investment is not declining. Total government spending on transportation and telecommunications in 43 developing countries increased by less than 7 per cent between 1980 and 1998 (Fan and Rao, 2003),[2] corresponding to an average 0.38 per cent increase per annum. At this pace, a given sub-Saharan country that, in 1980, aimed at doubling the mileage of its road network would not achieve its target until the year 2210.

Latin America is the region most affected by declining public investment (see Figure 3.2). In Brazil, for instance, public investment as a share of GDP fell from a 10 per cent record high in 1980 to 2.2 per cent in 2002 (Ferreira et al, 2005). In Argentina and Mexico, it reached a peak of 12 per cent of GDP in the late 1970s and early 1980s, to

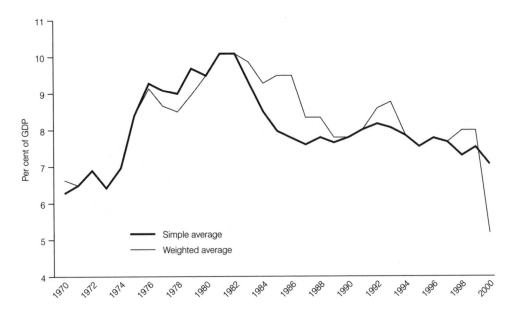

Source: Everhart and Sumlinski (2001)

Figure 3.1 *Public investment in developing countries, 1970–2000 (as a share of GDP)*

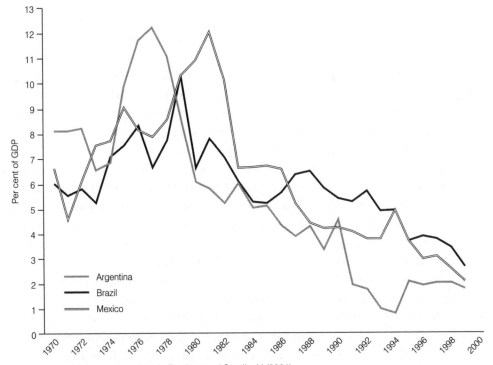

Source: Own elaboration from data in Everhart and Sumlinski (2001)

Figure 3.2 *Public investment in Argentina, Brazil and Mexico, 1970–2000
(as a share of GDP)*

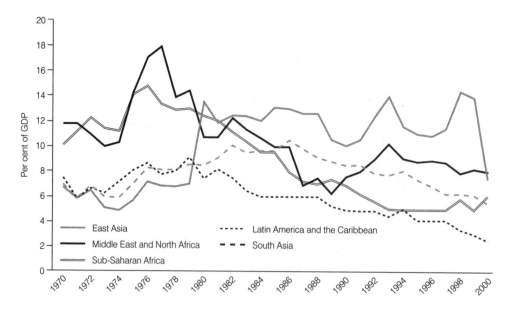

Source: Everhart and Sumlinski (2001)

Figure 3.3 *Public investment by developing region, 1970–2000*
(as a share of GDP, weighted averages)

fall over both subsequent decades, in spite of a slight and temporary increase at the end of the 1990s, to a low of 2 per cent in 2000 (IMF, 2004).

Similar trends are observable in East Asia, the Middle East and West Africa, and sub-Saharan Africa. In Asia as a whole, public investment over GDP decreased from 10 per cent to 7 per cent between 1980 and 2000, while sub-Saharan Africa experienced a drop from 9 per cent to 6 per cent over the same period (see Figure 3.3).

Declines are even more striking in the specific case of public investment in infra-structure. Between 1980 and 2000, the share of total infrastructure spending globally fell from 2.1 per cent (1980) to 0.81 per cent (2000) of GDP. Currently the public sector accounts for 75 per cent of total infrastructure investments in developing countries, with levels ranging, on average, between 2 per cent and 4 per cent of GDP. In Africa, public investment in infrastructure fell dramatically (see Figure 3.4) in the second half of the 1990s. Given the very low existing stock of infrastructure assets in sub-Saharan Africa, this causes 'critical bottlenecks to economic growth, poverty reduction and reaching the MDGs' (Development Committee, 2005). The access rate to electricity in the whole continent is as low as 15 per cent, while it is 9 per cent for telecoms, 36 per cent for sanitation and 64 per cent for clean water, with significant differences across countries as well as between urban and rural areas (Estache, 2005). While data are scarce and subject to caution, there is little doubt that the inadequacy and poor quality of infra-structure in Africa constitute a significant impediment to growth and development in that region.

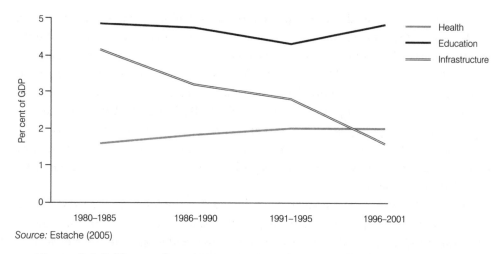

Source: Estache (2005)

Figure 3.4 *Public expenditure 1980–2001 (as a share of GDP) for 11 African countries*

The drop in public spending on infrastructure has been most significant in Latin America where the average ratio is only 1.6 per cent of GDP. The transportation sector was particularly hit in Brazil during the 1990s, since average public investments in roads in the 1990–1995 period amounted only to 25 per cent of the levels observed in the 1970–1975 period (Ferreira et al, 1998). This has resulted in significant 'infrastructure gaps' in these countries, in particular, when contrasted to the levels of infrastructure of the most successful East Asian economies (Calderón et al, 2003). According to the World Bank, logistics costs in the region represent 20 to 30 per cent of product value, in sharp contrast to an average 9 per cent for OECD countries, while the lack of adequate infrastructure services has direct detrimental effects on the poor's access to clean water and thus health (Development Committee, 2005).

Why has public investment spending declined?

Several related reasons are identified in the policy literature to explain these trends in public investment spending. The fiscal consolidation that took place in most developing regions in the 1980s and early 1990s as an outcome of the implementation of structural adjustment programmes (SAPs) is identified as a major causal factor for this decline. While SAPs were not specifically designed to curb public investment *per se*, it is argued that they typically had this effect. SAPs focused on securing macroeconomic stability and fiscal solvency by placing controls on fiscal deficits and on public debt. Empirically, constant or declining fiscal deficit/GDP ratios and debt/GDP ratios were used as overriding policy targets to be secured through fiscal consolidation. The choice of these policy priorities and fiduciary indicators greatly constrained the ability of governments to engage in public spending. This 'adjustment' fell disproportionately on public capital expenditures, including public investment in infrastructure. The IMF itself acknowledges that it 'has proved difficult to prevent public investment from bearing the brunt of the required fiscal adjustment' and that subsequently 'there is evidence that public investment has fallen because of fiscal adjustment', adding that on 'this count there are reasons to be concerned' (IMF, 2004, p9). The same report records that public investment cuts were 'on average more than three times larger than cuts in current spending during periods of fiscal adjustment in the 1980s' (IMF, 2004, p9). This point has also been noted in the policy literature on Latin America (Servén and Solimano, 1992; Calderón et al, 2003) where infrastructure investment cuts contributed to half or more of fiscal adjustment in five of the nine major Latin American countries over the 1980s and 1990s (Calderón et al, 2002).

Many policymakers and scholars have argued that the focus on the fiscal deficit, regardless of the composition of the expenditures, introduced a strong bias against expenditures characterized by high short-term costs and long-term returns, such as infrastructure projects. This view has also been expressed by heads of state such as President Lula of Brazil and President Musharraf of Pakistan, who underlined in 2004 'the need to find alternative solutions to fiscal adjustment that do not penalize infrastructure projects' (Estache, 2006, p15).

The argument is as follows. In the presence of fiscal rules that cap their fiscal deficit, governments are left with two options: either increase revenues or restrain expenditures. Increasing revenues is possible but is often not a plausible option in the short run, and it could also be associated with undesirable distortions resulting from increased tax rates. Reducing expenditures is thus the most straightforward and favoured means used to abide by the rule. The question is then, which expenditures should be cut or curbed?

The focus on the fiscal deficit in this circumstance 'puts both current and investment spending on an equal footing in the measurement of the deficit' (Perée and Välilä, 2005, p6). This directly affects the type of expenditure reductions that will be prioritized. On political considerations, governments have an incentive to protect spending on current programmes and transfers that ensure immediate economic and political benefits to their voters rather than invest in capital projects 'that yield social benefits for future voters' (Mintz and Smart, 2006, p3). Further, while interrupting an investment project appears relatively easy, 'it is neither a feasible nor in general a desirable option for wages, transfers, and interest payments which make up the bulk of current spending' (IMF, 2004, p13). Postponing the construction of an airport by one or two years, an investment that will only benefit the economy and voters in the long run, is obviously less politically costly than cutting civil servants' salaries.

A second set of factors is related to the level and patterns of foreign aid. Controversies about tied aid, concerns about corruption and evidence of 'white elephants' led to a growing scepticism among the donor community, and to a resulting shift away from infrastructure projects towards social development programmes (CARE International, 1999).

An important political economy discourse on the role of the development state had a major impact on mainstream views on the utility of public investment *per se* (Bhagwati, 1988; Lal, 1988; see Chang, 1994 and Roy, 1994 for a detailed review). This asserted that the state was generically incapable of operating 'at scale' and hence ambitious public investment programmes would be unproductive, as those in charge of the state would use the instruments at their disposal to maximize their own benefits and/or the benefits of the elites to whom they reported, rather than in the public interest. It was argued that the state would act as a 'predator' stifling and inhibiting private entrepreneurial energy.

In our view, the behavioural assumptions underlying the above paradigm fed into a central hypothesis underlying many SAPs: that private sector investment would compensate for the drop in public investment spending. SAPs, to a great extent, aimed to shape a macroeconomic framework that would better enable the private sector's involvement in areas hitherto reserved for the public sector. An obvious target was infrastructure, but, also, in many countries, capital spending for health and education. At the very least it was expected that the norm would be for the private sector to increasingly *provide* services with government stepping in to *purchase* these services where (as in the social sectors) such services exhibited public good characteristics.[3] In the case of infrastructure, the provider/purchaser distinction was absent, the focus was on 'unbundling' private provision of infrastructure (in electricity, for instance, separating the producer, transmitter and distributor of power) to allow competitive forces to enhance productive efficiency and 'signal' opportunities for increased investment in sectors where outputs were supply constrained. Unfortunately this did not happen, as we show below.

SAPs and IMF-supported programmes were also rooted in the belief in the 'crowding out' effect, which posits that public spending will negatively impact private sector investment through increased interest rates and a non-competitive business environment (Roy and Weeks, 2004), resulting in an overall decline in total investment. Again, it is by now well established that this has not happened in most developing regions as we show below. Cuts in aggregate public investment have not typically been compensated for by increases in aggregate private investment.

THE FAILURE OF THE OLD DOCTRINE AND THE NEW DEVELOPMENT CHALLENGE

The private sector does not fully take over from the public sector

Recent research shows that *the private sector did not compensate for the drop in public investment as it was hoped* (IMF, 2004). The 'Evaluation of Fiscal Adjustment in IMF Supported Programs' (IMF, 2003) stressed the consistent overestimation of aggregate investment in IMF programmes, which contradicts the hypothesis that public investment crowds out private investment. The report of the Commission for Africa (2005) concluded that the sharp reduction in infrastructure investment 'was a policy mistake founded in a new dogma of the 1980s and 1990s asserting that infrastructure would now be financed by the private sector' (p234). Both theoretical and empirical evidence show limited substitution between public and private investment (Calderón et al, 2003) and emphasize the critical importance of public investment to provide a more long-term durable basis for economic growth and human development (Roy and Weeks, 2004).

Roy and Weeks (2004) showed that the crowding out hypothesis is based on a series of assumptions that are implausible in the context of developing countries. Theoretically, the crowding out proposition follows from the hypothesis that financial markets are in equilibrium. If they are not, then the existence of supply-side bottlenecks and/or demand constraints greatly affects the relevance of the crowding out hypothesis. It is difficult to argue that such constraints do not exist in most developing regions, which greatly weakens the strength and relevance of the crowding out argument, and of policies based on its premises. The same paper cited UNDP-supported empirical research showing that the relationship between public and private investment appears complementary rather than conflictive in most countries in the Asia–Pacific region.

Recent IMF research also recognizes that '*public investment can crowd in private investment*', which reflects 'the complementarity of private investment with some components of public investment, especially infrastructure' (Gupta et al, 2006, pp26–27).

Public investment matters for human development

The debate on investment in infrastructure (IMF, 2004; Suescún, 2005) focuses on whether infrastructure investment has a significant positive impact on growth (see Chapter 2, section 'Definitions and uses of fiscal space'). The argument to specifically exclude infrastructure investments, as opposed to public investments, that directly impact upon human development from public expenditure ceilings (such as fiscal deficit and debt/GDP ratios) is self limiting. There are two main reasons why this is the case:

* The argument relies on the positive effect on growth of investments in infrastructure to make the case for relaxing public expenditure ceilings. This effect is empirically problematic to identify and limited in its analytical scope.
* The case for multisectoral public investment programmes based on human development paybacks (as measured by the MDGs) that can be quantified ex ante is both empirically easier to justify (given that the MDGs are quantitative targets) and analytically more consistent.

A key conclusion is, therefore, that a wide array of setting-specific public investments (including in infrastructure) can positively impact growth and human development. This is good for growth, both directly – through the provision of physical capital – and indirectly – through its impact on human capital (through developmental outcomes). It is also good for human development, both directly and through the 'trickle-down' effect.

In the rest of this chapter we therefore argue that the case for easing fiscal space for infrastructure investment is subsumed within the larger policy advocacy for a fiscal framework that recognizes the human development payback from a public investment-led strategy. The MDGs provide the basis for developing such a framework. We accept that existing fiscal rules focused on fiduciary solvency and sustainability are inadequate for this purpose and illustrate why this is the case in the following two sections, before discussing different issues involved in creating a more appropriate fiscal framework for this purpose in the final section.

Fiscal policy and public investment in the Bretton Woods approach

The Bretton Woods Institutions' (BWIs) approach to fiscal policy focuses on the overall fiscal balance and gross public debt as a measure of macroeconomic stability, within the timeframe of a standard BWI evaluation instrument, such as an IMF Article IV report or a World Bank CPIA. Within this approach BWI-supported programmes influence public investment through the funds disbursed to governments, the policy conditions they attach to their loans and, more generally, their policy advice (Dreher, 2005). The overall impact of BWI-supported programmes depends on the balance between the benefits of fiscal consolidation and the costs (to the economy) of lower levels of public expenditure.

This approach suffers from three serious shortcomings that, collectively, render the approach unsuitable for an assessment of the long-term needs of a typical developing country.[4] First, the narrow focus on growth and stability ignores the positive impact of public investment on competitiveness and the quality of growth. Second, the use of overall fiscal balance and public debt as the main empirical indicators of 'sound' fiscal policy limits the scope for a public investment-led strategy to achieve the MDGs. Third, there is reliance on conditionality-based programmes.

The model driving the BWIs' fiscal policy prescriptions inadequately recognizes the role of public investment for poverty reduction and economic growth. This approach implicitly considers public investment as an endogenous variable bound by strict fiscal deficit targets rather than a catalytic force for economic and human development. This is incompatible with an enabling medium-term development framework, such as that required to achieve the MDGs. As the Millennium Project report argues:

> *without public-led investment in infrastructure and human capital, the private sector simply stays away [because] many of the preconditions for growth… are public goods,*

meaning in shorthand that the social returns to providing them are much higher than the private returns. (Millennium Project, 2005, p49)

UNDP empirical research (Roy and Weeks, 2004) shows that the countries whose macro frameworks included strong public investment strategies enjoyed substantial and stable levels of economic growth with high poverty elasticities. In contrast, governments that sought to achieve deficit targets without reference to growth and poverty objectives suffered from economic stagnation. This demonstrates that the need to maintain sound fiscal policy to maintain macroeconomic stability goes beyond managing the fiscal deficit and public debt. The economic function of government is not merely to maintain a stable macro environment; its primary responsibility to its citizens is to foster the general welfare. A deficit target should not be set that undermines a government's ability to achieve the latter.

Liberating policy from a deficit target makes fiscal space for public investment. China and Vietnam are outstanding examples of robust public investment that has facilitated private investment, both domestic and foreign. Between 1990 and 2000, public investment grew from 35 to 38 per cent in China and 13 to 31 per cent in Vietnam. While in both countries the public sector accounts for a considerable share of output (more in Vietnam than in China), private investment has grown more rapidly than public. The share of FDI in gross capital formation in 2001 reached 8.3 and 12.8 per cent in China and Vietnam (Roy and Weeks, 2004).

In contrast, countries that have limited the investment role of the public sector during the same period – such as Indonesia, where it fell from 31 to 17 per cent – have experienced poor private sector investment performance. The share of FDI in gross capital formation in 2001 was negative (–13.2 per cent) in Indonesia (McKinley, 2003). In the case of middle-income countries, it is also important to note that Easterly (2001) and Calderón et al (2003) find that the impact of lower investment on the lack of competitiveness can worsen the fiscal deficit.

The instruments used to determine resource allocation to countries with IMF and World Bank programmes do not explicitly address public investment needs in a development context. The objective and design of the Poverty Reduction and Growth Facility (PRGF), Stand-By Arrangement (SBA) and Extended Fund Facility (EFF) programmes of the IMF are not intended to support public investment, but to preserve macroeconomic stability. The evaluation of fiscal adjustment in IMF-supported programmes (IMF, 2003; Development Committee, 2005) shows that stabilization has been established at the cost of public investment. World Bank programmes are more explicitly targeted at public investment. Following the launch of the Infrastructure Action Plan in 2003, total Bank lending for infrastructure in 2005 reached over $7.4 billion, representing 33 per cent of the Bank's total portfolio (Development Committee, 2005). Yet the Development Committee report on 'Infrastructure and the World Bank' (2005) stresses that 'the increase in support to infrastructure is still very small relative to needs' (pii). The direct impact of the money disbursed to governments appears to play a limited role in capital spending.

It has been argued that fiscal (and other) conditionalities of BWI-supported programmes adversely impact public investment. Assessing the impact (on public investment) of these programmes is undermined by some methodological difficulties. It is difficult to compare programme outcomes with what economic performance would have been with a different programme design or without a programme (Haque and Khan, 1998). However, it can be plausibly argued that more (and more broad-ranging and micro-level) conditionalities would constrain proposals for expanding public investment as there would be more restrictions on the types and magnitude of investments that would not affect conditionality compliance.

This would also reduce national ownership and, transitively, the effectiveness of public investment programmes further undermining the viability of proposals for public investment-led development strategies. In this context, a recent evaluation of IMF and World Bank conditionality in 20 countries (Eurodad, 2006; see also Buira, 2003) shows that, on average, poor countries face as many as 67 conditions per World Bank loan. Despite the IMF's new guidelines on conditionality in 2002, structural conditions in PRGF loans have risen. The average number of structural conditions contained within an IMF PRGF loan across the 20 countries that Eurodad assessed has risen from 10 to 11 per loan review between 2002 and 2006. This assessment contradicts the IMF's own review of conditionality, which concluded that structural conditions had been streamlined within PRGF programmes (IMF, 2005). This finding is complemented by that of an IMF 'Evaluation of Fiscal Adjustment in IMF Supported Programs' (2003) that shows that country programme arrangements projected a decline in investment rates in 25 per cent of the cases reviewed, while in reality investment rates fell in 50 per cent of the arrangements (IMF, 2003, p6).

The World Bank model also fails to account for country-specific public investment needs and their potential impact on economic growth and economic development. The World Bank CIPA considers public investment as a by-product, not a spearhead, of economic growth. The only reference to public investment in a World Bank CPIA is under the benchmark on 'Economic Management – Fiscal Policy', which assesses whether 'the provision of public goods, including infrastructure, is consistent with medium-term growth' (World Bank, 2005a, p7). Clearly public investment is little more than a footnote in the CPIA.

THE BRETTON WOODS RESPONSE TO THE
NEW DEVELOPMENT CHALLENGE

International partners, including the BWIs, have increasingly recognized the central role of fiscal policy in financing the provision of the public goods needed to achieve the

MDGs within a longer time horizon, such as that embodied in the Millennium Declaration (United Nations, 2000). The World Bank Group is committed to playing a major role in 'facilitating the international response to the call for expanded assistance to Africa by working in partnership with other development partners to help every African country to reach as many of the Millennium Development Goals as possible by 2015' (World Bank, 2005b, pi).

Has the acknowledgement of the MDG-based development paradigm resulted in a new approach to fiscal policy that addresses the concerns raised by previous critiques, as summarized in the previous section? The approach to the MDGs is best encapsulated in a report to the Development Committee for the IMF–World Bank meetings of spring 2006, titled 'Fiscal Policy for Growth and Development' (Development Committee, 2006, hereinafter 'The Report'). The Report focuses on 'how fiscal policy could be adapted to strengthen its role with respect to growth and the achievement of the MDGs' (Development Committee, 2006, pi).

The Report recognizes the cost of adjustment programmes on long-term economic growth: 'The success of fiscal policy in relation to its stabilization objective may have come at the cost of long-term economic growth... Across regions the pattern is that a disproportionate share of fiscal adjustment was borne by infrastructure' (p2). Figure 3.5 highlights the evolution of public capital formation between 1980 and 2005. Infrastructure investment cuts contributed to half or more of fiscal adjustment in five of the nine major Latin American countries over the 1980s and 1990s (Calderón et al, 2002). The Report stresses that the weighted average of public investment in infrastructure in Latin American countries fell from 3 per cent of GDP in 1980 to 2 per cent of GDP in 1990 and to less than 1 per cent of GDP in 2001. Estache (2005) finds comparable results for Africa where public capital formation has only been maintained in some countries, such as Uganda and Tanzania, through higher aid flows. Similarly, public capital expenditure on irrigation, power and transport fell by 3 per cent in India during the first half of the 1990s (Pinto et al, 2006).

The Report acknowledges that fiscal policy must better serve growth and poverty reduction objectives. It also acknowledges that private investment alone is insufficient to provide the levels of public goods and services necessary to secure long-term developmental objectives (such as those summarized by the MDGs). However, the Report confines its endorsement of this long-term developmental challenge by specifying that such investment should consist of 'some public infrastructure' that exhibits high returns and positive externalities. 'In a country where the Government can build and maintain infrastructure efficiently, increasing borrowing to finance new high return infrastructure would enhance government solvency' (p16). In consequence the fiscal framework presented remains subordinate to fiduciary rather than developmental concerns.

The Report presents a fiscal policy framework that is not significantly different from that used for short-term fiscal assessments by both BWIs, and fails to provide the

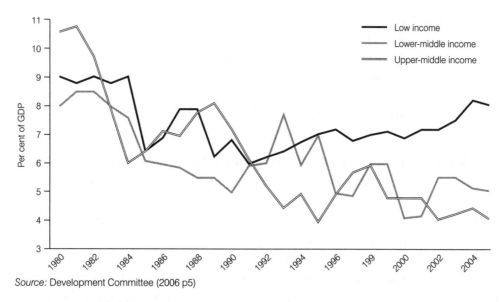

Source: Development Committee (2006 p5)

Figure 3.5 *Public capital formation by income group, 1980–2005 (as a share of GDP)*

substantial analytical reworking required by the initial acknowledgement of long-term objectives. The framework is of limited relevance for assessing the *developmental* (as opposed to *fiduciary*) implications of increasing fiscal space. It emphasizes the importance of considering the 'longer term effects' and 'long-term impact' of key elements of fiscal policy, such as fiscal deficit and public spending. The report further criticizes those 'short-sighted decisions', including cuts in public capital formation, that undermined 'long-term growth'. However, it is maintained that an expansion of public expenditures is only desirable when it does not compromise 'macroeconomic stability', which is further referred to as 'short-term macro-economic stability' (p19). Additionally, it is indicated that fiscal deficits 'with their short term impact on aggregate demand' will influence 'any decisions on public expenditure' (p19). Thus, the short term continues to act as a binding constraint on the long term (see Chapter 2, section 'Definitions and uses of fiscal space').

As a result, the Report's framework understates the possibility for enhancing fiscal space through debt-financed MDG-oriented public investments. For instance, the Report distinguishes between countries with(out) access to international borrowing and with(out) access to external grant aid (piii). It considers borrowing as a second best option, despite the potential rationale for using this financing instrument, even in the presence of other funding sources. Though the Report recognizes the potential crowding in between public and private investment, it does not then assess the implications of this shift for debt-financed public investment. *Ceteris paribus*, crowding in effects should enhance the net benefits from debt-financed public investment. This is not taken into account in the analysis used to assess 'solvency' with the result that only 'self-financing' projects are suitable for debt finance.

Further, this approach does not capture 'savings realization failures', that is, macroeconomic, social and political factors inhibiting the channelling of savings to public goods financing. It also makes no recommendations on instruments that could create an enabling environment to enhance savings mobilization for public investment. Addressing this issue should be an integral part of any analytical framework that seeks to secure fiscal space for achieving the MDGs (Roy and Heuty, 2005).

AN ENABLING FISCAL FRAMEWORK FOR PUBLIC INVESTMENT: ACCOUNTING, ANALYTICAL AND POLICY ISSUES

What, then, would be the desirable features of a fiscal framework that supports a human development-oriented public investment strategy, whose results can be measured in terms of quantifiable long-term development goals, such as the MDGs?

First, an MDG-based analysis should focus on the impact of public expenditures on aggregates and trends within the timeframe (ten years) for achieving the MDGs. This would imply that a deviation from the trend in the short run is acceptable if it translates into positive outcomes later in that timeframe.

Second, in a ten-year time period, public expenditure can have an endogenous effect on domestic resource mobilization. This effect can be positive or negative depending on the impact of public investment on the productive base, the capital accumulation process and savings behaviour. In this context, even if fiscal expansion results in a negative impact on macro-stability indicators in the short run, it is critical to assess whether this effect is temporary (short run) or structural and permanent. If macroeconomic instability is temporary, the desirability of fiscal expansion must be assessed by weighing the costs of this instability against the expected longer term benefits.

What would the details of such a strategy look like? This is the subject of our discussion in the rest of this section. First, we discuss proposals to develop better accounting rules for an enabling fiscal strategy. In the following sub-section, we discuss analytical and policy issues.

Accounting rules to increase fiscal space

Under the section entitled 'Trends in public investment spending and the development challenge' above, we noted the point made by several scholars and policymakers that restrictive fiscal targets used in fiscal reform programmes, chiefly the fiscal deficit and the debt/GDP ratio, were responsible for the observed decline in public investment/GDP ratios and, in particular, infrastructure/GDP ratios, globally. In this context, there have been several suggestions for alternative fiscal rules and associated institutional arrangements that would foster an enabling reform environment for scaled up public investments.

The generic technical argument can be summarized as follows. Existing fiscal indicators and targets do not account for the uniqueness of public investment 'which stems, obviously, from its potential to improve the economy's output potential and to benefit multiple generations' (Perée and Välilä, 2005, p5). Public spending creates public capital, 'an outlay of expenditure on assets that provide longer run benefits going beyond the current period' (Mintz and Smart, 2006, p9). While current expenditures, such as salaries or transfers associated with programmes, are *flow* variables, public investment increases the *stock* of public capital, whose payback impacts the economy in the long run (see Chapter 2, section 'Fiscal space for scaling up').

Most budgets classify current and capital expenditures separately. However, the fiscal deficit does not make this distinction, being defined as the difference between current revenues and current *and* capital expenditures.[5] A fiscal rule that recognizes the distinction between current and capital expenditure line items in the budget will ensure that fiscal restraint does not discourage growth in the aggregate public capital *stock* (the corresponding on-budget *flow* variable being gross public-sector capital formation). On this count, the current budget deficit/surplus would be a logical indicator to choose.

However, it is now commonly argued that financing gross public-sector capital formation entirely through current revenues makes little economic sense (Creel, 2003; Blanchard and Giavazzi, 2004; Fatás, 2005; Mintz and Smart, 2006) and that 'a rule... that introduces a financing constraint on investment expenditure is simply stupid' (Romano Prodi, former president of the European Commission, quoted in Blanchard and Giavazzi, 2004, p9). Consequently, there have been many proposals for alternative fiscal rules, inspired in their various forms by the UK's 'Golden Rule'.[6] All these aim to allow borrowing by the government for the sole purpose of financing net public investments.

It is important to understand the different arguments underlying these alternative proposals as to *why* (and consequently what type of) public investment should be debt financed (Mintz and Smart, 2006). The first argument pertains to intergenerational equity. Current generations should not be the sole financiers of investments that will also benefit future generations. Financing public investment through borrowing 'provides an opportunity to postpone taxes to the future', and it is therefore 'a means for future generations to help contribute to the cost of public investment' (Mintz and Smart, 2006, p8). Moral hazard questions aside, the intergenerational equity issue cuts both ways. Higher debt/GDP ratios would impose a cost on future generations, creating a reverse intergenerational inequity in the form of a higher debt service burden in the future.

The second, related argument pertains to tax smoothing. In summary, 'because the static marginal cost of public finance is an increasing function of the government tax take, there is a *prima facie* case for borrowing to finance public investment, thereby smoothing the associated tax burden over future years and future generations' (Mintz and Smart, 2006, p7). Given its focus on future tax revenues, the key policy implication is that while debt financing of tangible assets, infrastructures, in particular, with direct links to future private incomes is allowable, other forms of public capital (environmental, military, cultural) that do not generate future tax returns should have limited recourse to debt finance.

A third argument focuses on net debt and the value of assets. It posits that total debt does not matter as long as it is backed by assets whose value, if sold or leased to the private sector, would provide funds to amortize the debt. However, Mintz and Smart (2006) have argued that this analogy is false. Confidence in sovereign solvency in the perception of private agents, investors, lenders, financial markets and rating agencies, is important for fiscal sustainability. It would be difficult to convince these agents that rural roads or schools in remote areas, unlike power plants, could easily be sold or leased to the private sector.

Thus the tax smoothing and asset value arguments privilege some types of public investments, such as tangible infrastructure investments with a full private market value, over others. This epitomizes a major policy challenge for creating fiscal space for public investments, which we explain in the next section.

For accounting purposes, public investment can be decomposed into two distinct forms of 'public capital', public capital used as an input, 'used to produce goods and services directly', and public capital as an output, 'constructed by the public sector that provides longer term benefits to society over time' (Mintz and Smart, 2006, p14). An example from Mintz and Smart (2006) illustrates the argument. Health services use labour (doctors and nurses) and buildings (hospital, dispensaries) to produce health services (see Chapter 2, section 'Fiscal space of scaling up'). Hospitals 'are clearly capital inputs used in producing health services and should be amortized under capital budgets', while 'nurses' salaries should be expensed' (p15), that is, be financed out of current revenue.

Thus the distinguishing feature of a public investment is not the outcome of the investment, but its role in the capital accumulation process, which is that of a stock variable providing returns, in combination with recurrent inputs (flow variables), over a number of accounting years.

What conclusion do we draw from the above? First, while there are arguments for rules that treat infrastructure investments differently from other public investments, the reasons for doing so are principally fiduciary in nature. This may be problematic in a development context, as we shall elaborate below. Second, while there are cogent arguments for questioning the distinction between current and capital expenditures, we feel that there are sound economic reasons for treating these separately. This would imply our continued acceptance of the proposition that governments are not justified in running current deficits. Alternatively, we do not accept either the argument to privilege infrastructure investments over other types of public investments on tax smoothing or market valuation grounds.

Our argument finds support in a seminal paper by Blanchard and Giavazzi (2004). The contemporary debate about fiscal rules and fiscal space for public investment has been influenced by debates on the Stability and Growth Pact (SGP) adopted by the European Union in 1997. Blanchard and Giavazzi's paper finds the fiscal rules set by the SGP problematic. Under the SGP rules, member states must keep the ratio of the annual fiscal deficit to GDP below 3 per cent and the ratio of gross government debt to GDP must not exceed 60 per cent. In summary, they argue that borrowing should only be allowed to finance net investment, while the current fiscal deficit should be zero. This would include external grants in the context of developing countries. They expect three desirable outcomes. First 'it would remedy an obvious mistake in the way the Pact was written', as 'a private company does not attribute the entire cost of an investment project to a single year's account' but rather distributes its cost over time 'as [the] returns [to investment] accrue' (p3). Second, 'over time the debt-GDP ratio would tend to become equal to the ratio of public capital to GDP' (p4), a level that can reasonably be expected to be less than the debt ratios of many developing countries. Third, the modified rule would also 'introduce more transparency in the budget' and fight tendencies 'to shift borrowing off budget' (p4).

We can anticipate an objection to applying Blanchard and Giavazzi's proposal in a development context. It can be argued that what matters is aggregate capital accumulation, not its distribution between public and private capital, making it illegitimate to allow governments privileged access to resources for net public capital formation as opposed to other economic agents. However, the evidence cited above in the section 'Trends in public investment spending and the development challenge' does not support this argument. We observed there that current fiscal restraint rules inhibit public capital formation by governments with no compensating increase in capital formation by other agents. We also observed that empirical evidence indicated that 'crowding in' rather than 'crowding out' could be typically expected to hold in the case of developing countries.

Another concern is the fear of 'creative accounting' as governments would have an incentive to classify more and more expenditures as capital expenditures. Blanchard and Giavazzi agree and stress the need to define 'accounting rules' that would complement alternative fiscal rules and clearly specify what can and cannot be counted as 'investment' under the modified rule (Blanchard and Giavazzi, 2004; Creel, 2003). In this context we propose that expenditures on the following should *not* be classified as capital expenditures:

- outputs that are fully used up in the fiscal year in which the expenditure is incurred;
- inputs that are required to obtain desired outputs on a recurrent basis.

An enabling fiscal framework for human development:
Analytical issues and policy implications

In the sections 'Trends in public investment spending and the development challenge' and 'The failure of the old doctrine and the new development challenge' in this chapter, we reasoned that the argument for excluding infrastructure investments from public expenditure ceilings (based on benchmarks, such as fiscal deficit and debt/GDP ratios) is self limiting. We then argued in the sections 'Fiscal policy and public investment in the Bretton Woods approach' and 'The Bretton Woods response to the new development challenge' for a fiscal framework that recognizes the human development payback from a public investment-led strategy and that the MDGs provide the basis for developing such a framework.

Moving to a fiscal framework that is development centred from one that is grounded in a purely fiduciary logic raises several analytical issues. Perhaps the most important is what we term the '*fiscal space conjecture*' (see Chapter 2, section 'Fiscal space for scaling up').[7]

It can be argued that a public investment-led strategy, financed largely using external grants (ODA), relieves the fiduciary constraint by leaving the fiscal deficit and debt/GDP ratios unchanged. The Millennium Project report (2005) to the UN Secretary General sets out a practical plan to achieve the MDGs that calls for a major increase in ODA from 0.25 per cent of donor GNP in 2003 to 0.54 per cent in 2015 (Millennium Project, 2005). While the report also emphasizes the need for domestic resource mobilization, debt relief and trade, it focuses mainly on the role of ODA in breaking the poverty trap and financing a major scale up of public investment in developing countries to achieve the goals.

The issues that then arise on the macroeconomic front (like Dutch Disease) are important ones, but recent analytical work seems to indicate that these issues can be managed, over a ten-year horizon, so that they will not pose a binding constraint to scaling up to achieve the MDGs (Gupta et al, 2006; Chowdury and McKinley, 2006).

While such a scaling up in ODA would indubitably relieve the current binding constraint it does not obviate the need for an enabling fiscal framework in the long run. The success of the development strategies engineered by Chile, Korea, Malaysia, Singapore and Thailand has not been contingent on significant foreign assistance, though such assistance did play an enabling role in many ways. In low-income countries in developing Asia, such as the South Asian countries, aid supplies only a very small portion of investment needs and the growth in ODA would need to be of an order of magnitude that is simply unrealistic. In middle-income developing countries the question is obviously moot.

Analytical and policy conclusions

In Chapter 2, Section 'Fiscal space for scaling up' we discussed the principal issues on which attention needs to be focused, noting, first, that the fiscal space conjecture does not deny the possibility that a harmonious solution exists in which fiscal paybacks and development paybacks are simultaneously secured.

Second, as far as technical work on fiscal affairs goes, there have been very few systematic attempts to calculate the development payback of a scaled up public investment programme. Perhaps the first attempt needs to be at the international level, where it cannot continue to be the case that the chief dispenser of technical advice on fiscal affairs, the IMF, has neither the mandate nor the expertise to combine thinking on human development and poverty reduction with developing high-quality advice on enabling fiscal frameworks to secure these objectives. As at least one recent IMF paper (Gupta et al, 2006) shows, there is plenty of professional talent within the Fund to discharge such a mandate, but the mandate will need to be given, and the operational culture of the organization changed to one in which the phrases 'pro-poor' and 'MDG based' are as well understood and internalized as the phrases 'fiscal prudence' and 'fiduciary sustainability'. The exemplary impact of such a change on ministries of finance cannot be understated. If the IMF itself cannot take on such a role, then it would be important to devise an institutional arrangement in which long-term development payback assessments conducted by UN development agencies inform IMF technical and surveillance work, particularly Article IV activities, on a mandatory basis.

Third, the development discourse needs to more centrally take on board the fact that development is a risky business with potentially serious prudential and fiduciary consequences when things go wrong, as they all too often do. The fact that it is possible to achieve the MDGs by 2015, should donors make good on their ODA commitments, is in itself not a cause for celebration. Structural shocks, volatile financing for a scaled up public investment programme, and even natural disasters and political conflicts can detract from expected results. These risks and uncertainties have direct and tangible fiduciary impacts that can be of a magnitude that would threaten or even reverse achievements on the MDG front. Such shocks and volatilities, more generally, a combination of random events due to uncertainty that collectively have a negative structural impact on macro-fiscal fundamentals, such as the debt stock, can, over time, seriously reduce the capacity of a country to engage in structural transformation to achieve development results of the type called for by the MDGs. It is therefore important not to assume these away, but to devise instruments to mitigate their impact.

A good example of such an instrument is the proposed 'Stability and Social Investment Facility for High Debt Countries' (Dervis and Birdsall, 2006). The paper proposes a long-term facility (a stability and social facility – SSF) to provide a predictable source of development finance for high-debt emerging market economies. The paper focuses on the fact that in such economies, (a) the debt burden significantly constrains growth performance and, (b) growth when it occurs tends not to be pro-poor. The paper highlights an example of the fiscal space conjecture in the context of high-debt emerging market economies. In such economies, fiscal prudence requires either curtailing public investments altogether, or sanctions only investments that are consistent with providing adequate fiduciary payback. These are not likely to be chosen within a paradigm of human development within which growth would be demonstrably pro-poor.

The key innovation in the proposal is the advocacy of a long-term negotiated relationship focused on reducing the debt burden, thereby allowing for scaled up pro-poor public investments.[8] The proposal requires countries to have a medium-term growth programme with a path for the primary (or current) surplus and structural policies in support of growth. It would also require conditionality to be 'framed in terms of reductions in numbers of people living in poverty... and other such more easily measured indicators such as primary and secondary school completion rates and infant mortality rates' (Dervis and Birdsall, 2006, p11).

Finally, in the short term, the link between development results and public investment is exogenous and, in such a circumstance, it is analytically meaningless to distinguish between fiduciary and development paybacks. As the long-term emphasis of the SSF proposal above makes clear, it is important to recognize that the fiscal space conjecture is operational only in the medium- to long-term context. We argue that this involves devising an analytical framework in which the key fiscal impact variables, and, transitively the indicators to measure fiscal success, would focus more on the impact of the development process on domestic resource mobilization, savings and capital accumulation than is currently the case.

The Millennium Project report underlines the need for a framework that assigns a central role to the development of capital accumulation processes. 'The Goals are ends in themselves, [they] are also "capital inputs" [the means to a productive life] to economic growth and to further development... So, many of the Goals are part of capital accumulation defined broadly as well as objectives in their own right' (Millennium Project, 2005, p28). The identification of capital *accumulation* as the key economic process by which the Goals are to be achieved provides an innovative framework to understand the impact of a public investment-led development strategy. Economic models provide diverging explanations of the link between the capital accumulation process and the achievement of developmental outcomes (Solow, 1956 and 1988; Lucas, 1988). Yet all assume that investment in physical and human capital is a prerequisite for achieving development objectives, such as the MDGs.

Understanding the pursuit of the MDGs as a process of generating sustainable regimes of accumulation underscores the dual challenge of the international community to cope with the ambition of the Millennium Declaration, beyond the specific quantitative targets set for each Goal.[9] The first challenge is to foster a regime of capital accumulation at the national level so as to free developing countries from reliance on external concessional financing for the provision of public goods and to achieve their full integration in the world economy. The second challenge is to promote a country-specific process (mode of regulation) that sustains and perpetuates an enabling accumulation regime.

Thus, even if ODA-financed interventions to achieve the MDGs eventually lead to poverty reduction and foster capital accumulation, the sustainability of these virtuous outcomes is not automatically certain. The external and volatile nature of aid can undermine country ownership and increase vulnerability to shocks, which hinder the sustainability of regimes of accumulation. Substantial dependence on aid as the main financing source for the provision of public goods to achieve the MDGs will impact significantly on domestic patterns of consumption and production. An appropriate mode of regulation needs to be in place to build an adequate productive and economic base, which can sustain these achievements. There is evidence that, in Mexico for example, disparities in the wage–labour nexus and an economy prone to external shocks fostered extreme international dependence with domestic productive capacities weak or even absent in a number of critical areas of the economy, major impediments for building self-supporting growth regimes (Talha, 2002). In Mexico and Venezuela, the external financial constraints of the 1980s led to the complete destabilization of the regulation mode, with consequent slippages in development results (Aboites et al, 2002).

The BWIs' paradigm focuses on fiduciary measures and normative policy assumptions that are not sufficiently developed to assess the evolution of a capital accumulation process appropriate for securing fiscal space for sustainable human development. The CPIA[10] is an important tool used by the World Bank for the political economy and institutional assessment of a country. A country is identified as having 'good' policies if it receives a high score on the CPIA. This assessment includes subjective criteria, such as the presence of a 'competitive environment for the private sector', 'property rights and rule-based governance'.[11] The CPIA gives equal weight to each indicator, notwithstanding the preponderance of indicators linked to economic policies and outcomes and the relatively few indicators linked to social policies and outcomes. The instrument provides no long-term guidance.

New instruments need to be defined to address the political economy nature of the capital accumulation process that underpins the link between successfully securing human developmental outcomes, such as those embodied in the MDGs, and ensuring long-term fiscal sustainability. As our discussion above on the fiscal space conjecture indicates, the development challenge is to forge a credible instrument to quantify long-term fiscal payback from a public-investment programme with strong public good characteristics. While the process can be kickstarted using foreign aid (in low-income countries) or an SSF (in middle-income countries), fiscal sustainability would ultimately require 'closure'. That is, the development payback delivers, within a defined timeframe, a level of productive activity and savings mobilization that is compatible with long-term fiduciary sustainability.

The definition of political economy instruments to assess fiscal space and secure a sustainable capital accumulation process within the long term is meant to complement, not replace, existing fiduciary fiscal assessment tools (see Chapter 2, section

'Conclusions'). The chief economist of the World Bank recently noted the absence of 'an obvious policy framework within which to evaluate infrastructure investment options and tradeoffs' and called for further research in this area (Bourguignon, 2006, p5). As concluded in Chapter 2, a collaborative effort involving IMF expertise on fiduciary instruments and the UN system expertise in demonstrating the long-term human development payback from well-designed public investment programmes, in equal partnership with other development partners and developing country groupings, is therefore a matter of pressing urgency.

NOTES

1   This chapter has been peer reviewed by Paul Ladd, Policy Advisor, UNDP and Sanjay Reddy, Associate Professor of Economics, Barnard College, Columbia University. The authors would like to thank them for their comments from which this chapter has benefited. We would also like to acknowledge the contributions of Maria Davalos, UNDP, Elliot Harris, IMF and Olivier Blanchard, IMF. The views and interpretations in this chapter are those of the authors and do not represent the views and policies of UNDP.
2   All figures are in 1995 constant prices.
3   Defined in the section 'An enabling fiscal framework for human development: Analytical issues and policy implications' below.
4   The shortcomings apply in different measure to low- and middle-income countries. In the latter case, for instance, the competitiveness argument would be the most important. In the case of low-income countries, this critique is of particular importance for explaining and reversing public investment declines in the quest for a scaled up public investment-led strategy to achieve medium-term international development goals (most importantly the MDGs).
5   There is of course the issue of which expenditures fall under each category, a point we take up later in this section.
6   Since 1997, the UK government has been subject to a self-imposed 'Golden Rule', which states that, over the cycle, the government is to borrow only to finance capital and not current expenditures. This rule is augmented by a 'Sustainable Investment Rule', which stipulates that over the cycle the net debt to GDP ratio is not to exceed 40 per cent (where debt is defined as gross government debt less liquid assets). Taken together, they constitute the 'Modified Golden Rule'.
7   This is termed a conjecture pending a formal exposition, which is currently a work in progress. We are indebted to Sanjay Reddy for sharpening the analytical reasoning underlying the conjecture.
8   While the paper rightly emphasizes that the proposed facility would not be used to mitigate specific exogenous shocks, it can be argued that countries with persistently high levels of debt are in such a situation because of a combination of negative events that were not *ex ante* predictable.
9   For a detailed discussion of the role of capital accumulation in sustaining human development progress see Roy and Heuty (2005).
10   The CPIA assigns a value between 1 and 6 to capture perceived performance in 20 different aspects, ranging from macroeconomic management and factor market policies, to policies for social inclusion and public sector management (Burnside and Dollar, 2000).
11   Vandemoortele (2003, p14) stresses the subjectivity of evaluations concerning, for instance, whether a country has a distortionary minimum wage, excessive labour market regulations or too many public sector workers.

REFERENCES

Aboites, J., Miotti, L. and Quenan, C. (2002) 'Regulationist approaches and accumulation in Latin America', in R. Boyer and Y. Saillard, (eds) *Regulation Theory – The State of the Art*, Edition la Découverte, Paris, Routledge, London, pp280-287

Bhagwati, J. (1988) *Protectionism*, MIT Press, Cambridge, MA

Blanchard, O. and Giavazzi, F. (2004) 'Improving the SGP through a proper accounting for public investment', *European Economic Perspectives Newsletter*, no 1, Centre for Economic Policy Research (CEPR), London, UK

Bourguignon, F. (2006) 'Rethinking infrastructure for development. Closing remarks', Annual Bank Conference on Development Economics (ABCDE), Tokyo, Japan 29–30 May

Buira, A. (2003) 'An analysis of IMF conditionality', paper prepared for the XVI Technical Group Meeting of the Intergovernmental Group of 24, Port of Spain, Trinidad and Tobago, 13–14 February

Burnside, C. and Dollar, D. (2000) 'Aid, policies, and growth', *American Economic Review*, vol 90, pp847–868

Calderón, C., Easterly, W. and Servén, L. (2002) 'The output cost of Latin America's infrastructure gap', Central Bank of Chile Working Papers 186, Central Bank of Chile, Santiago

Calderón, C., Easterly, W. and Servén, L. (2003) 'Latin America's infrastructure in the era of macro-economic crises', in W. Easterly and L. Servén (eds) *The Limits of Stabilization: Infrastructure, Public Deficits and Growth in Latin America*, Stanford University Press and the World Bank, Palo Alto and Washington DC

CARE International (1999) 'Current donor approaches to urban development', UK Urban Briefing Notes, CARE, London

Chang, H.-J. (1994) *The Political Economy of Industrial Policy*, Macmillan Press, London

Commission for Africa (2005) *Our Common Interest*, Commission for Africa, London, www.commissionforafrica.org/english/report/introduction.html

Chowdhury, A. and McKinley, T. (2006) *Gearing Macroeconomics Policies to Manage Large Inflows of ODA: The Implications for HIV/AIDS Programmes*, UNDP, International Poverty Centre, Working Paper No. 17, May 2006, UNDP, Brasilia, Brazil

Creel, J. (2003) 'Ranking fiscal policy rules: The golden rule of public finance vs. the stability and growth pact', OFCE Working Paper 2003–04, OFCE, Paris

Dervis, K. and Birdsall, N. (2006) 'A stability and social investment facility for high debt countries', CGD Working Paper 77, Center for Global Development, Washington DC

Development Committee (2005) *Infrastructure and the World Bank*, Development Committee, World Bank and IMF, Washington DC

Development Committee (2006) *Fiscal Policy for Growth and Development – An Interim Report*, Development Committee, World Bank and IMF, Washington DC

Dreher, A. (2005) 'Does the IMF influence fiscal and monetary policy?', *Journal of Policy Reform*, vol 8, no 3, pp225–238

Easterly, W. (2001) 'Growth implosions, debt explosions, and my Aunt Marilyn: Do growth slowdowns cause public debt crises?', Policy Research Working Paper, World Bank, Washington DC

Estache, A. (2005) *What do we Know about Sub-Saharan Africa's Infrastructure and the Impact of its 1990s Reforms?*, The World Bank and ECARES, Université Libre de Bruxelles, Washington DC and Brussels

Estache, A. (2006) *Infrastructure: A Survey of Recent and Upcoming Issues*, World Bank, Washington DC

Eurodad (2006) *World Bank and IMF Conditionality: A Development Injustice*, Eurodad, Brussels

Everhart, S. and Sumlinski, M. A. (2001) 'Trends in private investment in developing countries. Statistics for 1970–2000 and the impact on private investment of corruption and the quality of public investment', IFC Discussion Paper No. 44, World Bank, Washington DC

Fan, S. and Rao, N. (2003) *Public Spending in Developing Countries: Trends, Determination, and Impact*, International Food Policy Research Institute (IFPRI), Washington DC

Fatás, A. (2005) 'Is there a case for sophisticated balanced-budget rules?', OECD Economics Department Working Papers No. 466, OECD, Paris

Ferreira, C., Maliagrios, P. and Maliagrios, T. (1998) 'Impactos produtivos da infra-estrutura no Brasil – 1950/95', *Pesquisa e Planejamento Econômico*, vol 28, pp315–338

Ferreira, C., Gonçalves do Nascimento, P. and Gonçalves do Nascimento, L. (2005) *Welfare and Growth Effects of Alternative Fiscal Rules for Infrastructure Investment in Brazil*, Fundação Getulio Vargas, Rio de Janeiro

Gupta, S., Powell, R. and Yang, Y. (2006) *Macroeconomic Challenges of Scaling Up Aid to Africa. A Checklist for Practitioners*, International Monetary Fund, Washington DC

Haque, N. U. and Khan, M. S. (1998) 'Do IMF supported programs work? A survey of cross-country empirical evidence', IMF Working Paper 98/169, International Monetary Fund, Washington DC

IMF (International Monetary Fund) (2003) *Evaluation of Fiscal Adjustment in IMF- Supported Programs*, IMF, Washington DC

IMF (2004) *Public Investment and Fiscal Policy*, IMF, Washington DC

IMF (2005) *Review of the 2002 Conditionality Guidelines*, IMF, Washington DC

Lal, D. (1988) *The Hindu Equilibrium 2 Vols, India c. 1500 B.C. – 2000 A.D.*, Oxford University Press, Oxford

Lucas, R. (1988) 'On the mechanics of economic development', *Journal of Monetary Economics*, vol 22, pp3–42

McKinley, T. (2003) *The Macroeconomics of Poverty Reduction, Initial Findings of the UNDP Asia-Pacific Regional Programme*, UNDP, New York

Millennium Project (2005) *Investing in Development: A Practical Plan to Achieve the MDGs*, report to the UN Secretary General, Earthscan, New York

Mintz, J. M. and Smart, M. (2006) 'Incentives for public investment under fiscal rules', Policy Research Working Paper 3860, World Bank, Washington DC

Perée, E. and Välilä, T. (2005) 'Fiscal rules and public investment', European Investment Bank Economic and Financial Report 2005/02, European Investment Bank, Luxembourg

Pinto, B., Zahir, F. and Pang, G. (2006) *From Rising Debt to Rising Growth in India: Microeconomic Dominance?*, World Bank, Washington DC

Roy, R. (1994) *The Politics of Fiscal Policy*, unpublished PhD dissertation, Faculty of Economics and Politics, University of Cambridge, Cambridge

Roy, R. and Heuty, A. (2005) 'Investing in development: The millennium development goals, aid and sustainable capital accumulation', *Journal of International Affairs*, vol 58, no 2, spring, pp161–176, www.undp.org/poverty

Roy, R. and Weeks, J. (2004) 'Making fiscal policy work for the poor', paper presented to G-24 Meeting, 27–28 September 2004, Washington DC

Servén, L. and Solimano, A. (1992) 'Private investment and macroeconomic adjustment: A survey', *World Bank Research Observer*, vol 7, no 1, pp95–114

Solow, R. (1956) 'A contribution to the theory of economic growth', *Quarterly Journal of Economics*, vol 70, pp65–922

Solow, R. (1988) *Growth Theory: An Exposition*, Oxford University Press, New York

Suescún, R. (2005) 'Fiscal space for investment in infrastructure in Colombia', Policy Research Working Paper Series 3629, World Bank, Washington DC

Talha, L. (2002) 'Théorie de la Régulation et Développement', in R. Boyer and Y. Saillard (eds) *Théorie de la Régulation, l'état des saviors*, La Decouverte, Paris, pp456–458

United Nations (2000) *United Nations Millennium Declaration. A/RES/55/2*, United Nations, New York

United Nations (2005) *2005 World Summit Outcome Document. A/RES/60/1*, United Nations, New York

Vandemoortele, J. (2003) *The MDGs and Pro-poor Policies. Can External Partners Make a Difference?*, UNDP, New York

World Bank (2005a) *Country Policy and Institutional Assessments – 2005 Assessment Questionnaire*, World Bank, Washington DC

World Bank (2005b) *Meeting the Challenge of Africa's Development: A World Bank Group Action Plan*, World Bank, Washington DC

4

The Fiscal Space Conjecture: Theoretical Reflections

Sanjay G. Reddy

The nineteenth century carried to extravagant lengths the criterion of what one can call for short 'the financial results,' as a test of the advisability of any course of action sponsored by private or by collective action. The whole conduct of life was made into a sort of parody of an accountant's nightmare. Instead of using their vastly increased material and technical resources to build a wonder city, the men of the nineteenth century built slums; and they thought it right and advisable to build slums because slums, on the test of private enterprise, 'paid,' whereas the wonder city would, they thought, have been an act of foolish extravagance, which would, in the imbecile idiom of the financial fashion, have 'mortgaged the future' – though how the construction to-day of great and glorious works can impoverish the future, no man can see until his mind is beset by false analogies from an irrelevant accountancy... The same rule of self-destructive financial calculation governs every walk of life... We are capable of shutting off the sun and the stars because they do not pay a dividend... But once we allow ourselves to be disobedient to the test of an accountant's profit, we have begun to change our civilization.

John Maynard Keynes (June 1933)

INTRODUCTION

Recent applied work in fiscal policy (for example, Roy et al, Chapter 2 in this volume) has advanced the so-called 'fiscal space conjecture'.[1] This conjecture states that:

> *For any public investment programme, the more the public good characteristics of the public investment outputs, the less the precision and predictability of the* fiduciary *payback calculation. The less the public good characteristics, the more the precision and predictability of the* fiduciary *payback calculation.*

And:

> *For any public investment programme, the more the public good characteristics of the public investment outputs, the more the precision and predictability of the* development *payback calculation. The less the public good characteristics, the less the precision and predictability of the* development *payback calculation.*

Although the conjecture is suggestive, its terms have not been fully defined and the conditions under which it is justified have not been fully identified. Since the conjecture may provide a useful framework for thinking about an appropriate approach to public investment, it may be deemed important to determine under what conditions it would hold true. In an attempt to explore the problem, it is necessary to begin with some definitions.

INITIAL DEFINITIONS: SOCIAL ACHIEVEMENTS, DEVELOPMENT PAYBACK AND FINANCIAL PAYBACK

Suppose that a society consists of n persons, $S = \{1,...n\}$. Let us also suppose that there is an 'individual achievement space', A, composed of l distinct dimensions $(1, ..., l)$ in relation to which cardinally measurable achievements are defined, so that $A: R_+^l$. Each member of the society, $i \in S$, possesses individual achievements $ai=(a_{i_1},...a_{i_l}) \in A$, which together compose a social achievement vector $a=(a_1,...a_n) \in A^n$. If a social achievement vector achieved in a given social state of affairs is designated by Φ, then by employing a corresponding superscript, it is possible to define a 'development ordering' by a reflexive and transitive binary relation, $>$, over the set of possible social achievement vectors $\{a^\Phi\}$. This development ordering reflects judgements about the manner in which social achievements are deemed to give rise to development. For simplicity, it will be assumed that $>$ is complete and strictly monotonic in social achievements, so that it can be represented by a real-valued 'development evaluation function' $D(a^\Phi)$ with the feature that higher values of the function correspond to greater development as defined by the relation $>$. The development evaluation function simultaneously encapsulates judgements concerning the relative significance of distinct dimensions of individual achievements and the distribution of these achievements across persons.

It is assumed that one of the achievements (without loss of generality, achievement 1) is defined by 'income'. Each individual then possesses income, $y_i=a_{i_1}$, and the total income of the society is given by $Y=\sum_{i=1}^{n} y_i$. As previously, the superscript Φ may be employed to refer to the incomes prevailing in a given social state of affairs.

Now, define a public investment as an action that may be undertaken by a government (at some cost, c) which has the effect of causing a change from one social achievement vector, $a^{\Phi 1}$, to another $a^{\Phi 2}$. The effect of this public investment is to bring about a change, $\Delta D = D(a^{\Phi 2}) - D(a^{\Phi 1})$, in the level of development. This may be referred to as the *development payback* of the public investment. It is determined by the initial social achievement vector, $a^{\Phi 1}$, the impact of the public investment on the social achievement vector (i.e. on $\Delta a = (a^{\Phi 2} - a^{\Phi 1})$) and the treatment of this impact by the development evaluation function. As such, the development payback cannot be determined without a composite assessment which integrates empirical observations and normative judgements.[2]

In contrast, the financial ('fiduciary' in the language adopted by Roy et al, Chapter 2) payback of the public investment may be defined as follows. The 'societal financial payback' is $\Delta Y = Y^{\Phi 2} - Y^{\Phi 1}$. If government imposes on each individual, $i \in S$, a proportionate tax rate of τ_i ($0 \le \tau_i \le 1$), in a given social state of affairs, Φ (designated as before by a superscript), then the 'governmental financial payback' is $\Delta Y' = \sum_{i=1}^{n} \tau_{1}^{\Phi 1} y_i - \sum_{i=1}^{n} \tau_{2}^{\Phi 2} y_i$. It is evident that the governmental financial payback is less than or equal to the societal financial payback. Henceforth, the focus will be on the societal financial payback, although the arguments may be readily extended to the case of the governmental financial payback.

Note that the marginal development payback (for example, that produced by 'small'[3] public investment projects) can be written as follows:

$$dD = \sum_{i=1}^{n} \sum_{j=1}^{l} \frac{\partial D}{\partial a_{ij}} = \sum_{i=1}^{n} \frac{\partial D}{\partial a_{i1}} da_{i1} + \sum_{i=1}^{n} \sum_{j=2}^{l} \frac{\partial D}{\partial a_{ij}} da_{ij}$$

$$= \sum_{i=1}^{n} \frac{\partial D}{\partial y_i} dy_i + \sum_{i=1}^{n} \sum_{j=2}^{l} \frac{\partial D}{\partial a_{ij}} da_{ij}$$

Even if a public investment project were to consist only of a financial payback (i.e. $\sum_{i=1, j=2}^{n, l} \frac{\partial D}{\partial y_i} da_{ij} = 0$), then the level of the development payback would still be potentially affected by the distribution of the societal financial payback across persons, since the financial payback, dy_i, received by each individual is valued to an extent that depends on the marginal social valuation $\frac{\partial D}{\partial y_i}$. In the special case where such distributional considerations play no role (either because the evaluator's normative judgements are distribution blind or because of the availability of lump sum tax and transfer instruments or similar means of achieving any desired distributional objectives), then:

$$dD = \sum_{i=1}^{n} dy_i + \sum_{i=1}^{n} \sum_{j=2}^{l} \frac{\partial D}{\partial a_{ij}} da_{ij}$$

that is, the marginal total development payback is equal to the marginal total financial payback plus the marginal non-financial development payback:

$$dD = dTFP + dNFDP$$

The discussion is specialized to this case for simplicity in the subsequent analysis, although it is not essential to do so.

PUBLIC GOOD CHARACTERISTICS OF PUBLIC INVESTMENTS

Public investments often possess 'public good characteristics'. How is this feature of public investments best understood within the current framework? Given a public investment project, for each individual and achievement it is possible to write:

$$\Delta a_{ij} = (a_{ij}^{\phi 2} - a_{ij}^{\phi 1}) = \theta_{ij}\delta$$

where δ is the largest increase in the achievement experienced by any of the individuals.

Let the matrix θ, consisting of the coefficients θ_{ij}, be called the impact coefficient matrix. These coefficients are assumed non-negative for simplicity. Consider a feasible public investment, P1, and suppose it has impact coefficient matrix θ. Now consider the set, J, of impact coefficient matrices θ' that is identical to θ with the exception that its coefficient vector, $\theta'_{ik}(k\in(1,...l))$, is less than the corresponding coefficient vector θ_{ik} for one or more $i\in(1,...n)$ and unchanged for the remaining $j\in(1,...n)$. Every element of this set must also correspond to a feasible public investment project if the original public investment, P1, features complete excludability, and if the benefits of the public investment project are perfectly divisible (which is assumed). This is because it must be possible for such a project to partially or wholly 'shut off' the benefits accruing to any individual without diminishing the benefits that accrue to others, even if these benefits are, in the first instance, jointly supplied. Alternatively, if there is not complete excludability, then at least some elements of the set J will be unfeasible. At the opposite extreme of complete non-excludability, all elements of the set J are unfeasible, implying that the only way to provide the good undiminished to one person is to provide it undiminished to all. The 'proportion' of elements in the set that are unfeasible, defined appropriately, provides a measure of the excludability of the benefits of a public investment. Let $\alpha\in[0,1]$ be such a monotonically decreasing index of the degree of excludability of a public investment, such that $\alpha=1$ when the benefits of the public investment are not excludable at all (corresponding to a public investment with maximal public good characteristics) and $\alpha=0$ when they are completely excludable (corresponding to a public investment with minimal public good characteristics). This is a definition that focuses on the benefits delivered by alternative public investments rather than on their physical or infrastructural features.

What about the assumption of non-rivalry in consumption? If the public invest-ment, P1, is efficiently produced, and if there is no rivalry in consumption, then 'shutting down' (or more generally diminishing) the benefits received by any individual cannot increase the benefits accruing to any individual who continues to receive them. Thus, there is no feasible public investment that has a distinct impact coefficient matrix such that its coefficients are identical to those of θ, with the exception that its coeffi-cients vector θ'_{ik} ($k \in (1,\ldots l)$) is less than the original coefficient vector for one or more $i \in (1,\ldots n)$, and its coefficient vector is greater than or equal to the original coefficient vector for all other $i \in (1,\ldots n)$ (and strictly greater for at least one). In contrast, if there is some rivalry in consumption, then there exist such feasible public investments. The magnitude of the trade-off between the lowered and the raised impact coefficients, appropriately defined, provides a measure of the extent to which there is rivalry in experiencing the benefits of a public investment.

Let $\beta \in [0,1]$ be a monotonically decreasing index of the degree of rivalry present in a public investment, such that $\beta=1$ when the public investment is such that there is no rivalry at all (corresponding to the case of maximal public good characteristics) and $\beta=0$ when there is the greatest rivalry (corresponding to the case of minimal public good characteristics). This is, once more, a definition that focuses on the benefits deliv-ered by alternative public investments rather than on their physical or infrastructural features.

It is important to note that whether a public investment possesses a high degree of public good characteristics does not appear to depend, in principle, on whether or not the payback generated by the public investment is predominantly financial or non-financial. Public investments that have paybacks of either type could vary in their public good characteristics. Of course, there may be an empirical relationship between the type of payback generated and the extent of public good characteristics. Whether this is the case would have to be empirically investigated.

DEFINING PREDICTABILITY AND PRECISION

Having presented these preliminaries, it is now possible to address the 'fiscal space conjecture' as described by Roy et al (Chapter 2). First, predictability and precision need to be formally defined. Roy et al define precision as the 'degree of expected error in *ex ante* calculations of payback' and predictability as 'the degree of observed error in *ex post* payback outcomes'. If the social decision-maker has 'rational expectations' the expecta-tion of the difference between predicted payback and actual payback is zero. It seems unappealing and implausible to *assume* that this difference is either systematically negative or positive. It seems more plausible that Roy et al have in mind a measure that penalizes greater deviation between expected payback and actual payback (such as the *variance* of the errors in prediction). It will therefore be assumed that predictability and precision both refer to such a measure, specifically the variance in the errors of prediction. Since the *ex ante* and *ex post* perspectives are equivalent in regard to such a measure, henceforth both terms can be referred to under the heading of 'predictability'.

PREDICTABILITY AND PUBLIC GOOD CHARACTERISTICS

Having defined these terms, can it be concluded that they vary in any systematic way with the public good characteristics of public investments?

If $dD = dSFP + dNFDP$

then the errors in prediction of the development payback ε_D, are defined by:

$$\varepsilon_D = (E(dD) - dD) = E(dSFP) + E(dNFDP - dSFP - dNFDP)$$

Further, predictability or precision of the development payback refers to:

$$\text{var } \varepsilon_D = \text{var} (E(dSFP) + E(dNFDP - dSFP - dNFDP)$$

$$= \text{var} (dSFP) + \text{var} (dNFDP) + 2\text{cov} (dSFP, dNFDP)$$

whereas errors in prediction of the financial payback are defined by:

$$\varepsilon_F = E(dSFP) - dSFP$$

and predictability or precision of the financial payback refers to:

$$\text{var } \varepsilon_F = \text{var} (dSFP)$$

It is interesting to note that var ε_D − var $\varepsilon_F =$ var $(dNFDP)+2\text{cov} (dSFP, dNFDP)$.

It follows that whether the predictability of the development payback is larger than that of the financial payback will depend jointly on var $(dNFDP)$ and cov $(dSFP, dNFDP)$. While it is straightforward to assume that the former is positive, the latter could, in principle, be of either sign, and would appear to depend on the exact nature of the interlinkages between financial and non-financial development achievements generated by the public investment.

In particular, given that var $(dNFDP)$ is positive, the predictability of the development payback is greater than the predictability of the financial payback (var ε_D − var $\varepsilon_F < 0$) if and only if the covariance between the non-financial development payback and the financial payback is *either* positive *or* negative and sufficiently small (possessing a magnitude that is less than half that of the predictability of the non-financial development payback). Note that both terms refer to properties of the outcomes generated by the public investment as assessed by the development evaluation function. As such, they each depend jointly on the empirical outcomes of the public investment and the normative assessments of these outcomes implicit in the function.

Consider the first (sufficient) condition – that the covariance between the societal financial payback and the non-financial development payback of a public investment project is positive. Is this likely to be the case? Whether investment projects that generate positive (negative) societal financial payback generate positive (negative) non-financial development paybacks will depend on whether there exist causal interconnections through which higher private incomes are translated into better (non-financial) development outcomes or vice versa. Much of the literature on development strongly suggests that such causal linkages, or 'spill-over', not only exist, but are pervasive. It is clear that the 'spill-over' that is present in the development process is likely to be largest when the public good characteristics of the development process are highest. (When the public good characteristics of an investment project are high then, from the definitions given above, it is not possible to design the projects alternatively so as to restrict the benefits to selected persons, and the benefits to particular persons cannot be increased by decreasing those available to others. However, this is precisely the case in instances in which there exist spill-over from financial to non-financial development outcomes, or vice versa.) It is sufficient to think of specific empirical examples, such as the income generation benefits of improving public health and sanitation, to see that this is very frequently the case. In contrast, there may be projects in which the pursuit of higher developmental payback is associated with lower financial payback and vice versa. Consider, for instance, the degree of success in collecting health service user fees from poor users. These diverse examples suggest that the sign and magnitude of the covariance between different kinds of paybacks in a given type of investment project are empirical matters. In particular, the greater public good characteristics of a public investment project may or may not be associated with the possession of higher covariance between the development payback and the financial payback of the project, and such covariance need not necessarily be positive.

So far the relative magnitudes of two concepts (the predictability of the development payback and the predictability of the societal financial payback) associated with any single public investment project have been explored. This, although interesting, is not the subject of the 'fiscal space conjecture' that, instead, involves comparisons *between* investment projects of each of the two concepts (predictability of development payback and the predictability of societal financial payback) individually.

THE FISCAL SPACE CONJECTURE

It is now necessary to formally define the 'fiscal space conjecture'. A first public invest-ment project (P1) is defined as having 'greater public good characteristics' than a second public investment project (P2) if $(\alpha_1,\beta_1) \geq (\alpha_2,\beta_2)$, where the subscripts denote the respective public investments and (α,β) are the measures of excludability and rivalry defined above.[4] The fiscal space conjecture (FSC1) then states that if P1 has greater public good characteristics than P2 (i.e.) $(\alpha_1,\beta_1) > (\alpha_2,\beta_2)$ then $\operatorname{var}\varepsilon_{D1} < \operatorname{var}\varepsilon_{D2}$ and $\operatorname{var}\varepsilon_{F1} < \operatorname{var}\varepsilon_{F2}$ where the subscripts 1 and 2 refer to the respective public investment projects.

It may be inappropriate to compare 'unlike' public investment projects, for instance those that have different levels of expected (overall) development payback. Taking this approach, it is possible to refine the fiscal space conjecture, for instance, as follows (FSC2): if P1 has greater public good characteristics than P2 (i.e. $(\alpha_1,\beta_1) > (\alpha_2,\beta_2)$) and P1 and P2 have the same expected overall development payback (i.e. $E(dD_1) = E(dD_2)$), then $\operatorname{var}\varepsilon_{D1} < \operatorname{var}\varepsilon_{D2}$ and $\operatorname{var}\varepsilon_{F1} > \operatorname{var}\varepsilon_{F2}$ where the subscripts 1 and 2 refer to the respective public investment projects.

It may be argued that this is not a sufficiently stringent conception of likeness. However, the variance of the financial payback and that of the overall developmental payback cannot be meaningfully compared unless the expected levels of these paybacks are *both* similar. Accordingly, it is possible to present the stricter definition (FSC3): if P1 has greater public good characteristics than P2 (i.e. $(\alpha_1,\beta_1) > (\alpha_2,\beta_2)$) and P1 and P2 have the same expected overall development payback (i.e. $E(dD_1) = E(dD_2)$), and the same expected financial payback (i.e. $E(dSFP1) = \sum_{i=1}^{n} E(dy_{i1}) = \sum_{i=1}^{n} E(dy_{i2}) = E(dSFP2)$), then $\operatorname{var}\varepsilon_{D1} < \operatorname{var}\varepsilon_{D2}$ and $\operatorname{var}\varepsilon_{F1} > \operatorname{var}\varepsilon_{F2}$ where the subscripts 1 and 2 refer to the respec-tive public investment projects.

It may be noted that, if the expected overall development payback and the expected financial payback are the same, then it follows that the expected non-financial develop-ment payback is also the same. That is:

$$E(dNFDP1) = \sum_{i=1}^{n} \sum_{j=2}^{l} E\left(\frac{\partial D}{\partial a_{ija}} da_{ija}\right) = \sum_{i=1}^{n} \sum_{j=2}^{l} E\left(\frac{\partial D}{\partial a_{ij2}} da_{ij2}\right)$$

$$= E(dNFDP2).$$

The stricter definition (FSC3), is taken as that being the most appropriate of the ones thus far considered. However, in any of these cases there are two required implications. Specifically,

$$\operatorname{var}\varepsilon_{D1} < \operatorname{var}\varepsilon_{D2} \tag{1}$$

which is true if and only if:

var $(dSFP1)$ + var $(dNFDP1)$ + 2cov $(dSFP1,dNFDP1)$ <

var $(dSFP2)$ + var $(dNFDP2)$ + 2cov $(dSFP2,dNFDP2)$

(Condition A*).

The argument above is that the covariance between financial payback and non-financial development payback for any given public investment project is likely to depend on the specific empirical features of that project (as well as the normative weights implicit in the development evaluation function). It follows that whether cov $(dSFP1,dNFDP1)$ < cov $(dSFP2,dNFDP2)$ is an empirical matter. The same would seem to be true of the relative magnitude of the variances of the developmental paybacks and the financial paybacks in the two cases. Nothing in the definition of a public good would seem to provide obvious guidance in assessing the relative magnitude of these variances.

Also:

$$\text{var } \varepsilon_{F1} > \text{var } \varepsilon_{F2} \text{ if and only if var } (dSFP1) > \text{var } (dSFP2) \tag{2}$$

(Condition B*).

Once again, the relative magnitude of the variances of the financial paybacks would seem to be a matter about which the definition of a public good would not seem to provide clear guidance. It is certainly possible that (1) and (2) are true for reasonable development evaluation functions under specific empirical conditions, but this would depend on empirical facts concerning the nature of public investments.

It is clear that it is necessary to place more structure on the problem if conclusions are to be derived. Returning to Condition A* above, and taking note of the earlier conclusion that there is no *theoretical* reason to assume that the covariance (between financial and non-financial development payback) is systematically different across projects with different public good characteristics, it is possible to specialize further to cases in which:

cov $(dSFP1,dNFDP1)$ = cov $(dSFP2,dNFDP2)$

If 'comparable' projects are defined as ones for which this 'equal covariance' condition holds, in addition to the previous conditions for likeness of projects (that the expected overall development payback and the expected financial payback of the projects are the same), then the fiscal space conjecture can be further refined to state (FSC4): if P1 has greater public good characteristics than P2 (i.e. $(\alpha_1,\beta_1)>(\alpha_2,\beta_2)$) and P1 and P2 are comparable projects, then var ε_{D1} < var ε_{D2} and var ε_{F1} > var ε_{F2} where the subscripts refer to the respective public investment projects.

From Condition A*, for this version of the fiscal space conjecture to be true it is required that:

$$\text{var}\,(dSFP1) + \text{var}\,(dNFDP1) < \text{var}\,(dSFP2) + \text{var}\,(dNFDP2),$$

(Condition A**) and, as before (Condition B*), that var $(dSFP1)$ > var $(dSFP2)$.

It is now possible to introduce an important feature of public goods, which has been considered to be central in the extensive empirical and theoretical literature on the subject. This is the idea that the financing and the provision of the optimal level of public goods is extremely challenging because of difficulties in eliciting the value that individual agents receive from a public investment that has high public good characteristics. The 'free rider problem' in public good provision has been widely viewed as being very serious.[5] Although there are, in principle, mechanisms for eliciting the required information, these are only available under very stringent theoretical conditions. In practice, in real situations, there are considerable uncertainties as to whether the optimal level of the public good can be provided and, more especially, as to whether the resources expended on public good provision can be recovered from those who benefit from them (which will directly affect the governmental financial payback and may indirectly affect the societal financial payback). Such difficulties in recovery may be important not only in creating obstacles to making the public investment initially effective, but in making it difficult to sustain the public investment over time and to generate an adequate ongoing stream of benefits. It might be argued from this fact that it is reasonable to characterize the variance of the financial payback expected from an investment with high public good characteristics as being greater than the variance of the financial payback expected from an investment with low public good characteristics. If this were true, then Condition B* would hold:

$$\text{var}\,(dSFP1) > \text{var}\,(dSFP2)$$

For Condition A** to hold it is necessary to require in addition that:

$$\text{var}\,(dNFDP1) < \text{var}\,(dNFDP2)$$

and that the difference in the predictability of the non-financial development payback of the two projects, var $(dNFDP2)$–var $(dNFDP1)$, be sufficiently large. In other words, projects with high public good characteristics must have relatively predictable non-financial returns as compared to projects with low public good characteristics. This assumption may be deemed not unreasonable if it is thought that certain public investment projects possessing high public good characteristics (for instance, public sanitation or immunization campaigns, or rural roads) are known to have fairly predictable beneficial effects on non-financial development objectives. In contrast, public investment projects possessing lower public good characteristics, such as toll bridges, contribute much less predictably to non-financial development objectives, because the causal interlinkages between the provision of such goods and non-financial development objectives are not well understood.

If these empirical hypotheses are correct then the fiscal space conjecture (FSC4) would hold true. Since the hypotheses required for the proposition to hold true are unverified, albeit plausible, it is correct to describe it as a conjecture.

CONCLUSIONS

In the interest of greater clarity, an attempt to make a formal statement of the fiscal space conjecture and to identify some empirical conditions under which it would hold true has been undertaken. The potential implications for public investment planning, especially in developing countries, are worth considering. The risk associated with receiving inadequate financial paybacks from projects that possess high public good characteristics may be high. That may not always be sufficient reason to avoid such projects, especially as the risk associated with the overall development payback of such projects is lower where the fiscal space conjecture holds true. A consequence is that a superficially rational, 'risk-averse' public investment policy may have considerable developmental costs, as it may give undue significance to the low predictability of a project's financial payback, which ought to be only one part of the overall assessment of the risks entailed in public investment.

NOTES

1   I am most grateful to Francisco Rodríguez for his helpful suggestions.
2   In this respect it is similar to many other economic and social measures, which involve 'thick ethical concepts' – see, for example, Putnam (2004).
3   This is not a restrictive characterization for most public investment projects, which must be viewed as either small relative to a national economy or possible to be disaggregated into small component projects. Moreover, the characterization is convenient but not crucial to the analysis that follows.
4   Excluded is 'jointness in supply', mentioned by Roy et al (Chapter 2, this volume), in keeping with current definitions of public goods.
5   See, for example, Cornes and Sandler (1995) for a survey. For an interesting view of the history of this discussion, see Tuck (2008).

REFERENCES

Cornes, R. and Sandler, T. (1995) *The Theory of Externalities, Public Goods and Club Goods*, Cambridge University Press, Cambridge

Keynes, J. M. (1933) 'National self-sufficiency', *The Yale Review*, vol 22, no 4 (June), pp755–769

Putnam, H. (2004) *The Collapse of the Fact/Value Dichotomy*, Harvard University Press, Cambridge, MA

Tuck, R. (2008) *Free Riding*, Harvard University Press, Cambridge, MA

5

Understanding Fiscal Expansions[1]

Francisco Rodríguez

INTRODUCTION

Suppose that a given country decides to increase government expenditures by more than 10 per cent in a given year. Suppose also that this increase is not a simple consequence of increasing per capita GDP, but was rather a result of an increasing participation of the public sector in the economy. What would you expect the long-run consequences of a fiscal expansion of this type to be?

Most economists would argue that, if such a fiscal expansion is not accompanied by a permanent increase in revenues, it would appear reckless and is unlikely to be sustained. Even if the expansion is financed by a temporary boom in incomes, coming, say, from an increase in resource rents or deficit financing, it is likely to collapse as soon as the source of revenue dries up. The reason is simple. An increase in spending without a consequent increase in revenues implies a long-run increase in the fiscal deficit, and high permanent fiscal deficits are, commonly, not sustainable. Even if the increase is accompanied by increases in tax revenues, or other apparently permanent sources of revenues, deep questions would remain about the long-run political sustainability of sudden and drastic tax increases of the magnitude necessary to sustain such fiscal expansions.

An alternative answer, however, can be given to this question based on equally solid economic theory. Whether *any* increase in expenditures is sustainable or not in the long run should depend on the uses to which the additional expenditure is put. If fiscal expansions are used to finance investment with high social returns, it could be argued that there is no reason for the fiscal expansion to be unsustainable because the expansion itself will be paid for by the revenue increase resulting from the payoff to these investments. If the society in question has the political institutions in place that allow it to choose socially optimal investments and for the state to reap a significant fraction of the gains from those investments in the form of higher revenues, then even deficit-financed expenditures can pay for themselves in the long run.

The latter argument is particularly pertinent in the context of the discussion regarding the MDGs. A number of economists, most prominently Sachs (2005), have argued that the social returns to investment in basic human capabilities in poor countries are sufficiently high to justify very large flows of development assistance. The underlying premise is that high injections of foreign aid will allow countries to transition to states in which the high payoffs realized from these investments make further foreign aid unnecessary. A not always explicit assumption behind this reasoning is the existence of multiple fiscal equilibria, in which the economy can either be in a low revenue-low investment situation or in a high revenue-high investment setting. Foreign aid plays the role of helping the economy transition between steady states, but the new situation can only be sustained without continuous flows of aid if it is in equilibrium.

More generally, the answer to this question is pertinent to the broader fiscal space debate (Hemming and Ter-Minassian, 2004; Heller, 2005). If fiscal expansions that are devoted to investments in human and physical capital can generate the revenues to pay for themselves in the long run, then the call for greater 'fiscal space' to carry out these investments on the part of developing countries would make sense. If, however, large fiscal expansions tend to be unsustainable in the long run, the scepticism often voiced by multilaterals on the prudence of raising spending without paying adequate attention to fiscal sustainability issues would be justified.

A typical approach to ascertain the sustainability of fiscal expansions is to estimate the expected social return to the investments into which the increased fiscal expenditures are directed. If the social returns are higher than the cost of investment, then there should be an appropriate set of taxes and transfers that make the government reap a net positive return on the investment directly into its fiscal accounts. Whether such a set of transfers is politically viable is a different question, and political constraints may well make socially optimal investments fiscally unsustainable. Nevertheless, these direct calculations of the return have the benefit of allowing an explicit consideration of the links between the microeconomic evidence on the returns of particular investments and the macroeconomic objective of fiscal sustainability.

The key strength of direct calculations is also one of its main weaknesses. To the extent that this approach relies on empirical estimates of the returns of particular investments, the results will be as strong as the underlying estimates that they are based on. Take, for example, the case of the effects of infrastructure investment on productivity. A vast literature has emerged attempting to estimate the elasticity of output (or productivity) to public investment in infrastructure. The estimates range from zero (Tatom, 1993; Hotz-Eakin, 1994) to highly positive (Aschauer, 1989; Easterly and

Servén, 2003; Pineda and Rodríguez, 2006). Direct calculations of the fiscal sustainability of investments in infrastructure will thus be heavily dependent on the choice of elasticity estimates.

This chapter takes an alternative approach. It studies the sustainability of fiscal expansions by examining how long these expansions last in the data. The central data set used is the IMF's *Government Finance Statistics* (2006a, 2006b), which allow the calculation of expenditure levels, as well as their decomposition, by type of expenditure for 109 economies since 1972. This chapter concentrates precisely on the type of phenomena that are referred to in the opening paragraph: substantial expansions of real per capita expenditures that are also accompanied by the growth of the share of the state in GDP. The basic question asked is, 'How often are these expansions sustained, and what makes them sustainable?' The dependent variable for most of the analysis will be the duration of these fiscal expansions.

The proposed approach contrasts with the widespread practice of evaluating fiscal sustainability through empirical tests of the present value budget constraint. This literature commonly appeals to testing for the existence of a long-run co-integrating relationship between expenditures and revenues.[2] While the results of that literature, which tend to show that governments must obey a long-run present value budget constraint, are certainly pertinent for the understanding of fiscal policy design, they form only a part of the answer to many questions of policy relevance. When deciding whether to carry out a fiscal expansion, countries usually lack information that would enable them to make a reasonably precise estimate about the expected evolution of their fiscal revenues. The relevant policy question faced by many of them is whether they should attempt to increase spending now in the hope that the revenues generated by infrastructure and human capital investment will enable them to sustain the higher expenditure levels in the long run, or whether they should wait until they can increase their sources of revenue through other means. This question can only be adequately addressed by studying the sustainability of expenditure levels, not of deficits.

The study of fiscal expansions poses some non-trivial econometric problems. In particular, the fiscal expansions that we are most likely to be interested in are precisely those expansions that do not end. However, an expansion that has not ended by the end of the sample will, by definition, be an expansion whose duration is not observed. Dropping these observations from the sample, a common and misguided way to deal with the problem, would significantly bias the results by systematically excluding successful fiscal expansions. In order to tackle this problem, a set of techniques from *survival analysis* is used that allows censored observations to be dealt with. Adequately interpreting the information in these regressions is fundamental for a complete understanding of the nature of fiscal expansions.

The analysis of fiscal expansions also allows reconsideration of the idea of multiple fiscal equilibria by explicitly studying the dynamics of the economy after fiscal expansions. If it is found that most fiscal expansions tend to die out after some time, this would reaffirm the idea that there exist unique fiscal equilibria, and that deviations from them will not be sustained in the long run. However, if it is found that the longer an expansion lasts, the lower the probability of returning to the initial equilibria, this would appear to confirm that some countries are able to move out of their 'fiscal poverty traps' by carrying out substantial increases in fiscal expenditures. Indeed, it can be shown that the existence of multiple equilibria can be evaluated by empirically estimating the probability of remaining at higher than initial expenditure levels given that an expansion has occurred, this is also known as the *hazard rate* of the duration model.

   The rest of this chapter proceeds as follows. In the next section, a theoretical model is developed that shows how the empirical evidence can be used to distinguish between single and multiple equilibria models of fiscal expansions. Then there is a discussion of the data sources as well as the construction of the measures of fiscal expansions. The following section presents the results of the empirical estimation exercise, and the chapter ends with some concluding comments.

THEORETICAL CONSIDERATIONS

Assume that an economy can produce with two different technologies, where the choice between these technologies depends on investment in a public good. If an investment of b is paid by the government, then output is $y = Bk^{\alpha}$; if it is not then production is carried out using the traditional technology and output is $y = Ak^{\alpha}$ with $B>A$. We assume that there is a fixed tax rate, τ, that is used to finance expenditures. There are two types of expenditures, current expenditures, C, and public goods investment, G. Note that G can take either the values b (if the investment is made) or 0. C, in contrast, can take any non-negative value. Governments face an intertemporal budget constraint:

$$\sum_{t=1}^{\infty} \left(\frac{1}{1+\rho}\right)^{t}(C_{t} + G_{t}) = \sum_{t=1}^{\infty} \left(\frac{1}{1+\rho}\right)^{t} \tau y_{t} \tag{1}$$

We use the conventional Solow closure for this model which is to assume that a fixed fraction, s, of net of tax income is used to accumulate capital:

$$k_{t} - k_{t-1} = s(1 - \tau)y - (n + \delta)k \tag{2}$$

where δ is the rate of depreciation, n is population growth, and s is the savings rate.

   We first investigate the situations under which the government can afford to pay for the public good. Note that in order for it to be feasible to pay for the public good, it must be the case that at the steady state level of income fiscal revenues are sufficient to at least pay for the public good, that is:

$$b < \tau B k_{ssb}^{\alpha} \tag{3}$$

where k_{ssb} is used to denote the steady state level of capital if the public good invest-ment is paid. Note that we can use the production function and the accumulation equation (2) to solve for k_{ssb} as:

$$k_{ssb} = \left(\frac{s(1-\tau)}{n+\delta} B \right)^{\frac{1}{1-\alpha}} \tag{4}$$

Similarly we can solve for the steady state level of the capital stock when the public good investment is not made as:

$$k_{ssa} = \left(\frac{s(1-\tau)}{n+\delta} A \right)^{\frac{1}{1-\alpha}} \tag{5}$$

It will also be assumed that the lower level of steady state income would not generate enough revenues to pay for the public goods investment. Putting this assumption together with (3), (4) and (5), we can summarize our parametric assumptions as:

$$\tau A \left(\frac{s(1-\tau)}{n+\delta} A \right)^{\frac{\alpha}{1-\alpha}} < b < \tau B \left(\frac{s(1-\tau)}{n+\delta} B \right)^{\frac{1}{1-\alpha}} \tag{6}$$

We are now ready to study two alternative fiscal scenarios. First consider an increase in current expenditures in the low-output steady state. Remember that at the low-level steady state, tax revenues are insufficient to pay for b, so that all expenditure is current expenditure.

Let

$$C' > C_{ssa} = \tau A \left(\frac{s(1-\tau)}{n+\delta} A \right)^{\frac{1}{1-\alpha}} = \tau y_{ssa}$$

be the level of expenditure after the fiscal expansion. Since current expenditures have no effect on output, then the intertemporal budget constraint can be rewritten as:

$$\sum_{t=1}^{T} \left(\frac{1}{1+\rho} \right)^t (C' - \tau y_{ssa}) + \sum_{t=T+1}^{\infty} \left(\frac{1}{1+\rho} \right)^t (C_t - \tau y_{ssa}) = 0 \tag{7}$$

Where T is the number of periods for which the fiscal expansion is sustained at C'. Since the first term on the left-hand side of (7) is negative, it follows that the second term must be positive and thus on net, after time t, the economy must generate fiscal surpluses to pay for the indebtedness incurred during the expansion. It follows that fiscal expenditures must go down below C_{ssa} at some moment and thus the fiscal expansion must end sooner or later. An analogous argument can be made about a fiscal expansion that is carried out when the economy starts out from a high income equilibrium. In that case, if a fiscal expansion occurs from the initial steady state to current expenditures $C''>C_{ssb}>C$, then equation (7) is replaced by:

$$\sum_{t=1}^{T} \left(\frac{1}{1+\rho}\right)^t (b + C'' - \tau y_{ssb}) + \sum_{t=T+1}^{\infty} \left(\frac{1}{1+\rho}\right)^t (C_t - \tau y_{ssb}) = 0 \quad (8)$$

with the same logic implying that C_t must fall below C_{ssb} at some moment in the future. When that moment occurs is, of course, indeterminate, as there are many paths that satisfy the intertemporal budget restriction and which one is chosen will depend on the political process used to take fiscal decisions. But, even without specifying that process, equations (7) and (8) allow us to predict that fiscal expansions that are concentrated on current expenditures are unsustainable.

Let us now suppose, in contrast, that an economy that starts out at the low-income equilibrium carries out a fiscal expansion in order to finance the acquisition of a productivity enhancing public good that allows the economy to shift to modern technology. In that case, current expenditures stay at C_{ssa} and public goods investment increases from 0 to b. Note, however, that the economy immediately shifts to using the superior technology once the public good investment is made. It follows that the budget constraint will now become:

$$\sum_{t=1}^{T} \left(\frac{1}{1+\rho}\right)^t (b + C_t - \tau y_t) = 0 \quad (9)$$

Note that, since the economy is now using the modern technology, as $t \rightarrow \alpha$, $\tau y_t \rightarrow \tau y_{ssb}>b$. Thus there exists a non-negative level of current expenditure such that the budget surplus can be made positive as time advances. Whether this will be enough to pay for the debt that was incurred when carrying out the investment will depend on the discount rate. For very high discount rates, the accumulation of budget surpluses, in the long run, will always be insufficient to pay for the debts incurred while carrying them out. But as the discount rate diminishes, the net present values of the net surpluses in the future become higher than any deficits that were incurred. Since as $\rho \rightarrow 0$ the sum of these surpluses tends to infinity, it follows that there is a positive discount rate ρ^* such that for all $\rho<\rho^*$ setting $G_t = b$ is consistent with the intertemporal budget constraint.

It is illustrative to observe the paths taken by the fiscal deficit, expenditures, and GDP in this scenario. Figure 5.1 simulates a typical path, in which we have assumed that

current expenditures stay at C_{ssa} until the debt accumulated to pay for the initial investment is paid off, and then increases to C_{ssb}. In this simulation we have set parameter
values that would be typical of a representative economy: $\tau = 0.2$, $s = 0.3$, $\rho = 0.015$,
$\alpha = 0.4$, $\delta = 0.02$, $n = 0.03$. We have also assumed that the benefit of public investment
is to double production at a given value of the capital stock ($B/A = 2$), given an investment cost equal to one year's production ($b = 1$).

As Figure 5.1 shows, the increase in total expenditure outweighs the initial increase
in output. Even after the initial gain in output (coming from the immediate increase in
productivity at current capital stock levels) is realized, the country still runs a deficit of
more than 7 per cent of GDP, and starts accumulating debt on what can easily be
perceived as an unsustainable path. The reason why the path is not sustainable is that
the accumulation of capital, which occurs as the result of the higher productivity levels,
allows for a longer run increase in per capita output that generates higher tax collection.
By period 34, the deficit turns negative and the debt starts to be paid off (after reaching
a peak of 115 per cent of GDP). Once the debt is totally paid off, a second fiscal expansion occurs, which allows the state to increase current expenditures by the amount of
resources that were previously devoted to paying off the debt.

This simple stylized model helps to underscore two points. The first is that even
deficit-financed fiscal expansions can be sustainable, whether they are financed by

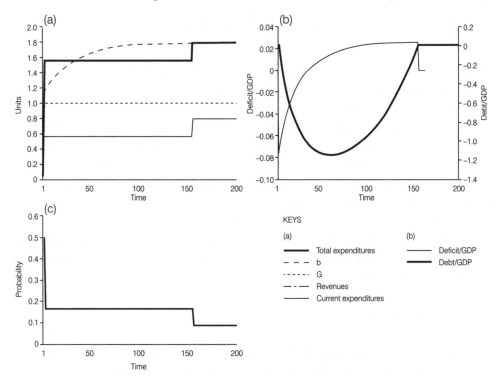

Figure 5.1 *(a) Expenditures and revenues; (b) deficit and debt to GDP ratios;*
(c) hazard rate of fiscal expansion

higher taxes or not. The example is precisely one of a deficit-financed fiscal expansion. A second point is that there are two key determinants of the fiscal sustainability of an expansion. One is the composition of government expenditures; whether the expansion can be sustained or not depends vitally on whether the increase occurs in the form of current expenditures or in the form of pubic investment. The second one is the set of policy choices that are undertaken to enable society to pay off the debt incurred by higher investment. Suppose, for example, that once the growth in productivity is realized, policymakers decide to raise current expenditures further in order to distribute the gains from the public investment among their cronies. This decision implies that there will not be enough revenues to pay back the debt that is accumulated during the start of the expansion. This may itself drive the economy on an unsustainable fiscal path. Policy choices and their determinants are thus key to understanding the sustainability of fiscal expansions.

The model can be slightly modified in another direction in order to derive an additional set of empirical predictions. Let us assume now that government expenditures are not deterministic but rather that they have a stochastic component. We will assume that this stochastic component takes the form of random changes in current expenditures. The intertemporal budget constraint will now be:

$$\sum_{t=1}^{\infty} \left(\frac{1}{1+\rho} \right)^t (C_t + \varepsilon_t + G_t) = \sum_{t=1}^{\infty} \left(\frac{1}{1+\rho} \right)^t \tau y_t \qquad (10)$$

where, now, there are two components of current expenditures, planned expenditures, C_p and the unplanned random component, ε_p which we will assume to be distributed according to a $U[-c,c]$ distribution. Note that this setup is particularly convenient because it enables us to calculate the economy's equilibrium independently of the path taken by the stochastic shocks, as we have assumed that current expenditures are simply waste.[3] A distinction will arise between *ex ante* sustainability, which requires that (10) holds in expectations, and *ex post* sustainability, which requires that (10) holds after a given set of shocks have been realized.

A particularly useful variable in our later analysis will be the *hazard rate*, which we define as the probability that a fiscal expansion will be cut back in this period (in the sense of returning to or below the pre-expansion level of expenditures). Given that it has not yet been cut back:

$$h_t = P(G_t < G_0 \mid G_{t-1} > G_0) \qquad (11)$$

What does the model predict to be the behaviour of the hazard rate? Let us think back to our possible three cases of fiscal expansions. First, we have the case of a fiscal expansion in current expenditures from the low-income equilibrium. We can now rewrite (7) as:

$$\sum_{t=1}^{T} \left(\frac{1}{1+\rho} \right)^{t} (C' + \varepsilon_t - \tau y_{ssa}) + \sum_{t=T+1}^{\infty} \left(\frac{1}{1+\rho} \right)^{t} (C_t + \varepsilon_t - \tau y_{ssa}) = 0$$

(12)

Note that this equation *still* implies that, if there is a fiscal expansion during the first T periods it must be counteracted by a fiscal contraction after period T. The only difference from the previous analysis is that an increase in expenditures from C_{ssa} to C' can now be thwarted by a set of negative shocks that make *realized* fiscal expenditures $C'+\varepsilon_t$ lower than C_{ssa}. However, in such a case we would not observe a fiscal expansion, since a fiscal expansion only occurs when C_t is greater than C_0. Although the exact form of the hazard rate will depend on the path of expenditure that is taken to restore *ex-post* sustainability, equation (12) does require that expansions today be counteracted by contractions tomorrow:

$$G_1 > G_{ssa} \rightarrow \ni J| G_J < G_{ssa} \rightarrow h_J = 1$$

(13)

so that the hazard rate must be one at some future moment of time. Since the symmetry of the $U[-c,c]$ distribution implies that at $t = 1$ the hazard rate is less than 0.5, then equation (13) implies that the hazard rate must be increasing over some range between $t = 1$ and $t = J$. A similar reasoning can be applied to an increase in expenditures for the high-income equilibrium.

What about an increase in investment that goes to finance the expansion of public investment? Here matters are a bit different, since there is no force that pulls expenditures back to their pre-expansion levels. Whether it does fall, in practice, will now depend on whether the path of expenditures is *ex ante* and *ex post* sustainable. Failure of either type of sustainability will force a reversion to pre-expansion expenditure levels and an increase in the hazard rate. A sustainable expansion, however, need not see an increase in its hazard rate.

We illustrate this result in Figure 5.1(c), where we track the hazard rate for the same example that we have used to build the first two panels, but now introducing the uncertainty component of equation (10). We calculate the *ex ante* expected hazard rate, that is, the expected probability of expenditures declining below g_0 at t, conditional on our expectation of the realization of $\varepsilon_1 \ldots \varepsilon_{t-1}$. As can be seen in Figure 5.1(c), the hazard function is now decreasing over time. The longer the fiscal expansion lasts, the lower its probability of returning to its initial level. This result gives us a useful empirical prediction regarding the contrast between sustainable fiscal expansions and unsustainable ones. In the former the hazard rate should decrease over time, whereas in the latter we know it will ultimately increase to one.

DATA AND CONSTRUCTION OF INDICATORS

The analysis in this chapter is based on the study of the durability of fiscal expansions. We define the start of a fiscal expansion as an increase in the real level of fiscal per capita incomes that exceeds a pre-specified level, $\alpha > 0$. We also require that these expansions be accompanied by an increase of $\beta > 0$ in the share of expenditures over GDP. This requirement ensures that the increase in expenditures is not a simple by-product of economic growth, but rather that it is generated by increases in the role of the state in the economy. Thus the per cent year-on-year increase in expenditures must be higher than the rate of GDP growth. We will also require $\alpha > \beta$. This ensures that the minimum expenditure growth must be higher than the minimum required growth in the share of expenditures. This is because $\alpha < \beta$ would imply a requirement of negative GDP growth. While we do not want to rule out that possibility, neither do we wish to restrict ourselves to countries that present negative growth.

An economy can be in one of two states, in the midst of an expansion or out of it. An economy is in the midst of an expansion whenever (1) a fiscal expansion has started, and (2) the level of real per capita expenditures is higher than its pre-expansion level. Thus a fiscal expansion ends as soon as an economy returns to its pre-expansion level of per capita real expenditures. It follows that an economy cannot enter into an expansion if it is already in one. In the baseline empirical tests, we adopt the thresholds $\alpha = 0.1$ and $\beta = 0.5$, thus classifying as a fiscal expansion an increase of more than 10 per cent in real per capita expenditures that is accompanied by an increase of more than 5 per cent in the expenditure share. (Experiments with alternative thresholds, available from the author upon request, give very similar results.)

The indicator of fiscal expansions is constructed using data from the IMF's *Government Finance Statistics* (IMF, 2006a and 2006b, hereinafter, GFS) combined with output data from their *International Financial Statistics* (IMF, 2006c, hereinafter *IFS*). Building this series (as well as the other expenditure series in the database) requires linking data from the *GFS Historical Statistics*, which cover the period 1972 to 1990, with those for the period 1990 to 2006. This is done using the guidelines set out in Wickens (2002). For the case of expenditures, this requires combining the post-1990 expenditure series with the sum of the pre-1990 current expenditure and capital transfer series. All series are expressed net of interest payments.

A set of analogous linking rules is used to construct series for the share of alternative components of expenditures. In particular, series are built for the share of defence, economic, education, health, housing, public order and safety, recreation, social protection and general public services in total expenditures (always net of interest payments). It is also possible to build indicators of the share of environmental expenditures in total spending, but these series are only available after 1990 and thus are of limited use.

These indicators of the composition of government expenditures will allow us to test the basic empirical hypothesis that comes out of the theoretical discussion in the previous section, that the durability of fiscal expansions should be inextricably linked with the type of expenditures that are carried out. However, as that discussion made clear, it is also the case that we should expect the sustainability of fiscal expansions to depend on a society's capacity to maintain policies consistent with fiscal sustainability. In other words, even a society that makes the right spending choices can make the wrong fiscal policy choices, thus making the expansion unsustainable. This can happen, for example, if a society decides to redistribute the increasing tax returns generated by productivity enhancing public investments through higher current expenditures instead of using them to pay back the debt incurred to finance its investment. We would, therefore, expect that the sustainability of expansions also depends on the social and political capabilities that societies have for adequately distributing the costs of alternative expansions.

There are several indicators that immediately come to mind if we think of measuring a society's capacity for distributing the costs of carrying out significant public investment expansions. One would be a society's level of democracy. As pointed out by Rodrik (1999), democracy indicators provide an adequate measure of the quality of a society's institutions for conflict management, which have significant predictive power in accounting for differential responses to adverse shocks. Thus an index of democracy, derived from the Polity IV data set (Marshall and Jaggers, 2004), is used as one of the key explanatory variables of interest. Other measures, which may have an impact on a society's capacity to sustain fiscal expansions, are used. Thus, a measure of society's human capital (total years of schooling, from Barro and Lee, 2000), as well as of its social and economic development (respectively, the urbanization rate and the log of per capita income from World Bank, 2006) are employed as general indicators of a society's possible capacity to manage fiscal expansions. Additionally, a control for financial development (the ratio of liquid liabilities to GDP from World Bank, 2006) is introduced as one may expect societies with a better-developed financial system to be more capable of financing the deficits necessary to carry on sustained expansions of public investment.

The control for an economy's openness deserves special mention. There exists a well-established correlation between openness and the size of government (Cameron, 1978; Rodrik, 1998). The reason behind this correlation has been alternatively attributed to greater need for social insurance expenditures in more open economies (Rodrik, 1998), or to the fact that more open economies also tend to be smaller in size and thus less able to take advantage of economies of scale in public goods' provision (Alesina and Wacziarg, 1998). Whatever the explanation, this correlation would imply that more open economies should be more capable of sustaining fiscal expansions.

One key problem in studying the duration of fiscal expansions is that many interesting expansions do not come to an end by the last observation of available data. But it is precisely those expansions, whose ends we do not observe – that we will henceforth call *censored* durations – that constitute what are, arguably, the most interesting subjects for our analysis. Indeed, not only are more than 45 per cent of our expansions censored but the distribution of their characteristics is very different from that of the uncensored observations. If we were to drop the censored observations from the sample, we would calculate a mean duration rate of 1.8 years for our expansions, whereas the average duration including the censored observations is actually 7.7 years. Even this duration is an almost certain underestimate of expected duration, since it includes the last observed duration for the censored regression. If we were to fit the simplest possible duration model (one with an exponential hazard function) to this data, we would calculate an expected unconditional duration time of 14.0 years.

The literature on survival analysis is referred to in order to deal with the problem of censored observations. Specifically, if we have n countries with $t_1, t_2, \ldots t_n$ expansion durations, we concentrate on finding the estimate of the probability density function, $f(t)$, with associated survival time, $S(t)$, that maximizes the likelihood function:

$$L = \prod_i f(t_i)^{\delta_i} S(t_i)^{1-\delta_i} \tag{14}$$

where δ_i is an indicator variable that takes the value 0 if the pre-crisis expenditures per capita have not been reached by the last observation in the sample. Broadly speaking, there are two approaches in the literature to estimating equation (14). One is to specify a parametric functional form for $f(t)$ and to estimate the parameters of that form. The second one is to use a nonparametric approach to estimation of $f(t)$. The latter is commonly associated with estimation of the Cox proportional hazards model. Although the nonparametric approach is more flexible, it can lead to more imprecise estimates of the hazard function than a correctly specified parametric form. Versions of both models are presented in this section.

Another key issue has to do with how to handle country-level heterogeneity in this framework. For reasons analogous to those of panel data estimation with binary dependent variables, fixed effects estimators are not consistent with duration models (Andersen et al, 1999). A common solution is to assume that countries have differing propensities to experiencing crises. These propensities, called *frailties*, are analogous to the random effects of panel data models. An alternative approach is to estimate different baseline hazard rates for different groups, say, by region, or *stratifying* the estimation. We examine results from both approaches below.

EMPIRICAL RESULTS

Our filter identifies 110 fiscal expansions occurring between 1972 and 2005. Nineteen (17.3 per cent) of these last longer than 20 years, while 44 (40 per cent) are over by the first year. The distribution of these expansions varies considerably by region. Latin America has the highest number of expansions in the sample, but their average duration is the second lowest in the sample at 4.1 years. In contrast, industrialized countries and

Asian countries share the highest average duration lengths (17.5 and 14.6 years) as well as the highest median durations (9.5 and 23 years). It is striking to note that the *minimum* duration of a fiscal expansion in an industrialized country is 12 years, so that short-lived substantial fiscal expansions are virtually unknown in industrialized countries.

One possibility is that our fiscal expansions are being generated by changes in the comparability, over time, of the national expenditure data. The *GFS* database maintains notes on the years during which these changes in comparability occur. Only two of our 110 fiscal expansions coincide with these changes. Colombia 1988 and St Kitts and Nevis in 1988. None of our key results are affected by excluding these observations from the sample.

The longest lived expansions are those of Indonesia (1972–2005), Singapore (1975–2005), Mauritius (1975–2005) and India (1975–2005). All of these are censored. Indeed, the percentage of censored observations is significantly related to the durability of the crises. In industrialized countries, 78.6 per cent of expansions and 64.3 per cent of those in Asia are censored, in contrast to only 22.0 per cent in LAC and 33.3 per cent in the Middle East and North Africa (MENA). The one exception is Central and Eastern Europe, for which the high per cent of censored observations appears to be a result of the shortness of its data span, which, for most countries in this region, only covers the 1990s.

Table 5.1 shows two alternative indicators of the magnitude of the expansion. The *cumulative spending expansion* is the cumulative gap, over the duration of the expansion, of the absolute difference between spending levels and the pre-expansion spending levels:

$$CE_{it} = \sum_{t \leq T} \frac{g_{it} - g_{i0}}{g_{i0}} \tag{15}$$

where we have introduced the i subscript to distinguish among countries and T is the period in which the spending expansion ends (we normalize the initial period to $t = 0$). Note that, in the same sense as duration, CE is a censored variable. An alternative indicator measures the yearly cumulative spending expansion:

$$CE_{it} = \frac{1}{T} \sum_{t \leq T} \frac{g_{it} - g_{i0}}{g_{i0}} \tag{16}$$

As Table 5.1 shows that the difference between the cumulative spending expansion indicators, whether the total measure or the yearly one, is substantial. Whereas the Latin American expansion is, on average, only 10.5 per cent of initial income, the average expansion in an Asian country is almost 80 per cent of initial income. This, however, is not a reflection of differences in magnitude of the initial expansion. The average initial expansion of an Asian country is 20.5 per cent of initial year GDP, which is very similar to that of a Latin American country (23.0 per cent). (Recall that these means are condi-

Table 5.1 *Summary statistics of fiscal expansions by region*

Region	Number of Expansions	Average	Standard Deviation	Minimum	Maximum	Percentiles 25	Percentiles 50	Percentiles 75
Duration								
Africa	16	6.313	9.844	1	30	1	1.5	6
Asia	14	14.643	13.545	1	32	2	9.5	28
Central and Eastern Europe	13	3.692	2.810	1	10	2	3	5
Industrialized	14	17.500	10.029	1	28	12	23	25
Latin America and Caribbean	41	4.122	5.900	1	29	1	1	3
Middle East and North Africa	12	6.000	8.312	1	26	1	2	6.5
All Regions	110	7.636	9.679	1	32	1	2	12
Fraction of expansions that are censored								
Africa	16	0.438	0.512	0	1	0	0	1
Asia	14	0.643	0.497	0	1	0	1	1
Central and Eastern Europe	13	0.769	0.439	0	1	1	1	1
Industrialized	14	0.786	0.426	0	1	1	1	1
Latin America and Caribbean	41	0.220	0.419	0	1	0	0	0
Middle East and North Africa	12	0.333	0.492	0	1	0	0	0
All Regions	110	0.455	0.500	0	1	0	0	1
Cumulative spending (as fraction of initial spending)								
Africa	16	3.284	8.150	0	25.360	0.000	0.023	0.523
Asia	14	21.505	27.893	0	86.813	0.014	7.312	37.452
Central and Eastern Europe	13	0.743	0.956	0	2.993	0.019	0.385	1.176
Industrialized	14	11.047	10.027	0	36.004	4.672	9.790	16.547
Latin America and Caribbean	41	1.443	3.542	0	17.324	0.000	0.000	0.286
Middle East and North Africa	12	1.761	4.505	0	15.649	0.000	0.024	0.654
All Regions	110	5.438	12.987	0	86.813	0.000	0.072	3.742
Cumulative yearly spending (as fraction of initial spending)								
Africa	16	0.133	0.273	0	0.874	0.000	0.012	0.089
Asia	14	0.794	0.938	0	3.100	0.007	0.456	1.338
Central and Eastern Europe	13	0.136	0.128	0	0.367	0.010	0.108	0.211
Industrialized	14	0.477	0.366	0	1.385	0.334	0.441	0.635
Latin America and Caribbean	41	0.105	0.201	0	0.710	0.000	0.000	0.073
Middle East and North Africa	12	0.105	0.223	0	0.782	0.000	0.008	0.113
All regions	110	0.248	0.459	0	3.100	0.000	0.036	0.340

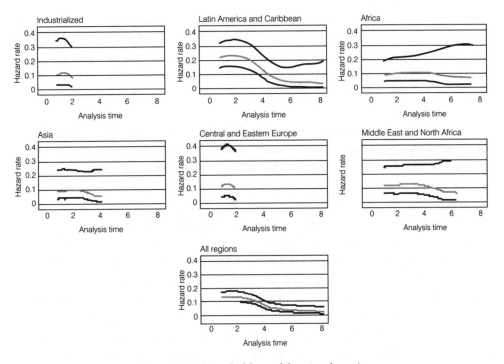

Figure 5.2 *Smoothed hazard function, by region*

tional on the expansion being larger than α, which we have set at 10 per cent.) Thus the data do not appear to signal that Latin American countries have less sustainable fiscal expansions because they are more reckless, at least as measured by the initial expansion magnitude, than their Asian counterparts, but rather suggest that we must look elsewhere to find the reasons for differences in sustainability.

One interesting initial approach that we can take to summarize the differences across countries on the sustainability of expansions is to study the unconditional hazard rates for different groups of countries. Since the results presented in Table 5.1 suggest that inter-regional variation is an important source of differences, in Figure 5.2 we present estimates of the unconditional hazard rate for six different regions, as well as a pooled estimate for all countries. The estimates presented in Figure 5.2 are derived as smoothed kernel density estimates of the Nelson–Aalen cumulative hazard function, and track the probability of exiting an expansion conditional on being in the set of countries that have not exited the expansion when *t* periods have elapsed since entering it.

Several factors are worthy of note in this figure. The first, is that for the group of industrialized and Central and Eastern European countries, as well as, to a lesser extent, those of Asia, the hazard rates are calculated only over very short intervals. This is nothing more than the reflection of the fact that in these regions most fiscal expansions are sustained. The fact that we seldom see fiscal expansions fail in these regions is the same as saying that there are very few failed expansions. But the unconditional hazard rate is based precisely on the information of countries that *exit* the expansion state. In the cases of Asia and the industrialized countries, this is truly a reflection of the long duration of fiscal expansions, whereas in Central and Eastern Europe it is again more a reflection of the lack of long spans of data (that leads most expansions in these countries to be censored).

An initial interesting observation is that all the hazard rates plotted in Figure 5.1 are downward sloping. In other words, the probability of exiting the expansion appears to be a decreasing function of the time spent in the expansion state. This observation would appear to confirm the intuition of the model set out above under the section 'Theoretical considerations', in particular, as represented in Figure 5.1(c), which predicts a declining hazard rate. It would, however, be hasty to jump from this observation to claim support for the existence of multiple equilibria, as there are simpler explanations that could be driving this pattern. In particular, country-level heterogeneity could generate decreasing unconditional hazard rates. If some countries have a higher propensity to sustain fiscal expansions, perhaps due to more prevalence of democratic institutions of conflict management, then these countries are likely to last longer in the crisis state and also to be less likely to exit it at any given moment (Hosmer and Lemeshow, 1999). This fact, known as the *frailty effect*, can be addressed by conditioning on country-specific effects, something we do below.

The third striking fact that comes out of Figure 5.2 is the large differences that exist in the shapes of these hazard functions by region. Despite the fact that the number of observations for any particular region is small, making the confidence intervals broad, it is apparent that there are substantial differences between a region that starts out with a high hazard rate that then drops abruptly (Latin America) and those that are low, but more stable (Africa and the MENA region), as well as with those that have a very short time span (industrialized, Central and Eastern Europe, and Asia). A more systematic way to identify the existence of these cross-regional differences is by statistically testing the hypothesis of equal hazard functions across regions. The results of these tests are presented in Table 5.2. Three distinct types of heterogeneity tests are carried out. Column 1 tests the hypothesis that all regions have the same hazard function. Column 2 groups industrialized and non-industrialized countries into two separate groups and tests for equality of the hazard functions of those two aggregate groups. Column 3 tests only for differences between non-industrialized regions.

A battery of tests for each of the three hypotheses is performed. The results are decisive, in that every single test rejects the hypothesis of equality of survival functions at a 1 per cent confidence level. The results thus point towards substantial heterogeneity across regions and suggest closer consideration of the reasons that could be driving these differences.

The theoretical discussion above emphasized the need to condition for the type of expenditures as a fundamental determinant of the sustainability of fiscal expansions.

Table 5.2 *Tests for equality of survival functions*

Test	All regions	Industrialized versus non-industrialized	Non-industrialized
Log-Rank	22.29***	7.03***	13.86***
Cox	17.87***	6.94***	11.02***
Wilcoxon	18.93***	5.84***	12.31***
Tarrone-Ware	20.85***	6.54***	13.40***
Peto-Peto	21.44***	6.78***	13.62***

Note: *** Significant at the 1 per cent level.

For the following analysis, information from *GFS* on the composition of expenditures according to an economic classification is used. This classification subdivides expenditures into ten subgroups: defence, economic, education, environmental, general public services, health, housing, public order and safety, recreation and social protection. Data for all but one of these categories, environment, are available before 1990. A further set of aggregate categories are built with the series that are available for the whole sample, spending on human capital (education and health), spending on the national economy (economic, recreation and housing) and transfers (social protection and general public spending net of interest). Defence spending and public order and safety are maintained as separate categories from any of these subgroups.

Before delving into regression analysis, Table 5.3 takes a first look at the data by calculating the characteristics of observed expansions both for the total subgroup of expansions and for those expansions that are accompanied by a positive growth of the share of each of the ten expenditure subgroups. The shortest lasting expansions are those that are accompanied by increases in public order and safety (5.06 years), defence spending (5.72 years) and general public services (5.81 years). By contrast, the longest lived expansions are those accompanied by increases in economic spending (11.11 years), housing (8.69 years) and recreation (8.32 years).

It is now appropriate to examine the hypotheses within the analytic framework of duration regressions. First, consider a well-known parametric duration model, which assumes the Weibull parameterization. Essentially, the hazard rate for country, i, is estimated as a function of a baseline hazard and the covariates:

$$h_i(t \mid X) = h_{0t} v_i exp(\beta X) \qquad (17)$$

where $h_{0t} = pt^{p-1}$. The parameter, p, characterizes the shape of the Weibull distribution, with $p < 1$ corresponding to a decreasing hazard function. An important distinction between equation (17) and a number of common duration models is that it allows for country specific effects, labelled v_i. These effects, also known as *frailties*, capture the country specific propensity to sustain a fiscal expansion. It is necessary to control for them in order to avoid the frailty effect discussed above.

Table 5.3 *Expansion characteristics by source of expansion*

	Duration	Censored Expansions	Cumulative Yearly Expansion
Total	110	110	110
	7.636364	0.4545455	0.2478288
Defence	25	25	25
	5.72	0.36	0.2165305
Economic	35	35	35
	11.11429	0.4857143	0.4159274
Education	30	30	30
	7.366667	0.4666667	0.2141707
Environmental	1	1	1
	2	1	0.1078913
General Public Services	37	37	37
	5.810811	0.4864865	0.1690469
Health	36	36	36
	6.25	0.4722222	0.1544963
Housing	48	48	48
	8.6875	0.4791667	0.2524268
Public Order and Safety	15	15	15
	5.066667	0.6	0.2088433
Recreation	37	37	37
	8.324324	0.5675676	0.2447608
Social Protection	32	32	32
	7.71875	0.34375	0.2302046

The estimates of the Weibull regression specification are presented in Tables 5.4, 5.5 and 5.6. First, controls for economy-wide characteristics are introduced in Table 5.4. In order to control for possible time specific effects, each regression controls for decade dummies. Note that the parameter estimates correspond to the effect of an increase in a unit of the dependent variable on the probability that the expansion ends. Thus a positive coefficient implies that the variable in question is *harmful* for fiscal sustainability, while a negative coefficient implies that it enhances fiscal sustainability. Columns 1, 2 and 3 show that there appear to be no simple correlations between duration and initial per capita income, democracy and openness. However, this changes once a control for human capital, as measured by the total years of schooling, is introduced. Now the *democracy* coefficient becomes significantly negative, indicating that democratic countries have greater capacity to sustain fiscal expansions. Education also has a strong significantly negative effect on the hazard rate, indicating that higher education levels enhance fiscal sustainability. In contrast, both openness and initial income enter with significantly positive coefficients. In other words, richer and more open economies are, *ceteris paribus*, less likely to sustain expansions. These results are striking, especially in light of the fact that almost all expansions occurring in industrialized economies are sustained. The explanation for this apparent contradiction is in the fact that equation (4) measures the effect of income *after controlling for democracy and*

Table 5.4 *Weibull duration regression, structural controls*

	(1)	(2)	(3)	(4)	(5)	(6)	(7)	(8)	(9)
Log of per capita GDP	−0.4326 (1.21)	−0.0071 (0.02)	0.0332 (0.09)	1.1984 (3.36)***	1.1329 (2.94)***	1.3711 (3.09)**	1.4928 (3.15)***	1.4928 (3.15)***	1.9627 (3.86)***
Democracy (polity)		−0.04 (1.37)	−0.0341 (1.58)	−0.0901 (3.02)***	−0.0875 (2.90)***	−0.0854 (2.78)**	−0.0843 (2.73)***	−0.0843 (2.73)***	−0.0618 (2.19)***
Openness			0.0051 (0.88)	0.0118 (3.22)**	0.0114 (3.02)**	0.0176 (3.40)**	0.0191 (3.48)**	0.0191 (3.48)**	0.0162 (3.07)**
Total years of schooling				−0.3303 (2.74)**	−0.3168 (2.56)**	−0.3667 (2.78)**	−0.3564 (2.65)**	−0.3564 (2.65)**	−0.4656 (3.25)**
Savings– investment rate					−0.005 (0.40)	0.0103 (0.62)	0.0138 (0.80)	0.0138 (0.80)	0.0193 (1.15)
Liquid liabilities/GDP						−0.014 (1.41)	−0.0174 (1.64)	−0.0174 (1.64)	−0.0018 (0.16)
Urbanization							−0.0087 (0.99)	−0.0087 (0.99)	−0.0058 (0.72)
Industrial country dummy									−2.6817 (2.95)**
Constant	1.5703 (0.52)	−1.3889 (0.39)	−1.9997 (0.64)	−10.6286 (3.76)***	−10.0895 (3.29)***	−11.1065 (3.44)**	−11.7648 (3.47)**	−11.7648 (3.47)**	−15.9413 (4.25)**
Observations	109	98	93	68	68	66	66	66	66
Number of groups	65	58	54	39	39	37	37	37	37

Note: Absolute value of z statistics in parentheses. All regressions include decade dummies. ** significant at 5 per cent; *** significant at 1 per cent.

schooling levels. Since GDP, democracy and education are significantly correlated, richer countries tend to be more democratic and more highly educated; what the regression is, in essence, saying is that after one controls for social and political development, economic development does not make it easier, and may actually make it more difficult, to sustain fiscal expansions. As regards openness, a possible interpretation is that more open economies are also more volatile and thus may have greater trouble sustaining stable fiscal policies.

The rest of Table 5.4 analyses a set of remaining potential explanations. First we look at the possibility that countries that are able to sustain fiscal expansions benefit from increases in domestic net savings that can be mobilized towards public investment. This hypothesis is tested by introducing the difference between savings and investment, which is of course equivalent to the current account surplus, as a per cent of GDP. This variable does not come out as significant in any of the regressions in which it is used. Next an indicator of financial depth (liquid liabilities/GDP) and a second indicator of social development (the urbanization rate) are added. Neither of these enter significantly, nor do they affect the sign and significance of GDP, democracy, openness and schooling. As a last control, a dummy for industrialized countries is introduced; this controls, in a parsimonious way, for inter-regional differences. This variable is strongly significant, implying that the economy-wide controls used in these

Table 5.5 *Weibull duration regressions, expansion characteristic controls*

	(1)	(2)	(3)	(4)	(5)	(6)	(7)	(8)
Human capital	−0.6745 (0.92)		−0.6993 (0.89)	−0.7875 (1.25)	0.0872 (0.07)	−0.0049 (0.01)	0.564 (0.64)	2.7009 (2.20)*
Education		−1.2056 (0.68)						
Health		−0.361 (0.31)						
National economy	0.1497 (0.79)	0.1623 (0.85)		0.1876 (1.03)	0.0227 (0.10)	0.1562 (0.88)	0.1674 (0.93)	0.0084 (0.04)
Economic			−0.191 (0.21)					
Recreation			0.8804 (1.43)					
Housing			0.1166 (0.45)					
Transfers	−0.3012 (0.31)	−0.3224 (0.34)	−0.2887 (0.28)		−0.1318 (0.10)	−0.5877 (0.62)	−1.4122 (1.21)	−1.4629 (0.70)
Social protection				−2.133 (1.58)				
General social spending				0.0407 (0.05)				
Defence	1.7116 (2.41)**	1.7196 (2.40)**	1.7041 (2.39)**	2.0585 (2.75)***	0.8561 (1.00)	0.3243 (0.23)	−0.0324 (0.02)	−1.4829 (0.81)
Log of initial GDP					−0.3159 (0.40)	−0.1567 (0.54)	−0.0757 (0.26)	1.0556 (1.35)
Democracy						−0.0302 (2.48)**	−0.0334 (2.65)***	−0.1371 (2.63)***
Openness							−0.0034 (0.40)	0.0162 (1.12)
Total years of schooling								−0.4977 (1.92)
Constant	−1.537 (2.37)**	−1.5287 (2.37)**	−1.5389 (2.37)**	−1.5838 (2.59)***	0.4022 (0.06)	0.4852 (0.20)	−0.7642 (0.30)	−8.5327 (1.45)
Observations	61	61	61	61	61	55	51	35
Number of groups	46	46	46	46	46	42	38	25

Note: Absolute value of z statistics in parentheses. All regressions include decade dummies. ** significant at 5 per cent; *** significant at 1 per cent.

regressions have not completely explained the reasons for inter-regional disparities in hazard rates.

In Table 5.5 an examination of whether the characteristics of fiscal expansions themselves have explanatory power to account for the duration of these expansions is explored. It commences with a simple subdivision of spending into its four basic components, spending on human capital accumulation, national economy spending, spending on transfers and defence spending. The logarithmic change in the ratio of spending to GDP for each category as our explanatory variables is used. Public order and safety is the category omitted. The only variable found to have a significant effect on sustainability is defence spending. The coefficient is positive, implying that the effect on sustainability is adverse. In other words, a shift towards defence spending increases the probability of making the expansion end sooner. One possible interpretation of this is that defence spending constitutes a particularly extreme example of wasteful government spending that is unlikely to enhance an economy's productivity and thus unlikely to have an effect on the sustainability of its fiscal expansions.

The next three columns test whether these results are due to the way in which we built the large aggregate spending categories. In each of these columns, each of the groups is subdivided into its subcomponents and they are inserted separately into the regression. There is no effect of the subcomponents of any of the three aggregate groups on the durations of the expansions when they are inserted separately into the regression.

The second part of Table 5.5 evaluates the effect of inserting both the expansion characteristics (that is, changes in the composition of spending) and the economy characteristics into the regression. The results are very interesting. The effect of most economy-wide characteristics goes away, as does that of defence spending. In other words, the data say that the economy characteristics appear to be closely associated with the patterns of spending, suggesting that their effect on fiscal sustainability comes precisely from the way in which they affect spending patterns. In contrast, the democracy variable remains strongly significant throughout. This result suggests that the effect of democracy on sustainability is not only due to its effect on spending patterns, but may be related to its effect on the capacity to implement adequate taxation policies that enable the expansion to become inter-temporally sustainable.

The theoretical discussion earlier in this chapter highlighted the importance of the hazard rate for understanding whether fiscal expansions would tend to be reverted over time or whether they would be sustained. A decreasing hazard rate suggests that the economy will, as time elapses, have a lower probability of returning to its initial level of spending, whereas an increasing hazard rate is suggestive of a single equilibrium model. It is thus enlightening to analyse the hazard rates derived from our estimation exercises. These are presented in Figure 5.3. All of them control for country-specific frailties, so that their declining pattern is not a result of country-specific heterogeneity. The upper right panel includes no other controls except for the frailty effects and is thus the best indicator of the frailty corrected unconditional hazard rate. This estimate is strongly declining, suggesting that the countries that have spent the most time in an expansion are less likely to see the expansion reverted. One possibility is that this is due to differences in the underlying determinants of duration. More democratic countries, or countries where the expansion is concentrated on non-defence expenditures, may have an easier time sustaining expansions. Note that, to the extent that these characteristics are country invariant, they will be captured by the frailty effects, but if some countries shift these characteristics within the sample, they will not. It is thus instructive to examine how the hazard rate varies once one controls both for economy characteristics and for expansion characteristics.

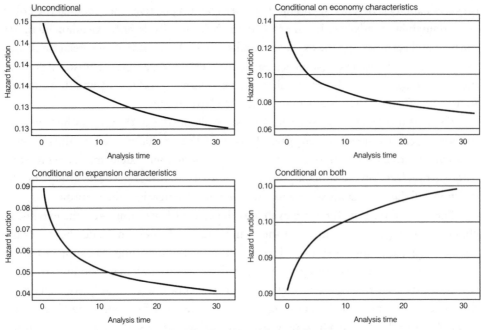

Figure 5.3 *Conditional hazard functions*

The remaining panels of Figure 5.3 illustrate the results. It shows that controlling only for economy characteristics or for expansion characteristics, does not make the hazard rate increase. Controlling for both, in contrast, makes the hazard rate virtually flat. This result confirms the idea that the reasons why some countries have longer expansion durations than others is precisely because they differ in the way in which the composition of spending changes over the expansion and in their structural characteristics. They are inconclusive with regards to the existence of multiple versus unique equilibria, in that, after controlling for these characteristics, the hazard rate is no longer declining. Note that the example in Figure 5.1(c) predicts that in a multiple equilibria setting the hazard rate can be flat over relatively long periods, so that the evidence does not contradict the multiple equilibrium model, but nor does it confirm it. Indeed, it is possible to design a fiscal policy with constant spending levels even in the context of multiple equilibria. However, the (slightly) increasing hazard rate is also consistent with a single equilibrium model. Therefore the data does not appear to have sufficient information to distinguish precisely between the two models.

One reason for the inconclusiveness of these results may be the inadequateness of the parametric specification of the Weibull model. An alternative to this approach is to use the nonparametric Cox regression model. The benefit of the Cox model is that the coefficient estimates are not dependent on parametric assumptions about the form of the hazard function. The drawback is that the estimates of the hazard function itself, in contrast to those of the parameter estimates, are generally not reliable. Heterogeneity in the Cox model is harder to deal with. Although, in principle, it is possible to use a frailty

Table 5.6 *Stratified Cox duration regressions*

	(1)	(2)	(3)	(4)	(5)	(6)
Log of initial GDP	−0.0187	0.0698	0.2495	0.8115		0.5574
	−0.12	−0.35	−1.4	(3.04)***		−1.73
Democracy		−0.008	−0.0099	−0.0337		−0.0246
		−0.96	−1.11	(2.02)**		(2.93)***
Openness			0.0051	0.0092		0.0127
			(2.68)***	(4.65)***		−1.29
Total years of schooling				−0.2236		
				(3.34)***		
Human capital spending					−0.6116	0.5194
					−1.26	−0.71
National economy spending					0.0814	0.0445
					−0.87	−0.37
Transfers spending					0.1384	0.1628
					−0.24	−0.19
Defence spending					0.5173	−0.4142
					−1.02	−0.41
Observations	109	98	93	68	61	51

Note: Absolute value of z statistics in parentheses. All regressions include decade dummies. ** significant at 5 per cent; *** significant at 1 per cent.

correction, in practice this is much more difficult, in terms of convergence of the maximized likelihood function, than in the parametric model when there are few observations per country, as is our case. Therefore, the solution of *stratifying*, that is, of estimating separate hazard rates, by region, while clustering the standard errors by country, is adopted.

The results of this approach are presented in Table 5.6. The estimation results appear to confirm the strong effect of democracy on expansion duration. The effects of GDP, openness and schooling are also present when controls for the composition of spending are introduced. Once controls for the composition of spending are included in the regression, again only democracy has some measure of independent explanatory power. Table 5.6 confirms that the main thrust of our results appears to be independent of the functional specification of the hazard rate.

We have concentrated on studying the impact of characteristics at the onset of the expansion on expansion duration. Although, in principle, it would be possible to study how the evolution of particular variables as the expansion evolves affects the probability of the expansion ending, this would exacerbate endogeneity problems that we can partially avoid by keeping to a set of predetermined variables, as we have. Nevertheless, it is instructive to study the evolution of certain variables throughout the duration of sustained fiscal expansions. Figure 5.4 does precisely this. In constructing this figure, the sample of expansions has been restricted to those that last at least ten years. This is a reflection of our interest in studying how key variables in the economy evolve during expansions that we know have succeeded.

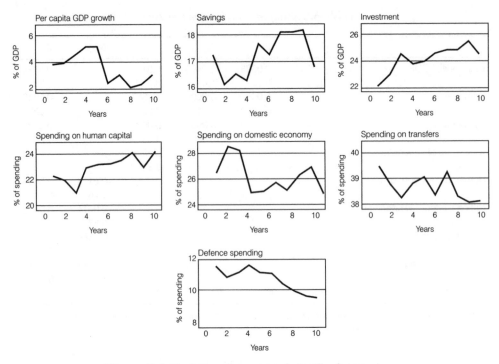

Figure 5.4 *Evolution of covariates during fiscal expansions*

The results display some interesting patterns. Real per capita GDP growth strengthens during the first years of the expansion and then declines. What is interesting is that the average levels, which oscillate between a maximum of 4.93 per cent after four years and 2.06 per cent after eight years, do not support the idea that very strong economic growth is the main explanation behind the sustainability of the expansions; average economic growth for *all* expansions is 3.07 per cent. Interestingly, the data do appear to show an upward trend in the investment rate during the expansions. The picture is not so clear cut for savings, although, on average, there appears to be some mobilization of savings; this occurs after year five and, if anything, appears to be a reaction to the increase in investment. The behaviour of spending patterns is also interesting. There is a clear upward trend in spending on human capital and a clear downward trend on defence spending, both of which are consistent with the idea that sustained fiscal expansions mobilize resources from unproductive to productive uses. There are somewhat less clear cut and more variable declines in spending on the national economy and transfers.

CONCLUDING COMMENTS

This chapter has studied the characteristics of fiscal expansions and the reasons why some are sustained and others are not. In contrast to the conventional approach to the study of fiscal sustainability, this approach has concentrated on the sustainability of fiscal expansions rather than the sustainability of deficits. There are two reasons why this makes sense. One is that expansions in spending may be very different phenomena than contractions in revenues. The second is that strong spending increases may coincide with low deficits if they are accompanied by temporary increases in revenues. Indeed, the typical policy choice facing a developing country seeking to expand spending in order to attempt to meet the MDGs is not necessarily the choice of whether to increase its deficit or not: it is a choice of whether to increase spending. A number of authors have expressed significant doubts about whether such increases in spending are prudent, given that the donor community is unlikely to maintain continued flows of financing in the long run. These doubts would be strengthened if we were to find that the strongest fiscal expansions end up becoming unsustainable.

In contrast, the evidence that we have found suggests that strong fiscal expansions, precisely defined as increases of more than 10 per cent in real per capita expenditures that are also accompanied by a substantial increase in the share of spending in GDP, are often sustained. Indeed, we find that 45 per cent of these expansions do not come to an end by the last year of available data. The mean time of duration until the last observation is 7.6 years for the world as a whole, but considerably larger in some regions, such as Asia (14.6 years) and industrialized countries (17.5 years).

Thus the data lend little support to the idea that strong fiscal expansions cannot be sustained. What the data do show is that whether these expansions are sustained or not depends, vitally, both on where the increase in spending is directed as well as the characteristics of the economy and society. We find that countries with more democratic systems and countries with higher education levels are more likely to sustain fiscal expansions. We also find that countries that devote more resources to defence spending are *less* likely to sustain fiscal expansions. As the expansion continues, the countries that are able to sustain the expansion increase the resources that they devote to human capital accumulation and further decrease those that are devoted to defence expenditures. They are also able to generate a sustained increase in national investment rates.

The results of this chapter have significant implications for the broader fiscal space debate. As the theoretical discussion has shown, countries following expansionary policies with similar deficit levels may be on completely different trajectories regarding the sustainability of their expansions, depending on whether the expansion is directed at uses that enhance productivity or those that do not. Furthermore, the sustainability of fiscal plans will depend on a society's capacity to enact relevant reforms during the expansion. While some of these facts form a standard motivation for the 'golden rule' approach to fiscal policymaking, there is considerable scepticism among academic economists and policymakers regarding the desirability of a golden rule approach in contrast to spending or deficit ceilings. What our analysis has shown is that countries that carry out the right types of expansions with the right types of institutions can, and often are able to, sustain permanent increases in the provision of public goods and services for their citizens.

NOTES

1   This paper was prepared for the Poverty Group of the Bureau for Development Policy of UNDP. The author thanks Antoine Heuty, Emmanuel Letouzé, Cameron Shelton and Rathin Roy for numerous discussions. The author is completely responsible for all remaining errors and mistakes.
2   Some classic examples are Hamilton and Flavin (1986), Wilcox (1989) and Hakkio and Rush (1991).
3   This is true given the choice of public investment. However, there is the possibility that a set of adverse fiscal shocks may force an economy that has undertaken the public investment to cut it back.

REFERENCES

Alesina, A. and Wacziarg, R. (1998) 'Openness, country size and the government', *Journal of Public Economics*, vol 69, September, pp 305–322

Andersen, P. K., Klein, J. P. and Zhang, M. J. (1999) 'Testing for centre effects in multi-centre survival studies: A Monte Carlo comparison of fixed and random effects tests', *Statistics in Medicine*, vol 18, no 12, pp1489–1500

Aschauer, D. A. (1989) 'Does public capital crowd out private capital?', *Journal of Monetary Economics*, vol 24, no 2, pp171–188

Barro, R. J. and Lee, J-W. (2000) 'International data on educational attainment: Updates and implications', CID Working Paper No. 42, April, Center for International Development at Harvard University, Cambridge, MA

Cameron, D. R. (1978) 'The expansion of the public economy', *American Political Science Review*, vol 72, pp1243–1261

Easterly, W. and Servén, L. (2003) *The Limits of Stabilization: Infrastructure, Public Deficits and Growth in Latin America*, World Bank, Washington DC

Hakkio, G. and Rush, M. (1991) 'Is the budget deficit too large?', *Economic Inquiry*, vol 29, no 3, pp429–445

Hamilton, J. and Flavin, M. (1986) 'On the limitations of government borrowing: A framework for empirical testing', *American Economic Review*, vol 76, no 4, pp808–816

Heller, P. S. (2005) 'Understanding fiscal space', IMF Policy Discussion Paper PDP/05/04, International Monetary Fund, Washington DC

Hemming, R. and Ter-Minassian, T. (2004) 'Making room for public investment: Possible new approaches to fiscal accounting', *Finance and Development*, vol 41, no 4, pp30–33

Hosmer, D. W. and Lemeshow, S. (1999) *Applied Survival Analysis*, John Wiley & Sons, New York

Hotz-Eakin, D. (1994) 'Public sector capital and the productivity puzzle', *Review of Economics and Statistics*, vol 76, pp12–21

IMF (International Monetary Fund) (2006a) *Government Finance Statistics Database and Browser on CD-ROM*, International Monetary Fund, Washington DC

IMF (2006b) *Government Finance Statistics Database and Browser on CD-ROM*, International Monetary Fund, Washington DC

IMF (2006c) *International Financial Statistics Database*, International Monetary Fund, Washington DC

Marshall, M. G. and Jaggers, K. (2004) *Polity IV Project: Political Regime Characteristics and Transitions, 1800–2002*, University of Maryland, College Park, MD

Pineda, J. and Rodríguez, F. (2006) 'Public investment in infrastructure and productivity growth: Evidence from the Venezuelan manufacturing sector', Wesleyan Economics Working Paper No. 2006-010, Wesleyan University, Middletown, CT

Rodrik, D. (1998) 'Why do more open economies have bigger governments?', *Journal of Political Economy*, vol 106, no 5, pp997–1032

Rodrik, D. (1999) 'Where did all the growth go? External shocks, social conflict, and growth collapses', *Journal of Economic Growth*, vol 4, no 4, pp385–412 (28)

Sachs, J. D. (2005) *The End of Poverty: Economic Possibilities for Our Time*, Penguin Group, New York

Tatom, J. A. (1993) 'Is an infrastructure crisis lowering the nation's productivity?', *Federal Reserve Bank of St. Louis Review*, November–December, pp3–21

Wilcox, D. (1989) 'The sustainability of government deficits: Implications of the present-value borrowing constraint', *Journal of Money, Credit, and Banking*, vol 21, no 3, pp291–306

Wickens, T. (2002) *Classification of GFSM 1986 Data to the GFSM 2001 Framework*, International Monetary Fund, Washington DC

World Bank (2006) *World Development Indicators CD-ROM*, World Bank, Washington DC

6

A Review of Four Cases on Fiscal Space: Morocco, Senegal, Thailand and Venezuela

Indira Rajaraman

INTRODUCTION

The year 2007 marked the midpoint between 2000, when the MDGs were announced, and 2015, the date by which they are to be achieved. Unfortunately not all countries are even halfway towards achieving the targets prescribed. It is now widely recognized that adequate fiscal space is a necessary, if not sufficient, requirement to reach these goals. The UNDP, therefore, commissioned a series of country studies to obtain a more contextualized understanding of what limits countries' ability to expand their fiscal space. This chapter reviews four country studies: Morocco, Senegal, Thailand and Venezuela. The scope of this review goes beyond fiscal space issues *per se* to consider the possible design and configuration of the goals themselves, so as to conform more closely to the ultimate objective, which is to reduce the incidence of deprivation in the world.

The studies are Brun et al (2006b; Chapter 7) for Morocco, Diaw et al (2006; Chapter 8) for Senegal, Jansen and Khannabha (2006; Chapter 9) for Thailand, and Moreno and Rodríguez (2005; Chapter 10) for Venezuela. Although the four countries are very disparate, they do not include the most undeveloped extremes in the MDG poverty spectrum. Even Senegal, with a poverty headcount of 26 per cent under a poverty line of one dollar a day per capita in 2003, was far ahead of other sub-Saharan African countries where the headcount stood at 46 per cent.

The next section summarizes the literature on fiscal space for the MDGs. As a result of the seminal studies by Sachs et al (2004) and Willoughby (2004),[1] there is now consensus on the need to direct fiscal space towards investment additionality. An implicit assumption underlying this, however, is that capital formation in the economy is efficiently deployed. In the subsequent section, therefore, the initial review of the four country cases is structured around two sets of cross-country comparisons. A sub-section examines the growth and investment rates in each country, and what they reveal of trends over time in the incremental capital output ratio. Another focuses on what has been achieved so far towards meeting the MDGs. Because poverty reduction is the first MDG and, in a sense, underpins the other goals that follow, most discussions of MDG achievement tend to start and stop at poverty.

The chapter then discusses the principles by which to identify fiscal slack along each of its four dimensions. The following three sections then examine performance in the four countries under review on three of these dimensions: own revenue, public borrowing and external financing. There is no separate section on expenditure reform since there is no systematic information in the country case studies on this issue. Finally the chapter concludes with 12 recommendations.

LITERATURE REVIEW

In the seminal paper by Sachs et al (2004), ODA is seen as the key source of funding for the capital accumulation needed for the MDGs to be achieved. But Roy and Heuty (2005) sound a much-needed cautionary note in Chapter 1, pointing out that external aid could undermine country ownership of progress towards the MDGs, and its potential volatility could increase vulnerability to external shocks. ODA is only one of the four points in the Cartesian space of the fiscal space diamond proposed by the Development Committee (2006). The fiscal space diamond is a useful descriptive tool for delineating the four dimensions along which developing countries can expand fiscal space to achieve the MDGs: own revenue, public borrowing, externally sourced financing (including but not confined to ODA) and expenditure restructuring.

There are two caveats with the diamond, one trivial and one more significant. The trivial point is that the diamond has to be seen as a purely descriptive and not an analytical tool, as the four points are not analytically calibrated to equivalents in terms of implications for fiscal sustainability. The more important point has to do with the potential danger of drawing battle lines in the development debate between MDG enthusiasts on the one hand, and what would be characterized by them as fiscal prudence enthusiasts, on the other. The MDGs were formulated in response to the impatience of the international community with the slow pace of human development in the world. The UNDP *Human Development Reports* have to be credited with having shifted the focus of the development debate to human outcomes on the ground. That

That said, there is a possibility that impatience with progress towards the goals could translate into impatience with fiscal prudence.

The conflict between MDG-driven fiscal expansion and fiscal prudence is resolved if human development translates into returns to the exchequer. In an interesting alternative approach to the issue, the paper by Rodríguez (Chapter 5) uses duration analysis, a technique widely used in the context of labour economics to study spells of unemployment (it is also widely used in the study of disease and survival). Kieffer (1988) has a useful review of methods and the literature. Rodríguez's chapter applies the technique to examining the duration of spells of public expenditure expansion since 1972 using data for 109 economies.

There are important differences between the unemployment context of duration analysis and its application to fiscal expansion spells. The unemployed state is an unchanged state of being, so that the probability of exit from that state as a function of duration in that state can be estimated after controlling for individual-specific characteristics. In contrast, spells of expenditure expansion are, by definition, a changing state. What happens during that change may both influence and be influenced by duration. The Rodríguez paper sets out a theoretical model in which the composition of expenditure is the basic explanation for duration. The mode of financing the expansion is recognized, though not formally modelled, as an important explicator, but that is instrumented through an unchanging, country-specific characteristic, by rating it on a measure of democracy.

Defence spending incrementally reduces duration but the effect of the composition of spending disappears when the democracy variable is added on. The democracy variable alone, of all the country characteristics, is robust and increases duration, from which the author infers its effect 'on the capacity to implement adequate taxation policies that enable the expansion to become intertemporally sustainable' (Chapter 5, section 'Empirical results').

When the hazard function for the probability of exit from an expenditure expansion spell is estimated after controlling for democracy alone, the hazard rate declines, showing that exit from expansion is less likely the longer the expansion spell. But, when changes in the composition of spending are additionally controlled for, the hazard function is flat.[2] This, together with the earlier regression results, suggests that democracy correlates with the composition of spending (in itself, a very interesting finding).

The principal problem with what is certainly a promising avenue of investigation of fiscal expansions is that the democracy variable is not something on which developing countries have a policy handle, whereas they do have a policy handle on mode of financing. If, at the end of the day, it is adequate taxation policies that are needed to make expansions intertemporally sustainable, then that is what countries have to aim towards through technocratic means, with or without democracy. But endogeneity makes it difficult to test directly for the impact of mode of financing on duration.

Chapter 2 deals with the tension between avenues of public investment that yield developmental outcomes and those that yield fiduciary outcomes. The country case studies do not provide a basis on which to test where the countries lie in terms of this choice. There may be no tension between the two at all, for example, if capital for providing water for irrigation or domestic consumption is paid for fully through user charges, but this is, paradoxically, most difficult to do in water-scarce regions of the world.[3]

The principal contribution of the paper is to define the conditions for exit from external aid financed investment. Clearly, if aid has enabled a higher investment rate than can be financed from domestic saving, then eventual exit from aid dependence is possible only if domestic saving can, in the long run, rise to sustain the higher investment level. They also define a public finance current account zero-deficit condition, to ensure that public borrowing goes into public capital formation rather than public consumption. These are useful and non-controversial guidelines to follow.[4]

On the focus on capital formation, the case study of Senegal sounds the important caveat that current expenditures also contribute to the achievement of the MDGs, and that overall investment rates do not capture the investments that are directed to the MDGs. The important issue though is the efficiency of investment, even if it is not necessarily MDG-directed. Efficient investment and growth are necessary, if clearly not sufficient, for the achievement of the MDGs, and have to inform the approach to fiscal space issues.

THE FOUR COUNTRY CASE STUDIES

Table 6.1 presents background information on the four countries under review. The periods covered in the papers vary: Venezuela from 1962 to 2004, Thailand from 1970 to 2004, Morocco from 1980 to 2005 and Senegal from 2000 to 2006.

Thailand is a major growth success story, sustaining high growth rates averaging 7–8.5 per cent over three decades until the structural break in 1997, when the exchange rate crisis occurred. The Venezuelan growth rates are averaged across volatile yearly figures. The essential characteristic of the country is political and economic turbulence centred around the struggle for control of oil, the principle underpinning both GDP and exports. The economy is therefore largely driven exogenously by the price of oil and by the domestic political-economy responses to those fluctuations.

Morocco, a middle-income country, and Senegal, a low-income country, are likewise subject to exogenous shocks, such as rainfall failure, with the added volatility of the international market for phosphate in the case of Morocco. Growth averages reported for Morocco are modest, at between 3 and 4 per cent from the 1990s until the present. The data for Senegal report growth rates only for 2000 onwards. There is higher growth from 2003, at around the 6 per cent level. If this is sustainable going into the future, the prospects for Senegal are good.

Table 6.1 *Basic indicators: Morocco, Senegal, Thailand and Venezuela*

Country and period considered	Years	Growth % GDP (ICOR)
Morocco 1980–2005	1990–1998	2.9 (7.60)
	1999–2004	4.0 (5.88)
Senegal 2000–2006	2000	4.3 (…)
	2001	4.7 (4.09)
	2002	1.1 (15.18)
	2003	6.5 (3.19)
	2004	5.6 (4.18)
	2005	6.1 (3.84)
	2006	5.0 (4.74)
Thailand 1970–2004	1970–1979	7.1 (3.35)
	1980–1989	7.3 (3.92)
	1990–1996	8.5 (4.79)
	1997–2003	1.7 (14.18)
Venezuela 1962–2004	1962–1972	5.7 (3.94)
	1973–1983	2.5 (11.05)
	1984–1994	2.2 (7.88)
	1995–2004	1.0 (22.59)

Note: ICORs (shown in parentheses) have been calculated from investment and growth rates as reported. The Moroccan growth rates have been calculated from average growth rates for the period 1990 to 2004 and 1999 to 2004 as reported in the text. Investment rates have been averaged from yearly data in Table 7.12 to yield the ICORs shown.

Source: Author's calculations from tables in the four country case studies. The periods are as reported in the chapters. Years of coverage are broadly defined and do not indicate the coverage of all data in the chapters.

Given the central importance of capital formation in the sustainable achievement of the MDGs, the first issue that arises in these countries is the productivity of investment in the years leading up to and into the MDG timeframe, 2000–2015. The next section therefore tries to construct incremental capital output ratios for the four countries, subject to the limitations of the data presented in the country case studies. The progress towards the MDGs, as indicated by the most recent data, is addressed in the subsequent sub-section ('Progress towards the MDGs').

Growth and the incremental capital output ratio

Thai growth, impressive as it was, shows steadily rising incremental capital output ratios (ICORs). These are calculated on the basis of the investment rates reported in the paper, for the period averages as shown in Table 6.1. The ICOR rose from 3.4 in the 1970s to 4.8 in the years just before 1997. In and of itself, this trend need not necessarily indicate that investment was increasingly inefficient in terms of growth outcomes. High ICORs could reflect high gestation infrastructure investment, and the rising ICORs could simply indicate that the capacity limitations caused by high growth called for a round of infrastructure additionality in the 1990s, perhaps an example of middle-income bottlenecks (Willoughby, 2004). However, with the hindsight of the 1997 crisis, it is now known that the push of easy externally sourced capital led to a number of ill-judged land development projects that led to a property price bubble. After the 1997 crisis, the growth rate crashed to an average of 1.7 per cent until 2003, and the ICOR rose to an astonishing 14.2, since investment remained at 24 per cent of GDP. The period averages provided in the chapter do not enable calculation of the ICOR for other than the full stretch 1997–2003, including the crisis year 1997 itself.

Issues remain, therefore, with the efficiency of capital formation in Thailand, and the reasons for the persistent low growth after 1997. If one of the reasons for the low growth post-crisis was high investment in the past and underutilized capacity, then the persistence of high investment is in itself puzzling.

The volatility in Venezuelan growth translates into volatility in ICORs around a sharply rising trend. The 1960s were the only period when the ICOR was at all reasonable, under 4. In the period after 1995, the ICOR is at 22.59, an implausibly high level, because of the low growth rates averaging out at 1 per cent, in conjunction with investment rates at above 20 per cent of GDP.

Morocco has had low average growth rates, subject to external weather shocks. At the high investment rates reported, the ICORs are high but have come down slightly from 7.6 in the 1990s to 5.9 in the period 1999 to 2004. This reflects some improvement in the efficiency of investment. The yearly figures for Senegal yield, except for 2002 when there was a negative growth shock, ICORs in the range of 3.2 to 4.5, which compare favourably with the pre-crisis ICORs for Thailand.

To conclude, the Thai and Venezuelan cases do not call for an immediate focus on raising investment because of very high ICORs. The Thai economy is more in need of structural reform and restoration of the growth rate and ICOR to pre-crisis levels. Likewise, Venezuela is more in need of obtaining a stable and higher growth yield from investment rates, currently at more than 20 per cent of GDP. Even in Morocco, despite an improvement in the efficiency of investment after 1999, there remains room for more growth at present investment levels. In Senegal alone, ICORs are currently at satisfactory levels, but investment is already at nearly a quarter of GDP. Thus, although the four countries are very disparate in terms of efficiency of investment, the need of the hour in general is for structural reform that will raise the growth dividend at existing rates of investment, rather than for an immediate focus on investment additionality. Only Senegal has present-day ICORs that compare favourably with pre-crisis ICORs for Thailand, showing good growth dividends from investment, and thereby suggesting a potentially strong payoff to investment additionality in terms of MDG outcomes.

Progress towards the MDGs

The MDGs are a vector of commitments distinguished by country-specific targets relative to a designated base year. The first of the MDGs, poverty, is to be halved by 2015 relative to the level in 1990. The measure of poverty most commonly used is a poverty headcount (expressed as a percentage of the population), but it could be a poverty gap or any of the other variants cited in the measurement literature. The poverty line is also left unspecified. It could be the international standard of either 2 dollars or 1 dollar per capita per day, translated into domestic currency by either purchasing power parity (PPP) equivalents or the official exchange rate. Alternatively it could be a country-specific line, developed from first principles, to measure the level of income that enables caloric sufficiency. The MDGs call for halving of extreme poverty, so countries are free to adjust the line downwards to accord with what would be extreme deprivation in their particular contexts. Cross-country comparisons have to factor in the nature of the poverty line in each country.

Similarly, other indicators need to be more fully specified in order to enable comparisons across countries. School enrolments when reported as gross look higher than net rates. The data in developing countries do not always permit a choice of indicators. However, all that is necessary is that each indicator reported should be fully specified so as to enable an understanding of cross-country differences.

Also, in view of the MDG goal of gender empowerment, it would be useful if school enrolment rates and other indicators could be broken down by gender. None of the country case studies supply such gender-disaggregated data, possibly because they are not available. But, if gender-disaggregated data are not available, it would be useful if this lacuna were explicitly mentioned as an incentive to develop such databases for assessment of progress towards the MDG.

Thailand is the major MDG success story, having already surpassed the poverty goal for 2015. The benchmark poverty headcount in 1990, with reference to an unspecified poverty line, was 27 per cent, notwithstanding two decades of high growth rates. By 2004, it had been brought down to 11 per cent, less than half the 1990 level. The government has now set an MDG+ target of 4 per cent for the poverty headcount in 2015. If this is achieved, poverty will essentially have been wiped out in Thailand.

Venezuela is altogether different. Comparable estimates of poverty over time begin only in 1995, when comprehensive household surveys were initiated.[5] The poverty headcount for 1995 was 15 per cent with respect to the 1 dollar per capita per day poverty line in domestic PPP currency equivalents. This is much lower than the starting point for Thailand. However, far from coming down, poverty in Venezuela actually increased to 16 per cent by 2005. Therefore, the gap between the starting point and the poverty goal has actually increased. In between, poverty went up sharply to 25 per cent in 2003, but came down thereafter. The year-to-year volatility in poverty is characteristic of Venezuela. At the same time, it has to be noted that it is the availability of annual data that permits this volatility to be observed. In other countries where data are available only every five or ten years, such volatility would be invisible.

In examining the Venezuelan figures, two facts have to be borne in mind. First, volatility is generally characteristic of the country, which means that single year points of comparison can be misleading. The period following the 2001 fiscal reform of the oil sector was particularly turbulent. Second, aside from sharp upward spikes in 1996 and again during the 2002–2004 turbulence, poverty headcounts have held at 15–16 per cent. Thus, there is no trend increase in poverty, as might be suggested by comparing headcounts in 1995 with headcounts in 2005. There is no decline in poverty either, but a poverty headcount of 15–16 per cent may not be unreasonably high from a developing-country perspective.

Where year-to-year volatility in growth and poverty is large, either because of the political and economic pulls and pushes related to a dominant natural resource (as in Venezuela), or where volatility is driven by external shocks such as weather, it is more important to configure the MDGs not in terms of a far-off terminal point like 2015, but in terms of annual targets along a path. These targets along paths could be simple annualized derivatives of the present terminal target and the initial starting point, but the mapping of a terminal target onto annual targets is more than just a matter of simple arithmetic.

What a path rather than a terminal target achieves is to focus attention on the central problem in a country such as Venezuela with respect to the goals, which may not be the poverty headcount itself, but the year-to-year movement of vulnerable segments of the population in and out of the state of poverty. If path targets are set with respect to the original distance to the terminal targets, and if the country has not advanced appreciably at the midway point, it follows that the original poverty reduction target will not be met. But the gain, in terms of focusing on the process of reduction rather than on some target several years into the future, may force immediate attention on the underlying problem.

Morocco has achieved commendable success in advancing towards the 2015 goals. Poverty came down from 21 per cent in 1985 to 14 per cent by 2004, a reduction of one-third and, therefore, more than halfway towards the eventual target of reduction by one-half. The Moroccan poverty line is specified at 2 dollars per capita per day. If the line was specified more stringently the poverty headcount would clearly be lower. Other MDG indicators, such as the school primary enrolment rate and the infant mortality rate, show that Morocco has progressed halfway or more towards the eventual target. Morocco is, therefore, clearly an MDG success story, although not an over-achiever like Thailand.

In Senegal, data for MDG indicators are available only for recent years and the starting poverty level in 1990 is not known. However, data on some of the instruments for achieving the MDG goals are provided (see Table 6.2). The percentage of under-weight children under three years of age does not show a substantial reduction from the starting figure of 21 per cent. The primary school enrolment rate, however, improved by over 9 percentage points to reach 91.1 per cent in 2004, and there was also good progress in vaccination for children under one year of age (not shown in Table 6.2).

A final point to note is that the starting point for the poverty level in Senegal was almost the same as the starting point in Thailand, despite their very disparate per capita income levels. What distinguishes the two, and makes fiscal space an urgent issue for Senegal, and a non-issue for Thailand, is the progress made towards the final targets.

Table 6.2 *Progress towards MDGs in Morocco, Senegal, Thailand and Venezuela*

Country	Year	Poverty (%)	Primary enrolment (%)	Infant mortality (per 1000 live births)	Underweight <3 years (%)
Morocco	1982–1991	...	...	57.0	...
	1985	21.0	...	...	...
	1994	...	60.2		...
	1994–2003	...	...	40.0	...
	2004	14.2	87.0	...	...
	2015 target	11.5	100.0	28.5	...
Senegal	2000	...	81.7	...	21
	2003	26.0	...	...	...
	2004	...	91.1	...	19
	2006	22.0	...	...	...
	2015 target	13	100.0	...	11
Thailand	1990	27	...	...	...
	2004	11	...	...	...
	2015 target	13.5	...	...	...
Venezuela	1995	15	...	...	...
	2005	16.4	...	...	...
	2015 target	7.5	...	...	...

Note: Because Thailand had already passed the MDG target for reducing poverty by 2004, the government is contemplating an MDG+ target of 4 per cent poverty by 2015. The poverty line is not defined. The Venezuelan poverty figure is the estimate from the INE, the national statistical agency, which in 1994 started including all sources of income in its official household surveys of individuals living on less than 1 dollar a day (PPP). The percentage of households at this per capita level is lower, indicating that households are larger at the lower end of the income spectrum. The figures shown for Senegal are reported as the latest available in the UNDP *Human Development Reports* for 2003 and 2006. The comparable 2003 figure for other sub-Saharan African nations is cited as 46 per cent. Further details about the poverty line are not reported. The Senegal chapter also reports data starting from 2000 on a number of other MDG instruments, such as the crude primary education rate, diphtheria-tetanus-pertussis (DTP) vaccinations and drinking water. The Moroccan poverty line is reported to be the hard core poverty line, not further elucidated. The primary school enrolment rates for Morocco are net, and gross for Senegal. The Venezuela paper reports gross primary enrolment rates exceeding 100 per cent. In Thailand, primary school enrolment is universal.

IDENTIFICATION OF FISCAL SLACK

This section deals with the principles by which fiscal slack is identifiable along each of its four dimensions: own fiscal revenue, public debt, external financing and expenditure restructuring. Actual country experiences on the first three of these dimensions will then be dealt with in the following three sections. There is no separate section on expenditure restructuring because the country cases do not provide enough information. The Morocco and Venezuela chapters deal with expenditure restructuring to some extent and the initiatives in these two countries will be examined at the end of this section.

An overall assessment of the existence or otherwise of unutilized fiscal space along any of its dimensions cannot be divorced from the efficiency of incremental capital formation. As the review of the country case in the previous section shows, where the efficiency of investment is falling, as in the case of Thailand, the need is to enhance the efficiency of investment rather than to look for investment and fiscal additionality. To characterize a country in this particular situation as fiscally underutilized is to ignore the macroeconomic imperative of the country at such a juncture, which is to restore the growth rate and lower the ICOR at what is a persistently high investment rate. The country has made a public policy commitment to achieve an MDG+ poverty level of 4 per cent. There may be enough slack in the economy to achieve this more ambitious goal even without exploiting fiscal slack, just by addressing the obstacles to lowering the ICOR.

A technique frequently adopted to assess fiscal slack in raising own revenue is to run cross-country regressions of fiscal indicators on GDP per capita, with or without controls for sectoral shares in GDP. A World Bank cross-country regression for 2002 shows, for example, that Thailand is below its estimated tax effort at its level of per capita GDP. Even the Brun et al (2006a) UNDP concept paper, which estimates a more sophisticated structural random effects model over panel data for 85 countries between 1970 and 2003, classifies Thailand and, to a lesser extent, Venezuela, as undertaxed countries. Cross-country regressions of this kind have to be used and interpreted with caution because they assign a determinism to GDP that is out of place. Indeed, the very formulation of the MDG essentially rejects GDP as the determinant of poverty or other human development failures. Likewise, tax/GDP ratios are a function of the public goods preferences of countries, as expressed through the voice of voters.

Therefore, a two-fold approach is adopted here. The historical experience of each country, in terms of own revenue as a percentage of GDP and assuming time-invariance in voter/citizen preferences for public goods, yields a very approximate measure of whether fiscal slack is increasing or decreasing over time. However, this has to be supplemented by a second approach, which is to examine the constituents of own revenue, partitioned into trade tax revenue and other revenue rather than into direct and indirect taxes as is more conventional, so as to estimate the fiscal cost of trade reform and the extent to which compensating revenue was found. Indirect taxes include both revenue from external trade and from domestic sales or value added tax (VAT), and therefore conceal the extent of the challenge posed by trade reform.

Trade reform by itself is a driver of efficiency and growth and cannot, therefore, be halted for fiscal reasons; indeed, some aspects of trade reform could even be revenue enhancing, such as tariffication of import quotas, and the elimination of tariff exemptions and tariff dispersion. Even with a decline in the effective tariff, there could be a sufficient response in import volume and, after factoring in exchange rate movements, there could, in principle, be no decline in trade tax revenue, at least over some phases of trade reform. However, the expectation is that there would be some decline and the scope for fiscal expansion, therefore, has to explore the prospects for enhancing revenue from domestic non-trade taxation. The two major instruments are income taxation and a non-cascading destination-based VAT on final consumption. The focus here has to be not on the amount raised alone, but on whether excessive reliance on one or other instrument has led to avoidable distortions in its functioning.

Natural resource taxation is in a category all by itself and is not a major source of revenue in most countries. Venezuela alone among the four countries reviewed has oil revenues. But, as the history of that country shows, there are severe political-economy problems in ensuring that the revenue from oil flows into the exchequer even when, as in this case, the oil sector is dominated by the public monopoly Petróleos de Venezuela, SA (PDVSA). This is a dimension of fiscal space not susceptible to purely technocratic solutions.

The tax data for any country typically refer to revenue raised by the national government, especially in a unitary political structure, which is the case in all four countries reviewed in this chapter. But local government revenues can be raised through effective property taxation, which generates supplementary revenue throughout the country as a whole. These local revenues can then be harnessed for the MDG effort, either through formal funding partnerships between national and local governments, or through one or more health or education delivery functions financed from local revenue.

The domestic fiscal space can also be enhanced through non-debt receipts from privatization. There is no systematic information in the country cases on privatization, but this, in any case, is merely an upfront present value of what in principle is a stream of dividends into the exchequer over time. The difficulty of ensuring dividend payments from PDVSA, the public sector oil monopoly, led the government of Venezuela to enhance royalty rates on production. Production is physically measurable, unlike the taxable profits of a company. Public borrowing is the second dimension of fiscal space but it is more treacherous. There is no theoretically underpinned optimum for public debt in terms of either levels (relative to GDP) or growth rates. There are only conditions that can be prescribed, with accompanying parameters on own tax buoyancy and the growth rate of public expenditure, which set the conditions for stabilising the debt/GDP ratio at any given level (see Rajaraman and Mukhopadhyay, 2005 for the derivation of these conditions). Needless to say, these debt stabilization conditions do not cap the debt stock in absolute terms, but merely curb the growth of the absolute debt stock at the rate of growth of nominal GDP. Most countries have some prudential limits on the public debt stock relative to GDP. A higher GDP nominal growth rate releases the cap on the growth rate of the absolute debt stock, for any given stock of debt/GDP, and this should preferably be through high real growth rather than high inflation.

Real growth therefore underpins the first two dimensions of fiscal space: own revenue and public borrowing. For a given buoyancy of domestic taxation, higher real growth yields higher incremental tax revenue. Likewise, for a given prudential cap on the (total) debt stock, higher real growth makes possible higher public borrowing.

External financing is linked, but not confined, to public debt. Ideally, the mix of domestic and ODA components in public debt should be determined by domestic policy rather than imposed externally. The mix should be based on objective parameters, such as the relative cost and maturity of debt from the two sources, with simulated exchange rate scenarios for servicing external debt. For low-income countries, external debt is available on concessional terms and is more attractive than domestic debt, which clearly will not be concessional. Domestic debt, notwithstanding, has its advantages. There is often excess liquidity in the risk-averse domestic banking system in developing countries, so that greater recourse by the government to domestic borrowing is unlikely to crowd out private investment. The reason this is not atypical today is that banking prudential norms have been tightening over the years, with restrictions on domestic banks lending outside the country, and poor risk assessment capacity within the banking system (see Summers, 2006 for a review of the evidence). In such countries, where financial intermediation is yet to cover the whole population, a certain measure of risk-free lending to government will, for a given measure of risk aversion within the banking system, increase the banks' willingness to lend with higher than zero risk. When there is less excess liquidity, banks will have an incentive to extend banking participation in the country. After factoring in these considerations, a higher share of domestically sourced public debt may be more conducive to growth and achieving the MDGs than is warranted by purely debt servicing considerations.

External financing not going into the public exchequer may also be sourced from worker remittances, which are a major support for external current accounts in Senegal and Morocco. The overall macroeconomic measure of the extent of external financing is the excess of national investment over national saving rates, where national saving rates include savings from worker remittances. The excess of investment over saving reflects the current account balance, with signs reversed, and is the final measure of the contribution of external savings to investment in the country, aggregated across ODA and private external capital.

Expenditure reform is the fourth dimension of fiscal space, and the one on which least information is usually available. There is, therefore, no separate section in this review on expenditure reform. But this is where cross-country regressions are at their most instructive, when used to identify factors that explain variations in health and education outcomes relative to public expenditure commitments to these sectors. Unfortunately, however, these kinds of analyses are not available in the literature, often because the necessary data do not exist.

The Morocco paper alone devotes considerable attention to this issue. The paper estimates public spending on education at 6 per cent of GDP (comparable figures are not available for the other three countries), but comments that the results are not commensurate with expenditure. The system is 'characterized by a high drop-out rate, a high unemployment rate for graduates and shortcomings as regards the teaching of basic skills' (see 'Policy of promoting human development' in Chapter 7 of this volume). Official recognition of this has resulted in the creation of the Agence de

Développement Social (Social Development Agency) (ADS), which coordinates the work of different ministerial departments and partner NGOs, raises supplementary funding from them on a project-specific basis, and mediates between them and the population. It also serves to expedite expenditure by intervening to reduce procedural delays. ADS itself is publicly funded and is subject to government auditing. The agency appears, from the evidence adduced in the paper, to function well. Its focus on arranging financing on a project basis (such as a rural tourism project with considerable promise of payback) has been sufficiently successful to have been adopted for the Initiative Nationale pour le Développement Humain (National Human Development Initiative) (INDH) started in 2005.

Another example of an attempt to improve the institutional mechanism for service delivery to the poor is the Venezuelan Literacy Mission (Misión Robinson), introduced on 1 July 2003, and followed by 13 other Misiones covering health and subsidized food for low-income consumers. The effectiveness of this and other experiments in modes of delivery is critically relevant to the whole issue of effective utilization of fiscal space. Total expenditure on the Misiones is estimated to have averaged 1.22 per cent of GDP over three years. Opinion surveys estimate that they reach 40 per cent of the population. However, the paper on Venezuela considers that government claims of their success are overblown, and cites a survey that exposed the unreliability of opinion surveys (20 per cent of the respondents declared having been reached by a fictional Misión Patria). In a laudable attempt to make an objective assessment of the effectiveness of the Misiones, within the limitations of the available database, the paper performs a test on the quality of dwellings as a function of the reach of Misión Mercales, which sold discounted goods. Moreno and Rodríguez argue in Chapter 10 that 'If Mercal raises the incomes of the poor significantly, one would expect part of that increase to be devoted to increasing the quality of dwellings'. The strength of this association will hinge on the magnitude of (real) income elasticities of demand, and upgrading of floors or roofs may not be at the top of the ranking. Also, there could be a lumpiness to improving dwellings that makes it happen only when the real income increase crosses a minimum threshold.

Finally, since progress towards the MDGs should be as much about monotonic movement towards the final target as about the overall direction of the trend, there may be non-fiscal instruments to cover for exogenous risk. These could be as important as fiscal instruments in achieving the MDGs in a monotonic way. Poverty risk can be either non-idiosyncratic (weather) or idiosyncratic (sickness or disability). In the context of climate change and the greater likelihood of disasters, the long-term need is paramount. Expanding the risk pool across regions with non-synchronized risk lowers insurance premiums for a specified degree of risk cover. Insurance also has to be configured to lower transaction costs, such as the costs of distinguishing real from fraudulent claims. Weather insurance fortunately carries no moral hazard and can be objectively verified from meteorological data.

In poor countries, a part or even the whole of weather or health insurance may need to be subsidized by the exchequer. Therefore, non-fiscal instruments may not be completely free of the need for fiscal support. But, given the difficulty of expanding the fiscal space in the poorest countries where starting poverty levels are the highest, fiscal resources need to be effectively leveraged, and risk pooling through standard insurance channels is a good way of doing so.

OWN FISCAL REVENUE

Overall performance

Thailand raised its tax/GDP ratio steadily from 11.6 per cent of GDP in the 1970s to a high of 16.2 per cent before the crash of 1997 (see Table 6.3). After that, the ratio dropped to 13.4 per cent of GDP. As argued in the previous section, the fact that a cross-country regression shows that Thailand lies below its normative value is not sufficient evidence of unused fiscal space. The fall in the tax/GDP ratio after 1997 is part of the macroeconomic change at that structural break. It is clear that the country is now around 3 percentage points below the averages for the previous decade and, in terms of the yearly figures (not reported in the country case study), possibly 5–6 percentage points below historically achieved rates.

In that sense, Thailand could aspire to higher levels of domestic tax revenue, simply in terms of levels achieved in the recent past. But the fiscal correction has to be part of a restoration of the earlier growth momentum of the economy.

Venezuelan non-oil tax revenue/GDP declined mildly from 6.7 per cent of GDP in the 1960s until the years 1999 to 2004 when it increased dramatically to a high of 8 per cent. Oil revenue has historically had far more potential than non-oil tax revenue for Venezuela, and it is the battle for control of the oil sector that has given the country its political and economic volatility. The fiscal potential of oil in Venezuela, as an example of resource taxation generally and the only example in the four cases reviewed here, is sufficiently important to be treated separately in the section 'Public debt', below.

Morocco has seen a substantial rise in tax revenue by 3.5 percentage points to 25 per cent of GDP since the early 1980s. Senegal has also achieved a steady and monotonic increase in tax revenue from 1995 by 5 percentage points of GDP to reach its estimated current level of 20 per cent. This is an impressive performance, but was essentially a restoration of tax revenues after they declined from 23 per cent of GDP in 1980 to 15 per cent in 1995.

What is impressive in the Senegal case is that the increase in tax revenue was achieved through administrative improvements, such as a special tax centre to handle tax payments by large companies, computerization of tax services, the introduction of a single tax and social identification number, a one-time tax amnesty to bring defaulters back into the tax system, and strengthening of the audit system. More personnel for tax

Table 6.3 *Ratios of tax revenues to GDP in Morocco, Senegal, Thailand and Venezuela*

Morocco	Year	Tax rev/GDP (%)
	1980–1984	21.8
	1985–1989	21.1
	1990–1994	23.7
	1995–1999	24.6
	2000–2003	25.2
Senegal	**Year**	**Tax rev/GDP (%)**
	1980	23.0
	1995	15.0
	2000	16.0
	2001	18.0
	2002	19.1
	2003	19.3
	2004	19.3
	2005	20.2
	2006	20.0
Thailand	**Year**	**Tax rev/GDP (%)**
	1970–1979	11.6
	1980–1988	13.6
	1989–1997	16.2
	1998–2003	13.4
Venezuela	**Year**	**Non-oil tax rev/ GDP (%)**
	1962–1973	6.7
	1974–1983	6.4
	1984–1988	5.9
	1989–1998	6.4
	1999–2004	8.0

Note: The Venezuelan estimates for non-oil tax revenue exclude revenue from the domestic tax on gasoline.

administration were recruited, and relations with tax payers improved through discussion forums. However, a 2004 tax reform that brought down rates of company taxation sharply will slow further increases in the tax/GDP ratio to a much lower trajectory.

To conclude, all countries saw a steady increase in tax revenue as a percentage of GDP, although only up to the 1997 crisis in Thailand, with non-oil revenue in Venezuela a late starter. The next section will go into the constituents of this increase, but to the extent that the increase in revenue has been based on strengthening the administrative network, prospects remain good for maintaining the own revenue achievement thus far, even in Morocco and Senegal. Morocco and Senegal will see further reductions in trade tax revenue with free trade agreements. What happens to overall tax revenue hinges critically on prospects for compensating revenue.

Privatization is a way to expand the domestic fiscal space without recourse to borrowing. It is not dealt with in any of the case studies but, in any case, is not a recurring revenue possibility. None of the countries under review has a really sizeable government presence in commercial activities, except for PDVSA, the oil sector behemoth, in Venezuela.

Leveraging of own revenue with funding from sub-national government revenue for achieving the MDGs is a way in which to expand the domestic fiscal space. Morocco has an example of such a partnership in the INDH, started in 2005. The national government contributes 60 per cent of INDH funding, local governments contribute 20 per cent, and the remaining 20 per cent is sourced from an unspecified source termed 'cooperation'.

Composition of own revenue

Table 6.4 breaks down overall tax revenue into two components: trade taxes and other taxes. The reason for this particular partitioning, contrary to the more usual partitioning into direct and indirect taxes, is that it shows to what extent the four countries have coped with the fiscal challenge posed by trade reform.

Table 6.4 shows the percentage of trade tax revenue at the first point in time covered for the country in question, and shows subsequent points in time with reference to the base period. Likewise, non-trade tax revenue is shown as a per cent of GDP for the first point, and as changes with respect to that constant base for all successive observations.

Table 6.4 *Composition of own revenue – ratios of taxes to GDP (%) in Morocco, Senegal, Thailand and Venezuela*

Morocco	Year	Trade taxes/GDP (%)	Other taxes/GDP (%)
	1980	5.7	13.0
		Change relative to 1980	*Change relative to 1980*
	1992	−0.7	+4.0
	2005	−3.0	+6.0
Senegal	**Year**	**Trade taxes/GDP (%)**	**Other taxes/GDP (%)**
	1996	5.9	9.1
		Change relative to 1996	*Change relative to 1996*
	2003	−2.8	+6.0
Thailand	**Year**	**Trade taxes/GDP (%)**	**Other taxes/GDP (%)**
	1970–1979	3.7	7.9
		Change relative to 1970–79	*Change relative to 1970–79*
	1980–1988	−0.5	+2.4
	1989–1997	−0.5	+5.2
	1998–2003	−2.0	+3.8
Venezuela	**Year**	**Trade taxes/GDP (%)**	**Other taxes/GDP (%) (non-oil)**
	1962–1973	1.2	5.5
		Change relative to 1962–73	*Change relative to 1962–73*
	1974–1983	+0.0	−0.3
	1984–1988	−0.1	−0.7
	1989–1998	+0.1	−0.4
	1999–2004	−0.1	+1.4

Note: The earliest reported figure in each country case study is taken as the base, with figures for subsequent years showing only changes with respect to that base. The Venezuelan figure for non-trade taxes are the residuals after subtraction of trade taxes from total non-oil tax revenue as reported in Table 6.3. The figures for Senegal pertain to central government alone and exclude local governments.

All four countries saw a drop in trade tax revenue as a percentage of GDP relative to their respective base periods. Thailand and Venezuela managed to find compensating revenue (Thailand concurrently and Venezuela eventually). It must be remembered that, in the case of Venezuela, these are non-oil revenues. Thailand, in particular, has been successful in finding compensating revenue despite a VAT rate of 7 per cent, which is among the lowest in the world. The scope for further success in finding compensating revenue in Thailand will clearly hinge on its success in restoring the growth momentum after the crash of 1997. In the case of Venezuela, it is basically the oil sector that has to be looked to for further fiscal reform.

Morocco's revenue from trade taxes declined from 5.1 per cent of GDP in 1992 to 2.7 per cent in 2005 but compensating revenue was successfully found, principally from direct taxation of company profits. The VAT and excise taxes in Morocco were not a source of incremental compensating revenue during this phase, but have yielded a stable 10 per cent or more of GDP, a high level of achievement. Even as far back as 1980, the revenue from VAT and excise taxes was around 8 per cent of GDP and, during the 1980s, the contribution of VAT and excise taxes grew to more than 10 per cent of GDP. That was a period when trade revenue fell by around 2 per cent of GDP, although not monotonically, and VAT and excise taxes were the source of incremental compensating revenue during that decade. It is expected that further partnerships with the European Union (EU) and with other countries will lead to a continuing decline in trade tax revenue in the future. The fiscal challenge therefore continues.

The Moroccan case study has an excellent treatment of the distortionary directions in which taxation can move under pressure to find compensating revenue for lost trade tax revenue. In company taxation there has been a mutually reinforcing process by which nominal tax rates are kept at high levels, leading to pressure for exemptions (by sector, region, product and destination), which then further lead to maintenance of high nominal rates. VAT reimbursement can also be delayed, which robs VAT of its non-cascading character and is tantamount to a breach of contract with the taxpayer. Delayed reimbursement also robs VAT of the inbuilt incentive for compliance. The normal VAT rate of 20 per cent is high relative to other countries, which usually fall in the 12–18 per cent range. The country paper sees the four non-zero rates plus a zero rate as non-neutral, although, if properly calibrated, it could reduce the regressive nature of the VAT in a developing country. In Morocco there is also a cut-off rule under which a net VAT credit can be reimbursed only in credit, never in cash. The credit has to be carried over and, if the rate structure is such as to lend permanence to the net credit, it never gets paid.

With the INDH, started in 2005, Morocco began a process by which national government revenues are leveraged. As mentioned in the previous section, the national government contributes 60 per cent of INDH funding, local governments contribute 20 per cent and the remaining 20 per cent is sourced from an unspecified source termed 'cooperation'. The country case study has an extended treatment of prospects for local taxation.

In Senegal too, the decline in trade tax revenue by 2.8 per cent of GDP in 2003 relative to 1996 was fully compensated, in this case through the successful introduction of VAT. Non-trade revenue rose by 6.0 per cent of GDP in 2003, compensating fully for lost trade tax revenue. The paper assesses that VAT was the principal source of buoyancy in own tax revenue, but fears that excessive dependence on VAT might lead to distortions, such as non-payment of reimbursements.[6] The proposed economic partnership agreement (EPA) with the EU is expected to further reduce tariff revenue substantially. A further increase in compensating revenue may be harder following the 2004 tax reform, which brought down the marginal rate of tax on capital from 40 per cent to 25 per cent by 2006, with dispensatory tax credits amounting to 40 per cent of investments. However, the 2004 reform is expected to raise local government revenues by lowering the threshold for exemption from land taxes, eliminating tax deductions and rationalizing the method of determining the base for the land tax. So it is possible that own revenue consolidated across national and local levels may not decline.

To conclude, the fall in trade tax revenue in these countries and the inevitability of further falls add to the difficulty of expanding the fiscal space along the domestic dimension. Although all four countries have successfully found compensating revenue so far, there has been excessive reliance on a single source, whether direct taxation or VAT. This has then led to further distortions in the pattern of taxation. The emphasis has to be on a balance between these two sources, supplemented by property-based local taxation as a third source of revenue additionality throughout the country. Venezuela has the added advantage of revenues from natural resources.

NATURAL RESOURCE REVENUES

Oil revenues outweigh all other revenue sources in Venezuela. Oil revenue, averaging 10.8 per cent of GDP between 1990 and 2003, yielded more than half the total central government revenue of 20.2 per cent. But this long period average conceals the year-to-year volatility visible in yearly data.[7] The coefficient of variation of the ratio of oil to non-oil central government revenue over the period 1990–2003 was 48.9 per cent, with the ratio itself ranging between a low of 0.5 in 1998, to a high of 3.3 in 1990.

There are three basic sources of oil revenue for the government. After PDVSA became a nationalized monopoly in 1976, the first source of oil revenue is the PDVSA dividends paid to the government, the sole owner. The government also wields control over the revenues of PDVSA itself as it makes the decision on whether or not to cooperate with the OPEC cartel. The government's second source of oil revenue is royalties on the oil produced, which are paid directly to the government (the country case study calls it a tax on production, but royalty is more commonly termed a non-tax revenue and is a part of the cost of production which is deducted to obtain the company's profit before tax). The third source of oil revenue is the domestic tax on consumption of gasoline and other petroleum products.

PDVSA dividends, paradoxically, started declining after nationalization. The company used its substantial surpluses to establish overseas subsidiaries, and transferred its assets abroad through transfer pricing, in preference to handing over dividends to the government, which was perceived to be corrupt and wasteful (Boudin et al, 2006).

A Hydrocarbons Law Reform in 2001 sought to stem this haemorrhaging by raising royalty rates from 16.7 to 30 per cent. The country case study concludes that this robbed PDVSA of investible surpluses, when the purpose had been precisely to secure for the government exchequer those surpluses which had earlier been transferred to overseas subsidiaries. The oil company strike that followed reduced oil revenues further, but these processes have to be understood in their proper context so as not to lead to the conclusion that the royalty rate hike was in itself counter productive.

In terms of membership of OPEC, the authors of the country case study suggest that it might be an advantage for Venezuela to follow the example of Ecuador in leaving OPEC because of the decline in market share of the cartel in the 1990s. But Figure 16 of the paper shows that, from 2003, the OPEC market share has risen again because of the turbulence in Iraq. In any case, it is difficult to argue in 2008 that price-cutting competition might yield revenue advantages, given the prospect of the hardening upward trend in oil prices.

Finally, the domestic price of gasoline has been set at a low level for fear of political repercussions if it were raised. There is a domestic tax on gasoline, but the revenue from it does not come close to compensating for the losses to PDVSA from selling oil domestically at below the cost of production. The authors' argument that this policy is wrong from both revenue and environmental standpoints is absolutely correct. The nominal price of gasoline in Venezuela has stayed constant since 1999, and is among the lowest in the world. The political economy constraints in this case obstruct what, from every perspective, is clearly the right thing to do.

Summing across all three sources of oil revenue, and notwithstanding the loss of revenue from underpriced domestic gasoline, the policy moves have served, on balance, to improve oil revenue prospects. The 2001 reform was an adroit move, given the difficulty of confronting an oil behemoth like PDVSA with multiple overseas subsidiaries and an opaque system of functioning, since it replaced uncertain dividends with the certainty of production-based royalties. Future oil revenue prospects for Venezuela are good, because of the buoyancy of the international price of oil, and the end of the production strike protesting the 2001 reform. The ratio of oil to non-oil revenue declined in the immediate aftermath of the 2001 reforms, because of the turbulence it touched off, but the coefficient of variation has declined, signalling greater stability. The policy moves of the last six years have, on balance, served to enhance oil revenue prospects rather than, as the authors seem to conclude, retard them, although prospects for higher revenues would clearly be better if the domestic price of gasoline were raised.

PUBLIC DEBT

Prudential limits on the public debt stock relative to GDP can be either self-imposed (Thailand, at 50 per cent, with some other limits that curb the growth of the debt stock; see Table 6.5) or externally imposed (Senegal at 70 per cent, as part of the 1999 Convergence, Stability, Growth and Solidarity Pact of the West African Economic and Monetary Union – WAEMU). There are also seignorage limits, as, for example, in Senegal, where there is a ban on direct advances from the central bank to the government.

The gap between development and prudence can be bridged with attention to payback, through user charges on publicly provided private goods such as water and electricity, and an attempt at partial recovery on public provision of developmental services, such as education and health (not public goods, but private goods with large externalities), although the Senegal study covers the impossibility of doing the latter in a low-income country.

Thailand is far below its prudential maximum, although debt did grow rapidly between 1996 and 2004. Venezuela saw a rapid reduction of public debt by 15 percentage points of GDP between 1989–1898 and 1999–2000, to a 35 per cent (average) level.

Table 6.5 *Public debt levels in Morocco, Senegal, Thailand and Venezuela*

Country	Year	Debt/GDP (%)
Morocco	1988	118.7
	1990	104.9
	1995	103.9
	2000	90.4
	2005	81.2
Senegal	1999	68.5
	2000	72.6
	2001	75.6
	2002	66.1
	2003	54.4
	2004	45.2
	2005	44.5
	2006	15.0
Thailand	1970	18.0
	1996	5.0
	2004	27.0
Venezuela	1962–1973	8.3
	1974–1982	23.3
	1983–1988	45.3
	1989–1998	51.5
	1999–2004	35.1

Note: The figures reported for debt are the sum of the external and domestic debts of the core government alone and do not include the wider public sector. Thailand places limits on the public debt at less than 50 per cent of GDP, the fiscal deficit at 20 per cent of government expenditure and debt servicing at 15 per cent of government expenditure. Senegal's debt is capped at 70 per cent of GDP by the 1999 Convergence, Stability, Growth and Solidarity Pact adopted by member states of the WAEMU. The public debt of Senegal is almost entirely externally sourced.

Even so, it is not necessary in either case to recommend an increase in debt, in Thailand because of MDG success, and in Venezuela, because of the far more prudential alternative of raising oil revenues. Venezuela appears to have achieved a decline in debt even without a fixed numerical ceiling, because of the Financial Administration Organic Law for the Public Sector (Spanish acronym LOAF) enacted in 1999. The law called for 'an annual maximum indebtedness level in accordance to fiscal sustainability requirements... the size of the economy, the economy's ability to raise fiscal revenues and to invest... (and) the stock of financial assets of the Republic' (Art. 25).[8] The task was entrusted to the Ministry of Finance and the Central Bank, and this annual limit was given legal rank (Law of Annual Macroeconomic Policy Agreement). From the evidence of the debt decline, this provision has had an impact, despite the involvement of the Ministry of Finance in setting the limit, and the latitude given to vary the limit by year depending on fiscal circumstances.

Moroccan debt levels have also come down, from a high of 118.7 per cent of GDP in 1988 to 81.2 per cent in 2005; very high by any prudential standards, but low by the historical standards of the country. The paper on Morocco details the history of public debt going back to 1974–1975, when international phosphate prices spiked upwards. On the strength of the consequent rise in non-tax revenue by 4 percentage points of GDP, supplemented by external debt, a major public investment expansion was launched. When phosphate prices fell in the late 1970s, that and rising international interest rates meant a sharp curtailment in spending. In Chapter 7 the authors cite the episode as demonstrating 'the adverse effect on fiscal space of any loss of control over the budget deficit'.

Public debt in Senegal, which is almost entirely externally sourced, has come down sharply from a high of 75.6 per cent of GDP in 2001, to a low of 45 per cent in 2005, and is projected to have fallen even further, to 15 per cent in 2006. But, this is an artificial decline driven by the heavily indebted poor country (HIPC) debt reduction process completed in April 2004 and, further, by the Multilateral Debt Relief Initiative of the IMF started in 2006. The dominant component of public debt was external. It is expected that new debt sustainability limits placed on Senegal could be between 30 and 45 per cent of GDP, and that the debt may be permitted to rise again to this level.

Senegal is an example of the kind of excess liquidity in the risk-averse banking system, referred to in the section titled 'Identification of fiscal slack', so that greater recourse by the government to internal borrowing is likely to have positive effects on the spread of financial intermediation and the availability of finance for small-scale enterprises. Even so, there are external conditionalities that explicitly discourage domestic borrowing. These unfortunate incentives are spelled out in the next section on external financing.

The mix of external and domestic borrowing is not reported in the other case studies. It is best from both an efficiency and prudential perspective if, within the overall cap on debt/GDP, the mix of sources is left to the in-country policy machinery to decide, without external interference. Domestic borrowing will certainly carry higher interest than the kind of concessional international development assistance (IDA) loans that Senegal is entitled to by virtue of being a low-income country, but that may be a cost well worth paying. The HIPC and other debt relief that Senegal has had from time to time carries a moral hazard, and, if the future prospects of borrowing are forcibly confined to external borrowing, the incentives for productive expenditure and fiscal management are removed from the system.

Thus, there is fiscal space for funding public investment from private domestic savings, which is presently constrained under the 1999 WAEMU Pact requiring that all public borrowing be sourced externally, as detailed in the next section. (Notwithstanding this constraint, the Senegalese government has issued small amounts of short-term and five-year bonds on regional financial markets.) In the other three cases, there is no necessity for increasing the public debt because of MDG success as in Thailand, or because of the more prudential alternative and scope for higher oil revenue as in Venezuela, or where, as in Morocco, public debt is still above 80 per cent of GDP after the heroic effort to reduce it following the borrowing spree of the early 1970s. The Moroccan experience is particularly noteworthy because the debt-financed public investment in dams and roads during the major fiscal expansion of the early 1970s was no guarantor against low growth on account of exogenous shocks (poor harvests or the international price of oil).

EXTERNALLY SOURCED FINANCING

Thailand had an excess of investment over saving in all decades leading up to the 1997 crisis and especially in the years immediately preceding the crisis. This indicates the high inflow of external savings into the economy in what (we now know in hindsight) were not efficient directions (see Table 6.6). In the case of Thailand, this was private capital rather than ODA. This flow became negative in the four years from 1997 to 2003. Clearly, notwithstanding the persistence of high domestic investment, domestic savings had to be invested outside the economy or in a reserve build-up, through a positive current account surplus.

The net flow of capital into Venezuela in the years leading up to the Hydrocarbon Reform of 2001 was negative and continued to be negative thereafter. For many decades PDVSA, the public monopoly over oil, had been transferring its surpluses out of the country into foreign subsidiaries, which paid no dividends into the state excheq-uer. The 2001 reform, which essentially gave primacy to royalties on production as the instrument of fiscal return to the exchequer, simultaneously raised public revenue while potentially stemming the outward flow of capital. It was, therefore, a successful attack on two points of the fiscal diamond. Even so, domestic investment remained below domestic saving, perhaps because of the political turbulence, and there would corre-spondingly have been large current account surpluses.

Table 6.6 *Contribution of external savings to national investment in Morocco and Thailand*

Country	Year	Investment – Savings (%GDP)
Morocco	1988	–2.3
	1990	–0.4
	1995	+3.6
	2000	+6.6
	2005	+5.3
Senegal	2001	+9.6
	2002	+11.1
	2003	+12.9
	2004	+13.7
	2005	+14.1
	2006	+13.8
Thailand	1970–1979	2.0
	1980–1989	3.5
	1990–1996	6.6
	1997–2003	–7.1
Venezuela	1962–1972	–1.30
	1973–1983	–2.35
	1984–1994	–1.59
	1995–2004	–6.37

Note: The excess of national investments over national saving rates yields the contribution to investment sourced from external savings, aggregated across public and private sectors of the economy, and equals the current account balance with signs reversed. The Moroccan country case study also reports a lower 'internal' savings ratio which is presumably residually obtained from the domestic rather than the national product, and therefore excludes remittance income. The savings rate used here to generate the external contribution is the national savings ratio.

Morocco had a negative excess of investment over saving until 1990, presumably reflecting the payback of the high external debt secured during the early 1970s. But, after 1990, the flow turned positive, and by 2000 was as high as 6.6 per cent of GDP. This is the total external financing coming into the country over and above worker remittances, which are already included in the national savings rate. The share of this going to the public exchequer is small because the external component of the public debt stock has been declining steadily (see Table 7.9, Chapter 7). The breakdown by equity and debt flows of external financing going into the private sector is not provided in the chapter. Equity inflows, on balance, pose fewer external liquidity risks than debt inflows.

Senegal is a country that historically has had a heavy dependence on external capital, shown in the data in Table 6.6, and, in particular, on ODA. However, the country case study points out that there are three features of ODA to Senegal that are of critical relevance. First, although the total volume of aid from a number of sources including the Millennium Challenge Account, expected over the period 2006 to 2010, amounts to 4.5 per cent of GDP, all this aid is not guaranteed. Uncertainty of funding is a disincentive for expenditures on MDG goals in education and health, which require a steady source of financing for salary and non-salary running costs of standing facilities.[9] To quote the study, 'The achievement of the MDGs is dependent on public expenditures in health and education, most of it current (notably payment of personnel in these sectors), whose numbers cannot be suddenly reduced' (Chapter 8, p265).

Second, as against CFAfr200 billion ($446 million) of ODA in 2005, Senegal received CFAfr345 billion ($770 million) in worker remittances. These receipts will clearly not go into the public exchequer, but there is a possibility of incentivizing this flow into MDG financing on a project basis (rather than a single borrowing pool). This is a way to leverage private participation in the development process and will also incentivize the need to examine payback for expenditure from remittance financing.

Third, the structure of commitments under the 1999 WAEMU Pact requires that the budgetary balance must be non-negative, where it is calculated:

> as the difference between the budgetary income and total expenditure (including interest on debt) with the exception of investment expenditures financed from foreign resources, which formally or in principle excludes the funding of public investments from domestic savings and thus, to some extent, encourages states to have recourse to external financing. (Diaw et al, 2006, p44)

Although this rule has been violated at the margin, through small amounts of securities issued by the Senegalese government on regional financial markets, it is clear that a rule of this kind seriously robs member states of sovereignty over an important macroeconomic policy instrument and must be amended. Sovereign countries cannot be constrained by such arbitrary directives on where to source public borrowing. Similar constraints were imposed on Senegal by the IMF facility during the period 2003 to 2005.

CONCLUDING RECOMMENDATIONS

Recommendation 1: The need to identify fiscal slack along any of its dimensions cannot be assessed independently of the efficiency of incremental capital formation and progress made so far towards MDG targets. Where the efficiency of investment is falling and MDG progress is satisfactory, the need is to enhance the efficiency of investment rather than to look for investment and fiscal additionality.
Identification of fiscal slack through cross-country regressions of fiscal indicators grounded in structural determinism of tax levels, ignoring voter (or more broadly citizen) preferences as the foundation of public choice is, in general, a poor guide to the existence of fiscal slack in any individual country. Thailand is a case in point. Thailand is assessed as having an excess of potential over realized own revenue on the basis of cross-country regressions of tax revenue/GDP ratios on GDP per capita. That, along

with its low level of public debt/GDP has led to Thailand's classification as a country with fiscal slack.

In Thailand, the MDG target for poverty was surpassed in 2004, but the ICOR spiked upwards after the 1997 crisis because of the persistence of high investment rates with low growth. To characterize a country in this particular situation as fiscally under-utilized is to ignore the macroeconomic imperative at such a juncture, which is to restore the growth rate and lower the ICOR. The need is not for more public resources and more investment, but for internal reform that raises the growth rate at existing levels of investment. The country has made a public policy commitment to achieve an MDG+ poverty level of 4 per cent, which may be possible without any investment additionality just by addressing the obstacles to lowering the ICOR.

Morocco shows satisfactory progress towards the MDGs. However, low growth rates of 3 per cent persisted all through the 1990s and up to the present. At the high investment rates reported, the ICORs are very high, but have come down slightly from 7.6 in the 1990s to 5.9 in the period 1999 to 2004. The principal macroeconomic issue here again is the low efficiency of investment, rather than low levels of investment. Public debt and debt servicing are still at unreasonably high levels after the imprudently debt-financed public investment of the 1970s.

Venezuela has made no progress towards even the MDG poverty target. Even so, the need of the hour is to obtain a higher and stable growth yield from investment rates, currently at more than 20 per cent of GDP. Structural reform is needed to even out the year-to-year volatility in growth and the concomitant volatility in poverty rates.

Of the four countries, Senegal most urgently needs to attend to fiscal space issues. There appears to have been some decline in poverty, from the *Human Development Report* figures of 22 per cent for 2006, as against 26 per cent for 2003, but the rate of progress is very slow. ICORs for Senegal compare favourably with pre-crisis ICORs for Thailand, showing good growth dividends from investment, and thereby suggesting a potentially strong payoff to investment additionality in terms of MDG outcomes.

Recommendation 2: Given the centrality of progress towards the MDGs in the assessment of unutilized fiscal space, it is necessary for case studies to develop a more multidimensional indicator of MDG achievement and for specifications of MDG indicators to be free of ambiguity.

All four studies largely document progress in terms of the first MDG, which is to reduce poverty to half its 1990 level by 2015. It may be useful in future work to include more information on other quantifiable elements of the MDG vector so as to get a more broad-based assessment of the extent of movement towards the terminal targets. Each indicator also has to be reported in a manner free from ambiguity. Even the poverty line, the most widely quantified and measured criterion, suffers from a number of ambiguities that are reflected in the poverty data presented in the chapters. The poverty line could be the international standard of either 2 dollars or 1 dollar per capita per day, translated into domestic currency at either PPP equivalents or market exchange rates. The differences between the various combinations could be very wide. Alternatively, a poverty line could be country-specific, developed from first principles to measure the level of income that enables caloric sufficiency. The MDG specifies halving extreme poverty, so countries are free to adjust the line downwards to accord with what would be extreme deprivation in their particular contexts.

Since gender empowerment is among the MDG goals, it would be useful if school enrolment rates and other indicators could be broken down by gender.

Recommendation 3: Fiscal space recommendations in the MDG context have to enable non-volatile and monotonic progression towards 2015 goals and to ensure no reversal beyond that.

The manner of financing fiscal expansion has consequences for the duration of expansion. So, the probability of an expansion ending could be less a function of the simple duration of the expansion (as in the unemployment context, where the probability could be either increasing or decreasing over time depending on what it does to job search efforts) and more a function of the manner of its funding. Sudden terminations of fiscal expenditure could not merely halt progress towards MDGs, but actually reverse achievements. This calls for close attention to the dimensions of expansion of fiscal space and will be addressed in the recommendations that follow.

There is, once again, a requirement for better data here. In order to examine volatility, it is absolutely essential to have annual data on the MDG indicators. Annual data on poverty permit examination of yearly volatility in Venezuela, whereas this is not possible in other countries where the data are available only at five or ten year intervals.

Recommendation 4: Own tax or non-tax revenue, or the domestic fiscal space more generally, has to be the key component of fiscal space expansion because of the potential volatility of ODA, and is possible even in low-income countries.

The focus on domestic fiscal space is necessary, even in countries such as Senegal with access to multiple sources of concessional ODA, because external aid is subject to budgetary approvals of donor countries and conditionalities, and is therefore unpredictable and potentially volatile. Uncertainty of funding is a disincentive for expenditures on MDG goals in education and health, which require a steady source of financing for salary and non-salary running costs of standing facilities. Senegal affords an impressive instance of a steady and monotonic increase in tax revenue in a low-income country, achieved through an expansion of the tax base and by streamlining the collection system, and not simply by increasing tax rates. The administrative improvements that enabled the increase in tax revenue in Senegal should be replicable even in other low-income country contexts and include:

- a special tax centre to handle tax payments by large companies;
- computerization of tax services;
- introduction of a single tax and social identification number;
- a one-time tax amnesty to bring defaulters back into the tax system;
- strengthening of the audit system;
- more trained personnel for tax administration;
- improved relations with tax payers through discussion forums.

The fiscal resources of the government can also be leveraged through partnerships with other levels of government or with private agencies. Morocco provides an example of such a partnership in the INDH. The national government contributes 60 per cent of INDH funding, local governments contribute 20 per cent and the remaining 20 per cent is sourced from ODA.

Recommendation 5: Own revenue performance and prospects are best understood by partitioning taxes between trade and non-trade taxes, rather than between direct and indirect taxes as is more usual, so as to understand the challenge posed by trade reform and the extent to which compensating revenue was found.

Indirect taxes include both revenue from external trade and from domestic sales or VAT and, therefore, conceal the extent of the challenge posed by trade reform. Trade reform by itself is a driver of efficiency and growth, and cannot, therefore, be halted for fiscal reasons; indeed, some aspects of trade reform could even be revenue enhancing, such as tariffs on import quotas, and elimination of tariff exemptions and tariff dispersion. But all four countries reviewed here, without exception, saw a decline in trade taxes as a per cent of GDP over the period for which figures are reported. Furthermore, Senegal and Morocco will see a further loss of tariff revenue with free trade agreements and programmed tariff reductions on other trade. This points to the central difficulty in mobilizing non-debt resources from the domestic fiscal space.

All four countries have successfully found compensating revenue so far. However, excessive reliance on either of the sources, direct taxation or VAT, that yield revenue additionality, can lead to distortions. Successful revenue additionality from direct taxation of company profits, as in Morocco, leads to pressure to keep up nominal tax rates, with countervailing pressure for exemptions and concessions, which then reinforce the pressure to keep up the nominal tax rate. The danger with relying on VAT for revenue, mentioned in both the Senegal and Moroccan studies, is that VAT reimbursements may not be paid at all, or may be delayed, which then robs the VAT of its non-cascading efficiency properties. This is tantamount to a breach of contract with the taxpayer, and removes the inbuilt incentive for compliance with VAT. The emphasis has to be on balancing taxation of income and domestic transactions. A third source of revenue additionality is property-based local taxation throughout the country. This can then be used to achieve MDG targets either through a formal link to national taxes, as in Morocco, or by assigning health or education functions to sub-national local government.

In Venezuela, the policy moves of the last six years have served to enhance oil revenue prospects rather than, as the authors of the case study seem to conclude, retard them. The 2001 reform was an adroit move, given the difficulty of confronting an oil behemoth like PDVSA with multiple overseas subsidiaries and an opaque system of functioning, since it replaced uncertain dividends with the certainty of production-based royalties. Future oil revenue prospects for Venezuela are good, because of the buoyancy of the international price of oil, and the end of the production strike protesting the 2001 reform. Prospects for higher revenues would be further improved if the domestic price of gasoline were to be raised.

Recommendation 6: Caps on the public debt stock relative to GDP illustrate the short-term conflict between developmental and prudential objectives, but violation of fiscal prudence threatens development in the medium term.

Prudential limits on the public debt stock relative to GDP can be either self-imposed (Thailand, at 50 per cent, and Venezuela, variably set for each year), or externally imposed (Senegal, at 70 per cent, as part of the 1999 Pact of the WAEMU). Although prudential limits of this kind cannot be theoretically underpinned, limits of some kind are better than none, and even the rate of expansion within the cap has to be controlled through path limits, such as on the annual fiscal deficit. With the sole exception of Senegal, there is no necessity to increase the public debt, either because of successful progress towards the MDGs (Thailand), the more prudential alternative of (and scope for) higher oil revenue, as in Venezuela, or where, as in Morocco, public debt is still above 80 per cent of GDP despite the heroic effort to bring it down from the borrowing spree of the early 1970s. The Moroccan experience is particularly noteworthy because the debt-financed public investment in dams and roads during the major fiscal expansion of the early 1970s yielded neither the growth nor revenue dividend with which to pay back the debt without painful curtailments of public expenditure. The gap between development and prudence can, potentially, be bridged through user charges on publicly provided private goods, such as water and electricity, and by partial recovery on public provision of developmental services, such as education and health, which are not public goods but private goods with large positive externalities. But attempts at recovery through user charges usually meet with low compliance.

Recommendation 7: Real growth critically underpins domestic dimensions of fiscal space.

For a given buoyancy of domestic taxation, higher real growth yields higher incremental tax revenue. Likewise, for a given prudential cap on the (total) debt stock, higher real growth makes possible higher public borrowing. The importance of real growth ties in with the first recommendation on improving the efficiency of investment. If structural reform raises the growth rate at existing levels of investment that, by itself, will yield the fiscal space from which to fund investment additionality.

Recommendation 8: It is best, from both an efficiency and prudential perspective, if within the overall cap on debt/GDP, the domestic/external mix is left to the in-country policy machinery to decide without external interference.

Senegal is a case in point. There is fiscal space for an increase in domestic borrowing in Senegal because of excess liquidity in the banking system (a standard phenomenon in developing countries). Domestic borrowing will carry higher interest than the concessional IDA loans that Senegal is entitled to by virtue of being a low-income country. But, the higher interest may be a cost well worth paying. A certain measure of risk-free lending to government will, for a given measure of risk aversion within the banking system, increase their willingness to advance credit with higher than zero risk. When there is less excess liquidity, banks will have an incentive to extend banking participation in the country. Low-income countries that can get external debt on concessional terms have to trade off these benefits against the higher cost of domestic debt. But this trade-off can only be determined within the domestic policy space. The kind of external requirements on Senegal under the 1999 WAEMU Pact, and similar constraints under the IMF facility of 2003 to 2005, essentially compel the country to fund public investment through external financing and debar investment financed from domestic savings. With future prospects of borrowing forcibly confined to external borrowing, the incentives for productive expenditure and fiscal management are removed from the system because of the moral hazard accompanying HIPC and other debt relief that Senegal has received from time to time.

Recommendation 9: Externally-sourced financing may be enabled as much from worker remittances and returning flight capital as from ODA.

Senegal is again a case in point. In contrast to the CFAfr200 billion (446 million dollars) of ODA awarded in 2005, Senegal received CFAfr345 billion (770 million dollars) in worker remittances. These receipts will clearly not go into the public exchequer, but there is a possibility of providing incentives for them to flow into MDG financing on a project basis (rather than into a single borrowing pool). This is one way by which to leverage private participation in the development process and will also provide the incentives needed to secure payback for projects financed through remittances. Morocco also receives substantial worker remittances, and already has a project-based structure for financing (through the agency of ADS, see next recommendation) whereby remittance financing could be factored in. An example of a successful ADS initiative of this kind is a rural tourism project with considerable promise of payback.

Recommendation 10: Expenditure side reforms are as much or more about reforming public delivery as about reallocations of sectoral shares of expenditure.
Morocco is a case in point. The creation of ADS is a Moroccan special initiative that coordinates the work of different ministerial departments and partner NGOs; it also raises supplementary funding from them on a project-specific basis, and mediates between them and the population. ADS also serves to expedite expenditure by intervening to reduce procedural delays. ADS itself is publicly funded and is subject to government auditing. From the evidence provided in the country case study, the agency appears to function well, and its focus on arranging financing on a project basis has been sufficiently successful as to have been adopted for the INDH.

Recommendation 11: At this midpoint in the 2000 to 2015 timeframe the MDG targets should be configured towards the annual path targets implicit in the earlier terminal targets.
Venezuela is a case in point. Where there is huge year-to-year volatility in growth and poverty levels because of either a dominant natural resource (and the political economy pulls and pushes related to that resource), or where the volatility is driven by external weather shocks, it is more important to configure the MDG not in terms of a terminal year such as 2015 but in terms of annual path targets. These paths could be simple annualized equivalents of the original starting points and terminal targets, but the mapping of terminal onto annual targets is more than just a matter of simple arithmetic. Such a reconfiguration would serve to focus attention on the need to smooth the year-to-year fluctuations in and out of the state of poverty.

For a country that is not already halfway towards the MDGs, annual path targets in terms of the original starting points and terminal targets will mean that the original terminal targets will not be achieved. This does imply a softening of the initial goals but it will retain movement along the path initially envisioned, and will be more realistic in view of the clear evidence of difficulties being encountered on the ground.

Recommendation 12: Non-fiscal instruments
Following on from the previous recommendation, there is a great need to establish extended cover for poverty risk. This could be as important as fiscal instruments in achieving the MDGs in a monotonic manner. Poverty risk can be either non-idiosyncratic (weather) or idiosyncratic (sickness or disability). In the context of climate change and the greater likelihood of disasters, the long-term need is paramount. The difficulty is the computation of actuarial risk when historical weather patterns may be subject to change.

Insurance premiums for a given level of risk cover are lower when the risk pool is expanded across regions with non-synchronized risk. Insurance also has to be configured so as to lower transactions costs, such as the costs of distinguishing real from fraudulent claims. Weather insurance fortunately carries no moral hazard and can be objectively verified from meteorological data.

In poor countries, a part or even the whole of weather or health insurance may need to be subsidized from the exchequer. Therefore, non-fiscal instruments may not be completely free of the need for fiscal support. But, given the difficulty of expanding the fiscal space in the poorest countries where starting poverty levels are the highest, fiscal resources need to be effectively leveraged, and risk pooling, through standard insurance channels, is a good way of doing so.

NOTES

1   Notwithstanding the rather inconclusive survey of studies on the impact of growth of additional investment (IMF, 2004).
2   Since 45 per cent of the durations were truncated at the point of observation (expansion was continuing at the time of observation), the paper uses both parametric (Weibull) and non-parametric methods to deal with this incomplete spells problem.
3   This is, however, unlikely because of low compliance with water charges on the one hand, and the inefficiently high costs of providing water on the other (Rajaraman, 2006). The best that can be done is to configure the water supply so as to achieve efficiency of use while at the same time conceding the necessity for public subsidy. Subsidies can be progressively reduced by increasing the efficiency of supply and raising water charges.
4   A caveat that has to be kept in mind is that grants taken from the current account to finance capital expenditure could make the current deficit an inadequate measure of the imbalance on account of non-capital current expenditure alone.
5   The paper cites a number of poverty estimates, by the United Nations Economic Commission for Latin America and the Caribbean (ECLAC), by the World Bank, and by the national statistical agency Instituto Nacional de Estadística (INE) for 1990, but declares that none of them are very reliable because regular household surveys covering all sources of income by INE began only in 1994.
6   The central VAT rate in Senegal of 18 per cent is also at the high end of the cross-country range.
7   Data supplied on request by authors of the Venezuelan study.
8   Personal communications from authors of the Venezuelan study.
9   Rajaraman (2008) deals with funding uncertainty in the Indian federation and how this has discouraged expenditure on health and education at the sub-national level, which is where responsibility for these functions is constitutionally vested.

REFERENCES

Boudin, C., Gonzalez, G. and Rumbos, W. (2006) *Venezuelan Revolution: 100 Questions, 100 Answers*, Thunder's Mouth Press, New York
Brun, J-F., Chambas, G., Combes, J-L., Dulbecco, P., Gastambide, A., Guerineau, S., Guillaumont, S. and Rota Graziosi, G. (2006a) 'Evaluation of fiscal space in developing countries' (mimeo), UNDP, New York
Brun, J-F., Chambas, G. and Mourji, F. (2006b) 'Guaranteeing fiscal space for human development in Morocco' (mimeo), UNDP, New York
Diaw, A., Guerineau, S. and Guillaumont Jeanneney, S. (2006) 'Guaranteeing fiscal space for human development in Senegal' (mimeo), UNDP, New York
Development Committee (2006) 'Fiscal policy for growth and development – an interim report', paper presented at the Development Committee Meeting, 23 April 2006, Washington DC

IMF (International Monetary Fund) (2004) *Public Investment and Fiscal Policy*, IMF, Washington DC

Jansen, K. and Khannabha, C. (2006) 'The fiscal space of Thailand: An historical analysis' (mimeo), UNDP, New York

Kieffer, N. (1988) 'Economic duration data and hazard functions', *Journal of Economic Literature*, vol 26, pp646–79

Moreno, M. A. and Rodríguez, F. (2005) 'Plenty of room? Fiscal space in a resource abundant economy' (mimeo), UNDP, New York

Rajaraman, I. (2006) 'Fiscal perspective on irrigation water pricing: A case study of Karnataka, India', *Water Policy*, vol 8, no 2, pp171–181

Rajaraman, I. (2008) 'The political economy of the Indian fiscal federation', *India Policy Forum*, (Brookings and NCAER), vol 4, forthcoming

Rajaraman, I. and Mukhopadhyay, A. (2005) 'Sustainability of public debt', in A. Bagchi (ed) *Readings in Public Finance*, Oxford University Press, New York, pp320–338

Rodríguez, F. (2006) 'Understanding fiscal expansions' (mimeo), UNDP, New York, www.undp.org/poverty/e-discussions/fiscalspace/docs/Fiscal%20Space%20II.doc

Roy, R. and Heuty, A. (2005) 'Investing in development: The MDGs, aid and the sustainable capital accumulation', *Journal of International Affairs*, vol 58, no 2, pp161–176

Roy, R., Heuty, A. and Letouze, E. (2007) 'Fiscal space for what? Analytical issues from a human development perspective', paper for the G-20 Workshop on Fiscal Policy, Istanbul, July

Sachs, J., McArthur, J., Schmidt-Traub, G., Kruk, M., Bahadur, C., Faye, M. and McCord, G. (2004) 'Ending Africa's poverty trap', *Brookings Paper on Economic Activity*, 1, pp117–240

Summers, L. H. (2006) 'Reflections on global account imbalances and emerging markets reserve accumulation', L.K. Jha Memorial Lecture, Reserve Bank of India, New Delhi

Willoughby, C. (2004) *How Important is Infrastructure for Pro-Poor Growth?*, OECD, Paris

7

Guaranteeing Fiscal Space for Human Development in Morocco

Jean-François Brun, Gérard Chambas and Fouzi Mourji
with the assistance of the Office of Studies and Financial Programming
(Ministry of Economy and Finance, Morocco)

INTRODUCTION

Morocco is a middle-income country with a population of 30.5 million (according to 2006 census data) and a per capita income[1] of 2346 dollars. Although it has made progress in the past few decades, it continues to be held back by considerable poverty, especially in rural areas; 22 per cent of the population lives in poverty.

Starting in the early 1980s, the Moroccan authorities embarked on a wide-ranging programme of economic reforms in order to offset the difficulties resulting from an inward-looking economic policy (based on extensive government intervention including in the areas of production) and pro-cyclical management of the phosphate shock. Although they did stabilize the economy, the reforms have not yet produced the strong growth that could have led to a rapid reduction in poverty. Thus far, the supply of public goods is not sufficiently directed at the most underprivileged and, moreover, it remains inadequate.

Since the end of the 1990s, a variety of reforms has been introduced with a view to bringing about political and democratic transition. These reforms have already led to the definition of a democratic legal framework that affirms the primacy of the rule of law and is conducive to economic and social development and to safeguarding the rights of those categories of persons that have traditionally been disadvantaged, such as women and children. The adoption of the MDGs in 2000 is an essential element in the shift by the authorities towards development benefiting the greatest number.

The shift in economic policy should not only be an essential tool in the fight against poverty and for human development, but should also strengthen growth. The thinking on the subject of endogenous growth theory (Romer, 1986) is that the supply of public goods and services (education, health, and road, transport and telecommunications infrastructures[2]) is a basic element for accelerating growth. The MDGs raise the question of how to mobilize an adequate level of additional resources. In other words, how to find all the resources that make up fiscal space that can, potentially, be mobilized to finance the government spending needed to produce public goods in order to achieve the MDGs. The goal is, therefore, to expand the existing fiscal space in order to create the optimum fiscal space.

Brun et al (2006) show that the resources that can be used to finance public goods in order to achieve the MDGs fall into three categories:[3] (1) domestic public resources (tax and non-tax); (2) domestic financing (domestic borrowing, seignorage); and (3) external financing (grants, external borrowing). Increasing the effectiveness of government spending is tantamount to mobilizing additional resources, for it makes it possible to finance a greater supply of public goods with the same amount of public resources or financing.

In order to prevent a loss of collective resources, Brun et al (2006) stress the need for optimal mobilization of fiscal space resources. This means equalizing marginal costs for the various components of fiscal space. Moreover, creation of fiscal space must be part of the poverty reduction strategy. This means encouraging the mobilization of resources that will help reduce poverty. Finally, mobilization of resources, using the financing component of fiscal space (external borrowing or domestic financing) must be compatible with the long-term sustainability of the principal macroeconomic balances.

The next section of this chapter is devoted to the linkage between fiscal space and social spending in Morocco, and then a specific analysis is made of each component of fiscal space using the method adopted by Brun et al (2006). To this end, while remaining within the context of optimal mobilization of fiscal space resources, the remainder of the chapter is divided into sections that each attempt to answer one of the following four questions:

- What would be the optimal level of public resources (tax and non-tax) for Morocco in light of the MDGs and what are the resources that can be mobilized using the other components of fiscal space?
- What level of domestic financing (domestic borrowing, seignorage) and external financing (grants, external borrowing) is adequate?
- What resource space could be achieved by enhancing the effectiveness of government spending?
- What are the medium-term prospects for Morocco's fiscal space?

FISCAL SPACE AND HUMAN DEVELOPMENT: THE OVERALL LINKAGE

This section evaluates Morocco's current levels of social development in such areas as employment, health and education. It then analyses various programmes that have been implemented to try to combat issues in the area of human development, attempting to determine the best ways to increase and utilize fiscal space to combat poverty and other social ills in Morocco.

Despite considerable efforts, including implementation of the 1993 social development strategy (access to basic social services, employment opportunities, social welfare programme), Morocco still lags behind in the area of social development. For example, its overall school enrolment rate was just 56.3 per cent for the period 2003 to 2004, as compared to more than 70 per cent in Algeria, Egypt and Tunisia. This situation has arisen, notwithstanding the goals of the government authorities, partly as a result of an insufficient mobilization of fiscal space resources, and it has many consequences. Slow development of the factors determining the level of human capital results in lower competitiveness and therefore less growth. However, sustained growth is one of the basic prerequisites for poverty reduction.

In order to overcome these difficulties, Morocco has adopted major initiatives in recent years, making it all the more necessary to press ahead with the mobilization of fiscal space resources. Not only has it endorsed the MDGs, but recently (18 May 2005) His Majesty King Mohammed VI announced the Initiative Nationale pour le Développement Humain (INDH), which reflects the commitments made by Morocco at the Millennium Summit in 2000 and is also designed to give new impetus to finding a solution to the challenges of poverty reduction.

The Millennium Development Goals

In 2000, Morocco pledged to achieve the MDGs and it is already moving ahead in that direction. It has focused, in particular, on reducing bias affecting the place of women in development. However, progress remains uneven and varies according to sector.

Progress towards attainment of the MDGs

The MDGs outline a series of targets, to be attained between 2000 and 2015, concerned with the following:

- Poverty reduction;
- Achievement of universal primary education;
- Promotion of gender equality (education, employment, political representation, legal provisions);
- Reduction of child mortality (reduction by two thirds between 2000 and 2015);

- Improvement of maternal health;
- Combating HIV/AIDS, malaria and other diseases;
- Promotion of environmental sustainability (by preserving biodiversity, reducing emissions of harmful gases, increasing access to safe drinking water, improving habitat[4]);
- Establishment of a global partnership for development (commitment to good governance to deal with the debt problems and to implement strategies to facilitate access to work for young people).

The national report on the MDGs (Haut Commissariat au Plan, 2005a) contains a detailed analysis of the various goals, an assessment of progress made towards attaining them in 2004, and the target for 2015. Given the progress made since the reference period (1994 in most cases), it is very likely that all the goals will be met. However, the cost of the investments needed in order to fully attain these goals will be very high, given that the marginal cost of intervening increases (Burn et al, 2006) the closer one gets to attaining the MDGs (or the elasticity of response decreases). Clearly, given the ambitious nature of the MDGs and the INDH, the fiscal space to be created will have to be sizeable. Considerable thought will, therefore, have to be given to its potential components, especially since the only way to balanced government finances in the medium or long term is by pursuing a coherent strategy for optimal development of all the components of fiscal space.

Considerable gender bias

Since the early 1980s, the Moroccan government has been giving priority attention to the advancement of women within the context of its social development strategy (UNDP, Morocco Office, 2006). This is because, despite a variety of innovative initiatives, girls and women are still discriminated against, especially in the areas of education, health and employment. These biases are generally most pronounced in rural areas, which, as noted above, are also the most impoverished.

Disparities in the area of education

During the period 2003 to 2004, overall school enrolment for the population as a whole was 31.9 per cent. In 2004, in urban areas the rate was the same for girls as for boys (52.3 per cent and 51.4 per cent). Also in 2004,[5] the overall primary enrolment rate was 87 per cent, as against 64.5 per cent in 1994. Yet while the gap in primary enrolment rates has been decreasing, it remains high in rural areas (roughly 10 per cent).

At the secondary level, geographical and gender disparities are particularly evident in rural areas. In the period 2003 to 2004, the school enrolment rate at the secondary level was 68.8 per cent overall, but in rural areas the rate for girls was very low (8.9 per cent). The school enrolment rate for girls in rural areas was one-fifth that for girls in urban areas.

In higher education, the overall enrolment rate rose from 10.4 per cent to 12.8 per cent between 2001/2002 and 2005/2006. The bias against girls is less pronounced at this level with girls accounting for 46.2 per cent of the students in the period 2003 to 2004.

Disparities in the area of health

The gender bias in the area of health is particularly significant for women living in rural areas. In 2002, their life expectancy was just 68.4 years as compared with 75.6 years for women in urban areas. Furthermore, the difference in life expectancy between women and men in urban areas is 4.4 years, whereas in rural areas it is only 1.9 years.

The maternal mortality rate for Moroccan women was 227 per thousand live births in the period 1999 to 2003, or double the rate of Egypt or Tunisia. It is even higher in rural areas: 267 as compared with 187 per thousand in the cities. However, the growing ability to control fertility is having an impact on the status of women. The total fertility rate (average number of children born to a woman over her lifetime) has fallen from 7 in 1962 to 2.5 in 2004.

Other disparities

In 2004, the employment rate was 59.6 per cent for men and 15.1 per cent for women in urban areas. In the 15 to 34 years age group the disparity was still there, but was smaller: 26.4 per cent of men in that age group were unemployed as compared with 33.9 per cent of women. In urban areas, 60.7 per cent of women are housewives, whereas in rural areas this rate is 38.8 per cent. Many women living in rural areas are employed as family aides.

In recent years, significant steps have been taken to reduce discrimination against women. The new Family Code, which was adopted on 3 February 2004, made significant changes to the legal status of women in society. The new Nationality Code, which changed the conditions whereby children acquire nationality, has had a similar effect.

Unequal poverty reduction and marked inequalities

Evaluation of poverty

Morocco has devoted considerable resources to analysing poverty. In 2004, the department of planning, Haut Commissariat au Plan (HCP), with the assistance of the World Bank, drew up a poverty map that identified poverty, inequality and vulnerability down to the municipality level (HCP, 2004, 2005a, 2005b).[6] The map makes it possible to identify the causes and manifestations of poverty and provides information concerning access to public goods or collective infrastructure (roads, electricity and water, education and health).

According to the definition used by HCP, poverty has decreased (see Table 7.1). Whereas in 1985, 21 per cent of the population lived in poverty, by 2004 the rate had fallen to 14.2 per cent. The decrease has been much greater in the cities than in rural areas and by 2004 poverty was increasingly a rural phenomenon: 22 per cent of the population in rural areas lived in poverty compared with 7.9 per cent in the cities. The bias against the rural population is also reflected in the vulnerability index. Whereas, overall, 39.3 per cent of the country's population was considered to be vulnerable in 2004, more than half of the rural population (51.1 per cent) was considered to be vulnerable.

Morocco is experiencing rapid urbanization. The urbanization rate increased from 42.5 per cent in 1982 to 55.1 per cent in 2004. Although the situation is relatively more favourable in urban areas, there are still large pockets of poverty in the cities and a large proportion of city dwellers lack access to certain basic services. Some 8 per cent of the urban population lives in precarious housing, 17 per cent lack access to water and 10 per cent lack access to electricity. In urban areas, the unemployment rate among secondary school graduates was 20.8 per cent in 2006.

Although the Human Development Index (HDI) increased from 0.479 in 1980 to 0.642 in 2004, Morocco still ranks 123rd overall even though, in terms of per capita GDP, it ranks 108th.

Slow growth: Recovery to be confirmed

The low level and irregularity of growth is one of the leading factors working against a speedy elimination of poverty. Over the long term, the annual average growth rate of 3.2 per cent between 1990 and 2006 is not sufficient to reduce poverty; moreover, it is too dependent on agriculture, which is vulnerable to the vagaries of the weather. Morocco's GDP grew at a relatively sustained rate during the 1980s, slowed in the 1990s, and then accelerated between 1999 and 2006 to an average annual rate of 3.6 per cent. However, growth remains irregular. In 2005, it fell to 1.6 per cent because of the drought. Thanks to an excellent growing season, growth was high in 2006 (8.1 per cent).[7]

Table 7.1 *Poverty, vulnerability and HDI, 1985–2004*

	Total population		Urban population		Rural population	
	1985	2004	1985	2004	1985	2004
Relative poverty (HCP definition)	21.0%	14.2%	13.3%	7.9%	26.8%	22.0%
Vulnerability (HCP definition)		39.3%				51.1%
Poverty: international definition $2/day PPP	16.8% (1990)	9.7%	7.8% (1990)	4.3%	24.8% (1990)	16.4%
Poverty: experiencing hunger	4.6%	1.8%		3.7%		
Human Development Index (overall)	0.515	0.642		0.721		0.537
Human Development Index (men)		0.665		0.739		0.566
Human Development Index (women)		0.621		0.704		0.509

Source: HCP (2005)

The increase in per capita GDP has been facilitated by the slowdown in population growth, which averaged 2.4 per cent for the period 1994 to 2006. Morocco could benefit in the coming years from a demographic structure particularly favourable to growth. Much of the population is of working age, expenses for the elderly are relatively low since the elderly are relatively few in number, and expenses for the younger generations are decreasing in relative terms since the fertility rate has declined.

Inadequate supply of public goods

Access to basic public goods (education and health services) is still inadequate in relation to comparable countries (see the following section). Moreover, access to essential collective services (water, electricity and the road network) is not yet widespread, particularly in rural areas.[8] Priority has been given to large-scale projects, such as large dams, and a goal was set (and has been nearly reached) of irrigating one million hectares, while other areas have been somewhat neglected. The Water Act of 1995 introduced changes to the way in which water is managed.

Policy for promoting human development

The government plays a lead role in human development. Despite the results achieved, government action has not yet been sufficiently effective. This is due to a variety of factors: lack of participation by the people, programmes of action not properly followed, poor decision making, lack of evaluation and, as yet, insufficient accounting. Better governance and increased effectiveness of government spending are essential.

Human development: A diagnosis

Human development and education

In 2006, the illiteracy rate of the population aged ten years and older was 38.5 per cent, as compared with 42.8 per cent in 2004 and 54.9 per cent in 1994. Although illiteracy is declining, it is still relatively high[9] when compared with neighbouring countries. In 2006, illiteracy was particularly high in rural areas, affecting roughly 54.4 per cent of the population (as compared with 75 per cent in 1994) (see Table 7.2).

Table 7.2 *Illiteracy rate and net primary school enrolment, 1994–2004*

	Total population			Urban population			Rural population		
	1994	2004	2006	1994	2004	2006	1994	2004	2006
Illiteracy rate (over 10 years) (%)	54.9	42.8	38.5	37.0	29.4	27.2	75.0	60.5	54.4
Net primary school enrolment (%)	64.5	92.9	93.0	(M) (F) 84.2 79.8	(M) (F) 91.2 89.8	94.4	50.3	89.0	91.6
Girls	55.1	90.1	90.5					84.3	87.2

Source: Institut National de la Statistique (Population and Housing Census), 2004

Table 7.3 *Infant and under-5 mortality rates, 1982–1991 and 1994–2003, and maternal mortality rates, 1987–1991 and 1999–2003*

	Total population		Urban population		Rural population	
	1982–1991	1994–2003	1982–1991	1994–2003	1982–1991	1994–2003
Infant mortality rate (%)	57	40	52	33	69	55
Under-5 mortality rate (%)	76	47	59	38	98	69
Maternal mortality rate	1987–1991	1999–2003	1987–1991	1999–2003	1987–1991	1999–2003
(per 100,000 live births)	332	227	284	187	362	267

Source: Population and housing census, 2004

Human development and health

The infant mortality rate is one of the best indicators of a country's health situation. The infant mortality rate in Morocco is high (40 per 1000 in the period 1994 to 2003), and the situation is particularly bad in rural areas (55 per 1000) as compared with urban areas (see Table 7.3). The picture given by maternal mortality rates, which stand at 267 per 1000 in rural areas as against 187 per 1000 in urban areas, leads to the same conclusion.

Instruments to promote human development

Government spending and education

In 2006, government spending on education[10] accounted for 6.3 per cent of GDP (approximately 19 per cent of overall government spending). Government spending on education is high relative to similar countries but the results achieved are lower. The educational system is, therefore, ineffective. It is characterized by a high drop-out rate, a high unemployment rate for graduates and shortcomings in the teaching of basic skills. The relative cost of secondary education is particularly high.

In 1999, Morocco adopted the National Charter, an ambitious project for the renewal of the educational system. Education was declared to be the nation's highest priority, next to the absolute priority given to integrity of the national territory. The goal of the School Charter is to reduce the illiteracy rate to 10 per cent by 2010 and to wipe it out altogether by 2015. A plan for the period 2000 to 2004 provided for a series of measures to extend education, including at the preschool level. The Commission Spéciale Education-Formation (COSEF), which is responsible for evaluating progress, carried out a midterm evaluation in 2005. The Charter has resulted in significant progress.

Government spending and health

Overall, spending on health amounts to approximately 5 per cent of GDP; 54 per cent of that amount is financed directly by households, 25 per cent by the government budget, 16 per cent by health insurance and 5 per cent by other sources of financing. In 2006, government spending on health amounted to 1.2 per cent of GDP and accounted for 3.6 per cent of overall spending in the budget. Of the ordinary government spending on health, four-fifths goes for hospitals as compared to one-fifth for basic health services and preventive care in rural areas. One important aspect of the health strategy is the introduction of compulsory health insurance. There is no efficient linkage as yet between the public and the private health care systems.

Targeted programmes: Social Priorities Programme BAJ 1

The barnamaj al awaliyat al ijtima`iya (BAJ) 1 programme, which was run during the period 1996 to 1997, offers a partial solution to the problem of human development by focusing on the areas of education, health and unemployment in several poor rural areas. BAJ 1 targets 14 provinces that were chosen because of the high incidence of poverty and the extent of their unmet fundamental needs. The programme, which is designed to operate for six years, consists of three parts:

- Basic education – this has made it possible to improve the school supply and has had positive results for girls in rural areas.
- Basic health – the goal has been to increase the supply of care in seven provinces by establishing infrastructure.
- National advancement, coordination and follow-up of social programmes – the aim is, essentially, to reduce unemployment and increase the supply of basic infrastructure, such as roads, schools and health facilities.

The programme presents four difficulties:

- It affords only partial coverage for the poor, since the provinces chosen for the programme contain only 37 per cent of the poor people of Morocco and 48 per cent of the rural inhabitants.
- There are limitations in terms of the targeting of poor people between provinces and the interior portions of the provinces.
- Programme resources are insufficient to reduce poverty.
- More generally, there are questions about the effectiveness of adopting an approach through specific programmes as opposed to acting through the general budget (see below).

A general approach: INDH

INDH seeks to be a more general and more effective solution to human development needs than programmes such as BAJ 1. The King announced the initiative's implementation in a speech to the nation on 18 May 2005. INDH seeks to introduce a human development dynamic using a decentralized approach that respects the principles of participation, partnership, convergence of actions and strategic planning. By affirming these principles, INDH seeks to make up for the frequent ineffectiveness of the supply of public goods. It emphasizes the need to remedy, by means of innovative actions,[11] the traditional ineffectiveness of public action. The intention is to coordinate public action in order to adhere to schedules, to implement projects fully and to achieve a pace of reform that will bring about irreversible change.

A participatory approach with elected representatives and civil society. INDH seeks to promote sensitization with a view to mobilizing all available energies and resources and overcoming the usual stumbling blocks. It is broadly based on a participatory approach that pools the skills of members of the administration, elected officials and representatives of civil society (see also the section 'Participation, decentralization and effectiveness of government spending').

INDH has four levels: local, provincial, regional and central. Local committees are made up of elected representatives, the president of the commission responsible for economic, social and cultural development, representatives of civil society organizations, and decentralized state technical services. The local committees are usually composed (based on a sample of 404 such committees) of staff from government services (30 per cent), elected representatives (of whom 85 per cent are representatives of municipal councils) (31 per cent), and representatives of civic organizations (39 per cent). The mission of these committees is to draw up the local human development initiatives (ILDH) and also to implement the projects agreed on at the local level. Local committees see to the follow-up and implementation of actions on the spot.

Provincial committees are chaired by the governor and have 15 members who include elected representatives, the staff of decentralized administrations and representatives of civil society. Their tasks include approving local initiatives (ILDH), drawing up financing agreements and releasing funds for projects that have been approved. They also report follow-up indicators of what has been implemented to the central level. They are, therefore, in charge of oversight and implementation of the ILDH and management and follow-up of projects. Provincial committees are responsible for identifying which urban districts and rural municipalities are to be targeted. The priority areas for action are determined by means of municipal poverty maps.

Regional committees, which are chaired by the *Wali* (regional governor), consist of provincial governors, the chairpersons of the regional councils, the chairpersons of the provincial councils, staff of the decentralized government services and representatives of civil society. Their main role is to ensure that provincial initiatives are consistent and that the programmes of the government, public establishments, local governments and the actions of INDH are all convergent. If there is an extreme poverty component, the regional committees draw up the regional scheme for combating extreme poverty on the basis of proposals from the provincial committees.

At the central level, the role of the Inter-Ministerial Committee and the Steering Committee is to define the budgetary framework, to allocate resources and to encourage international support.

INDH financing. The establishment of the Fund to Support the Human Development Initiative (Prime Minister's Trust Fund) is an innovative approach in terms of financing. The resources are delegated to the *Walis* and the governors and are allocated according to a specific analysis of needs. The government contributes 60 per cent of INDH financing, local governments contribute 20 per cent, and cooperation provides for another 20 per cent.

In 2005, a total of 250 million Moroccan dirhams (MAD; US$1 = MAD0.128 on 7 February 2008) was mobilized to finance a priority programme having the following components: rural poverty reduction (30 per cent), reduction of urban exclusion (39 per cent), and reduction of precariousness (31 per cent). The funding came from contributions from the central government (MAD50 million), local governments (MAD100 million) and the Hassan II Fund for Economic and Social Development (MAD100 million). Each province received MAD1.5 million for human development, and each of the regional capitals received an additional amount of MAD2 million. In the case of the six largest cities, that additional amount was increased to MAD3 million.

INDH expenditures. INDH expenditures are set forth in the Human Development Initiative Trust Fund.[12] For the period 2006 to 2010, the MAD10 billion allocated for INDH is divided among four areas, each of which will get MAD2.5 billion. The areas are rural poverty reduction, reduction of urban exclusion, reduction of rural precariousness and a cross-cutting programme.

Rural poverty reduction: The 403 rural municipalities (3.75 million people) where the poverty rate is more than 22 per cent (348 municipalities have a poverty rate in excess of 30 per cent) will each receive a total of MAD5 million over 5 years (MAD1 million each year).

Reduction of urban exclusion: Some 264 districts in 30 towns will receive MAD8 billion over a 5-year period (again receiving 20 per cent each year). The amount they receive will depend on the size of the town. Casablanca, with 54 districts, will receive a total of MAD432 million). Rabat-Salé, which has 30 districts, will receive MAD240 million, and so on. The population affected (some 2.5 million people) accounts for 22 per cent of the population in the 30 towns and 16 per cent of the total urban population. The districts involved are experiencing significant problems (lack of basic social infrastructure, high drop-out rates, large-scale unemployment, unhealthy habitat, high rate of exclusion of women and so on).

Reduction of precariousness: This covers 16 regions, each of which will receive MAD20 million over the five years, plus an additional amount depending upon the size of the urban population. It involves setting up regional poverty reduction plans based on reviews of the numbers of people living in precarious situations and of the infrastructure. The regional committee is responsible for executing the plan of action to reduce precariousness, but it may entrust this to those for whom the projects are designed. The cross-cutting and reduction of rural precariousness categories have made it possible to increase the number of persons benefiting from INDH.

Cross-cutting: This covers 70 provinces and prefectures, each of which is to receive MAD10 million for the 5 years, plus an additional amount that will depend upon the size of the urban population living below the poverty line. The aim is to prolong INDH by calling for projects designed, *inter alia*, to improve access to basic services, develop income-generating activities, strengthen local capacities and develop social and cultural leadership. Projects submitted by local governments, professional chambers, trade unions, cooperatives and associations are selected and financed by the provincial committees. Those for whom the projects are designed will be encouraged to also help finance them, possibly through contributions in kind. Another aim is to provide training and to strengthen local capacities (local government administrators and employees, local committees and so on). Yet another aim is to create a network of experts.

In addition to existing programmes, funding in the amount of MAD10 billion over five years is reserved for major projects.

INDH achievements. Currently, there are plans for 1104 projects (apart from the cross-cutting activities), of which 570 are intended for rural areas, 364 for urban areas and 170 to reduce precariousness. By the end of December 2006, of these 1104 projects, 987 had been completed and 197 were being implemented. INDH has had a multiplier effect inasmuch as the overall amount allocated to this initiative came to nearly MAD600 million. The financial contribution of the partners thus accounted for 59 per cent of this amount.[13]

A gender-sensitive budget

The characteristics of the supply of public goods stem from the structure of government spending and contribute, in large part, to determining the level of human capital (education, health) and how it is distributed. It is by no means far fetched to suggest that government spending is a major instrument for reducing gender bias. Thus far the 'gender' dimension of government policies has been small.[14]

However, in 2001, Morocco took the initiative of integrating gender into national budgets in order to reflect the priority given to the advancement of women. Piloted by the Ministry of Finance and Privatization, the initiative is the focus of the authorities' concerns (see, for example, the speech by His Majesty the King of 20 August 1999). It is one of several initiatives regarding legal matters, planning and preparation of statistics, participation of women in public life and, finally, education (equal access to education). Gender in this context is taken to mean the socio-cultural factors that determine the specific situation of men and women in society. The initiative seeks to introduce gender into the programming and execution of the budget[15] to promote equitable and sustainable development characterized by a lack of gender bias (Ministry of Finance and Privatization, 2005a). In short, the goal is to satisfy the needs of women and men in an equitable manner.

To this end it will be necessary not to assume that the situations of men and women are the same, but, rather to take specific account of the differences between the situations of men and women and to evaluate, in terms of equity and effectiveness, the consequences thereof. It will be necessary to start by analysing the situation according to gender and it is, therefore, essential to have statistical information disaggregated by gender in order to be able to identify inequalities and anomalies. It will then be possible to target budgetary interventions and to evaluate their impact (Burn et al, 2006). Gender analysis tools are fundamental for enhancing budgetary effectiveness, transparency and equity.

Section summary

In order to compensate for the inefficiency of conventional government spending, particularly evident in the area of spending on education, Morocco has embarked on two types of action. First, it has adopted major programmes that are largely independent of traditional government spending and are designed to accelerate poverty reduction efforts (the BAJ 1 social priorities programme and the important INDH). Basically, these programmes have shortcomings related to the partial nature of the quest for optimum solutions. One risk is that partial solutions will be adopted that do not necessarily correspond to the global solution that could have been devised through global management of the various components of fiscal space. Another risk is that, when adopting partial solutions, the global reforms essential for improving the efficiency of traditional government spending will be postponed and reform measures will be reserved for more specific programmes. For example, the obstacle connected with cumbersome public accounting procedures is partially eliminated through the INDH. It would be more useful to eliminate this type of difficulty for all government spending. Likewise, remedying the lack of coordination between various categories of spending is an action that should apply to all government spending. Lastly, implementation of specific or sectoral expenditure management programmes in parallel with traditional global budget management results in higher administrative costs for government intervention.

The second type of action has been taken specifically in order to reduce the widespread gender bias, which is not only prejudicial to development but also undermines women's equality. Morocco has decided to mainstream gender in budgetary procedures through what we will call 'gender budgeting'. In principle, this approach should make it easier to find a better solution, since the strategy of reducing bias against women is an integral part of the general budget negotiations. A global solution can be found by following this procedure.

EVALUATION OF TAX REVENUE SPACE

The goal of this section is to determine, within the context of a partial equilibrium approach, the optimum level of public resources, or tax revenue space, within Morocco's fiscal space. Here, tax revenue space is taken to include tax and non-tax revenue.[16] In order to determine the optimum level of public resources it is necessary to take into account the actual public resources and the tax effort. A political economy analysis makes it possible to evaluate the requirements for achieving an optimum level of public resources.

Optimum public resource mobilization

As demonstrated in Brun et al (2006), assessment of the optimum level of public resources depends on optimization of the various components of fiscal space. Within the context of an initial partial equilibrium approach it is possible to use different criteria for evaluating what resource space may be available in the public resources component. The analysis is based, first of all, on a review of the actual level of revenues collected and then on the notion of fiscal effort. Lastly, budget balances are taken into account.

Analysis based on actual taxation level

Morocco's potential public resource space can be evaluated by analysing the ratio of public resources to GDP, which allows comparisons both in time and with other countries. Figure 7.1 shows a trend towards an increase in public revenue. During the 1980s, this never exceeded 23 per cent of GDP.[17] Starting in 1991, the figure stabilized above this level, except during the period 2001 to 2004, which immediately followed the liberalization of tariffs.[18] There was significant growth in 2006 when the rate reached 25.3 per cent of GDP. Despite relatively important short-term shocks (droughts, oil shocks and cyclical reversals) during the 1980–2006 period, Morocco's public revenue was less unstable when compared with many developing countries, and

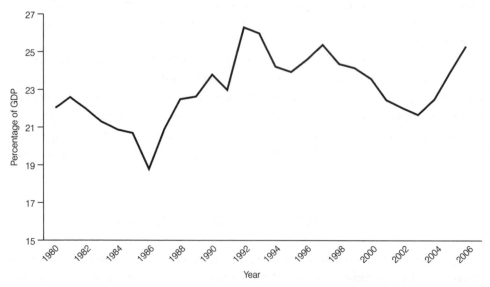

Source: Ministry of Finance and Privatization and IMF (compilation of data for many years)

Figure 7.1 *Trends in public revenues as a percentage of GDP*

Table 7.4 *Morocco's tax effort and tax potential: International comparisons, 1980–2003*

	1980–1984 (% GDP)	1985–1989 (% GDP)	1990–1994 (% GDP)	1995–1999 (% GDP)	2000–2003 (%GDP)
Morocco	21.8	21.1	24.7	24.5	22.4
MENA	29.1 (10)	26.1 (11)	25.9 (11)	28.3 (12)	28.0 (13)
Middle-income countries	23.8 (42)	25.3 (41)	24.8 (42)	24.9 (43)	24.3 (45
Developing countries	21.3 (82)	24.1 (83)	20.8 (87)	20.6 (92)	20.8 (99)
Asia	19.3 (12)	22.1 (110	20.8 (13)	19.1 (16)	18.5 (19)
Low-income countries	18.7 (40)	17.5 (42)	17.0 (45)	16.9 (49)	17.8 (54)
Morocco tax effort	–2.7	–2.9	0.3	–0.1	2.9
Morocco tax potential	24.5	24.0	24.3	24.6	25.3

Note: The number in brackets is the sample size. The data are the unweighted arithmetic averages calculated over the five-year periods of 1980–1984, 1985–1989, 1990–1994 and 1995–1999, and the four-year period of 2000–2003.

Source: GFS (International Monetary Fund), country data; authors' calculations

this is conducive to the good management of government finances.[19] Public revenue seems close to the average for middle-income developing countries (see Table 7.4) particularly in the year 2000 and beyond. Admittedly, it is lower than the level of 28 per cent found in the group of countries in the MENA region, but many of these countries derive considerable public resources from minerals, particularly oil, whereas minerals and, in particular, phosphates, currently contribute little tax revenue to Morocco's budget.

Tax effort analysis

However, an analysis conducted solely on the basis of effective taxation[20] is not entirely satisfactory because a significant portion of tax revenues is dependent on structural factors, which economic policy is unable to address in the short term, while the balance (tax effort) is determined by factors that depend largely on economic policy.

The rate of taxation observed can be broken down into two elements, a rate of structural taxation (tax potential, capacity to contribute), which is dependent on structural factors unrelated to economic policy, and tax effort, which is determined by the tax mobilization policy. In other words, a country's tax potential can be defined as the rate of taxation one would normally expect given the country's structural features. The difference between the observed rate of taxation and this tax potential is attributed to economic policy. It is thus similar to a tax effort measure.

The rate of structural taxation is determined by a set of structural variables. Among these variables is the level of development viewed in terms of three variables: per capita GDP, the sectoral origin of the income measured by the share of agricultural value added and, lastly, the degree of monetarization of the economy measured by the ratio of aggregate money supply (M2) to GDP (see, for example, Stotsky and Wolde Mariam,

1997). One can, in fact, suppose that the higher a country's level of development, the greater will be its capacity to collect revenue. There are several possible explanations for this. On the demand side, the rise in the level of development entails an increase in and diversification of the demand for public goods that may reduce taxpayer resistance to taxation. On the supply side, an increase in the level of development definitely increases the economy's capacity to contribute. Moreover, administrative capacities, particularly when aimed at lifting taxes, most likely improve with the level of development. This is chiefly a result of the existence of economies of scale in tax administration and a more favourable environment (high-quality infrastructure, skilled administrators and overall educational level of the population).

The rate of structural taxation is also positively affected by the extent to which trade is open. In fact, revenue from international trade is more easily taxable than domestic earnings or consumption. The effect of openness on tax potential is reinforced, in some countries, by a high proportion of mining and petroleum products among the total exports, for this category of exports can give rise to substantial revenues in the form of taxes or fees.

Measuring tax effort thus makes it possible to obtain a preliminary assessment of fiscal space that can be mobilized on the basis of the (actual) rates of public resources observed. A positive tax effort suggests that there are difficulties in mobilizing additional public resources, while a negative effort indicates an underutilized public resource space. The method of analysis based on an evaluation of tax effort makes it possible to assess the potential and tax effort of individual countries, including Morocco (see Table 7.6).

Determining whether additional fiscal space can be identified in a particular country leads one to consider the following question, 'Where do actual public revenues stand in relation to the level of taxation determined by structural factors?'. As can be seen from the following two hypothetical cases, a given level of actual taxation can correspond to radically different situations insofar as the utilization of tax space is concerned.

In the first case, structural factors determine that the tax potential is higher than the actual level of taxation. This translates into a negative tax effort in which the economic policy that the country is implementing is the cause of tax demobilization.[21] This suggests that a more favourable economic policy should make it easier to mobilize additional public resources and thus broaden the public revenue component of the budgetary space. Total taxation thus reinforced would then lead to admissible tax distortions, as they would be similar to those occurring in the other countries.

In the second case, structural factors determine a tax potential that is lower than actual taxation. The level of public resources is, thus, partly attributable to an economic policy favourable to tax mobilization (positive fiscal effort). One can thus conclude that the public revenue space is well utilized and the identification of additional revenue space would require the implementation of a revenue mobilization policy more vigorous than the one generally pursued by other developing countries. It would then seem

Table 7.5 *Econometric equation for determining developing country tax potential*

Explanatory variables	Coefficients	Student t	p value
Constant	4.01	1.00	0.31
Imports M/GDP	3.85	7.97	0.00
Per capita product, retarded	0.95	2.10	0.04
Mining and petroleum exports as a share of all exports	0.03	3.12	0.00
Agricultural value added/GDP	−0.16	5.73	0.00
$R^2 = 0.33$			

Sources: GSF (International Monetary Fund), national data, authors' calculations

Table 7.6 *Tax effort of selected countries*

	1980–1984 (% GDP)	1985–1989 (% GDP)	1990–1994 (% GDP)	1995–1999 (% GDP)	2000–2003 (%GDP)
Morocco	−2.7	−2.9	0.3	−0.1	−2.9
Senegal	1.5	1.1	−0.9	−1.1	−0.1
Thailand	0.8	0.4	0.7	−1.8	−3.8
Venezuela	4.7	1.4	−4.2	−4.3	−1.8

Note: The data are the unweighted arithmetic averages calculated over the five-year periods of 1980–1984, 1985–1989, 1990–1994 and 1995–1999, and the four-year period of 2000–2003.

Source: GSF (International Monetary Fund), national data, authors' calculations

possible that any new economic policy measure adopted to increase public resource mobilization would probably lead to a worsening of economic distortions deriving from taxation[22] and result in undesirable social effects. In such a situation, notwithstanding the fact that the taxation levels are identical in both cases, one must conclude that there is no underutilized revenue space.

As the tax potential can only be evaluated on the basis of an econometric evaluation covering all developing countries (see Table 7.5 and Box 7.1 for an explanation of the method), the quality of tax mobilization (or tax effort) is evaluated in terms of the average policy for the entire sample. The measurement is thus a relative one.

The econometric evaluations show a tax effort very close to zero[23] during the 1990s (see Tables 7.4 and 7.6). During this period, Morocco adopted an economic policy with an efficiency level similar to the average for all developing countries. Using the criterion of tax effort, the conclusion is that Morocco's public resource space is fully utilized.[24] Any attempt to further develop its public resource space would create a risk of excessive tax distortions.

Beginning in 2000, when tariff liberalization was expanded further, the tax effort became very negative (−2.9 per cent during the period 2000 to 2003). However, this situation was an ephemeral one. As of 2004, as the result of a tax reform programme and enhanced administration, the situation recovered. In 2006, the actual rate of taxation was similar to the tax potential, which was thus fully utilized.

> ### BOX 7.1 A METHODOLOGY FOR ASSESSING TAX EFFORT
>
> The method for calculating tax effort consists of estimating (see Table 7.6) an explanatory equation for the rate of taxation in terms of the variables listed above using relative data from a broad sample of countries over a considerable period of time (panel data for 85 developing countries for the period 1970 to 2003). The estimate uses an econometric analysis of panel data (random country effects impacting an unobserved heterogeneity constant over time). The balance of the equation, which can be calculated for a specific country or a group of countries, thus makes it possible to measure tax effort. If p is the rate of taxation, $\hat{p}$ the public revenue level, and $\hat{\varepsilon}$ tax effort, then $p = \hat{p} + \hat{\varepsilon}$.
>
> As the mean of residuals, $\hat{\varepsilon}$, for the total sample is nil, tax effort must be interpreted relatively. The benchmark is the average behaviour of the country-year panel selected. Thus for a particular country a negative balance means that the country's tax effort is below the norm, with the reverse being true in the case of a positive balance. Finally, if the balance is nil, the country's tax effort is consistent with the sample mean. Thus a situation in which a tax effort is nil does not signify a flawed policy, but a tax mobilization policy the efficacy of which is comparable to the panel mean.

Level of taxation and budget deficit. The period prior to 1986 was marked by a severe budget imbalance, resulting in a heavy debt servicing burden. Since 1986, the budget deficit has been contained. As a result, it was possible to stabilize debt servicing over the period 1983 to 2000 at between 5 and 6 per cent of GDP. Since 2000, the debt service to GDP ratio has been less than 5 per cent of GDP and has been declining slowly.

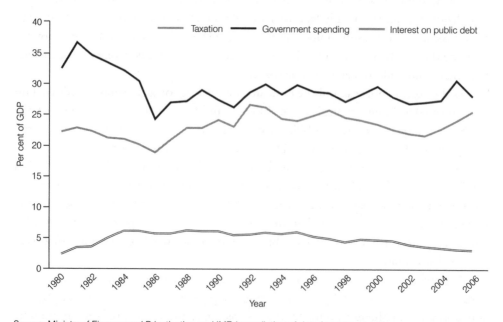

Source: Ministry of Finance and Privatization and IMF (compilation of data for many years)

Figure 7.2 *Changes in the balance of government finances*

**BOX 7.2 SHOCKS, MANAGEMENT OF GOVERNMENT FINANCES
AND FISCAL SPACE**

In the early 1970s, Morocco's government finances were characterized by a low rate of taxation (17.7 per cent of GDP), a low level of public debt (interest payments representing 0.8 per cent of GDP in 1974) and a moderate budget deficit of about 3 per cent of GDP. In the period 1974 to 1975, at the time of the first oil shock, Morocco enjoyed a phosphate boom following a sharp increase in international phosphate prices. Non-tax revenue then increased sharply by four percentage points of GDP.

Morocco took advantage of this public resource boom to embark on major public investment programmes, particularly in the area of public infrastructure (dams and roads). Government capital expenditure increased rapidly from 5.9 per cent of GDP in 1970 to 11.6 per cent of GDP in 1980. Like most countries that enjoyed a mineral boom (illustrating the general nature of the Dutch Disease), Morocco funded most of the increased capital expenditure by borrowing abroad.

The international boom did not last. By 1977, phosphate prices were declining. However, in order to continue its capital expenditure programmes, and probably in the hope that the phosphate market would recover, Morocco intensified its policy of borrowing abroad. In 1981, its budget deficit reached 14 per cent of GDP and net external borrowing represented 9.1 per cent of GDP. Thus considerable public debt was accumulated over a very short period of time and this continues to have an impact on the level of fiscal space resources that can be mobilized.

Starting in the late 1970s, Morocco embarked on a policy of stabilization and then of structural adjustment in which improved government finances were an essential component. The cost of this policy of adjustment of government finances was increased by the public debt burden. This forced Morocco, in an unfavourable economic climate (years of low growth, oil shock and bad harvest), to reduce non-debt spending particularly drastically because debt servicing problems had been aggravated by an exchange rate decline and an international rise in interest rates (interest payments alone on the public debt represented more than 5 per cent of GDP). This fiscal policy episode, which permanently reduced the resource space available for government spending on development, demonstrates the adverse effect on fiscal space of any loss of control over the budget deficit.

Currently, Morocco is in danger of seeing its public resources decline because of the dismantling of tariffs following free trade agreements. In 1996, it signed a free trade agreement with the EU. The agreement came into force in March 2000 and was followed by other agreements with Turkey and the US. Having opted for open trade, Morocco will eventually see its customs revenue (currently accounting for some 15 per cent of tax revenue) dwindle to almost nothing. In order to make up for the loss of tariff revenue and avoid an imbalance of government finances that would be unsustainable, Morocco has embarked on the road to fiscal transition. The increase in current government spending, excluding interest on debt, which has been under way in recent years, must also be kept under control (see below).

A decrease in the burden of interest payments on debt accelerated after 2000 due to three essential factors: (1) there was a resumption of growth; (2) although still high, budget deficits have been contained at about 5.0 per cent of GDP since 2000; and (3) privatization has reduced the debt.

Improved structuring of the public debt and more efficient management of its financing (see the section 'Evaluation of financing space') have enhanced the favourable effect of the decline in interest rates. However, this debt servicing burden remains the reason why the fiscal space available to finance spending has shrunk. In

Table 7.7 *Overall trends in government finances in Morocco, 2002–2006 (% GDP)*

Government finances (including local governments)	2002	2003	2004	2005	2006
Total revenues (*)	22.0	21.7	22.5	21.9	25.3
Tax revenues	20.4	20.8	20.2	21.9	22.2
Total expenditure (**)	26.6	26.9	27.3	30.4	28.1
Wages as a component of expenditure	10.9	11.2	1.3	11.9	11.0
Investment as a component of expenditure (***)	4.6	4.2	3.8	3.8	4.1
Budget deficit (****)	4.6	5.2	4.7	6.5	2.9
Current GDP (MAD billions)	447	477	500	523	580

Note: (*) Including earnings from special Treasury accounts; (**) Including balance of special Treasury accounts; ((***) Including Special Highway Fund; (****) Excluding revenue from privatizations.

Source: Ministry of Finance and Privatization (DEPF database) and authors' calculations

recent years, even though there has been a reduction, government spending on debt servicing alone is close to capital expenditure levels. In addition, the deficit level in recent budget years, which has remained relatively high (see Table 7.7), means that the recent decline in debt servicing payments is vulnerable[25] to an unexpected event (declining growth or rising interest rates).

The budget deficit in recent years is still high.[26] This could indicate a need for additional public resources. This solution would be optimal (World Bank, 2006b), provided that the social cost of mobilizing public resources was equal to the costs associated with mobilizing other elements of fiscal space (financing resources). Another condition to be met is to ensure that the social benefit derived from public expenditure should at least equal the social cost, including the costs entailed by the mobilization of other elements of fiscal space (public resources, financing resources and resources released due to enhanced efficiency of government spending). However, it should be noted that studies on government spending in Morocco, including those carried out by the World Bank, seem to indicate that there is room for significant improvement in the efficiency of government spending.

Structure of government spending and fiscal space
Since the 1990s, the pressure on government finances has not prevented the public wage bill from increasing from 10 per cent of GDP in 1980 to 11.0 per cent of GDP in 2006. Mention must be made of the sharp decrease in capital expenditure since the early 1980s: from 10 per cent in 1980 to less than 5 per cent since 2002. The efforts to rationalize[27] government spending have certainly improved the quality of capital expenditure, however, if in the future capital expenditure is consistently below 5 per cent of GDP, this would undoubtedly have adverse effects on development (see the following

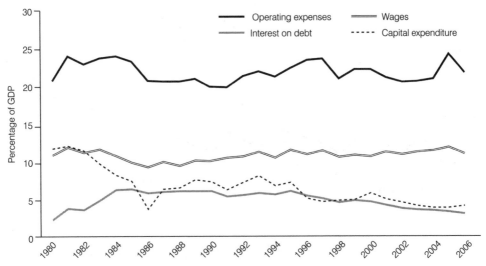

Source: Ministry of Finance and Privatization and IMF (compilation of data for many years)

Figure 7.3 *Changes in the levels of government spending as a percentage of GDP, 1980–2005*

sections). Global analysis indicates that the preservation of government capital expenditure should be emphasized, and this undoubtedly requires action to modify the spending structure.

Tax transition and public resource space

Morocco's tax transition policy has two goals. The first is to stabilize and improve the level of public resources, which involves providing ongoing resources to offset the gradual disappearance of tariff revenue (see Figure 7.4) and of revenues from privatization. The second[28] is to reduce the distortions inherent in taxation with a view to making the economy more competitive.

Tax transition and level of taxation
If the level of Morocco's public resources is to be maintained in the coming years, the tax structure will have to undergo a major transformation, and a substantial increase in non-tariff public resources will be required.

As Figure 7.4 shows, since 1992 there has been a considerable decrease in the ratio of tariff revenue to GDP (2.1 per cent of GDP in 2006 as compared with 5.1 per cent of GDP in 1992). Since 2003, tariff revenue has been about 2.5 per cent of GDP. The increase in 2001 was due to the efforts of the Customs Administration to become more efficient, but does not reflect a countertrend. Ongoing trade liberalization, particularly as regards tariffs, under the partnership agreement with the EU[29] and also under agreements with other countries (Egypt, Jordan, Tunisia, Turkey, US) decreases tariff revenue further (see Table 7.8 for an example).

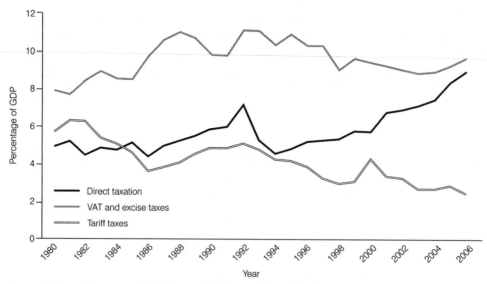

Y-axis: Percentage of GDP (0, 2, 4, 6, 8, 10, 12)

- Direct taxation
- VAT and excise taxes
- Tariff taxes

X-axis: Year (1980, 1982, 1984, 1986, 1988, 1990, 1992, 1994, 1996, 1998, 2000, 2002, 2004, 2006)

Source: Ministry of Finance and Privatization and IMF (compilation of data for many years)

Figure 7.4 *Changes in tax structure as a percentage of GDP, 1980–2006*

Since 1994, the decline in tariff revenue has been offset by a considerable increase in revenue from direct taxation, particularly on company profits (corporation tax[30]). In contrast, revenue from domestic indirect taxation, particularly VAT, has not noticeably increased (see Figure 7.4). This form of tax transition, based on revenue from direct taxation, is atypical; usually, the transition is towards domestic indirect taxation, including VAT (Chambas, 2005). The lopsided nature of the Moroccan VAT system (four positive rates and one of zero, plus broad exemptions) is a major obstacle to a tax transition centred on domestic indirect taxation. Moreover, one relatively important sector of modern companies provides relatively fertile ground for increased contributions from direct taxation. The Moroccan tax authorities have managed, in recent years, to substantially increase their control over what can be taxed in the case of modern companies.

The fact that the structure of public resources is moving, atypically, towards a greater contribution from direct taxation of companies is creating several problems.

Table 7.8 *Estimate of losses resulting from the implementation of the EU Association Agreement, 2003–2009)*

Cumulative revenue losses	2003	2004*	2005*	2006*	2007*	2008*	2009*
MAD billions	2.26	2.66	3.06	3.46	3.86	4.26	4.66
As % of non-agricultural GDP	0.64	0.75	0.86	0.97	1.09	1.20	1.31

Note: *Forecast, base year 2003.

Source: Directorate General of Customs and Excise (DGDDI) and IMF calculations (compilation of data for many years)

First, revenue from a profits tax, based on the profit margin, is more unstable than revenue from indirect consumption taxes (VAT or excise taxes).[31] Second, the potential additional revenue that could be mobilized from domestic indirect taxation is substantial. However, in order to tap this potential additional revenue, particularly from VAT, it will be necessary to introduce major reforms, including a drastic broadening of the VAT base. Some of these reforms, which are central to the success of the tax transition, will be introduced over the next three years (see overleaf). Finally, the yield from direct taxation of personal income (wages, professional income and miscellaneous income) inevitably has a ceiling because its basis of assessment is narrow. In 2004, wages accounted for 76 per cent of the income tax basis of assessment.

Tax transition, revenue structure and tax distortions

Tax distortions are now being reduced by modifying the structure of taxation, reducing the relative importance of the resources causing the greatest tax distortions (especially tariff revenue). The goal of this policy is to reduce the social cost of taxation[32] and thus enhance the social effect of government finances. In fact, the change in the tax structure, following the sharp decrease in tariff levels, has not produced the reductions in tax distortion that might have been expected because of the lack of neutrality of the various taxes, the relative contributions of which have increased during the tax transition.

For example, the economic neutrality of the corporation tax has been reduced by the increasing complexity of this tax, in which numerous exemption and reduction regimes (by sector, region, product and destination) coexist. The resulting erosion of the basis of assessment encourages the maintenance of high nominal tax rates, whereas many of Morocco's competitor countries are currently reducing their rates significantly. The risk involved is a slippage between the rate of taxation on earnings in Morocco and that applied in other countries, such as Ireland, or certain countries of Eastern Europe.

Under the General Tax Code,[33] income tax applies to all income (wages, professional earnings, farming income, income from land and income from capital, including interest, dividends and capital gains). In fact, wages account for most of the income tax base of assessment (76 per cent in 2004, see above). The low rate of contribution by self-employed persons is aggravated by the system of exemptions. This creates considerable economic distortions that are detrimental to wage-earners and the companies that employ them (high labour costs, particularly for executives). Moreover, wage-earners feel they are being discriminated against.

Because of extensive exemptions, the cut-off rule[34] preventing reimbursement of credits after VAT, and the complexity of the VAT system, Moroccan VAT is a source of considerable economic distortion.[35] Its lack of economic neutrality is aggravated by enforcement problems (excessive delay in the repayment of VAT credits eligible for reimbursement).

The current budget yield of VAT is partly the result of certain tax distortions and in particular of legal and actual[36] obstacles to VAT credit reimbursement. That is why, notwithstanding the complexity and imperfections of its legislation, including the narrowness of its base because of the many exemptions and reductions, Morocco's VAT income accounts for roughly 6 per cent of GDP, which is considerable.

The change in the structure of public resources is certainly not producing the expected improvement in the economic neutrality of taxation because of the considerable distortions caused by the various categories of revenue replacing tariff revenue. Reduction of these distortions is therefore an essential goal of tax transition. In the context of the quest for an optimal solution it could, because of the resulting reduction of distortions, be instrumental in achieving an increase in public resources and thus result in a greater contribution to fiscal space from this component.

Tax transition, equity and poverty

The distribution of the tax burden is determined both by the nature of the taxes and by their characteristics. The replacement of tariff taxes by domestic taxes (direct and indirect) is currently producing, and will continue to produce throughout the process of tax transition, considerable changes in the distribution of the tax burden. In addition, the revenue of producers, particularly farmers, depends on the incentive system of which taxation is one of the basic factors. The characteristics of income distribution and poverty are profoundly altered by tax transition reforms.

The social effect is therefore a major issue and the effects of tax transition reforms are, of course, particularly sensitive politically. As shown below in the section entitled 'Political economy of fiscal transition reform', the promotion of sweeping multi-year reforms in a democratic framework can be facilitated by scientific impact studies, particularly studies on the social impact of tax transition.

Morocco should be able to conduct such studies quite easily, since it has efficient statistical machinery (see, for example, the poverty map) and simulation instruments are already available, such as the one for evaluating the distribution impact of removing the tariffs on cereals (World Bank). In particular, the simulations should include the impact of broadening the VAT base[37] in addition to the impact of tariff dismantling. This would make it possible to identify transmission channels, give an accurate picture of the social impacts of tax transition and, in particular, recognize pockets of vulnerability. The authorities would then be able to provide the appropriate social safety nets or the necessary investments to mitigate the negative effects of tax transition. Clearly, this is an essential component of successful tax transition reform.

Political economy of tax transition reform

An analysis of the level of public resources leads to the conclusion that there is a need to stabilize the current rate of tax revenues in relation to GDP while, at the same time, continuing the tax transition reform stemming from the trade and economic liberalization policy adopted by Morocco. An analysis of the political economy of the reforms can identify the various obstacles that need to be overcome in order to attain these goals. Moreover, such an analysis can help to generate instruments for the promotion of reform.

To achieve these objectives, the following four questions must be answered:

1   What are the goals of reform?
2   What are the obstacles to reform?
3   What are the prerequisites for the implementation of tax transition?
4   What are the instruments for the promotion of reform?

Goals of tax transition reform

Essentially, Morocco's tax policy is aimed at achieving tax transition now and in the years ahead. This involves reducing tariff taxation, which produces major distortions, while safeguarding the level of public resources. Stabilization of the overall level of resources should be obtained through an increase in domestic tax revenue. Of course, the substitution of domestic tax revenue, particularly VAT, for tariff revenue is justified only if domestic tax revenue produces fewer[38] distortions than tariff revenue. It will then be possible, following the reform, for a given level of revenue to suffer fewer tax distortions.

The tax transition strategy has four main themes:

1   Strengthening VAT, which is to play the central role in tax transition;
2   Reducing tax exemptions and exemption regimes;
3   Formulating a medium-term income tax strategy;
4   Continuing the efforts to strengthen the tax administration.

VAT reform

VAT reform should enable VAT to fully play the role of a general tax on final consumption, both as a basic purveyor of tax revenue and as an instrument of tax neutrality. It constitutes an essential phase of tax transition. The analyses conducted at the request of the Moroccan authorities showed the need for a thoroughgoing reform of VAT. Despite its many defects, which result from its lack of economic neutrality and transparency of its impact, current VAT revenue is around 6 per cent of GDP. A superficial reform would be unlikely to provide substantial increases over an already high level of VAT revenue, especially as some measures needed to restore its neutrality (for example, calling the cut-off rule into question, see below) will entail losses of VAT revenue.

A substantial boost in VAT revenue requires a drastic broadening of the VAT base, which up to now has been heavily eroded by exemptions. The VAT base should be broadened as much as possible and, in particular, extended to all basic consumption that has until now been exempt. Such a broadening of the base would result in a gain of around two percentage points of GDP, even with the revenue losses that the implementation of a neutral VAT would entail (elimination of the obstacles to reimbursement of VAT credits and, essentially, of the cut-off rule[39]). Special attention should be paid to the consistency of such broadening with poverty reduction goals.

Broadening the VAT base (hence decreasing exemptions) will reduce the creation of VAT credits, which up to now have been residual[40] because of exemptions. Thus, it will facilitate the gradual transition to a modern VAT, initially with two rates and then, over time, with a single rate.[41] The establishment of a uniform liability threshold that is sufficiently high will be an essential step towards improving the effectiveness of VAT management and simplifying the tax obligations of small enterprises. Lastly, the long-term elimination of the cut-off rule and the removal of all obstacles to rapid reimbursement of VAT credits will improve the economic neutrality of VAT.

Reducing tax exemptions

The tax exemptions freeze that has been in place since 2004 has been followed by the publication of tax expenditure assessment reports (Ministry of Finance and Privatization, 2006)[42] and by a decrease in exemption regimes. Thanks to this report, which will be issued regularly and is available on the Ministry of Finance and Privatization website, legislators and the authorities are fully informed of the cost of exemption measures. As a result of having more relevant information, the state's actions should be better targeted, more effective and more transparent, especially through the use of budget subsidies instead of tax exemption measures. Moreover, the decrease in exemptions would help to safeguard the level of public resources and would have the advantage of avoiding the need to raise tax rates. The reduction of exemptions in all categories is, without doubt, essential to maintaining the current level of government revenue space while pursuing a policy of tariff liberalization.

Formulation of an income tax reform strategy

While the Tax Code provides for a progressive tax on all income, the income tax in Morocco is, in practice, mainly a tax on wages; non-wage income (particularly self-employment income and real-estate income) is largely under-taxed. Moreover, the nominal wage increase, combined with the failure to amend income tax brackets, has led to an increase in the tax burden that is particularly resented by wage earners. The income tax study that the authorities are planning will help them to identify a programme to reform this tax and make it more equitable, improve its yield, and thus strengthen tax reform in the medium term.

Continuing the efforts to modernize the tax administration

Lastly, continuing the efforts to modernize the tax administration is a prerequisite for successful tax reform. Such modernization, which among other things requires that all revenue administrations use a single tax identifier,[43] should help to streamline the structure of the tax administration and ensure better tax collection and audits, while

improving the services provided to taxpayers. What is involved, in particular, is a continued reduction of the social costs of public resource mobilization to the government
and enterprises. The tax transition programme constitutes a major reform for the long-
term sustainability of government finances in Morocco. This programme is supported
by the EU and a three-year (2006 to 2008) agreement for its continuation was signed on
27 April 2006.

Obstacles to the implementation of tax reform
In comparison with the more limited reforms of the past, tax transition is a large-scale
reform, comprising politically and socially sensitive aspects. Thus, the challenge to a
traditional policy of incentives and/or exemptions will mean a profound shift in the
distribution of the tax burden and the system of incentives. While necessary, this
reform faces various obstacles.

One obstacle is the probability of conflicts between groups related to the distribution of the benefits of reform (Alesina and Drazen, 1991). Potentially affected groups
will oppose reforms that run counter to their interests. Thus, in the Moroccan case, it is
not surprising that heavily protected business groups, or those benefiting from strong
incentives (such as the housing construction sector), are the most recalcitrant.
Moroccan businesspeople are highly organized and their representative organizations
have been quite effective in the past in obtaining protection measures, incentives and
exemptions. Groups that have been adversely affected will oppose the reforms or will
seek some form of compensation. The risk may be a flagging of the Moroccan authorities' commitment to the reform when they have difficulty resisting pressure groups that
seek to maintain existing exemptions or waivers. A strong and sustained commitment to
the reform on the part of the government would constitute a decisive advantage.

Uncertainty as to the impact of the reform measures and the distribution of their
benefits (Fernandez and Rodrik, 1991) is another obstacle to reform. Opposition arises
within certain groups, including those that should be in favour of the reform, because
of this uncertainty (Drazen, 1996). This leads to a bias in favour of the status quo,
which results in the postponement of reforms (Laban and Sturzenegger, 1994). A
precondition for reform, therefore, is to have a capacity for credible analysis of the
effect of the reforms and to disseminate the results of this analysis, thus reducing the
uncertainty perceived by various groups.

The prospect of a new government taking office is another potential difficulty.
Political change could occur with future elections. The political group that has been in
power could be forced to bear the political cost of difficult reforms, while a group with
different sensitivities could reap the benefits. Yet, clearly, the group in power has
embarked on the road to reform, particularly with the three-year agreement concluded
with the EU in 2006 despite the perspective of a possible change with the 2007
elections. This seeming paradox can be explained by the hope of the current group of
remaining in power, but also by a sense that the government relies on its permanence,

which is fostered by the monarchy. The government's sense of its staying power is also explained by the influence of senior policymakers. The Moroccan authorities clearly have the capacity to project themselves into the future, as shown by numerous forward-looking analyses (see, for example, Comité Directeur, 2006).

A decline in public resources could also occur. Clearly a large-scale reform designed to strengthen domestic tax revenue (particularly in order to achieve a substantial broadening of the tax base) is essential to mitigate this hazard. Without thoroughgoing domestic tax reform, there would be a risk of growing tax revenue losses and, accordingly, a budgetary imbalance that would become intolerable, calling into question not only the reform as a whole but also the sustainability of government finances.

Prerequisites for the implementation of tax transition

In addition to a favourable institutional environment, the Moroccan authorities must be provided, through the administrations concerned, with instruments for the promotion of reform (the capacity to assess and formulate a reform strategy and the adoption of an appropriate communication programme).

Political and institutional framework for the promotion of civic responsibility regarding taxes

The optimal use of fiscal space calls for action with regard to certain institutions, particularly those defining and managing government spending, in order to promote pro-tax behaviour (tolerance of the tax burden). What is at issue, in other words, is taking into consideration the institutional determinants of the demand for tax effort, such as inequality, as well as the consent to pay taxes (Frey, 1997). Effective programmes to reduce poverty or inequality can promote civic responsibility regarding taxes.

Similarly, consent to pay taxes is better assured if an additional supply of public goods is offered in exchange for any additional tax. In this regard, the Moroccan authorities' current commitment to the MDGs through the INDH can be thought of as helping to improve consent to pay taxes. The trend towards greater democracy in the Moroccan political system is another encouraging factor (Acemoglu et al, 2005).

National capacity for assessment and long-term reform

To promote tax transition reform, the authorities can diminish the risk perceived by different groups by mobilizing the skills needed to credibly predict all the consequences of the reform. The continuity of the reform policy over time and the apparent low risk of a turnaround also contribute to diminishing the perceived risk.

Credible assessment capacity. The goals of tax transition reform include mitigating the medium-term risk of the budget imbalance being exacerbated by the impact of liberalization and by the disappearance of some exceptional resources (privatization revenue). This concept requires an appropriate national analytic capacity to identify and quantify a medium-term budget risk and then formulate and implement an adequate reform programme.

Clearly, to mobilize such capacity, the national administrations must be able to call upon senior managers who have been released from day-to-day management and are thus able to contribute to the assessment and formulation of a reform strategy. In Morocco's case, this requirement has been met. The tax administration has been provided with a significant number of senior managers who have been given sufficient freedom from daily operational tasks. Likewise, various divisions of the Ministry of Finance have the expertise and the high-performance information system required to make medium-term forecasts of government finances.

Long-term reform strategy: Anticipation and reduction of perceived uncertainties. In the short term, the Moroccan authorities should not face major difficulties in maintaining the solvency of government finances. The risk of imbalances in government finances arises in the medium term. Despite these risks in the medium term, what is needed here is a rather favourable situation, for any reform of government finances is difficult[44] and socially costly in a crisis situation (a large budget deficit combined with a debt crisis; see Box 7.2).

The fact that the Moroccan authorities have embarked on the road to reform in a period typified by the absence of immediate threats to the balance in government finances shows that they have a genuine capacity for taking a medium-term and a long-term view. It should therefore be possible to avoid overly painful budget trade-offs; now that the debt burden is under control, trade-offs on other expenditure items are becoming less constraining. In a situation of relative budget affluence, consideration can also be given to implementing compensatory measures or adjustment mechanisms, particularly for vulnerable groups whose situation has deteriorated as a result of the reform and who would, in the absence of compensation, become de facto opponents of the reform.

The Moroccan authorities have clearly opted for the gradual implementation of reform. This is certainly the more rational choice, for it builds on the gains made through previous reforms. Thus, it is possible to benefit from these gains and minimize the costs and risks associated with the reform. Lastly, continuity of the reform over time helps to ensure its credibility.

Instruments for promoting reform

For the authorities to be able to promote a large-scale reform, it is certainly in their interest to rely on three basic instruments: (1) scientific studies that provide an accurate diagnosis of the situation at the outset and a thorough quantified assessment of the budgetary, economic and social impacts of the proposed reform; (2) a pertinent communication strategy concerning the reform; and (3) development partners that can provide decisive support.

Assessment of the effects of reform

In the past, many countries, including Morocco, implemented tax reforms without having conducted the scientific studies that provide accurate diagnoses of the situation at the outset and a thorough quantified assessment of the budgetary, economic and social impacts of the proposed reform. In some cases, especially for occasional measures, the lack of relevant information, particularly impact assessments, has had a surprise effect; confronted with a *fait accompli*, taxpayers have not been able to challenge the actions taken.

Such a 'shock' strategy does not rule out effective communication campaigns addressed to economic stakeholders and legislators, but it has the disadvantage of conflicting with Morocco's institutional development, which affords wide scope for debate and participatory processes. Accordingly, it cannot be the most appropriate choice for a fundamental reform continuing over time and being implemented in a democratic framework.

Given the diversity of measures and their multi-year nature, affected pressure groups will have time to react and form alliances against the reform; their strategy will make use of the lack of clear assessment of the impact of the proposed reform. It would seem preferable, therefore, to play the cards of scientific assessment and transparent information, especially since the highest authorities have clearly signalled their commitment to an open debate (see the King's speech of 20 August 2003 and the report entitled *L'avenir se construit et le meilleur est possible* (Comité Directeur 2006).[45]

Communication strategy targeted at pressure groups and public opinion
More transparent information on tax expenditure and the effects of tax transition reform in all its aspects, and a stronger communication policy should facilitate the implementation of reform.

Need for a communication strategy. Assessment of the impact of reform and the adoption of a pertinent reform strategy are insufficient to bring about support for the reform. Indeed, one obstacle to reform is that the maintenance of the status quo would benefit groups that are often well informed and well organized. These groups, which benefit from protection and tax incentive measures, are extremely active in producing information that supports the maintenance of their acquired benefits. Furthermore, owing to the nature of their activities, these pressure groups receive support from the sectoral ministries associated with these activities (industry, agriculture, public housing construction and so on).

In contrast, the groups that would benefit from reform are dispersed, heterogeneous and often ill informed. As has been noted in many developing countries (Chile, Taiwan and Turkey), groups of economic stakeholders or consumers not benefiting from the system of exemptions or incentives that are being challenged have an inverse tendency to remain in the background, owing to uncertainty about the distribution of the costs and benefits of reform (Fernandez and Rodrik, 1991). The reformers, especially a segment of the civil service administration and some policymakers, then lack support in asserting the need to challenge the acquired benefits. These characteristics foster free-rider attitudes that undermine the influence of groups benefiting from the reform. Furthermore, poor information is a source of uncertainty that is unfavourable to any reform.

Communication and reduction of uncertainty. Appropriate information is essential for reducing uncertainty about the impact of reform and mobilizing groups that stand to benefit from reform. Morocco's experience has shown the advantage of implementing substantial communication programmes. Thus, in recent years, the various administrations (Directorate General of Taxes, Directorate of Customs and others) have held direct conversations with economic stakeholders on a regular basis. These conversations provide information on the proposed reforms and their impacts. They have the effect of reducing the uncertainty perceived by economic stakeholders. Dispersing information about the tax expenditure assessment has been very effective. In particular, the greatest care has been taken in drafting the Arabic language version of the tax expenditure assessment and in launching numerous communication efforts targeted at various audiences.

More broadly, the large number of 'addresses' given by the Director-General of Taxes, particularly to business owners, should be stressed. These occasions are meticulously planned by a seven-person communication division of the Directorate General of Taxes. The authorities have also taken into account the important role of the electronic and print media in the adoption and implementation of the reform. Some Moroccan media outlets are demonstrating a real grasp of the reform. The press and all the media should be essential participants in the progress of the reform.

Assessment of the effects of reform bolsters the communication strategy. The production of grounded arguments and the formulation of a communication strategy addressed to the public are certainly essential. In the tax area, in particular, it is possible to put forth arguments to pave the way for reform, forestall some opposition and propose compensatory measures following consultation. However, in the absence of such communication based on assessments of the effects of the reform, it is very difficult, as the 2005 Niger experience in particular has shown (Brun et al, 2006), to overcome arguments that are sometimes irrational and combined with hidden political agendas. With the repetition of simplistic slogans that exploit often negative views of taxation, public opinion may become deaf and may then show systematic opposition to reform. The conflict between public opinion and reformers then hardens and, quite often, the reform proposal has to be shelved or at least heavily amended. Sometimes earlier measures that had hitherto been entirely accepted have had to be withdrawn (as in the case of VAT imposed on rice in Niger).

Intervention of external partners: Conditionality matrix and financial support for reform
2004: Major obstacles to tax reform. Like most developing countries wishing to undertake tax reform and, more recently, tax transition reform, Morocco has benefited on several occasions, particularly in 2000, from advice and technical assistance provided by the

IMF. The joint IMF-EU technical assistance mission of 2004 revealed that the reform measures had made relatively modest headway since 2000. Despite Morocco's substantial capacity to design and grasp the reforms needed to achieve tax transition, three basic obstacles stood in the way.

The first obstacle lies in the uncertainty (Laban and Sturzenegger, 1994) arising from the lack of key reform instruments, such as the tax expenditure assessment. As indicated above, uncertainty affects not only taxpayer behaviour, but also the behaviour of government offices and the political authorities, who are often extremely risk averse. Uncertainty can be at least partially overcome, however. In 2005, for example, no developing country had a tool for systematically and credibly evaluating its tax expenditure, a tool that until then had been the privilege of the countries belonging to the OECD. Although in Morocco the obstacles seemed very large (lack of knowledge of the practical modalities of implementing the methodology; difficulty of risk assessment), the country managed in a very short period of time to assess the tax expenditure arising from exemptions.

The second obstacle, which is of an institutional nature and certainly not specific to Morocco, is the difficulty of combining the expertise of divisions belonging to different administrations. In this respect, the Directorate General of Taxes quickly emerged as the structure best able to manage the reform.

The third obstacle is the difficulty of ensuring that the reform adheres to international best practice in the matter. Experience shows that a strong demand for validation by internationally recognized experts is a prerequisite for the acceptance and success of the reform. In this respect, Morocco has regularly called upon internationally recognized experts.

Coordinated intervention of external partners. A key factor of progress in tax transition reform is close coordination between the IMF and the EU, the main external partners involved in such reform. The participation of these two institutions is closely complementary. The former has internationally recognized expertise in tax matters, while for the latter, tax transition is largely a concomitant of the EPA between the EU and Morocco. Coordination has promoted the consistency and hence the credibility of reform.

The participation of an external technical assistance monitoring mission, in close coordination with the IMF and based, in particular, on the outcome of the 2004 joint IMF-EU mission, certainly bolstered the credibility of the effort under way. The preparatory work for the reform advanced quickly, owing to the exchanges between the Moroccan administration and the technical assistance mission. This point can be illustrated by the tax expenditure assessment, a key instrument for the advancement of reform (see above). During a two-day workshop in March 2005, seasoned practitioners presented the methods specifically used by the OECD countries, pointing out, in particular, acceptable simplifications of theoretical principles. This facilitated the publication, in November 2005, of a first annual tax expenditure report annexed to the 2006 Finances Act.

Preparation of the reform matrix. Tax transition reform requires a programme of diverse and complex actions that are appropriately coordinated in a multi-year setting. In Morocco's case, this programme is presented mainly through a matrix describing the stages of the process and the performance criteria enabling disbursement of the various portions of financial support for the reform. Preparation of the matrix has provided an opportunity for an intensive mobilization of expertise to generate a coherent and realistic programme for coming years. The content of the matrix was the subject of a 2006 agreement between the Moroccan government and the EU Commission based on various studies carried out since 2004.

The experience of joint work with external experts having extensive knowledge of the subject and of the various constraints (administrative, socio-political and so on) created favourable conditions for the drafting of a coherent technical document that became the basis for a final political negotiation. Clearly, the swift preparation of a complex matrix revealed a high degree of ownership of the reform.

The achievement of a coherent and solid matrix signals a deep commitment on the part of the national authorities. The partnership between Morocco and the EU is, moreover, based on the adoption of *actual* measures and not on commitments to *proposed* reform measures, which are items included in the budget proposal without any guarantee that the measures would be included in the version of the budget approved by parliament. This, too, shows the strength of the authorities' commitment to reform. They undertook to actually implement the reform measures and will therefore have to promote them, especially in parliament, the membership of which was affected by the 2007 elections. Although the final goals are set, the specific path or schedule to reform is flexible.

Lastly, the matrix is a bet on the future. It should generate a momentum that, based on the first beneficial results of the reform, should promote the continuation of the process towards successful tax transition.

The role of the context for reform
The 2005 budget year was characterized by the sustained growth of tax revenue, a trend that has continued, due in large part to excellent agricultural conditions. This trend legitimized the major reform measures already adopted and was certainly favourable to the continuation of actions to promote tax transition. However, the 2007 election perspective was probably a handicap to the continuation of the reform.

Section summary

An analysis that relies on assessments of the actual tax ratio based on international comparisons as well as on the notion of tax effort leads to the conclusion that there is a lack of significant tax resource space. This conclusion converges with the approach favouring stabilization of the tax ratio as contained in the report by the Comité Directeur (2006). However, this conclusion could be called into question by the optimization of government finances as a whole. The need for the expansion of public resource space could arise from the following factors:

- The cost of alternative financing sources other than public resources, which could become particularly high (see the next section);
- The reduction of tax distortions for a given level of public resources;
- Higher taxation could also be justified by greater effectiveness of government spending (see the section 'Participation, decentralization and effectiveness of government spending'). The social benefit of government spending would then be greater than the social cost of the new level of taxation.

A political economy analysis has highlighted the requirements that would need to be met to promote a reform as complex and sensitive as tax transition reform:

- National capacity to design a modern and coherent reform mechanism coupled with the capacity to envision the reform in a multi-year setting;
- Promotion of the reform, taking into account the existence of a democratic framework. Scientific assessments of the effects of reform (assessment of the tax expenditure arising from exemptions; analysis of the effects), an appropriate communication policy targeted to various interest groups and rational management of media relations;
- The participation of external partners, facilitating ownership of the reform and serving as a catalyst for all available expertise.

EVALUATION OF FINANCING SPACE

Financing space is characterized by several elements. First, there is clearly a wish to substitute internal debt for external debt. Second, the state's borrowing needs have been covered by internal resources in an environment typified by a lower borrowing cost. Third, while total investment (especially private investment) has remained at historically high levels (contrary to the opinion frequently expressed), state investment has been redirected towards local communities and state enterprises and institutions, which have accounted for a greater share. Appropriations have reached significant levels (approximately 17 per cent of GDP in 2007 and 16.2 per cent in 2006).

In the 2000s, external savings have inflated national savings (sustained by economic growth) to the point of generating a positive net financing capacity, in which saving exceeds investment. These savings could possibly finance additional public investment. In addition, while central bank advances to the government are prohibited (apart from the granting of short-term credits), the government is generating substantial amounts of resources through virtuous seignorage that should be perpetuated.

Replacement of external financing by internal financing

Changes in the structure of budget deficit financing

In the light of Table 7.9, the strategy pursued by the Moroccan authorities can be seen clearly: replace external debt with internal debt. This operation is taking place, as Table 7.9 shows, in the context of a reduction in the public debt ratio (and the treasury debt ratio). This strategy is explained by three elements; first, the wish to reduce the exchange risk inherent in a consistent amount of external debt; second, the existence of liquidity within the economy that can be mobilized more easily, and third, the desire to bring the debt ratio down to levels that offer more leeway in the medium term.

Thus, the Treasury's internal debt ratio rose in 2006 to 46.2 per cent of GDP. This ratio has risen steadily since the early 1990s (it was 26.9 per cent in 1990). It reflects a desire to make better use of internal resources to meet the government's borrowing needs. This strategy is being carried out at the same time that there is concern about reducing dependency on external sources. In this respect, the share of external treasury debt is decreasing, standing at 50 per cent of GDP in 1990, it dropped to 11.2 per cent of GDP in 2006.

During the same period, secured debt, which had accounted for 25.7 per cent of GDP in 1990, accounted for only 8.8 per cent in 2006. Overall, while official external debt accounted for roughly 80 per cent of GDP in the early 1990s, by 2006 it represented only 20 per cent of GDP, which is a significant drop.

The distinguishing feature of internal debt, beyond the increase in its stock, is the extension of its average life. Long-term debt (5 to 20 years) represented 52 per cent of the stock in 2006 (as compared with 47 per cent in 2005), medium-term debt represented 32 per cent (as compared with 40 per cent in 2005), and short-term debt (less than a year) was 16 per cent (as compared with 13 per cent in 2005). The average life of the debt was thus six years and nine months in 2006 as compared with six years and five months in 2005. Auctions represented 97.8 per cent of the stock of internal debt in 2006. In 2006, 28 per cent of treasury bonds were held by insurance companies, 27 per cent by banks, 24 per cent by mutual funds (in Organisme de Placements Collectifs en Valeurs Mobilières (OPCVM), 11 per cent by the Caisse des Dépôts et de Gestion (CDG) deposit and management fund, and 10 per cent by other stakeholders.

The decline in resources made available by investors on the auction markets in 2005 (MAD202 billion as compared with MAD274 billion in 2004) should prompt a degree of caution. In 2005, there were 2.7 times more subscriptions than bids, as compared with 3.6 times more in 2004. A margin still exists, of course, which reflects a certain confidence in Morocco's capacity to honour its commitments. The decline seen in 2005 is attributable to two phenomena: a liquidity outflow (MAD6 billion) linked to an exchange transaction by Vivendi following a transfer of Maroc Télécom securities to Société de Participation dans les Télécommunications (SPT) that was financed on the domestic market; and the decline in banking system liquidity geared to the exchange market owing to rumours of a possible devaluation of the dirham.[46]

Table 7.9 *Public debt indicators*

										Public debt indicators									
	1988	1989	1990	1991	1992	1993	1994	1995	1996	1997	1998	1999	2000	2001	2002	2003	2004	2005	2006
Stock in MAD billions																			
Treasury internal debt	51.4	58.7	57.1	58.9	67.2	76.8	93.8	101.5	110.5	121.5	131.0	136.7	149.4	175.9	191.6	211.5	223.9	258.5	265.9
Total public external debt	164.9	169.0	165.8	172.5	193.6	201.4	195.3	191.9	188.1	184.6	179.4	177.5	170.9	163.1	142.3	126.0	115.3	115.9	115.2
Treasury external debt	119.7	122.8	111.1	120.2	141.0	144.1	136.3	132.0	131.0	129.3	125.0	124.1	119.3	119.3	92.6	79.0	70.4	69.2	64.5
Secured debt	45.1	46.2	54.7	52.2	52.6	57.3	59.0	60.0	57.1	55.2	54.3	53.4	51.6	52.0	49.8	47.1	45.0	46.6	50.7
GDP	182.4	191.4	212.5	241.4	244.0	250.0	279.6	282.5	319.4	318.3	384.5	389.8	393.8	426.9	446.0	477.0	500.1	522.6	575.3
Ratio to GDP (per cent)																			
Treasury internal debt	28.2	30.7	26.9	24.4	27.5	30.7	33.6	36.0	34.6	38.2	34.1	35.1	37.9	41.2	42.9	44.3	44.8	49.5	46.2
Total public external debt	90.4	88.3	78.0	71.5	79.3	80.5	69.9	67.9	58.9	58.0	46.7	45.5	43.4	38.2	31.9	26.4	23.1	22.2	20.0
Treasury external debt	65.6	64.1	52.3	49.8	57.7	57.6	48.8	46.7	41.0	40.6	32.5	31.8	30.3	26.0	20.8	16.5	14.1	13.2	11.2
Secured debt	24.8	24.2	25.7	21.6	21.6	22.9	21.1	21.2	17.9	17.4	14.1	13.7	13.1	12.2	11.2	9.9	9.0	8.9	8.8
Ratio relative to Treasury debt (per cent)																			
Treasury external debt	69.9	67.7	66.0	67.1	67.7	65.2	59.2	56.5	54.3	51.6	48.8	47.6	44.4	38.7	32.6	27.2	23.9	21.1	19.5

Source: Ministry of Finance and Privatization (DEPF database) and authors' calculations

---

BOX 7.3 THE TREASURY BOND AUCTION MARKET

Since 1989 the Treasury has financed the budget deficit through a system of treasury bond auctions, the purpose of which is to encourage competition among subscribers. These auctions are open to a large number of stakeholders: banks, financial institutions, insurance companies, enterprises (private and public) and individuals. Non-residents can also be subscribers. The bond categories are short-term (13, 26 and 52 weeks), medium-term (2 and 5 years) and long-term (10, 15 and 20 years). Stimulation of the markets (primary and secondary) rests with Intermédiaires en Valeurs du Trésor (IVT) chosen from among the financial institutions. Their role is to assess market demand and purchase 8 per cent of the volumes allotted each quarter in the three categories of treasury bonds.

The bidder can offer a single amount at the corresponding rate or price, or divide it into several segments at different rates or prices. It is possible to submit bids expressed in prices for bonds having the same rate and term characteristics as previous issues to which they are attached. This entails issue by assimilation to encourage the growth of the secondary market created in 1996.

Submissions are received by Bank al Maghrib, which draws up a table of anonymous bids that it transmits to the Ministry of Finance; it in turn sets the cut-off rate or cut-off price for the auction. Bids with a rate lower than or equal to the cut-off rate (or a price higher than or equal to the cut-off price) are accepted. The amount of the bids can also be accepted in whole or in part. In the latter case, the distribution is made in proportion to the bids received. It should be noted that Bank al Maghrib widely disseminates the principal results of each auction session (every Tuesday for short-term bonds, twice per month for medium-term bonds and once per quarter for long-term bonds). Auction settlements take place on the Monday following the auction sessions.

Source: Quarterly Bulletin No. 89, September 2001, Bank al Maghrib, Rabat

---

Interest charges and fees rose in 2006 to MAD16.2 billion. The weight of these charges and fees represents 12.9 per cent of tax revenue as compared to 13.6 per cent in 2005. The weight of the charges is decreasing as the stock of internal debt increases. This phenomenon is attributable to lower interest rates (see below). Thus, in 2006, interest rates on long-term debt fell by 212, 162 and 132 basis points, respectively, on 20-, 15-

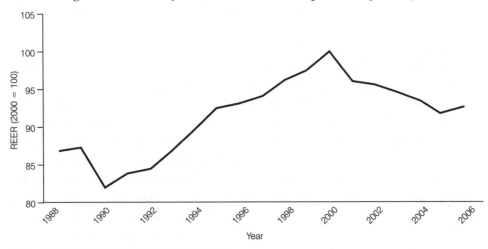

Source: IMF (TCER routinely calculated for Morocco)

Figure 7.5 *Trends in the real effective exchange rate*

and 10-year bonds. With regard to shorter maturities, the decline in interest rates was relatively moderate in the medium term and, in fact, quite low in the short term. Overall, interest rates on internal debt trended downward, and thus the average rate on 15-year bonds dropped from 6.93 per cent in 2002 to 5.69 per cent in 2004, 5.34 per cent in 2005 and 4.91 per cent in 2006.

Repayment of principal amounted to MAD36.3 billion in 2006. Short-term maturities represented 38 per cent of this total. As the total amount of subscriptions reached MAD38.8 billion, the stock of debt increased by MAD7.3 billion in 2006. This compares with MAD34.6 billion in 2005, with MAD79.6 billion in subscriptions and repayment of MAD49.7 billion.

Treasury external debt in 2006
International development institutions hold 50 per cent of the external debt, bilateral creditors 37 per cent (including the Paris Club, which holds 32 per cent) and commercial banks 13 per cent. The debt is denominated in Euros (65 per cent) and US dollars (16 per cent). Fixed-rate debt accounts for 70 per cent of the total. Debt service rose in 2006 to MAD18 billion – MAD13.8 billion for principal and MAD4.2 billion for interest – representing a total of 12.5 per cent of tax revenue (including VAT from local governments).

Coverage of the government's borrowing need
The strategy of replacing external debt by internal debt is, of course, seen in the coverage of the government's borrowing need (see Table 7.10). As grants are practically nil there is no difference between financing need and borrowing need. Beginning in 1993, net external financing became negative, reflecting the decline in dependence on external sources. At the same time, net internal financing was consistently positive and higher (in absolute terms) than the government's conventional financing need, reflecting the build-up of internal debt. Borrowing need remained at relatively high levels.

Lower financing resource costs for the government
External debt was replaced by internal debt in a context of lower internal interest rates (see Table 7.11a) and hence lower borrowing costs. The gap between nominal lending rates and borrowing rates has, however, tended to increase on average since 1993. This may be attributable to insufficient competition in the banking system, which thus increased its margins. Moreover, real loan rates have tended to decline more slowly than borrowing rates, producing a spread that tends to increase over time (see Table 7.11b).

Internal resource taxation aimed at covering the government's borrowing need and lowering external debt did not lead to a rise in interest rates. On the contrary, increased internal financing was accompanied by lower interest rates. The average cost of internal debt declined appreciably between 1998 and 2006, from 8.91 per cent in 1998 to 5.87 per cent in 2006 (see Figure 7.6). The lack of pressure on interest rates provides the first argument for the lack of a crowding-out effect on private investment.

Table 7.10 *Coverage of the government's borrowing need*

	1988	1989	1990	1991	1992	1993	1994	1995	1996	1997	1998	1999	2000	2001	2002	2003	2004	2005	2006
											Public debt indicators								
MAD millions																			
Financing needs	1237	9343	8999	7759	5176	7426	9465	9430	10,247	9674	5962	8575	8466	18,837	17,282	15,934	13,030	28,529	11,022
Internal financing	5559	5994	−539	2123	4898	8383	1363	11,541	12,913	180,720	11,342	12,844	15,035	28,698	28,480	24,680	19,447	29,986	11,560
External financing	4678	3349	9538	5627	278	−957	−4425	−2111	−2666	−8398	−5380	−4269	−6319	−9861	−11,199	−8746	−6417	−1457	−538
GDP	12,390	191,399	212,518	241,356	244,041	250,023	279,584	282,467	319,390	318,342	384,452	389,786	393,786	426,871	446,044	477,000	500,100	522,600	575,300
Ratio to GDP (percentage)																			
Financing needs	5.61	4.88	4.23	3.21	2.12	2.97	3.39	3.34	3.21	3.04	1.55	2.20	2.15	4.41	3.87	3.34	2.61	5.46	1.92
Internal financing	3.05	3.13	−0.25	0.88	2.01	3.35	4.85	4.09	4.04	5.68	2.95	3.30	3.82	6.72	6.39	5.17	3.89	5.74	2.01
External financing	2.56	1.75	4.49	2.33	0.11	−0.38	−1.58	−0.75	−0.83	−2.64	1.40	−1.10	−1.60	−2.31	−2.51	−1.83	−1.28	−0.28	−0.09

Source: Ministry of Finance and Privatization (DEPF database) and authors' calculations

Table 7.11a *Changes in nominal interest rates (%)*

	1993	1994	1995	1996	1997	1998	1999	2000	2001	2002	2003	2004	2005	2006
Invitations to bid			7.00	6.50	6.50	6.00	5.00	5.00	4.25	3.25	3.25	3.25	3.25	3.25
Passbook savings accounts	8.50	7.00	7.00	7.00	7.00	6.00	6.00	4.48	4.72	3.42	2.95	2.35	2.49	2.49
Long-term debtors Creditors	14.00	13.00	12.50	11.25	10.25	9.00	8.50	8.50	8.50	8.25	8.25	7.50	7.50	7.50
6–12 months	11.49	8.80	8.30	8.29	7.62	6.52	5.42	4.95	4.69	3.88	3.58	3.37	3.48	3.69
Spread	2.51	4.20	4.20	2.96	2.63	2.48	3.08	3.55	3.81	4.37	4.67	4.13	4.02	3.81

Source: Ministry of Finance and Privatization (DEPF database) and authors' calculations

Table 7.11b *Changes in real interest rates (%)*

	1993	1994	1995	1996	1997	1998	1999	2000	2001	2002	2003	2004	2005
Invitations to bid			0.85	3.4	5.45	3.11	4.27	3.04	3.63	0.44	2.03	1.72	1.92
National savings accounts	3.14	1.71	0.85	3.88	5.94	3.11	5.26	2.53	4.1	0.6	1.73	0.59	0.22
Long-term debtors Creditors	8.37	7.41	6.03	8.01	9.16	6.03	7.75	6.48	7.85	5.3	6.97	5.91	6.12
6–12 months	5.98	3.42	2.07	5.14	6.55	3.62	4.69	2.99	4.07	1.05	2.35	1.84	2.08
Spread	2.39	3.99	3.96	2.87	2.6	2.41	3.06	3.48	3.79	4.25	4.61	4.07	4.04

Source: Bank Al-Maghrib

Internal financing by the government and financing of economic activity

Table 7.12 shows that there is a consistent gap between the internal savings ratio and the national savings ratio, which has increased since 2000. Several observations can be made. Net internal financing capacity remained negative during the period 1988 to 2005. Net national financing capacity was practically negative from 1988 to 2000 (it was positive in 1988 and 1996); then it became positive owing to increased external savings linked to large remittances from expatriate Moroccan workers, but also in conjunction with economic growth. The gross national savings ratio thus jumped 5.4 percentage points of GDP in 2001 and has since remained high, oscillating around 25 per cent of GDP.

The gross investment ratio for the period 1988 to 2005 ranged from 19.6 per cent (1996) to 25.9 per cent of GDP (2005). Thus, during the 2000s, it has tended to be at the top of the range. The public investment ratio has decreased from the early 1990s to the 2000s (6.1 per cent of GDP in 1993 as compared to 4.6 per cent of GDP in 2005). Two questions, therefore, arise. Is it possible to increase the public investment ratio? And can this increase be financed by national savings, particularly by their external component?

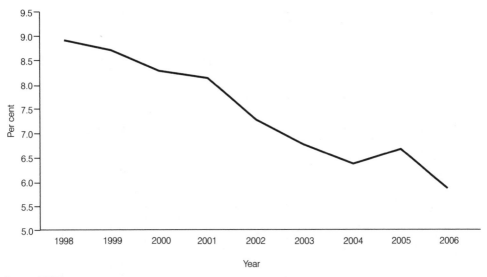

Source: DEPF

Figure 7.6 *Trend in the average cost of internal debt (%)*

Since 2002, the public investment ratio has oscillated between 4 and 4.8 per cent of GDP. There is probably some leeway for achieving an investment ratio of around 6 per cent of GDP, moreover, such a level was nearly reached in 2000. To this end, the public investment ratio should be increased by 1 to 1.5 per cent of GDP. However, the classification of government spending as current expenditure and capital expenditure is not always very pertinent. It would probably be desirable to equate some current expenditure to investment, particularly in the education and health sectors. The projects could certainly be placed in the context of the INDH, that is, they seek to reduce poverty and, in the long run, strengthen fiscal space.

The possibility of financing additional public investment through gross national savings (see Table 7.13) boils down to the question of the sustainability of external savings flows. If these flows are sustainable, then there is certainly some leeway to finance additional public investment. If, however, the flows are transitory, at their current level it becomes difficult to use them as a cushion. Nevertheless, the nature of the investment being financed could bolster the sustainability of these transfers and thus help to strengthen fiscal space. The funds could be allocated on a priority basis to sectors with high visibility (rural poverty reduction, for example, or project execution in the areas that expatriate workers come from), in which the impact is easily verifiable. A targeted investment strategy is likely to perpetuate the flows transferred by workers living abroad. In the long run, therefore, it helps to strengthen fiscal space.

Assuming that the external savings flows are sustainable, the risk of crowding out private investment appears unlikely, because there is still some leeway to finance increased private investment of approximately 1 to 1.5 per cent of GDP.

Table 7.12 *Changes in savings and investment ratios*

									Public debt indicators (% of GDP)										
	1988	1989	1990	1991	1992	1993	1994	1995	1996	1997	1998	1999	2000	2001	2002	2003	2004	2005	2006
Gross domestic savings ratio	20.9	19.0	20.0	17.8	17.1	17.2	15.3	14.0	15.7	16.9	17.6	18.8	17.1	19.4	19.4	19.9	18.4	18.3	
Gross national savings ratio	23.3	20.8	24.9	21.6	22.0	20.8	18.9	17.1	19.7	20.4	21.8	22.6	22.3	27.6	26.8	27.7	27.0	28.4	
National/internal savings gap	2.4	1.8	4.9	3.8	4.9	3.6	3.6	3.1	4.0	3.5	4.2	3.8	5.1	8.3	7.4	7.8	8.6	10.0	
Gross investment ratio	21.0	24.0	25.3	22.7	23.1	22.4	21.3	20.7	19.6	20.7	22.2	23.1	23.7	22.9	22.7	24.1	25.0	25.9	
Public investment ratio	6.4	7.5	7.3	6.2	7.0	7.8	6.8	7.0	5.2	5.3	6.0	5.1	5.0	5.3	4.8	4.4	4.5	4.1	4.4
Internal financing capacity	-0.1	-5.0	-5.3	-4.9	-6.0	-5.2	-6.0	-6.7	-3.9	-3.8	-4.6	-4.3	-6.6	-3.5	-3.3	-4.2	-6.7	-7.6	
National financing capacity	2.4	-3.2	-0.4	-1.1	-1.1	-1.5	-2.4	-3.6	0.1	-0.3	-0.4	-0.5	-1.4	4.8	4.1	3.6	1.9	2.4	

Source: Ministry of Finance and Privatization (DEPF database) and authors' calculations

Table 7.13 *Structure of gross national savings*

	Structure of gross national savings (%)																	
	1988	1989	1990	1991	1992	1993	1994	1995	1996	1997	1998	1999	2000	2001	2002	2003	2004	2005
External savings	10.3	8.8	19.7	17.7	22.3	17.4	19.1	18.2	20.3	17.2	19.2	16.9	23.1	30.0	27.6	28.1	31.9	35.4
Gross domestic savings	89.7	91.2	80.3	82.3	77.7	82.6	80.9	81.8	79.7	82.8	80.8	83.1	76.9	70.0	72.4	71.9	68.1	64.6
Government savings	7.7	6.9	15.0	14.3	21.8	26.1	18.6	10.6	11.1	18.6	9.8	31.0	7.9	23.6	5.3	8.4	9.3	2.2

Source: Ministry of Finance and Privatization (DEPF database) and authors' calculations

Financing through virtuous seignorage

Under article 27 of Act No. 76-03, the Central Bank 'may not grant financial assistance to the Government, nor act as guarantor of commitments entered into by it, except in the form of short-term credits'. Such 'short-term credits shall be limited to 5 per cent of the tax revenue collected during the previous budget year'. It should be noted that 'the amounts actually used under this facility shall be remunerated at the base refinancing rate that commercial banks pay to the Bank'.

Therefore, there are no direct advances from the Central Bank to bridge a gap in the government's borrowing needs. However, money creation remains a financial resource for the government, since, through the Central Bank, it exercises its prerogative of issuing cash currency, the manufacturing cost of which is lower than the face value of the banknotes. What is involved is seignorage (in the absence of advances, returned in principle to the government budget in the form of dividends).

Seignorage comprises two elements, virtuous seignorage and the inflation tax. The first element represents an increased demand for actual cash related mainly to revenue growth by way of economic growth. The second element results from an increase in excess base money relative to the demand for currency. This excess causes inflation.

According to Table 7.14, Morocco benefits from considerable virtuous seignorage, which, on average, represented 2.6 per cent of GDP between 2000 and 2005. Conversely, the inflation tax remains relatively modest (0.4 per cent of GDP, on average, from 2000 to 2005). The independent status of the Central Bank (prohibition against advances and mission of ensuring monetary stability) (Kingdom of Morocco, 2006) limits seignorage almost exclusively to its virtuous component. The Moroccan situation is therefore sound and should be perpetuated. From a conservative standpoint, it is reasonable to count on income from virtuous seignorage of around 1.5 per cent to 2 per cent of GDP. This can be used in the context of increasing and more efficiently using fiscal space in order to achieve the MDGs.

Section summary

Financing space offers considerable leeway. First, it offers the capacity to finance increased public investment through external savings flows. This leeway, which represents 1 per cent to 1.5 per cent of GDP, can, however, decrease if the external savings flows change direction. Second, it promotes the existence of virtuous seignorage linked not to inflation but to the country's health in terms of economic growth. This leeway represents 1.5 per cent to 2 per cent of GDP and appears relatively stable.

Table 7.14 *Seignorage and inflation rate*[47]

	1988	1989	1990	1991	1992	1993	1994	1995	1996	1997	1998	1999	2000	2001	2002	2003	2004	2005
									Public debt indicators (% of GDP)									
MAD billions																		
Central currency	26.2	30.8	38.3	47.8	44.0	47.8	50.7	53.4	57.6	62.6	67.0	75.9	78.4	95.1	98.6	114.6	129.0	141.3
GDP	182.2	193.9	212.8	242.4	244.0	250.0	279.6	282.5	319.4	318.3	384.5	389.8	393.8	426.9	446.0	477.0	500.1	522.6
Per cent																		
Inflation rate	2.31	0.04	7.0	8.0	5.7	5.2	5.2	6.1	3.0	1	2.8	0.7	1.9	0.6	2.8	1.2	1.5	1.3
Ratio to GDP																		
Seignorage	2.27	2.55	3.87	4.47	-1.58	1.55	1.18	0.94	1.45	1.59	1.40	2.32	0.63	4.27	0.80	3.59	3.03	2.46
Inflation rate	0.33	0.42	1.04	1.33	1.06	0.89	0.94	1.04	0.55	0.18	0.54	0.14	0.41	0.13	0.68	0.29	0.40	0.37

Source: Bank Al-Maghrib; IMF international financial statistics; national authorities (data sourced from multiple years)

PARTICIPATION, DECENTRALIZATION AND EFFECTIVENESS OF GOVERNMENT SPENDING

Morocco is pursuing a policy of decentralization and local government reform in parallel with the civil service reform, the objective of which is to improve its effectiveness in budgetary and human resources management (Dahri, 2005). As the objective is to mobilize growing resources on behalf of local governments, it is gradually modernizing local tax systems. Morocco's objective is also to expand its fiscal space through more effective government spending. The next sub-section deals with local finances and their conceivable potential, and the following sub-sections analyse the ways in which partnerships between development agencies, NGOs and local governments can promote the optimal use of public resources for local development and thereby lead to the mobilization of additional resources.

Local development and fiscal space

Annex 7.1 (page 237) presents tables that are relevant to this section, with ratios breaking down the size of each of the revenue and expenditure items in each main category under overall revenue and expenditure. The breakdown was prepared for 2003 to 2005, based on data supplied by the Ministry of Finance, Directorate of Local Governments, for each type of local government, urban and rural municipalities, provinces and prefectures, and regions.

Resources of local governments and tax revenue space

The revenue dimension of local finances has been undergoing renewal since the 1970s and a reform project is currently under way. The complexity inherent in the large number of local taxes and the frequent lack of expertise within the municipalities reduces their efficiency. The characteristics of the resources of local governments and the proposed reform measures and their anticipated impact are analysed below. The probable effects on the investment financing possibilities of local governments are then examined.

Tax resources of local governments

The tax resources of local governments consist of tax resources collected by the government and passed on to the municipalities, some in consideration of their territorial base (business licence tax, municipal tax and town council tax) and others that are distributed according to predefined criteria (VAT) and own tax revenue. Act No. 30-89, amended with regard to local taxation, determines local taxes.

Own resources. In accordance with Act No. 30-89 governing taxation by local governments, local tax rates fall into three categories: rates or tariffs set by the Act that applies to all local governments; maximum rates or tariffs that allow for some leeway; and rates or tariffs that local governments are free to choose.

Local governments are responsible for only 13 out of 39 taxes.[48] However, the difficulties faced by municipalities with regard to the execution and operation of their projects make it necessary to delegate responsibility to local elected officials at: (1) the tax level (where some decisions should be left to their discretion to enable them to moderate the tax burden and assume the corresponding loss of revenue), and (2) the fiscal level (to enable them to assess the fiscal revenue available for investment).[49]

Transfers by the government. The 1976 reform introduced two lines of subsidies for the benefit of local governments. One line consisted of 'infrastructure subsidies' (development funds for local governments), allocated on a case-by-case basis by each technical division of the Ministry of the Interior and giving rise to a budget line in the accounts of the Direction Général des Collectivités Locales (DGCL) (Directorate General of Local Governments); this measure was comprehensive in nature. A second line consisted of 'operating subsidies' that were to serve as an occasional contribution to budgets. This measure had a demotivating effect on local governments, as they relied on this grant to balance their budget. These two subsidies were abolished in 1996 and replaced by a grant consisting of 30 per cent of the overall VAT yield, or approximately 2 per cent of GDP.

The system of distribution of the local government share in the VAT yield is based on principles designed to: (1) guarantee a minimum block grant to all local governments, regardless of size or tax wealth; (2) ensure equalization among local governments to mitigate their excessive tax inequalities; and (3) 'reward' efforts by local governments to collect their own resources. These principles give rise to the following procedures: (1) a block grant that provides a guaranteed equal minimum for all local governments; (2) a grant linked to tax potential, a criterion based on the resources of the taxes levied (municipal tax, town council tax and business licence tax); and (3) a grant based on fiscal effort to encourage resource collection. It is indexed to local taxes and therefore largely controlled by the municipalities. Table 7.15 shows the share associated with each of these criteria in the formation of the overall VAT grant for each local government category. Urban communities are treated as a category of municipality; in reality they form an association of municipalities constituting a town (see SCET-URBA Systems (2003).

The prefectures and provinces have their own resources that are limited to three taxes. They receive no permanent transfers other than VAT. Universal distribution of

Table 7.15 *Criteria for determination of the overall VAT grant (%)*

Criteria	Urban Municipalities	Urban Communities	Rural Municipalities
Block grant	15	20	30
Tax potential	70	60	60
Fiscal effort	15	20	10
Total	100	100	100

Source: Ministère de l'Intérieur, Directorate General of Local Governments (data from multiple years)

the VAT allocation has freed local governments from their former dependence on 'balance and investment support', with its unpredictable changes. Their financial autonomy has been significantly strengthened as a result. In short, the external divisions of the Direction Générale des Impôts (DGI) (Directorate General of Taxes) collect the bulk of local taxes. These are delegated taxes, the urban tax,[50] the town council tax and the business licence tax. The DGI divisions ensure censuses, issuance and settlement of disputes. In return, the DGI receives 10 per cent of the sums collected. Until now these taxes have been collected by the regional treasury departments (which are subordinate to the General Treasury of the Kingdom).

Of local government revenue, 75 per cent consists of grants from the general budget (30 per cent from overall VAT revenue and 1 per cent from corporate tax revenue). The 39 local taxes provide around 25 per cent of local government revenue. Henceforth the DGI will collect the corporate tax, VAT and, soon, income tax. This change constitutes an efficiency factor for the municipalities given the support provided to them by the DGI external divisions (establishment of the tax base, that is, conducting a census of taxpayers and setting the rates and amounts owed).

Currently, collection by local governments is basically spontaneous; reassessments are sometimes performed and transmitted to the municipal tax collector. Underpayments are dealt with through correspondence between the regional treasury department and the regional audit office (with a copy to the president of the municipality).

Growth prospects of local government resources. Following broad consultations, a local tax reform proposal will soon be introduced in the legislature. The general principle of the reform is a reduction in the number of taxes and a simplification and harmonization of the systems for determining the basis of assessment. The objective is to ensure stable revenue for local governments without driving away taxpayers or dissuading investors. The 39 local taxes generate less than MAD4 billion. For some taxes, the collection cost is higher than their yield (Kubota, 2005). The potential benefits of the reform reside in: (1) greater stringency in setting rates and understanding the tax base, and (2) better organization of collection.

Elected officials have the latitude to set rates for some taxes and charges. There has never been a decree, for example, that proposes to raise the rents on shops or houses belonging to local governments. There is an unutilized potential here as revenue of this type is diminishing in real terms because of inflation. Officials in charge of local finances believe that they could achieve MAD7 billion in revenue.

In a similar vein, local government assets are not properly valued. Transfers are made at prices that do not reflect market reality (underestimated land sales, for example). The legal framework regulating the management of local government assets, which dates from 1924, should be re-examined. Asset revenue represents slightly more than 3 per cent of local government resources (MAD500 million out of MAD15 billion). In addition, taxes are currently collected both by the managers of the municipalities and by regional treasury agents. This overlap of jurisdictions has led to a piling up of arrears. The current local tax reform provides for the consolidation of some taxes, the abolition of those that cost more to collect than they yield, and the designation of a single collection entity.

Distributions of the share that is not part of the block grant (earmarked for payment of local government staff) are determined by circulars from the Ministry of the Interior. This sometimes poses a risk of discriminatory treatment depending on the influence of the local government concerned. It is noteworthy that nearly 40 per cent of the VAT grant benefits the six largest cities (Casablanca, Rabat, Marrakesh, Fez, Salé and Agadir).

If the distribution of the 'special grant' was covered by the act, then even impoverished local governments, lacking management capacity, could be coached in optimizing the use of resources. Moreover, this would help to reduce inequality, as well as poverty. A more equitable distribution would perhaps push affluent municipalities to mobilize more of their own resources.

Local government revenue in general should also be consolidated in the years ahead as a result of the tax transition reform (see the section 'Evaluation of tax revenue space', page 177). In the context of tax transition, the reform of VAT and the elimination of its exemptions will enable VAT to fully play its role as a general tax on consumption.

Investment financing resources of local governments
The VAT equalization system has strengthened the finances of local governments and enabled them to generate significant resources for investment. The improvement has benefited rural municipalities in particular. Local governments also have recourse to investment loans from the DGI Municipal Infrastructure Fund (FEC).[51]

Analysis of FEC financing trends and approaches to optimization of operations. Table 7.16 tracks the sectoral changes in FEC disbursements. The loans granted for the urban planning and unclassified sectors account for more than 59.2 per cent of disbursements (34.7 per cent and 24.5 per cent).[52] The other items financed are highways, sanitation and sports and tourism infrastructure. Commercial infrastructure is not always used in an optimal fashion. It would be preferable for such infrastructure to be entrusted to private operators on the basis of a set of terms and conditions. The same could apply to outsourcing the management of services. Some large municipalities (Casablanca and Rabat) have already outsourced drinking water distribution, sanitation and electricity. The results are satisfactory from the standpoint both of services to users and of the government (an end to recurrent subsidies).[53] Mixed companies can also be created for waste management.

Analysis of disbursements by type of client. FEC practices have changed. Previously, the principle of equality among local governments prevailed. Currently, as a public service agency, the FEC is developing a policy adapted to each category of local government.

Table 7.16 *Sectoral changes in disbursements (MAD millions)*

Sectors	1996–2000	2001–2005	Overall
Urban Planning	1629	1537	3166
Liquid Waste Disposal	259	184	442
Drinking Water	127	61	188
Electricity	448	259	707
Commercial Infrastructure	529	331	860
Special Infrastructure	139	49	188
Sports and Tourism Infrastructure	288	125	413
Unclassified	179	1083	1262
Rolling Stock	367	75	442
Highways	137	651	788
Urban Transport	101	71	173
Total	4202	4426	8627

Source: FEC (various activity reports sourced from multiple years)

The study of FEC disbursements by type of client shows a change in loan beneficiaries and a rebalancing to the benefit of impoverished municipalities.

Table 7.17 shows a strong increase in loans to rural municipalities (97 per cent growth in the periods 1996–2000 and 2001–2005); their relative share went from 17 per cent to 33 per cent. This trend is in line with poverty reduction efforts, which are especially prevalent in rural areas (see the section 'Fiscal space and human development: The overall linkage' above). The provincial and regional councils, many of which were impoverished and not playing a significant role, are also beginning to be financed (their share went from 1.7 per cent to nearly 8 per cent). The decline in numbers (45.5 per cent) and proportion of disbursements to operating authorities reflects the growing role of private operators in the water, electricity and transport sectors.

FEC commitments to local development programmes. FEC financing was promoting a growing role for local governments in poverty reduction programmes long before the human development initiative was launched.

Management of local government financing. Local governments' access to loans depends upon the existence of a well-defined project and its feasibility and profitability, all of which are assessed by the FEC. For greater effectiveness, local government loans

Table 7.17 *Changes in disbursements by type of client (MAD millions)*

Type	1996–2000	2001–2005	Overall
Urban municipalities	3103	2378	5481
Rural municipalities	743	1470	2213
Provincial and regional councils	73	354	426
Association of municipalities	22	0	22
Water, electricity and transport authorities	123	67	190
Other	138	157	295
OVERALL	4202	4426	8627

Source: FEC (various activity reports sourced from multiple years)

BOX 7.4 FEC SECTORAL PROGRAMMES

The FEC participates in several programmes. One is Programme d'Electrification Rurale Global (PERG), the comprehensive Rural Electricity Programme. This is a participatory programme, the financing of which is provided by three partners, local governments, beneficiary households and the Office National d'Electricité (ONE) (National Electricity Board). When the participation of the FEC is requested, it takes charge of the local government investment. In view of the specific features of this type of operation, the FEC loan granting and disbursement procedures were simplified. Loans granted in this framework by the FEC total nearly MAD405 million to about 181 local governments.

The purpose of the Programme d'Approvisionnement Groupé en Eau potable des populations Rurales (PAGER) (Programme for Connected Supply of Drinking Water to Rural Populations) is the rehabilitation of collection, storage and distribution works, as well as the installation of pumping infrastructure and the construction of drinking fountains – four projects totalling MAD6.6 million.

The Programme National Coopératif de Recherches Routières (PNCRR) (National Programme for Construction of Rural Roads) is being carried out in the context of a partnership between the municipalities and the Ministry of Infrastructure. The local government share of support for FEC financing is around 10 per cent. The loans granted in this framework to nearly 370 beneficiary local governments exceed MAD 205 million. Here, too, the FEC assessment, loan granting and disbursement procedures were simplified.

The Ministère de l'Education National (MEN) (Ministry of Education) has another important programme. In October 1999 the Ministry of the Interior, the Ministry of Finance, FEC and MEN signed a framework agreement for the rehabilitation and upgrading of school infrastructure in rural and suburban areas. Under this agreement, local governments assume responsibility for launching and carrying out works financed by FEC loans, and MEN annually allocates to the local governments a financial grant covering the costs of the FEC loan. Loans granted in this framework to 94 beneficiary local governments total nearly MAD954 million.

---

should be based on their overall financial capacity to honour their debt, while the municipal council should have sole responsibility for the assessment of the projects. Such an adjustment in the operation of credit to local governments is conceivable because the FEC is capable of assessing the borrowing capacity of local governments, particularly due to its access to DGCL data. The principle of automatically recording the due dates of payments to the FEC in local government budgets should be maintained. This reform of procedures should be accompanied by the elimination of prior approval from the supervisory authorities.

The advantage of these adjustments would be to reduce the time needed for execution of the projects and hence their cost. However, they would require strengthening the expertise of elected officials and local government staff (for example, by training officeholders in fiscal management). In an intermediate phase, expanded cooperation with agencies, such as the ADS (see below), or support from regional treasury departments, could make up for the gaps in expertise. The regional treasury departments are already working with local governments and thus are quite familiar with their finances. The scope of their support for local governments should, therefore, be widened. The goal is to provide reliable fiscal estimates with a cost–benefit analysis of the projects.

FEC is considering ways to adjust its participation. The new methods of managing services (particularly the delegation of services to private companies) will require new financing methods.

In short, the 1996 reform had a significant impact on municipal fiscal management. Informing the municipality of the amount allocated to it, prior to the preparation of its budget, enabled local government administrators to improve their forecasting ability. It also helped them to make more rational choices in terms of expenditure.

Expenditure of local governments and fiscal space

Universal distribution of the VAT allocation has lessened the tendency on the part of the municipalities to artificially inflate costs, so as to benefit from 'balance and investment' support. This has slowed the growth of operating expenditure and bolstered the savings of local governments.

The external divisions of the treasury fulfil the functions of financial controller and paymaster for local governments (the payment authorization officer is the elected official). Treasury accountants monitor commitments and payments. In each location, the tax collector acts as the accountant for the local governments in his district. This task of administrator of local finances leads to a role as adviser, which could be expanded, as suggested above.

Characteristics of the expenditure of local governments

The merger of the treasury divisions with those of the Contrôle des engagements et dépenses (CED) (Oversight of Commitments and Expenditure) at the central government level was extended to local governments. At the same time, consultations are underway to change the oversight of expenditure. The legislation being drafted provides for 'hierarchical oversight of expenditure', first in stages, depending on the amounts, or second varying according to the management capacities of local governments.

In the past, some public expenditure authorization officers viewed approval by the controller as a release from responsibility. The current draft tends, on the contrary, to view each authorization officer as 'responsible for the actions he has taken, approved or executed'. Municipal policymakers will need to be more vigilant to facilitate the shift towards ex post oversight, as the central government oversight system is being extended to the municipal councils. The elimination of oversight of commitments and expenditure will also apply to the municipalities.

This change would entail a risk, however, if the expertise of municipal policymakers is not strengthened. In their role as 'advisers' to local governments, the governments' external divisions publish annual operating tables showing (1) debt ratios at the national, provincial and regional levels, and (2) deviations from the forecasts. The same applies to the share of wages in total expenditure. Moreover, a chart of accounts was designed for local governments.

Modernization of oversight calls for energizing the regional audit offices. Under article 98 of the Constitution, the regional audit offices are responsible for overseeing the accounts and the management of local governments and their associations. However, the reports examined do not mention the results of any investigations carried out. Furthermore, the Inspectorate General of Finances only conducted around 50 audits between 1970 and 2005. The Inspection Générale de l'Administration Territoriale (IGAT) (Inspectorate General of Territorial Administration) also does not seem to exercise its prerogatives.

Local expenditure and effectiveness of the supply of public goods
Overall, wages absorb MAD6 billion of the local government budgets; the governments had to resort to mass recruitment to reduce the unemployment rate among university graduates. Currently, there are 150,000 employees on the local government roster, with a management ratio of less than 8 per cent. It is estimated that two thirds of the staff are redundant. At the time of the mass recruitment, the posts that were filled were often on the lower rungs of the administrative ladder. Once recruited, however, the young graduates rejected their posts. Redeployment became necessary leading to overstaffing of some divisions (which induced absenteeism) and staff maladjustment. As a consequence, staff productivity fell and the budget of local governments was overburdened by wage expenditure.

Currently, there is talk of a scenario involving a 'voluntary separation' programme modelled after the one that was organized for the staff of the ministries. If this scenario is adopted, it will be crucial to rely on the experience gained and to proceed as follows. First, require actual presence in the divisions. Thus, some of the absentees, who have outside jobs, will be forced to resign. Second, take a poll to identify the optimal amount of the separation allowance, and finally, avoid the departure of skilled staff.

Social Development Agency: An innovative approach to local development and the supply of public goods

The experience of the Agence de Développement Social (ADS) (Social Development Agency), inaugurated in 1999, shows that its success is due to: (1) an approach involving the populations benefiting from the projects to be financed, (2) a cross-cutting approach, and (3) flexible operating procedures coupled with stringent governance.

Participatory approach and effectiveness of government spending
Three principles underlie the activities of ADS. It does not execute tasks falling under the jurisdiction of the ministerial departments and their external divisions. Instead, it works with these departments and other partners (national NGOs) recognized as being in the public interest, such as the Mohammed V Foundation, or again, local governments to ensure that the projects best meet the needs of the populations. And finally, it compensates, where necessary, for the failure of some participants. ADS participates

directly on an exceptional basis. For instance, if houses are too far apart to make electrification possible under conditions that are financially sustainable for ONE, ADS will then mobilize the population to devise solutions suited to their environment, needs and incomes. It provides the direct support necessary. For this reason, it is a model for the projects developed in the framework of INDH.

Duplication of the work of ADS and other agencies is thus avoided and ADS helps to increase the effectiveness of the projects executed by the ministries (GRET, 2005). ADS acts as an interface between the various participants and the population. It also plays a role in raising their awareness, delegating responsibility to them and educating them. Thus, in all the projects in which it is involved, the populations usually contribute 25 per cent to 35 per cent of the overall cost.[54] For some projects, however, ADS mobilizes the total financing in which case the populations contribute in kind (labour or logistical contributions). The search for effectiveness has led ADS to involve the populations or project stakeholders in all stages of the project, including: (1) formulation of the request, (2) design, (3) financing contribution, and (4) oversight of execution.

Support and negotiation of contributions are made easier by the fact that ADS increasingly works with partners that request its participation (this is particularly true of local governments far removed from large urban centres, as they lack the senior staff needed to design and implement development programmes). The agency is often sought out solely for its engineering services or to skirt administrative red tape.

Other actions of the authorities also benefit from the successful practices and experiences of ADS. For example, ADS is in the habit of operating in partnership with associations, from which it requests project descriptions which should be simple, but sufficient to establish the credibility of the projects submitted. Such project descriptions were recently adopted as part of INDH.

Integrated/cross-cutting approach and effectiveness of government spending

ADS operates largely with a cross-cutting approach. For example, if a department is planning to build a school, ADS draws the attention of other participants to the need to provide roads and electricity. The cross-cutting approach is also embedded in the agency's institutional procedures. Thus, in its cooperation with the municipalities, in order to expedite project execution, ADS uses 'local development funds'. For a given project, the municipality could put in MAD1 million and ADS would do the same. The amount is placed in the ADS account and released as the project progresses. This procedure avoids the red tape inherent in the dual oversight of local governments (Ministry of the Interior/approval of invitations to bid by the governor and the Ministry of Finance). To ensure the quality of the operation, ADS involves the Provincial Directorate of the Ministry of Infrastructure for the design of the invitations to bid.

Generally speaking, projects are executed in partnership with the ministries (education, housing, infrastructure and health), offices (such as the Office National de l'Eau Potable (ONEP) (National Bureau for Drinking Water)), NGOs recognized as being in the public interest (and having access to sizeable public funds, such as the Mohammed V Foundation), regional development agencies,[55] and sometimes even individuals.[56] After an agreement is signed, ADS sets up a coordinating structure at the local level, solicits contributions from NGOs and/or calls upon development consultants/agents.

The cross-cutting approach promotes consistency among the actions of the various participants, as shown by the support for the Villes sans bidonvilles (VSB) (Cities Without Slums) programme. This programme, initiated by the Ministry of Housing with the support of the World Bank, for which the government has established a guarantee fund (Fonds de Garantie pour les Revenus Irréguliers et Modestes – FOGARIM), had encountered problems in achieving its goals. This was because of a lack of expertise, such as knowing how to approach the target populations. The ADS team working in one of the locations (Douar Kora), which was supervising the project design and construction, put the Association for Mountain Parks Protection and Enjoyment (AMPPE) (an NGO promoting income-generating activities) in charge of coaching the slum residents in facilitating the transfer of their activities. In other locations, the teams are raising the awareness of the municipalities concerning the efforts to establish public infrastructure (markets and transport) and to get the populations concerned to accept its transfer, where necessary.

Mindful of the advantages of the ADS approach, the Directorate of the Budget requested it participate in a cross-cutting manner in the 'argan tree' programme (ADS, Projet Arganier, 2007). The Forest Administration showed that it had an exclusively 'environmental' conception of this project (forest preservation), while other partners (cooperatives) saw only its financial aspects (income from timber cutting).

The agency's image of being 'close to the ground' and its capacity to work in cooperation with various partners has led it to expand the scope of its participation. Thus, in addition to the infrastructure projects in which it participates, it helped to initiate a health insurance service. This initiative was developed with the support of the World Health Organization (WHO). At the outset, ADS, while working in a region or neighbourhood to promote income-generating activities, realized that with the growth in their income, micro-entrepreneurs were generating additional savings. ADS urged the creation of community funds to mutually protect their savings against health risk. This experiment is currently being tested in two pilot areas, Fez (an urban and suburban setting) and Azilal (a rural setting).

The cross-cutting approach is consistent with the membership of the agency's board of directors, which includes representatives of (1) the government administration (the Ministries of Infrastructure, Interior and Finance), (2) the private sector, and (3) civil society (development NGOs).

Operating procedures, method of governance and effectiveness of government spending
ADS was designed as an instrument to fight poverty. As it was financed by public funds, the legislators wanted to make it a flexible and 'responsive' organization; thus,

the oversight it receives is *ex post*. But since the agency also has recourse to foreign funds, it is subject to two audits. The first one is carried out by the Inspectorate General of Finance, which checks the regularity of the spending procedures. The second audit (Auditgroup, 2005), conducted by a well-known firm,[57] is an accounting audit. For 2006, the agency requested a socio-economic assessment of the projects (ADS, 2006).

The strict procedures for the implementation of ADS projects have been noted. For example, for a project worth MAD24 million, which it is executing on behalf of the UNDP, ADS began by drafting a procedures manual specifying the schedule for each action. Thus, it is breaking with the widespread practices of administrations that often operate without deadline constraints[58] or efforts to simplify procedures.

As far as possible, ADS softens the procedures for the beneficiaries of its services; it does not systematically require authenticated signatures or certified true copies. For the implementation of the projects, ADS works directly with the promoters and/or NGOs (without intermediaries). Moreover, the engineering service that has been developed delegates responsibility to decentralized teams at the local level.

The ADS approach seeks to ensure the effectiveness of government spending. Audits are conducted to ensure the regularity of the operations and use of funds. Likewise, impact studies are initiated to optimize the reach of the operations among the populations who are involved in the projects.[59] These studies are now familiar and have been adopted in some NGO programmes. They have a twofold objective, 'prove and improve'. The first stage consists of verifying whether the goals that were set have actually been achieved among the populations initially targeted (and not other segments), and the second stage consists of measuring the degree of satisfaction experienced by the populations, and any expectations they may have.

In accordance with good governance practices, the agency's structure is typified by the presence of an internal auditor who continually monitors observance of the procedures and the handling of any failures. In practice, it would seem even more appropriate for the auditor to report to the board of directors (relationship to the mission) and not to the management. The agency's management ratio is 80 per cent. Managers have their own personal computers and manage all the project tasks directly. In addition, ADS has ample recourse to contractual consultants (development agents) for limited periods (six months) or on a project fee basis. Such procedures lessen the risk of recruitment of part-time staff.

The agency's mode of operation (governance, participatory approach and cross-cutting perspective) also facilitates the mobilization of additional resources. For example, Agence française de développement (AFD) (French Development Agency), which has procedures similar to those of a bank, relied on ADS for a programme to support the construction of guesthouses for rural tourism development (€1.5 million), having a 30 per cent contribution from the EU. The same was true for a programme carried out with the Spanish cooperation agency.[60] The transparency of the agency's budgetary and accounting procedures, coupled with its status as a government agency, is a guarantee of confidence and expedites the implementation of commitments.

Civil society initiatives

Since the early 1990s, with the publication of the results of the household income survey and the liberalization of conditions for the establishment of NGOs, Morocco has witnessed a genuine explosion of development associations. This movement accelerated in the 2000s with awareness of the social risk that economic fragility entails. At the same time, large corporations began to support these initiatives, particularly in the context of commissions formed by professional associations.

There was, for instance, a commission formed by the Confédération Générale des Entreprises du Maroc (CGEM) (General Confederation of Moroccan Enterprises) that was tasked with 'establishing a relationship between a corporation and a neighbourhood association'. Based on the observation that these small associations did a great deal of work, the results of which fell short of the effort invested, the idea was to support them, for example, to overcome their lack of expertise in the organization of projects. The chairperson of the commission insisted that what the associations were looking for was not financing ('handing over a cheque'), by 'coaching'. The commission set itself the task of mobilizing small- and medium-sized enterprises and industries for these efforts.

For economic stakeholders, such action should favourably alter the image of the corporation in a neighbourhood and an environment in which calm is an essential factor. It is important that the corporation not be perceived solely as a 'profit-making machine'. Accordingly, the efforts to be made and the actions to be carried out should lead to 'mutual benefits'. These actions consist of the execution of social and cultural projects (holding children's festivals, sporting events and so on).

Each year the commission organizes a forum with selected corporations and associations. The theme of the next forum will be sustainable development, and it will be supported by the World Bank. On this occasion the associations will present projects. The projects are managed by the associations on behalf of youth and women with limited budgets (MAD50,000–100,000) so that they are both manageable for the corporations and compatible with the absorption and management capacity of the target small associations. The commission organizes training for the associations and the World Bank underwrites the cost of holding other workshops with a grant of MAD500,000. Local governments are pulled in to provide premises for the associations.

This example highlights the spontaneous contributions of corporations to local development. The efforts that they are making in kind or in financing terms can be equated with taxes, since the contributions fall in areas that are usually delegated to the authorities (the central and local governments). It follows that working in close proximity to neighbourhood associations promotes efficiency and frequently makes up for the lack of expertise at the level of both the municipalities and the associations.

Section summary

With the reform providing for the transfer of a portion of the corporate tax yield, and especially of 30 per cent of VAT revenue, local governments have relatively sizeable and stable revenue at their disposal. The rules on sharing these resources have made for equalization between local governments. The tax transition reform currently underway at the central level (see the section 'Evaluation of tax revenue space', page 177), which should be reflected in an increase in the relative VAT contribution, will, therefore, work in favour of strengthening the resources of local governments. Access to borrowing by local governments is currently being hampered by red tape and by the lack of qualified staff, especially in rural communities where the populations are mostly poor. A simplification of procedures should facilitate the mobilization of lending resources on behalf of local governments with sufficient repayment capacity.

Local government spending that is weighed down by excessive wage costs is ineffective. The cross-cutting participation by ADS compensates, at least in part, for the failures in coordination between the various ministerial departments. ADS is relatively free from the handicaps of administrative procedures (where these do exist they are in the process of being reformed, for example, spending oversight). This promotes a participatory approach that has long been neglected in traditional government interventions. It helps to increase the effectiveness of government spending and therefore to expand fiscal space without duplicating governmental efforts.

Civil society can also, through its numerous associations, help to mobilize resources for development. The accomplishments of the CGEM (CGEM, 2005) show that it is possible to mobilize human and material resources for poverty reduction while improving the image of the corporation among impoverished populations.

Supported by innovative actions on the government's part, local development and the growth of associations should make for an expansion of fiscal space, both through the mobilization of additional resources and, especially, through better use of available resources. The expansion of fiscal space is difficult to assess, but it represents the essence of the possible margin for progress in this area. See Annex 7.1 (page 237) for data and further information relating to the structure of local government revenue and expenditure.

MEDIUM-TERM PROSPECTS FOR BUDGETARY SPACE

Efforts by the public authorities in recent years in the area of taxation and rationalization of expenditure suggest the probability of a significant improvement in Morocco's tax and budgetary space. This trend towards an enhanced public finance profile will be followed up in the future to consolidate growth and social development. The current tax reform is part of a larger effort characterized by an acceleration of the opening up of the country's economy and the institution of financial, economic and social reforms that require a large volume of resources.

To create additional budgetary space it will be necessary to further reduce tax distortions and stabilize tax returns at the 2006 level at the very least. In particular, an effort should be made to bring expenditure under control and make it more efficient. Thus, the tax reform seeks to consolidate the rationalization, simplification and harmonization of the existing tax system. From this standpoint, important reform measures have been taken, while still others remain to be taken. These reforms have given concrete shape to the recommendations made during the national meeting on taxation held on 26 and 27 November 1999. They are the result of a gradual movement towards modernization of the tax system and its harmonization with the tax laws of partner countries. Moreover, the Moroccan authorities have always made budgetary policy a major strategic tool for achieving economic and social development at a level commensurate with expectations in order to overcome existing social inadequacies. From this standpoint, for a number of years, emphasis has been placed on bringing spending under control and enhancing governance. These two vectors play a crucial role in the allocation of resources and in building the country's economy.

Future projects and reforms in the tax and budgetary sphere are aimed at ensuring the conditions needed for vigorous economic growth that stimulates employment, consolidating macroeconomic stability and improving the situation of public finance. These reforms give due weight to the national and international context in which they are being undertaken. Some thoughts on the risks inherent in mobilizing additional resources to finance the MDGs through economic and social development in order to better serve the population are set out in the boxes below. They have to do with increasing public expenditure for the implementation of the MDGs and the impact of this on private investment and long-term growth; broadening fiscal space and its implications for the sustainability of public finance; and the mobilization of additional resources and the impact thereof on reducing inequalities.

Enhancing the profile of public finance

Above and beyond macroeconomic stability, the objectives of budgetary and fiscal policies are better management of state finances, the creation of conditions for economic recovery and development of the social sectors.[61] The budgetary and fiscal policies being pursued are designed to achieve these objectives while maintaining the budget deficit at a sustainable level despite internal and external constraints. Thus, while tariffs have been dismantled and there have been the high budgetary cost of the reforms and the assumption of certain exceptional expenses, implementation of the finance acts has been characterized by a reduction in the budget deficit. Excluding revenues from privatization, the budget deficit was reduced from 4.6 per cent of GDP in 2002 to 2.9 per cent in 2006, an adjustment equivalent to 1.7 per cent of GDP (see Table 7.7). Forecasts in the 2007 Finance Act reflect this trend notwithstanding the impact of a reworking of the income tax rate schedule and a significant increase in investment spending.

These accomplishments occurred in a context marked by several constraints, including an increase in subsidies for basic foodstuffs and petroleum products as well as the cost of efforts to combat locusts, the earthquake in the Al Hoceima region, which generated costs associated with a recovery programme of MAD2.7 billion, and a heavier wage bill, which amounted to MAD63.4 billion in 2006 due to measures taken in the context of social dialogue since 1995. To reduce this bill the government launched Operation Intilaka, which resulted in the voluntary retirement of some 38,600 individuals.

Significant growth in revenue

Tax revenues, not including corporate tax, income tax and VAT from local governments, have been consolidated, rising from 20.4 per cent of GDP in 2002 to 22.2 per cent in 2006 (see Table 7.7). This improvement is largely attributable to the significant increase in direct taxes, which has made it possible to offset the relative drop in earnings from customs duties (see above). Overall, tax revenues have largely exceeded forecasts, chiefly because of the performance of the tax and customs administrations, the improvement in taxpayer returns, linked to awareness and recovery measures, and more effective customs oversight. This is also attributable to increased tax bases and the impact of business-related reforms. Thus the structure of tax revenues has seen an increase of 5.7 per cent derived from direct taxation between 2002 and 2006.

Non-tax revenues, excluding privatizations, have also shown a positive trend, averaging roughly 2.1 per cent of GDP for the period 2002 to 2007. This can be explained by the increase both in revenues from state enterprises and in other revenues, such as the gas pipeline fees and miscellaneous contributions from various administrations. Income from privatizations amounted to MAD2.4 billion in 2006, as compared with MAD6.9 billion in 2005, MAD5.2 billion in 2004, MAD6.3 billion in 2003 and MAD0.6 billion in 2002. An amount close to the sum of these figures was contributed to the Hassan II Fund for Economic and Social Development. Income from privatizations was just 0.4 per cent of GDP in 2006 and was limited to 0.8 per cent of GDP on average during the period 2002 to 2007. The forecasts in the 2007 Finance Act reflect this trend, which is indicative of the gradually increasing autonomy of the budget vis-à-vis this category of income.

Efforts to bring non-recurrent expenditure under control

Regular expenses have been characterized by diverging trends showing, on the one hand, an increase in spending on goods and services, including subsidies, and, on the

Table 7.18 *Trends in expenditure as a percentage of GDP (2002–2006)*

	2002	2003	2004	2005	2006	Average 2002–2006
Regular expenditure	20.2	20.2	20.6	23.9	21.2	21.3
Goods and services	15.7	16.0	15.9	18.8	16.1	16.5
Personnel	10.9	11.2	11.3	11.8	10.9	11.2
Other goods and services	4.8	4.8	4.6	7.0	5.2	5.3
Debt interest	3.9	3.6	3.5	3.3	3.2	2.5
Subsidies	0.5	0.6	1.1	1.7	1.8	1.2
Investment	4.3	3.9	4.0	3.6	3.8	3.9

Source: Ministry of Finance and Privatization and IMF (data sourced over multiple years)

other hand, a decrease in debt interest. During the period under consideration, the state budget for goods and services has been subjected to a number of exceptional operations, including, in particular, the inherent costs of various social programmes, the voluntary retirement operation (payments to beneficiaries and compensation of the pension fund) and the increase in international energy prices. At the same time, the one-time nature of these operations, together with the reduction in the wage bill deriving from the voluntary retirement programme, suggests that fairly significant savings can be achieved as from 2007.

The rate of growth in personnel costs was relatively high between 2002 and 2005 because of a re-evaluation of salaries for certain categories of government employees (nearly 6.6 per cent on average per year). However, the voluntary retirement programme has meant that this line of expenditure, which grew by 2.4 per cent in 2006, should not exceed 1.4 per cent in 2007, taking into account normal personnel movements.

During the period 2002 to 2007, state subsidies totalled nearly MAD50 billion, of which MAD25.4 billion was spent on petroleum products. Total cost of subsidies was MAD8.3 billion in 2007, as compared to MAD10.6 billion in 2006 and MAD2.4 billion in 2002. In contrast, interest on debt declined, falling from the equivalent of 3.9 per cent of GDP in 2002 to approximately 3.2 per cent of GDP at the end of 2006 (see Table 7.18). This was a decrease of roughly 0.7 per cent of GDP, which must be viewed in conjunction with the success achieved in the active management of both external and internal debt. Investment spending under the state budget represented roughly 3.9 per cent of GDP between 2002 and 2006.

In fact, this expenditure should be viewed as including spending by state enterprises and institutions, including the Hassan II Fund for Economic and Social Development and local governments.

Reducing the debt burden
With regard to debt, the consolidation of fundamental balances has made it possible to bring Treasury needs for financing within dimensions compatible with the government's objectives. This has made it possible to bring the debt ratio down significantly

and to enhance the overall profile. Thus total Treasury debt went from 63.7 per cent in 2002 to 57 per cent in 2006, or a drop of 7 percentage points of GDP in four years. This decrease comes primarily from efforts to actively manage external debt through early reimbursement by the Treasury and the conversion of debt into investments. It is also the result of net negative flows of external debt and the effects of the depreciation of the dollar against the dirham. External debt has thus shrunk to 11 per cent of GDP, as compared with 21 per cent in 2002.

At the same time, taking into account the regularization of State arrears vis-à-vis the Caisse Marocaine de Retraite (CMR) (Moroccan pension fund) and subsidies for the voluntary retirement programme, internal debt showed an increase of nearly 4 per cent of GDP, rising from 43 per cent at the end of 2002 to 46 per cent at the end of 2006. This increase results from a deliberate choice based on a strategy of arbitrage between internal and external resources aimed at providing the Treasury with optimum financing conditions in terms of costs and risks, and emanates from a desire to modernize and revitalize the domestic financial market.

Medium-term fiscal and budgetary policy: Towards a more efficient and rational approach

The government's activities and reforms seek, in the medium term, to enhance the profile of public finance, revitalize the financial sector, restructure the public sector and expand private sector activity. Thus financial policy reform is to be carried out while seeking to consolidate state resources and enhancing the effectiveness of public spending. In this context, gradual reform and modernization are intended to give increased responsibility to the parties concerned. Such strategies help adapt public action to developments in the national and international economic environments and optimize the government's contribution to accelerating economic growth, macroeconomic stabilization and improving the financing of the economy and the well-being of the people of Morocco.

Fiscal policy: Development incentives

The principal measures recently implemented in the area of fiscal policy have to do with extending an economic and social policy designed to create the conditions for sustainable development. The desire to modernize the tax system and bring it into line with best international practices has been spelled out in the most recent finance acts. These reforms and measures take into account Morocco's commitments under free-trade agreements concluded with the EU, Arab countries of the Mediterranean, US and Turkey. The adverse consequences in terms of state revenues in the wake of this aperture have led to a search for alternative resources to offset the failure to meet expected goals, ensure a more equitable distribution of the tax burden and consolidate change in the area of taxation. This course of action is based on a strategy aimed at broadening the tax base and establishing a simpler, more transparent and more rational tax system that can generate additional income without creating any inequities.

The principal tax reforms planned for the next four or five years focus chiefly on efforts to simplify and harmonize the tax system, strengthen international cooperation and strengthen the tax administration. The reform of VAT should be aimed at achieving greater simplicity and harmonization in order to gradually reduce distortions. The same holds true for the tax thresholds applicable to all activities and enterprises liable to be affected by VAT and income tax. Reform will also focus on other taxes with a view to a gradual reduction of the tax burden together with a broadening of the tax base.

With regard to the broadening of the tax base, a special effort will be made to facilitate the integration of the informal sector into the organized economy, largely by means of the tax system. The desired objective is to guarantee an environment characterized by open competition favourable to the development of the enterprises, investments and businesses of citizens. The system of tax exemptions will be studied further in order to assess its impact on the budget and the economy from the standpoint of optimizing the use of such incentives.

In the area of international cooperation, Morocco will continue to implement the organizational and free-trade agreements it has signed (with the EU, US, Turkey and so on). This strategic choice will be accompanied by the implementation of reforms relating to the elimination of double taxation and the consolidation of efforts to combat under-reporting, tax fraud and counterfeiting. In addition, there are plans for a reform of customs tariffs aimed at gradually reducing the differences between taxes on imports covered by organizational and free-trade agreements and those imposed under ordinary law.

All of these undertakings will be supported by efforts to modernize the tax and customs administrations, enhance their effectiveness and the quality of their services, and more effectively combat tax fraud and evasion as well as under-reporting and counterfeiting. Such efforts will involve strengthening controls, developing an information system, deploying the necessary material and human resources, developing human resources and setting up performance evaluation systems. In addition, making widespread use of electronic declarations and payments will help to improve collection of the main taxes.

Budgetary policy: Controlling expenditure and improving public management

The main strategies of the budgetary policy designed by the ministry are centred on control of public expenditure, enhancing public management and modernizing control.

Bringing public expenditure under control

From the standpoint of consolidating public investment, efforts to bring public spending under control are being made in the medium term by slowing the growth rate of the wage bill, restructuring public institutions and enterprises and seeking to remove subsidies and actively manage the country's debt.

BOX 7.5 MOBILIZING ADDITIONAL RESOURCES WITHOUT CREATING ECONOMIC DISTORTIONS THAT PENALIZE GROWTH

Economic growth: A determining role in terms of income

The sensitivity of income to level of activity can be analysed by studying the elasticity that exists between taxation and economic growth. As economic theory suggests, elasticity over a long period is close to 1. As evaluated for the Moroccan economy for the period 1988 to 2006, this sensitivity is nearly 1.3, which suggests that apart from administrative factors, economic growth is increasingly a generator of income. Consequently, changes in tax revenues have occurred more rapidly than those in economic activity, with the result that taxation, which currently accounts for 20 per cent of GDP, has shown an upward tendency since 2004.

The evaluation of the impact of economic growth on income is also linked to the origin of the growth. Because they are taxed unequally, the various components of economic activity and their contributions to growth play a determining role. Economic growth driven by household consumption is income rich, while growth driven by foreign trade generates less income. The simulations carried out show that a slowdown in growth of 1 per cent of GDP could have different effects. The drop in income would be 0.7 per cent GDP if the slowdown was due to a decline in consumption, 0.3 per cent GDP in the event of a decline in public investment, and minimal if it resulted from a decline in exports. This shows the importance of taxation linked to domestic demand, which has become an engine for economic growth in recent years.

Fiscal spending: Potential resources that can be mobilized

Encouraging economic actors and activities through tax incentives is one of the tools used by the public authorities to achieve their growth and development objectives. Tax incentives take the form of exceptions, usually comprising exemptions and waivers, partial or total, or abatements and deductions at the taxable level. Unfortunately, this leads to a shrinking of the tax base, given that various sectors of the economy do not participate, or do so only slightly, in the financing of the budget. Enhancing the contribution of tax revenues to economic growth requires a tax burden that is distributed equitably among taxpayers and the various sectors of economic activity. A multiplicity of exemptions and systems of exceptions to tax schedules thus runs counter to improving the financing of public expenditure, particularly as the informal sector plays a major role in the economic life of Morocco, and this tendency toward exceptions should be curtailed.

The Moroccan government has in recent years been making efforts to modernize the country's tax system, with the objective of providing the country with appropriate fiscal tools, which can then fully play their political and economic roles. In order to determine the significance of tax exceptions, Morocco has, like developed counties, been carrying out estimates for a number of years of the loss of budgetary income from fiscal spending, evaluating these expenditures by type of tax, sector of activity and beneficiary. This has led to several conclusions.

Some 405 tax exceptions were identified in 2006, as against 337 such measures in 2005. Among the measures identified, 39.3 per cent were subject to budgetary evaluation in 2006, as compared with 30.3 per cent in 2005. The cost of these measures was estimated at MAD21.5 billion in 2005, or 4.3 per cent of GDP, including 52 per cent for VAT and 18 per cent for the corporate tax. In 2005, the cost was evaluated at MAD15.5 billion, accounting for 3.4 per cent of GDP, including 54 per cent attributable to VAT and 24 per cent to the corporate tax. International comparisons show that the weight of fiscal spending evaluated in Morocco is comparable to that of France (3 per cent of GDP) and lower than that of such countries as Spain and US (6 per cent of GDP) and Canada and UK (15 per cent of GDP).

Activities related to real property are the primary beneficiaries of indirect assistance (17 per cent of all fiscal spending), followed by agricultural products and fisheries products (each with 11 per cent of the total). A breakdown of fiscal spending by beneficiary shows that enterprises receive 60 per cent of the total, as opposed to just 22 per cent for households.

BOX 7.6 OPPORTUNITIES FOR MOBILIZING ADDITIONAL RESOURCES WHILE REDUCING INEQUALITIES

The importance of inequalities in the structure of household expenditure in Morocco and the existence of a range of VAT rates (five different separate rates) are the main reasons underlying the study of equity of VAT and its effectiveness in the income redistribution policy. The use of VAT as a redistribution tool is largely based on the notion that different rates make it possible to favour low-income households by taxing the goods largely consumed by this group at the lowest level, while taxing the goods consumed by high-income households at a higher level. While this redistribution function is played by income tax in Morocco today, there are several theoretical and practical objections that significantly limit the role of VAT as a redistributing agent.

Proportionality of VAT

A review of the weight of VAT paid against household consumption[62] by class of expenditure shows that this cost is only slightly graduated. This suggests that VAT is a tax that is quasi-proportional to household consumption notwithstanding the existence of different rates. It would thus seem that VAT cannot be used as an effective tool for reducing inequalities. Hence, a reform aimed at creating two rates or even a single rate seems important.

Different VAT rates do not benefit the state or those who pay the tax

The difference between household consumption structures by rate is not large. Accordingly, the use of a reduced VAT rate for certain goods is considered to be an ineffective means of redistribution. Given a specific budgetary cost, the greatest share benefits wealthy households, which are not the target of the measure.

Given a situation in which there is a single VAT rate of 20 per cent, the application of rates of 7 per cent and 10 per cent results in a saving in expenditure for the poorest quintile of MAD272 million, as opposed to MAD1,354 million for the wealthiest quintile; five times more than that of the poorest quintile. VAT policy thus does not benefit disadvantaged groups because the

Table 7.19 *Estimates of loss of state revenues deriving from a tax rate of 7% instead of 20%*

	Class of annual per capita expenditure				
	1	2	3	4	5
Loss of state revenues per quintile (MAD millions)	185.3	271.7	336.9	429.4	677.4
TOTAL (MAD millions)			1900.7		

Source: Office of Financial Studies and Forecasting, Ministry of Finance and Privatization (data sourced over multiple years)

Table 7.20 *Estimates of loss of state revenues deriving from a tax rate of 10% instead of 20%*

	Class of annual per capita expenditure				
	1	2	3	4	5
Loss of state revenues per quintile (MAD millions)	86.7	130.6	182.7	257.4	676.5
TOTAL (MAD millions)			1333.9		

Source: Office of Financial Studies and Forecasting, Ministry of Finance and Privatization (data sourced over multiple years)

poorest quintile benefits from only 8.5 per cent of the tax expenditure at these two rates. As for the state, the loss in revenues is approximately MAD3.23 billion, while the cost of the social objective does not exceed MAD272 million for the poorest quintile and MAD457 million for the two poorest quintiles. There is thus a need to redesign the VAT system together with a policy targeting the most disadvantaged segments of the population.

At the same time, the use of VAT to effect redistribution poses problems of horizontal inequality between households having the same income, but different consumption patterns. Some preliminary results of a study by Direction des Etudes et des Prévisions Financières (DEPF), the directorate of financial studies and forecasts, are showing that indirect taxation, particularly VAT, is virtually neutral as a tool for redistributing income, the redistribution of income should be carried out by graduated rates of direct taxation or through direct transfers, and the adoption of a single rate of VAT guarantees neutrality and equality, and reduces the vulnerability of VAT to sectoral claims. It also makes it possible to control management costs for both the administration and the taxpayer.

Controlling the wage bill will be achieved by limiting the creation of new budgetary posts to the priorities set by the administration, making the filling of posts a competency-based exercise and organizing the voluntary retirement of local government staff and staff in public bodies of an administrative nature. A forecast model for the civil service wage bill will also be introduced. This tool will make it possible to study the impact of human resources management reform and the enhancing of tools for forecasting personnel-related spending as part of a system of multi-year expenditure planning. This model will be subsequently introduced into all ministries, the senior managers of which will be given responsibility for managing personnel credits.

The search for a better allocation of public expenditure should do more to limit state transfers to public enterprises and institutions, chiefly by restructuring these bodies and enhancing their economic and financial situations.

In pursuing active debt management, the ministry will implement activities to bring official debt under control and mobilize concessional external financing for reforms and priority projects (housing, roads, waste management, health, water supply, education and so on). In addition, the ministry will encourage the active management of domestic debt and optimize management of the Public Treasury by modernizing the Treasury securities market. Planned activities relate primarily to expanding Treasury involvement in the currency market.

Modernization of the management of public monies
Morocco plans to extend the new approach of results-based budgeting by credit globalization measures, improving performance indicators and developing a budget performance report. In addition, it will encourage decentralization through the establishment of more appropriate budgeting and expense monitoring procedures, and will further pursue consolidation of formalized relations between central administrations and their subsidiary services. Support will be provided for results-based budgeting by extending the use of the Medium-Term Expenditure Framework (MTEF) to all

ministries. This will make it possible to ensure the coherence of sectoral policies with viable objectives in the macroeconomic context, to control the budget deficit, and to better allocate resources in keeping with the priorities identified by the Moroccan authorities. This approach to budgeting will also be reinforced by integrated expenditure management, which seeks to optimize the process of public expenditure.

Modernization of oversight

In order to meet the demands for a simplification of oversight procedures and to make these procedures less costly and more flexible and fluid, oversight reform will be integrated with tax reform at the local level. Another process that will help to achieve modernization of the oversight of public expenditure is the consolidation of transparency (Cherkaoui, 2001).

Oversight reform, which began in 2006, will continue with a view to ensuring that the oversight function is better adapted by decreasing compliance monitoring and increasing performance monitoring. Specific activities include consolidating the principle of a single spokesperson at the directorial level, the implementation of modular monitoring of expenditure and a total redesign of information systems and processing. At the level of public enterprises and institutions, there will be a reform of state financial oversight, the development of a management monitoring system based on performance indicators and the preparation of a frame of reference for good governance. Efforts will also be made to consolidate the accounts of different public entities.

In the area of transparency consolidation, efforts will be made to generalize the obligation of accountability. This reform will take account of the development of the actors' roles, the linkages between internal controls at the director level and external oversight by the General Ministerial Inspectorate, as well as *a posteriori* monitoring by the Inspectorate General of Finance and the Court of Auditors. In addition, tools for monitoring resource management will be introduced, which will ensure respect for the objectives set by the authorities and the means of achieving them.

Pursuing privatization policy and public–private partnerships

In the area of privatization, state disengagement from certain activities in favour of private agents will continue, whether in the form of actual privatization or delegated management. The medium-term plan of action seeks to identify new opportunities for privatization, the opening of equity and delegated management of public services and so on, in conjunction with sectoral liberalization. Privatization or the opening of equity in enterprises in such competitive sectors as ports, ground and air transport, phosphates and housing will be undertaken. There are also plans for the widespread adoption of delegated management in such services as urban transport, water supply, electricity, sanitation and irrigation. In the context of agricultural and agro-industrial partnerships, the second offering of partnerships in farmland managed by the Société de Développement Agricole (SODEA) (Agricultural Development Corporation) and

Société de Gestion des Terres Agricoles (SOGETA) (Agricultural Land Management Corporation) has begun, and an ad hoc committee entrusted with the monitoring and evaluation of partnerships in this area is to be created.

Medium-term economic and financial prospects

Until the recent economic downturn, the prospects for the global economy suggested, rather, an improvement in macroeconomic balances and the pursuit of structural and sectoral reforms. The fruits of these were already being observed, particularly in terms of wealth and job creation, and in an upturn in national economic indicators and the well-being of the population. The development of a medium-term macroeconomic framework is based on year-end prospects for 2007 and on a number of scenarios linked to the national and international environment.

International and national prospects

National prospects for foreign trade in goods and services should be bolstered in the future by the implementation of the Agadir Declaration, the simplification and reduction of customs tariffs and the anticipated positive effect of organizational and free-trade agreements. These latter will help to strengthen Moroccan exports by increasing business opportunities and reducing supply costs. Foreign trade should also benefit from a strengthening of the tourism and industrial sectors, which should make tourism one of the main sources of hard currency income, the development of the programmes forming the 'Emergency Plan' and the development of new niches of activity.

The macroeconomic context also takes into account the hypothesis relating to the average price of crude oil, which should remain stable on the world market at roughly US$60 a barrel, and the price of phosphates at US$42 a ton, with a relatively promising environment for phosphate derivative exports in conjunction with ongoing partnerships in the construction field.

With regard to the national environment, it is assumed that grain production will continue at the rate of an annual harvest of 6 million tonne (60 million quintals). National economic activity should also benefit from the pursuit of sectoral and structural reforms, which strengthen the productive structures of the national economy and ensure the conditions for greater integration in the global economy.

Medium-term economic forecast

On the basis of the aforementioned national and international economic prospects, national economic activity should benefit from a promising international environment, continued reform effort, measures to promote private initiative, increased domestic demand and sustained growth of productive activities, particularly in the light of a voluntary policy aimed at consolidating this growth through structural reform and sectoral strategies. National productive activities would also benefit from foreign demand for national products and the improvement in exportable offerings.

Accordingly, GDP would increase by 5.6 per cent in real terms. This consolidation of economic activity would derive chiefly from growth at the rate of 5.7 per cent in non-agricultural activities. In the primary sector, value added would grow to 4.6 per cent in the wake of satisfactory performance in livestock, industrial farming and market gardening, and the positive effect of hydro-agricultural equipment and modern methods of irrigation.

At the level of supply, household consumption at current prices would continue to drive economic growth, with an average annual increase of 7.7 per cent. This vitality would be spurred chiefly by consolidation of the labour market, an increase in household income, an increase in the volume of transfers from Moroccans living abroad and the maintenance of household purchasing power, abetted by inflation kept under control.

Growth in investment (at current prices) should follow the present increasing trends, which should bring the rate of investment to 33.5 per cent of GDP in the medium term instead of approximately 28.5 per cent, where it stood in 2006. This increase should, in essence, derive from the continuation of the strong trend in investment, both public and private. The increase in investment would also be stimulated by foreign investment flows in the wake of major efforts to attract greater volumes of foreign capital. These prospects would also be encouraged by continued gross national savings at a sufficiently high rate, 36 per cent of GDP as opposed to 32 per cent in 2006.

In the area of foreign trade, despite a persistent trade deficit hovering around 17.7 per cent of GDP in the medium term (compared with 16.3 per cent of GDP in 2006), the current account balance would continue to post a surplus, at around 3 per cent of GDP on average (2.5 per cent of GDP at the end of the period). This situation would follow on the heels of a strengthening of exports in services, and especially earnings from tourism, coupled with satisfactory performance in the tourism sector.

In addition, along with an invigoration of global demand directed at Morocco, and taking into account the opportunities afforded by organizational and free-trade agreements, the current rate of increase in exports should reach 9.7 per cent. This increase would be driven largely by exports of manufactured goods, which should register an average annual growth of 10.4 per cent, largely as a result of efforts to post a satisfactory performance in sales of electronic goods and revitalized textile and clothing exports.

Global imports of goods would increase in the medium term at an average annual rate of 9.4 per cent. Apart from energy and lubricants, this increase would be 10.9 per cent and include a 12.1 per cent increase in purchases of capital goods and a 14 per cent increase in semi-finished goods, together with a projected upturn in non-agricultural activities. Stable prices for imported oil and raw materials over the forecast period should not lead to significant imported inflation. Moreover, the pursuit of an accommodating monetary policy and the introduction of a modern currency exchange system, management of the budget deficit and factor costs could keep inflation at a level comparable to that of Morocco's partners. This should promote the maintenance of household purchasing power and make the national economy more competitive.

Public finance prospects

Public finance projections in the medium term reflect a continuation of recent trends, taking into consideration the effects of measures and actions already being implemented or planned. They show a continued improvement in public savings and a continuation of the overall deficit at less than 3 per cent, despite a significant increase in investment spending in terms of GDP and a steady decline in fiscal pressure at a level of roughly 20 per cent.

Income trends

Increased public revenue would be attributable to a satisfactory performance by tax revenues, chiefly from direct taxation, which would stabilize at 8.5 per cent of GDP. Tax revenues from indirect taxation in the broad sense (VAT, the domestic consumption tax, customs duties and so on) would evolve at a slower pace than income from direct taxation due to a moderate change in domestic consumption taxes and the effects of liberalization on customs revenues. The latter would show a loss of earnings of nearly 0.2 percentage points of GDP a year, accounting for roughly 1.3 percentage points in the medium term.

Non-tax revenues would continue to increase steadily, particularly revenues from monopolies, in connection with the regularization of the economic and financial situations of public enterprises and institutions. However, the share of total revenue and of GDP would drop slightly, while the share of income from privatizations would represent an increasingly marginal share of overall earnings.

Changes in expenditure

Public expenditure would increase at a slower pace than GDP. In keeping with observed trends, efforts by the state to reduce ordinary expenditure will be particularly important over this period and would result in savings of more than 3 percentage points of GDP. This forecast takes into account an average annual growth in personnel costs of 4 per cent. Thus the weight of this expenditure, in terms of GDP, would be at least 9 per cent in the medium term. Spending on other goods and services would rise by 8 per cent a year. Conversely, the net cost of subsidies would continue to weigh heavily on the budget, largely on account of the butane gas subsidy and the failure to index petroleum products in their entirety. The narrowing gap between income and regular expenditure indicates that public savings are likely to rise steadily, accounting for 44 per cent of investment spending by 2012.

Alongside structural reforms and sectoral policies, efforts by the state in the area of investment would be of increasing significance. Spending in this area would grow steadily to exceed the equivalent of 3.8 per cent of GDP in 2006 and 5 per cent in 2012.

Taking into account this investment spending, these movements as a whole would create a situation in which the global deficit would be brought under control, as it would stand at approximately 2.8 per cent of GDP, on average, by 2012.

In addition, calculation of the prime rate indicates that the public finance picture is likely to improve significantly in the coming years. Indeed, this rate stays constant across the entire projection period. This shows that apart from the debt interest arising from financial obligations assumed in the past, current fiscal and budgetary policy will continue to improve the public finance situation. This indicator is an essential factor for the sustainability of state finances in the next few years to the extent that the real interest rate is lower than the rate of economic growth. In other words, the constraint imposed by official debt makes a prime surplus necessary in the future.

This improvement in the medium-term public finance situation could be more evident with the releasing of additional margins. To this end the state will continue to implement reforms, particularly in the area of financial policy.

Evolution of the rate of indebtedness

Reduction of the rate of indebtedness is an essential step in absorbing the impact of the various external shocks on public finances. In addition to bringing the budget deficit under control, which is to be achieved by revitalizing growth and controlling expenditure, reduction of the rate of indebtedness also involves other factors. These include debt management capacity, the nature of the outstanding balance and the loan market.

To highlight the room for manoeuvre in terms of sustainable budgetary policy, simulations were carried out over a medium-term period to assess the viability of the results using a sensitivity analysis based on fluctuations in the different components of the rate of indebtedness. Even with a nominal average annual GDP growth rate of 5.2 per cent, which is lower than the cost of domestic debt by 0.8 percentage points, it is possible to bring down the rate of direct Treasury indebtedness by approximately 0.9 percentage points a year thanks to a prime rate higher than that needed for debt stabilization. Thus, in the medium term, the rate of indebtedness would stand at 52.5 per cent of GDP and official debt would thus be on a sustainable track. Given an average economic growth rate that was 1 per cent lower than that of the reference scenario, if a shock should occur, the rate of indebtedness would increase by nearly 1 point of GDP, to stand at over 55.2 per cent of GDP in the medium term.

A second scenario simulated a primary balance against the benchmark scenario. Interest payments would gradually increase, entailing a deepening of the overall deficit and a resurgence in the debt ratio, which would reach 57.5 per cent in the medium term. These simulations show that Morocco has an increasingly large budgetary space, as demonstrated by the fact that government finances are more resistant to various external shocks.

BOX 7.7 PROSPECTS FOR EXPANDING BUDGETARY SPACE WITHOUT COMPROMISING THE SUSTAINABILITY OF PUBLIC FINANCES

The outstanding balance of direct Treasury debt has followed a downward curve since 1993, having gone from 66.8 per cent of GDP in 1998 to 57 per cent in 2006. In 2005, a downward trend was observed due to a series of events that impacted public finances in general. However, certain factors that would seem to be ephemeral have persisted, such as the oil bill. These factors are reflected in a ballooning of debt stock, which represented 62.6 per cent of GDP in 2005 as opposed to 58.9 per cent in 2004.

This development with regard to debt, contrary to the concerns it might seem to evoke, has not had any significant crowding-out effect or any negative effects on household behaviour. In fact, over a relatively long period of time, the Moroccan economy has remained largely unaffected, unlike certain other countries' economies, where the increase in domestic debt has been generally accompanied by an increase in interest rates. This is primarily because of a positive trend with regard to the underpinnings of the economy, excess liquidity and a relaxing of interest rates, and this is in addition to active debt management.

Moreover, domestic debt in 2005 was held by banks (roughly 29 per cent), insurance companies (30 per cent) and investment companies (19 per cent). The remaining 22 per cent was held in equal parts (11 per cent each) by CDG and other institutions. The Treasury bond and state fund portfolio represented, on average, 20 per cent of all bank assets in recent years, as against 60 per cent for loans. This structure of bank appropriations shows that the Treasury is far from exercising a noticeable crowding-out effect on the private sector. Furthermore, the results of surveys of the financial structure of Moroccan enterprises show that self-financing accounts for an increasing share of investment.

Furthermore, while during the period 1998 to 2002 an average primary surplus of 1.9 per cent of GDP was needed to leave the ratio of debt to GDP unchanged, during the period 2003 to 2006 a primary deficit of approximately 0.5 per cent of GDP was enough to achieve the same result. This led to an increasingly significant easing of state budget constraints, as the sustainable budget deficit was of the order of 3.9 per cent of GDP from 2003 to 2006, as opposed to 2.4 per cent of GDP for the period 1998 to 2002.

Despite the growing effort of the state in respect of future investment along with structural reforms and sectoral policies, control of financing flows would make it possible to continue the downward trend of the rate of direct Treasury indebtedness, which would not exceed 52.2 per cent of GDP in 2012.

Section summary

The Moroccan authorities are engaged in a policy of expanding budgetary space through two essential tools. The first is reduction of distortions while increasing the level of public resources. The level of demobilization of public resources achieved in 2006 would seem to correspond to an optimal use of fiscal space, but the level of public resources should be maintained, at the very least, while pursuing a policy aimed at improving the taxation structure. This improvement will be achieved through various tax reform measures, one of the most important of which is the modernization of VAT, which is going ahead.

The second tool is control of public expenditure levels, particularly where personnel expenses or debt-related expenses are concerned. The expansion of budgetary space to incorporate public expenditure should result from a significant increase in its effectiveness. Results-based modern management and oversight of public expenditure are already being carried out with a view to achieving this goal. They are based on the use of tools such as the MTEF and integrated expenditure management. Medium-term economic projections show that giving such an orientation to an economic policy, based on an expansion of budgetary space and making optimal use of the various elements of this space, holds out much promise.

CONCLUSION

This chapter has highlighted the need for an increase to an optimal level of Morocco's fiscal space, which will then be used to further pursue the achievement of the MDGs. It has been demonstrated here that although Morocco's system of revenue gathering is not less efficient than that of other comparable countries, there is still room for improvement. This can best be done by increasing Morocco's level of public resources, which can be accomplished through major tax reform and through increased regulation of public expenditure.

The second section ('Fiscal space and human development: The overall linkage') showed that Morocco can use its fiscal space in various ways, some more effective than others, to address various social problems such as gender biases, low levels of education, health issues and unemployment. It concluded that the most effective programmes are those that utilize global rather than partial solutions, since global solutions have the advantages of being able to use higher numbers of resources and of being able to address all sides of an issue more efficiently than more narrowly-focused or sectoral programmes.

Next (see section 'Evaluation of tax revenue space', page 177), the chapter addressed the question of whether or not optimal levels of tax and non-tax resources are now being reached in Morocco. Although conventional studies have concluded that there is no significant room for increases in the tax resource space, there is justification for increasing tax resources within the context of optimization of public resources. This justification would rely on government financing being optimized and made more effective; it also relies on the fact that private resources are much more costly than public resources such as taxes. Care would need to be taken to ensure that tax reform did not result in tax distortion. Perhaps more importantly, the Moroccan authorities would need to ensure compliance with tax reform through scientific measurement of its probable effectiveness, transparent and open dialogue, and dissemination of information to the public as well as to the press and media.

The section entitled 'Evaluation of financing space' discussed the financing space resources of domestic financing, such as domestic borrowing and seignorage and external financing, such as grants and external borrowing, finding that there is considerable room in both types of resources for optimization of Morocco's fiscal space.

Under the heading of 'Participation, decentralization and effectiveness of government spending', the chapter analysed the potential effects on resource space of improvement in the effectiveness of government spending, focusing particularly on local governments and also on the successes of the ADS programme. Local governments, especially those in impoverished rural areas, now have difficulty with funding, effective management and gaining access to borrowed funds. Tax reforms now being carried out will hopefully have a positive effect on local governments' revenues due to an increase in what they will receive from VAT contributions. In addition, ADS is an agency that works with local governments and has proven in many cases more effective in mobilizing resources for local development; it could serve as a model for future such measures.

'Medium-term prospects for budgetary space' was the section that looked at Morocco's medium-term prospects, in particular, at measures that the Moroccan government is already taking towards optimizing its fiscal space. It is currently using the tools of reduction of tax distortions and control of public expenditure levels, both with the overall goal of increasing the level of public resources. This seems to mean that Morocco is on the right path in terms of optimization of its fiscal space, and that its long-term prospects in the context of achieving the MDGs are promising.

ANNEX 7.1 — STRUCTURE OF LOCAL GOVERNMENT REVENUE AND EXPENDITURE

Table 7.A1 *List of the major categories used for the breakdown of local government revenue and expenditure*

Codes	Categories
D1	I - Operating revenue (1)
D2	Allocated tax revenue
D3	Local revenue
D4	II - Operating expenditure (2)
D5	Staff
D6	Equipment and supplies
D7	Debt service
D8	Estimated surplus (3)
D9	III - Investment revenue (4)
D10	Estimated surplus
D11	N-1 surplus
D12	Investment VAT
D13	Loan
D14	Other revenue
D15	IV - Investment costs (5)
D16	Securities purchases
D17	Major renovations and new construction
D18	Real estate purchases
D19	Overall revenue (1)+(4)-(3)
D20	Overall expenditure (2)+(5)

Source: Directorate of Local Government

Codes (D1 to D20) were introduced in order to calculate the ratios needed for the analysis. It will be noted (Table 7.A2) that the revenue earmarked for operation consti-tutes the bulk of the total revenue (84 per cent and 78 per cent for 2004 and 2005). Within this category, local revenue represents one-fifth. This reflects the dependence of local governments on the revenue allocations (74 per cent). For urban municipalities, under revenue earmarked for investment, 74 per cent comes from estimated surpluses (18 per cent) and prior surpluses (56 per cent). This shows the fragility of investment programming: the amounts are determined by the bottom line and their use takes time (see the section 'Participation, decentralization and effectiveness of government spend-ing' above). Overall, 56 per cent of expenditure goes to pay staff (73 per cent for rural municipalities).

Revenue earmarked for operation continues to weigh heavily on local government budgets; 78 per cent (68 per cent for provinces and prefectures). Revenue from the VAT grant represents the largest share (56 per cent) of the revenue allocated (45 per cent for urban municipalities); municipal taxes account for only 6 per cent. On the expenditure side, operations take up between 85 per cent for urban municipalities, and 78 per cent

Table 7.A2 *Significant ratios for analysis of the structure of local government revenue and expenditure*

Operating Revenue	Urban Municipalities		Rural municipalities		Provinces and prefectures		Regions	
	2004	2005	2004	2005	2004	2005	2004	2005
D1/D19	84	79	100	100	73	58	66	76
D2/D1	72	74	72	69	91	90	42	43
D3/D1	28	26	28	31	9	10	58	57
D9/D19	20	25	38	38	32	47	78	72
Investment revenue								
(D10+D11)/D9	74	83	100	100	39	33	81	95
D12/D9	6	5	0	0	57	63	0	4
D14/D9	4	4	0	0	4	3	0	0
D19/D9	495	393	265	266	312	215	129	139
Expenditure								
D4/D20	83	82	80	81	69	56	25	37
D15/D20	17	18	20	19	31	44	75	63
D1/D20	87	87	129	129	75	61	73	101
D19/D20	103	110	129	129	102	105	111	132
Structure of expenditure								
D5/D4	49	50	73	73	56	68	22	17
D6/D4	38	38	22	23	42	31	71	69
D7/D4	13	12	4	4	1	1	7	14
D8/D4	5	6	61	60	8	9	193	173
D16/D15	11	11	0	0	7	5	4	6
D17/D15	85	83	0	0	89	95	95	93
D18/D15	4	5	0	0	4	1	1	1

Source: Calculations based on data over multiple years from the Ministry of Finance and Planning, Directorate of Local Government

Table 7.A3 *Breakdown of revenue and expenditure items for urban municipalities, provinces and prefectures, and regions*

	Items
D1	I - Operating revenue (1)
D2	Allocated tax revenue
D3	VAT (operation)
D4	Town council tax
D5	Business licence tax
D6	Municipal tax
D7	Corporate tax/general income tax
D8	Local revenue
D9	II - Operating costs (2)
D10	Staff
D11	Equipment and supplies
D12	Debt service
D13	Operating budget balance (3)
D14	III - Investment revenue (4)
D15	Estimated surplus
D16	N-1 surplus
D17	VAT (Investment)
D18	Loan
D19	Other revenue
D20	IV - Investment costs (5)
D21	Securities purchases
D22	Road systems
D23	Sanitation
D24	Electrification
D25	Water supply
D26	Construction
D27	Planning and development
D28	Real estate purchases
D29	Integrated investment
D30	Other expenditure:
D31	Pager
D32	Total resources (1)+(4)−(3)
D33	Total expenditure (2)+(5)

Source: Directorate of Local Government (data sourced from multiple years)

for all local governments (rural municipalities not included in Table 7.A4[63]); with the exception of Table 7.A2, we observed 73 per cent for these municipalities. The ratio of 'revenue earmarked for investment' to 'investment costs' is greater than 100 per cent (146 per cent); this testifies to the time lags in the programming of investment (as was noted for the use of FEC loans), and expresses the lack of expert staff in local government, as referred to earlier.

The following is a list of taxes and local taxes with 'maximum rates' and rates that local governments are free to choose from:

Table 7.A4 *Ratios for analysis of revenue and expenditure items for urban municipalities, provinces and prefectures, and regions*

Revenue	Urban Municipalities			Provinces and prefectures			Regions			Total		
	2003	2004	2005	2003	2004	2005	2003	2004	2005	2003	2004	2005
D1/D32	86	84	81	73	73	68	79	69	79	83	80	78
D2/D1	73	72	74	84	91	95	41	42	43	73	75	76
D3/D2	44	44	45	100	100	100	0	0	0	56	58	56
D3/D1	32	32	33	84	91	95	0	0	0	41	43	43
D4/D1	20	20	21	0	0	0	0	0	0	15	15	16
D5/D1	15	14	14	0	0	0	0	0	0	11	10	10
D6/D1	6	6	6	0	0	0	0	0	0	5	4	5
D7/D1	0	0	0	0	0	0	41	42	43	2	2	2
D8/D1		28	26	16	9	5	59	58	57	27	25	24
D15/D14	32	20	19	19	17	15	71	56	71	34	25	25
(D15+D16)/D14	70	74	85	36	39	40	97	81	98	64	65	74
D17/D3	1	5	3	33	27	33				14	15	15
D8/D14	120	116	92	35	20	8	63	49	63	87	77	65
D19/D14	7	4	4	2	4	4	0	0	0	4	3	3
D1/D33	92	878	90	74	75	71	89	96	110	88	83	86
D2/D33	67	62	66	63	68	68	36	40	48	64	62	66
(D4+D5+D6+D7)/D33	37	35	36	0	0	0	36	40	48	28	26	29
(D4+D5+D6+D7)/D20	250	198	238	0	0	0	52	40	80	133	111	133
D13/D14	32	20	19	19	17	15	71	56	71	34	25	25
D9/D33	85	83	85	68	69	65	30	33	41	79	76	78
D10/D9	49	49	50	62	56	68	22	22	17	51	50	53
D11/D9	36	38	38	36	42	30	71	71	69	37	39	37
D12/D9	15	13	12	2	1	1	6	7	14	12	10	10
D20/D33	15	17	15	32	31	35	70	100	59	21	24	22
D20/D1	16	20	17	43	41	49	79	104	54	24	29	25
D14/D20	142	120	165	105	107	113	119	114	167	125	115	146
D21/D20	10	11	12	5	7	7	11	4	7	9	9	10
D22/D20	22	28	21	9	15	18	24	22	15	18	23	19
D23/D20	4	2	3	1	2	1	1	0	0	3	2	2
D24/D20	5	5	4	2	5	4	2	0	7	3	4	4
D25/D20	1	1	1	1	4	4	5	3	4	2	2	3

Source: Authors' calculations based on data from the Directorate of Local Government

- Tax on street vendors;
- Tax for late closings or early morning openings;
- Tax on drinking establishments;
- Slaughtering fees;
- Fees on markets and retail outlets;
- Contribution of frontage residents to infrastructure and development expenses (following calculation of costs incurred);
- Tax on admission tickets to sporting events and private swimming pools open to the public (with a minimum rate of 15 per cent of the ticket price exclusive of taxes);

- Tax on mineral water and table water (with a minimum rate of MAD0.10 per litre or fractional litre approved for use);
- Tax on construction operations, including the fee on overhangs situated in public spaces (with a maximum rate for each type of construction);
- Tax on parcelling operations (with a maximum rate of 5 per cent of the market value of the land);
- Tax on subdivision operations (with a maximum rate of 5 per cent of the site development cost);
- Fee for temporary occupation of municipal public space for construction purposes (with a maximum rate of MAD40/m^2 per quarter);
- Fee for temporary occupation of municipal public space for commercial, industrial and professional purposes.

NOTES

1   Gross national income per capita according to updated figures.
2   Using a diversified sample of developing countries, Easterly and Serven (2003) confirm the crucial role played by municipal infrastructures in growth.
3   'Budgetary margins for manoeuvre', according to managers of government finances.
4   The goal is to expand the access of the largest number of people to habitat through social habitat programmes.
5   In 2005/2006 the overall primary enrolment rate was 93 per cent (90.5 per cent for girls).
6   For the cities and provincial capitals, the poverty maps are drawn at the intra-municipal (district) level.
7   According to the latest figures.
8   The issue is one of approach to the supply of certain public goods, such as water and electricity (see Comité Directeur, 2006). The desire of all the population to have access to a standard service and the lack of a participatory approach have resulted in uniform and inflexible supplies.
9   For example, in Morocco the adult literacy rate in 2002 was 63 per cent for men and 38 per cent for women. The figures for Algeria were 79 per cent and 60 per cent, and those for Tunisia were 93 per cent and 65 per cent (World Bank, 2005a).
10 Including higher education.
11 ADS has introduced similar innovations. Its role is analysed in the section entitled 'Participation, decentralization and effectiveness of government spending'.
12 In order to facilitate effective management, several provisions setting out exceptions to the traditional rules of accounting have been adopted. It is now possible to use imprest accounts, up to MAD1 million. Likewise, the ceiling on restricted calls for tender has been raised (MAD1 million). The signature of the Inspector of Commitments (with or without comment) has no effect on when a payment is due. Payment must be made within ten days of receipt of the order. Operations are audited jointly by IGF and IGAT); this gives them broad powers to intervene (see the section 'Participation, decentralization and effectiveness of government spending').
13 The amount for 'human development' totalled MAD168 million, two-thirds of which was used to support basic services. The amount for 'precariousness', which came to MAD76 million, was distributed according to the size of the urban population (for example, MAD16 million went to Greater Casablanca). Some 59 per cent of this was used to upgrade reception centres.
14 Given the lack of information concerning gender and the fact that little thought has been given to how best to structure government spending so as to reduce gender bias, it has not been possi-

ble to take effective action in order to reduce discrimination against women.

15   Steps are being taken to introduce 'gender budgeting' into local budgets.

16   The concept of global public taxation (public resources) is chosen in preference to the concept of tax revenues, in the strictest sense, since an indicator based on overall taxes is not subject to any influence from major categories of public revenues, an accounting device that may sometimes affect significant amounts. Thus, in some countries, the change in the system of taxing publicly owned mining companies has led to substitutions between dividend earnings (non-tax revenues) and tax on profits (tax revenues), which has an effect on movements in tax revenues without affecting the overall level of public revenues (public taxation).

17   Prior to the phosphate boom of 1974 to 1975, the tax rate was between 16 per cent and 18 per cent of GDP. After 1974, public revenue settled at above 20 per cent, despite the fact that the contribution to tax revenue from phosphate had declined considerably.

18   The APE partnership agreement with the EU came into force in 2000.

19   In the early 1970s, Morocco experienced a boom in public resources. This led to a grave crisis in government finances due to the development of a Dutch Disease (see Box 7.1). This crisis placed a major constraint on Morocco's fiscal space, which was deprived of the resources allocated to debt servicing, which continued to account for more than 4.5 per cent of GDP from 1983 to 2000.

20   Observed (or effective) taxation, as opposed to levels of taxation, estimated in terms of structural factors (tax potential).

21   This is an assessment relative to the mean of the reference panel (see Box 2.1).

22   Given a similar tax effort, the level of tax distortions is dependent on the characteristics of the actual taxation, which largely determines its economic neutrality. Furthermore, the importance of admissible tax distortions by a particular country depends on the effectiveness of public expenditure. Public spending that is highly useful in social terms can justify significant tax distortions, whereas, conversely, less effective expenditure should imply a lower level of taxation and/or a reduction in tax distortions intended, at unchanged levels, to reduce the social cost of public expenditure.

23   The negative tax effort observed during the 1980s suggested that there was significant space for public resources that was capable of being mobilized.

24   In the most recent period, the tax effort was negative by 0.6 per cent of GDP. Taking into account the methodology used and the margin of uncertainty affecting the estimate of a particular country's tax effort, one may consider that the tax effort is almost non-existent.

25   This vulnerability has, however, been reduced by the policy of domestic financing using long-term financing (see the section 'Evaluation of financing space').

26   It will not be possible to achieve the authorities' goal of reducing the deficit to 3 per cent of GDP by 2009, which had been achieved in 2006 because of strong growth and the positive impact of reform efforts, unless far-reaching reforms are carried out. These include fiscal transition reforms and government spending reforms.

27   These efforts have been pursued in a conventional manner in order to enhance the efficiency of government spending procedures (reformed oversight of spending). They have also been undertaken with the assistance of INDH and ADS.

28   This goal is also mentioned in the report by Comité Directeur (2006).

29   The partnership agreement with the EU was signed in 1996 and came into force in March 2000.

30   The corporation tax applies to all commercial companies, public establishments and other artificial persons. It is currently 35 per cent with a special rate of 39.6 per cent for financial institutions. A minimal assessment of 0.5 per cent of turnover is applicable (this minimal contribution is reduced to 0.25 per cent for sales of petroleum products, gas, butter, oil, sugar, flour, water and electricity). This assessment is chargeable to the corporation tax up to the third year following payment of 61 per cent of the corporation tax revenue from large corporations.

31   Company profits, namely the margin between turnover and expenses is traditionally subject to wide fluctuations. In the event of a drop in turnover, businesspeople may wait a while before

adjusting their expenses (rigidity of expenses) that then results in a sharp drop in profits. The opposite may happen in the event of a rapid and unexpected increase in turnover which sometimes occurs without any significant increase in expenses. In contrast, the consumption basis for VAT is on a much more stable basis. In order to maximize their well-being, consumers try to even out their level of consumption by consuming their savings in periods when available income is on the decline. Conversely, households save more at times when their income is increasing, and this then reduces the relative amount of taxable consumption.

32   In the context of optimizing the resources-spending of total government finances, reducing tax distortions, by lowering the social cost of taxation, can also encourage mobilization of additional public resources.

33   The graduated income tax scale has undergone very little change since 1990. The minimum taxable income has been increased from MAD12,000 to MAD20,000 and the top marginal rate has been lowered from 52 per cent to 44 per cent on incomes of MAD60,000 and over.

34   The cut-off rule, which was included in the initial VAT legislation and, after 1955, in the French legislation, was devised in order to safeguard the state's budget interests. Legislators adopted this conservative measure, which is contrary to VAT's fundamental principle of neutrality, because they feared that the system of reimbursement of VAT credits would not be properly handled. The cut-off rule prevents people who have a net VAT credit from being reimbursed. They have no choice, but to carry over their VAT credits. Sometimes, and this is common in Morocco, a taxpayer's activity is subject to reduced rates whereas the intermediate inputs or consumption are taxed at a higher VAT rate. VAT credits pile up and the taxpayer bears the VAT tax burden indefinitely, which is contrary to the principle of neutrality of VAT vis-à-vis production activities. Instead of being a tax on consumption, VAT thus becomes in part a tax on production.

35   The characteristics of VAT considerably reduce its neutrality. For example, there are four VAT rates (a normal rate of 20 per cent and three reduced rates of 14, 10 and 7 per cent) and a zero rate.

36   Excessive delays, as compared with Morocco's other trading partners, for review of requests for reimbursement.

37   In this connection, it would seem desirable to use the Computable General Equilibrium (CGE) Model, which is tailored to evaluating the impact of reducing the tariffs on cereals. The advantage of this approach is that it is possible to identify several categories of household, whereas other approaches are based on a representative household. Available means of evaluation have made it possible to assess the impact on poor people in rural and in urban areas according to which cereal tariff reduction region they belong to.

38   This condition is not met automatically (Emran and Stiglitz, 2005); it depends, in particular, on the VAT legislation and the conditions under which VAT is applied.

39   Elimination of the cut-off rule would imply a prior decrease in the number of VAT rates – if possible, convergence towards a single VAT rate – to avoid the creation of massive new VAT credits. One problem with eliminating the cut-off rule has to do with the large amount of VAT credits involved (this amount has not been accurately assessed to date).

40   As a rule, it is not possible to carry over VAT credits on exempt products. However, the Moroccan Tax Code atypically provides for a zero-rate taxation and hence the possibility of carrying over VAT credits for certain goods or services, particularly for intermediate agricultural inputs. This mitigating provision, adopted to safeguard agricultural competitiveness, contributes to the complexity and opaqueness of the Moroccan VAT.

41   Some 72 per cent of the countries that introduced the VAT in the past ten years opted for a single rate. The single rate considerably simplifies the management and oversight of VAT and is conducive to its effective application.

42   The report, entitled *Tax Expenditure*, is annexed to the 2006 and 2007 Finances Act. Tax expenditures for 92 of a total of 327 tax exemption measures are assessed. These tax expenditures for 92 measures are assessed at around MAD15 billion, or 16 per cent of tax revenue, which corre-

sponds to 3.4 per cent of GDP. 60 of the 92 measures involve VAT and account for 60 per cent of the assessed tax expenditure. The housing construction sector is the primary beneficiary of the exemption measures. In 2004, it received 25 per cent of tax expenditure. In general, the exemption measures chosen for assessment are those on which tax expenditure is probably highest. Measures were also chosen on the basis of the available data and instruments for assessment. This report on tax expenditure had a resounding impact and is a key instrument for reform of government finances.

43   The adoption of a single identifier by all revenue administrations (particularly the tax and customs administrations) is the prerequisite for an automatic exchange of data in real time between these administrations. In this way it is possible to ensure that all importers known to the customs authorities are also known to the tax authorities. Such exchanges are particularly necessary for data cross-checks, which are essential to tax audits, especially VAT audits. VAT is collected mainly by the customs administration (VAT on imports collected at customs control). Most of the amounts collected by customs are subject to a deduction on VAT declarations filed with the revenue administrations. The cross-checking of data between the two administrations is, therefore, particularly useful for auditing taxpayer declarations effectively (that is, in ensuring in particular that taxpayers do not deduct fictitious VAT credits).

44   Nevertheless, the extremely heavy cost of some crises makes it possible to cement an agreement on stabilization measures that would never be possible in the case of lower costs (Drazen and Grilli, 1993).

45   This involves emphasizing a gradual approach that makes the reform more politically acceptable (Dewatripont and Roland, 1995).

46   Figure 7.5, which traces the evolution of the real effective exchange rate, indicates that the rate has depreciated somewhat in recent years. The devaluation hypothesis thus appears implausible.

47   Seignorage (SG) is calculated as the ratio of variation in the central currency (MC), or monetary base, to the previous year's GDP: $SG = (MC_t - MC_{t-1})/GDP_{t-1}$. The rate of inflation (TI) corresponds to the per cent loss in real value of the central currency supply, which is expressed as a share of GDP: $TI = [\pi_t/(1 + \pi_t)] \times [MC_{t-1}/GDP_{t-1}]$, where π is the rate of inflation.

48   See Annex 7.1 (page 237) for the list of taxes for which local governments are responsible. It will be noted that these taxes involve a high degree of technical complexity and require expertise that is not always available in local governments.

49   Section 'Participation, decentralization and effectiveness of government spending', on the financing resources of local governments, shows how the delegation of responsibility could also be extended to borrowing strategies.

50   The urban tax represents 13 per cent of the rateable value of properties; when this is combined with the business licence tax, the cost to operators is high.

51   Established in 1959, this agency was first conceived as a 'specialized financial agency', a division within the CDG. Following an initial reform in 1992, it became autonomous, with dual supervision by the Ministry of the Interior and the Ministry of Finance and a mandate to finance infrastructure only for local governments. In 1996 it acquired the status of a bank to guarantee permanent access by local governments to infrastructure financing resources. Subject since then to the rules of the Banking Act, the fund has generated resources to increase its own funds. It also has access to financial markets.

52   The unclassified sector absorbed only 4 per cent during the period 1996 to 2000.

53   The process began in the 1980s with urban transport; poor management by the transport authorities had made it a financial black hole. Currently, many municipalities have granted licences for the operation of part or all of the urban transport lines and systems by private companies.

54   It is important to point out that these contributions can be equated with taxes, except that the purpose is specified, as it corresponds to a specific project. This encourages support from the population, as people receive direct benefits from their contributions. Such procedures can be an effective means of educating the population (whose illiteracy rate is over 45 per cent) about

the fiscal effort, in that they have a better understanding of how the money paid to the tax agencies helps to finance public goods.

55   For example, a saffron-growing project with the southern development agency, a small-scale fishing project with the northern development agency and a project to protect routes and promote livestock breeding with the eastern development agency.

56   There is the example of a sponsoring physician who wanted to build a boarding school in a rural area, and another project to promote income-generating activities by establishing a dairy cooperative. While the amounts at stake are modest (MAD500,000 and MAD200,000), this is an interesting experiment, as it shows that a credible agency can also mobilize funds from the public. It should also be noted that sums arising from the 'zakat' could transit through ADS.

57   For example, Klynveld Peat Marwick Goerdeler, Masnaoui-Mazard.

58   A royal letter to the prime minister was necessary to mitigate these practices, which tend to discourage investors. In order to compel the administrations to observe a time limit of two months for responding to requests from citizens, it was announced that after that period, stakeholders could assume that they had implicit authorization to proceed. In many other cases, however, there is no time limit for responding or taking action.

59   It is known that 'involving the population is not enough', as community elites may subvert the goals (F. Bourguignon, GDN, January 2006). The elites 'screen out' the population from which they emerge, steering actions in their own interests; the risk is particularly great in that the target populations are illiterate. Yet promoters often appeal to these elites as spokespersons, knowing that the populations will fall into line more easily that way.

60   In fact the grants are never intended for ADS, they are awarded in the context of partnerships for well-defined projects. This project financing approach has also been introduced into the Directorate of the Budget (which manages the general budget in the framework of the Budget Act). As the point is to ensure, to the extent possible, a return-seeking approach to government spending, this directorate has introduced the concept of a programme contract into its selection criteria. In the same way, INDH has adopted the project description approach for its financing.

61   The relevant data are to be found not in the Ministry of Finance, Directorate of the Budget, but in the Treasury of the Kingdom.

62   See details in the section entitled 'Medium-term fiscal and budgetary policy: Towards a more efficient and rational approach'.

63   A study of the weight of VAT against household income shows a certain bias, given that income includes savings, whose growth increases as income does.

REFERENCES

Acemoglu, D., Johnson S. and Robinson J. A. (2005) 'Institutions as the fundamental cause of long-run growth', in P. Aghion and S. Durlauf (eds) *Handbook of Economic Growth*, North Holland, Amsterdam, pp386–472

Alesina, A. and Drazen, A. (1991) 'Why are stabilizations delayed?', *American Economic Review*, vol 81, December, pp1170–88

Bank al Maghrib (2004) 'Annual report, presented to H.M. The King', Bank al Maghrib, Rabat

Bank al Maghrib (various dates) 'Quarterly report', Bank al Maghrib, Rabat

Brun, J-F., Chambas, G., Combes, J-L., Dulbecco, P., Gastambide, A., Guérineau, S., Guillaumont, S. and Rota Graziosi, G. (2006) 'Evaluation de l'espace budgétaire des pays en développement', Concept Paper, CERDI and UNDP, Clermont-Ferrand and New York

Burn, N., Fazouane, A. and Lamrani, N. (2006) *Estimation des coûts de mise en œuvre des objectifs du Millénaire pour le développement 'gendérisés' au Maroc*, MFP-UNIFEM

CGEM (Confédération Générale des Entreprises du Maroc) (2005) Commission Entreprise et Proximité Sociale, Le Réseau des associations de quartier de Casablanca (RESAQ); Réseau Al

Amal d'Al Hoceima; Deuxième forum Entreprises Associations 'Catalogue of projects, 2005', CGEM, Palmier-Casablanca

Chambas, G. (ed) (2005) *Afrique au Sud du Sahara. Mobiliser des ressources fiscales pour le développement*, Economica, Paris

Cherkaoui, M. (2001) *Institutional Reform and Efficiency of the Budget Process: A Case Study of Morocco.* Université Mohammed V, Rabat, Morocco

Comité Directeur (2006) '50 ans de développement humain et perspectives 2025. L'avenir se construit et le meilleur est possible', Discussion Paper and Report, www.rdh50.ma, accessed 30 January 2008

Dahri, M. (2005) *Le financement du développement local au Maroc. Comment améliorer le rôle des collectivités territoriales?* Centre d'Etudes Financières, Economiques et Bancaires, Marseille

Dewatripoint, M. and Roland, G. (1995) 'The design of reform packages under uncertainty', *American Economic Review*, vol 85, December, pp1207–1223

Drazen, A. (1996) 'The political economy of delayed reform', *Policy Reform*, vol 1, pp25–46

Drazen, A. and Grilli, V. (1993) 'The benefit of crises for economic reforms?', *American Economic Review*, vol 83, June, pp598–607

Easterly, W. and Serven, L. (eds). (2003) *The Limits of Stabilization: Infrastructure, Public Deficits, and Growth in Latin America*, Stanford University Press and World Bank, Palo Alto, CA and Washington DC

Emran, M. S. and Stiglitz, J. E. (2005) 'On selective indirect tax reform in developing countries', *Journal of Public Economics*, vol 89, no 4, pp599–623

Fernandez, R. and Rodrik, D. (1991) 'Resistance to reform: status quo bias in the presence of individual-specific uncertainty', *American Economic Review*, vol 81, no 5, pp1146–55

Frey, B. S. (1997) 'Do people care about democracy, comment', *Public Choice*, vol 91, no 1, April, pp53–55

GRET (Groupe de recherche de recherche et d'échanges technologiques) (2005) 'Analyse du rôle de l'ADS', GRET, Nogent-sur-Marne

Haut Commissariat au Plan (2004) 'Recensement général de la population et de l'habitat', Haut commissariat au plan, Rabat

Haut Commissariat au Plan (2005a) 'Objectifs du Millénaire pour le développement', National Report, Haut commissariat au plan, Rabat

Haut Commissariat au Plan (2005b) 'Pauvreté, développement humain et développement social au Maroc' (cartographic and statistical data), Haut Commissariat au Plan, Rabat

International Monetary Fund (2005) 'Morocco: report on observance of standards and codes - fiscal transparency module', Country Report no 05/298, IMF, Washington, DC

Kingdom of Morocco (2006) 'Bulletin officiel 2 mars 2006 No. 5400', Statut de la Bank el Maghrib, Rabat

Kubota, K. (2005) 'Fiscal constraints, collection costs and trade policies', World Bank Policy Research Working Paper 2366, World Bank, Washington, DC

Laban, R. and Sturzenegger, F. (1994) 'Distributional conflicts, financial adaptation and delayed stabilisation', *Economics and Politics*, vol 6, pp257–276

Ministry of Finance and Privatization (2005a) Direction du budget et UNIFEM. Guide de la réforme budgétaire. La nouvelle approche budgétaire axée sur les résultats et intégrant la dimension genre', Ministry of Finance and Privatization, Rabat, CD-ROM

Ministry of Finance and Privatization (2005b) Rapport sur la dépense fiscale annexé à la Loi de Finances 2006, Ministry of Finance and Privatization, Rabat

Romer, P. (1986) 'Increasing returns and long growth', *Journal of Political Economics*, vol 94, no 5, October, pp1002–1037

SCET-URBA Systems (2003) 'Étude sur le financement des collectivités territoriales marocaines et la réforme de la fiscalité locale, synthèse stratégique', document prepared for the World Bank, SCET-URBA Systems

Stosky, J. G. and Wolde Mariam, A. (1997), 'Tax effort in sub-Saharan Africa', IMF Working Paper, 97/107, IMF, Washington DC

UNDP Morocco office (2006) 'Rapport sur le développement humain: femmes et dynamique du développement', UNDP, Rabat

World Bank (2005a) 'La performance macroéconomique et sectorielle des politiques du logement dans les pays de la région MENA: une étude comparative' World Bank, Washington, DC

World Bank (2005b) 'Projet d'appui à l'Agence de développement social (ADS)', Follow-up mission aide-mémoire, 5–9 September, World Bank, Rabat

8

Securing Fiscal Space for the Millennium Development Goals in Senegal

Adama Diaw, Samuel Guérineau and Sylviane Guillaumont Jeanneney

INTRODUCTION

The MDGs are directed at achieving a significant reduction in poverty in developing countries by the year 2015. It is now useful to review the achievements to date, and the means used to achieve them, in order to determine what additional resources will need to be mobilized in order to reach the goals by 2015.

The purpose of this chapter is to determine whether it is possible for Senegal to increase its domestic fiscal space. In other words, is it possible for the government to mobilize additional domestic resources, that is, its own resources, borrowed or reallocated, to finance the attainment of the MDGs? The response to this question must, therefore, be based on a specific diagnosis of Senegal that takes into account both the progress to be made between now and 2015 and the financing constraints associated with the country's economic situation.

A review of the core indicators associated with the MDGs clearly shows that Senegal's starting point was more favourable than that of other sub-Saharan African countries in 2000/2001.[1] The proportion of the population living on less than $1 a day is 26 per cent in Senegal and, on average, 46 per cent in other sub-Saharan African countries. Similarly, the infant/juvenile mortality rate (145 deaths of children under 5 years per 1000 live births compared with 174) and the proportion of underweight children under the age of 3 years (19 per cent compared with 33 per cent) are lower in

Senegal when compared to other sub-Saharan African countries. Access to potable water (67 per cent compared with 58 per cent) and the crude primary school enrolment rate (71 per cent compared with 62 per cent) are also higher in Senegal. Although Senegal faces significant challenges to achieve the MDGs, the objectives are nevertheless more attainable there than in most sub-Saharan countries.

From the point of view of financing, the situation in Senegal is marked by a number of contradictory elements. On the one hand, good macroeconomic performance and liquidity in the banking system seem to offer good prospects for an increase in domestic resources, while on the other, the recent increase in tax levels and the scale of external aid raise questions about the prospects and need for this additional mobilization of domestic resources. Moreover, the rapid increase in resources allocated to the attainment of the MDGs in Senegal during the last five years, particularly by the state itself, raises questions about its capacity to effectively utilize these additional resources.

This chapter is divided into three sections that seek to respond, successively, to three questions.

- Is it useful to expand domestic resource mobilization in Senegal?
- What domestic resources can be mobilized to accelerate the attainment of the MDGs?
- What are the risks associated with expediting this effort?

Is EXPANSION OF THE FISCAL SPACE NECESSARY IN ORDER TO FINANCE THE MDGs?

In order to determine whether it is necessary to mobilize additional domestic resources, we first undertake a review of the status of the implementation of the MDGs in Senegal and then identify the various stakeholders involved in this effort. Lastly, we discuss the value of mobilizing domestic resources for a country that benefits from a significant level of official development aid.

Progress towards attainment of the MDGs

The MDG initiative identified eight goals that are broken down into targets (see Annex 8.1, page 300), which, in turn, are associated with one or several indicators. The most significant indicators are the final outcomes, such as the incidence of poverty, the literacy rate, infant and juvenile mortality rates and the maternal mortality rate (children and pregnant women constituting vulnerable populations). These indicators are associated with others that are closer to the tools used, such as school enrolment rates, vaccination rates, or the proportion of births attended by medical personnel. It is striking to note that, in Senegal, it is not possible to monitor progress towards the achievement of the MDGs on the basis of final outcome indicators, as these are not available for recent

Table 8.1 *Main strategic approaches of the Senegal Poverty Reduction Strategy Papers (PRSPs)*

PRSP 1 (2001–2005)	PRSP 2 (2006–2010)
Line 1: Wealth creation	Line 1: Wealth creation – growth targeted at the poor
Line 2: Capacity building and improvement of basic social services	Line 2: Easier access to basic social services
Line 3: Improved living conditions for vulnerable groups	Line 3: Social protection, risk and disaster prevention and management
	Line 4: Good governance and decentralized and participatory development

dates. It would, therefore, be useful to increase the frequency of those surveys that can provide data for the calculation of these final indicators (Senegalese Household Surveys (ESAM) for poverty and Demographic and Health Surveys (DHS) for health), rather than compiling a series of intermediate indicators.

Achievement of the MDGs must be pursued both by stimulation of growth and by improved access to social services. This dual concern is at the core of Senegal's PRSP 1 and PRSP 2, since wealth creation is their first strategic approach (see Table 8.1), while approaches two and three are concerned with social policies.[2]

Growth and poverty

The first MDG is the reduction of poverty, and specifically the eradication of extreme poverty. The scope and severity of poverty are, however, difficult to measure using the standard statistical systems of states and must generally be measured through targeted surveys.

In the case of Senegal, there are two poverty surveys dating from 1994/1995 and 2001/2002. The poverty threshold was fixed at 2400 calories per adult equivalent per day, and the proportion of the poor in the population – the incidence of poverty – was estimated at 67.9 per cent in 1994/1995 and at 57.1 per cent in 2001/2002. The incidence of poverty in rural areas (65.2 per cent) is significantly higher than that in urban areas (50.1 per cent), particularly in Dakar (42.0 per cent). More recent data are not available. Estimates of the current incidence of poverty are calculated using a ratio of poverty elasticity to per capita GDP of 0.9, which gives a rate of 54 per cent for 2004 and 52.7 per cent in 2005 (for average increases in GDP and in population growth of 5.3 per cent and 2.5 per cent).[3]

Even though measuring poverty reduction on the basis of its elasticity to growth is imperfectm, developing countries' experience clearly shows that sustained growth is a necessary condition for the sustainable reduction of poverty. It also appears that macroeconomic stability is a factor that is conducive to poverty reduction. In particular, the maintenance of a moderate level of inflation is important, insofar as it is the poor who suffer the most from high inflation, since their incomes are not protected against the reduction in value caused by inflation.

Table 8.2 *Macroeconomic indicators of Senegal, 2000–2006*

	2000	2001	2002	2003	2004	2005	2006
Nominal GDP (current prices in billions of CFAfr)		3343.00	3473.00	3725.00	4243.00	4582.00	4846.00
Rate of increase in real GDP (%)	4.30	4.70	1.10	6.50	5.9	5.6	2.30
Rate of increase in consumer price index (inflation) (%)		3.00	2.30	0.00	0.50	1.70	2.10
Tax receipts (% GDP)	16.10	17.30	18.10	18.20	18.30	19.20	19.90
Current expenditure (% GDP)		15.5	13.8	13.3	13.3	13.8	17.10
Total non-grant budget balance, (% GDP)		−4.4	−1.8	−3.3	−5.2	−4.6	−7.3
Gross domestic investment (% GDP)		19.2	16.7	20.7	26.0	29.5	28.7
Goods and services imports (billions of CFAfr)	951.6	1047.1	117.9	1200.5	1318	1524	1661
Goods and services exports (billions of CFAfr)	654.9	735.3	743.4	730.6	797.4	832	833
Real effective exchange rate IMF (base 100=1995)	85.2	86.7	89.0	91.6	92.1	90.9	90.7

Source: Ministry of Economy and Finance (2005d); IMF (2005a, 2006b, 2007, 2008)

From this perspective, Senegal's macroeconomic performance since 2000 can be considered to be good (see Table 8.2). The annual growth in real GDP was, on average, 4.8 per cent between 2000 and 2006 (with only one year, 2002, of low growth) and was even greater than 5.5 per cent in 2003, 2004 and 2005. This sustained growth relied not only on the strong performance of the construction sector (in particular, in the Dakar metropolitan area), but also on the new technologies introduced and the agro-food industries that helped to diversify production. Senegal experienced a slight reduction in 2006 (to about a 2.3 per cent annual growth rate), mainly as a result of the increase in oil prices, which also builds inflationary pressures. Average annual inflation was 2.1 per cent in 2006 (IMF, 2008).

Despite this good overall performance, two problems arise. First, while growth has been rapid, the rate has not been fast enough to achieve the MDGs. The second PRSP (March 2006) set a growth target of 7 to 8 per cent of real GDP, which would enable a per capita increase in GDP of 5 per cent to be achieved, sufficient to significantly reduce poverty. In order to achieve this target, a strategy for accelerated growth has been launched.

Second, there is a problem with the quality of growth in Senegal. At an identical rate, growth could make a greater contribution to the reduction of poverty and, more generally, contribute more effectively to the achievement of sustainable development. Current growth relies too heavily on housing construction and consumption made possible by the increase in remittances from migrant workers and is, no doubt, too heavily concentrated in the urban sector. If it was more broadly derived from productive investments, especially in agriculture or in infrastructure, the growth would have a more sustainable impact on poverty. From this perspective, the second PRSP (2006–2010) identifies a number of conditions that must be met in order to achieve a 'qualitative' improvement in growth: 'an increase in public and private investments... better targeting of investment, improved quality of investments and a greater contribution by the agricultural sector to growth based, in particular, on product diversification and plant modernization' (Ministry of Economy and Finance, 2006e, p27). Few figures are available on infrastructure development. The percentage of villages with access to paved roads (bitumen or laterite) was only 47 per cent in 2000 and no figures are available for the period since then. The rate of electrification of rural households has remained low, increasing from 8 per cent in 2000 to 12 per cent in 2003.

The benefit to be derived from expanding the domestic fiscal space becomes evident when one looks at the rate of investment in Senegal (see Table 8.3). The rate of public investment in 2005 was 9.8 per cent and the rate of private investment was 13.6 per cent, which corresponds to an overall rate of 23.4 per cent. This rate is within the average range for low-income countries and above average for Africa, but is well below the average rate for the countries of East Asia and the Pacific, where it is more than 30 per cent. Even if this rate has been growing over the past several years, a further increase still seems necessary both to increase the rate of growth and to improve the capacity of this growth to reduce extreme poverty and, generally speaking, to achieve the MDGs. From this perspective, the PRSP plans a gradual increase in the rate of overall investment, which should rise to 25 per cent in 2010. This increase in the rate of investment risks widening the gap between domestic investments and domestic savings,

Table 8.3 *Savings–investment balance, 2003–2006*

(Percentage of GDP)	2003	2004	2005	2006
Gross domestic investment	25.9	26.0	29.5	28.7
Government investment	8.5	9.7	9.9	9.8
Non-governmental investment	17.4	16.3	19.6	18.9
Gross domestic savings	13.8	13.4	14.1	11.2
Government savings	8.3	8.4	7.9	3.5
Private savings	5.5	5.0	6.2	7.7
Savings–investment balance	−12.1	−12.6	−15.4	−17.5
Public	−0.2	−1.3	−2.0	−6.3
Private	−11.9	−11.3	−13.4	−11.2

Source: IMF (2006b, 2007, 2008)

which has been growing in recent years. This is why it is important to examine how the expansion of the fiscal space can be accompanied by an increase in the savings rate.

Basic social services and poverty

It is evident that poverty reduction cannot be achieved through growth alone. It also requires targeted policies aimed at improving basic social services. It is, therefore, useful to evaluate the progress achieved in the sectors of education (MDGs 2 and 3), health (MDGs 4 5, and 6) and water (MDG 7), based on the MDG indicators incorporated into Senegal's PRSPs (slightly amended at times). The latest progress report on the strategy for reducing poverty by the IMF (2006a), measures the progress achieved in the period from 2000 to 2004. Table 8.4 contains a list of selected indicators.

Education

The average rate of primary school attendance has increased sharply since 2000, climbing from 68.3 per cent to 79.9 per cent in 2004. The primary school enrolment rate was 91.1 per cent in 2004 (compared with 81.7 per cent in 2000). In 2004, the enrolment rate for girls was 93.9 per cent (compared with 78.9 per cent in 2000), while it was only 90.4 per cent for boys (compared with 84.6 per cent in 2000). This has brought the school attendance rate for girls, which was 77.3 per cent in 2004 (compared with 63 per cent in

Table 8.4 *Selected indicators associated with the MDGs (%)*

Sector	Indicators		2000	2004	2010	2015
Education	Crude primary	National	68.3	79.9	98.0	100
	education rate	Girls	63	77.3	>90	>98
		Boys	73.5	82.40	>95	100
	Primary education	National	81.7	91.1	100	100
	enrolment rate	Girls	78.9	93.	100	100
		Boys	84.6	90.4	100	100
	Primary education completion rate	National	n.a.	48.7	85.0	100
Health	Rate of DTP 3 vaccination of children under the age of 1 year	National	41	75	80	80
	Underweight children under the age of 3 years	National	21	19	13	11
	Births attended by medical personnel	National	38	59	70	75
Water and sanitation	Rate of access to safe drinking water	Urban	78	83	87	89
		Rural	56	58	70	78
	Urban population served by a sanitation system		56	60	70	78
Infrastructure	Dirt road network classified as 'average' or 'good'		n.a.	25	60	>75

Source: Ministry of Economy and Finance (2006e) and Ministry of Planning and Sustainable Development (2004)

2000) closer to the rate for boys (82.5 per cent compared with 73.5 per cent in 2000). If the trend towards higher school enrolment rates continues, the goal of universal education for all will be achieved by 2010.

However, a full six-year primary school cycle seems to be the minimum needed to ensure irreversible literacy and the rate of completion of the primary cycle remains low (calculated at 48 per cent in 2004 and estimated at 54 per cent in 2005). It is therefore necessary to focus not only on access to education, but also on improving its quality.

Health

The infant and juvenile mortality rate increased slightly between 1992 (140 per thousand) and 2000 (145 per thousand) (*Demographic and Health Survey*, Ministry of Economy and Finance, 2006e, drawn from Demographic and Health Survey (DHS III)), but indicators for the years since then are not available. Therefore it is necessary to rely on output indicators that are more accurate than budget allocations to approximate final outcomes – improvements in health. It should thus be noted that the proportion of underweight children below the age of three years has declined only slightly, from 21 per cent to 19 per cent between 2000 and 2004. It is still far from the goal for 2015, which is 11 per cent. In contrast, the DTP 3 vaccination rate for children under the age of one year rose rapidly from 41 per cent to 75 per cent between 2000 and 2004, so that the goal of 80 per cent should have been met by 2006. Lastly, the proportion of births attended by medical personnel rose from 38 per cent to 59 per cent, while the goal for 2015 is 75 per cent. It should be recalled that the rate of prevalence of the HIV/AIDS virus remains low (1.4 per cent), even though a slight increase has been recorded since 2000. It is currently lower than the MDG target of less than 3 per cent. This low incidence of the virus is, no doubt, partly due to the result of a long-standing policy of providing information to the population about the dangers of the epidemic.

Water and sanitation

During the period from 2000 to 2004, the rate of access to potable water rose from 78 per cent to 83 per cent in urban areas and from 56 per cent to 58 per cent in rural areas, while the respective targets are 89 per cent and 78 per cent. During the same period, the proportion of the urban population with access to a sewage system rose from 56 per cent to 60 per cent, with a 78 per cent target for 2015. The relatively limited progress in this sector shows that a considerable effort will be needed to achieve the targets for 2015. It should be noted that these average figures mask significant disparities between Dakar and other cities and between the central areas of cities and the outskirts. Moreover, the price of water at supply points, which affects the poorest sectors of the population, is sometimes higher than the rate charged for those sectors that have access to piped water.

Despite the progress achieved since 2000, the targets set by the MDGs are far from having been achieved at the current time. Further, it should be noted that the results are generally more modest on the indicators of outcomes than on the indicators of means, which means that considerable efforts must be made to achieve the 2015 goals for the first indicators, which are the most relevant ones. Moreover, the level and quality of growth must be improved in order for these goals to be accessible.

Stakeholders in the achievement of the MDGs

Diversity of stakeholders involved in the achievement of the MDGs

The achievement of the MDGs is dependent on the participation of several categories of stakeholders: (1) the national government, (2) the local governments, (3) development partners (donors), and (4) the private sector.

The national government is naturally the lead actor in the strategy for reducing poverty, both in terms of promoting growth (Strategic Approach 1 of the PRSP) and in the provision of social services (Strategic Approaches 2 and 3 of the PRSP). The Government can stimulate growth through public investment and by favouring private investment (subsidies, fiscal policy and legal frameworks). With regard to the production of social services, wages account for a large part of the expenditures, of which the state bears most of the cost. Moreover, in the education and health sectors, public investment decisions are prepared through national action plans, the ten-year Education and Training Programme (PDEF) and the National Health Improvement Plan (PNDS). Despite the national government's pivotal role, the other actors are closely involved in the achievement of the MDGs. The PRSP places emphasis on this aspect through the principle of 'making each person do his/her job'.

In particular, local governments have seen their role in the achievement of the MDGs expand as part of the trend towards decentralization and devolution that began in Senegal over ten years ago. This trend, moreover, was more marked in the sectors directly involved in the production of social services, in accordance with the principle of proximity established in the PRSP. According to this principle, 'the centres where decisions are taken concerning the implementation of measures in keeping with the Poverty Reduction Strategy must be as close as possible to the beneficiaries and their place of residence in order to ensure better targeting of action' (Ministry of Economy and Finance, 2006e, p51). The expanding role of local governments justifies a more detailed study of this issue in the section entitled 'Tax revenues of local governments' below.

Naturally, the donors, who are at the origin of the MDGs, are also actors in achieving the goals. On the one hand, they provide technical support to Senegal for the elaboration of its poverty reduction strategy, in particular the UNDP, which participated in the review of the PRSP in 2005, and which, generally speaking, contributes to the coordination of the various development programmes (MDGs, PRSPs, the Strategy for Accelerated Growth (SCA), New Partnership for Africa's Development (NEPAD) and the Common Country Assessment-United Nations Development Assistance Framework (CCA-UNDAF)). On the other hand, donors also finance a part of the cost of implementing this strategy. They do so by funding the social sectors (health and education infrastructure and programmes to combat epidemics)[4] and also by funding infrastructure and productive projects (either directly or through microfinance institutions) that contribute to growth.

Donors have played a very important role in the process of decentralization. The World Bank, for example, has funded two very important programmes, the Municipality Support Programme (PAC), launched in 1997, which was also assisted by the AFD, and the National Rural Infrastructure Programme (PNIR), launched in 2000. The aim of PAC was twofold: to strengthen urban municipalities[5] though better mobilization of their resources and their management, and to increase the supply of urban infrastructure and services. It was implemented by measures aimed at institutional development and capacity building and by investments identified in a participatory process. These two functions were entrusted to a new agency, the Municipal Development Agency (ADM). The PNIR seeks, at the same time, to build capacity in rural communities by providing both institutional support and by financing local infrastructure (construction and equipment of classrooms, health centres, rural maternity clinics and health outposts, and by building latrines, drilling equipment, drinking water supplies, and building or rehabilitating rural roads). There again, the participatory approach is at the heart of the programme. Lastly, while PAC was targeted at all urban municipalities, PNIR was concerned only with some rural communities (69 at the outset). UNDP-UNCDF is also involved in the promotion of local development, notably through the Local Development Fund (FDL), which has helped to develop the capacities of local governments by training locally elected officials and community leaders and financed basic infrastructure.

Contributions by the private sector (broadly speaking, households, civil society and businesses) to providing access to basic services take a number of different forms. For households, this contribution takes the form of a financial contribution for the use of certain social services and the consumption of water, energy or medicines, but also, at times, as a contribution to the construction of local infrastructure. This funding of local infrastructure often benefits from remittances from immigrant workers, which are quite substantial in Senegal and have been on the increase in recent years. A number of large companies themselves bear the cost of the production of social services in the area where they are located, mainly through neighbourhood health clinics, or share in the cost of investments in these social services. Lastly, through its credit activities, the banking sector participates in the provision of social services by financing private clinics or private schools (from primary to high school) and by financing the studies of pupils, mainly through study savings plans.

The key role of local governments

Senegal has long experience with administrative and territorial decentralization. At the time of its independence, Senegal had 34 municipalities concentrated in urban areas. Later, a number of reforms were introduced to strengthen the power of local governments. In 1960, all municipalities were granted the status of full-fledged local government.[6] In 1972, the establishment of rural municipalities extended decentralization to rural areas,[7] and in 1990, an additional step was taken with the transfer of responsibility for the management of the budget to local governments, granting them authority over expenditures.[8]

The reform of 1996 marked a major step forward in the decentralization process.[9] First, it transformed the region into a local government, but above all it transferred to the three types of local governments (regions, municipalities and rural municipalities) nine areas for which they would thenceforth be responsible. These were environment and the management of natural resources, health, population and social action, youth, sport and recreation, culture, education, land use planning and management, and town planning and housing. Currently in Senegal there are some 441 local governments, 11 regions, 110 municipalities (urban) and 320 rural municipalities with overall responsibility for designing, planning and implementing economic, educational, social and cultural programmes at the regional, municipal or rural levels.[10]

Local governments operate according to three principles: (1) they are independently managed by elected bodies; (2) the transfer of the nine areas of responsibility to them is to be accompanied by a transfer of funds (the Decentralization Allocation Fund (FDD) was created for this purpose); and (3) responsibilities must be exercised at a level closest to citizens, given that actions are much more effective when carried out on the basis of partnerships and formal contracts (the principle of subsidiarity). At the same time, the regional development agencies (ARD) and local development support centres (CADL)[11] were designed to provide assistance to local governments in all areas concerned with local development.

The transfer of responsibilities has increased the responsibility of the local governments in respect of access to social services by the population. Health and education, along with the justice system and the environment, are four of the areas of responsibility transferred. These are areas for which the central state provides a financial contribution corresponding to the responsibility that has been transferred. Insofar as the national government is still responsible for paying the salaries of teachers and for most investments (according to the education and health maps), the expenses borne by the local governments have, so far, been limited to operating expenses, the purchase of medicines, payment of water and electricity bills of health centres and schools, and rehabilitation of classrooms. Because of the heavy involvement of the central state in the education and health sectors, local governments have concentrated their investments in the water supply sector, 44 per cent of local public investments, as opposed to only 20 per cent for health and 10 per cent for education and in business infrastructure. It should be noted, however, that the biggest cities, in particular Dakar, have their own health personnel. A decision has just been taken to expand the role of local governments through the gradual decentralization of certain expenses under the Consolidated Investment Budget (BCI). Starting in 2006, this primarily concerns expenditures for investments in primary education.

Why mobilize additional domestic resources?

Having described the modalities of financing the MDGs thus far, we now look at the best way in the future of financing the achievement of these goals.

How have the MDGs been financed in Senegal since 2000?

The financing of the MDGs, both in terms of growth promotion and increased access to social services, has been based both on an increase in the State's domestic resources and on an increase in external aid. Unfortunately, the most recent review of the first phase of the PRSP is not yet available. According to the second progress report on PRSP I (2001–2004) (Ministry of Economy and Finance, 2005d, p19), the resources mobilized to finance investments related to the poverty reduction strategy were estimated in 2004 at CFAfr236 billion, of which 39 per cent were domestic resources. These resources represent 58 per cent of capital expenditures in the Tableau des Opérations Financières de l'Etat (TOFE), the 'table of government's financial operations'. They underestimate the public effort to implement the MDGs for two reasons. First, certain current expenditures contribute to the achievement of the MDGs and, second, it is difficult to isolate the investments that contribute to the achievement of the MDGs.

This is why it is useful to globally consider the trend in government resource allocation and in foreign assistance with reference to TOFE and the balance of payments (see Table 8.5, overleaf, and Annex 8.2, page 301). During the first phase of the PRSP, between 2001 and 2005, total government revenues rose by 45.8 per cent while the amount of foreign aid channelled through the budget doubled (+101.6 per cent). It should be noted that the increase was due mainly to loans, which tripled in value. A review of the balance of payments data shows an estimated increase in official development assistance of 51.5 per cent, but a certain inconsistency is also noted between TOFE and the balance of payments, since the level of foreign aid under the latter heading should be higher than the level indicated in TOFE.[12]

This increase in financing has led to a more rapid rise in public expenditures (7 per cent per annum) than in GDP, with a trend in expenditures that is favourable to the realization of the MDGs. Thus, a relatively greater share of expenditures has been allocated to basic services, health, education and access to safe water, and capital expenditures have increased at a faster pace than current expenditures. The budgetary effort in the field of education has been the most remarkable: 40 per cent of operating expenses in the 2005 budget were allocated to education (including HIPC expenditures), 46 per cent of which was allocated to primary education. The effort in the health sector has also been significant, with a share of 8.25 per cent of the operating budget. It should also be noted, that current expenditures increased more slowly than tax revenues and the Senegalese government was, therefore, able to devote a larger share of its income to investments. Domestic financing allocated to capital formation thus

Table 8.5 *Changes in financing during the first phase of the PRSP*

| | Billions of CFAfr | | % of GDP | | Variation |
	2001	2005	2001	2005	2001–2005
					%
Government revenues (TOFE)	602.7	879	18.0	19.3	45.8
Foreign loans and grants (TOFE)	116.6	235.1	3.5	5.2	101.6
External financing (loans)	54.9	168.5	1.6	3.7	206.9
Grants	61.7	66.6	1.8	1.5	7.9
Capital expenditures (TOFE)	232.3	425.6	6.9	9.3	83.2
from domestic financing	118.5	198.8	3.5	4.4	67.8
from external financing					
(including HIPC)	113.8	226.8	3.4	5.0	99.3
Total public assistance (BP)	131.5	199.3	3.9	4.4	51.5
Total private assistance and					
migrant remittances (BP)	172.8	345.1	5.2	7.6	99.7

Source: Authors' calculations based on TOFE and balance of payments (BP) data (cf Annex 8.2)

increased by 67 per cent. It can therefore be seen that as a percentage of GDP, government revenues and public external funding, in the form of loans and private transfers, increased between 2001 and 2005. Only the grant portion declined.

It would also be useful to measure the contribution of private financing to the achievement of the MDGs. The amount of the private sector's contribution is unknown.[13] It is possible, however, to determine the amount of private transfers, which are essentially remittances of funds by migrant workers and grants from NGOs. It is not possible to distinguish between the use of these funds for consumption or for investment, or to assess the proportion of these transfers that contributes to the reduction of present or future poverty. The balance of payments indicates that these private transfers have increased very rapidly, from approximately CFAfr100 billion in 2000 to CFAfr345 billion in 2005. This figure is significant when compared with the amount of official development assistance (approximately CFAfr200 billion in 2005; IMF, 2008).

Deciding between internal and external resources
We first evaluate the future need for financing linked to the achievement of the MDGs, then look at the prospects for external financing and later demonstrate the value of expanding the domestic fiscal space independently of any gap in funding projections.

Financing requirements to the year 2010
While it is very difficult to conduct a prospective evaluation of financing needs for the achievement of the MDGs (see Table 8.6), the projections contained in the PRSP 2 for the period 2006–2010 may be a useful starting point. This chapter envisages an increase in annual investments from CFAfr530 to CFAfr720 billion through an effort culminating in 2007–2008 (12 per cent of GDP). The operating budget concerns only the additional expenditures and therefore provides for lower amounts (approximately 1 per

Table 8.6 *Projected financing requirements linked to actions under the PRSP (CFAfr billions)*

Investment budget	2006	2007	2008	2009	2010	Total	Average/year
Amount of PRSP Triennial Public Investment Plan	530	640	721	661	719	3271	654
	457	414	325	258	198	1653	331
Government	210	172	141	104	99	726	145
Donors	251	252	181	161	102	947	189
Donors + shortfall	324	477	576	564	623	2565	513
Financing gap	73	226	395	403	521	1618	324
Operating budget education-health (additional expenditures)	79	74	80	87	17	327	65
Share of external financing (not including gap)	54	59	56	61	51	57	57
External financing (gap included)	61	74	80	84	86	78	78
GDP (optimistic scenario)	4929	5358	5851	6410	7043	29,591	5918
PRSP capital (% of GDP)	10.7	11.9	12.3	10.3	10.2	11.1	11.1
Gap (% of GDP)	1.5	4.2	6%	6.3	7.4	5.5	5.5
Additional operating expenditures (% of GDP)	1.6	1.4	1.4	1.4	0.2	1.1	1.1
Total PRSP expenditures	12.4	13.3	13.7	11.7	10.4	12.2	12.2

Source: Ministry of Economy and Finance (2006e) and authors' calculations

cent of GDP on average for the period). Financing for these expenditures is expected to be shared fairly evenly between the government and donors (43 per cent and 57 per cent over the total period).[14] However, the financing gap increases towards the end of the period (from 1.5 per cent to 7 per cent). If it is felt that this gap should be filled by the donors, in the spirit of the commitments undertaken within the framework of the MDGs, then the share of external financing would increase from 61 per cent to 86 per cent between 2006 and 2010, which would be considerable.

This evaluation of the costs included in Senegal's PRSP may be compared with that contained in the report on the Millennium Project (Millennium Project, 2005). The report estimates that per capita financing needs for low-income countries such as Senegal amount to approximately $100 in 2010 (which corresponds approximately to the average need between 2006 and 2015 based on a fairly steady increase in the regime). Per capita GDP in Senegal may be projected at $890 in 2010,[15] which gives us an order of magnitude of the expenditures needed to achieve the MDGs of approximately 11 per cent of GDP, a figure that is consistent with the projections for Senegal (12.2 per cent). The report suggests a breakdown in expenditures of approximately 10 per cent from households, 30 per cent from the government and 60 per cent from donors.

Any evaluation of funding needs, however, must be used with a great deal of caution insofar as these estimates are subject to sizeable margins of error. Moreover, the breakdown between expenditures on investments and operating expenses is not always very clear. Moreover, the Millennium Project report makes it clear that no distinction should be made between investments and operating expenses in development assistance,[16] but presents in its tables funding needs entitled 'MDG investment needs'. Generally speaking, the measurement of needs relies on a somewhat artificial distinction between so-called 'PRSP' or 'MDG' expenditures and other budget expenditures. The question is whether to include sectors that have an indirect impact on poverty reduction, as the Senegalese PRSP does, or to restrict it to the social sectors, education, health and water. Must all expenditures in the selected sector be considered MDG investment expenditures (as Senegal does), or should they be limited to additional expenditures, and in that case what benchmark should be used? Should operational expenditures include only recurrent charges resulting from new investments, as is done in the PRSP for Senegal, or all expenditures?[17]

Even though overall needs assessments are useful in promoting political mobilization for the securing of additional resources, it must be remembered that the reliability of estimated data is very low and that it must therefore be recognized that we know very little about the real size of funding needs.

In Senegal the following trends can be identified:

- A massive increase in investments is necessary; the amount of PRSP investments alone, or 11 per cent of GDP, is approximately equal to the total sum of all current public investments (9 to 10 per cent);
- During the initial years, the increase in domestic resources should permit Senegal to finance approximately half of its needs;
- After 2008, the financing gap is likely to increase significantly and to justify an expansion of the domestic fiscal space, unless there is greater recourse to external financing.

Prospects for substantial but uncertain financial resources
The Senegalese government secures its external resources from three different sources, debt forgiveness, support from multilateral institutions and bilateral support and assistance from the EU, mainly in the form of grants (see Table 8.7). External resources should be provided on favourable terms, since Senegal has pledged to the IMF not to seek any new external loans on non-concessionary terms (minimum grant component of 35 per cent). Past experience and statements of intention of the different donors suggest that the level of these resources will remain significant or even increase, but we do not have comprehensive projections for this category of resources, and even if these were available to us, they would be very uncertain because of the conditions that are likely to be attached to any new disbursement.

Table 8.7 *Projections of average annual flows from several external donors, 2006–2010*

	Billions of CFAfr	% average GDP for the period
Exceptional Highly Indebted Poor Countries (HIPC) financing (World Bank, African Development Bank, Paris Club and Kuwait)	85	1.4
Debt service reduction (MDRI cancellation)	47	0.8
Reimbursements to IMF (to 2009) (pre-MDRI)	−15	−0.25
Credit available from World Bank	32	0.54
Budget support grants	118	2.0
TOTAL	267	4.51

Source: third and fourth IMF reviews of the IMF (2006a, 2006b)

Senegal reached the completion point of the HIPC initiative on 19 April 2004, which should qualify it for a total inflow of funds in the amount of $488.3 million. According to balance of payments projections (latest IMF report: IMF, 2006b, p29), this financing, not including the cancellation of debt to the IMF, for the period 2006 to 2010 should be on average CFAfr85 billion. These amounts should be supplemented by cancellations under the Multilateral Debt Relief Initiative (MDRI) (which has been evaluated by the IMF at approximately $47 million per year or 0.8 per cent of GDP).

Where the BWI are concerned, Senegal should have reimbursed funds to the IMF in the absence of any cancellation of its multilateral debt and should have received funds from the World Bank. Some $309 million remains available from the World Bank credits granted until 26 July 2005. The World Bank, moreover, proposed to establish a new Country Assessment Strategy (CAS) in December 2006. Between 2006 and 2010, Senegal expects to receive budget support in the form of grants amounting to the equivalent of 1.9 per cent or 2 per cent of its GDP (see Table 8.11). Senegal has, in the past, also borrowed from the European Investment Bank, the African Development Bank, the West African Development Bank, the Islamic Development Bank and the Kuwaiti Fund for Arab Economic Development, but estimates of their future contributions are not available.

The total volume of external resources that could be quantified (4.5 per cent of GDP), which is set out in Table 8.7, is greater than the level of external financing projected in the PRSP (CFAfr189 billion, or 3.2 per cent of GDP) (Ministry of Economy and Finance, 2006e, p54). However, the difference (corresponding to 1.3 per cent of GDP) is not sufficient to cover the funding gap identified in the PRSP (5.5 per cent). It is known, however, that new sources of financing could emerge in the next few years – for instance, the sale of the state's minority share in the capital of Sonatel, the sale of the cellular telephone new licence, or Chinese and Arab funds. These exceptional resources are likely to be increased by loans from other development banks.

Since the education and health sectors will presumably be the main beneficiaries of the assistance from donors, it is possible that these sectors will not suffer from funding gaps. According to Robert (2006), it seems that in the education sector, donor contributions (especially under the Fast Track Initiative) can cover the additional financing needs in order to achieve the MDGs. The health sector is likely to benefit from adequate resources in view of its absorptive capacity. However, this does not mean that funding needs will be covered for all of the components of the poverty reduction strategy, particularly wealth creation programmes, which are the first justification for seeking to expand the domestic fiscal space.

Because of the uncertainty as to the amounts that still remain effectively available, even for the short term, it is proposed to prepare a supplementary budget for 2006. The unpredictability of external aid flows is one of the reasons that, as we shall see later, justifies the expansion of the domestic fiscal space.

Justification for expansion of the domestic fiscal space in Senegal
Senegal is a good example of a country where expansion of the domestic fiscal space is justified, either by raising taxes or by domestic borrowing. The magnitude of funding needs for the attainment of the MDGs is the primary justification for expanding the fiscal space. However, the very measurement of these needs, and of the gap between needs and predictable funding resources, is very uncertain, as we have seen in the preceding section. It should be noted here that there are other justifications for expanding the domestic fiscal space that have to do with certain characteristics of development aid.

Development aid is made available either in the form of grants (aid from most bilateral donors and from the EU) or in the form of loans on conditions that are more or less advantageous. The terms of the World Bank's International Development Association loans are particularly favourable: 50-year repayment periods with a 10-year grace period and a 0.75 per cent rate of interest. Current loans from the Kuwaiti Fund are repayable over a period of 20 to 45 years with an average rate of interest of 2 per cent, while those from the Islamic Development Bank are repayable over 15 to 25 years at an average rate of interest of 3.7 per cent. The terms of the loans granted by the European Investment Bank and the West African Development Bank are less favourable, with minimum repayment periods of 10 years and average interest rates of 5.1 per cent and 5.7 per cent (see Annex 8.6 on public debt in Senegal, page 312). From the point of view of the beneficiary states, ODA, even when it takes the form of grants, is still not free. It carries high administrative management costs arising from the negotiation procedures and complex disbursement methods that are specific to each donor. It also includes more subjective costs that have to do with the conditionality attached to budget support, and sometimes with the definition and shared implementation of projects. The costs of such aid must be compared with the costs of domestic financing. An increase in taxes, particularly when it takes the form of higher rates rather than an expansion of the tax base, is not always desirable, since it causes distortions and reduces the incentive for the private sector to produce, which could, in turn, reduce economic growth. Domestic borrowing, for its part, can only be done at market rates. We see later that the financial situation of Senegal enables it to obtain relatively advantageous terms on the regional financial market (between 2.5 per cent and 5 per cent depending on the length of the repayment period). However, these financial conditions are less favourable than those that apply to most development aid flows.

Aid volatility and unpredictability further justifies an expansion of domestic fiscal space. This unpredictability of aid is due to the budgetary procedures followed by donors that are not conducive to long-term commitments, as well as to the aid conditionality. These result in disbursements either being delayed or even cancelled if the beneficiary country fails to fulfil the conditions. The efforts of donors to harmonize their aid and their tendency to consider the IMF as a leader, increase the risk of a simultaneous suspension of payments by a large number of donors on the sole grounds that the country has failed to meet the conditions negotiated with the IMF. It is therefore important for the government of Senegal to retain a margin of domestic manoeuvrability in order to meet its public expenditure needs or, at any rate, the expenditures that are critical for the achievement of the MDGs. Moreover, even though the international community recognizes that poor countries need the international aid they receive to cover a part of the recurrent expenditures that are incurred in social investments, coverage of this component will never be in full, which is an argument for states to increase the level of domestic resources.

It should be noted, first of all, that short-term loans in the form of treasury bond issues are indispensable to the management of the state treasury, since the Central Bank of West African States (BCEAO) no longer makes advances, even temporary ones, to African public treasuries. This is the condition to ensure that the state no longer has excessive delays in payment, which pushes up public expenditures. Beyond this question of short-term cash flow, the unpredictability of aid disbursements creates a problem for the inter-annual smoothing of public expenditures. The achievement of the MDGs is dependent on public expenditures in health and education. Most of these are current expenditures, notably the payment of personnel in these sectors, whose numbers cannot be suddenly reduced. The delay or extension of the timeframes for the execution of investment projects is a well-known cause of the increase in costs and, therefore, of lower returns. In order to avoid a situation in which the state accumulates arrears in payments or is forced to put a sudden stop to development projects, it is important for the state to be able to build up a reserve (see, for example, Heller, 2005). This can be done either in the form of deposits in the Central Bank or by securing domestic lines of credit. This requires the creation of the conditions for recourse to domestic borrowing, while retaining an available margin in the event that the level of aid declines.

Lastly, and from a more socio-political standpoint, excessive reliance on aid risks creating an 'aid dependency' that is not without institutional consequences (see Moss et al, 2006). Attention is often drawn to the risk that generous aid might make the government less willing to work on improving the effectiveness of their expenditures, notably by reorienting them towards the MDGs, and on boosting its tax effort. Much has been written recently about the possible negative impact of aid on the tax effort (Brautigam and Knack, 2004; Ghura, 1998, Remmer, 2004). The results of econometric analyses are somewhat inconclusive. It seems clear, however, that grants have a more negative impact than loans on the tax effort (Gupta et al, 2004). We shall see that this risk has not materialized in Senegal over the last few years.

It is doubtlessly more important to emphasize the danger that, given the very generous aid it receives, the government no longer feels genuinely responsible for its economic and social policies and thus not fully accountable to its citizens for its actions. This risk is clearly not independent of the modalities of aid and, in particular, of the conditions that accompany it. This is why it would be desirable to reform aid conditionality by substituting results-based conditions for the tools or economic policy measures-based conditions currently implemented by most donors. The objective of the reform is to return to the beneficiary country government control over its policies, so that it can freely decide its policies, with the pursuit of aid depending on the final results of its policies and not on the implementation of this or that economic policy measure.[18] The expansion of the domestic fiscal space, by creating greater freedom of manoeuvre for the government, is an additional response that has the advantage of being within its power.

The justification for an expansion of the domestic fiscal space in Senegal leads us to examine which modalities are required for its implementation and then to analyse the limits and risks associated with such an expansion.

PROSPECTS FOR EXPANSION OF THE INTERNAL FISCAL SPACE

Internal fiscal space is potentially comprised of three elements: increased tax revenues (central and local), greater recourse to seignorage and increased domestic borrowing. In the case of Senegal, it is easy to demonstrate that, unlike domestic borrowing, the first two elements will not offer a broad margin for manoeuvre in the future. Lastly, it is no doubt possible for certain categories of MDGs to rely more on private financing in order to relieve the pressure on public financing.

Potential increase in tax revenues

Below we analyse the prospects for an increase in tax revenues at the state and local levels, relying in each case on an analysis of the trends at these levels.

National government tax revenues

The increase in tax revenues in Senegal and its explanation
While Senegal had experienced a decline in tax revenues as a proportion of GDP between 1980 and 1995, from 23 per cent to 15 per cent, there has been a significant upturn since then with the rate rising to 19.3 per cent in 2004 and a projected rate of

more than 20 per cent in 2005 (see Table 8.2 and Figure 8.1). In absolute terms, revenues increased from CFAfr700 billion in 2000 to a projected CFAfr1360 billion in 2006. If the level of tax revenues in Senegal is within the average for sub-Saharan African countries, it is well above the average for the member countries of the West African Economic and Monetary Union (WAEMU), which was 15.1 per cent in 2004 (Comité de Convergence, 2005). Senegal is the only country in the zone to exceed the threshold of 17 per cent, which is one of the Union's second tier criteria. Senegal's tax potential for the period 2000 to 2003 has been estimated at 18.4 per cent of GDP,[19] which shows that Senegal is currently making a positive tax effort. The gap between actual tax revenues and their estimated potential is approximately 1 per cent of GDP.

This increase in tax revenues has been achieved within the framework of a very clear tax transition, with a lowering of the share of import taxes, from 39 per cent of total revenues in 1996 to only 17 per cent in 2003, and a gradual increase in indirect domestic taxes, from 39 per cent to 59 per cent of total revenues over the same period (see Table 8.8[20] and Figure 8.2). The level of VAT revenues is high at 7.7 per cent of GDP in 2003, corresponding to an effectiveness coefficient of 0.43 based on the Keen calculation of the ratio between VAT receipts as a percentage of GDP and the nominal VAT rate (18 per cent in Senegal).[21] By way of comparison, this coefficient is approximately 0.30 to 0.35 for developing countries.

The rapid rise in tax revenues in Senegal was as a result of the expansion of the tax base and the streamlining of the collection system. Significant reforms were introduced to register and identify the owners of land, thereby ensuring more effective coverage of potentially tax paying households and businesses. The effort to identify taxpayers has been so successful that the problem is now one of capacity to manage the new taxpayers.

The rate of collection has increased thanks to numerous supplementary measures. These include the following: the establishment of a special tax centre to handle tax payments by large companies; computerization of the tax services; introduction of a single tax and social identification number; tax amnesty on unpaid taxes to bring taxpayers back into the system (in particular, those in the liberal professions, such as architects, lawyers and so on); and the establishment of programmes for the periodic auditing of declarations. An effort to recruit tax base agents (150), tax recovery officials (150) and tax inspectors has accompanied these measures over recent years. In order to improve their relations with taxpayers, the tax services have expanded their advisory services by organizing drop-in seminars and a discussion forum for businesses, the Presidential Council for Investments. At the same time, in 2004, Senegal introduced broad fiscal reforms also covering local taxes, the effects of which on the level of tax revenues is still difficult to quantify.

The success of this tax transition is attributable to a number of inter-related factors of which the most important is, evidently, the relatively steady and sustained economic growth that Senegal has enjoyed since 1994. Another factor, of a more political nature, is that Senegal had a democratic change in government in 2000, which has helped create a

Table 8.8 *Structure and trends in tax revenues of Senegal, 1996–2003*

				Billions of CFAfr				
	1996	1997	1998	1999	2000	2001	2002	2003
Tax revenues	389.4	408.6	440.8	491.2	537.3	576.8	627.3	677
Direct taxes	85	94.3	107.2	107.5	128.7	130.6	145.9	159.3
Taxes on goods and services (a)	151.3	177.3	209.6	265.9	324.5	338.1	367.5	402.6
Of which VAT (a)	125.8	149.5	164	182.2	231.7	241.8	265.4	285.8
Import taxes (a)	153.1	137	124	117.8	84.1	108.1	113.9	115.1
GDP	2591	2727	2968	3167	3332	3343	3473	3725
As a % of total taxes								
Direct taxes	21.8	23.1	24.3	21.9	24.0	22.6	23.3	23.5
B&S taxes	38.9	43.4	47.5	54.1	60.4	58.6	58.6	59.5
Of which VAT	32.3	36.6	37.2	37.1	43.1	41.9	42.3	42.2
Import taxes	39.3	33.5	28.1	24.0	15.7	18.7	18.2	17.0
As a % of GDP								
Tax revenues	15.0	15.0	14.9	15.5	16.1	17.3	18.1	18.2
Direct taxes	3.3	3.5	3.6	3.4	3.9	3.9	4.2	4.3
B&S taxes	5.8	6.5	7.1	8.4	9.7	10.1	10.6	10.8
Of which VAT	4.9	5.5	5.5	5.8	7.0	7.2	7.6	7.7
Import taxes	5.9	5.0	4.2	3.7	2.5	3.2	3.3	3.1

Note: (a) Data include oil related taxes.
Source: IMF (2005a)

climate of confidence for economic actors. Lastly, the progress achieved by the tax admin-istration is, no doubt, linked to the recruitment of new staff and to the increase in their real remuneration. It should be noted that net public transfers expressed as a percentage of GDP declined in Senegal over the long term, from 11 per cent in the period 1980 to 1984 to only 4 per cent in the period 2000 to 2003 (Gupta et al, 2006). We have also noted

Source: Chambas (2005)

Figure 8.1 *Changes in rate of public taxation in Senegal, 1970–2003 (% of GDP)*

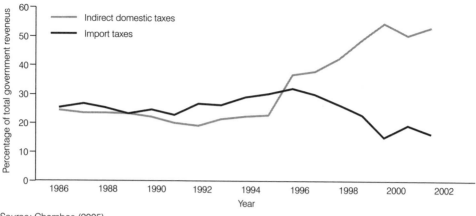

Source: Chambas (2005)

Figure 8.2 *Changes in the structure of public revenues in Senegal, 1986–2002*
(% of total government revenues)

that the share of grants in total official development assistance has decreased from 53 per cent in 2001 to 38 per cent in 2006. It is assumed that these different elements tempered the potential disincentive of aid on the tax effort described above.

Prospects for government tax revenues
The 2004 tax reform was aimed, primarily, at promoting investment and the competitiveness of companies operating in the territory of Senegal (Ministry of Economy and Finance, 2006d). A study (Ministry of Economy and Finance, 2006d, p6) conducted in 2000 showed that the effective marginal tax rate on capital (the tax on the last unit of capital invested) was of the order of 40 per cent. The main idea was, therefore, to bring about a substantial decrease in this marginal tax rate in order to bring it more into line with international standards. The measures concerned both the tax regime, under ordinary law the Standard Tax Code, and the dispensatory provisions contained in the Investment Code. With regard to income taxes, the principal measure has been the lowering of the rate of corporate tax from 35 per cent to 33 per cent, and later to 25 per cent in 2006. Note should also be taken of the introduction of a tax incentive, the Collective Investment Scheme, which provides, in particular, for the exemption of the Variable Capital Investment Company from corporate tax in order to 'promote the mobilization of savings and to expand financial and stock market activities' (Ministry of Economy and Finance, 2006d, p10). Moreover, in order to adapt the tax system to the needs of small businesses, a common tax, the global single tax, was introduced for companies with an annual turnover of less than CFAfr50 million. The global single tax covers six individual taxes (trading license, income taxes on industrial and corporate profits, minimum tax, VAT, license and flat payroll tax, and the employer's payroll tax for training), and it is expected that a portion of the proceeds (60 per cent) will be returned to the local governments.

With regard to the dispensatory provisions, the Investment Code provides for a company tax credit equal to 40 per cent of approved and effectively realized investments to be deducted over five consecutive fiscal years from taxable profits.

With regard to indirect taxes, VAT has undergone a reform that modifies its field of application. The introduction of the notion of export services and that of 'own services' provides a legal basis for the right to deduct these operations with the purpose of strengthening the competitiveness of Senegalese businesses. Moreover, companies recognized under the Investment Code are now governed by the suspension, which means that they are no longer exempt from VAT but that VAT becomes payable only after the first business operation, in other words after the business activity has begun. Lastly, banks are exempt from taxes on bank operations payable on interest and commissions on loans and advances made to the government. Likewise, taxes on transfers of wealth have been reduced (a 50 per cent reduction in the applicable rates).

Since they were only recently introduced, the impact of these measures on government revenues is difficult to assess. According to an estimate by the General Department of Taxation and Property (Ministry of Economy and Finance, 2005b), a 25 per cent cut[22] in corporate tax would reduce government revenues by CFAfr19 billion in 2005 and by CFAfr21 billion in 2006. This represents a reduction of approximately one-quarter in company taxes and of 1.5 per cent in overall revenues, compared with a scenario in which the corporate tax rate is kept at 33 per cent (see Annex 8.3, page 303).

The increase in revenues from the global single tax is naturally much more modest (CFAfr1.8 billion in 2004, rising to CFAfr2.2 billion in 2005). Lastly, tax revenues in Senegal are likely to be affected in the short term by two adverse external shocks. First, given the still quite heavy dependence on tariff income, the proposed implementation of the EPA with the EU could have a serious negative impact. Second, the negative impact of rising oil prices on economic growth will have implications for company tax and VAT receipts.

Given the recent increase in tax to GDP ratio and the reforms that have just been described, it is unlikely that government tax revenues will increase significantly in the years ahead without jeopardizing growth. VAT, which accounts for a large share of revenues, is economically much less neutral than it might have been because of the likelihood that the proportion of VAT collected that should be reimbursed, will not be and also because of the exemptions granted. It is important to reduce the existing distortions by limiting exemptions and expanding the base for property taxes, which could compensate for the loss of revenues that result from the desirable increase in the reimbursement of VAT credits. This effort to reduce distortions by expanding the tax base also concerns income taxes, insofar as employees are subject to much tighter controls than the liberal professions. Likewise, certain types of income, such as rental income, are poorly integrated into the tax revenue base because of the widespread practice of verbal lease contracts.

The 2004 tax reforms, as was mentioned above, were designed to stimulate economic growth and should therefore contribute to the reduction of poverty. However, their aim was not to redistribute resources. At the present time no study has been carried out to determine the direct impact of these reforms on the situation of the poor.

Tax revenues of local governments

Overview of tax revenues of local governments

Local governments receive three streams of revenue: their own resources (tax and non-tax revenues); transfers from the state (FDD, FECL and decentralization of the consolidated investment budget); and grants and loans from donors. Tax revenues include local taxes and shared taxes. Local taxes are specific to local governments, are calculated by the tax services and collected by the Treasury Department, but are then directly credited to the account of the local government. In Senegal, these are mainly land taxes and professional taxes (trading taxes and licenses). Shared taxes are national taxes, a part of which is returned to the local governments (a refund) in proportion to the amount collected from the municipality. The 2004 tax reform limited shared taxes to the new global single tax. From the standpoint of the local governments, the problem with shared taxes is the uncertainty about the amount that would be effectively refunded by the national government and the time it would take for the amount to be credited to the local government's account in the treasury. This is because (unlike local taxes) the funds collected are first paid into the Ministry of Economy and Finance.

Local governments are also in receipt of non-tax income obtained from the sale of their assets, referred to as property income, such as income derived from the sale of lumber from municipal forest. Other examples are income from services produced from their assets, referred to as income from operations or payment for services rendered, such as market taxes or payment for the use of coach stations.

Local governments in Senegal also benefit from three types of different transfers from the national government. First, FDD finances the operating expenses associated with the transfer of responsibilities under the 1996 law. The amount of this fund is determined as a proportion of VAT, according to a percentage fixed each year by the law on finances. There is no provision for the indexing of this fund to VAT receipts. The value of the FDD rose from approximately CFAfr5 billion in 1997 to approximately CFAfr13 billion in 2005 (see Table 8.9), which represents a slower growth than the growth in VAT receipts. Moreover, the Local Collectivity Capital Development Fund (FECL), which is included in the BCI of the state, is intended to fund investments in municipalities. The amount of the FECL increased significantly in 2003 (from CFAfr4 billion to CFAfr6 billion), when the national government substituted itself for the local governments, whose savings were insufficient to provide local counterpart funding for donor-financed projects. As in the case of shared taxes,

Table 8.9 *Resources transferred by the central state to local governments (CFAfr billions)*

	2000	2001	2002	2003	2004	2005*	2006*
FDD	6.6	7.3	8.1	9.1	10.1	13	14
FECL	3.5	3.8	4.0	6.0	4.0	6	7
TOTAL	10	11	12	15	14	19	21

Note: * Estimated.
Source: World Bank (2005) and interviews at FECL

making funds effectively available to local governments is often a slow process. Lastly, the decentralization of the BCI, which began in 2006 in the education, health, justice and environment sectors, represents a third transfer from the central state to local governments, the scope of which is potentially much greater. In the education sector, the decentralized BCI amounted to CFAfr4 billion. This is the total budget of the central state for primary education, which should be enough to fund the construction of approximately 1000 classrooms out of the 2700 classrooms needed to achieve the MDGs. Again, there is the problem of the slow rate at which the corresponding funds are made available to the local governments. For example, the 2006 credits were not disbursed until it was too late to have new classrooms ready for the beginning of the 2006 school year.

The third source of financing is donors, who have significantly increased the level of their support to local governments in Senegal over the last few years. As already indicated, the principal programmes of support to local governments have been PAC and PNIR, which are financed, respectively, by the World Bank and AFD, and by the World Bank alone. The municipalities have also benefited from contributions from other donors, such as UNDP and the United Nations Capital Development Fund (UNCDF), the German technical cooperation agency GTZ and the EU.

It is difficult to have an overall view of the resources of local governments in that donor funds are not included in the budgets of local governments. Moreover, the financial data on rural communities are not systematically aggregated at the national level. With regard to urban municipalities, for which more precise data are available (see Observatoire des Finances Locales, 2003), half of all current income (not including investment capital and donor assistance) in 2003 was derived from local tax receipts, while non-tax income accounted for 22 per cent and state contributions only 8 per cent.[23] Tax receipts are comprised mainly of professional taxes, while land taxes represent a smaller percentage. In 2003, the total income of local governments represented only 0.9 per cent of GDP, or 4.9 per cent of national government revenues, which is clearly inadequate when compared with the responsibilities that have been placed on them.

Prospects for tax revenues of local governments

It seems that it may be possible in the relatively near future to increase the overall tax revenues of local governments, not just tax and property income, but also transfers from the national government.

The fiscal reform of 2004 was also concerned with local taxes[24] and was aimed at reducing taxes on production, simplifying the calculation of taxes and promoting greater equity by restoring the integrity of the tax base. In this spirit, the main changes introduced by the new law are as follows:

- Lowering of the threshold for exemption from land taxes from CFAfr1 million to CFAfr500,000;
- Reduction in the temporary exemption period from 10 or 15 years to 5 years;
- Elimination of tax deductions and establishment of a general tax rate of 7.5 per cent for factories and 5 per cent for other buildings;
- Determination of the tax base from the rental value, with priority given to the cadastral method.

Moreover, as indicated above, the taxes on informal businesses were considerably simplified by the introduction of a common global singe tax.

The impact of these reforms on local tax revenues cannot yet be assessed, but, given the reduction in tax relief and exemptions, it should be generally positive. The increase in tax revenues could be even greater if the management of the local tax system is improved. The first area of progress concerns the establishment of the tax base. Given the shortcomings of the land survey and owner identification systems, the identification of economic activities taking place in local governments and, generally speaking, of potential taxpayers, was quite inadequate, which was reflected in a severe underestimation of the tax base. The operation to identify owners, which was conducted within the framework of PAC, and the cross-comparison of owners with the activities being carried out, enabled many taxpayers to be identified. The cadastral Land Survey Modernization Support Project (PAMC) was also launched in certain towns. The new tax code has placed greater responsibility on mayors by giving them control over licenses and the global single tax collected in the municipality. It would appear that many mayors now have a keen interest in this issue and closely follow trends in the size of the local tax base, while previously they were more concerned with collecting taxes. The tax services are also regularly updated by the municipalities on activities in their localities that are unregistered (for instance, unit of Senelec, gas stations) or poorly located (Sonacos de Diourbel).

There has also been some improvement in the collection of local taxes, which has traditionally been ineffective. Indeed, treasury officials who are responsible for the collection of central and local taxes mainly recovered taxes owed to the national government, on which greater value was placed by their supervisors (notably in the form of bonuses). In order to reduce this problem, a reform aimed at the decentralization of collection services (Treasury) in the regions was implemented with the objective of extending it to the localities. Moreover, ADM simultaneously sought to improve the relationship between local tax collectors and the services of the local governments, and proposed the signing of agreements with the ministry responsible for the agents of the decentralized services. The main idea is to strengthen the relationship between municipal officials (in particular the mayor's office), tax officials (tax services) and recovery agents (from the decentralized treasury services). In a number of cities, the campaign to collect trade taxes (*patente*) in advance is first discussed at a coordination meeting and the collection is done jointly by the agents of the local government, tax officials, treasury agents and public security officials.

The strengthening of local tax collection also requires the recruitment of agents in the decentralized services. The municipality of Dakar, for example, has made 60 base agents available to the tax services to work towards expanding the tax base.

It should be possible to increase tax revenues by increasing the volume of resources coming from the assets of the municipalities. Indeed, the municipality support programmes have enabled municipalities to build or rehabilitate business infrastructure, such as markets and coach stations, which are used to generate operating income. Moreover, there are prospects for increasing property resources by developing partnerships with the private sectors. ADM is seeking to encourage local governments to identify interesting projects for private actors, particularly in the tourism sector, and to offer municipal land for lease to businesses. Lastly, in addition to generating income from their assets, local governments could obtain resources by streamlining their expenses, particularly by reducing their wage bills, which are swollen by excess personnel as a result of nepotism in hiring practices.

The experiences of a number of municipalities show that the prospects for increasing the revenues of local governments are good in large cities. A study (interview at the Agence de Développement Municipal) of the municipality of Saint-Louis has assessed the value added created in the municipality at CFAf58 billion for a local tax of approximately CFAfr300 million, which represents a tax rate of only 0.6 per cent. If this tax rate were to increase to 5 per cent, income could then rise to CFAfr3 billion. Within the framework of PAC, Rufisque has seen a massive increase in ordinary tax revenues, which rose from CFAfr700 million in the early stages of the project (1997) to CFAfr4 billion in 2006. In rural areas, the tax potential is much lower. Nevertheless, the experience of PNIR has shown that an improved supply of public goods would increase civic mindedness in tax matters. In view of the low level of administrative capacity in rural communities, an increase in their income would also require significant institutional support.

A reform of the rules governing FECL and FDD has also been proposed. Indeed, the resources now being transferred are not sufficient to enable local governments to correctly exercise their new activities, and donors are urging the government of Senegal to increase the level of funding. The increase in the volume of resources transferred to local governments is part of the explicit objectives of the PSRP, since it provides for the size of the FDD and the FECL[25] to be increased to at least CFAfr15 billion and CFAfr8 billion, respectively, and for the relative share of the government's financial transfers (depending on its total resources) to local governments to be greater than 3 per cent, as compared with only 1.9 per cent in 2004. This increase in the volume of resources transferred still remains very limited, since it represents only 0.2 per cent of GDP.

In conclusion, several of the officials with whom we spoke were of the view that it would no doubt be possible to double or even triple the municipality's own resources, given the low level of their existing resources (0.9 per cent of GDP) compared with the level of local economic activity, especially in towns. This would mean continuing to improve the management of local taxes. Even doubled, the level of these resources would remain modest as a percentage of GDP and in no way commensurate with the level of responsibility entrusted to the municipalities. This means that the municipalities would remain dependent on transfers from the state, which is a risk that we examine below in the section 'Risks and conditions for the successful expansion of the fiscal space'.

Seignorage

The precise level of income from seignorage in Senegal is not known, but it is thought to be low and will remain so in the future.

Seignorage is limited in Senegal owing to its membership in WAEMU

Seignorage is the revenue that a state derives from the creation of currency. In Senegal, seignorage is necessarily limited because of the country's membership of WAEMU, and this is for several reasons.

First, the advances that the BCEAO may grant national governments are limited by its statutes (Articles 14 to 16). Cumulative advances cannot exceed 20 per cent of budgetary income for the year just ended. Moreover, following the transformation (in 1994) of the Monetary Union into the Economic and Monetary Union, the governments pledged, in 1998 to bring to zero by the year 2001 the negative current account balances owed by public treasuries to the Central Bank. However, in light of the difficulties encountered by all of the governments (with the exception of Benin) in honouring this commitment, the Council of Ministers decided in September 2002 to consolidate statutory advances at their level of 31 December 2002 and make them repayable over a ten-year period, beginning on 1 January 2003, at a rate of interest set at 3 per cent. Senegal is honouring this commitment and is gradually reducing its reliance on statutory advances, which declined from CFAfr68.7 billion on 31 December 2003 to CFAfr 55.4 billion on 31 December 2005 (see Annex 8.4, Table 8.A6, page 304).

However, even without direct advances from the central bank to the public treasury, a state may benefit from seignorage revenues in the form of profits from the central bank that are refunded to the state. Indeed, an increase in the base money (currency and commercial bank reserves in the central bank) as a result of an expansion of the money supply results in more profitable assets on the balance sheet of the central bank (external assets and domestic credits). This source of seignorage is itself restricted in Senegal in two ways: (1) by the low level of the amount of this seignorage throughout the WAEMU, and (2) by the rule requiring distribution of the profits of the BCEAO among the states of the Union.

Since seignorage is derived from expansion of the money supply, its volume depends on the increase in the demand for real balances as a consequence of economic growth (the so-called virtuous seignorage) and on the excess nominal balances tied to inflation (or inflation tax). This is why it is usual to associate seignorage during a given period to the increase in the base money according to the following formula:

$$\frac{\delta Mc}{p} = \frac{\delta Mc}{Mc} \times \frac{Mc}{P} = \left[\frac{\delta Y}{Y} + \frac{\delta P}{P}\right] \times \frac{Mc}{P} = \left[\frac{\delta Y}{Y} \times \frac{Mc}{P}\right] \times \left[\frac{\delta P}{P} \times \frac{Mc}{P}\right]$$

where Mc represents money issued by the central bank, P the general price level, and Y the national income, at constant prices. In the last expression of the equation, the first term between square brackets represents the increase in real demand for base money tied to economic growth (virtuous seignorage), while the second term represents the inflation tax. The level of real base money, Mc/P, constitutes the tax base and the rate of inflation determines the tax rate.[26] The low levels of growth and inflation in member states of the WAEMU (over the course of 2000–2005, roughly an average of 3.0 per cent and 2.6 per cent per annum, respectively) limits the potential for seignorage in the Union (UEMOA, 2005). Considering that in the WAEMU, the base money[27] represents approximately 11.8 per cent of GDP (see Annex 8.4, Table 8.A11, page 307), an increase in this product by about 6 per cent would result in a seignorage potential of 0.71 per cent. This is well below the average amount of seignorage in developing countries or even in sub-Saharan Africa (between 2 and 3 per cent), depending on the period (see Chambas et al, 2006).

It should be recalled, however, that this measure of seignorage imperfectly reflects the profits that the central bank derives from the creation of money. According to the above equation, the assimilation of the increase in the base money to the benefit of the central bank would assume that the rate of interest charged on its assets (in the absence of interests paid by the central bank on banks' reserves) is equal to the nominal economic growth rate (real growth rate plus rate of inflation), which is not necessarily the case.[28] The profitability of the Central Bank is high because it provides no remuneration to banks for their required or free reserves in their accounts and because its assets, comprised mainly of foreign assets (78 per cent in December 2005), are relatively well remunerated. At present, most of the external reserves of the BCEAO are held in its operating account with the French Public Treasury, which pays interest at the marginal facility rate of the European Central Bank. This rate is a ceiling rate for the refinancing of banks in the EU and is 100 points higher than the tender rate. After fluctuating between 4.25 per cent and 4.75 per cent during the period 2000 to 2001, it gradually declined and settled at 3 per cent between June 2003 and December 2005, then rose steadily to 3.75 per cent in June 2006. This rate is attractive and is higher than the three-month deposit rate in Europe (Euro Interbank Offered Rate).[29] Since 2002, the BCEAO has followed the trend of the benchmark rates of the Central European Bank and has thus gradually lowered its rates so that the rate on its pension fund holdings is currently 4 per cent (see Annex 8.4, Table 8.A7, page 305). A rate of return on assets of the Central Bank in the order of 4 per cent would yield an amount of seignorage that would still be lower than the amount previously estimated.

Lastly, the seignorage collected by the Central Bank does not go directly to Senegal, which benefits only from the distribution of a portion of the Central Bank's profits. However, allocation of the profits of BCEAO is within the purview of the Council of Ministers of WAEMU. Before being distributed among the states, a portion may be placed in reserve or used to finance joint projects or regional financial institutions. The distribution of the amount allocated to states (Article 67 of the statutes of BCEAO) is on an equal basis, in proportion to each country's stake in the Bank's capital, and does not correspond to the seignorage generated in each state, in relation to the relative size of its money supply and the growth of its national product. The fact that the currencies circulating in Senegal represent a large proportion of that of the Union (30 per cent), and that growth in Senegal has been higher than in other countries of the union over the past few years, would not lead to an increase in its revenues from seignorage. There is no likelihood that the rule governing the distribution of profits would be modified in the future, since it reflects the solidarity of the states belonging to the Union to which the member governments attach great value.

Difficulty of precisely measuring income from seignorage in Senegal
The amount of profits payable by the BCEAO to Senegal is not known precisely for two reasons. First, the amount paid by the BCEAO to Senegal does not correspond to the gross amount of the profits due, but to a net amount that is equal to the difference between this profit and Senegal's liabilities to the BCEAO. These liabilities are three-fold: (1) interest payments on the consolidated advances from the BCEAO; (2) the salaries of BCEAO officials seconded to ministries; and (3) funds owed by Senegal to regional institutions pre-financed by BCEAO. Moreover, the payment of this balance is considered to be a treasury operation and is, therefore, not reflected in the budget and not explicitly identified in the amendment to the Finance Act. This accounting procedure is regrettable, since it does not conform to the rule of an exhaustive budget. In any event, for the reasons mentioned above, the sums in question are not very large.

Unlike tax and seignorage revenues, there seems to be potential in Senegal for expanding the fiscal space by recourse to domestic borrowing.

Potential increase in domestic borrowing

The monetary situation in Senegal suggests that there is a domestic source of funds that can be mobilized for implementation of the MDGs. After examining this situation,[30] we look at the potential role of the two public actors, the state and local governments, in the mobilization of supplementary resources.

Excess liquidity of the Senegalese economy and surplus external reserves

Two characteristics of the monetary situation of Senegal suggest that there is room for additional financing. The first is the excess liquidity in the Senegalese banking system, as there is in the WAEMU consolidated system. Next is the size of foreign reserves held by the BCEAO for the Union as a whole and of foreign reserves reflecting the monetary situation of Senegal. Those reserves are the counterpart of bank liquidity.

a) Excess liquidity in the banking system in Senegal and in the Union as a whole Excess liquidity is reflected in the absence of any refinancing of Senegalese banks by the BCEAO and in the high required and free reserve rates (see Table 8.10). In Senegal, the rate of required reserves (required for sight deposits, short-term loans, including agricultural loans, and bank assets held abroad) is 9 per cent. For the Union as a whole, accumulated reserves over and beyond the required reserves, including instruments representing the consolidated debts of the states, averaged CFAfr358 billion during the period 2000 to 2004. Of these, CFAfr63 billion was owned by Senegalese banks, corresponding to 144 per cent and 98 per cent, of the required reserves. At the end of 2004, the free reserves for WAEMU stood at CFAfr430 billion, including CFAfr79 billion for Senegal (excess amounts of 123 per cent and 76 per cent, respectively). At the end of 2005, the free reserves in WAEMU were only CFAfr204 billion, of which CFAfr67 billion were for Senegal. Despite this decline, the level of free reserves remains considerable. The rate of required reserves set by the BCEAO is high because of the size of the free reserves and could be lowered if necessary. The excess liquidity of the banks shows the reluctance of banks to take risks by making loans to the private sector. This reluctance, the causes of which we will examine later, is not conducive to a more intensive mobilization of resources to promote growth by public or private enterprises. Given the excess liquidity in the banking system, both in Senegal and in the Union as a whole which constitutes a single financial market, a greater recourse by the government of Senegal to domestic borrowing is unlikely to crowd out private investment.

Large size of the Union's and Senegal's external reserves

The prohibition on banks placing their excess liquidity outside the Union is the reason why the excess liquidity in the banking system of the Union takes the form of banks' reserves in the Central Bank, and results in the high levels of external reserves of the Central Bank (see Table 8.10 and Annex 8.4, Table 8.A11, page 307). Excess liquidity

Table 8.10 *Free reserves of banks and foreign reserves of the Central Bank*

Free bank reserves	Senegal		West African Monetary Union	
	Billions of CFAfr	As a % of required reserves	Billions of CFAfr	As a % of required reserves
Average 2000–2004	63	98	358	144
December 2004	79	76	439	123
December 2005	67 (a)	-	204	49
Central Bank foreign reserves	Billions of CFAfr	Months worth of imports	Billions of CFAfr	Months worth of imports
2005	666	4.5	3769	4.5

Note: (a) IMF estimates.
Source: data provided by BCEAO

and large reserves are therefore closely linked. Paradoxically, the banking system of Senegal places savings abroad,[31] even though the Senegalese economy is characterized by a need for financing since its current account is in deficit. If banks increased their lending, that would automatically reduce foreign reserves. Are the foreign reserves of the Union and of Senegal, in particular, excessive?

Academic studies on the adequate level of a country's reserves refer to the purpose for the foreign reserves held by the Central Bank. When faced with a temporary negative external shock on the balance of payments, the existence of sizeable reserves averts a brutal adjustment of the economy that would lead to a drop in economic activities. However, the accumulation of reserves has an economic cost insofar as it requires a balance of payments surplus, which means that the economy is not using all of the resources derived from exports, from revenue net of factors and from net inflows of capital. It also includes a financial cost, which must be balanced against the security that they bring if the yield from foreign investments is lower than the return on domestic loans. We have seen above that for BCEAO this gap is small (-0.26 per cent).

This problem, which concerns the purpose of reserves, does not fully apply to WAEMU. Indeed the security which the monetary authorities of other countries are tempted to seek in a broad cushion of foreign currency reserves is already achieved by the agreement governing the operating account that links the French Public Treasury to BCEAO and which permits the bank's foreign reserves to become negative when faced with an adverse external shock. The objective of the franc zone agreements is, in fact, to ensure that African states do not have to brutally adjust their exchange rates and suspend the convertibility of their currency in the face of negative shocks, knowing that they would then be required to take the measures necessary to gradually improve their balance of payments position (Article 51 of the statute of BCEAO).

If, however, the criteria that are traditionally used to judge 'an adequate level' of reserves are applied to the reserves of WAEMU, these would appear to be relatively high. Since the main source of vulnerability of the balance of payments of countries that maintain control of changes in capital movements (which is the case of WAEMU) lies in the trade balance, it is usual to compare the amount of reserves available for imports. In the WAEMU, the gross exchange reserves held by the BCEAO corresponded, in 2005, to six months of imports and in the case of Senegal, to four and a half months, while it is generally considered that they should cover three to four months. We recognize, however, that many countries have higher levels of reserves, for example, on average, nine months of imports in the emerging countries of Asia and in Latin America (IMF, 2004).

It is also common to compare reserves to the money supply because of the risk of an exchange crisis triggered by a rush on bank deposits. While this risk is quite low in WAEMU, the ratio of gross reserves to money supply is 59 per cent (December 2005) and 47 per cent for Senegal. This is comparatively higher than in Asia (30 per cent, on average) and at roughly the same level as Latin America (50 per cent) (IMF, 2004). Moreover, according to the statutes of the BCEAO (Article 51), the rate of coverage of monetary issues (in other words, the ratio between gross exchange reserves and Central Bank's sight instruments) should not fall below 20 per cent. This percentage is evidently not optimal, but nevertheless constitutes a floor that would activate restrictive monetary measures. However, this ratio was 120 per cent in December 2005, a figure that is often cited to justify the higher level of reserves, but which has no major significance for our purposes.

These various ratios would seem to indicate a level of foreign reserves that is at least comfortable. However, this judgement must be tempered by the fact that the accumulation of reserves has been accompanied by an accumulation of payment arrears by Côte d'Ivoire and, to a lesser extent, by Togo. Moreover, the accumulation of reserves would be much lower if the external position of the banks was not limited by regulation.

How can the excess liquidity of the economy contribute to the fiscal space?

The question of concern is to what extent the government of Senegal can borrow domestically to fund increased expenditures. The question applies mainly to the central government, since most local authorities have not developed an adequate administrative and financial basis. However, it would be desirable, as we shall see in the next section, for companies to be able to benefit simultaneously from additional financing from the local financial system.

Potential for government borrowing

The expansion of the fiscal space through government borrowing comes up against administrative and economic constraints. Two administrative constraints must be examined, the first resulting from Senegal's membership of the West African Monetary Union (WAMU), and the other from its simultaneous membership in the WAEMU.

We have noted in connection with seignorage that the BCEAO no longer makes direct advances to the Senegalese government, which is also required to gradually repay previous advances. The only instrument through which the Senegalese government can channel private savings is, therefore, an issue of public securities to which banks may subscribe. A second institutional constraint that affects the issuing of government paper is related to the criteria set out in the Convergence, Stability, Growth and Solidarity Pact adopted in 1999 by the member states of WAEMU. Two of the main criteria of convergence deserve a closer look.

The first is the maximum domestic and external debt, as a percentage of GDP, aimed at preventing over-indebtedness by states. That maximum is set at 70 per cent and there is, *a priori*, no reason to change that level. Adherence to this criterion, moreover, poses no problem for Senegal, whose rate was 50 per cent in 2004, mainly as a result of reaching the completion point of the HIPC initiative on 19 April 2004, and 48.2 per cent in 2005 (UEMOA, 2005). This ratio should decline even further because of Senegal's eligibility for the MDRI following the IMF review of December 2005. Its external debt therefore declined from 42 per cent of GDP in December 2005 to 17.8 per cent in 2006 (IMF, 2008).

The second, considered more important by the WAEMU authorities, is a base budgetary balance that must be zero or positive. Curiously enough, this balance is calculated as the difference between the budgetary income and total expenditure (including interest on debt) with the exception of investment expenditures financed from foreign resources. This latter requirement formally, or in principle, excludes the funding of public investments from private domestic savings and thus, to some extent, encourages states to have recourse to external financing, which is understandable in the case of grants or financing obtained on very concessional terms. Therefore, the financing of public investment through domestic borrowing can take place only by violating, supposedly on a temporary basis, the rule that has been adopted, or by amending the rule. If the Convergence Pact is to retain any credibility, it would be better to improve the criteria than to accept their routine violation. Since currently only Senegal and Togo have positive balances and Mali and Côte d'Ivoire have zero balances and seemed, in 2005, to be adhering to these criteria (just four states out of the eight in the Union), some relaxation should be easily accepted by the ministers of the Union.

We suggest two solutions. The first would be to no longer account for the share of investment from domestic resources, beyond the 20 per cent of tax revenues, as part of expenditures retained for calculating the balance. (One of the 'second tier' criteria to be observed is to allocate 20 per cent of tax revenues to investment.) Another modification would be to exclude from investment expenditures from domestic resources directed at regional projects.

It should be noted that under a different framework of the EU, consideration has been given to modifying the Growth and Stability Pact. The suggestion has been made to exclude the minimum budgetary balance to be observed (–3 per cent of GDP) from the calculation of certain investment expenditures, on the grounds that because of the future income from the investment its cost should be distributed over time (see Conseil d'analyse économique, 2004).

Consideration should also be given to the commitments entered into with the IMF. Within the framework of the PRGF granted to Senegal for the period 2003 to 2005, Senegal has been obliged to maintain a positive base budgetary balance. This is calculated differently from that used in the Convergence Pact, by subtracting expenditures, with the exception of capital expenditures financed from external resources, the temporary cost of structural reforms, and expenditures financed from HIPC Initiative resources. Senegal has also had to respect a ceiling on loans from the banking system to the state, which was negative in 2005 (CFAfr-17.5 billion) as a result of repayments to the BCEAO. Lastly, Senegal, which has benefited from the HIPC Initiative, was not authorized to receive new loans on non-concessional terms from foreign lenders, with loans from financial institutions of the Union being exempt from this prohibition. The IMF will no doubt set similar criteria in the future. Senegal confirmed with the IMF, in February 2006, that it was working towards the implementation of the new economic policy support programme (not financed by the IMF), which nevertheless includes conditions and reviews at regular intervals.

In addition to these institutional constraints, the expansion of the fiscal space through domestic borrowing evidently comes up against economic constraints. The risk from an increase in government borrowing that is most often highlighted is that it discourages private investment. At the present time this risk seems low given the substantial banking liquidity in Senegal, in particular, and in the WAEMU as a whole, and the regional scope of the financial market (see the previous section). Moreover, it seems that in many low-income countries, public and private investments complement each other because of the lack of infrastructure, which is an obstacle to private investment (Gupta et al, 2006). This argument seems valid in Senegal, where some observers believe that the problems of severe congestion in the Dakar peninsula have discouraged foreign investors. Similarly, the current shortages of electricity are clearly an obstacle to the expansion of private activity.

The main question is the cost of these loans. In 2004, Senegal issued, on the regional financial market, 12-month treasury bonds in the amount of CFAfr45.3 billion on attractive financial terms (an interest rate of from 2.05 per cent to 3.4 per cent). It renewed the operation in September 2005 with an issue of CFAfr35 billion for a term of 12 months and at slightly higher interest rates (2.5 to 4 per cent). In July 2005, it also issued five-year bonds at a 5.5 per cent interest rate, which is lower than the rate for the loans of other member states of WAEMU, with Togo and Côte d'Ivoire securing a rate of 6.5 per cent and Burkina Faso 7 per cent. These bonds are issued with technical support from the BCEAO. As we have shown above, these rates are not very different from those obtained from multilateral development banks, with the obvious exception of the International Development Association. Since these rates are not negligible, because they are, by definition, market rates, the funds borrowed should be allocated mostly to productive projects, or to use the terminology of the PRSP, must contribute to the first objective of 'wealth creation'

The conditions for future issues will depend on the demand for and supply of funds in the regional market. In 2005, government issues, through public offerings for savings, account for only 13.7 per cent of such issues in the Union as a whole. If issues by other Senegalese entities (banks and companies) are added, outstanding instruments in Senegal would represent 23.3 per cent of the total. This percentage is of the same order of magnitude as the proportion of the money supply of Senegal in that of the Union, which was 24.4 per cent as of 31 December. Overall bank liquidity is excessive and thus provides additional scope for borrowing in Senegal. However, if future demand became excessive on account, notably, of possible competition from other members of the Union, that would lead to an increase in interest rates that would disrupt the balance of public finances and discourage private sector activity. This risk justifies action to promote the expansion of financial savings and, more particularly, savings earmarked for investments on the Abidjan market (Annex 8.5 on page 310 presents the situation of the regional financial market).

Generally speaking, there is a large gap between domestic investment and domestic savings, as we have seen in the above section entitled 'Is expansion of the fiscal space necessary in order to finance the MDGs?' (see Table 8.3). Senegal, like many developing countries, is characterized by a low rate of banking participation by households, which is not conducive to the growth of monetary savings. Indeed, currencies still represent 24 per cent of the money supply (as opposed to only 8.5 per cent in the Euro zone)[32] while bank money and quasi-money represent 39 per cent and 37 per cent of the money supply. The aim should be, first, to increase the participation in the banking system of poor households, whose level is not only low, but the savings of such households are held mainly in the form of cash or goods (grain, herds of animals and land) and, second, to retain the savings of high-income individuals, which are often exported to more developed financial markets.

In Senegal, the number of lending institutions is relatively high (12 banks and 3 financial institutions), which guarantees a certain amount of competition. Interest rates are set freely, apart from savings deposits on which the rate of interest is 3.5 per cent, thereby ensuring a positive rate of real remuneration, since inflation has stayed below 3 per cent since 2001. The Senegalese economy, therefore, does not suffer from financial repression. Even though the banking sector evidently covers few low-income households, it should be noted that the micro-credit institutions have been rapidly expanding their operations in Senegal and, indeed, throughout the WAEMU. From 2000 to 2003, the expansion of outstanding credit by micro-finance institutions was increasing 3.3 times faster than that of bank credit (IMF, 2004b).

Given the number of banks and micro-credit institutions, and the absence of financial repression, increased use of banking services by households probably depends on improvements to the existing financial system in order to increase the confidence of households. Senegal's financial system may be considered to be generally healthy and depositors have never had their deposits frozen as in other WAEMU countries.

However, the level of non-performing loans and the excessive concentration of loans are sources of vulnerability in the system (IMF, 2006b; and for a detailed analysis of the Senegalese financial system see Financial System Stability Assessment - Update, IMF, 2005c). Indeed, the share of non-performing loans in the total remains significant (13 per cent in September 2005), even though it has declined since 2002 (18 per cent in 2002). Loans granted to the five largest borrowers still account for 140 per cent of the capital of banks. Moreover, not all banks exercise normal prudence, especially as regards the risk-weighted capital asset ratio (CAR). The government of Senegal is aware of these problems and requested the Council of Ministers of WAEMU in October 2005 to strengthen the rules governing banking prudence, by increasing the minimum capital asset ratio and by enacting a law on bank failures in line with best international practices.

Naturally, it is not sufficient to increase financial savings. It is also necessary to channel these to the state. This channelling of capital to the public sector must be based both on a strengthening of confidence in the financial stability of the state and on the modernization of the financial techniques used in government borrowing.

The confidence of potential investors depends on the control of public deficits and on improvements in budgetary procedures. Indeed, Senegal has been able to benefit on the regional market from a rate lower than that of other countries of WAEMU partly as a result of the initiative of UNDP, which helped secure a Standard and Poor's rating of B+ for Senegal. It is also the result of the strict management of public finances and of the successful completion of the agreement signed with the IMF. Indeed, the year 2005 was marked by a decline in the overall budget balance from -3.1 per cent of GDP in 2004 to -4 per cent in 2005 (not including grants, respectively -5.2 per cent and -5.8 per cent). For its part, the wage bill increased by 14.6 per cent. The request for a new agreement (without financing) should help to strengthen Senegal's credibility in the eyes of the region's financial institutions. The prospects for the future are thus good, even though certain financial difficulties faced by companies that are important to the Senegalese economy constitute a threat to public finances. In February 2006, the company Chemical Industries of Senegal was unable to honour its matured commercial paper. The company SONACOS is feeling the effects of the low price of peanuts on the international market, and SENELEC has not been authorized to increase the price of electricity following the rise in oil prices. A significant reform would be to improve budgetary transparency, in accordance with the recommendations contained in the budget module of the report on the observation of standards and codes. The main objective is to increase awareness of budget transfers to agencies, to expand the expenditure tracking software system (SIGFIP), and to strengthen the role of the Audit Court.

In the area of debt management, the main aim is to diversify the paper issued. For example, it would be useful to issue indexed bonds (on a price index or the Euro value), as do many developed countries (such as France and the US). Such an arrangement could overcome reluctance on the part of those, especially non-residents, who fear becoming victims of a devaluation of the CFA franc.

If, following an increase in domestic debt, the total government debt of Senegal becomes unsustainable, that would necessarily lead to an increase in interest rates. This hypothesis is unlikely to be realized, given the current level of the debt. Indeed, while it rose between 1999 and 2001, the ratio of debt to GDP has been declining steadily since then. In 2005, Senegal's external debt represented only 44 per cent of its GDP, compared with 75 per cent in 2001, a drop of nearly 40 per cent (see Table 8.11). The level of domestic debt, depending on the data sources, varied between 3.6 per cent (2004 figure) (see Annex 8.3, page 303) and 7 per cent of GDP (see Table 8.11). The total debt of Senegal, therefore, represents approximately 50 per cent of GDP, with domestic debt accounting for a low per cent of the total. The foreign debt to export ratio has shown a similar trend. It fell sharply between 1999 and 2005, from 244 per cent to 160 per cent. Annex 8.6 (page 312) presents a detailed analysis of the current debt situation.

After the implementation of MDRI, which provides for 100 per cent cancellation of the debt owed to the International Development Association, the African Development Fund (FAD) and IMF, the external debt ratio, according to preliminary estimates, should be 15 per cent of GDP and the total debt ratio between 19 per cent and 22 per cent. The IMF is currently preparing a debt sustainability analysis of the volume of future new debt that Senegal could reasonably contract in light of the quality of its economic policies, as measured by the CPIA indicator. For a country like Senegal, which is considered to have a reasonably sound policy, the debt sustainability threshold, expressed as net present value (NPV), could be between 30 per cent and 45 per cent of GDP, using the IMF and World Bank methodology (IMF and IDA, 2005), while the current value is approximately 13 per cent.[33] It is evident that this level reveals a potential for a significant level of new borrowing (cf. IMF, 2008).[34]

Using the most prudent estimate of the level of sustainable debt (30 per cent of GDP), and assuming that the level of current debt, internal and external, could be equal to 20 per cent of GDP, yields a margin for additional borrowing of approximately 10

Table 8.11 *Trends in selected indicators of external public debt (%)*

Years	Debt/GDP	Debt/exports	Debt service/ Exports	Debt service/ tax revenue
1999	68.5	244	11.7	21.3
2000	72.6	260	12.8	23.5
2001	75.6	247.2	10.0	17.7
2002	66.1	217	11.2	18.8
2003	54.4	189	10.1	15.9
2004	45.2	163	6.9	10.7
2005	44.5	160		

Note: The debt service considered here is debt after rescheduling and cancellations under the HIPC Initiative.
Source: Ministry of Finance and Economics, Directorate for Debt and Investment, internal database

per cent of GDP to be distributed between internal and external debt. It is, therefore, not unreasonable to conclude that Senegal could increase the level of its domestic debt by an annual amount of 0.5 per cent of GDP over the next ten years. This percentage corresponds to about one tenth of the present budget deficit (see Table 8.2) and of the funding gap projected for the second phase of the PRSP (see Table 8.6).

Potential borrowing by municipalities
Within the framework of Senegal's PAC 1998–2005, urban municipalities that offered adequate guarantees for success, after a detailed audit of their financial situation, have been able to finance their investments in the following proportions:

- 70 per cent through subsidies from the Municipal Development Agency;
- 20 per cent through loans from that Agency;
- 10 per cent from their own contributions.

The term of the loans granted was 12 years at an interest rate of 4.2 per cent, payable in monthly instalments. Some 48 of the 67 municipalities in Senegal have used this loan/subsidy combination. It is important to note that the municipalities have honoured their commitments to a remarkable extent. The repayment rate for loans was 95.07 per cent, even though 18 municipalities fell behind in their payments by between 4 and 18 months. With regard to the municipalities' own contributions, these were made in 99.52 per cent of cases and only four municipalities fell behind in their payments by between one and four months. It should be noted, however, that the government has been forced, in certain cases, to substitute for the local governments in providing the 'own funds' component.

These good results have led the World Bank and AFD to continue the experiment and, in the case of municipalities in the Dakar metropolitan area, whose financial capacity is superior to that of the other municipalities, to increase the proportion of loans to 30 per cent (Programme for the Strengthening and Equipment of Local Governments).

These results are very encouraging and, as the evaluation report of the World Bank loan allocated to this programme indicates, municipalities in Senegal have developed a culture of financial discipline. However, this does not mean that municipalities are ready to borrow from banks or that banks would be prepared to grant them loans. The excellent loan repayment rates are attributable both to the mix of subsidy to loan and to the technical support available to municipalities for evaluating their financial situation and for concluding 'municipal contracts' with ADM and, thus, selecting their own investments. According to certain officials responsible for the implementation of the new programme, it will be a dozen or more years before most municipalities will be able to borrow freely and directly from the banking system.

In order for banks to be willing to lend to municipalities, they must be in a position not only to assess the their financial situation (the audits carried out by ADM are a good starting point), but also to estimate future flows of resources from municipalities and to secure guarantees. Municipalities wishing to borrow could conceivably be subject to rating by an independent entity (ADF, 2005b). However, it is currently difficult to estimate the level of municipal resources owing to the ongoing reforms of local tax systems and of the arrangements for the transfer of funds from the state (see above), as well as to the uncertainty about the returns on recently installed business infrastructure. Stabilization of the rules for the financing of municipalities, taxes and government transfers could increase their borrowing capacity. With regard to guarantees, a number of innovative mechanisms can be envisaged, such as tax revenues, after these have been placed on a sound footing, or fees, as surety for loans and municipal assets, particularly land as a mortgage. Access to bank credit for the largest urban municipalities is more likely.

In the shorter term, it is possible that ADM, which is financed by the state from its own resources and from grants and loans from donors, might be converted into an autonomous agency for the financing of local governments, which could itself borrow from the banking system. This change would bring the conditions under which local governments borrow more into line with market conditions.

In conclusion, unlike the state, the borrowing potential of the municipalities appears weak in the short term.

Financing of the MDGs by the private sector

As discussed above, private actors are in a position to make significant contributions to the achievement of the MDGs. Their contributions are, by nature, difficult to measure, since they are not subject to programming or to systematic surveys. The potential contributions of households and of the financial system are explored qualitatively here.

Possibility of cost recovery

Where efforts are being made to provide poor populations with social services as quickly and as widely as possible, the possibility of making such groups pay for a part, even a small part, of the cost of the services is a controversial issue. It seems that a distinction must be made here between services that have short-term economic value for populations and those with long-term benefits.

Prospects for cost recovery for services with immediate returns

Certain basic social services have economic value for populations and at the same time improve their well-being. For example, access to drinking water from standpipes or from individual connections has a direct impact on the health of the population, and it also frees women from the burden of fetching water, thereby making more time available to them for productive activities. Another example is connection to an electricity supply network. Cost recovery for commercial services teaches the lesson that it is necessary to avoid waste (of water and energy) and to provide a minimum of resources for the maintenance of facilities to ensure the sustainability of the services. The extremely high demand in Senegal for micro-credit, at very high rates of interest and with excellent repayment rates, shows the capacity of poor people to seize opportunities to invest in projects that yield immediate returns. Naturally, this requires a participatory approach to investment decisions.

Cost recovery will be made easier if rural and semi-urban populations increase their participation in the banking system, which would enable them to safely and beneficially accumulate the real cash resources needed to fulfil their obligations.[35]

Importance of free education and primary healthcare services
It does not seem fair to ask families to pay a part of the monetary cost of educating their children, since the costs they already bear for transportation, school supplies and in the time of children who can no longer be used for domestic tasks, are already high. This high cost is probably one of the reasons, together with the poor opinion parents have about the quality of education, for the low demand for education in certain regions in relation to supply (Robert, 2006). The same type of argument against cost recovery seems to apply to expenditures on primary healthcare, including all prevention-related expenditures, such as vaccinations and prenatal check-ups. As a result, the Ministry of Health plans to reduce the current level of cost recovery, which is considered by many to be prohibitive. This concerns, in particular, primary healthcare and services to vulnerable groups, children, pregnant women and the elderly. In the absence of a social security scheme, the state is forced to assume the basic risks by providing healthcare services at little or no cost.

Role of the financial system in the attainment of the MDGs
Banks could contribute to the attainment of the MDGs by funding more productive activities in two complementary ways: first, by financing SMEs, and second, by increasing the proportion of medium-term loans for the financing of productive investments. Indeed, bank loans appear to be concentrated in large companies. Moreover, the increasing availability of micro-credit has given very small companies relatively easy access to credit. The rationing of credit, therefore, concerns mainly the intermediate segment of SMEs. The Regional Solidarity Bank (BRS) was established in 2005 mainly for the purpose of addressing this shortcoming. In view of the difficulties encountered by these companies in using land guarantees, alternative systems of collateral, particularly mutual sureties, must be developed.

The second characteristic of bank credit is its concentration on short-term loans: an average of 63.9 per cent of loans to the economy during the period from 2003 to 2005 (see Table 8.12). These loans are granted not only to importers but also to large companies. Indeed, even if these large companies obtain sizeable loans, they lack sufficiently rigorous accounting systems for banks to take the risk of lending them a significant proportion of long-term loans. Incentive measures, such as selective exemptions from taxes on bank transactions for medium-term loans or loans in sectors requiring significant investments, may be envisaged. The scarcity of medium-term loans is also linked to the lack of long-term bank resources. One possible solution to this constraint, which is attributable to the structure of bank liabilities, is the use of the external medium-term credit lines granted by the multilateral institutions (World Bank, European Investment Bank, West African Development Bank and African Development Bank). From this viewpoint also, the third component of the 'Compact' programme, associated with the Millennium Challenge Account, establishes a financing facility to alleviate the shortage of long-term bank resources. For reasons of prudence, however, the share of sight or short-term resources converted to medium- or long-term ones cannot exceed a ceiling of 25 per cent.

With respect to medium-term financing, the basic problem is the absence of risk capital companies whose long-term resources would enable them to make this type of loan, while banks' liabilities, comprised mainly of sight deposits, do not predispose them to take this risk. Financing of these risk capital companies can be done through the Collective Investment Schemes (OPCVM) that would have shares in the companies. In order to attract investors to these OPCVM, it is possible to incorporate foreign instruments, but a higher proportion of foreign instruments than is permitted under current regulations would have to be authorized. Generally speaking, an increase in the liquidity of the regional market would favour the mobilization of long-term resources by companies.

Another potential contribution of the banking sector to the achievement of the MDGs is related to the distribution of banks throughout the territory. A wide distribu-

Table 8.12 *Structure of bank credits in Senegal and in WAEMU, 2003–2005*

	Banks of Senegal Millions of CFAfr			Average	WAEMU banks Millions of CFAfr			Average
	2003	*2004*	*2005*	*2003–2005*	*2003*	*2004*	*2005*	*2003–2005*
Short-term credits	513.2	548.2	659.0		2324.5	2431.0	2679.7	
Farm credits	3.6	14.0	10.1		128.2	114.0	167.0	
Ordinary credits	509.6	534.2	648.9		2196.4	2317.0	2512.7	
Medium-term credits	235.3	268.8	359.6		781.1	936.9	1110.3	
Long-term credits	33.6	36.8	45.4		117.1	135.3	132.5	
Total	782.1	853.9	1064.0		3222.7	3503.2	3922.4	
Percentage								
Short-term credits	65.6	64.2	61.9	63.9	72.1	69.4	68.3	69.9
Farm credits	0.5	1.6	0.9	1.0	4.0	3.3	4.3	3.8
Ordinary credits	65.2	62.6	61.0	62.9	68.2	66.1	64.1	66.1
Medium-term credits	30.1	31.5	33.8	31.8	24.2	26.7	28.3	26.4
Long-term credits	4.3	4.3	4.3	4.3	3.6	3.9	3.4	3.6
Total	100.0	100.0	100.0	100.0	100.0	100.0	100.0	100.0

Source: BCEAO (2006a) and previous years

tion could facilitate the payment of teachers and health personnel in rural areas, in particular. Indeed, the need to travel to a payment centre to collect one's salary is very costly in terms of the time spent by civil servants stationed in remote areas. Their absence during these periods of travel reduces the supply of basic social services. An indirect impact of the expansion of banking services on the achievement of the MDGs, by developing mobile banking centres for example, would be a reduction in this absenteeism. It should be noted that Senegal is not the country in which these potential gains are the greatest, insofar as villages are rarely more than one day's travel away from the nearest payment centre.

Expansion of the domestic budgetary space in Senegal appears not only to be justified (see the section 'Is expansion of the fiscal space necessary in order to finance the MDGs?' above), but possible. It should be achieved mainly through the increase in the resources of the municipalities and expanded borrowing by the state. It would be useful at this stage to examine the risks and conditions for the success of this expansion.

RISKS AND CONDITIONS FOR THE SUCCESSFUL EXPANSION OF THE FISCAL SPACE

There are currently two conflicting theses in the international community. The definition in 2000 of the Millennium Goals, the objective of which is to eradicate a large part of the poverty in the world by the year 2015, and the delay in the implementation of which, over the past five years, have led to the idea that it was necessary to massively and quickly increase public expenditures, particularly those earmarked for basic services for the poor population. That, in turn, gave rise to a commitment on the part of the industrialized countries to significantly increase the level of their aid. At the same time, however, there is doubt as to whether it is possible to quickly and effectively increase public expenditures, whether financed from domestic resources or from foreign assistance. These two theses are linked to the analyses of earlier authors of development economics, the first to the theory of the big push (Rosenstein-Rodan, 1943, 1961) and the second to that of absorption capacity (Millikan and Rostow, 1957, and again Rosenstein-Rodan, 1961).[36] It is this second theory that needs to be examined here, since it points to the difficulties that would follow from an acceleration of expenditure. These difficulties are of two kinds. There are physical and administrative constraints to the rapid mobilization of additional financing. Second, a massive increase in public expenditures creates a difficult problem of macroeconomic management, insofar as it risks endangering competitiveness.

Risk of low utilization and limited effectiveness of additional resources

As was seen in the section 'Is expansion of the fiscal space necessary in order to finance the MDGs?', public expenditures aimed at reducing poverty are shared between the state and the local authorities. The problem of capacity to manage additional resources is posed at both levels, but clearly with particular severity at the local level because of the fact that decentralization is relatively recent in Senegal.

Administrative constraints to effective execution of the budget

Poor execution of expenditures in basic services

When reading the second PRSP review, for the year 2004 (Ministry of Economy and Finance, 2005a), one is struck by the huge difference between the rate of execution of expenditures under the national budget from internal resources and those from external aid. These rates are, respectively, 80.3 per cent and 45.1 per cent. The same rates, relative to expenditures funded from external aid are, however, 92 per cent and 96 per cent. The low rate of execution of investment expenditures from domestic resources in the second strategic approach mainly concerns the education sector (32.5 per cent) and, to a lesser extent the health sector (65.8 per cent), while the resources allocated to education account for 72.6 per cent of total domestic resources under the second main line.

The slow pace of execution of expenditures is attributable to the shortcomings of the budgetary procedures, which were highlighted in the Country Financial Accountability Assessment-Country Procurement Assessment Report (CFAA-CPAR). For a number of years now, Senegal has improved its budgetary procedures, an important goal of its policy. It has introduced an expenditure tracking software system (SIGFIP) that reveals at any given time the status of expenditures. The question could also be asked whether or not the recent decision to decentralize the BCI will help to ensure the rapid execution of expenditures. Initially, the fear is that the delays will be even greater (see below). Lastly, Senegal has adopted a new public procurement code and introduced a plan for procurement throughout the year under which bids could be invited before the credits were opened. This reform is all the more important as Senegal has pledged to significantly reduce the share of no-bid contracts (without succeeding in 2005 in fully respecting its commitment).

The problem of the quality of executed expenditures

The improvement in the rates of execution would not be desirable at the price of a decline in the effectiveness of expenditures. In its review of public expenditures, the World Bank (2005) noted the low productivity of public investment expenditures. Improvement in the quality of expenditures requires, at the outset, better planning of expenditures to clearly establish the costs and benefits, even if it is not evident in the social sectors how to define and collect good indicators of results. This is the objective of the Medium Term Expenditure Framework (CDMT), which, in practice, began to be implemented in the education and health sectors from 1998 and should be extended to all public investments (see Ministry of Economy and Finance, 2005b).

The question of the quality of expenditures was certainly exacerbated by the expansion of the goals and resources in the area of social services. A good example is found in the education sector. As was seen in the section 'Is expansion of the fiscal space necessary in order to finance the MDGs?', the gross rate of school attendance increased from 68 per cent in 2000 to 80 per cent in 2004, which ranks Senegal above the average for low-income African countries (75 per cent). At the same time, the gross college attendance rate rose from 23.1 per cent to 29.4 per cent and the expansion of secondary education was also rapid: 333 students per 100,000 people in 2001, against 555 in 2004. Only the numbers of students attending high schools and technical and vocational schools registered no increases. These results have been achieved with increased resources. The share of expenditures on education in GDP, 4 per cent, is higher than the upper threshold of indicative values in the Fast Track Initiative indicative framework (3.6 per cent) (see Annex 3, Table 2 of Robert, 2006). Senegal's eligibility for the Fast Track Initiative should create the impetus for further acceleration of expenditures in primary education.

A series of elements suggests that the quality and scope of primary education have not improved or may have even declined. The proportion of children completing six years of primary schooling, which is no doubt necessary in order to achieve effective literacy, has not improved since 2001 (rate of completion of primary school lower than 50 per cent). While there have been no recent tests of standardized evaluation, the 2002 evaluation ranks Senegal very low among African countries (see UNESCO, 2006).[37] The high school dropout rate is due to the high incidence of repeats and the fact that the education system does not always meet the expectations of families, who often view the quality of schools as poor. This underscores the importance of improving the pedagogical management of primary education and its local administration (see Robert, 2006). Note should be taken, in particular, of the urgent need to increase the number of effective teaching hours (hours spent by the teacher 'chalk in hand'), especially by reducing teacher and student absenteeism (reform of the school calendar), developing an elementary school curriculum (programmes, pedagogical tools, testing) and establishing mechanisms for monitoring teaching practices.

It seems, moreover, that the recruitment of volunteers as teachers in primary schools who are paid one-third of the salary of fully-fledged qualified teachers has not led to a decline in the quality of teaching. The reason for this is the large number of unemployed graduate students who took up these posts for which they were overqualified. It remains true, nevertheless, that the high level of unionization of teachers makes it difficult to ensure an optimal geographic distribution.

The question of the absorption of additional resources also arises in the health sector. The share of health expenditures in GDP has risen steadily to 8.25 per cent in 2003 (PNDS). However, the IMF noted (IMF, 2006b, p12) with regret, that the funds allocated to health declined in 2006, due apparently to a shortage of new projects to be funded, which indicates the existence of limited absorption capacity, at least in the short term. According to the Minister of Health, the principal bottleneck is currently the difficulty of quickly training health personnel (nurses, midwives and laboratory workers). In response to this problem, three regional schools have been established to train nurses and midwives and three more are due to be opened in 2006. A project is in place to open new decentralized medical faculties. Only an increase in the supply of health personnel could enable them to be deployed throughout the national territory, particularly in remote rural areas.

Administrative weaknesses of technical ministries

These absorption difficulties are due in part to the administrative weaknesses of the technical ministries. The Ministry of Education is certainly an important example in this regard. This becomes evident from a reading of the report on the technical evaluation of the candidacy of Senegal for the Fast Track Initiative (Robert, 2006). This report underscores the difficulty of precisely measuring resources in terms of personnel and of effective expenditures.[38] The severity of this problem can be seen from the fact that many donors sponsor projects aimed at improving the management capacity of the Ministry of Education[39] at the risk of creating a problem of coordination between the different initiatives of donors.

Management weaknesses are also reflected in the difficulty of producing the many follow-up indicators for their actions. This poses a problem, especially since donors are increasingly conditioning their disbursements on the achievement of a certain number of results. Taking the education sector again as an example, our view is that the indicators chosen[40] are too numerous, they inadequately target primary education alone and are too focused on resources instead of being centred on the final impact of primary education policies.[41]

Constraints and prospects for decentralization

Opinions as to the capacity of local authorities to achieve the MDGs in the areas of their responsibility seem rather divided. On the one hand, the transfer of responsibilities to the municipalities discussed above should lead to better targeting of expenses to the real needs of the population, while, on the other hand, it raises the issue of the management capacity of local governments and the proper functioning of the budget process.

Thus in its Country Report No. 05/155, the IMF (2005a) considered that the Senegalese authorities have major challenges to meet in increasing the management capacities of local authorities and reducing the opacity of the budget process, simplifying the expenditure process, better regulating procurement, improving accountability and developing ex post control systems. Furthermore, the weight of the government in decisions on the allocation of the investment budget carries the risk that the real needs of the population at the local level would not be adequately taken into account.

The view of the World Bank (2005) seems to be less pessimistic insofar as it has contributed through its PAC to the improvement of management capacity in the municipalities. Under this programme, local officials have undergone training courses (1741 officials).[42] However, many municipalities have still not managed to reduce the number of ineffective personnel and to recruit the required expertise, perhaps because no assistance has been provided to help retrain dismissed workers. Under the city contracts that were required prior to any ADM funding, municipalities were accustomed to basing their decisions on a systematic audit of their financial situation and an analysis of the economic and financial viability of planned investments. The sustainability of this approach was strengthened by the training of local consultants for municipality support missions (23 audit companies underwent training sessions). It also appears that the cost of investments is significantly lower (about 20 to 30 per cent) when invitations to tender are managed by the local governments than when they are managed by the sectoral ministries. This is because of the too small size of the projects for companies based in Dakar and the social control which can be exercised on local companies (interview with Christian Fournier, UNCDF). Even though a great deal remains to be done to strengthen management capacity in the municipalities, the World Bank believes that progress has clearly been made (see World Bank, 2005).

The municipalities have come up against three main problems: (1) the lack of available land on which to carry out investment projects; (2) insufficient funds allocated in their budgets for the maintenance of infrastructure (the solution to this problem is clearly critical to the continuity and quality of services provided); and (3) the lack of structures (outside the Dakar and Rusfique urban agglomerations, which were recently put in place) capable of managing inter-municipal infrastructure.

The FECL reform project, described earlier, should improve the quality of expenditures by the municipalities. From this perspective, a number of measures have been proposed. These include modification of funding mechanisms, rationalization of the criteria for the allocation of financing, reduction in the time taken for disbursement to local governments, and establishment of mechanisms for the monitoring and control of the use of the Fund. In addition to the necessary increases in the amounts, the fundamental problem for local governments is the unpredictability of the resources transferred by the state. The establishment of clear rules for the distribution of the FECL is a move in that direction. In the same vein, a project is underway to inform local governments of the future amounts that will be transferred to them so that budgets could be voted on this basis.

The main risk for the future of decentralization, and thus of the achievement of the MDGs, lies in a loss of autonomy by the local governments or ADM in favour of the national government. This could jeopardize the earlier initiative, which was based on 'city contracts' aimed at locally identifying the needs of the populations and at providing investments in the capacity of municipalities to absorb new projects. This could also jeopardize the development of ADM as an agency for the financing of municipalities. The new programme to promote the municipalities, which must be negotiated by the World Bank and AFD for the five-year period ahead, takes account of these risks.

The risk of loss of competitiveness

Dutch Disease theory

It is known that a sudden influx of external resources, due, for example, to a marked improvement in the terms of trade, to the discovery of natural resources, to FDI or to foreign aid, could give rise to a 'Dutch Disease' effect.[43] The reasoning is simple. If the inflow of external resources is not completely absorbed by additional imports, it leads to an increase in demand for goods that are not internationally tradable. If there is no unutilized production capacity in this sector, this increase in demand leads to a relative price increase in these goods, in other words a rise in the real exchange rate (or real appreciation in the national currency) and a loss of competitiveness.[44] This real appreciation is manifested in ways that include a rise in real wages for qualified labour, which is a rare factor of production in developing countries. It therefore risks affecting, in particular, the industrial sector or commercial services that use modern technology that is particularly demanding of qualified labour (Rajan and Subramanian, 2005).

An increase in the public domestic debt can have a similar effect when the borrowing is done in the regional (and no longer national) financial market and/or in an over-liquid economy, so that this reliance on domestic savings to effect additional public expenditures does not bring about a reduction in private expenditures. If the increase in public expenditures is allocated to imported goods, it will have no impact on the price level of these goods in an economy like Senegal's where the currency is convertible. It will merely lead to a reduction in foreign reserves whose level we have deemed to be excessive. In contrast, if the additional public expenditures are allocated to non-tradable goods, they can lead to an increase in the prices of those goods, a rise in the real rate of exchange and a loss in competitiveness of the economy as a whole, since the nominal rate of exchange is fixed and established at the level of the Union.

However, the real appreciation of the currency poses a problem of competitiveness only if it is not accompanied by an increase in productivity. If the additional public expenditures increase the production capacity in the sector of non-tradable goods, they help to stop the rise in prices. If they improve the productivity of the sector of export or import substitution goods they help to offset the impact of the real appreciation in the competitiveness of the economy. That is why it is important for the state to ensure that a balance is maintained between public expenditures aimed at expanding productive capacity and improving the productivity of factors (communication infrastructure, worker training and dissemination of new technologies, for example) and those allocated to the social sectors. Current expenditures or investment in child health and education have only long-term impacts on labour productivity. In the short term, increased hiring in these sectors tends to increase the cost of qualified labour. Care should also be taken to avoid sudden changes in the pattern of expenditures that are likely to provoke instability in the real rate of exchange. Where this is not anticipated by economic agents, it results in the reallocation of resources between sectors, which is costly and unjustified over the long term. Even where it is anticipated, it can lead to the cessation of activity in the face of credit market imperfections that would be difficult to reverse. The negative consequences of instability in the real rate of exchange on the expansion of foreign trade and more generally on growth are now well established (Guillaumont et al, 1998; Bleaney and Greenway, 2001).

Changes in competitiveness in Senegal

Given the economic trends of recent years, there is little fear of a loss of competitiveness in Senegal as a result of the increase in the fiscal space brought about by an increase in aid and recourse to domestic borrowing. Over the past five years inflation has been low (average annual rate of 1.5 per cent, see Table 8.2) and the macroeconomic strengthening of the second phase of the PRSP suggest that the level of this increase will be kept above the community threshold (2.2 per cent compared with 3 per cent). The IMF (2006b) recently expressed concern at the risk of inflation that might result from an increase in the budget deficit for the year 2006. The moderate increase in inflation recorded in 2005, however, seems linked in particular to the increase in the price of oil and there is currently little evidence of inflationary tendencies.

The change in the real exchange rate calculated by the IMF (Table 8.13) indicates a real rate of depreciation of approximately 10 per cent since the devaluation of 1994, and a very slight appreciation since 2000 due in large part to the appreciation of the Euro against the dollar. Moreover, in view of the marked increase in per capita GDP since 2000, this low rate of real appreciation should have been partially offset by an increase in productivity. In addition Senegal has experienced a change in its competitive position that is much more favourable than the other countries of the WAEMU since 1994 (see IMF 2006b and Figure 8.3). Indeed, while Senegal has experienced real depreciation over this period, all the other countries of the Union have had a real appreciation of between 10 per cent and 35 per cent. It therefore seems that Senegal's competitiveness has not declined in recent times and that it has even increased in comparison with its partners in the Union.

The change in relative prices in the Senegalese economy can be seen from the secondary nomenclature of the price index provided by the Department of Economic Estimates and Statistics (Ministry of Economy and Finance, 2006a). During the period 2002 to 2005, the rise in prices of local goods has been only slightly higher than the increase in prices of imported goods (1 per cent per annum compared with 0.1 per cent, respectively). During this same period, price increases in the tertiary sector (comprised mainly of non-tradable goods) is not markedly higher than increases in the secondary sector (comprised mainly of tradable goods), since the annual inflation rates were 0.8 per cent and 0.5 per cent. There is, therefore, no change in the cost of production in relation to the price of internationally traded goods. These figures confirm the thesis of the maintenance of a satisfactory level of competitiveness in Senegal in recent years. It is true, however, that the continued nominal appreciation of

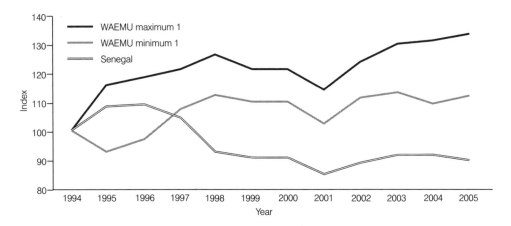

Source: IMF (2006b)

Figure 8.3 *Index of real rate of exchange in Senegal and comparison with other member countries of WAEMU, 1994–September 2005*

the Euro vis-à-vis the dollar could jeopardize this good performance of the country's competitiveness.

The other positive element to consider is the strategy for reducing poverty that has been adopted by Senegal (IMF, 2006a). It should be recalled that this strategy is based on three main approaches: wealth creation, capacity building and the expansion of basic services, and improvement in the living conditions of the most vulnerable sectors of the population. Some 36 per cent of all domestic and external resources, not including HIPC resources, have been allocated to this first component.[45] This percentage would be somewhat lower if HIPC resources (a fifth of the total), which are no doubt concentrated in the sector of basic services,[46] were included. If we consider

Table 8.13 *Nominal and real effective exchange rate in Senegal, 1994–2004*

	TCEN	TCER
1994	100.0	100.0
1995	104.9	108.3
1996	105.5	108.9
1997	101.8	104.9
1998	104.1	92.7
1999	102.4	90.9
2000	97.3	85.2
2001	98.5	86.7
2002	100.8	89.0
2003	106.1	91.6
2004	108.0	92.1

Notes: TCEN is the French acronym for nominal effective exchange rate (taux de change effectif nominal), while TCER stands for real effective exchange rate (taux de change effectif reél).
Source: IMF (2006b)

expenses that are effectively disbursed, the percentage rises in favour of expenditures on wealth creation (to 47 per cent), since the rate of execution is higher in this component. It is all the more important to maintain the balance[47] between productive and social expenditures as, in order to achieve the Millennium Development Goal of a reduction in extreme monetary poverty, an annual rate of economic growth of at least 7 per cent is necessary.

At the level of the municipalities, the same balance between investment expenditures yielding quick economic returns and social expenditures with more long-term benefits should also be maintained. A review of the structure of projects deemed to be priorities and carried out by the municipalities under the PAC shows that 65 per cent have been basic and market infrastructure projects. The rest consist of projects in the fields of health and education, administrative and social infrastructure, and environmental projects or projects for the preservation of the country's historical patrimony (Gorée Island) (World Bank, 2005).

CONCLUSION

The question posed by this study is whether it is possible to expand the domestic fiscal space in Senegal, or, in other words, to mobilize additional domestic resources (own, borrowed or reallocated resources) in order to finance the achievement of the MDGs. The situation of Senegal is exemplary in many respects, both in terms of the justifications for this expansion and the resources to be employed.

The progress still to be made to achieve the MDGs justifies the mobilization of additional financing in the years ahead, since the actions provided for under the second PRSP (2006–2010) represent approximately 12 per cent of average GDP for the period. However, the level of external resources should increase significantly in the years ahead, probably by more than 4.5 per cent of average GDP, and it is possible that this would be sufficient to cover most of the needs for financing in the education and health sectors. However, poverty reduction has other dimensions, including, in particular, basic infrastructure, access to water, access to electricity, and development of environmentally friendly sources of energy. Moreover, expansion of the domestic fiscal space would enable Senegal to be less dependent on foreign assistance. Such dependence, which is currently high in Senegal, is dangerous to the extent that the unpredictability of aid sources is a threat to the sustainability of its strategy for combating poverty. Moreover, studies have highlighted the institutional difficulties created by over dependency on aid, which can lead to less responsibility on the part of the political authorities, who would then be little inclined to be accountable to their citizens. Donors are no doubt studying ways of changing the modalities of aid to attenuate this unfavourable impact. By increasing the freedom of action of the Senegalese Government, expansion of the domestic fiscal space is another possible response.

Expansion of the fiscal space can, in theory, be achieved through tax revenues (central and local), seignorage, borrowing, and private sector contributions. Senegal appears to have limited fiscal room for expanding government tax revenues. Indeed, the recent increase in fiscal pressures has enabled Senegal to exploit its tax potential with satisfactory results and the reforms introduced since 2004 have had the overall effect of reducing taxes on companies and thereby promoting growth. Additionally, local tax reform and improvements in the administration of local taxes should enable local governments to increase their tax revenues. The reallocation of a part of government revenues to local governments through transfers (FDD, FECL and decentralization of the BIC) could further increase the revenues of local governments.

Given Senegal's membership in the WAEMU, seignorage cannot play a major role in increasing the level of resources available to the state. Alternatively, Senegal should be able to increase its borrowing on the regional market because of the good handling of its public finances and the liquidity in the Senegalese economy or, more generally, in the Union. The cost of this debt should remain reasonable in the medium term, particularly if measures to encourage savings are simultaneously implemented. Since these resources will be obtained at market prices, they should be targeted at investments that stimulate growth.

Lastly, the private sector can contribute to the financing of the MDGs through selective cost recovery for only those services that have immediate economic returns (and not education and basic healthcare services). By expanding medium-term financing, which is currently very limited, the financial system should be able to stimulate growth and thereby bring about a reduction in poverty.

The increase in the level of resources mobilized to finance the achievement of the MDGs carries risks that Senegal should be able to overcome. The first of these risks lies in the capacity to absorb the resources mobilized. The aim is both to guarantee a good rate of realization of planned expenditures (which requires, in particular, the streamlining of budgetary procedures), and to improve the quality of expenditures executed. It also requires an evaluation of the constraints existing in each sector. Improvement in the quality of expenditures in education appears to be closely linked to a strengthening of the capacity to manage and control the education system. Improved capacity to train medical personnel is, without doubt, the major challenge in the health sector. The transfer of financial resources to local governments should help improve the quality of expenditures, since local governments are best placed to identify the needs of their populations, but this improvement can be achieved only if the management capacity of local governments is significantly strengthened. Another risk frequently discussed in the literature on large increases in public expenditure is the risk of provoking macroeconomic imbalances and lessening the competitiveness of the economy. This risk did not appear to be high in Senegal, given the trend in the real effective exchange rate and in relative prices, provided however that a balance is maintained between social expenditures and expenditures to stimulate growth.

ANNEX 8.1 — MILLENNIUM DEVELOPMENT GOALS
AND RELATED TARGETS

Goal 1: Eradicate extreme hunger and poverty

Target 1: By 2015, halve the proportion of people whose income is less than $1 a day.
Target 2: By 2015, halve the proportion of people who suffer from hunger.

Goal 2: Achieve universal primary education

Target 3: Ensure that by 2015 children everywhere, boys and girls alike, will be able to complete a full course of primary schooling.

Goal 3: Promote gender equality and empower women

Target 4: Eliminate gender disparity in primary and secondary education by 2005 and in all levels of education no later than 2015.

Goal 4: Reduce child mortality

Target 5: By 2015, reduce by two-thirds the under-five mortality rate.

Goal 5: Improve maternal health

Target 6: By 2015, reduce by three-quarters the maternal mortality ratio.

Goal 6: Combat HIV/AIDS, malaria and other diseases

Target 7: By 2015, have halted and begun to reverse the spread of HIV/AIDS.
Target 8: By 2015, have halted and begun to reverse the incidence of malaria.

Goal 7: Ensure environmental sustainability

Target 9: Integrate the principles of sustainable development into country policies.
Target 10: By 2015, halve the proportion of people without sustainable access to safe drinking water.
Target 11: By 2020, have achieved a significant improvement in the lives of at least 100 million slum dwellers.

Goal 8: Develop a global partnership for development

Target 12: Develop a more open financial system that includes good governance and poverty reduction.
Target 13: Address the special needs of the least developed countries (relief from, and cancellation of, official bilateral debt, more generous official development assistance).
Target 14: Address the special needs of landlocked developing countries and small island developing states.
Target 15: Deal comprehensively with the debt problems of developing countries.
Target 16: Create productive work for youth.
Target 17: Provide access for all to essential drugs.
Target 18: Make available to all the benefits of new technologies.

ANNEX 8.2 — BALANCE OF PAYMENTS AND TOFE DATA

Table 8.A1 *Balance of payments of Senegal (CFAfr billions)*

	2000	2001	2002	2003	2004	2005*
Exports free on board (FOB)	654.9	735.3	743.4	730.6	797.4	810.1
Including other WAEMU countries	61.3	85.0	125.1	165.1	183.2	186.1
Imports FOB	−951.6	−1047.1	−1117.9	−1200.5	−1318.5	−1507.8
Including other WAEMU countries	−47.0	−59.7	−43.4	−56.2	−56.3	−64.3
Trade balance	−296.7	−311.8	−374.6	−469.9	−521.1	−697.7
Services balance	−12.9	−11.4	−12.7	−13.0	−14.8	−16.3
Including freight and insurance	−125.4	−138.7	−146.9	−158.4	−173.9	−204.4
Net revenues	−79.3	−76.8	−90.6	−79.1	−69.0	−71.9
Including interest on debt	−57.9	−45.4	−47.5	−45.7	−47.4	−41.0
Balance on current transfers	152.3	220.0	256.9	308.3	333.9	403.0
private	100.1	172.8	192.2	241.0	269.6	345.1
public	52.2	47.2	64.8	67.3	64.3	57.9
Balance on current transactions	−236.6	−179.9	−220.9	−253.8	−271.0	−382.9
Financial capital and operations account	234.4	249.8	311.2	301.1	368.4	377.6
Capital account	59.4	107.1	88.4	87.4	396.2	101.7
Including debt relief	4.2	21.6	22.0	20.7	322.1	32.6
Financial operations	175.0	142.7	222.8	213.7	−27.8	275.9
Direct investments	44.3	28.6	30.7	29.0	33.8	52.7
inflows	62.6	75.5	69.9	77.9	91.4	108.2
outflows	−18.3	−46.9	−39.2	−48.9	−57.6	−55.5
Portfolio investments	9.8	10.2	2.1	12.8	−14.7	−11.6
inflows	20.8	20.4	15.7	26.3	15.9	14.6
outflows	−11.1	−10.2	−13.6	−13.5	−30.7	−26.2
Other investments	120.9	103.9	190.0	171.9	−46.9	234.8
Public	40.7	62.7	61.9	38.7	−176.4	108.8
draw downs (budget support loans and project loans)	88.0	116.5	120.7	90.9	156.6	153.5
amortization	−94.5	−99.8	−112.6	−113.2	−380.8	−74.1
rescheduling	47.2	46.0	54.8	62.0	46.2	29.4
variation of arrears	0.0	0.0	0.0	0.0	0.0	0.0
other (including investments yet to be secured)	0.0	0.0	−1.0	−1.0	1.6	0.0
Private	80.2	41.1	128.1	133.2	129.5	126.0
Net errors and omissions	−6.3	6.1	21.4	8.7	9.1	0.0
Total before adjustments	−8.5	76.0	111.7	56.0	106.4	−5.3
Adjustment of cash in circulation (CF)	–	–	–	164.4	–	–
Total after adjustments CF	−8.5	76.0	111.7	220.4	106.4	−5.3
Rate of coverage: export/imports (%)	68.8	70.2	66.5	60.9	60.5	53.7
Degree of openness (import + export)/GDP (%)	51.6	53.3	53.7	51.8	52.5	51.1
Current account balance/GDP (%)	−7.6	−5.4	−6.4	−6.8	−6.7	−8.4
Current account balance not including grants/GDP (%)	−9.3	−6.8	−8.2	−8.6	−8.3	−9.7
Current account balance not including grants	−288.8	−227.2	−285.6	−321.0	−335.3	−440.8
GDP	3.1	3342.7	3472.7	3725.5	4029.2	4537.1
Total/GDP	−0.3	2.3	3.2	1.5	2.6	−0.1

Note: *Estimation.
Source: BCEAO, Balance of Payments; Republic of Senegal (2005) and previous years

Table 8.A2 *Table of TOFE in Senegal (% of GDP except where otherwise indicated)*

	2001	2002	2003	2004	2005	2006
Total Revenue and Grants	19.9	20.9	21.4	21.5	22.0	21.9
Revenue	18.0	19.1	19.3	19.3	20.2	20.0
Tax revenue	17.3	18.1	18.2	18.3	19.3	19.1
Non-tax revenue	0.8	1.0	1.2	1.0	0.9	0.9
Grants	1.8	1.8	2.1	2.2	1.8	1.9
Total expenditure and net lending	22.3	21.6	23.1	24.5	25.6	25.8
Current expenditure	15.5	13.8	14.2	13.7	15.1	15.0
Wages and salaries	5.3	5.7	5.5	5.4	5.9	5.7
Interest payments	0.9	1.1	1.2	1.2	1.0	1.0
Other current expenditure	9.2	6.9	7.5	7.2	8.3	8.3
Goods and services	3.9	...	3.8	3.7	3.6	3.9
Transfers and subsidies	5.3	...	3.8	3.4	4.5	4.2
Capital expenditure	6.9	7.9	9.1	10.2	9.8	10.1
Domestically financed	4.0	4.3	5.1	5.5	5.9	6.3
Externally financed	3.0	3.7	4.0	4.7	3.9	3.8
Treasury special accounts and correspondents (net)	...	...	...	...	...	...
Net lending	−0.2	−0.2	0.3	0.2	0.2	
Temporary costs of structural reforms	0.0	0.0	0.0	0.3	0.1	0.3
Selected public sector entities balance[1]	−0.2	0.6	0.3	−0.2	0.0	0.0
Primary fiscal balance[2]	−1.5	0.5	−0.5	−1.9	−2.5	−3.0
Overall fiscal balance						
Payment order basis, excluding grants	−4.4	−1.8	−3.5	−5.5	−5.3	−5.8
Payment order basis, including grants	−2.6	0.0	−1.4	−3.3	−3.5	−4.0
Basic fiscal balance (programme definition)[3]	−0.8	2.1	1.3	0.8	0.9	0.0
Financing	2.6	0.0	1.4	3.3	3.5	4.0
External financing	1.6	2.0	1.8	3.5	3.9	3.1
Domestic financing	0.3	−2.1	−0.3	−0.2	−0.3	0.8
Errors and omissions	0.6	0.2	0.0	−0.1	0.0	0.0
Financing gap	0.0	0.0	0.0	0.0	0.0	0.0
Memorandum items:						
Basic fiscal balance (WAEMU definition)[4]	−1.3	2.0	0.6	−0.2	−0.8	−1.5
HIPC Initiative expenditure	0.5	0.1	0.8	0.7	1.6	1.1
Health expenditure	2.1	1.7	1.8	2.1	...	...
Education expenditure	4.3	4.4	5.0	4.9	...	...
Wages and salaries (in per cent of fiscal revenue)	29.4	30.0	28.3	28.0	29.0	28.5
GDP (CFAfr billions)	3343	3473	3725	4029	4346	4600

Notes: 1 Local governments, autonomous public sector entities (for example, hospitals, universities), and the civil servants' pension fund (FNR). 2 Defined as total revenue and grants minus total expenditure and net lending, excluding interest expenditure. 3 Defined as total revenue minus total expenditure and net lending, excluding externally financed capital expenditure, on-lending, cost of structural reforms and HIPC expenditure. 4 Defined as total revenue minus total expenditure and net lending, excluding externally financed capital expenditure, and on-lending.
Source: IMF (2006b)

ANNEX 8.3 — IMPACT OF 2004 TAX REFORMS ON TAX RECEIPTS

Table 8.A3 *Local and national governments' direct tax receipts, 2000–2006 (CFAfr billions)*

	2000	2001	2002	2003	2004	2005	2006
Direct central government taxes							
Company taxes	46.8	52.6	52.8	53.8	71.4	88.6	
Other taxes on income	13.1	7.6	7.3	8.8	6.2	10.6	
Total	59.9	60.2	60.1	62.6	77.6	99.2	
Local direct taxes							
Tax on household garbage disposal	3.4	3.4	3.5	4.3	3.5	4.1	4.1
Land taxes	6	7.2	6.4	7.1	6.7	6.8	5.8
Minimum tax	0.02	0.04	0.04	0.05	0.01	0.01	0.01
Single global contribution (CGU)					1.8	2.2	2.2
Licenses	0.02	0.02	0.04	0.02	0.01	0.01	0.01
Trading taxes	9	12.7	14	12.8	21.2	24.3	24.1
Total	18.44	23.36	23.98	24.27	33.22	37.42	36.22

Source: Ministry of Economy and Finance (2005e)

Table 8.A4 *Estimate of the impact of reduction in the corporate tax rate*

	2000	2001	2002	2003	2004	2005	2006
Profits before reduction	155.8	152.9	155.6	156	220	242.8	266.7
Company tax	39.6	46.5	52.5	52.6	72.7	79.9	87.8
Company tax at 25%	39	38.2	39	39	55.2	60.7	66.7
Gap at 25%	−0.6	−8.3	−13.5	−13.6	−17.5	−19.2	−21.1
Company tax at 30%	46.7	45.9	46.7	46.8	66.3	72.8	80
Gap at 30%	7.1	−0.6	−5.8	−5.8	−6.4	−7.1	−7.8

Source: Ministry of Economy and Finance (2005e)

ANNEX 8.4 — MONETARY AND BANK SITUATION

Table 8.A5 *Summary accounts of the Central Bank at 31 December 2003–2005 (CFAfr millions)*

	Senegal			WAMU		
	2003	2004	2005	2003	2004	2005
Net foreign assets	351,581	471,142	486,468	2,894,468	3,029,828	3,195,388
Gross foreign assets	577,347	658,924	665,616	3,735,286	3,729,418	3,768,896
Foreign liabilities	225,766	187,782	179,148	840,818	699,590	573,508
Credit to government	262,157	226,096	203,754	1,130,891	972,223	869,553
Claims on banks	0	0	0	1687	1212	10,534
Claims on other institutions	0	0	0	6258	1247	1110
Total assets	613,737	697,237	690,222	4,033,303	4,004,510	4,076,584
Currency in circulation	337,497	344,346	388,503	1,847,876	1,799,736	2,046,258
Government deposits (including cash)	86,638	118,060	120,724	429,717	413,763	332,106
Bank deposits (including cash)	185,510	233,843	178,628	707,942	819,608	670,745
Other deposits	1475	303	490	113,904	111,152	84,625
Other net categories	2618	686	1877	933,864	860,250	942,850
Total liabilities	613,737	697,237	690,222	4,033,303	4,004,510	4,076,584
Credit/liabilities reconciliation	0	0	0	0	0	0

Source: BCEAO (2006a) and previous years

Table 8.A6 *Central Bank interventions (CFAfr millions)*

	Bank of Senegal			WAMU		
	2003	2004	2005	2003	2004	2005
Support to banks and financial institutions	0	0	0	7945	2459	11,644
Money market	0	0	0	0	0	0
Pensions	0	0	0	7945	2459	11,644
Advances on government instruments	0	0	0	0	0	0
Consolidation	0	0	0	0	0	0
Other support	0	0	0	0	0	0
Support to treasury	75,260	66,509	57,860	396,984	372,506	354,834
Security warranty discount	0	0	0	0	0	0
Current account deficit	68,760	62,209	55,460	379,900	356,043	340,733
Government securities discount (Art.15)	0	0	0	0	0	0
Government securities	6,500	4,300	2,400	17,081	16,462	14,099
Compte cheques postaux	0	0	0	2	1	1
Total interventions	75,260	66,509	57,860	404,928	374,965	366,478

Source: BCEAO (2006a) and previous years

Table 8.A7 *Changes in Central Bank intervention rates (%)*

Date of change	Discount rate	Pension rate	Money market rate	Invitations to tender Injections	Recovery
31 December 2002	6.50	6.00	4.95	4.95	5.00
1 July 2003	6.50	6.00	4.95	4.95	5.00
7July 2003	5.50	5.00	4.95	4.95	5.00
13 October 2003	5.50	5.00	4.95	4.95	5.00
20 October 2003	5.00	4.50	4.95	4.95	5.00
15 March 2004	5.00	4.50	4.95	4.95	5.00
22 March 2004	4.50	4.00	4.95	4.95	5.00
30 June 2006	4.50	4.00	4.95	4.95	5.00

Source: BCEAO (2006a) and previous years

Table 8.A8 *Summary accounts of commercial banks at 31 December 2003–2005 (CFAfr millions)*

| | Senegal | | | WAMU | | |
	2003	2004	2005	2003	2004	2005
Net foreign assets	199,246	199,156	173,168	166,538	155,416	131,645
Gross foreign assets	25,4805	296,956	297,898	430,639	444,448	499,305
Foreign liabilities	–55,559	–97,800	–12,4730	–264,101	–289,032	–367,660
Reserves	185,510	233,843	178,628	700,220	827,659	640,930
Credit on government	69,075	71,334	69,093	775,925	851,419	882,674
Credit to the private sector	782,062	853,889	1,063,990	3,222,702	3,503,191	3,922,449
Short-term loans	51,3159	548,226	658,980	2,324,516	2,431,002	2,679,660
Farm loans	3600	14,040	10,050	128,164	114,012	166,957
Ordinary loans	509,559	534,186	648,930	2,196,352	2,316,990	2,512,703
Medium–term loans	235,267	268,820	359,635	781,068	936,882	1,110,259
Long-term loans	33,636	36,843	45,375	117,118	135,307	132,530
Total assets	1,235,893	1,358,222	1,484,879	4,865,385	5,337,685	5,577,698
Individual and company deposits	933,169	1,088,342	1,168,634	3,625,270	3,993,096	4,210,486
State enterprises	50,635	91,621	72,730	282,299	328,971	308,571
Sight	36,553	42,600	30,331	164,829	159,802	168,458
Term	14,082	49,021	42,399	117,470	169,169	140,113
Individual and private companies	882,534	996,721	1,095,904	3,342,971	3,664,125	3,901,915
Sight	448,935	507,426	555,941	1,740,031	1,924,613	2,002,574
Term	433,599	489,295	539,963	1,602,940	1,739,512	1,899,341
Government deposits	186,313	165,120	191,683	783,369	766,202	755,766
Claims of the Central Bank	0	0	0	1714	1212	11,610
Other net items	116,411	104,760	124,562	455,032	577,175	599,836
Own funds	125,266	139,527	165,971	576,515	641,455	696,717
Losses	0	0	11168	8151	5999	16796
Total liabilities	1,235,893	1,358,222	1,484,879	4,865,385	5,337,685	5,577,698
Total assets – total liabilities	0	0	0	0	0	0
Recap						
Foreign assets	254,805	296,956	297,898	430,639	444,448	499,305
Foreign liabilities	55,559	97,800	124,730	264,101	289,032	367,660

Source: BCEAO (2006a) and previous years

Table 8.A9 *Summary of West African Monetary Union inter-bank market transactions, 31 May–6 June 2006 (CFAfr billions)*

	7 day		15 day		1 month		3 month		9 month		Total	
	L	B	L	B	L	B	L	B	L	B	L	B
Benin	0	15,000	0	1000	1500	0	2000	0	700	0	4200	16000
Burkina	0	4000	1000	0	0	1000	0	2000	0	0	1000	7000
Côte d'Ivoire	12,000	0	0	0	0	500	0	0	0	700	12,000	1200
Guinea-Bissau	0	0	0	0	0	0	0	0	0	0	0	0
Mali	8000	0	0	0	0	0	0	0	0	0	8000	0
Niger	0	2000	0	2700	0	1000	0	0	0	0	0	5700
Senegal	7000	8000	0	0	0	0	0	0	0	0	7000	8000
Togo	3000	1000	2700	0	1000	0	0	0	0	0	6700	1000
WAMU	30,000	30,000	3700	3700	2500	2500	2000	2000	700	700	38,900	38,900
Average weighted rate (%)	4.31		5.00		5.40		5.75		5.00			
Minimum rate (%)	3.00		5.00		5.00		5.75		5.00			
Maximum rate (%)	5.50		5.00		6.50		5.75		5.00			

Note: L = loans; B = borrowing; WAMU = West African Monetary Union
Source: BCEAO (2006b)

Table 8.A10 *Breakdown of West African Monetary Union inter-bank market operations, 31May–June 2006 (CFAfr billions)*

Institution	Country of lending institution	Type	Amount	Rate (%)	Borrowing institution	Country of borrowing institution
BDM	Mali	Loan	3000	4.40	CLS	Senegal
ECOBANK	Togo	Loan	2000	5.00	ECOBANK	Burkina
ECOBANK	Mali	Loan	1000	5.15	ECOBANK	Niger
ECOBANK	Mali	Loan	1000	5.15	ECOBANK	Benin
ECOBANK	Mali	Loan	2000	5.15	ECOBANK	Benin
ECOBANK	Mali	Loan	1000	5.15	ECOBANK	Niger
CBAO	Senegal	Loan	3000	4.00	ECOBANK	Senegal
BHS	Senegal	Loan	2000	3.00	CLS	Senegal
CBAO	Senegal	Loan	2000	5.00	BIB	Burkina
ECOBANK	Togo	Loan	1000	5.00	ECOBANK	Benin
BIAO	Côte d'Ivoire	Loan	1000	5.50	BIA	Togo
SGBCI	Côte d'Ivoire	Loan	5000	3.80	SGBBE	Benin
SGBCI	Côte d'Ivoire	Loan	6000	3.80	SGBBE	Benin
ECOBANK	Togo	Loan	1700	5.00	ECOBANK	Niger
BOA	Burkina	Loan	1000	5.00	BOA	Niger
ECOBANK	Togo	Loan	1000	5.00	ECOBANK	Benin
BOA	Benin	Loan	1000	5.00	BOA	Niger

Table 8.A10 *continued*

Institution	Country of lending institution	Type	Amount	Rate (%)	Borrowing institution	Country of borrowing institution
BSIC	Benin	Loan	500	6.50	VERSUS BK	Côte d'Ivoire
ECOBANK	Togo	Loan	1000	5.25	BACB	Burkina
BOA	Benin	Loan	1000	5.75	BACB	Burkina
BOA	Benin	Loan	1000	5.75	BACB	Burkina
BOA	Benin	Loan	700	5,00	CITIBANK	Côte d'Ivoire

Source: BCEAO (2006b)

Table 8.A11 *Monetary survey of Senegal at 31 December 2003–2005 (CFAfr millions)*

	Senegal			WAMU		
	2003	2004	2005	2003	2004	2005
Net foreign assets	550,827	670,298	659,636	306,1006	3,185,244	3,327,033
Central Bank	351,581	471,142	486,468	2,894,468	3,029,828	3,195,388
Commercial banks	199,246	199,156	17,3168	16,6538	155,416	13,1645
Domestic credit	848,795	880,973	1,032,055	3,988,228	4,223,972	4,660,410
Net credit to the government	64,239	24,085	−34,905	740,385	705,863	71,8928
Credit to the economy	784,556	856,888	1,066,961	3,247,843	3,518,109	3,941,482
Crop credit	3,600	14,040	10,050	128,164	114,012	166,957
Other credit	780,956	842,848	1,056,911	3,119,679	3,404,097	3,774,526
(including questionable and disputed loans)	14,904	14,43	18,604	112,036	143,737	184,818
Total assets	1,399,621	1551270	1691691	7049234	7409216	7987443
Money supply	1,280,593	1,445,825	1,565,253	5,652,588	5,979,842	6,413,866
Currency in circulation	337,497	344,346	388,503	1,847,876	1,799,736	2,046,258
Deposits in CCP accounts	8,452	12,834	7,625	28,838	35,319	30,159
Deposits in Caisse Nationale d'Epargne (CNE) accounts	0	0	0	36,700	40,539	42,338
Bank deposits	934,644	1,088,645	1,169,124	3,739,174	4,104,248	4,295,111
State enterprises and industrial and commercial public institutions	51,123	91,819	73,102	374,272	434,279	387,627
Demand deposits	37,041	42,798	30,703	256,802	265,110	247,514
Time deposits	14,082	49,021	42,399	117,470	169,169	140,113
Individuals and private enterprises	883,521	996,826	1,096,023	3,364,902	3,669,970	3,907,484
Demand deposits	449,922	507,531	556,060	1,761,962	1,930,458	2,008,143
Time and saving deposits	433,599	489,295	539,963	1,602,940	1,739,512	1,899,341
Other net items	119,029	105,445	126,439	1,396,646	1,429,374	1,573,577
Total liabilities	1,399,621	1,551,270	1,691,691	7,049,234	7,409,216	7,987,443
Total assets – total liabilities	0	0	0	0	0	0
Recap						
Short-term loans	515,653	551,225	661,951	2,349,657	2,445,920	2,698,693
Medium- and long-term loans	268,903	305,663	405,010	898,186	1,072,189	1,242,789
Bank deposits/loans (%)	132	135	120	110	109	103

Source: BCEAO (2006a) and previous years

Table 8.A12 *Net foreign assets of Senegal at 31 December 2003–2005 (CFAfr millions)*

| | Bank of Senegal | | | WAMU | | |
	2003	2004	2005	2003	2004	2005
Net foreign assets of BCEAO	351,581	471,142	486,468	2,894,468	3,029,828	3,195,388
Gross foreign assets	577,347	658,924	665,616	3,735,286	3,729,418	3,768,896
Gold	0	0	0	238,084	244,807	315,539
IMF	7000	4971	6314	32,803	28,612	47,981
Foreign currency holdings	1411	998	812	3,464,400	3,455,999	3,405,377
Operations account	0	0	0	3,443,244	3,445,309	1,831,382
Other	1411	998	812	21,156	10,691	1,573,995
Available foreign assets	568,936	652,956	658,490	0	0	0
Foreign liabilities	225,766	187,782	179,148	840,818	699,590	573,508
Foreign currency liabilities	0	0	0	0	0	0
Recourse to IMF credits	131,545	104,803	82,487	669,929	521,345	424,912
Special drawing rights allocated	19,950	19,500	19,441	96,737	94,554	94,268
Other	74,272	63,480	77,221	74,151	83,692	54,328
Net foreign commercial banks assets	199,246	199,156	173,168	166,538	155,416	131,645
Banks and subsidiaries	93,489	63,688	49,447	279,299	273,599	292,078
Other WAMU countries	25,437	23,864	5483	0	0	0
Rest of the world	68,052	39,824	43,964	279,299	273,599	292,078
Medium- and long-term liabilities	19,468	25,484	29,558	41,423	41,881	41,398
Other WAMU countries	2566	5311	12,910	0	0	0
Rest of the world	16,902	20,173	16,648	41,423	41,881	41,398
Other	125,225	160,952	153,279	−71,338	−76,302	−119,035
Other WAMU countries	117,017	148,432	150,154	0	0	0
Rest of the world	8208	12,520	3125	−71,338	−76,302	−119,035
Total net foreign assets	550,827	670,298	659,636	3,061,006	3,185,244	3,327,033
Sight money liabilities	632,003	710,893	708,657	3,123,880	3,179,450	3,133,275
Gross foreign assets/sight money liabilities (%)	91	93	93	120	117	120

Source: BCEAO (2006a) and previous years

Table 8.A13 *Net government position vis-à-vis banking system at 31 December 2003–2005 (CFAfr millions)*

| | Bank of Senegal | | | WAMU | | |
	2003	2004	2005	2003	2004	2005
Bank notes and coins	1435	1763	3247	16,794	17,641	19,285
Central Bank deposits	85,203	116,298	117,477	412,923	396,122	312,822
Bank deposits	186,313	165,120	191,683	783,369	766,202	755,766
Guaranteed bonds	2494	2999	2971	18,883	13,671	17,923
Total assets	275,445	286,179	315,378	1,231,969	1,193,636	1,105,796
Central Bank support	75,260	66,509	57,860	396,984	372,506	354,834
Discount on Guaranteed bonds	0	0	0	0	0	0
ARTICLE 16 support	68,760	62,209	55,460	379,900	356,043	340,733
CCP	0	0	0	2	1	1
Government securities	6500	4300	2400	17,081	16,462	14,099
Bank support	69,075	71,334	69,093	775,925	851,419	882,674

Table 8.A13 *continued*

| | Bank of Senegal | | | WAMU | | |
	2003	2004	2005	2003	2004	2005
Plan d'Epargne Populaire (PEP) deposits in CCP accounts	8452	12,834	7625	28,838	35,319	30,159
CNE deposits	0	0	0	36,700	40,539	42,338
IMF support	133,467	110,446	88,984	680,477	550,577	457,809
Other support	53,430	49,140	56,910	53,430	49,140	56,910
Total debt	339,684	310,264	280,472	1,972,354	1,899,499	1,824,724
Net position	64,239	24,085	-34,905	740,385	705,863	718,928

Source: BCEAO (2006a) and previous years

ANNEX 8.5 — SITUATION OF THE REGIONAL FINANCIAL MARKET

Table 8.A14 *Market issuance of negotiable securities (CFAfr millions)*

Issuer (Active securities)	Amount	Date of issue	Term (months)	Interest rate (%)	Outstanding
A – Issuances					
1 Treasury bills					
Industries Chimiques du Sénégal (ICS)	15,000	09/02/04	24	5.30	15,000
2 Financial institution bonds					
LOCAFRIQUE Sénégal	180	01/01/05	48	5.50	135
3 Regional financial institutions bonds					
West African Development Bank	7855	04/01/02	84	5.85	7855
West African Development Bank	20,000	24/03/03	84	5.48	20,000
West African Development Bank	25,000	07/11/03	84	5.34	25,000
West African Development Bank	17,300	05/11/04	84	5.35	17,300
4 Treasury bills					
Treasury of Senegal	35,500	28/09/05	6 & 12	2.50 to 4.0	17,750
Treasury of Guinea-Bissau	6000	17/10/05	6	4.0 to 5.50	2400
Treasury of Burkina Faso	13,100	13/01/06	6	2.9 to 5.0	13,100
Treasury of Benin	20,150	27/02/06	6	3.5 to 5.5	20,150
Treasury of Niger	8300	01/06/06	6	3.95 to 5.0	8300
Treasury of Burkina Faso	17,275	02/06/06	3	3.0 to 4.25	17,275
Total	185,660				164,265
B–Pending issues					
Malian bonds	20,000	21/06/06	3		

Source: BCEAO (2006c)

Table 8.A15 *Public savings bond market issuance*

Issuer (Active securities)	Amount (CFAfr millions)	Date of issue	Term (years)	Interest rate (%)	Outstanding (CFAfr millions)
A – Issues					
West African Development Bank	20,120	1/02/99	10	6.25	8051
SGBS-Senegal	10,000	99	7	6.80	3333
West African Development Bank	17,100	16/11/99	8	6.30	8354
West African Development Bank	11,947	4/01/02	5	5.85	9558
West African Development Bank-Benin	5,004	10/01	7	6.60	3704
SAGA Côte d'Ivoire	3,000	1/01/02	5	7.50	1500
BHM Mali	9,398	20/01/03	5	7.50	3759
SHELTER Afrique Sénégal	3,500	01/03	7	6.25	2800
Treasury of Burkina Faso	25,000	03/03	4	7.00	8334
SENELEC Senegal	15,000	03/03	5	7.50	9375
Communauté Electrique du Bénin (CEB)	16,000	06/03	7	6.50	16,000
Treasury of Côte d'Ivoire	40,403	1/09/03	3	6.50	40,403
BNDA Mali	3,500	12/04/04	5	6.50	2100
Port Autonome de Dakar Senegal	30,000	15/07/04	7	6.50	30,000
CEB	9,000	16/06/04	7	6.50	9000
West African Development Bank	22,700	5/11/04	7	5.35	22,700
Société Béninoise d'Energie Electrique	22,765	14/04/05	7	6.85	22,765
SONATEL Burkina Faso	16,000	04/05	6	6.65	16,000
Treasury of Senegal	45,000	25/07/05	5	5.5	45,000
Treasury of Côte d'Ivoire	86,133	15/07/05	3	6.50	86,133

Table 8.A15 *continued*

Issuer (Active securities)	Amount (CFAfr millions)	Date of issue	Term (years)	Interest rate (%)	Outstanding (CFAfr millions)
West African Development Bank	18,595	11/05	8	5.00	18,595
West African Development Bank	6405	11/05	6	4.50	6405
Treasury of Togo	36,300	28/02/206	5	6.50	36,300
TOTAL	472,870				410,169

Source: BCEAO (2006c)

Table 8.A16 *Breakdown of active public savings securities or securitized instruments (CFAfr millions)*

Type	Amount issued	Amount outstanding
Negotiable bills	185,660	164,265
Securitized public debt	667,078	61,656
Bonds	472,870	410,169
TOTAL	1,325,608	636,090

Source: BCEAO (2006c)

ANNEX 8.6 — MACROECONOMIC ANALYSIS OF
PUBLIC DEBT IN SENEGAL[48]

The macroeconomic analysis of the public debt in Senegal can be performed in the following three stages:

- First determine the profile of the public debt;
- Next study the changes in selected indicators – critical to evaluating the sustainability of the foreign debt;
- Lastly, examine the country's prospects for debt relief.

Profile of public debt

As of 31 December 2004, Senegal's public debt stood at CFAfr2,013.8 billion or 50 per cent of GDP and comprised CFAfr1,865.1 billion of foreign debt and CFAfr149.7 billion of domestic debt. The level of the total public debt rose by an average of 5.7 per cent per year during the period 1995 to 2001. Since 2002, the upward trend in the debt has been reversed. Indeed, the debt declined from CFAfr2,743.6 billion in 2001 to CFAfr2,014.8 billion in 2004, a decrease of CFAfr729.8 billion in absolute value, and of 9.8 per cent in average relative value per year.

Table 8.A17 *Size of public debt (CFAfr billions)*

DEBT	1995	1996	1997	1998	1999	2000	2001	2002	2003	2004
Foreign	1718.6	1900.7	1984.3	2114.5	2169.5	2418.7	2530.6	2316.4	2028.9	1869.1
Domestic	245.7	238.2	235.6	234.5	196.5	153.5	213.9	158.2	156	149.7
Total	1964.3	2138.9	2219.9	2349	2366	2572.2	2744.5	2474.6	2184.9	2014.8

Source: Directorate of Debt and Investment Internal, Ministry of Economy and Finance

Level of domestic public debt

The domestic public debt comprised, on average, 8.7 per cent of total public debt over the period 1995 to 2004. As Table 8.A17 shows, the level of the domestic public debt declined by an average of 5.4 per cent per year between 1995 and 2004. This steady downward trend in the debt is largely due to the good health of public finances which has made it possible to make payments on time and to maintain the level of domestic debt at moderate levels. In 2004, the domestic public debt was CFAfr 149.7 billion and comprised of CFAfr144.9 billion in bank debt (including CFAfr 45.3 billion in treasury bonds) and CFAfr4.8 billion of non-bank debt.

Level of the external public debt

Senegal's external public debt was estimated at 31 December 2004 to be CFAfr1,865.1 billion (or $3.5 billion). It has declined steadily since 2001, despite the marked increase in 2005 (CFAfr1,944 billion in that year).

Tables 8.A18 and 8.A19 show the trends and structure of Senegal's external debt. They indicate that multilateral debt accounts for most of the country's foreign debt. The relative share of this type of debt increased steadily, rising from two-thirds of total debt early in the decade to more than 80 per cent of the total by the end of 2005. The World Bank Group is the principal creditor, followed, in order of importance, by the African Development Bank group and IMF. These three creditors account for most of Senegal's multilateral debt. Table 8.A20 shows the loan conditions of the main multilateral donors in relation to the term of the loan, deferment period and interest rate. The conditions seem to be quite favourable and non-demanding.

Table 8.A18 *Structure of foreign public debt (CFAfr billions)*

Donor categories	1999	2000	2001	2002	2003	2004	2005
Loans from multilateral agencies	1383.3	1650.4	1642.0	1503.4	1367.2	1509.6	1574.2
IMF	154.0	154.1	163.0	157.4	124.5	110.4	89.0
IDA/IBRD	896.7	1191.9	1023.0	964.7	868.6	1040.4	1112.0
EIB/FED	50.4	48.8	74.6	50.6	57.1	7.0	8.0
AfDB/IFAD	214.1	204.3	251.0	224.7	185.1	218.3	219.3
OPEC/BADEA/BID/FASA	47.5	41.7	85.3	72.0	70.7	74.2	74.4
Other	20.7	9.7	45.1	34.0	61.2	59.3	71.5
Bilateral loans	786.2	768.4	897.0	791.5	657.5	355.5	369.8
OECD countries	482.1	520.4	474.0	504.9	384.9	87.6	80.3
Arab countries	195.1	185.4	291.8	228.4	164.5	216.8	228.7
Other	109.0	62.6	131.2	58.2	108.1	51.1	60.9
Total foreign public debt	2169.5	2418.8	2539.0	2294.9	2024.7	1865.1	1944.0

Source: Directorate of Debt and Investment Internal, Ministry of Economy and Finance

Table 8.A19 *Structure of foreign public debt of Senegal (%)*

Years	Multilateral debt	Bilateral debt
1999	63.76	36.24
2000	68.23	31.74
2001	64.67	35.33
2002	65.51	34.49
2003	67.52	32.48
2004	80.93	19.07
2005	80.97	19.03

Source: Directorate of Debt and Investment Internal, Ministry of Economy and Finance

Public bilateral debt is the second type of debt. During the period under review, it represented on average some 30 per cent of the total external debt. The size of the debt declined by more than 80 per cent between 2003 and 2004. The share of bilateral debt in total public debt decreased from 32 per cent in 2003 to less than 20 per cent in 2004 and 2005.

Table 8.A20 *Loan conditions of donors*

Donors	Loan conditions		
	Term (years)	Grace period (years)	Interest rate (%)
International Development Association	40	10	0.75
	50	10	0.75
African Development Bank	15	7	8.00
	10	3	0.50
	12	4	0.50
	12	3	6.00
	13	3	10.00
	15	5	6.50
	15	4	5.50
	17	5	6.80
	25	7	2.00
Average	14.9	4.6	5.1
European Investment Bank	10	3	8.00
	12	4	8.00
	12	4	8.00
	12	1	5.50
	13	3	6.50
	15	4	8.50
	15	5	3.00
	15	5	8.00
	18	3	2.28
	20	5	2.00
	20	5	3.00
Average	14.7	3.8	5.7
Islamic Development Bank	15	0	5.10
	15	2	6.00
	25	7	0.00
Average	18.3	3.0	3.7
Kuwaiti fund for Arab economic development	17	4	1.00
	20	4	3.00
	23	4	3.00
	24	4	1.50
	25	5	2.00
	30	10	3.00
	40	16	0.50
	40	5	2.00
	45	10	2.00
Average	29.3	6.9	2.0
Saudi fund for development	2	5	3.00
	19	5	3.00
	20	5	2.00
	22	5	3.00
	25	5	3.00
	30	6	1.00
	46	11	2.00
	50	10	1.00
	50	10	1.00
Average	29.3	6.9	2.1
Export-Import bank of India	20	5	1.75
African Development Bank/FAD	50	10	0.75
	40	10	0.75

Source: Directorate of Debt and Investment Internal, Ministry of Economy and Finance

Trend in core indicators relative to foreign debt

Trends in the profile of the foreign debt are usually determined based on a comparison between the debt level and the debt service with certain indicators that reflect the solvency and liquidity of the economy in question. The indicators selected for this purpose are the following ratios:

• Public debt/GDP;
• Public debt/exports of goods and services;
• Debt service/exports of goods and services;
• Debt service/tax revenues.

The change in these indicators is shown in Table 8.A21.

Table 8.A21 *Trends of selected foreign public debt indicators (%)*

Years	Debt/GDP	Debt/ Exports	Debt service/ Exports	Debt service/ Tax revenues
1999	68.5	244	11.7	21.3
2000	72.6	260	12.8	23.5
2001	75.6	247.2	10.0	17.7
2002	66.1	217	11.2	18.8
2003	54.4	189	10.1	15.9
2004	45.2	163	6.9	10.7
2005	44.5	160		

Note: The debt service in question is the servicing after HIPC rescheduling and cancellations.
Source: Directorate of Debt and Investment Internal, Ministry of Economy and Finance

After rising between 1999 and 2001, the debt/GDP ratio has declined steadily since then. In 2005, the foreign debt of Senegal was only 44 per cent of its GDP compared with 75 per cent in 2001, a decline of nearly 40 per cent. This ratio is well under the community ceiling of 70 per cent for the member countries of the WAEMU.

The trend in the debt/export ratio has shown a similar pattern, declining sharply between 1999 and 2005 from 244 per cent to 160 per cent. This ratio is one of the principal warning signals of a debt crisis. Using empirical data on developing countries, Cohen (1986) has calculated the probability of a debt crisis (in other words, difficulties for a debtor country to honour all of its commitments) as a function of the level of its debt to export ratio (see Table 8.A22).

Table 8.A22 *Probability of a debt crisis*

Debt/exports (%)	Probability (%)
200	60
250	69
300	93

Source: Cohen (1986)

These results may suggest that up to 2001, the probability of a debt crisis in Senegal was quite high, at between 60 per cent and 69 per cent. At the present time, because of the change in the debt to export ratio, this probability should be well below 50 per cent. Throughout the period 1999 to 2004, the average debt service to export ratio was approximately 10 per cent, or half the critical threshold of 20 per cent from which point the repayment difficulties may become severe. This ratio has declined steadily. The same is true for the debt service to tax revenues ratio which declined by nearly 40 per cent between 1999 and 2004, from 21.3 per cent to 10.7 per cent. The weight of the debt service on government resources thus declined markedly.

The changes in these different ratios tend to reflect a sustainable level of foreign debt. These remarkable results are due to the country's economic performance and to the considerable efforts made to implement economic and structural reforms that have been acknowledged by the creditor countries. They are also due to the debt cancellations and rescheduling granted by the donors.

Cancellations and rescheduling of the foreign public debt

Senegal became eligible for the enhanced HIPC Initiative in June 2000. It reached its completion point in April 2004. Table 8.A23 gives the figures on HIPC debt rescheduling and cancellations from 1999 to 2004.

Table 8.A23 *Rescheduling of foreign debt and HIPC debt cancellations (CFAfr billions)*

1999	2000	2001	2002	2003	2004
32.1	50.1	58.8	45.6	48.2	92.6

Source: Directorate of Debt and Investment Internal, Ministry of Economy and Finance

In June 2004, the member countries of the Paris Club decided to cancel an amount of $94 billion in net present value debt, representing the effort falling to them under the Initiative. In addition to this amount, most creditors pledged to grant bilateral relief of additional debt in the amount of $336 million in net present value. Multilateral creditors, some of which had even granted interim assistance, also granted their share of debt relief. Thus the implementation of the decisions taken at the Paris Club meeting of 9 June 2004 granted Senegal substantial debt relief.

In nominal terms, this relief amounted to $708.6 million or CFAfr362 billion. In net present value, it was equal to $450.4 million and CFAfr234 billion. Thus, the entire debt of the government of Senegal to France, Italy, Japan, the UK, The Netherlands, Canada, the US and Norway had been cancelled (Directorate of Debt and Investment Internal, Ministry of Economy and Finance).

The impact of this debt relief is the achievement of a sustainable level of foreign debt. Thus, the net present value of the foreign public debt as a share of export earnings, the standard for which was set in the context of the Initiative at 150 per cent, was 132 per cent in 2004 compared with 141.7 per cent in 2003 (Directorate of Debt and Investment Internal, Ministry of Economy and Finance).

In 2005, many creditor countries cancelled debt in addition to debt under the HIPC Initiative. This was true of France, Japan, the US and others. The ratio of sustainability of the debt for that year was 117 per cent for a net present value of the foreign public debt to export earnings, or a net decline compared with its 2003 level. In 2006, the implementation of the G8 initiative for granting relief from multilateral debt, provided for the cancellation of 100 per cent of the debt stock to the International Development Association, FAD and IMF for HIPC countries. This action eased the weight of debt on the economy significantly. The debt ratio would be less than 15 per cent of GDP. As a result, savings on the servicing of the debt are projected to be CFAfr62.2 billion.

The strategy for getting out of debt

As part of the agreement following the meeting of the Paris Club on 9 June 2004, the member countries of the Paris Club all granted not only the relief that had been agreed on, but also applied (except for Belgium for legal and regulatory reasons) the recommendations to go beyond the Initiative. They cancelled the entire stock of non-concessional rescheduled debt and the concessional debt resulting from the consolidation agreements of the 11th and 12th Paris Clubs. Germany, to whom Senegal owed no rescheduled debt stock, cancelled a number of loan repayment deadlines (after 1983).

Bilateral debt owed to creditors not members of the Paris Club

For debt owed to creditors not belonging to the Paris Club, only one agreement was signed, which was the agreement with the Kuwaiti Fund for Development. The other creditors took into account the prevailing situation, leading to suspension of debt servicing payments to the Abu Dhabi and Oman Fund pending the fulfilment of the cancellation pledges, and maintenance of the status quo for the Kuwaiti deposit pending the conclusion of the renegotiations under way with the Kuwaiti Investment Authority.

Multilateral debt

The treatment of this category of debt is based on two modalities of relief that are currently being applied. The following modalities have thus been applied:

* International Development Association: reduction of debt servicing to 2010 for delivery of total due;
* IMF: assistance continues in the form of reduction of the debt servicing due up to 2006;
* African Development Bank/FAD: reduction in debt servicing up to the amount of the balance that would permit relief to be granted for the amount due up to 2006;

- European Investment Bank/FED: additional relief up to the amount of the assistance envisaged and account taken of additional cancellations of debt granted within the framework of the assistance given to least developed countries, which Senegal became a member in November 2002;
- West African Development Bank: interim relief already granted in 2001, supplementary relief granted through reduction of debt servicing from the completion point.

The International Fund for Agriculture Development (IFAD), the Nordic Development Fund (FND) and the Arab Bank for Economic Development in Africa (BADEA) have not granted interim relief, but have begun to provide assistance from the completion point still in accordance with the modalities that they themselves have defined and which are as follows:

- IFAD: relief that could be as much as cancellation of 100 per cent of the debt service due for a period equal to the assistance envisaged;
- FND: relief from a part of the debt service in the amount of the assistance envisaged;
- BADEA: a rescheduling agreement was concluded and concerned four loans. A rescheduled loan over 27 years with a 1 year grace period and an interest rate of 1 per cent, and 3 loans rescheduled over 26 years with a 1 year grace period and an interest rate of 1 per cent.

For the OPEC Fund, all assistance was disbursed in November 2001 in the form of a new loan of $6.9 million at a rate of 1 per cent over 15 years with a five-year grace period. The grant element of this loan was considered by OPEC as its contribution to HIPC debt relief (Directorate of Debt and Investment Internal, Ministry of Economy and Finance).

NOTES

1   The data for Senegal are taken from Ministry of Economics and Finance (2005d) and those on the average for sub-Saharan countries in Africa are taken from the Millennium Project (2005).
2   The second PRSP identifies an additional component that concerns institutions.
3   Estimates of the annual rate of increase in real GDP vary from one source to the other and are, in any case, approximations.
4   WHO and UNDP are two major actors in the fight against AIDS in Senegal.
5   Before the launching of PNIR, during the period from 1997 to 2000, PAC was only marginally concerned with rural communities.
6   Act No. 66-64 of 30 June 1964 on the Municipality Administrative Code.
7   Act No. 72-25 of 25 April 1972.
8   Acts Nos. 90-35 and 90-37 of 1990.
9   Acts Nos. 96-06 and 96-07 of 22 March1996.

10   Article 3 of the Local Collectivity Code.

11   Formerly known as multipurpose rural development centres (CERP).

12   The evaluations are hardly any more consistent if reference is made to the balance of payment figures published by the IMF (2006b).

13   For example, there is currently no aggregate in the national accounts that covers all health expenditures (public and private). The Ministry of Health is planning to prepare such an aggregate that will include household expenditures on pharmaceuticals, estimated at approximately CFAfr50 billion in 2005, household expenditures in private clinics and so on.

14   A gap exists between the total amount in the Triennial Public Investment Plan and the total of the amounts financed by the government and donors. Unfortunately, this marginal difference, approximately 1 per cent, is not explained.

15   Based on a per capita GDP increase of 3 per cent per year up to 2010, which is a relatively optimistic scenario, but consistent with the projections on which the overall strategy is based.

16   'We stress that no distinction should be made between funding capital and operating costs through Official Development Assistance, since poor countries cannot afford to fund operating expenditures, which account for a large share in health, education and other sectors' (Millennium Project, 2005, p246).

17   Must these targeted expenditures include, for example, the total remuneration of teachers or only the increase in the wage bill resulting from the increase in school enrolment rates, or again only the construction of new classrooms?

18   This point is not the object of the chapter. It has been developed in Guillaumont and Guillaumont Jeanneney (2006) and in Adam et al (2006).

19   This potential is calculated on the basis of the level of the structural variables that determine the long-term tax capacity of a state (GDP, share of value added of agriculture in GDP, degree of monetarization of the economy, degree of commercial opening) based on a method described in Chambas, 2005.

20   The data on the structure of tax revenues in the period since 2003 have not been included in the subsequent reports of the IMF.

21   In other words, a 1 per cent increase in the VAT will yield an increase in VAT receipts of 0.4 per cent of GDP.

22   The reduction in the rate of corporate tax to 25 per cent is greater than the international standard and it had, therefore, been thought that this decrease should at first be conditioned on the reinvestment of the tax savings. This conditionality has been abandoned in favour of retaining only a 'moral commitment'. However, an increase in the distribution tax revenues has been noted (taxes on dividends), which shows that the after tax benefits obtained from the lowering of corporate taxes have not been broadly reinvested, contrary to one of the objectives of the reform.

23   The remainder (20 per cent) corresponds to various municipal taxes and other unidentified resources.

24   Law of 6 February 2004 on local tax reform.

25   It has also been suggested that the FECL should be transformed into an investment fund.

26   The above equation assumes that the ratio of the money supply to the money base (M/Mc), commonly referred to as the credit multiplier, is stable, as is Y/M, the rate of circulation of money, in order to give $\delta Y/Y + \delta P/P = \delta Mc/Mc$.

27   The monetary base is calculated as the sum of currencies and bank deposits held by the BCEAO in 2004 and expressed as a proportion of the GDP for that same year.

28   In other words, with i being the rate of interest charged by the Central Bank, i
$Mc/P = (\delta Y/Y + \delta P/P)Mc/P$.

29   As a result of the depreciation of the Euro against the special drawing rights, the French Treasury in the period 2000 to 2002 compensated the central banks of the franc zone to an amount of more than €450 million in the form of development assistance. See the memorandum of France to the DAC Secretariat (2004). This compensation, however, is in response to a specific situation and should not be payable again in the near future. It should also be noted that under the new agreements, the French Treasury no longer guarantees the value, in special drawing rights, of assets in the operating account except for the portion of required deposits, which declined to 50 per cent from 65 per cent. Interest rates higher than the benchmark rate do not apply, except to required deposits.

30   This situation, however, is not peculiar to Senegal. It is also the case in numerous countries, mainly in Asia (Summers, 2006). The countries of the franc zone are rather an exception in Africa.

31   It should be added that, according to Article 12 of the Treaty establishing WAEMU, the monetary and credit policy of the Union is set by the Council of Ministers 'to ensure the safety of the common currency and to provide funding for activities and economic development of the members of the Union'.

32   By using the monetary aggregate M2 so that the data could be compared.

33   The threshold for the debt/export NPV criterion is 150 per cent for a ratio of 73 per cent, and the threshold for the debt service/export criterion is 20 per cent for a ratio of 5 per cent.

34   The monitoring of sustainability should be significantly strengthened by the fact that, in accordance with the terms of an agreement with the donors, this debt will be analysed before it is contracted. Moreover, certain institutional constraints are put in place to prevent over indebtedness. These include a requirement that authorization to contract debt must be given by the parliament, and a prohibition against contracting loans with a grant element lower than 35 per cent.

35   This may be compared to the McKinnon conduit effect, according to which the possibility offered in developing countries to poor populations to have bank accounts helps to promote self-financed investments. We have shown elsewhere that an increase in bank deposits as a proportion of GDP helps to reduce monetary poverty (Guillaumont Jeanneney and Kpodar, 2006).

36   Guillaumont (1971, pp16–30) provides a summary of writings on the capacity to absorb aid. For a more recent analysis of the problems associated with the 'Big Push' and absorption capacity, see Guillaumont and Guillaumont Jeanneney (2005).

37   50 per cent of correct answers.

38   For example, Robert (2006) points out that the data on the number of elementary school teachers and their distribution at the different levels are different according to officials of the ministry (DPRE or DRH). Similarly, the Ministry of Finance was unable to provide data on the execution of expenditures. This is why it is possible that the rates of execution of expenditures provided in the CSLP study are approximations.

39   ACDI (Can$14 million), World Bank (US$5 million), French Ministry of Foreign Affairs (€2.55 million) and AFD (€3 million). The Senegalese authorities have expressed interest in retaining in this field of capacity building an aid project that is different from budgetary assistance, since it would allow travel allowances (transportation and per diems) to be set at levels that reflect actual costs.

40   Within the framework of the Education for All Fast Track Initiative.

41   It should also be pointed out that indicators can be easily manipulated. It was noted that in order to respect the wage ceiling in total expenditures, a portion of the salaries of volunteer teaching staff is counted under the budget head 'Material'.

42   It should also be recalled that in order to address the weakness of administrative capacities in local governments (particularly of the mayors), the Union of Associations of Local Elected Officials (UAEL) established an administrative service, the Support Unit for Local Elected Officials (CAEL), the role of which is to reinforce the management capacities of municipalities,

particularly through training programmes for locally elected officials.

43 Studies on the Dutch Disease abound (see, in particular, Collier and Gunning, 1999).
44 There are two ways of calculating the real rate of exchange. The first, found mainly in the litera-
    ture on developing countries, is the price of internationally tradable goods relative to the price
    of non-tradable goods in the country in question. The second is the ratio of general price
    indices abroad and in the country in question expressed in the same currency (by conversion at
    the exchange rate). For a given productivity level, an increase in these two indices thus defined,
    or a real depreciation of the national currency, corresponds to an improvement in the competi-
    tiveness of the country in question. Conversely, a decline in these two indices, presumed here to
    be caused by an increase in the price of non-tradable goods, leads to deterioration in the
    country's competitiveness.
45 Authors' calculations based on IMF (2006a).
46 The same distribution of expenditures by strategic approach is not available for HIPC resources.
47 The idea of dividing in half obviously has no precise scientific basis.
48 This annex is written by Adama Diaw.

REFERENCES

Adam, C., Chambas, G., Guillaumont, P., Guillaumont Jeanneney, S. and Gunning, J. W. (2006)
    'Performance-based conditionality: A European perspective', *World Development*, vol 32, no 6,
    pp1059–1070
AFD (Agence Française de Développement) (2005a) *Évaluation du programme d'appui aux collectivités
    locales (PAC)*, AFD, Paris
AFD (2005b) 'Financer les investissements des villes des pays en développement – synthèse des
    travaux du groupe de travail "Financement des investissements des collectivités locales" de
    l'AFD', AFD Research Department, Notes and Documents series, No. 24, 109 pages, AFD, Paris
Bleaney, M. and Greenaway, D. (2001) 'The impact of terms of trade and real exchange rate volatil-
    ity', *Journal of Development Economics*, vol 65, no 2, pp491–500
Brautigam, D. and Knack, S. (2004) 'Foreign aid, institutions and governance in sub-Saharan Africa',
    Economic Development and Cultural Change, vol 52, pp255–285
Chambas, G. (ed) (2005) *Afrique au sud du Sahara. Mobiliser des ressources fiscales pour le développement*,
    Economica, Paris
Chambas, G., Brun, J-F., Combes, J-L., Dulbecco, P., Gastambide, A., Guérineau, S., Guillaumont
    Jeanneney, S. and Rota Graziosi G. (2006) 'Evaluation de l'espace budgétaire dans les pays en
    développement', Mimeo prepared at the request of UNDP
Cohen, D. (ed) (1986) *Money, Wealth and Debt of Nations*, CNRS, Paris
Collier, D. and Gunning, J. W. (eds) (1999) *Trade Shocks in Developing Countries*, Clarendon Press,
    Oxford
Comité de Convergence (2005) *Report to the Ministers of the Franc Zone*, Comité de Convergence, Paris
Conseil d'analyse économique (2004) *Réformer le pacte de stabilité et de croissance*, La documentation
    française, Paris
Ghura, D. (1998) 'Tax revenue in sub-Saharan Africa: Effects of economic policies and corruption',
    IMF Working Paper 98/135, IMF, Washington DC
Guillaumont, P. (1971) *L'absorption du capital*, Cujas, Paris
Guillaumont, P. and Guillaumont Jeanneney, S. (2005) 'Efficacité, sélectivité et conditionnalité de
    l'aide au développement', in Conseil d'analyse économique (ed) *La politique d'aide au développement de
    la France*, La Documentation Française, Paris
Guillaumont, P. and Guillaumont Jeanneney, S. (2006) 'Big push versus absorptive capacity: How to
    reconcile the two approaches', United Nations-Wider Conference, 'Aid: Principles, Policies and
    Performances', Helsinki, 16–17 June

Guillaumont, P., Guillaumont Jeanneney, S. and Brun, J-F. (1998) 'How instability lowers African growth', *Journal of African Economies*, vol 8, no 1, pp87–107

Guillaumont Jeanneney, S. and Kpodar, K. (2006) 'Développement financier, instabilité financière et réduction de la pauvreté', in P. Plane, B. Decaluwe, A. Diaw and F. Mourji (eds) *Le développement face à la pauvreté*, Economica, Paris, pp48–74

Gupta, S., Clements, B., Pivovarsky, A. and Tiongson, E. (2004) 'Foreign aid and revenue response: Does the composition of foreign aid matter?' in S. Gupta, B. Clements, G. Inchauste (eds) *Helping Countries Develop. The Role of Fiscal Policies*, IMF, Washington DC

Gupta, S., Powell, R. and Yang, Y. (2006) *The Macroeconomic Challenge of Scaling Up Aid to Africa*, IMF, Washington DC

Heller, P. S. (2005) 'Pity the finance minister: issues in managing a substantial scaling up of aid flows', *World Economics*, vol 6, no 4, pp69–110

IMF (International Monetary Fund) (2004) *Chile: Selected Issues*, IMF, Washington DC

IMF (2005a) 'Selected issues and statistical appendix', IMF Country Report No. 05/155, IMF, Washington DC

IMF (2005b) *Senegal: Memorandum of Economic and Financial Policies for 2006*, IMF, Washington DC

IMF (2005c) *Senegal: Financial System Stability Assessment Update*, IMF Country Report No. 05/126, April 2005, Washington DC

IMF (2006a) 'Senegal: Poverty reduction strategy paper – second annual progress report- joint staff advisory note', February, IMF Country Report No. 06/69, IMF, Washington DC

IMF (2006b) 'Third and fourth review under the three-year arrangement under the poverty reduction and growth facility and request for waiver of performance criteria: Poverty reduction strategy paper', IMF Country Report No. 06/127, IMF, Washington DC

IMF and IDA (2005) *Operational Framework for Debt Sustainability Assessments in Low-Income Countries – Further Considerations*, 28 March, IMF, Washington DC

Millennium Project (2005) *Investing in Development: A Practical Plan to Achieve the Millennium Development Goals*, UN, New York

Millikan, M. and Rostow, W. W. (1957) *A Proposal: Keys to an Effective Foreign Policy*, Harper, New York

Ministry of Economy and Finance (2005a) *Progress Report on Implementation of the Poverty Reduction Strategy*, MEF, Dakar

Ministry of Economy and Finance (2005b) *Note de synthèse du cadre des dépenses de moyen terme 2006–2008 (CDMT)*, Direction du budget, MEF, Dakar

Ministry of Economy and Finance (2005c) 'La réforme de la fiscalité locale au Sénégal, Partenariat pour le développement municipal (PDM)', *La Revue Africaine de Finances Locales*, vol 8, p15-17, Direction générale des impôts et des domaines, MEF, Dakar

Ministry of Economy and Finance (2005d) *Poverty Reduction Strategy Paper (PRSP I), Progress report on the implementation of the Poverty Reduction Strategy Paper – 2004, Cellule de suivi du programme de lutte contre la pauvreté (CLSP)*, MEF, Dakar

Ministry of Economy and Finance (2006a) *Évolution annuelle des prix à la consommation en 2005*, Direction de la prévision et de la statistique, MEF, Dakar

Ministry of Economy and Finance (2006b) *Nomenclature secondaire de l'Indice harmonisé des prix à la consommation du Sénégal (IHPC)*, Direction de la prévision et de la statistique, MEF, Dakar

Ministry of Economy and Finance (2006c) *Situation économique et financière en 2005 et perspectives en 2006*, MEF, Direction de la prévision et de la statistique, Dakar

Ministry of Economy and Finance (2006d) *Atelier de présentation de l'expérience des réformes fiscales de 2004 et 2005*, Direction générale des impôts et domaines, MEF, Hotel Méridien Président, 3 May

Ministry of Economy and Finance (2006e) *Document stratégique de réduction de la pauvreté (PRSP II). Cellule de suivi du programme de lutte contre la pauvreté (CLSP)*, MEF, Dakar

Moss, T., Pettersson, G. and van der Walle, N. (2006) 'An aid-institution paradox? A review essay on aid dependency and state building in sub-Saharan Africa', Working Paper No. 74, Center for Global Development, Washington DC

Observatoire des Finances Locales (2003) *Partenariat pour le développement municipal (PDM), Finances locales au Sénégal: 2001 et 2002*, Observatoire des Finances Locales, Dakar

Rajan, R. and Subramanian, A. (2005) 'What undermines aid's impact on growth?', NBER Working Paper No. 11657, National Bureau of Economic Research, Cambridge, MA

Remmer, K. (2004) 'Does foreign aid promote the expansion of government?', *American Journal of Political Science*, vol 48, no 1, pp77–92

Robert, F. (2006) *Rapport sur l'évaluation technique de la candidature du Sénégal à l'initiative Fast-Track*, consultancy report, www.poledakar.org/IMG/SEN-FTI-EXESUM_ROBERT_08_fevrier_2006.pdf

Rosenstein-Rodan, P-N. (1943) 'Problems of industrialization of eastern and south-eastern Europe', *Economic Journal*, vol 53, pp202–213

Rosenstein-Rodan, P-N. (1962) 'Notes on the theory of the big push', in H. S. Ellis and H. Wallich (eds) *Economic Development for Latin America, Report on a Conference organized by the International Economic Association*, St Martin's Press, New York

Summers, L. H. (2006) 'Reflections on global account imbalances and emerging markets reserves accumulation', L. K. Jha Memorial Lecture, Reserve Bank of India, Harvard University, 24 March

UEMOA (2005) *Rapport semestriel d'exécution de la surveillance multilatérale*, UEMOA, Ouagadougou

UNESCO (2006) 'L'efficacité de l'éducation au Sénégal: Une analyse économique', Note Pays No. 3, UNESCO, Dakar

World Bank (2005) 'Implementation completion report – urban development and decentralization program, Senegal (PAC)', No. 32408, World Bank, Washington DC

9

The Fiscal Space of Thailand: A Historical Analysis

Karel Jansen and Choedchai Khannabha[1]

INTRODUCTION

The MDGs and fiscal space

The concept of 'fiscal space' has emerged in the context of the MDGs. It is clear that enormous efforts are required from international donors and governments and societies in developing countries to achieve the goals. Whether a poor household can escape poverty and malnutrition, send its children to school, get access to safe water and good housing, live a healthy life and so on, depends on three factors: (1) whether its income increases sufficiently; (2) whether the government provides the required services and support; and (3) whether the international community assists where necessary.[2]

The achievement of the MDGs, in most countries, is going to be a heroic task. It should be recognized that the success of this endeavour depends mainly on economic growth that will put income into the hands of the people to reduce poverty and improve their health status, educational participation, housing and so on. Without growth it will be impossible to attain the MDGs. Growth is also necessary to generate the additional government revenue to finance government activities. Government spending will be required to create the conditions for growth, but growth will not be enough. There is also likely to be a need for special government spending programmes directly aimed at achieving the MDGs.

It is for these reasons that the discussion around fiscal space takes on the notion of 'finding fiscal space', that is, mobilizing resources to finance the government activities that are needed to achieve the goals. In general, four sources of finance can be identified. These are taxes, domestic borrowing, aid and redirecting existing resources away from low-priority areas towards the MDGs. In this chapter we concentrate on the first two sources. However, fiscal space is not just about raising taxes and borrowing; it is the entire process of fiscal intervention and its interaction with the rest of the economy. The main concern is whether these fiscal interventions create a domestic regime of capital accumulation that promotes human development. This is not easy. Increasing taxes may run into economic bottlenecks, political resistance and problems of tax administration. Moreover, high tax rates may create negative incentives. High domestic borrowing may lead to excess demand that may result in inflation and current account deficits. Domestic borrowing by the government may make it difficult for the private sector to borrow on domestic financial markets. And the accumulation of government debt will raise questions about the longer run sustainability of this way of financing. At the same time, when government intervention fails to create the right institutions and incentives, and when government provision of infrastructure and social services falls short of what is required for productive private investment, growth will falter and human development will stagnate. This chapter analyses how, in the case of Thailand, the interaction between the state and the private sector led to a successful accumulation strategy that contributed significantly to human development and to the achievement of the MDGs.

Poverty reduction depends on economic growth. If the benefits of growth are equally spread, all income groups will gain. Of course, if a growth strategy can be engineered that is pro-poor, or if effectively targeted poverty alleviation programmes are implemented, poverty can fall faster. In some countries, such distributive pro-poor strategies have been effective, but in many other cases the contribution of pro-poor growth strategies, or of redistributive efforts for the reduction of poverty, has been modest. This finding complicates the discussion of fiscal space. Any fiscal space should be used in such a way that it enhances the growth potential. Economic growth is crucial to the achievement of the MDGs (World Bank, 2005) and any fiscal action that may threaten growth should be considered with extreme caution. Government spending can contribute to growth, but such a positive interaction will only take place when the infrastructure and human capital is used by producers. Any additional infrastructure or human capital that is financed in ways that reduce private investment incentives and opportunities may actually lead to stagnation and may block achievement of the MDGs. We know that private investment is sensitive to macroeconomic conditions (inflation, current account balance, debt overhang), to cost (interest rate, tax rates) and to the availability of credit. Fiscal actions that cause deterioration in these investment conditions are likely to take us further away from the MDGs. We are thus faced with a dilemma: government spending is required but should be financed in a cautious way. This interaction explains why finding fiscal space is like walking a tightrope.

Apart from being an economic tightrope, finding fiscal space is also a political struggle. Increasing fiscal space means that people have to pay and people do not like to pay. Powerful people and vested interests will use their positions to prevent, avoid and evade taxes. Government interventions create institutions and incentives that induce and direct private action.

This chapter analyses how Thailand has walked this tightrope. In the historical analysis that follows in the rest of this chapter we show how Thailand has successfully secured fiscal space that not only sustained growth, but, more importantly, provided the basis for a sustainable capital accumulation process. In this analysis we focus not so much on conventional concerns with short-term solvency and stability, but on the long-term impacts of fiscal interventions.

The case of Thailand

Thailand provides an interesting case study. Economic growth has been rapid over the last 50 years and poverty has fallen sharply, making Thailand one of the most successful developing countries. Table 9.1 brings together some basic data.

Growth was strong until the Asian crisis hit in 1997.[3] Behind the growth was an investment ratio that increased over the years to a high level. The investments were financed by high domestic savings. In the periods before the crisis, however, domestic savings always fell short of investment and a part of investment was financed by foreign capital. The rapid growth was supported by macroeconomic stability that was reflected in the modest rate of inflation.

The rapid economic growth meant a seven-fold increase in per capita income between 1950 and 2000 and resulted in a sharp fall in poverty (see Table 9.2). Also other social indicators showed rapid gains. Life expectancy at birth was around 50 years in the early 1950s and increased to over 71 years by 2005. Infant mortality in 1960 was 103 per 1000 live births; now it has fallen to 20. Primary school enrolment is now universal, but at the secondary level, performance was rather poor compared to other countries in the East Asian region. The gross enrolment rate for lower secondary education was only 40 per cent in 1990, but active government policy since then led to a sharp increase, up to 86 per cent in 2005. There is gender equality in schooling. In 2000, the ratio of girls to boys in primary schools stood at 0.93, in secondary schools, at 1.01 and in tertiary

Table 9.1 *Main economic indicators (%)*

	1950–1959	1960–1969	1970–1979	1980–1989	1990–1996	1997–2003
Growth rate real GDP	5.4	8.0	7.1	7.3	8.5	1.7
Savings/GDP ratio	11.5	20.6	21.8	25.1	34.1	31.2
Investment/GDP ratio	13.6	20.8	23.8	28.6	40.7	24.1
Inflation rate	5.1	2.2	8.0	5.8	5.1	2.1

Source: Ingram (1971); National Economic and Social Development Board; Bank of Thailand

Table 9.2 *Poverty and income distribution*

	Total	Poverty incidence Rural	Urban	Gini Coefficient
1962	57	61	38	0.41
1975	32	36	21	0.43
1990	27	34	2	0.52
2000	14	22	3	0.53
2004	11			0.50

Source: Krongkaew (1993); Warr and Sarntisart (2004); World Bank (2005)

education, at 1.12. In addition, Thailand registered significant success in controlling the spread of HIV/AIDS and reducing the incidence of malaria (Jansen, 2001; NESDB/UN, 2004; National Statistical Office; UNESCO).

Table 9.2 shows that the poverty target of the MDGs has already been achieved. Poverty fell sharply with the economic boom of the 1990s. The crisis of 1997 provided a set back, but only temporarily changed the trend of falling poverty. Table 9.2 also makes it clear that the fall in poverty is fully due to growth; there was no redistribution and the Gini coefficient is high. In fact, over the years, income distribution in Thailand has become increasingly uneven and income inequality now is at a relatively high level.[4]

The rapid growth since 1990 implies that the MDGs have already been achieved, or are close to being achieved (NESDB/UN, 2004). The Thai government has now issued a set of MDG+ targets for 2015, which go beyond the MDGs. For instance, poverty incidence is to be brought below 4 per cent and universal secondary schooling is to be achieved by 2015.

The Thai political economy is dominated by the interaction between (big) business interests and the state. As we show later, the size of the Thai state, as measured by the government expenditure to GDP ratio, is relatively small. But that does not mean that the state is inactive. Phongpaichit and Baker (1998) present an interesting perspective on the role of the Thai state. Behind the rapid growth of the Thai economy are dynamic Chinese businesspeople and the rapid integration of Thailand into the regional and global economy, but also a cautious and determined state. Phongpaichit and Baker emphasize that the state was hardly passive. It made economic development a crusade and it created the institutional structures for it. Development was considered necessary to deal with the communist threat. Communist groups were winning in neighbouring countries and there was a communist insurgency in various parts of the country. In other East Asian countries a similar threat pushed governments to actively seek economic advancement (Campos and Root, 1996).

A number of offices were created in 1959 to steer the development process, the National Economic and Social Development Board (NESDB), the Board of Investment (BoI) and the Budget Bureau. In 1961 the first development plans were published. These comprised a list of public sector investment plans. Phongpaichit and Baker (1998, p62) claim that 'at the heart of Thailand's economic policy making there is one long term constant. The policy makers believe that Thailand must grow through trade'. From the late 1950s, this strategy focused on agricultural exports. Intensive state investment in roads opened up all parts of the country to commercial farming and investment in irrigation expanded the irrigated area. The taxation of rice helped to bring about diversification into other export crops. Banks were under an obligation to reserve a part of their credit for agricultural/rural activities. This ensured the private sector of funds to invest in agriculture and agribusiness.

The industrial policy was less structured and tariffs remained comparatively low. Tariff structures were haphazard, not the reflection of a coherent industrial policy. Changes in tariffs were driven more by revenue needs than by changes in industrial policy. Gradually, in the 1980s, BoI shifted investment incentives towards the export industries, but the big boost for industrial exports came after the mid-1980s when the appreciation of the Japanese yen led to an investment boom of Japanese export industries in Thailand. Real trade liberalization, in the form of a significant reduction in tariffs, came only after that boom, in the 1990s (Jansen, 1997).

Thus Phongpaichit and Baker's (1998) claim that the Thai government was hardly passive is based more on its agricultural policy than its industrial policy. Even in the agricultural sector, a main element of state intervention was the traditional government task of providing infrastructure. The Thai state never engaged in detailed sectoral policies, it just set overall conditions and let the private sector decide on the details. There are three types of government policies that have been important to growth: (1) the maintenance of macroeconomic stability, (2) the provision of infrastructure and education, and (3) the control of labour.

An aspect of government policy that has had a significant impact on development is the government's concern for macroeconomic stability. Warr and Nidhiprabha (1996) see this as the main factor underlying the Thai economic success. The priority for maintaining macroeconomic stability has historical roots. During the colonial period, the Thai state feared that financial instability might invite external intervention. Hence, very cautious fiscal and monetary policies ensured that international reserves remained high, inflation low and the exchange rate stable.

Structures were created to insulate macroeconomic policymaking from the political process by giving it into the hands of independent technocrats. The main institutions involved were the Budget Bureau within the Prime Minister's Office, the Office of Fiscal Policy in the Ministry of Finance, the Bank of Thailand and NESDB. These institutions were staffed with well-educated technocrats and were given a high degree of independence. The budget law strictly regulated the budget process. The Budget Bureau, in consultation with the Office of Fiscal Policy, the Bank of Thailand and NESDB, would set ceilings for budget expenditures in line with expected revenue and politicians could not change these ceilings (Warr and Nidhiprabha, 1996; Root, 1998).

The Bank of Thailand was given a great degree of autonomy in deciding on monetary policy. In recent years, however, these arrangements have not worked so well. Under governments democratically elected since 1988, the independence of the bureaucracy and of the economic technocrats has been reduced. Also the quality of these economic agencies is said to have fallen as, during the boom, their best staff were lured to the private sector. NESDB is sidelined in major government investment decisions. It is argued that increased political interference at the Bank of Thailand is one of the factors behind its loss of control over the financial system that led to the financial crisis of 1997 (Phongpaichit and Baker, 1998).

The record of the Thai state in the provision of physical and social infrastructure is not impressive. Investments in ports, roads, transport systems and communications have not kept pace with economic growth (Dixon, 1999). Social infrastructure is also far from adequate. It has already been noted that participation in secondary education is far below regional standards, and below the standards required for a country of Thailand's level of development. Secondary education, and, in particular, vocational education, is essential for the development of modern sectors of the economy. Tertiary education enrolment rates are well in line with those of other countries in the region. Thailand has an unbalanced educational structure with universal primary education, underdeveloped secondary education and a well-developed tertiary education. This pattern is understandable from political reasons. Mass education at the primary level extends government control and helps to instil a national identity, and good university education is necessary for the children of the elite. But economically the pattern makes no sense as Thailand found out during the growth boom when skilled workers were in short supply. The recent spurt in secondary enrolments is an answer to that need.

The coalition between the state and the capitalist class has been very successful in controlling labour. Thailand has a long history of labour repression. The 1975 Labour Relations Law seemed to bring improvement, but its implementation has been stilted and it did not help workers much (Brown, 1997). Unger (1998) links the absence of effective trade unions to the lack of social capital, but unwilling employers and a repressive government have had much to do with it.

There is a legal minimum wage, but this is only irregularly revised and very poorly enforced. Some studies suggest that it is paid in less than one third of firms, covering about half of all unskilled workers (Warr and Nidhiprabha, 1996). A compensating factor is that the government policy to tax rice helped to keep the local price of rice, the main staple food, low, thus keeping the urban cost of living under control.

During the boom of the 1990s the tight labour market exerted an upward pressure on wages, which led Dixon (1999) to observe that at the end of the 1990s Thai industry faced the problem that its labour costs were too high for labour intensive industries, but that skill levels were too low for skill-intensive industries.

The record shows that, on the whole, the Thai state has been successful in stimulating development. The political dominance of business interests is translated into a preference for relatively small government, into little political support for redistribution, and into a concern for macroeconomic stability. Thai policymakers have always placed economic growth as their top priority and economic growth is seen as being mainly driven by exports. The main task for the government is to provide infrastructure and basic social services and to ensure macroeconomic stability. 'The prevailing view in Thai political circles is that the government should play only a limited role in the economy' (Warr and Nidhiprabha, 1996, p96).

The concern for stability is reflected in generally cautious fiscal and monetary policies. The development strategy that makes exports the engine of growth has resulted in a rapid integration with global markets for goods, investment and finance. This globalization may have further limited policy options.

Outline of this chapter

This study explores Thailand's 'fiscal space'. We interpret fiscal space as the total of government activities and their financing. In line with the UNDP project, of which this country study is part, the focus will be on government revenue and deficit financing. We trace the experience of Thailand on these issues over the period since 1970.

In the fiscal space there are a number of significant players that share the same properties of using resources for public purposes, and/or function for some public purposes. Fiscal operations are identified with activities of public sector agents in matters relating primarily to the provision of public goods and services.

The fiscal space can be viewed, at least in Thailand, from four vantage points, namely:

1   the central government;
2   the local governments;
3   state enterprises;
4   non-budget public sector funds set up to carry out specific tasks.

Each of the four components of the fiscal space can perform in its own context and work milieu to help attain the aims of the country, whether reducing poverty, empowering women, taking good care of the environment, containing and fighting deadly diseases and so on.[5]

The next section of the chapter concentrates on the analysis of trends in central government revenue, but also has sub-sections on the fiscal activities of local government and state enterprises. Government in Thailand is relatively centralized; only recently have there been serious attempts at decentralization. Revenue collection and other financing by local government have been almost negligible. In our analysis we concentrate on the central government finances, but in light of the discussion on decentralization, we analyse the role of local governments. Some of the state enterprises in Thailand play a role in the fiscal space. There are two brief sections, one on administrative issues in the revenue system, and the other to track some recent fiscal innovations.

The chapter then focuses on deficit financing by the central government. This section explores the use of monetary financing and of domestic and foreign borrowing. It was the debt financing that led to concerns about debt sustainability. The final section of the chapter draws some conclusions and tries to assess whether the way Thailand has used its fiscal space has contributed to the achievement of the MDGs.

GOVERNMENT REVENUE

It is instructive to start with a review of government finances in Thailand. Figure 9.1 shows the expenditure and revenue to GDP ratios since 1950. Thailand had always remained independent but international treaties with the colonial powers had considerably limited its fiscal freedom before 1950. The Bowring Treaty of 1855 had fixed tax rates that the Thai government could impose at low levels. In 1926 these treaties were renegotiated and fiscal autonomy was considerably increased. This led to a considerable change in the tax structure, in particular, the contribution of import duties increased from 7 per cent of total revenue in 1926 to 27 per cent in 1950 (Ingram, 1971). While the regained fiscal autonomy changed the tax structure, it is less clear whether it changed the level of tax revenue. Data on revenue from Ingram (1971) and estimates of GDP in Manarungsan (1989) suggest that around 1926 the revenue to GDP ratio may have been approximately 11 per cent, that is, not much different from the 1950 level shown in Figure 9.1.

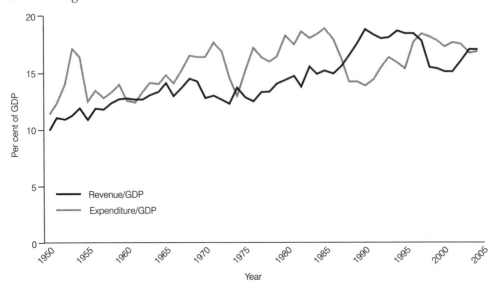

Source: Bank of Thailand, Quarterly Bulletin, various issues

Figure 9.1 *Revenue and expenditure ratios for Thailand (% of GDP)*

Figure 9.1 shows government spending, as a percentage of GDP, gradually rising from 1950 to the early 1980s. There are sometimes very sharp short-term fluctuations, which suggest an active use of short-run fiscal policy (see Jansen, 2004). The long-term trend is upwards from an expenditure ratio of between 12 and 14 per cent in the 1950s to a level of around 18 per cent in 1971. The first oil crisis led to a fiscal retrenchment but later on the expenditure ratio climbed back to around 18 per cent in the early 1980s. During the growth boom of the 1990s, the expenditure ratio declined and in recent years the ratio recovered to a level of around 17 per cent. The revenue ratio followed this trend at some distance. In the 1950s the revenue ratio was between 10 and 12 per cent of GDP. It rose to a level of around 14 per cent by the late 1960s and stayed around that level until the early 1980s. In the late 1980s and the 1990s the revenue ratio climbed to around 18 per cent of GDP, driven by the booming economy. The Asian crisis brought a sharp fall, back to around 15 per cent, in the period 1998 to 2001. The most recent years have seen a recovery to around 17 per cent (in the period 2003 to 2005). The higher levels of the early 1990s have not been regained and it seems as if fiscal space has been lost.

The balance between the expenditure ratio and revenue ratio was quite small until 1970, then the budgets showed a small deficit. The 1970s and the first half of the 1980s show considerable deficits. The economic boom that began in the late 1980s, driven by foreign capital inflows, gave a boost to government revenue. This contributed to the substantial fiscal surpluses of the period 1988 to 1996. It is remarkable, however, that the surpluses of this period are not only due to buoyant revenue but also to a significant decline in the expenditure ratio.

The Asian crisis led to a new fiscal situation. In 1996 and 1997, fiscal policy was strongly expansionary to compensate for the decline in export demand. But once the crisis occurred, revenue fell sharply, the IMF imposed extremely tight fiscal policy conditions and government expenditure declined considerably. This is not so much reflected in the expenditure ratio in Figure 9.1 because in that ratio both the numerator (government spending) and the denominator (GDP) declined. Table 9.A1 in Annex 9.1 (page 393) gives government spending at constant (1988) prices and shows that total spending declined from a peak of Bt604 billion in 1997 to Bt500 billion in 1998. This was totally due to a collapse in capital spending. Revenue at constant prices fell from Bt550 billion in 1997 to Bt425 billion in 1998. As revenue fell more sharply than expenditure, fiscal deficits returned during the period 1997 to 2002, but since 2003 fiscal balance has been restored.

The 'size' of government in Thailand

In international terms, the revenue to GDP ratio in Thailand is relatively low. The scatter diagram of Figure 9.2 brings together data for a group of 72 developed and developing countries for 2002. The data show a clear relationship between economic development and the revenue ratio, as reflected in the trend line. At the same time, there

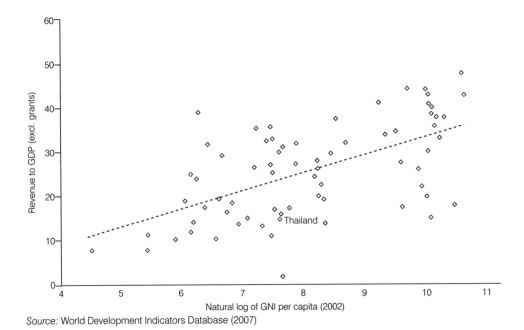

Source: World Development Indicators Database (2007)

Figure 9.2 *Revenue ratio and economic development*

is considerable variation around the trend line; individual country characteristics, other than their income, play a large role in determining the level of the revenue ratio. Thailand lies below the trend line. Given its per capita income, one would have expected a revenue-to-GDP ratio close to 24 per cent. In fact Thailand's 2002 ratio was just over 15 per cent. Of course, the revenue ratio in 2002 was unusually low in the aftermath of the financial crisis. However, even at the historical peak levels of the ratio (at just over 18 per cent), it would be considerably below the average pattern suggested by Figure 9.2.

Moreover, the trend line in Figure 9.2 would suggest that as over time per capita income rises, so too would the revenue to GDP ratio increase. In fact, the trend line indicates that the income growth that Thailand experienced since 1950 would result in an increase in the revenue to GDP ratio of close to 10 percentage points. In fact, as Figure 9.1 shows, the revenue ratio increased from a level of around 11 to 12 per cent in the 1950s to a level of just over 18 per cent in the early 1990s, but since then has fallen back to around 17 per cent in recent years.

The evidence from cross-country data in Figure 9.2 is confirmed by time series data. Over the last 100 years, the economies of the advanced countries of the world have grown and government spending has increased faster than GDP. As a result, the ratio of government expenditure to GDP has increased (see Table I.1 in Tanzi and Schuknecht, 2000; and Table 3.9 in Maddison, 2001).[6]

The fact that the revenue ratio of Thailand lies far below the regression line of Figure 9.2, and the fact that over time the revenue ratio did not grow as fast as that of other countries, could be taken to indicate that there is unused fiscal space. Still, such a conclusion would be unfounded. Figure 9.2 shows a clear and significant trend line, but it also shows a considerable dispersion around that line. Clearly there are, at each income level, countries with 'big' governments and countries with 'small' governments, and Thailand appears to be a country with a relatively small government. A number of reasons can be suggested to explain this:

- As noted above, from a historical perspective, the size of government revenue had been restricted by international treaties during the colonial era. When, however, greater fiscal autonomy was obtained in 1926, this was not used to sharply increase revenue. The available evidence suggests that the revenue to GDP ratio in 1950 was not much different from its 1926 level. It could be hypothesized that the historical experience had instilled a habit of low taxes.
- The historical experience did not just instil a habit of low taxes, it also instilled a habit of cautious fiscal policy. The budget process in Thailand is driven very much by the revenue side. Estimates are made of available revenue and that determines the level of government spending that can be undertaken. An alternative approach to budgeting, in which necessary or desired government spending would determine the level of revenue that would be required, would give rise to a more active revenue policy. But this is not the way fiscal policy in Thailand has operated. Tax rates in Thailand are relatively low and politically difficult to increase, and there are legal ceilings to the level of an acceptable deficit.
- Political power in Thailand is in the hands of a small elite of military, business and bureaucratic interests. This elite has no desire for high taxes that would eat into their incomes or increase the costs of production. As a result, corporate and personal income taxes have remained fairly low, as have the indirect taxes that could have increased cost of living and labour costs.
- This elite, and the general public, may also find that the public sector is rather inefficient in providing services and that, therefore, the role of government and of state enterprises best remain small. A government that is seen as inefficient and highly corrupt will find it difficult to see high taxes accepted. In the 2005 Corruption Index of *Transparency International*, Thailand scored just 3.8 (10 being the best score) and ranks fairly low (the 2005 Corruption Index of Transparency International can be accessed online at www.transparency.org/policy_research/surveys_indices/cpi/2005). Thai newspapers regularly report on corruption in government projects.
- Globalization is another factor that may keep government revenue in check. Figure 9.1 shows how the revenue ratio slowly increased from 1950 to a peak in 1990, but since then has stagnated and declined. This coincides with the acceleration of the process of integration of Thailand into the global economy. Since 1988 FDI in Thailand increased sharply. Since 1990, financial markets were liberalized and integrated with global financial markets. Trade liberalization increased in the 1990s.

Table 9.3 *Structure of government expenditures – period averages (% of GDP)*

	Capital Expenditure	Social Services	Total Expenditure
1970–1979	4.1	4.6	15.9
1980–1989	3.0	5.3	17.7
1990–1997	5.1	6.0	16.2
1998–2003	4.2	8.0	17.6

Source: Bank of Thailand, *Quarterly Bulletin*, various issues

As we see in more detail later, these processes reduced revenue from taxes on international trade and may have reduced the ability to tax capital income.

Government expenditure and revenue ratios are comparatively low in Thailand, but size is not all. The relevant question is whether government activities are supportive of the process of capital accumulation and growth. Not all government spending is equally important in this context. Generally, capital expenditures and expenditures on social services are considered instrumental in the process of capital accumulation. Government investment is crucial because it creates the infrastructure required to sustain efficient and profitable private investment, production and competitiveness. Government spending on social services is paramount because it helps create the human capital that is crucial for increasing productivity and incomes. Apart from that, government spending on social services contributes directly to the achievement of the MDGs. Table 9.3 gives some period averages for these important categories of government spending.

Sturm (2001) uses a sample of 37 developing countries with data over the period 1975 to 1993 to calculate the median ratio of central government capital spending to GDP. The median ratio was around 4.5 in the period 1975 to 1981 and then declined to around 3 per cent in 1990, after which it recovered somewhat in the early 1990s, but has stayed below 4 per cent. Capital spending in Thailand seems to follow the same pattern and to be around a level similar to other developing countries.

Fan and Rao (2003) give data for Asian developing countries that indicate that, for 1980, social services spending accounted for 4.4 per cent of GDP and that, by 1998, this ratio had fallen to 4.1 per cent. Compared to these numbers, the level of spending on social services in Thailand seems high.

It can thus be concluded that, while the overall spending ratio of Thailand is rather low, spending on crucial items such as infrastructure and social services is not low in a comparative perspective. Such spending has supported a dynamic accumulation process and contributed to human development.

The structure of revenue

The revenue structure, as a percentage of GDP, has been relatively stable over the last

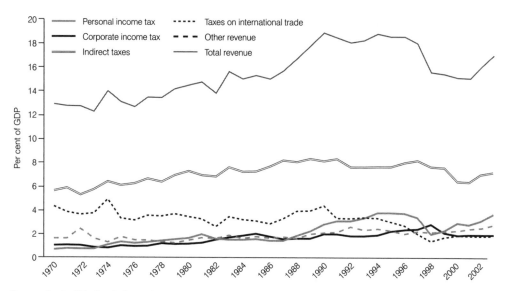

Source: Bank of Thailand, *Quarterly Bulletin*, various issues

Figure 9.3 *Revenue structure, 1970–2003 (% of GDP)*

35 years, as Figure 9.3 shows. The increase in the overall tax ratio from 1970 to 1990 was driven mainly by the growing importance of income and indirect taxes. The share of trade and other revenue in GDP did not change much.

From 1990 onwards, a systematic decline in the revenue from taxes on international trade occurs. While these taxes still generated an income equivalent to 4.3 per cent of GDP in 1990, by the early 2000s this share had fallen to below 2 per cent. This is also the main reason for the stagnation and decline of the overall revenue ratio since 1990.

The share of other taxes in GDP has not changed significantly since 1990. Of course, during the crisis that occurred after 1997, all revenue sources suffered from the sharp fall in incomes and expenditures and, by 2003, the shares of personal and corporate income taxes and indirect taxes in GDP had not fully returned to the levels of the early 1990s.

Total revenue is composed of:

$$Rev = PIT + CIT + Ind + Trade + Other \tag{1}$$

Where Rev = total revenue; PIT = personal income tax revenue; CIT = corporate income tax revenue; Ind = indirect taxes (business taxes and excise duties, and since 1992, VAT); $Trade$ = taxes on international trade; and $Other$ = other revenue.

We can express (1) as a fraction of GDP (Y):

$$\frac{Rev}{Y} = \frac{PIT}{Y} + \frac{CIT}{Y} + \frac{Ind}{Y} + \frac{Trade}{Y} + \frac{Other}{Y} \tag{2}$$

Table 9.4 *Revenue structure – period averages (% of GDP)*

	1970–1979	1980–1988	1989–1997	1998–2003
Personal income tax	0.9	1.5	2.0	2.0
Corporate income tax	1.0	1.5	3.2	2.7
Indirect taxes	6.0	7.3	7.9	7.0
Taxes on international trade	3.7	3.2	3.2	1.7
Other revenue	1.5	1.5	2.1	2.3
Total revenue	13.1	15.1	18.3	15.7

Source: Bank of Thailand, Quarterly Bulletin, various issues

The long-term picture of Figure 9.3 suggests a number of sub-periods (see Table 9.4). The period 1970 to 1988 shows a slow but steady increase in the overall revenue ratio from 12.7 per cent of GDP in 1970 to 16.6 in 1986. This rise was driven by small gains in both the personal and corporate income tax ratios and a somewhat stronger increase in the indirect tax ratio. These gains compensated for a slow decline in the contribution of trade taxes. The next period is that from 1989 to 1997, the pre-crisis period of rapid growth. The overall revenue ratio increased rapidly from 1988 to 1990 and then stabilized at the peak level of over 18 per cent of GDP. This rise was driven by the good performance of the income taxes. The shares of indirect taxes and of taxes on international trade were stable over these years. In the post-crisis years the total revenue ratio first collapsed but then recovered and now seems to be stabilized at a level around 17 per cent of GDP, that is, below the peak level of the early 1990s. By the end of the period, in 2003, revenue from taxes on international trade had fallen to a significantly lower level. The ratios of personal income tax revenue and of indirect taxes have recovered but stay below their pre-crisis peaks, while the corporate income tax ratio has come back to the pre-crisis level.

Zee (1996) provides comparative data on tax structures in developing countries.[7] Table 9.5 reproduces the data from Table 2 of Zee (1996) and adds to this the information for Thailand. The table suggests that Thailand has an unusual tax structure. The share of income taxes in total tax revenue is considerably lower than that of the other countries included in the table. However, while the share of income taxes is fairly stable over the period covered by the table in the other country groups, for Thailand there is an increasing trend for this share. But even at the end of the period the share is far below that of the other countries. In contrast, the share of indirect taxes on consumption is relatively high in Thailand. While for most countries this share is somewhere between 25 and 40 per cent of total taxes, for Thailand it brings more than half the total tax revenue. The share of taxes on international trade is comparable to that of the other countries.

It would thus appear that Thailand's tax structure is biased against income taxes and towards indirect taxes. It should be noted, however, that since the years covered in Table 9.5, the Thai tax structure has changed. In recent years the share of income taxes in the

Table 9.5 *Comparative tax structure (% of total tax revenue)*

	Income taxes			Indirect taxes			Trade taxes		
	1975–1979	1980–1984	1985–1989	1975–1979	1980–1984	1985–1989	1975–1979	1980–1984	1985–1989
OECD	38.7	39.4	38.6	27.3	27.9	29.2	4.2	2.9	2.2
Developing countries	32.3	31.9	31.2	29.5	30.9	32.5	29.6	27.4	26.5
Africa	33.3	32.3	34.5	25.5	28.5	29.3	36.4	34.8	32.5
Asia	32.8	34.0	32.6	36.7	37.6	39.2	26.5	24.8	23.8
Middle East	40.7	37.3	31.9	22.1	17.8	20.7	31.0	30.7	31.5
Latin America	26.0	26.4	25.3	31.2	34.1	35.8	23.8	19.3	19.2
Thailand	18.3	22.0	22.1	52.4	52.9	53.0	28.0	23.6	22.6

Source: Zee (1996, p1661); for Thailand, Bank of Thailand, Quarterly Bulletin, various issues

total tax revenue of Thailand has increased to around 35 per cent, a proportion more in line with the data in Table 9.5. The share of taxes on international trade has fallen to around 12 per cent of total tax revenue and the share of indirect taxes has fallen to just below 50 per cent of total tax revenue.[8]

The World Bank (2000) compares Thailand's revenue structure to that of other Southeast Asian nations. Compared to these neighbouring countries, Thailand has a relatively low overall revenue ratio. A comparison of the revenue structures confirms the above findings. The shares in total revenue of corporate income tax and of taxes on international trade are comparable to those of other Southeast Asian countries, but the share of the personal income tax is smaller and that of indirect taxes significantly higher.

Tax elasticity, or tax buoyancy, links changes in tax revenue to changes in GDP (see, for example, Warr and Nidhiprabha, 1996; and World Bank, 2000). Long-run elasticity for total tax revenue is typically just above one. The personal and corporate income taxes are elastic with respect to GDP (elasticity estimates for personal income tax centre on 1.3, and for corporate income tax on 1.5), while the elasticity for indirect taxes is lower (around 1), and for import duties below 1. Such elasticity estimates give an indication of how tax revenue will develop as GDP grows.

A CERDI study by Brun et al (2006) performs a standard tax effort analysis. Tax revenue is explained in a cross country regression by structural characteristics of the country (GDP per capita, import/GDP ratio, share of mineral exports and share of agriculture in GDP). The regression predicts, for each country, a level of the tax/GDP ratio and the difference between that predicted value and the actual tax ratio reflects the 'fiscal effort' of the country, that is, its ability to create fiscal space. Results of this exercise suggest that Thailand's tax effort is rather poor. In the last decade, its tax revenue has lagged behind what could be expected (see Table 2-5 in Brun et al, 2006).

We prefer to use another method to show the impact of structural change on tax revenue. To get more insight into the factors underlying the changes reflected in Table 9.4 we assume some simple proportional relationships:

$$PIT = a\,W$$
$$CIT = b\,Pr$$
$$Ind = d\,C$$
$$Trade = e\,M$$
$$Other = h\,Y$$

PIT, the personal income tax revenue, is a proportion of wage income (W) in the formal sector of the economy. This will be approximated by the 'compensation of employees' of the National Income Statistics. *CIT*, the revenue from corporate income tax is proportional to the profits (*Pr*) of corporations. This will be approximated by the 'savings of corporations and government enterprises' of the National Income Statistics. *Ind*, the revenue from indirect taxes is proportional to private consumption expenditure (*C*). Data are taken from National Income Statistics. *Trade*, the revenue from taxes on international trade is proportional to expenditure on imports of goods and services (*M*). Data are taken from National Income Statistics. *Other*, other revenue is simply assumed to be proportional to GDP(*Y*). The variables W, Pr, C, M, Y constitute the tax base for each particular revenue source, while the coefficients a, b, d, e, h can be interpreted as the effective tax rates.

These assumptions allow us to rewrite (1):

$$Rev = a\,W + b\,Pr + d\,C + e\,M + h\,Y \tag{3}$$

Again, we can express (3) as a fraction of GDP. The change in the total revenue ratio over the period can be decomposed as follows:

$$\Delta\left(\frac{Rev}{Y}\right) = (a_t - a_0)\left(\frac{W}{Y}\right)_t + a_0\left[\left(\frac{W}{Y}\right)_t - \left(\frac{W}{Y}\right)_0\right]$$

$$+ (b_t - b_0)\left(\frac{Pr}{Y}\right)_t + b_0\left[\left(\frac{Pr}{Y}\right)_t - \left(\frac{Pr}{Y}\right)_0\right]$$

$$+ (d_t - d_0)\left(\frac{C}{Y}\right)_t + d_0\left[\left(\frac{C}{Y}\right)_t - \left(\frac{C}{Y}\right)_0\right]$$

$$+ (e_t - e_0)\left(\frac{M}{Y}\right)_t + e_0\left[\left(\frac{M}{Y}\right)_t - \left(\frac{M}{Y}\right)_0\right]$$

$$+ (h_t - h_0) \tag{4}$$

Equation (4) shows that the change of the revenue to GDP ratio over the period can be decomposed (the subscript *t* indicates the value of the variable at the end of the period,

Table 9.6 *Decomposition of changes in the revenue ratio (% of GDP)*

Period	Structural change	Tax effort	Total change revenue ratio
1970–2003	9.598	−5.274	4.324
1970–1979	2.217	−0.891	1.327
1979–1988	0.600	1.355	1.955
1988–1997	1.499	−0.138	1.360
1997–2003	2.711	−3.549	−0.087

while 0 refers to its value at the beginning of the period). For each of the revenue sources the change in the tax ratio can be attributed to:

1   changes in the coefficients $(a_t − a_0)$, and so on. This is the change in the effective tax rate or in the tax intensity and will, normally, be the result of changes in tax policy. This could be interpreted as the 'tax effort';
2   changes in the structure of GDP (W/Y, Pr/Y, C/Y, M/Y). The changes in these ratios reflect structural changes in the economy. For instance, increases in W/Y and Pr/Y reflect the increasing role of the formal sector in the economy and the increase in M/Y, the steadily rising openness of the Thai economy.

Table 9.6 shows the result of the decomposition (Table 9.A2 on page 394 provides more detail). Table 9.6 makes clear that the gradual increase in the total revenue to GDP ratio from 1970 to 1997 was, to a large extent, due to changes in the structure of the economy. Three changes are particularly important. First, as the Thai economy developed, the organization of production became more formal. The small, unincorporated, household businesses lost out to the modern and large corporations. The National Income Statistics show that 'Income from Unincorporated Enterprises' accounted for 52 per cent of GDP in 1970. By 1996 that share had fallen to 23 per cent.[9] The share of corporate profits and of wage payments in the formal sector of the economy increased, thus widening the tax basis for corporate and personal income taxes. The revenue from personal and corporate income taxes together increased from 1.5 per cent of GDP in 1970 to 6.0 per cent in 1996 and fell to 5.5 per cent in 2003. Table 9.A2 (page 394) shows that the effective rates for personal income tax increased little over the period and the effective rates for corporate income tax increased by a bit more. For both taxes, their increasing share of the tax base in GDP made an important contribution to the increased revenue.

The second important structural change was the opening up of the economy. The share of imports of goods and services in GDP stood at 19 per cent in 1970. By 1996 the share had increased to 46 per cent and it continued to rise to 59 per cent by 2003. The effective tax rate on international trade (the 'e' of the model) showed a steady and steep decline. The rate fell in the 1970s, then stabilized in the 1980s and continued its decline in the 1990s. The outcome of these two trends is shown in Figure 9.3 on page 337. The share of taxes on international trade in GDP remained high and relatively stable during the 1970s and the 1980s. Trade liberalization, as reflected in the decline of tariffs, was leading to a decline in trade tax revenue, but the rapid increase in the volume of international trade compensated for this. In the 1990s, trade liberalization advanced further and the fall in tariffs could no longer be fully compensated for by the increase in the trade volume. As a result the revenue from taxes on international trade declined from around 4 per cent of GDP at about 1990 to 1.9 per cent in 2003.

The third structural change relates to private consumption. The share of private consumption in GDP was 70 per cent in 1970. In the period up to 1990 this share declined as private savings increased. By 1990 the share had fallen to 55 per cent, a level at which it has stabilized in the years since. The relative decline of private consumption reduced the tax base for indirect taxes. Over the period 1970 to 1990 this was more than compensated for by an increase in the effective indirect tax rate, so that the share of indirect taxes in GDP increased from 5.5 per cent in 1970 to just over 8 per cent by about 1990. Since 1990 the share of private consumption in GDP has been fairly constant while the effective indirect tax rate has shown a slight decline. The result is that the share of indirect taxes in GDP has fallen back to a level of around 7 per cent in recent years.

The remarkable conclusion of this analysis is that 'fiscal space' is created as much by the structural changes that come with economic development as by an active revenue policy. If we interpret the changes in the effective tax rates in the model (that is, the tax effort column in Table 9.6) as the outcome of policy changes, the conclusion will have to be that fiscal policy worked to reduce revenue over the long run.

Table 9.A2 presents a more detailed picture than Table 9.6. It shows that, over the entire period from 1970, effective tax rates for income and indirect taxes increased, albeit not by much. The overall decline in 'tax effort' is caused by the sharp fall in the effective rate of trade taxes due to the process of import liberalization. It is worrying that in the most recent period, since the Asian crisis, the effective tax rates of all types of taxes have fallen. Table 9.A2 can be used for making some comments on individual revenue sources.

Personal income tax
If we look at the pattern of the personal income tax revenue over time in Figure 9.3 we observe that the share was stable at around 1 per cent of GDP in the 1970s and started to rise in the 1980s reaching a level of around 2 per cent of GDP in the early 1990s. Before the 1997 crisis, the revenue ratio increased somewhat more, driven by the booming economy, but after the crisis the ratio of personal income tax revenue to GDP stabilized at around 2 per cent. The downward adjustment of the top rates in 1986 and 1991 resulted in a small and short-term dip in the revenue to GDP ratio, but it appears that the revenue from the tax is not so dependent on the tax rates. It is probably driven

more by the changes in the exemptions, allowances and deductions and the efforts of the tax administration.

As noted above, the contribution of personal income tax to total tax revenue is comparatively small in Thailand. Personal income tax is generally judged to be inefficient and inequitable. Different types of income are treated in different ways and there are many exemptions, allowances and deductions that introduce an element of arbitrariness and possible inequity and distortion (see, for example, World Bank, 2000; and Sahasakul, 1993).

Data from the Ministry of Finance show that in 2004 close to 6 million persons filed tax returns. This is out of a labour force of 35 million, of which about 15 million are public and private sector employees.[10] Of the almost 6 million tax returns, just over 2 million actually paid some tax, most of them in the low brackets. But the bulk of personal income tax is paid by a small group of big earners, a group of about 100,000 people with incomes over Bt1 million per year paid about two-thirds of the total personal income tax revenue in 2004.[11]

The personal income tax has a progressive rate structure. The top rate used to be 65 per cent, but in 1986 it was reduced to 55 per cent and in 1991 it was further reduced to 37 per cent. Over the years the income brackets have also been adjusted. At present the rate structure contains six brackets ranging from 0 to 37 per cent. It should be noted that the progressivity of the rate structure does not necessarily lead to progressivity in actual tax payments, the many exemptions, deductions and allowances may reduce the incidence of payment. Available studies conclude that personal income tax in Thailand has a progressive incidence (World Bank, 2000; Warr and Sarntisart, 2004), but the impact on income distribution is only marginal. As observed above, a very small group of high income earners pay most of the personal income tax and most of the population pays nothing; therefore personal income tax only affects incomes in the top income decile.

In terms of fiscal space, one could consider it unfortunate that the drastic change in the labour force is not reflected in a more significant change in personal income tax revenue. From 1970 to 2004 the number of formal sector employees, the type of person most easily tracable for tax administrators, increased from 2.6 million to 15 million, or from 15 per cent of the labour force to 43 per cent. Over the same period the share of personal income tax in GDP increased from 1 to 2 per cent. However, one should recognize that most of these formal sector workers earn low incomes out of which they cannot really afford to pay much tax. The poverty of the personal income tax is thus closely linked to the very unequal income distribution that Thailand has. Most workers in agriculture, industry and services earn a modest income out of which they cannot pay any tax. The very small group that earn a high income, on which they should make considerable tax payments, also have the political power and influence that helps to turn the available exemptions, deductions and allowances to their advantage.

Corporate income tax

Corporate income tax made a very small contribution to revenue in the early 1970s. In the 1980s the share rose to around 1.5 per cent of GDP and the economic boom of the late 1980s and 1990s lifted the share further to over 3.5 per cent in the period 1994 to 1996. The Asian crisis was reflected in a considerable drop in revenue as most firms recorded losses, but in recent years the share has returned to the level of 3.5 per cent of GDP.

Over time, the rate structure has changed. In the 1970s the tax rate depended on the size of profits. Until 1977, companies making small profits (less than Bt500,000) paid 20 per cent while those making large profits (over Bt1 million) paid 30 per cent. Since 1978 a uniform rate has been applied, although now firms listed on the stock market pay less (30 per cent) than unlisted firms (35 per cent). This was done to encourage listing and to help develop the stock market. Over the years there have been small variations in these rates. At present the basic tax rate is 30 per cent, but there are (small) variations for different types of companies (for example, for small firms or firms newly listed on the stock market). These small changes in the tax rates are not the root cause of the fluctuations in tax revenue. The ups and downs of corporate income tax revenue follow closely the ups and downs of the economy. The growth in the 1970s was accompanied by a rapid increase in corporate income tax revenue as a percentage of GDP. The recession of the early 1980s is reflected in stagnation and even a small decline in the ratio and the boom of the late 1980s and 1990s results in a rapid growth of the ratio. The Asian crisis lead to a sharp fall and the economic recovery of recent years is reflected in a recovery of the ratio.

Like personal income tax, corporate income tax is paid by only a few corporations. Warr and Nidhiprabha (1996) mention that close to half of all companies declare losses and do not pay taxes, and that in 1984 less than 1 per cent of all corporations paid 77 per cent of all corporate taxes. These data suggest that compliance is rather poor.

Indirect taxes

Thailand depends relatively heavily on revenue from indirect taxes. Until 1992 the main elements were business taxes (sales tax) and excise taxes. In 1992 VAT was introduced to replace the business taxes, which were rather inefficient. There were 14 categories of business tax with rates ranging from 1 to 50 per cent (Sahasakul, 1993), but the effective tax rate depended on the structure of the sector. In highly segmented sectors, cascading of business taxes could lead to high effective rates. VAT removed these distortions.

VAT was introduced in 1992 with a uniform rate of 7 per cent. In 1997, in the context of the IMF conditionality after the Asian crisis, this was raised to 10 per cent. But the tight fiscal policy of that year turned out to be a mistake and contributed to an even faster economic downturn, so in March 1999 the rate was reduced temporarily to 7 per cent. Since then many deadlines have passed for the government to bring the rate back to 10 per cent, but so far this has not happened. At 7 per cent, the VAT rate is rather low. Tanzi and Zee (2000) list VAT rates for 30 developing countries, and Thailand has one of the lowest.

The share of indirect taxes in GDP has steadily increased from around 5.5 per cent in the early 1970s to a peak of 8.2 per cent in 1990/91. The introduction of VAT was associated with a small fall in the ratio (to 7.6 per cent). The Asian crisis undermined private spending, and revenue from the indirect taxes fell to a low level from which it is now recovering. However, in recent years the revenue from indirect taxes amounts to about 7 per cent of GDP, which is considerably below its peak of the 1990s.

In our decomposition model the revenues from indirect taxes are driven by the trend in consumption spending and the effective tax rate. From 1970 to the 1990s the share of consumption in GDP gradually declined, from 70 per cent to around 55 per cent, while the effective indirect tax rate gradually increased. Over this period the increase in the share of indirect taxes in GDP is due to the increase in the effective tax rate, resulting from shifts in the tax rates and shifts in consumption patterns. In the 1990s both the consumption share and the effective tax rate were rather stable and so was the share of indirect tax revenue in GDP. Since the Asian crisis the effective tax rate has been declining.

Taxes on international trade

In most countries trade taxes are import duties, but in the case of Thailand we also have to consider export taxes. Until 1986 Thailand operated a rice premium, an export tax on rice as well as export taxes on other products, such as rubber. The premium varied over the years in order to stabilize the domestic rice price. The rice export tax was not important in terms of revenue. It brought in little revenue in most years, but it was important in that it created a wedge between the world market price of rice and the local rice price, with considerable distributional consequences. The export tax shifted income from rice producers to rice buyers and can be interpreted as shifting resources from agriculture to industry and services, or from rural to urban areas. In September 1985 the rice export tax was suspended.

The main revenue from taxes on international trade comes from import duties. Tariffs are determined by considerations of trade and industrial policy and by revenue concerns. In Thailand they have also been used for short-term macroeconomic management. On several occasions import tariffs were raised or lowered depending on the macroeconomic and balance of payments situation rather than revenue considerations. For instance, in 1983 a surcharge of 10 per cent was introduced to manage the current account deficit that was caused by the overvalued exchange rate. When the exchange rate eventually depreciated in 1984, the surcharge was lifted. Also, in 1997 a 10 per cent surcharge was introduced to deal with the Asian crisis (it was dropped again in 1999).

It is difficult to give a precise picture of the rate structure because there are so many rates for different products and, at the same time, there are many exemptions, for example, for firms receiving BoI privileges, or for export firms that can get tax rebates. The effective import tax rate of our decomposition model fell rapidly in the 1970s (from 22 per cent to around 12 per cent), then stabilized in the 1980s, to continue the decline in the 1990s. By the early 2000s, the rate has fallen to a fairly low level (3 per cent). Over the years, imports have been gradually and selectively liberalized. Particularly during the boom in the 1990s, Thailand was fully integrated into the global economy and import duties came down quickly. In 1991 and 1994 there were significant reductions of tariffs.

It is remarkable that the decline of the effective import tax rate in the 1970s was not reflected in the decline of trade tax revenue as a percentage of GDP. In the 1970s the decline in the effective tax rate was compensated for by the steady increase in the import/GDP ratio (from 19 per cent in the 1970s to around 30 per cent in 1980). In the 1980s, both the effective tax rate and the import/GDP ratio were rather stable. As a result, the ratio of trade taxes to GDP was also rather stable over these two decades; it fluctuated in a range between 3 to 4 per cent of GDP. In the 1990s the import/GDP ratio increased further (to around 45 per cent) and the effective trade tax rate declined with import liberalization. Now the increase in the import/GDP ratio was not sufficient to compensate for the fall in the effective tax rate, consequently the revenue from trade taxes fell to below 2 per cent of GDP. Recent years have seen a further increase in the import/GDP ratio (to close to 60 per cent in the 2000s), but now the import tariffs have fallen to very low levels and there is no effect on the trade tax revenue.

The role of local government in the Thai fiscal space

Local governments are agents in the fiscal space. Until very recently, the Thai government was highly centralized, with local government playing only a marginal role in government spending and an even smaller role in revenue collection. In the 1990s the central government spent 93 per cent of all general government expenditure and collected 95 per cent of all revenue and only 25 per cent of municipal revenue was locally collected and retained (World Bank, 2000). There would thus be little reason to devote much attention to local government were it not for the fact that in the last few years a rapid process of significant decentralization has started. This process will give greater responsibility to local governments for the management of revenue and the delivery of economic and social services. Local governments receive a substantial review here because their use of resources, which has a direct impact on people's daily activities and their functions, logically identifies with the poverty reduction objective and the attainment of the MDGs.

Before the Constitution of 1997, local governments were treated rather like a department in the Ministry of the Interior, so budget and financial data were not clearly separated. The creation of the Tambon Administration Organizations as a group in 1992 (they number 6622 today, see Table 9.7) overwhelmed the local government sector. Overall supervision of the local government sector became focused in these

Table 9.7 Categories of Thai local governments

Type	Number of Units
1 Bangkok Metropolitan Administration	1
2 Pattaya City	1
3 Provincial Administration Organizations	75
4 Municipalities	1156
5 Tambon Administration Organizations	6622

newly created Tambon Administration Organizations, which delayed the refinement of the other sub-sectors of local governments.

The new Constitution of the Kingdom of Thailand of 1997 is the basis for the legal and constitutional definitions of the roles of local government. Part 9 of the Constitution, comprising 9 articles, defined the basic framework for local governments. Fiscal space is affected by local government functions as prescribed in Article 284 of the Constitution (determination of local fiscal and monetary measures, management of local public service provision, and obtaining an allocation of tax revenues from the national total), in Article 289 (preservation of local art, customs, culture and learning) and in Article 290 (management, maintenance and use of local natural resources and the environment).

Two years after the Constitution came into force, a law based on these provisions in the Constitution, the Decentralization of Power to Local Governments Act (1999), was passed. This law defined the status and scope of responsibilities of five categories of local government (see below) in Articles 16, 17 and 18. Their revenues are set out in Section 3 (Articles 23 to 30). Article 30 sets a framework for the decentralization of power to local governments, stating in Paragraph 4 that, by 2006, local governments shall get budget allocations equivalent to 35 per cent of the central government's revenues. In Thailand, there are 7855 local governments that are grouped into five categories (see Table 9.7).

Each category of local government has its own law defining the basic framework for that type of local government. The fiscal functions of the local government and the management of budget and revenue sources are also defined in each of these laws.

To grasp the actual roles and performances of Thai local governments in delivering local public goods and services and carrying out their other functions, it is instructive to turn to their flows of revenues and expenditures. Table 9.8 contains the relevant summary data for the total local government sector in recent years. From this table, there are a number of interesting observations which can be made. First, until the late 1990s the role of local government in revenue collection was small. A considerable part of the taxes received by local government was collected locally by central government agencies and handed over to local government. Second, another major source of revenue was the grants received from the central government. Since the decentralization law, the share of local government revenue from central government revenue increased

rapidly to 24 per cent in 2006, but this increase was largely driven by the growing importance of transfers from the central government (grants). This ratio is higher than it used
to be, but is still low and is lower than the legal requirement. Part of the reason for this
small ratio is the relatively small collections of revenues by local governments
themselves. Given their political and constitutional mandates to provide certain public
services locally, there is a question of the effort put into raising revenues by local
governments. This issue is dealt with below. Third, given the letter of the law concerning local governments' receipt of resources, questions arise concerning the allocation of
the necessary funds by the central government to local governments. The
Decentralization of Power to Local Government Act (1999), Article 30, specifies that
by 2006 35 per cent of the revenues of the government must be allocated to local
governments. As far as Thai fiscal space is concerned, one may view this problem as, on
the surface, a non-issue because what does not get spent through the local governments
will be spent through the central government. However, activities by the local governments are deemed to be important in themselves for expanding the fiscal space or for
improving the quality of delivery of public services through local governments (see
Brun et al, 2006, p57 on devolution). The problem of Thai local governments not
getting the targeted allocations raises the issue of whether the fiscal space is efficiently
and effectively used.

In the preceding paragraphs we spelled out the broad constitutional basis for the
operation of local governments. Now, it is necessary to turn to specific laws that underlie and justify greater roles for local government. Realizing these mandated roles would
add to the fiscal space, as well as improving the quality of the public services that are
delivered to the population. To concretely grasp the issues of fiscal space and local
governments here, the following discussion is undertaken using the statistics of municipalities to supplement statements, but the analogies apply to all of the other local
governments.

The municipalities are a very important group of local governments in Thailand.
There are 1156 municipalities in Thailand today (Table 9.7). The origin of the present
day form of the municipality in Thailand can be traced back to the Public
Administration Act of 1933. From 1898, local governments, in a form called
sukhapiban, were experimental institutions and they were not institutionalized until the
passing of the Local Government Act of 1914. The Municipality Act of 1953, however,
set out the present day legal basis for the operations of and for matters related to the
current-day municipalities.

Municipalities are classified into three groups according to the size of their population. The largest, with populations over 50,000, are the *tessabaan nakon*; the next group,
with populations between 10,000 and 49,999, are the *tessabaan muang*; and the smallest,
those with populations between 7000 and 10,000, are the *tessabaan tambon*. The responsibilities of this last group, as specified in Articles 50 and 51 of the Municipality Act,
include waste disposal, fire fighting, water treatment and provision, slaughterhouse

Table 9.8 *Financial transactions of local governments (Bt million)*

	1996	1997	1998	1999	2000	2001	2002	2003	2004	2005	2006
1 Revenues	83,677	94,427	96,588	107,015	94,285	127,846	165,037	183,880	225,308	293,915	327,113
1.1 Taxes	46,046	50,675	57,568	50,436	55,177	65,631	69,853	82,984	97,744	110,983	n.a.
1.1.1 Taxes on property	6736	8079	8027	8459	12,711	17,201	18,887	22,441	28,646	50,844	n.a.
1.1.2 Taxes on goods and services	39,310	42,596	49,541	41,977	42,466	48,431	50,966	60,543	69,098	60,140	n.a.
1.2 Other revenues	12,008	13,890	7858	10,859	7301	6215	7671	7793	8228	11,831	n.a.
1.3 Grants	25,623	29,862	31,162	45,720	31,808	56,000	87,513	93,104	119,336	171,101	n.a.
2 Central Government revenues	854,235	849,208	732,351	712,960	747,873	834,141	871,700	1,045,580	1,168,655	1,320,998	1,360,137
3 Ratio of 1 to 2 (%)	9.8	11.1	13.2	15.0	12.6	15.3	18.9	17.6	19.3	22.2	24.1

Source: Fiscal Policy Office, Ministry of Finance, and the Office of Local Government Decentralization, Prime Minister's Office

operations, waterway and land access maintenance, provision of public transportation, piers operations, marketplace operations, hospital and first-aid operations, electricity provision and general commerce. For the second category of municipality, their functions are augmented over and above what had been listed above, as specified in Articles 53 and 54 of the Municipality Act, to include the operation of pawn shops and public utilities, vocational schools, sports facilities, public parks and zoos, and maternity and child care. For the *tessabaan nakon*, the functions are further expanded, under Articles 56 and 57 of the Municipality Act, to include supervision of food vending, cinemas and other service provision outlets, tourism promotion, city planning and the supervision of construction.

The mandate to provide public services is not solely limited to what is presently specified in the law. The appropriateness of using local governments to provide public services is determined by suitability, convenience and ability to serve real needs. The national government can be left to perform tasks which are truly 'public' and nationally relevant. Other public services, which may be location specific and very much locally determined, should then be applied by and through local governments. These possibilities, and the likelihood of the actual situation developing so, are however presently reduced by the central government's unwillingness to devolve more of the power it now exercises. Thailand has been facing this dilemma for years since the decentralization policy was implemented under the Constitution of 1997. In one respect, there has been duplication of provision in some public services in Thailand because of this tug of war between the various levels of government concerning the devolution of power. This is deemed to be wasteful in resource use. The duplication of functions occurred because the central government held on to the power that should have been decentralized (for example, over environmental pollution, water provision and much more). Those who resisted the decentralization process argued that they did not believe local governments were ready to take over such functions.

What are the revenues of the local government? Again the use of municipality data is meant to provide concreteness and clarity for the reader; analogous situations apply to the other local government forms.

Article 66 of the Municipality Act specifies that the revenues of municipalities may be derived from:

1   taxes and tariffs, as mandated in the laws;
2   fees, permit charges, and fines, as specified in the laws;
3   incomes from municipal assets;
4   incomes from public utilities and municipal commercial enterprises;
5   bonds and loans, as specified in the laws;
6   loans from government agencies, organizations and other corporate bodies – such loans can be acquired only after approvals given by the relevant municipal councils and the minister of the interior;
7   grants from the government or the Provincial Administration Organization (PAO);
8   contributions, whether in cash or in kind;
9   other revenues, as specified in the laws.

Observations can be made about most or all of the listed revenue sources of municipalities, but it would be more useful to elaborate on the more important items, namely: (1) taxes and tariffs, (2) bonds and loans, (3) loans from government agencies, and (4) grants.

Where taxes and tariffs are concerned, reference to the data in Table 9.A3 (page 394) helps one to understand better the actual situation confronting local governments in Thailand today. Tax revenues of local governments can be grouped into three categories: (1) taxes collected by the local governments themselves, such as land and building taxes, (2) local government taxes collected by the central government and turned over to local governments, such as vehicles taxes, VAT, excises on tobacco and alcohol beverages, and (3) revenues allocated from the central government and grants. Category (1) revenues have never been greater than 10 per cent of local government revenues. Lack of effort, and perhaps of interest and other related factors, are very clear here. Category (2) revenues invite questions as to why local governments are not collecting many of these revenues themselves. If local governments have the right to collect levies on values created in their jurisdiction, such as personal income and corporate income, why are they not collecting such revenues? Category (3) revenues have been facing political volatility and the central agencies' resistance to comply with existing relevant legislation, namely, the Decentralization of Power to Local Government Act of 1999. This law set a target for the allocation of revenues to local governments of

35 per cent of government's revenues to be achieved by 2006. There is, presently, a shortfall of about 11 per cent in this 35 per cent that is still withheld by the government.

Local governments have essentially not tapped the bond and loan markets to finance their activities. Instances of capital market resource mobilization or debt incurrence by local governments have occurred only in a very limited context and in, essentially, a highly controlled environment. Given the myriad tasks that should be performed by local governments in the MDG context and in the matter of poverty reduction, this failure to access an important set of resources is, to say the least, very regrettable. The absence of resource mobilization in the money and capital markets by local governments signified losses of opportunities to grow and develop faster.

There are certain limitations on loans from government agencies and others that are put on local governments. One concern is the excessively conservative rules that are imposed on such borrowings, that is, the delivery of security collateral in the form of cash deposits. Another concern is the overlapping and crossing of central government power and local government power, in that approval has to be given by the minister of interior. This last point creates a rather ambiguous context: the minister approving borrowings as a regulatory authority of local government. If the loans are correctly secured financially, it is not usual market practice for regulators to have to also directly approve such transactions in order for them to be executed. Government regulations on this matter are very unclear and have effectively blocked local governments from mobilizing borrowed resources from the money and capital markets for developmental as well as for other tasks.

As far as grants are concerned, the government had withheld part of the allocations decreed by the Decentralization Law of 1999 and established the funds as grants for local governments (see Table 9.A3). This difference in treatment raises issues about controls and rightful ownership of the funds for the purposes of budget setting and fiscal planning.

It would seem from the above, that there is unused fiscal space at the local government level. Not only is there a limited allocation of funds from the central government, but also local taxes do not raise much revenue and borrowing opportunities are not exploited.

Being public financial entities, local governments should also perform other public functions apart from the provision of public goods and services. Some of these other functions are performed at the national government level, or are more suited to be performed by the national government. However, this raises questions as to whether local governments also have proper reasons to be involved and to take actions. For example, in environmental pollution control and prevention, there are responsibilities at the national level (for example, commitments to the Kyoto Protocol on Climate Control), but there are also responsibilities at the local level. This is the case of negative externalities and, logically, coverage by local governments should extend to positive externalities too. When resources are used in sub-optimal, non-sustainable situations, government action is called for, and this includes action by local governments. Such involvement by governments will increase the fiscal space, by prompting appropriate government measures to deal with the externalities that arise, subsidizing where externalities are positive, taxing where externalities are negative. Local governments in Thailand may have certain tools that can be used to take such action, but the local governments have not yet tabled such policies nor proposed integrated strategies to deal with these phenomena in their localities. The issues are usually left to the central government to handle. Examples include the Songkla Inland Water pollution, the Borapet Lake pollution in Nakon Sawan Province, and Kwan Payao Lake pollution in Payao Province.

Another common task of a public financial entity concerns income redistribution and poverty reduction. A government should strive, where possible, to achieve a more equitable distribution of income for its population and local governments may be more effective at this task as they know local conditions best. Measures that can be taken toward this end are numerous. Performing this task adds to expanding the fiscal space. The consequences of implementing a redistribution measure are long term and multidirectional in nature, but as the impacts work out, the end results would provide benefits through the reduction of poverty and the attainment of many of the MDGs.

Given their responsibilities and power, it is clear that Thai local governments have not maintained the desired fiscal space as intended by the law. They have under collected the taxes that are within their power to collect (for example, the Buildings and Land Tax and Local Development Tax), they have kept away from taking the initiative to collect taxes which are theirs, but have relied on Ministry of Finance agencies to collect those taxes for them. Examples include VAT on expenditures in their locality, excise taxes for consumption in their locality and vehicle registration fees. And they are lacking initiatives to claim taxes for activities that are clearly in their jurisdiction that could be taxed, for example, local income tax, as is now practiced in many countries and, property tax. There are risks in a decentralization process that devolves spending tasks but does not devolve the responsibility for revenue collection.

Administrative issues in the revenue system

Improving the fiscal space would involve improving the quality of the fiscal machinery. The qualitative aspects of improving the tax system are important in bringing the system inline with the levels of change and development in the economy. For Thailand, at present, the important issues in this regard are the rationalization of the tax system and the reform of property, income, excise and customs taxes, as discussed below.

Rationalization of the tax system
Because of changes in the economy, the collection of customs duties has declined steadily from its previous dominant position. Discussions have been conducted from time to time to merge the excise and customs collection authorities, as is the case in

many other countries, to rationalize tax administration. Idealism here clashed with pragmatic (and bureaucratic) stances. The issue has not been permanently decided, so it may come back in the future.

On this same logic about tax-agency modernization, the Revenue Department, which collects both VAT, an indirect tax, and the income tax, a direct tax, was to be organized on an independent basis in 1993, similar to the US Internal Revenue Service (that is, more independent and distant from the reach of the government). The proposal was not further pursued, however.

The rationalization of the tax collection authorities arises in policy discussions from time to time. A more far reaching proposal would be to bring all the operational aspects of collection under one administration, which would have no policy units at all, unlike the present tax collection agencies that have their own in-house policy units.

Actions in this respect, along whatever line is chosen, would change the qualitative aspect of the Thai fiscal space and may affect (in positive ways) tax collection itself.

Overhaul of the taxes on property

Existing taxes on properties are not systematic or uniform. The logic behind taxing properties is not made clear, except for the potential that targeted properties offer for some tax collection. Tradition also plays a part in keeping some of these taxes alive, even if they produce very little revenues. The basic drive for wanting a bigger role for property taxes has been the examples, seen in other countries, where property taxes are collected to finance local authorities' budgets. Since the decentralization of power to local governments in Thailand is still limited in actual scope, this should explain why a new property tax regime has not been implemented. The issues of property taxation lead to further consideration of wealth taxation. So far, the discussion on this subject has revolved around estate taxation or inheritance tax. The line of policy choice is not clear on this matter and if it is to be pursued, it will take more time before any policy conclusion can be reached.

Reform of income tax

Income tax is an important tax for the whole tax system as well as for the economy. Its use over the years has raised many important questions about its character and structure. Perhaps the more important question is whether there should be a global or a partial tax. Many features existing in the present system, which seems to suggest a global character, are evidence of the partial approach to taxation. The most important instance is the taxation of interest income, which can be separated from global income and is subject to a maximum tax rate of 15 per cent, different from the 37 per cent on taxable global income. Other instances of this partial approach do exist but the greatest flaw in the logic of income taxation is the exclusion of a large part of the national income. Of the 38 million people in the labour force in the country, the Revenue Department required filings from about 6–7 million taxpayers. Categories of income excluded from income taxation include agricultural income and income from stock trading on the national exchange. Further, petroleum income is separately taxed and no meaningful discussions are raised about the need for this, or how it may be better done.

Income tax holidays are important fiscal incentives given to investors to encourage them to invest in the country. Although this task is supervised by an agency, the fiscal implications of this 'tax expenditure' are not known outside of this agency, even though taxpayers have to bear additional taxes because the government's budget has to be financed. It is not transparent what the additional taxes incurred for these investors are exchanged for, exchanges that should be accurately monitored and calculated, and that should be reported to the power that passed the laws to tax the population. Rational decisions can be made if the information is publicly available and these may lead to improved resource allocation for the economy, and for the poor, if these 'tax expenditures' are spotlighted.

Double taxation agreements (DTAs) are important instruments for the management and development of the economy, and the promotion of commerce and prosperity. Thailand has established DTAs with many nations. The issue is that rarely are the details and implications of the DTAs brought to the knowledge of the public and properly used to further the objectives of society and the economy, including promoting the causes of the poor.

Exemptions from the income tax assessment lead to unequal tax rewards to different taxpayers and promote an unequal distribution of income. The inequity feature of the use of exemptions can be reduced by using and giving equal tax credit to each qualified person. Reform here is straightforward, but political acceptance is difficult.

Reforms of the excise tax
Excise taxes were originally based on consumption behaviour that is considered luxurious and hence should be subject to taxation. Also, the penalty to be put on the consumption of 'public bads', such as alcohol and cigarettes, was considered best done through excise taxes. Today, with the need to collect more money to finance the budget, the thinking has become rather desperate in that the authorities justify taxing various 'handles' citing, for example, environmental protection, health protection and the like, without a clear logic or mandate as to why that should be so. Certainly, excise authorities are not health experts, nor are they environmental experts, but collections are decreed anyway. A rationalization of this process and the associated taxation would be reassuring to taxpayers.

Reforms of customs taxes
Customs taxes and duties cannot be collected without regard to their consequences on commercial and production competitiveness. The increasing number of free-trade arrangements that Thailand has entered into, and expects to conclude, plus the country's subscription to multilateral trade talks in the past, present and future, imply

a change of responsibilities for customs authorities. Past mechanisms and practices that are not in line with this change in the way of doing business, for example, the arbitrary use of the General Agreement on Tariffs and Trade (GATT) valuation approach and heavy-handed imposition of bonded warehouse regulations, lead to missed opportunities for the country in creating value added, employment, foreign-exchange earnings and income, all of which are important variables for the country's prosperity. But none of them are important indicators of the performance of the customs authorities. An overhaul of the customs collection machinery will greatly benefit the economy and help in gearing up for a better competitive position in world trade and production.

The roles of state enterprises in the fiscal space of Thailand

The roles of state enterprises are relevant to the analysis of fiscal space for three reasons. First, state enterprises may provide goods and services that are relevant to the achievement of the MDGs, for example, water and electricity supply, public transport, rural credit and housing. Second, state enterprises are owned by the government and, on top of any taxes paid, transfer dividends to the owner. Third, some state enterprises may require subsidies from the government because the prices they charge do not fully cover costs (public transport, for example) or because they are inefficient.

In connection with its state enterprises, every country has to decide on which goods and services have to be delivered through the public sector, and which have to have the flexibility not to be treated strictly like a public good or service. The flexibilities involved are properties that relate to pricing. Consumers pay according to the units or amount consumed. This makes these public goods and services similar in some sense to private goods and services, which are allocated by the rules of the market. Think of transportation services, potable water, public utilities and similar items. These goods and services are usually delivered to society by entities in the form of 'enterprises', albeit public ones. Some of these services are 'natural monopolies' and they are provided through state enterprises to prevent the abuse of market power. Governments may also choose to use state enterprises to ensure that all have access to the services at affordable prices. There is no fixed rule on how public/private sector demarcation is done in different societies and across countries. Even the choices made in a particular country are not always the same. It is generally true to say that this realm of public goods and services (not the strictly public type) exists between the pure public goods and services realm and the private sector economy.

The use of state enterprises to deliver goods and services to the public is widespread. In Thailand, the practice expanded in the years after the Second World War. In the 1950s the government set up a host of state enterprises to carry out tasks not necessarily related to public services. State enterprises in that period used the word 'organization' in their names, and many still remain in existence today, such as the Battery Organization, the Zoo Organization and the Express Transport Organization.

Table 9.9 *Operations of non-financial state enterprises (Bt million)*[1]

		1984	1985	1986	1987	1988	1989	1990	1991
1	Revenue	179,410	206,977	218,131	235,924	270,492	308,561	370,568	433,257
2	Of which, capital transfer from central government	1810	2494	378	528	924	1488	1922	2207
3	Expenditure	150,792	173,278	181,613	189,749	214,733	234,249	276,054	330,317
4	Corporate income tax	1075	738	955	1155	2676	3244	3167	2271
5	Profit (or loss)	17,107	12,629	15,173	22,288	30,785	42,318	52,679	64,828
6	Dividend and distribution	4315	6469	6546	7488	8384	12,775	16,988	19,411
7	Retained income	21,946	25,271	27,818	35,815	42,559	55,818	71,062	77,157
8	Capital expenditure	32,986	35,715	35,444	32,436	48503	48,669	77,085	99,263
9	Financing requirement (-)	−11,040	−10,444	−7626	3379	−5944	7148	−6023	−22,106
10	Financing	11,040	10,444	7626	−3379	5944	−7148	6023	22,106
11	External borrowing (net)	9379	9785	4094	−2384	−3288	2746	12,073	5460
12	Domestic borrowing (net)	926	7080	6618	8839	16,043	6631	10,110	35,971
13	Others[2]	735	−6421	−3086	−9834	−6812	−16,525	−16,160	−19,325
	As a percentage of GDP:								
20	Revenue	18.2	19.6	19.2	18.1	17.3	16.6	17.0	17.3
21	Of which, capital transfer from central government	0.2	0.2	0.0	0.0	0.1	0.1	0.1	0.1
22	Expenditure	15.3	16.4	16.0	14.6	13.8	12.6	12.6	13.2
23	Corporate income tax	0.1	0.1	0.1	0.1	0.2	0.2	0.1	0.1
24	Dividend and distribution	0.4	0.6	0.6	0.6	0.5	0.7	0.8	0.8
25	Retained income	2.2	2.4	2.5	2.8	2.7	3.0	3.3	3.1
26	Capital expenditure	3.3	3.4	3.1	2.5	3.1	2.6	3.5	4.0
27	Financing requirement (-)	−1.1	−1.0	−0.7	0.3	−0.4	0.4	−0.3	−0.9
30	Net govt position (23+24−21)	0.4	0.4	0.6	0.6	0.6	0.8	0.8	0.8

Notes: (1) Comprising 43 non-financial state enterprises by fiscal year; (2) Inclusive of changes in working capital and changes in cash and deposits, and so on.

Source: Bank of Thailand, Annual Economic Report, various issues

Also, state enterprises were set up more for delivering public utilities and for infrastructure development. At that time, the preference for state enterprises was part of a nationalistic policy that tried to prevent the domination of the economy by Chinese and foreign businesses. In the late 1950s, when many of these state enterprises turned out to be inefficient and unable to deliver the expected results, policy shifted (Ingram, 1971). Since then the private sector has dominated the productive sector and the roles of state enterprises have been comparatively limited, although significant. There are, at present, 68 state enterprises, some of which have been partially privatized. Table 9.9 gives a historical perspective on the roles that state enterprises have played in the Thai economy and fiscal space since 1984.

State enterprise expenditures have grown almost tenfold over the 21-year period shown, while their operating and non-operating revenues had similar growth over the same timeframe. The government gave them capital transfers over this period (1984 to 2004) amounting to Bt135 billion. State enterprises had, in turn, paid Bt123 billion in corporate income taxes over this period, and Bt628 billion in dividends out of total profits of Bt1379 billion. The dividends paid to the government were incorporated into the annual national budget, thus supporting national expenditures. The net profits, after payment of dividends, went to the financing of expansion and necessary investments,

1992	1993	1994	1995	1996	1997	1998	1999	2000	2001	2002	2003	2004
464,628	503,256	568,818	683,856	786,843	914,677	957,156	943,249	1,185,183	1,328,059	1,720,715	1,564,262	1,718,315
3552	10,316	8872	9978	9303	9827	12,822	5760	7840	11,168	8941	10,436	14,787
346,058	379,429	419,585	505,812	589,002	744,214	773,193	766,690	1,015,971	1,105,405	1,456,606	1,282,042	1,422,375
1836	91	1938	2429	3125	1623	4266	5037	4409	6667	12,756	29,781	32,541
67,879	69,522	75,316	88,319	103,446	73,802	84,108	−21,922	65,983	95,071	145,873	126,551	147,430
27,194	29,859	31,372	37,288	39,266	47,712	56,022	49,406	39,213	58,167	49,481	51,515	56,550
84,841	87,920	108,788	132,187	148,335	113,719	116,138	118,255	123,128	155,323	200,330	197,528	201,706
120,365	127,751	121,989	148,113	137,073	194,356	193,937	176,037	202,318	171,744	100,957	132,945	182,905
−35,524	−39,831	−13,201	−15,926	11,261	−80,637	−77,800	−57,782	−79,190	−16,421	99,373	64,583	18,800
35,524	39,831	13,201	15,926	−11,261	80,637	77,800	57,782	79,190	16,421	−99,373	−64,583	−18,000
16,233	−759	1347	9386	12,924	−7834	−8849	52,009	6063	−7152	−34,571	−47,633	−58,802
17,894	35,583	45,234	27,882	20,826	34,000	31,053	28,858	80,847	15,350	−22,841	−15,133	78,031
1397	5007	−33,380	−21,342	−45,011	54,471	55,596	−23,086	−7720	8223	−41,961	−1,817	−37,229
16.4	15.9	15.7	16.3	17.1	19.3	20.7	20.3	24.1	25.9	31.6	26.4	26.4
0.1	0.3	0.2	0.2	0.2	0.2	0.3	0.1	0.2	0.2	0.2	0.2	0.2
12.2	12.0	11.6	12.1	12.8	15.7	16.7	16.5	20.6	21.5	26.7	21.6	21.9
0.1	0.0	0.1	0.1	0.1	0.0	0.1	0.1	0.1	0.1	0.2	0.5	0.5
1.0	0.9	0.9	0.9	0.9	1.0	1.2	1.1	0.8	1.1	0.9	0.9	0.9
3.0	2.8	3.0	3.2	3.2	2.4	2.5	2.6	2.5	3.0	3.7	3.3	3.1
4.3	4.0	3.4	3.5	3.0	4.1	4.2	3.8	4.1	3.3	1.9	2.2	2.8
−1.3	−1.3	−0.4	−0.4	0.2	−1.7	−1.7	−1.2	−1.6	−0.3	1.8	1.1	0.3
0.9	0.6	0.7	0.7	0.7	0.8	1.0	1.0	0.7	1.0	1.0	1.2	1.1

which over the period, totalled Bt2421 billion. The difference of Bt 275 billion had to be borrowed from the markets.

Profits steadily increased up to 1996 then wobbled in the period 1997 to 2001, before reverting to the usual level. Since total profits were mostly positive, it can be said that state enterprises, as a group, helped to accumulate capital. Profits are not necessarily an indication of efficient use of capital because some state enterprises enjoy monopolistic positions. Their dividend payments remitted to the government were funding national budget programmes. Finally, in making capital expenditures, state enterprises directly performed the task of mobilizing capital, tapping the financial markets and adding to the fiscal space in accumulating capital. The extent of this capital accumulation and expenditure, which went toward benefiting the poor or reducing poverty, must be looked for in the pricing practices, products and services that applied to the poor, and at the special efforts the enterprises made for the poor.

In accumulating capital, state enterprises had to use the capital markets as well as the banking system to obtain financing. When state enterprises incur debt, they usually look to the government to provide guarantees or to obtain other special treatment. Financially weak enterprises do get some 'sympathy' from the government, and usually get some deals in the banking and capital markets. As a group, state enterprises are

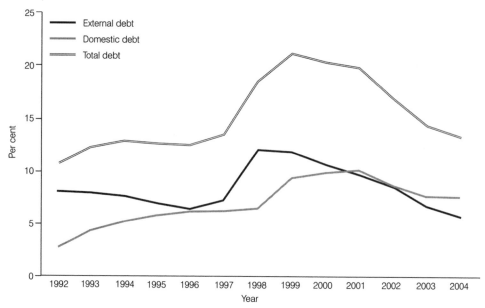

Source: Bank of Thailand, Quarterly Bulletin, various issues

Figure 9.4 *State enterprise debt*

significant participants in the financial markets, following the private corporate sector, but leading the government in terms of the real volume of finance obtained.

Historical data on the indebtedness of state enterprises are not complete. Figure 9.4 presents debt ratios since 1992. There were periods when a weak economy and weak public sector conditions reduced the amount of financial resources mobilized, for example, in the period 2002 to 2004. The instruments of indebtedness used by state enterprises include bonds, loans and notes, but bonds were by far the most extensively used instruments. This accords well with the objective of building a deep and wide domestic debt market. However, when state enterprises ask the government to guarantee their bonds, market development is stunted. One sees the medium-term bond market as playing an important role in the maturity structure of state enterprise debts, perhaps because state enterprises want to reduce costs, but the shying away from the long-term end of the market does not reflect well on the true development intentions of the state enterprises themselves, or else the bond market has not been properly developed yet.

Given the conceptual positioning of the state enterprise sector, it is necessary to establish the actual role of the Thai state enterprises in the economy. There are currently 68 state enterprises. This relatively small number reflects the predominance of the private sector in the Thai economy. The enterprises can be grouped roughly into three categories as follows:

- Near-public good/service type. This type of state enterprise will enjoy a separate existence for the foreseeable future. Their legitimacy is not seriously under question. Falling into this category are entities such as the Tourism Authority of Thailand and the Thailand Institute of Scientific and Technological Research.
- Market compatible goods/services type. In today's ever-evolving economies, goods and services, which used to be provided through public entities, are now being provided through market regulated bodies, and therefore are subject to competition and other market disciplines. Goods and services such as electricity, potable water supply, education, transportation services, communication and telecommunication are nowadays provided through market compatible enterprises. In Thailand there are many state enterprises falling into this category, such as the Electricity Generating Authority of Thailand, the Provincial Electricity Authority, the Metropolitan Electricity Authority, the Metropolitan Waterworks Authority, the Provincial Waterworks Authority, Thai Airways International, the Transport Company, Bangkok Mass Transit Authority, CAT Telecommunications, Krung Thai Bank and Petroleum Authority of Thailand. In recent years, the Thai government has drawn up plans for the privatization of some of these enterprises, joining a worldwide privatization drive. There are many philosophical, policy and operational issues arising from the existence of these types of state enterprises. For example, in the market, one sees the co-existence of private entities providing similar and identical goods and services: Ban Pu Company, Lanna Lignite, Sahacogen, Eastern Water, Bangkok Airways, Bangkok Expressway, Bangkok Mass Transit System (BTS), Juta Maritime, among others. Questions then arise about the abilities of the state enterprises to compete, the quality of the governance of their organizations, their abilities to appeal to investors to raise inexpensive funds (and not use state power to guarantee low-cost funds), and so on. A compelling benchmark is the raising of resources by other (private) enterprises, which is based on performance, governance and management excellence. Should state enterprises, which provide similar or identical goods and services, be permitted to ignore such discipline when tapping society's resources? One possible reason for maintaining such state enterprises would be to correct for market failures and to guarantee that the poor will have access to essential services at affordable prices.
- Superseded type. There are state enterprises, which, for obvious reasons, do not have much ground for continued existence because, for example, the duplication of tasks and total ineffectiveness. In this category, entities like the Battery Organization, Tannery Organization, Provincial Waterworks Authority, Provincial Electricity Authority and the Thai Navigation Company, can be placed. The justifications for having and keeping these organizations do not make any economic sense today.

The budget implications of state enterprises are not very large. State enterprises pay income tax on their profits and the dividends paid by state enterprises are also part of government revenue. Table 9.9 shows that, on average, over the period 1984 to 2004 government income from state enterprises averaged around 1 per cent of GDP. There were some changes over time: in the early 1980s the income amounted to around 0.5 per cent of GDP, from which it increased to around 1 per cent during the 1990s and somewhat over 1 per cent in recent years. It seems that the state enterprise reforms in the 1980s had significant revenue effects. However, the government also provides subsidies to state enterprises to compensate for losses or to help finance investment. If we deduct these subsidies, the net fiscal contribution of state enterprises remains positive but small at below 1 per cent of GDP (on average 0.8 per cent over the period 1984 to 2004).

Employment data for the entire state enterprise sector are available for the period 1996 to 1999, as shown in Table 9.10. The table helps to make two points. First, state enterprise employment is rather small, compared to the total labour force. And, second, most of the employees work in the public transport sector. State enterprise employees have an influence beyond their numbers as they are well organized in unions, which have an impact on the state enterprises themselves and on setting some of the agendas on national welfare issues, as well as job security issues for labour in general. State enterprise employees lead in pushing for the general goals and welfare of members of the labour force. Because of their organization, state enterprise employees wield some political leverage, not least because they can assemble their members to make a visible physical presence or demonstrate for policy or political gains.

This cursory picture of the state enterprise sector necessarily does not yield reasonable useful details for a thorough analysis. Can these enterprises be utilized to further the goals of poverty reduction, equity promotion, social welfare and justice, which are elements in the MDGs?

It should be noted that some state enterprises are active in areas that are crucial to the process of capital accumulation and poverty alleviation. The electricity authorities

Table 9.10 *Employment in state enterprises, 1996–1999 (thousands of persons)*

Sector	1996	1997	1998	1999
1 Agriculture	9.2	8.9	8.8	8.7
2 Manufacturing, Mining	17.1	16.8	13.1	13.0
3 Transportation, Communication	148.6	147.2	148.6	149.2
4 Commerce, Tourism	2.4	2.4	2.4	2.4
5 Science, Technology, Energy	82.4	81.5	80.5	78.5
6 Education	0.3	0.3	0.3	20.3
7 Social Services	18.1	18.2	19.4	19.4
8 Banking	42.1	39.9	40.1	14.3
TOTAL	320.1	315.2	313.2	285.7

Source: Bureau of the Budget

played a role in rural electrification. Water authorities provide access to safe water. The Bank of Agriculture and Agricultural Cooperatives (BAAC) provided many rural households with credit. Mass transport organizations provide cheap transport for low-income groups. The current government is using state-owned financial institutions to channel resources to villages, to low-income groups, to cheap housing and to small enterprises.

It must also be realized that the MDGs are mostly society-oriented ends, whereas running enterprises as businesses can conflict with achieving social objectives. This is the point where society must intervene to minimize economic loss and to maximize the achievement of social goals. This intervention point is crucial to the attainment of the MDGs, but it is also very complex. Political machineries may not deliver the desired goals, as is well known. Ruling 'classes' may not enact laws that will bring economic harm to themselves, or they may implement privatization of state enterprises only to increase the wealth of the members of the elite. In practice, what occurred in resource mobilization was not much related to the theories of public goods and services provision through state enterprises. Often, sound economic management of the enterprises was ignored because political controls dictated a management that served more political ends. Expenditures continued to benefit the immediate areas/jurisdictions of politicians who influenced the policies of the state enterprises. Resource mobilization is undertaken more for political expediency than for the progressive development of the enterprises, so the demand for guarantees by the state enterprises is still rampant; bankrupt enterprises are perpetuated because their bleedings feed some political tills. State enterprises continue to ignore market discipline. Often, their status as an 'enterprise' rings hollow because the management and employees of the enterprise continue to behave no differently from ordinary civil servants staffing regular state agencies. Productive interactions between the boards of directors and management do not exist because collusion and/or dominance take over this relationship, and it is therefore not subject to the cleansing discipline of the market. This places the enterprises under narrow subjective controls. Most of these misdirected outcomes occurred because of the dominance and influence of the politicians and political machines. Corrections can be made but this will take time and needs citizens to take control of the political machineries. There needs to be a healthy meaningful participation by the public in determining state enterprises' policies and activities. For the MDGs to be achieved, effective public watchdogs, whether these are the media, citizens' action groups or other organizations, must function to achieve the desired targets.

New developments: Fiscal innovations

The Thaksin government that came to power in 2001 introduced a number of fiscal innovations that have created some controversies. Although the perspective of this chapter has been historical, it is relevant to briefly comment on these recent developments.

Following the elections and the formation of the new government, a number of measures were announced. A village fund was created from which each of the over 70,000 villages in the country would receive Bt1 million for local development purposes. A debt moratorium was announced for farmers. A 'People's Bank' was created to run a micro-credit scheme. And the Bt30 health scheme was introduced under which people can obtain a health card that gives them the right to medical treatment at a fixed cost of Bt30 per visit.

These initiatives are interesting for a number of reasons. First, they were part of a plan for fiscal stimulus. After the slow recovery from the 1997 crisis, the Thai economy needed a push and measures to put money in the hands of people with a high propensity to spend. Second, the measures were aimed at a segment of the population that was not used to being spoiled by the government, the rural population. This populist strand of 'Thaksinomics' changed the political economy of Thai politics. And finally the measures were financed in innovative ways. It is this last aspect that is of interest to us.

The revolving village fund is financed by loans from the Government Savings Bank (GSB). The burden of the farmers' debt moratorium is on the BAAC. The People's Bank was also established by the GSB. Other public sector financial institutions were engaged in new programmes of lending to small enterprises. The Bt30 health scheme is financed from the budget. It is clear that state enterprises play a dominant role in financing and organizing these new initiatives.

The off-budget financing was clearly attractive at a time when concerns about public sector debt were high. It enabled the government to increase expenditure without raising taxes or increasing the budget deficit and the government debt. But critics have questioned whether this way of financing really increases fiscal space. To some extent, the initiatives just meant a shifting of resources over time. The government will eventually have to pay or compensate GSB and BAAC.[12] The financing of the health scheme has created some problems. Health providers get a fixed sum per person registered but the actual cost of treatment is higher. Also the scheme is popular, with almost three-quarters of the population registering. The result is complaints about substandard treatment and overburdened state hospitals, particularly in rural areas. Work overload means that doctors are leaving state hospitals and inadequate budgets mean that hospitals are rapidly accumulating debt. According to Ministry of Finance data, health outlays now amount to 7.4 per cent of total government spending, a share that is similar to the share before the scheme.

The initiatives of the Thaksin government are directly aimed at that part of the population that is the focus of concern when discussing the MDGs. Providing health care for the poor and moving resources to indebted farmers and small enterprises can make a significant contribution to the alleviation of poverty. At the same time, the initiatives are also a calculated populist ploy, trying to win the rural vote. This ploy paid off. Thaksin's party won the elections in 2005 by a wide margin. There is, of course, a danger in populist policies without sustainable financing. Current evaluations are too recent or too partial to come to a firm conclusion on these fiscal innovations.

Section summary

In this chapter we have analysed the pattern and trends of government revenue in Thailand over the period 1970 to 2004. Over this period the economic performance of Thailand has been excellent. During these 35 years, the per capita GDP increased more than 4 times and the structure of the economy changed radically. As we have shown, it is particularly the changes in the structure of the economy that explain the changes in the level and the composition of government revenue.

Historical experience of developed countries, as well as cross-country comparisons would lead us to expect an increase in the revenue/GDP ratio as income rises. This did indeed happen in Thailand, although to a lesser extent than might have been expected. The current level of the revenue ratio is low when compared to countries with a similar level of development. Moreover, the current level of the revenue ratio is below historical peaks. All these findings together suggest that Thailand has unused fiscal space or, even, that fiscal space that had been occupied has been lost again.

However, taxation is a political process and in Thailand there is clearly a preference for a relatively small government. The business and political elite overlap to a considerable extent in Thailand and they have no use for higher taxes that would increase costs.

It should be noted that a stable revenue to GDP ratio, or government expenditure to GDP ratio, together with a rapidly growing per capita GDP, imply that government spending and revenue per capita is growing fast. Per capita government expenditure at constant (1988) prices increased from around Bt2200 in 1970 to around Bt9500 in 2003. The success of Thailand in achieving the MDGs can be attributed to the rapid growth that put income in the hands of people. They could use it to improve their living standards. It also increased the real resources available to government to provide the necessary services. Moreover, within government spending there has been a shift of resources towards social spending that has certainly helped to achieve the MDGs. While the overall government expenditure and revenue ratios are not high, the ratios of capital spending and of social services spending to GDP are relatively high. Thailand thus concentrates government spending in areas that support the private sector accumulation process and that promote human development.

Thailand has gone through a fiscal transition in the period under study. Taxes on international trade in 1970 still accounted for 37 per cent of total revenue. By 2003 that share had fallen to 12 per cent. This fall was compensated for by an increase in the contribution of income taxes (from 13 per cent of revenue in 1970s to 36 per cent in 2003). The share of indirect taxes has remained the same over the period. From a comparative perspective, the Thai tax structure is unusual in that the share of income tax, and particularly personal income tax, is rather small while that of indirect taxes is relatively large. The share of income tax has been increasing over the years, thus bringing Thailand somewhat closer to the average pattern. The structure of the tax system has important implications for income distribution. The incidence of indirect taxes is normally neutral; any progressivity in taxation has to come from income taxes. The small role of the personal income tax implies that taxation is not used in Thailand to redistribute income.

Another fiscal transition, that has just begun, is decentralization. The role of local government has been relatively small in the past but is now rapidly increasing. Another element of the public sector, state enterprises, does not play a very prominent role, but some of them are directly involved in activities that support private production and poverty alleviation. It is thus important to note that the activities of these enterprises have increased significantly over time.

DEFICIT FINANCING

Figure 9.5 shows the budget balance for the national government since 1950. The figure shows that, up to 1988, deficits were the norm, but since that year a period of surpluses occurred which came to an end with the Asian financial crisis.

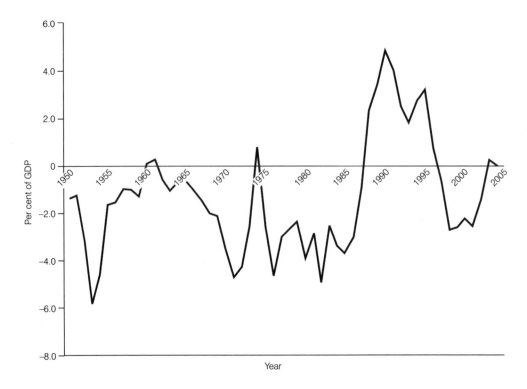

Source: Bank of Thailand, *Quarterly Bulletin*, various issues

Figure 9.5 *Budget balance (% of GDP)*

The deficits were never excessively large. The average deficit over the period 1950 to 1987 was 2.3 per cent of GDP. Deficits tended to occur in peaks (such as in 1953 and 1971/72) but were then quickly corrected. The only period of sustained considerable deficits was 1976 to 1986. Then, for ten consecutive years, substantial budget deficits were recorded. This period came to an end when, after 1986, substantial fiscal adjustment took place. Figure 9.1 shows how, after 1986, the expenditure to GDP ratio declined and the revenue to GDP ratio increased, leading to a period of fiscal surpluses.

The financing of the deficit can come from three sources: monetary financing, domestic borrowing and external borrowing. Thailand has used all three.

Monetary financing

Seignorage is a real resource that the government can mobilize through its ability to create money. It is measured by the increase in the monetary base (or high powered money):

$$\frac{\Delta M}{P} = \frac{M_t - M_{t-1}}{P_t} = \Delta\left(\frac{M}{P}\right) + \frac{M_{t-1}}{P_{t-1}}\left(\frac{\pi}{1+\pi}\right)$$

The first term on the right-hand side, $\Delta\left(\frac{M}{P}\right)$, reflects the increase in the demand for real balances.

The second term, $\frac{M_{t-1}}{P_{t-1}}\left(\frac{\pi}{1+\pi}\right)$, is the inflation tax ($\pi$ is the rate of inflation).

The real resources the government can obtain from seignorage are determined by the increase in the demand for money, which, in turn, depends on the growth of income, and by the inflation tax levied on outstanding money balances.

Figure 9.6 shows the contribution of seignorage in Thailand. The average revenue from seignorage over the period 1970 to 2004 is 1.8 per cent of GDP, and most of that is due to the growth in the demand for real balances (1.4 per cent). The inflation tax accounts for just 0.4 per cent of GDP over the period. The growing demand for real balances is fully determined by the growth in income, while the inflation tax depends on the level of inflation.[13]

Thailand is a country with a low appetite for inflation. The average inflation over the period 1970 to 2005 was only 5.6 per cent. In Figure 9.7 it is clear that this average is pushed up by high inflation in some special years.

The peak in 1974 was due to the first oil crisis and the peak in 1980 to the second oil crisis. The lower peak in 1997 was due to the pass through effect after the large depreciation of the baht. In all these instances inflation was very quickly brought down after the shock. For instance, inflation jumped to 24 per cent in 1974 but was back at 5 per cent in 1975, and similarly it fell from 13 per cent in 1981 to 5 per cent in 1982. If we remove these peak years from the series the average rate of inflation in Thailand falls to around 4 per cent per year, which is rather low for a country going through a period of rapid structural change.

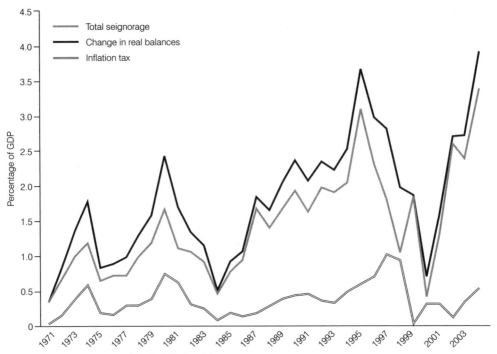

Source: Calculated on basis of Bank of Thailand data

Figure 9.6 *Seignorage in Thailand (% of GDP)*

Source: Bank of Thailand, *Quarterly Bulletin*, various issues

Figure 9.7 *Inflation, 1970–2005*

In 2000, the Bank of Thailand adopted inflation targeting as its monetary policy regime. The target is to keep inflation below 3.5 per cent that, in view of historical experience, is ambitious.

Thailand's revenue from seignorage is relatively modest compared to the average seignorage revenue for developing countries and for Asian developing countries as recorded in Table 3-5 of Brun et al (2006). This can be related to two factors. First, Thailand is a low inflation country. The average inflation is much lower than that of most other developing countries (see Brun et al, 2006, Table 3-7).[14] Figure 9.6 shows spikes in inflation tax revenue in 1974, 1980 and 1997 when external shocks pushed up inflation, but outside these peaks the revenue from the inflation tax was quite low. The second factor is that the Thai financial system is relatively well developed, with the banking system taking care of a large share of payments. This implies economizing on base money (the most significant part of which is currency in circulation). This implies the monetary base as a percentage of GDP is relatively low and that economic growth leads to modest demands for additional base money. In the period 1970 to 1985, the increase in real money balances produced seignorage revenue of around 1 per cent of GDP. In the late 1980s and 1990s the rapid growth lifted this revenue to around 2 per cent of GDP.

The Bank of Thailand expands the monetary base and thus controls seignorage. The revenue from seignorage flows to the government in two ways. First, the Central Bank may print money to pay for the government bonds that it buys from the government (this flow is included in government borrowing). Second, the Central Bank transfers profits to its owner (this is recorded in the non-tax revenue on the budget).

Debt financing

The main way to cover fiscal deficits is by the government borrowing at home and abroad. As Figure 9.8 shows the Thai government debt (as a percentage of GDP) follows closely the pattern of the deficits of Figure 9.5. In the 1970s total government debt stood at around 20 per cent of GDP. But the sustained deficits in the 1980s led to a rapid rise in the debt/GDP ratio to a peak of over 36 per cent in 1986.

The period of budget surpluses from 1987 to 1996 created the resources to pay down the government debt and the debt ratio fell to below 5 per cent of GDP in 1996.[15]

Debt financing is regulated by law. The fiscal deficit is limited to 20 per cent of planned expenditure (World Bank, 2000).[16] Recently, the Public Debt Management Office has been created for more effective public debt management. Rules for borrowing (for example, by state enterprises) are clarified and debt management plans are formulated. The Ministry of Finance has now formulated the following objectives: (1) the public debt should not exceed 50 per cent of GDP; and (2) government debt service payments should not exceed 15 per cent of budgeted expenditure (Bank of Thailand, 2004).

Source: Bank of Thailand, *Quarterly Bulletin*, various issues

Figure 9.8 *Government debt (% of GDP)*

To judge the acceptability and sustainability of government borrowing the public finance literature suggests some simple criteria. A first criterion is that prudent govern-ments should only borrow to finance investment. The rationale is that investment leads to an increase in output and income and thus an increase in future government revenues, out of which the debt can be serviced. Borrowing to finance current consumption spending will require a cut in future consumption spending to service the debt. Such borrowing may be acceptable as a short-run adjustment measure but is not sustainable in the medium term. If the government would only borrow to finance investment, government savings (defined as total revenue minus government consump-tion spending) would be equal to or larger than zero.

Simple debt sustainability models focus on the relationship between the interest rate and the growth rate:

$$\Delta D = D_t - D_{t-1} = G + iD_{t-1} - Rev$$

or

$$D_t = (G - Rev) + (1 + i)D_{t-1}$$

D is government debt, G is non-interest government expenditure, iD is interest payments, Rev is total revenue and $(G\text{-}Rev)$ is the primary budget balance. Dividing by GDP (Y) and using $Y_t = (1+g)Y_{t-1}$ gives:

$$\frac{D_t}{Y_t} = \frac{(G - Rev)_t}{Y_t} + \frac{(1 + i)D_{t-1}}{(1 + g)Y_{t-1}}$$

The debt ratio will increase when the government keeps running primary deficits and/or when the interest rate on government debt exceeds the growth rate of GDP.[17] These simple approaches give us three measures for judging the borrowing situation: government savings, the primary budget balance and the relationship between the interest rate and growth rate.

In most years over the period 1970 to 2004 government savings were positive. In 1982 and in the period 1984 to 1986 government savings were negative, but, as a percentage of GDP, not very high at an average of -0.68 per cent of GDP over these four years.

Thailand experienced primary deficits in the years 1970 to 1973, 1975 to 1985 and 1997 to 2002, that is, in the years in which there were also overall budget deficits. And, comparing the effective interest rate on government debt to the growth rate of nominal GDP shows that in 1971, 1976, 1984 to 1986, 1997 to 1999 and 2001 the interest rates were higher than the growth rates. Judged by these criteria, danger signals were flashing, particularly in the early 1980s and after the Asian crisis.

However, these indicators are only partial and incomplete. Fiscal balances have to be judged in the wider context of the state of the entire economy. One role of fiscal policy is stabilization, or demand management. If the economy is in recession, fiscal deficits may be required to maintain economic activity and to stimulate the recovery. The early 1980s were certainly a difficult period for Thailand. In 1979 oil prices had sharply increased again. As a result, by 1981, oil imports cost three times the 1978 level.[18] The government attempted to reduce the impact of oil costs on domestic prices through subsidies on retail prices and through cuts in taxes on oil products. Oil and energy prices were only gradually allowed to increase. This was one factor behind the fiscal deficits. In 1979 global interest rates started to rise and local interest rates followed, increasing the cost of debt service. The oil shock and the rise of global interest rates resulted in a global recession. In the period 1981 to 1983 world trade fell. Thailand, as a strongly export dependent economy, suffered. In 1982 export earnings stagnated and in 1983 they actually declined.

It could thus be argued that there was a need for fiscal stimulation. To analyse the role of fiscal policy in this period it is useful to refer to the macroeconomic balance equation:

$S - I = CAB$

The gap between savings (S), and investment (I), is equal to the current account balance (CAB). The overall savings/investment balance can be split up into sectoral balances, the private sector and the public sector, with the public sector further divided into government and state enterprises:

$$(S_g - I_g) + (S_s - I_s) + (S_p - I_p) = CAB$$

The current account balance is the sum of the saving investment balances of the government, the state enterprises and the private sector. The equation can be used to analyse fiscal policy. Suppose that private sector confidence falls and thus private investment and consumption declines. The result will be a decline in aggregate demand and a savings surplus of the private sector. To compensate for the fall in demand, an expansionary fiscal policy is appropriate. The increase in government spending (or the fall in revenue) is likely to lead to a budget deficit, but this can be easily financed as the private sector has idle savings. Figure 9.9 gives the three sectoral balances.

Figure 9.9 shows that in the early 1980s private investments were at a reasonable level and that, up to 1987, private sector savings and investment were always close together. This implies that there were few domestic resources available to finance government deficits.

The figure also shows that the government savings gap in the period 1975 to 1986 was accompanied by a substantial savings gap of the state enterprise sector over the same period. This led to a rather high aggregate public sector gap. Over the period 1976 to 1986 the public sector savings/investment balance was -4.7 per cent of GDP with peaks of over 6 per cent in 1981/82. As the private sector was in balance, the savings gap of the public sector was fully reflected in the current account deficit and in foreign borrowing and external debt.

Figure 9.10 shows the close relationship between the public sector savings/investment balance and the current account. Over the period 1970 to 1987 the two graphs were almost identical. The large public sector deficits of the period 1976 to 1986 were associated with large external gaps. To some extent this reflects the attempt of the public sector to provide compensation for the external shocks that were hitting the economy. But there is also something else behind these patterns.

In these years there was an important shift on the international financial markets. After the first oil shock of 1973/74 the recycling of petrodollars resulted in very high liquidity on international financial markets. International banks started lending to developing countries on a significant scale, preferably to governments and public sector entities that could obtain government guarantees for the debt service. For the public sector a new source of financing opened up and it looked quite attractive as, in the 1970s, global interest rates were low. And it was used. The total external debt of Thailand increased from around $1 billion in 1973/74 to $10 billion in 1983/84. As a percentage of GDP, external debt increased from 8.5 per cent in 1974 to a peak of 39.2

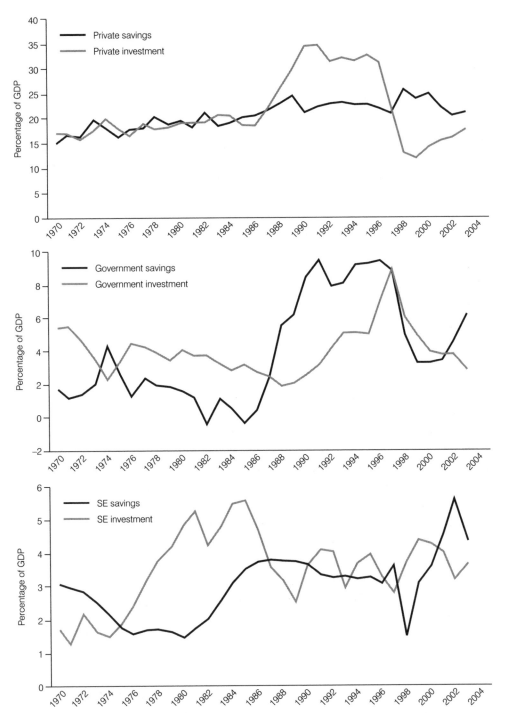

Source: Calculated on basis of Bank of Thailand data and the National Accounts of the National Economic and Social Development Board

Figure 9.9 *Accumulation balances (% GDP): (a) Private sector saving investment balance; (b) government saving investment balance; (c) state enterprises saving investment balance*

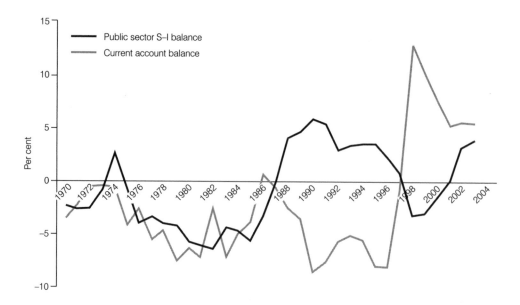

Source: Calculated on basis of Bank of Thailand data and the National Accounts of the National Economic and Social Development Board

Figure 9.10 *External and internal balance*

per cent in 1985 (or as a percentage of the export of goods and services, from 40 per cent in 1974 to 162 per cent in 1985).

In the early 1980s problems emerged. As global interest rates rose to high levels and domestic rates followed, the cost of servicing debt quickly increased. Interest payments by the government increased from 7 per cent of total government spending in 1978 to more than 15 per cent in 1985. While external debt service was rising, export earnings were stagnating in the early 1980s, so that debt servicing capacity came under stress.

The debt crisis erupted in 1982 in Mexico, which was quickly followed by a number of other countries that were no longer able to service their debt. The debt crises served as a warning to other countries, such as Thailand, and action was taken. The adjustment required action on the trade side (the devaluation in 1984) and on the fiscal policy side. Figure 9.9 shows that after 1982 there was a gradual decline in government investment. Government savings only improved after 1986, but savings by state enterprises increased after 1981 as a result of increases in the tariffs and rates charged by some big enterprises.

In the context of our fiscal space perspective, this period provides some important lessons. While government borrowing to finance investment is perfectly acceptable, its sustainability depends on the efficiency of the investment made. If the investment contributes to the growth of output and income, the debt can be serviced without problem, but if the investments are inefficient and do not lead to growth, the debt burden will increase. In the case of Thailand, growth has generally been rapid, thus making it possible for the government to borrow to finance its investment.

A second lesson is that the sustainability of government borrowing depends on the situation in the rest of the economy. The state enterprise sector is of obvious importance, its profits provide revenue to the government and its investments may require government subsidies and transfers. But it is also important to note that its external borrowing carries an explicit or implicit government guarantee that could affect the budget in times of crisis. In general, the macroeconomic balance equation gives us a good handle with which to assess the situation. It links the government balance to those of the state enterprises and the private sector and to the external balance. The configuration of these balances implied that in the early 1980s government and public sector deficits were leading to large current account deficits and a rapid growth of external debt.

The third lesson is that assessing sustainability is difficult in the face of uncertainty. The external borrowing that looked perfectly attractive in the 1970s, when global interest rates were low and exports rising fast, became highly problematic after 1979, once global interest rates increased sharply and global trade and Thailand's export earnings stagnated. In some countries, such as Mexico, this led to a full blown debt crisis. In Thailand such a crisis was avoided because the external debt was more moderate, but there were significant problems that required fiscal adjustment.

However, it should be recognized that fiscal adjustment can be an illusion (Easterly, 1999). Table 9.A1 (page 393) and Figure 9.9 show that the period of fiscal adjustment in the 1980s was characterized by stagnating real capital expenditure and a declining government spending to GDP ratio. Government investment in infrastructure suffered from adjustment. The investments by state enterprises, many of which provide infrastructure and public utilities, had risen to high levels, financed by debt, but then fell sharply between 1985 and 1990. When the private sector boom started in the late 1980s it quickly ran into infrastructure bottlenecks, requiring a sharp increase in government investment (see Figure 9.9). It could thus well be argued that the concern with short-term stability during this period led to a public sector adjustment that endangered the capital accumulation process in the longer run.

The second period when fiscal danger signals were flashing was after the Asian crisis. The crisis itself was not caused by fiscal factors. As Figure 9.5 shows, there were fiscal surpluses up to and including 1996 and Figure 9.8 shows that government debt had fallen to a very low level, below 4 per cent of GDP. In July 1997, the combination of the overvaluation of the exchange rate and stagnating exports, the large current account deficit and rapidly growing external debt, the weakness of the financial system and the volatility of international financial markets, led to the collapse of the currency and the ensuing crisis (see Jansen, 2000). Once the baht was floated, the large outflow of capital led to a precipitous depreciation with disastrous effects on externally indebted corporations and financial institutions. The result was a rapid decline in demand and output.

The IMF came to the rescue and in the first Letter of Intent (LOI) of August 1997 a very tight fiscal and monetary policy was imposed, aiming at a fiscal surplus of 1 per cent of GDP through increased revenue (for example, the VAT rate went from 7 to 10 per cent) and restrained expenditure. The second LOI (November 1997) observed that economic conditions had turned more negative than expected. Aggregate demand was declining faster and the exchange rate was depreciating more than expected. Still, the targeted fiscal surplus of 1 per cent of GDP was maintained and additional expenditure cuts and tax rises were introduced. This, it was said, was necessary to offset the cost of financial sector restructuring and to provide a clear signal to the market of the government's intent to implement the economic programme.

The fiscal surplus that was foreseen in the first two LOIs never materialized. The sharp fall in output led to a decline in revenue. Table 9.A1 shows that real government revenue declined sharply in 1998 and even though the government cut its capital expenditures deeply, fiscal deficits re-emerged.[19]

In early 1999 funds became available from the Japanese Miyazawa Plan that enabled some fiscal expansion. Thailand also reduced, temporarily, the VAT rate from 10 per cent to 7 per cent. Around that time, Thailand stopped drawing on the IMF facility (after about $14 billion of the available $17 billion had been used).

The fiscal balance was in deficit in 1999, 2000 and 2001, but still these years do not show the expansionary impulse that would have been appropriate. Table 9.A1 shows that real primary expenditure actually contracted in 1999 and 2000 as government investment was kept at very low levels.

In 2002, the fiscal expansion was stronger and is credited with reviving the economy (see, for example, *Far Eastern Economic Review*, 11 July 2002). The Thaksin government that came to power in 2001 adopted a different type of fiscal policy. First of all, it formulated a *dual track* approach to macroeconomic management under which fiscal stimulus is used when other elements of demand, such as exports or private investment, are weak, but when exports recover the fiscal stimulus should be held back. The government introduced an explicit *contingency fund* in the budget to be spent when economic conditions required it, for example, to cope with the impact of the Severe Acute Respiratory Syndrome (SARS) crisis. Fiscal stimulus was provided through a number of grassroots programmes. These included the programme in which each of the 77,000 villages received Bt1 million for village projects, a public works programme, subsidized health care, a moratorium on farmers' debt and so on.[20] These initiatives aimed to put money straight into the hands of the people rather than spending it through government agencies. Some of the new initiatives of the Thaksin government were financed outside the budget. For instance, the directed lending programmes aimed at providing micro-credit for the poor, at the housing sector or at SMEs were channelled through state-owned financial institutions, such as the Government Savings Bank, the Government Housing Bank and the Krung Thai Bank. The burden of the moratorium on farmers' debt is mainly carried by BAAC. Many are worried about the future impact of these off-budget items. Still, Table 9.A1 shows the rapid increase in real primary expenditure in 2001 and 2002. However, the recovery of the economy also led to an increase in government revenue and the fiscal deficit was falling in 2002.

With the fiscal deficits, government borrowing increased and government debt increased as well. The steep increase in government debt, shown in Figure 9.8, is not so much due to the fiscal deficits; these were initially (in 1998 and 1999) mainly financed by running down Treasury cash balances that had accumulated during the years of surpluses. The debt is mainly due to the bonds issued to finance the restructuring of financial institutions. The cost of this turned out to be quite substantial.

In this context there was a debate, in 2002, on the sustainability of the fiscal deficits and of the public debt. Total public sector debt had peaked at over 57 per cent of GDP in 2000 and 2001 and, by the end of 2002, stood at 54 per cent of GDP. The concern was that public debt may rise to 60 per cent of GDP, a limit above which, according to many, it would be dangerous to go and many studies questioned whether the level of public sector debt was sustainable (see, for example, IMF, 2002; Sawitree et al, 2002; Fiscal Policy Research Institute, 2003). In some contributions to this debate it seems as if the only role of fiscal policy is to bring budgets back into balance and to reduce public debt, but that position is extreme and premature for a number of reasons.

First, to limit government debt at 60 per cent of GDP is arbitrary; the number may have been borrowed from the EU that used it in the stability pact that was formulated with the introduction to the common currency, but even in Euroland there are countries with still larger ratios. Some have argued that when 60 per cent is the ceiling for rich countries it should be lower for emerging markets. In countries such as Thailand, government revenue ratios are lower and revenue may be more volatile, the domestic financial markets are not as deep, corporate governance poorer, and many financial institutions weaker. Access to international financial markets is not always ensured and countries cannot borrow abroad in their own currency; as a result they always face currency mismatches. All these factors contribute to lowering the debt carrying capacity.

The IMF (2003) observes that 55 per cent of the debt defaults in emerging markets occurred in countries with public debt to GDP ratios below 60 per cent. In 35 per cent of the defaults the debt ratio was even below 40 per cent. The median public debt to GDP ratio was about 50 per cent in the year before default. But the report notes that there are also countries with high debt ratios that never defaulted. It is thus difficult to pitch a ceiling. The IMF (2003) uses several methods to assess the sustainability of public debt. It runs a fiscal policy reaction function in which changes in the primary deficit are regressed against a number of variables, including the public debt ratio, in order to establish whether policymakers respond to the level of the debt ratio. The result shows that this is indeed the case. When the public debt ratio gets higher, the primary balance improves. However, this positive relationship breaks down around a public debt ratio of 50 per cent. Apparently, when public debt becomes too high, authorities lose control over fiscal variables. Of course, the pattern observed is an average and there is a lot of variation around this average, and individual countries have their own fiscal policy rules. Another method applied is to calculate the present value of future primary surpluses. It is assumed that past primary surpluses are the best indicators of future ones. On the basis of the present value, a benchmark level of public debt can be assessed and compared to the actual level to see whether the country has been over borrowing. The benchmark for the public debt ratio of emerging markets that results from this exercise is as low as 25 per cent, but this low level is mainly due to poor fiscal balances in Latin America. For the Asian emerging markets the benchmark is close to 75 per cent (see IMF, 2003).

The Euro norm of 60 per cent relates to government debt. In the case of Thailand, the focus was on public debt, defined very broadly. It appears that the various studies are not fully consistent; they seem to be using slightly different definitions. The public debt includes the following:

- The domestic and external debt of the government. It should, however, be noted that only the debt of the central government is included. There is no central record of local government debt, but it is known that the level of this debt is presently very low. This could change in the future with fiscal decentralization.
- The domestic and external debt of state enterprises (bonds issued). It is not clear whether loans from domestic commercial banks are also included. Most studies only include the debt of non-financial state enterprises. It should be noted that the majority of state enterprise debt is issued by perfectly healthy and profitable enterprises and can be serviced from their cash flow and is backed by the assets of these enterprises (Fiscal Policy Research Institute, 2003). The public debt problem is overstated by including this part of the debt. One study also included the debt of the Central Bank, incurred with the IMF package of 1997. But this raises the question about what to do with the international reserves. Should we consider the external debt on a net basis (foreign liabilities minus foreign assets, such as the Central Bank's reserves) or on a gross basis?
- The debt incurred to salvage financial institutions. This debt is in the form of bonds issued by the Financial Institutions Development Fund (FIDF), but the government has the obligation to finance the servicing of these bonds.

It is clear that public debt is a flexible concept. For instance, if we assume that half of the state enterprise debt is held by commercially viable companies that will never bother the government, and if we include the net foreign position of the Central Bank in the calculation, the 2001 public debt to GDP ratio would be just 27 per cent and not the 57 per cent that was the subject of debate.

However, public debt may be understated as there may be contingent liabilities that in the future could increase government debt. The concept of contingent liabilities is clear from the FIDF debt. These bonds were issued to raise the funds necessary to salvage the banks after the Asian crisis had made them insolvent. The majority of these banks are privately owned; still the government felt it had to intervene to keep financial intermediation going and not make the crisis worse. More contingent liabilities may arise from further losses of financial institutions for which the government may have to assume responsibility, but it is also possible that some of the losses can be recouped when bad loans turn good again with the recovery of the economy, or when the assets of closed financial institutions can be sold above the purchase price paid by the asset management companies. The financing of some of the new initiatives of the Thaksin government may also lead to future contingent liabilities. But there can be too much attention paid to contingent liabilities while contingent assets are ignored.

A second point to note is that public debt is composed of domestic and foreign debt. Presumably, the external debt is more worrying, as too high a level may reduce access to foreign funds, or would increase the risk premium. About 70 per cent of public debt is domestic, only 30 per cent is external debt. Total (public and private) external debt by the end of 2002 was $59 billion or 46 per cent of GDP, down from a peak of $109 billion in 1997. These numbers are relatively low, particularly when taking into account that the net foreign assets of the Central Bank were about $33 billion at that time. Moreover, almost all public debt is long term, and only 17 per cent is short term.

Third, the domestic public debt would only constitute a problem if the conditions on financial markets were tight. This was not the case. Figure 9.9 shows that private investment was low in these years and far below private savings. Financial institutions are thus awash with funds and there is a ready market for government bonds. Despite the high level of government debt, the yield on government bonds is very low. The liquidity on financial markets makes monetary policy rather ineffective and, despite the low loan rate, the demand for credit is small. This leaves fiscal policy as the only instrument to stimulate the economy. But the emphasis on debt sustainability, based on an excessively broad measure of public debt and a pessimistic assessment of possible contingent liabilities, made fiscal expansion suspect. In 2003 there was only a small increase in government spending and the government expenditure to GDP ratio declined (see Figure 9.1). As revenues were increasing, 2003 had already recorded a small fiscal surplus and the public debt ratio had been declining rapidly.

As noted above, debt sustainability depends on how the borrowed funds are used. If debt is financing public investment, the resulting growth will generate the revenue to service the debt. This requires an efficient allocation of the public investment and avoidance of crowding out. Debt to finance infrastructure may have that effect. In this respect it is worrying that so much of the current debt is accumulated to bail out financial institutions, which is not a very productive investment. However, if the government had allowed the financial system to collapse, the economic consequences would have been disastrous.

It should be noted that, at the time of the debt sustainability debate, various studies engaged in model simulations to assess sustainability (World Bank, 2000; IMF, 2002;

Sawitree et al, 2002; Financial Policy Research Institute, 2003). All came to the conclusion that, under reasonable assumptions with respect to economic conditions, the public debt was sustainable, fiscal deficits would come down and the debt ratio would decline.

One significant impact of the rising government debt is the rising level of debt service payments. In the 1980s, when the debt was high and interest rates were high, interest payments on government debt increased to over 15 per cent of total government spending. In the early 2000s, government debt was again high, but interest rates were rather low. Still, interest payments on government debt took more than 7 per cent of government spending in the period 2000 to 2002, up from the 1 per cent in 1996. In a budget that is under pressure, such a claim easily crowds out other government activities.

Again we can draw some lessons from this period. The first lesson is that, if a country wants to keep autonomy and control over its fiscal policy it is best to stay out of the hands of the IMF because that institution has a strong predilection for tight fiscal policy. Thailand has been fortunate in this respect. During the early 1980s there were two SBAs, in 1981 and 1985. The fiscal reforms demanded in the 1981 SBA were largely unsuccessful and the 1985 SBA was interrupted halfway through by the Thai government, due among others reasons to disagreement on fiscal policy. In these years the Thai government was not really dependent on the IMF; it had access to other sources of finance (see Jansen, 1997). In 1997 Thailand was more dependent on the IMF and, as we have seen, there was again disagreement on fiscal policy.

A second lesson is that the sustainability of fiscal deficits, or of public debt, are extremely fuzzy concepts. There is no agreement on how public debt should be measured, what to include and what not. When we looked at the debt situation in the early 1980s it was noted that one should not only consider government debt, but also the debt of state enterprises. In recent years the problems of private sector financial institutions directly affects fiscal balances and public debt. More of such 'contingent liabilities' can be imagined. But the inclusion of contingent liabilities also opens the door to arbitrary and farfetched arguments. Fiscal policymakers find it difficult enough to deal with today's problems and it is not very realistic to expect them to take into consideration any possible future problems that may arise.

There is also no agreement on the standard for sustainability. The 60 per cent norm is totally arbitrary and attempts to establish analytically based norms showing that country-specific conditions are crucial and that acceptable levels will differ from country to country. Moreover, any number that is proposed is subject to a wide range of uncertainty. Sustainability is a forward looking concept and depends on future growth of output and exports, in terms of trade, on future inflation and interest rates and so on. All these variables may show unexpected variations. In the end, fiscal sustainability is based on the market perception of what is acceptable, and market perceptions are subject to sudden changes of mood, contagion or shocks.

The result of all this is that sustainability is an almost unworkable concept. Still, it is equally obvious that this does not mean that anything goes. Fiscal space through borrowing is constrained, only we do not and cannot know precisely how. One way out is to set an arbitrary norm, like the Ministry of Finance has now done, stating that public debt should not exceed 50 per cent of GDP. Such a norm helps the Minister of Finance to contain spending pressures and to prioritize expenditure, but it may not be an appropriate guide under all circumstances.

Macroeconomic impact of deficit financing

The fiscal space that can be created by deficit financing is, in the end, determined by its macroeconomic effects. Deficit financing has direct and indirect effects on economic growth. Growth of output is determined by the rate and efficiency of investment, and fiscal policy and deficit financing can impact on both.

Deficit financing is generally used to finance public investment in infrastructure and it is recognized that adequate infrastructure is instrumental in stimulating private investment and growth. But excessive deficit financing may harm growth.

It has been widely established that macroeconomic stability is a prerequisite for growth and, to the extent that fiscal policy undermines stability, it negatively affects growth. These stability links can be assessed through the analysis of the relationships between fiscal balances and inflation, current account balance and debt overhang. Excessive fiscal expansion will threaten stability. The excess demand will translate into inflation and current account deficits and the financing of the current account deficits will result in an accumulation of external debt. The debt overhang will eventually affect creditworthiness and reduce access to credit or increase its cost. Macroeconomic instability may negatively affect private sector confidence and private spending and it may change the system of incentives and distort the allocation of investment.

Fiscal policy would directly affect growth when fiscal expansion leads to a decline in private investment. This is the issue of crowding out. Deficit financing on domestic financial markets may lead to an increase in the interest rate or to a rationing of credit for the private sector. As a result, the level of private investment that can be undertaken declines. According to standard open economy macro models, under a flexible exchange rate and capital mobility, fiscal expansion will lead to an appreciation of the exchange rate. Under a fixed exchange rate, the inflation caused by fiscal expansion will lead to an appreciation of the real exchange rate. In both cases, the profitability of the traded goods sector declines and investment falls.

To assess the impact of fiscal policy we need to study the links between the fiscal variables and inflation, current account balance, debt burden, interest rates, private credit and the real exchange rate. This is what we will do in the following pages.

Inflation

Figure 9.7 shows that, on average, inflation in Thailand has been modest and that the spurts of inflation that did occur were due to external shocks. It is not possible to establish a link between the budget balance and inflation. Theoretically, one would expect a negative relationship – a larger deficit associated with higher inflation. However, the correlation coefficient between the budget balance (as a percentage of GDP) and inflation is positive and very low at 0.08.[21]

In another study (Jansen, 2004) it was shown that in fact the relationship is the other way around. It is not fiscal policy that leads to inflation; rather, fiscal policy responds to changes in inflation. In Jansen (2004) we constructed an indicator for the fiscal impulse (or the fiscal policy stance) and saw it quickly respond to changes in inflation. One of the reasons for the low inflation in Thailand is this cautious fiscal policy.

Current account balance and debt overhang

Figure 9.10 shows the link between the public sector savings/investment balance and the current account. In the period 1975 to 1986 there was a substantial gap in public sector savings that was fully reflected in the current account deficit, since private sector saving and investment were in balance in this period (see Figure 9.9). In these years there were concerns about the current account deficits and the debt that was accumulating. For instance, in its report covering 1985 the Central Bank stated:

> *The government has faced chronic financial problems for many years... The problem is one of overspending, giving the government persistently high deficits and state enterprises continuing operating losses. The result of this overspending is cumulatively high government debt, both domestic and international, which, if not resolved, will have profound repercussions on both the economic and the financial stability of the country.*
> (Bank of Thailand, 1985, p13)

The recovery of the world economy and the fiscal adjustment measures together helped to solve this problem. It should be noted that the debt problem in Thailand did not become as serious as in some other countries: Thailand always remained able to fully service its debt obligations and maintained its access to international financial markets.

In the subsequent period, 1987 to 1996, these balances turned upside down. As Figure 9.9 shows, in these years the private sector had a very large savings gap. This was caused and financed by very substantial inflows of private international capital. The saving investment balance of state enterprises was, on average, in balance. The government now had a savings surplus (and a budget surplus), with government savings far exceeding government investment. The fiscal policy at this time tried to dampen the sharply expansionary effects of the private sector boom. Here again we see an illustration of the generally cautious nature of fiscal policy in Thailand. While the government had ample revenue available, and while there was no shortage of desirable public sector expenditure (for example, in infrastructure), the government controlled spending to cool down the overheating economy.

Crowding in or out

Crowding in or out is usually analysed as the link between government investment and private investment. When an increase in government investment is followed by a fall in private investment, this is called crowding out. Note that there may also be crowding in, with government investment inducing private investment. Government investment can not only affect the level of private investment, it may also affect its efficiency. Crowding in or out are complex processes as there are many channels through which public and private investment may interact:

- Government investment creates infrastructure that reduces the production costs of the private sector. The increase in private profitability or competitiveness will induce a higher level of private investment (crowding in) and may increase the efficiency of investment.
- An increase in government investment will increase aggregate demand that may induce more private investment (crowding in). Such an interaction would particularly be expected when the economy is in a recession and the government uses fiscal policy to improve economic conditions. In countries like Thailand, fiscal policy is mainly implemented through variations in government investment spending. In the other phase of the business cycle, the interaction between public and private investment may be negative. During a boom, when private investment is at (too) high levels, the government may reduce its spending to cool down the economy.
- The high tax burden to finance government spending reduces private profits. Government borrowing on domestic financial markets pushes up interest rates or reduces the availability of credit for the private sector. As a result, private investment falls (crowding out).
- Fiscal expansion may lead to an appreciation of the real exchange rate that reduces the profitability of the traded goods sector. This may result in a fall in investment in this sector.

The first two points suggest crowding in. Public investment generates infrastructure and demand that makes private investment possible and profitable. If there is crowding in, a higher level of public investment invites a higher level of private investment and the correlation between the two would be positive. In contrast, crowding out would mean that more public investment is associated with lower private investment: a negative relationship.

One of the main ways in which public investment could crowd out private investment is through the claims the government makes on the financial markets to finance its expenditures. If there is a strong government demand for funds, credit markets could become tight, leading to either higher interest rates or a rationing of credit for the private sector.

Thailand has fairly well-developed financial markets, dominated by commercial banks. The M3/GDP ratio has steadily increased over time from 32 per cent in 1970 to 47 per cent in 1980, 86 per cent in 1990 and 112 per cent in 2004. Financial institutions used to hold most of the government debt. For instance, 85 per cent of total domestic borrowing was financed by financial institutions in the fiscal year 1985. Particularly since the Asian crisis, the Central Bank and the Ministry of Finance have been consciously planning the development of the bond market. An active bond market will contribute to financial stability as it will provide firms with opportunities for longer term financing. The Ministry is issuing bonds with varying maturities to establish a benchmark yield curve against which corporate paper can be priced.

In recent years, the share of government debt held by the general public and non-financial entities has increased, but still the majority is held by financial institutions. These bond market development plans are an interesting case where government debt management is placed in the service of financial market development, which could improve private financing and so, indirectly, contribute to investment and growth.

At the regional level, there is the Asian Bond Market Initiative (ABMI). Here East Asian governments work together to develop local and regional bond markets. The purpose is to contribute to financial stability by creating long-term financing opportunities and by creating the possibility of issuing international bonds in the local currency, thus removing the currency mismatch and exchange rate risk. If the ABMI is successful it would enhance financing opportunities for the public and private sectors in the region.

There is some suggestion of crowding out through financial markets. Figure 9.11 traces the local loan rate against the international interest rate (the London Inter-Bank Offered Rate – LIBOR). In general, the local market rate follows the trend in the global interest rate quite closely. The loan rate tends to be above the global prime rate. In the early 1980s, when public sector borrowing was heavy, the gap between the two rates became marginally wider. However, in the period 1990 to 1998, when the government was not borrowing at all, the gap between the two rates was even wider. It may well be that the gap between the two interest rates in Figure 9.11 does not so much reflect fiscal pressures but more the tight monetary policy that was implemented in the early 1980s (to fight the current account deficit and to defend the exchange rate) and in the 1990s (to cool down the economy during the private sector boom).

Another indicator of financial crowding out is the availability of domestic credit for the private sector. Figure 9.12 shows the change in private domestic credit as a percentage of GDP.

From 1970 to the mid-1980s the ratio hovers between 2 and 12 per cent, with an average of 6.7 per cent per year. Against that, average private credit growth in the early 1980s is not particularly poor. There is even a peak in 1983 after which credit growth falls to a low level in 1986. Following the slump, there is a boom in private credit expansion, fuelled by capital inflows but also facilitated by budget surpluses, which implied that the government did not need to borrow.

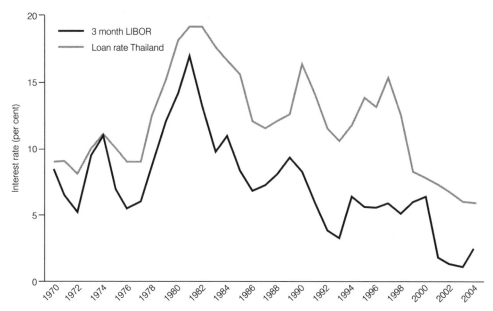

Source: Bank of Thailand, *Quarterly Bulletin*, various issues

Figure 9.11 *Thai and global interest rates*

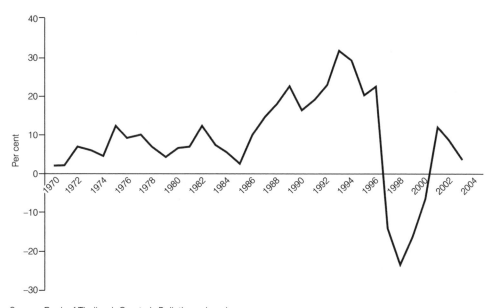

Source: Bank of Thailand, *Quarterly Bulletin*, various issues

Figure 9.12 *Private credit expansion*

It is difficult to judge whether the low level of private credit growth in 1985/86 is due to a crowding out of the private sector by public sector borrowing, or by a low demand for credit in the private sector. The economy was doing rather poorly in these years and it is thus likely that credit demand was low.

Figure 9.1 shows how the government spending ratio fell from its high level, around 18 per cent, in the mid-1980s to a much lower level, between 14 and 16 per cent, in the late 1980s and the first half of the 1990s. This period recorded substantial fiscal surpluses and rapidly declining government debt. In Figure 9.9 we see how government investment, which had fallen to a very low level by 1988, recovered to a more normal level but government savings increased sharply as current spending stayed behind the rapid growth of revenue. The fiscal policy of this period was very clearly aimed at compensating for the private sector boom. Private investment was very high in this period (Figure 9.9), financed by large capital inflows and a very rapid expansion of domestic credit (Figure 9.12). The government was worried about the inflationary pressures and the large current account deficits that the private sector boom engendered and used fiscal policy to reduce demand pressures. The fiscal policy in this period could be interpreted as a case of *reverse crowding out*, a private sector investment boom crowding out government spending. If such a situation persists over time problems may arise. The growing private sector needs government services and infrastructure and, when cautious fiscal policy prevents the adequate provision of such services, private growth may falter.

A final channel for crowding out would run through the exchange rate. Fiscal expansion could lead to an appreciation of the real exchange rate which, in turn, will reduce the competitiveness of the traded goods sector, and reduce production of and investment in this sector. Figure 9.13 traces the trade weighted real exchange rate index. The index is so constructed that a rise in the line is a depreciation of the country's currency and a fall in the line marks an appreciation.

In the early 1980s there was a mild appreciation of the real exchange rate. It could be argued that, in that period, the public sector expansion pushed up domestic prices and this, together with the fixed nominal exchange rate, implied an appreciation of the real exchange rate. It is good to remember that this was a period of extreme shocks. Domestic prices soared after the second oil shock and the authorities were slow to adjust the nominal exchange rate to the new situation. There was a minor devaluation in 1981, but strong resistance against further adjustment. Only by November 1984 was it obvious to all that further action could no longer be avoided; the baht was devalued by almost 15 per cent.

The fiscal deficits after the Asian crisis did not affect the exchange rate. At that time the exchange rate was driven by the outflow of capital and there was a strong depreciation of the real exchange rate between 1996 and 2001, after which it stabilized. As noted above, the fiscal deficits of these years did not cause any domestic demand pressures because they were mainly due to sharply falling revenue. In conclusion, there

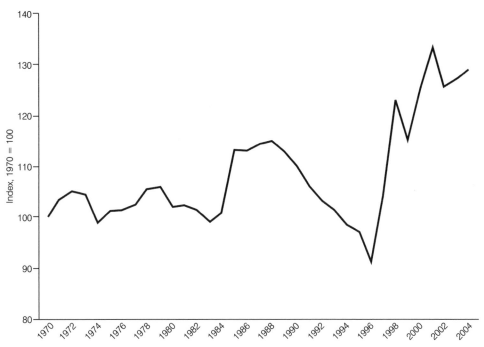

Source: Calculated on basis of Bank of Thailand data

Figure 9.13 *Real exchange rate index*

is little evidence of crowding out. None of the channels for crowding out (interest rate, credit supply and real exchange rate) show a strong relationship with the fiscal balance.

A number of econometric studies have tried to establish the link between public and private investment in Thailand. World Bank (2006) contains a single equation regression analysis of the determinants of private investment in Thailand and concludes that public investment has a positive impact. More complete macroeconometric models have estimated the relationship between public and private investment and found evidence for crowding in, private investment is stimulated by public investment (see, for example, Jansen, 1995, and Jitsuchon and Sussangkarn, 1993).[22] We can, therefore, conclude that, in general, there has been a positive relationship between public investment and private accumulation. Government investment has, through this mechanism, significantly contributed to the high level of investment and the rapid growth of the economy.

Section summary

This section of the chapter has analysed deficit financing in Thailand. Historically, Thai fiscal policy has been cautious in nature and this is reflected in a limited use of deficit financing.

Seignorage has made a significant contribution to government revenue, but the use of the inflation tax has been minimal. The majority of government borrowing is done on domestic financial markets. The rapid financialization of savings implied that it has been easy to place government debt. There was concern in the early 1980s about the rapidly increasing domestic and external debt of the government and state enterprises. It is possible that, at that time, private investment was crowded out to some extent as the combination of fiscal borrowing and tight monetary policy pushed up interest rates. But the increasing interest rates were also caused by high global rates and it is more likely that the slow expansion of private credit in these years is due to low demand as the economy was doing poorly. Private investment did not fall very much in this period (see Figure 9.9).

This period showed the dangers of deficit financing in an open economy like Thailand's. Global interest rates are volatile and may change suddenly, as for example, happened after 1979. Local interest rates in open markets with relatively developed financial systems tend to follow global trends. This can thus lead to sudden changes in the cost of deficit financing. In the 1980s this led to a rapid increase in government spending on interest payments, crowding out other government activities. Where external debt is concerned, the borrower faces an exchange rate risk: the cost of external debt service increased after the devaluation of 1984. In response to these shocks the gradual fiscal reform improved the finances of the government and state enterprises. But the brunt of fiscal adjustment was on public investment and this had a negative impact on the infrastructure supply.

The cautious nature of fiscal policy was further illustrated in the 1990s when the government was running substantial budget surpluses for a period of ten years. It could be argued that during, this time, desirable government expenditures were postponed in order to maintain the stability of the economy.

The crisis of 1997 and its aftermath renewed the discussion about the sustainability of public sector debt. Unfortunately, in this debate the concept of public debt was stretched to such an extent that it became useless for analysis. It is not meaningful to include all elements of public sector debt, including commercial debt of profitable state enterprises. Moreover, the insistence on considering all possible types of contingent liabilities takes the discussion away from the reality of day-to-day policymaking.

The correct conclusion is that we do not know what the sustainable level of public sector debt is. This is not only because of definition and measurement problems, but also because of uncertainty; what looks sustainable today may be unsustainable tomorrow once some serious and unforeseeable shock occurs. Sustainability is a forward looking concept and the future is always uncertain. What to do? The reaction of the Thai government seems to be that it is better to err on the safe side. In the last few years the government has been running balanced budgets, the public debt is rapidly declining and the Central Bank has accumulated a huge stock of international reserves.

Was there, in the period under study, unused fiscal space? Could Thailand have borrowed more to finance public investment? The answer is difficult to give. It could be argued that Thailand could have obtained more resources from the inflation tax; other Asian countries did so without ending up with runaway inflation. It is also possible to argue that Thailand could have borrowed more. The public debt never became excessively high, there were never any problems with servicing the debt and there is no evidence of crowding out.

At the same time, the fiscal caution paid off. Fiscal policy has been very much concerned with maintaining macroeconomic stability and this stability is seen as one of the main factors behind the strong performance of the economy. This rapid growth has, in turn, helped Thailand to achieve the MDGs.

FISCAL SPACE AND THE MDGS

This chapter has analysed the fiscal space of Thailand in the context of poverty reduction and the MDGs. Poverty has fallen sharply and most of the MDGs are already achieved, well before the 2015 target date. In this final section we want to assess the relationship between fiscal interventions and this outcome.

Human development first of all depends on rapid and dynamic accumulation and growth. Fiscal interventions can support this process in two ways. By creating institutions, incentives and infrastructure, government can induce rapid and efficient private investment. Moreover, fiscal policy underlies the macroeconomic stability that is required for sustained growth. Fiscal interventions can also directly support human development and the achievement of the MDGs through the provision of essential social services and through the redistribution of income.

In this final part of the chapter we summarize our findings under the familiar headings of growth, stabilization and distribution.

Fiscal interventions and growth

In Thailand, economic growth has been rapid over the last 50 years and is the main force behind the phenomenal decline in poverty that occurred. The economic growth literature is not very clear about the role of fiscal variables in economic growth. Various cross-country regression studies have included fiscal variables among the explanatory variables. The results are not robust. Different studies, using different methods and country samples and covering different periods, find different results. A number of studies find a negative relationship between the level of government spending (total spending or current spending as a percentage of GDP) and growth. Some studies also find a positive relationship between the budget balance and growth. If we accept these findings we can conclude that Thailand's record of a low level of government spending and, on average, good budget balances has promoted growth. But this conclusion may be too quickly reached, and not only because the statistical basis for it is not very robust.

There is a contradiction in the growth studies. Many studies have concluded that good infrastructure and human capital promote growth. Government spending is required to produce these. One could thus imagine a growth regression in which growth is positively influenced by infrastructure and human capital, but negatively influenced by the government spending that created this infrastructure and human capital. But one cannot have one (infrastructure and human capital) without the other (government spending), and one could thus argue that, even when government spending ends up with a negative coefficient in the regression, its impact on growth is positive. While it is obvious that excessive and inefficient government spending will never be good for growth, reasonable levels of efficient and well-allocated expenditures are likely to promote growth. This suggests that it is not so much the level of government spending, as reflected in expenditure or tax ratios, that explains growth but the composition and quality of the government spending.

In Thailand, the government and state enterprises have been active in the provision of infrastructure, such as roads, electricity and water, and the general level of service is good. Still, there have been periods when the supply of infrastructure ran behind the rapid growth of the private sector. Also human capital formation has been far from exemplary. Until 1990 Thailand had one of the lowest secondary school enrolment ratios in the region. It is thus well possible to argue that more public investment should have been undertaken to support growth.

Growth is mainly generated in the private sector of the economy, but fiscal policy can affect the incentives the private sector faces. In the public finance literature there is a concern about the 'distortions' that government action will create. Government regulation, spending programmes and taxation affect decisions of economic agents and thus change economic outcomes. Theoretically, the economic reason for government intervention is to correct for market failures and such interventions would thus be expected to improve economic outcomes. Government intervention is necessary to provide the public goods and merit goods that the market cannot provide and to regulate the market in the case of externalities. The taxes required to finance the government interventions will, of course, distort economic incentives as they inevitably change relative prices. The tax literature is full of analyses on how to minimize such distortions. Inevitably taxation in Thailand has affected incentives but there is reason to believe that distortions through taxation have become less over time. In 1992 Thailand shifted to VAT, which is supposed to be less distorting than the preceding cascading sales tax. The import tariffs, which according to the trade and development literature have a strong anti-export bias, have been declining in Thailand over time and have now reached fairly low levels, but there have been many inequities in the administration of income taxes and these may well have increased over time.

There is a widespread concern that governments are rather inefficient or captured by special interests, and that the interventions would lead to a less efficient allocation of resources and to rent seeking. It is our impression that the reputation of the Thai government with the population is not very strong in this respect. Thailand scores fairly high on the corruption index and Thai newspapers regularly carry stories of alleged corruption in government projects. State enterprises are perceived to be rather ineffi-cient, dependent on government protection and resistant to change.

It is difficult to assess the impact of the microeconomic distortions that are inher-ent in government interventions in the economic performance of the country. Clearly, the impact cannot have been very negative, otherwise private investment and growth would not have performed so well. Presumably distortions could lead to low productiv-ity and to low productivity growth, but productivity growth in Thailand has been quite good. In growth accounting studies, growth is explained from the accumulation of production factors, capital and labour, and from total factor productivity growth (TFP). TFP has made a significant contribution to growth in Thailand. In the studies summa-rized in Jansen (2001), productivity growth accounts for 20 to 50 per cent of total economic growth. In the East Asian comparative perspective, the contribution of TFP to growth is relatively large in the case of Thailand. This would support the conclusion that the inefficiency caused by the various government interventions has not been too serious.

We may thus conclude that fiscal interventions have, on balance, supported the dynamic growth process. Governments have been supportive of private business, have provided infrastructure and human capital at workable levels and have kept the number and level of distortions at a relatively low level.

Fiscal policy and stabilization

One of the factors behind the rapid growth is the macroeconomic stability ensured by the conservative fiscal and monetary policies. As we have shown, inflation was always kept low and, when the public sector debt approached dangerous levels in the early 1980s and around 2002, corrective action was taken. During the late 1980s and early 1990s fiscal surpluses tried to counterbalance the private sector boom. Short-run fiscal policies were driven by a concern for macroeconomic stability. In another study, it was shown that fiscal policy has been actively used to stabilize the economy (Jansen, 2004).

Over time, fiscal policy has consistently been used to stabilize the economy in the face of external and internal shocks. When the country was faced with the collapse of the Bretton Woods system of fixed exchange rates in 1973, the baht was tied to the US dollar. This practice had the main consequence of hitching the country's fortunes to the fortunes of the dollar. Business cycle volatilities in the period were thus very much linked to how the dollar fared. These volatilities caused a pursuit of fiscal policies to seek adjustments which would restore economic stability. The fiscal space was used up more in this period for the purpose of economic stabilization rather than for develop-ment or for poverty reduction/eradication. This period of high economic volatility saw the country faced with currency devaluations in 1981 and in 1984, and this came to a close when the currency was linked to a basket of currencies (1984) for better stability

of the baht and of the economy. Fiscal policy was devoted to correcting macroeconomic instability while the monetary policy was very constrained by financial fragility.
The financial crisis of 1984 saw the collapse of a bank and about 16 finance companies,
whereby, the authorities turned to the 'life boat' method of rescue for those institutions.
A new mechanism, the FIDF was set up to administer this support tool. The burdens
that arose were partially channelled to the fiscal space.

Thailand accepted structural adjustment loans from the World Bank from 1981 to
1986, and the country implemented, through its development plan, some structural
adjustments. The Plaza Agreement currency realignment of 1985 did the rest in carrying the Thai economy into a new era.

In this period, the country was awash with capital inflows, not because of the implementation of particular domestic policies (fiscal policies included), but because of the
world currency realignment. The resultant monetary changes in the country brought a
period of boom (1987 to 1995) whereby many people became suddenly wealthy
because of rapid growth and asset inflation. Investments (from outside, mostly) were
very strong. International reserves increased in leaps and bounds, and revenue collections did likewise. An important change then occurred when, in 1990, the country
liberalized the capital account. This freedom reinforced Thai external economic activities with consequent foreign exchange abundance, hence driving monetary policy into
an expansionary posture for the years up to 1996. The fiscal space certainly benefited
from this economic expansion. The eventual rejection of the sales tax in favour of the
value added tax was part of the fiscal reforms of this period. Fiscal practices and
budgetary procedures were also reformed to modernize the fiscal space. Finally, in the
financial system, an offshore banking variant was introduced into the Thai system,
called the Bangkok International Banking Facility (BIBF), to further link the financial
sector to international financial markets, just as the domestic commerce and economy
were opened up and linked to international trade and businesses.

From 1990 onwards, the fiscal space became copious in relation to resource use.
The expanding economy post-1987 generated such plentiful taxes that the treasury
surplus balance kept rising to higher levels for the period 1990 to 1997. At the peak of
this tide, the level of the surplus balance reached Bt400 billion. The plentiful revenues
of the day were not usefully employed in the economy. The high treasury balance was
mainly used to keep and maintain macroeconomic stability, that is, to counter the
expansionary monetary policy (because foreign exchange inflows kept the liquidity level
relatively high throughout this period). Neither was the copious Treasury surplus used
to carry out a redistribution policy. On reflection, it can be said that opportunities were
lost to undertake meaningful activities such as reforming the total tax system and
making it progressive, installing needed infrastructure in the economy to reinforce real
growth, carrying out further structural adjustments of the economy and so on. The
great lesson from this period was the under-utilization of the fiscal space to further
society's important goals. Expansionary monetary policy and a mismanaged exchange

rate regime finally brought disaster to the whole economy. Facing the crisis, in the period 1997 to 1999, in the same way as in the period 1981 to 1984, the fiscal space was mobilized to the economy's rescue. A big difference in 1997 was the much bigger role taken on by the IMF.

For the period post-1997, the country faced numerous reforms and changes, as the economy struggled to adjust from an overvalued uncompetitive position to normal competitiveness. The conditions imposed by the IMF were severe and led to widespread popular discontent. The fiscal space was confined to helping big banks instead of being allowed to underwrite the future for the rest of the economy. Resources from the fiscal space were devoted more to rescuing private assets than to laying down fresh infrastructure and other needed foundations for new changes that were taking place in the international scene.

Redistribution

The public sector can contribute to poverty reduction through redistribution. We have observed that the level of government spending, as reflected in the government expenditure to GDP ratio, is relatively low in Thailand. This limits the resources the government can use to directly attack poverty. At the same time, the very rapid growth of GDP translated into a rapid growth of government revenue and this has implied that expenditure per capita could rapidly increase. Moreover, within total government spending over the years, the share of expenditure on social development, education, health, social services and agriculture, which are presumably crucial for poverty alleviation, have increased significantly. While such expenditure constituted only 10 per cent of total government spending in 1970, this share increased to over 40 per cent by 2003.

Were government taxation and spending pro-poor? World Bank (2000) reviews available studies on tax incidence. Different studies use different methods and come to different conclusions, but there is agreement that:

- The overall effects of taxation on income distribution, if any, are very small.
- Personal income tax is progressive, but this tax generates only a small part of total government income and, hence, the effect on income distribution is negligible. As we have seen, the top income decile pays almost all of this tax.
- Indirect taxes are either neutral or regressive.

The conclusion is, therefore, that the overall tax system is neutral and income distribution after tax is not more equal than that before. The World Bank report also concludes that government expenditures on education, health and agriculture do not particularly benefit the poor; it is the middle- and high-income groups that benefit more (World Bank, 2000).

Warr and Sarntisart (2004) also go into detail on the incidence of government expenditure. They first review an existing study that finds that government spending benefits the rich more than the poor and they then go into an analysis of the provincial allocation of government spending. They find that total per capita government spending increases with the per capita income of the province, and the per capita spending has no relationship to the incidence of poverty in the province. Per capita expenditure on education and health are not significantly related to provincial income or poverty. Focusing specifically on the anti-poverty programmes of the government, Warr and Sarntisart (2004) first of all observe that spending on such programmes has been relatively low; before 2001 it amounted to around just 4 per cent of total government spending. Poverty-related expenditure has increased a bit in recent years, but they observe that the allocation of poverty-related spending over the provinces is not in proportion to the incidence of poverty in the provinces.

From these studies we can conclude that fiscal policy has not been used to improve income distribution. Moreover, direct anti-poverty spending has been very low and not well targeted. The conclusion must thus be that the main contribution fiscal policy has made to poverty reduction is through its support for growth and stability. The rapid growth of income meant also a rapid increase in government revenue, and a growing share of these resources was spent on social development. This will have helped the poor even when the distribution of these social expenditures was not particularly pro-poor.

ANNEX 9.1

Table 9.A1 *Government expenditure and revenue at constant 1988 prices (Bt billion)*

| | Primary Expenditure | | | | | |
	Current Excl. Interest Payments	Capital Expenditure	Total Primary	Interest Payments	Total Expenditure	Total Revenue
1970	50.1	25.5	75.6	5.2	80.8	60.4
1971	54.7	27.2	81.9	6.4	88.3	62.8
1972	50.2	23.7	73.9	13.3	87.2	65.5
1973	56.0	20.0	76.0	7.8	83.8	69.0
1974	53.9	13.5	67.4	7.5	74.9	82.8
1975	62.9	20.8	83.7	9.0	92.7	81.2
1976	74.5	30.3	104.7	8.5	113.2	85.5
1977	81.9	31.5	113.4	9.1	122.5	100.0
1978	99.0	32.1	131.1	9.0	140.1	110.3
1979	100.9	30.0	131.0	11.5	142.5	122.5
1980	116.8	36.7	153.5	13.4	166.9	131.8
1981	116.7	35.9	152.5	17.3	169.8	142.3
1982	132.4	37.7	170.1	20.1	190.2	140.5
1983	135.6	34.8	170.4	24.9	195.3	167.6
1984	149.5	32.0	181.4	28.5	209.9	170.8
1985	153.6	37.3	190.9	34.6	225.5	181.1
1986	153.7	34.1	187.8	38.8	226.6	188.5
1987	152.5	33.0	185.4	39.1	224.5	214.0
1988	154.2	28.7	182.9	40.2	223.1	258.2
1989	171.6	35.5	207.0	41.6	248.6	308.3
1990	185.6	49.1	234.6	35.7	270.3	365.5
1991	208.2	65.8	274.0	29.6	303.6	387.7
1992	239.6	93.1	332.7	23.9	356.6	411.9
1993	264.4	122.8	387.2	19.4	406.6	448.7
1994	277.4	136.3	413.6	16.3	429.9	505.1
1995	296.3	146.0	442.2	9.4	451.7	546.2
1996	330.7	215.8	546.6	6.2	552.7	575.8
1997	322.3	271.9	594.2	10.1	604.3	549.8
1998	325.0	163.5	488.5	11.1	499.6	425.4
1999	344.9	140.9	485.8	30.2	516.1	441.7
2000	366.5	118.2	484.8	36.6	521.4	455.4
2001	391.0	114.4	505.4	38.7	544.1	464.5
2002	406.3	121.1	527.4	40.6	568.0	521.3
2003	443.9	98.6	542.5	38.7	581.2	590.8

Table 9.A2 *Decomposition of the changes in revenue*

	$(a_i - a_0)\left(\frac{W}{Y}\right)_i$	$a_0\left[\left(\frac{W}{Y}\right)_i - \left(\frac{W}{Y}\right)_0\right]$	$(b_i - b_0)\left(\frac{Pr}{Y}\right)_i$	$b_0\left[\left(\frac{Pr}{Y}\right)_i - \left(\frac{Pr}{Y}\right)_0\right]$	$(d_i - d_0)\left(\frac{C}{Y}\right)_i$	$d_0\left[\left(\frac{C}{Y}\right)_i - \left(\frac{C}{Y}\right)_0\right]$	$(e_i - e_0)\left(\frac{M}{Y}\right)_i$	$e_0\left[\left(\frac{M}{Y}\right)_i - \left(\frac{M}{Y}\right)_0\right]$	$(h_i - h_0)$
1970–2003	0.56	0.51	1.38	1.52	2.62	−1.06	−11.01	8.62	1.17
1970–1979	0.01	0.23	0.58	0.21	1.67	−0.39	−2.78	2.17	−0.38
1979–1988	0.38	0.08	−0.42	0.77	2.01	−0.88	−0.45	0.63	−0.16
1988–1997	0.47	0.32	1.50	0.12	0.42	−0.29	−3.17	1.35	0.64
1997–2003	−0.36	−0.04	−1.80	1.93	−1.27	0.30	−0.68	0.52	0.56

Note: This table is based on the decomposition model presented in the text.

Table 9.A3 *Local governments' revenue structure (2005) (Bt million)*

	Municipalities	TAO	Pattaya	PAO	BMA	Total	%
Revenues Collected by LG	8987.2	5570.8	239.3	2290.0	9931.7	27,019.0	9.2
Taxes Collected by LG	4665.9	2837.4	150.1	1837.5	7833.5	17,325.0	5.9
Land and Building Tax	3913.7	1833.3	126.0	-	7173.2	13,046.1	4.4
Non-Tax Revenues	3504.3	2226.9	66.9	385.7	1195.3	7397.1	2.5
Charges, Fines, Permits	1556.4	747.9	47.5	68.1	658.1	3078.1	1.1
Efficiency Improvement	817.0	506.4	21.8	66.7	902.9	2314.8	0.8
Revenues Collected by CG	15,913.9	42,167.9	383.9	15,887.0	28,167.6	102,520.3	34.9
VAT	4901.6	12,905.2	96.4	4440.0	11,552.5	33,895.6	11.5
Alcohol Tax	1638.4	5903.3	12.0	-	778.5	8332.2	2.8
Excises	3748.6	13,543.4	26.3	-	1772.8	19,091.0	6.5
Vehicle Tax	-	-	-	10,914.5	5998.1	16,912.6	5.8
Land Registration Fee	5161.9	8351.0	240.6	-	6298.5	20,052.0	6.8
Allocations from CG	19,634.2	23,416.7	608.0	3052.9	2288.2	49,000.0	16.7
Sub-total before Grants	44,535.4	71,155.3	1231.3	21,229.9	40,387.4	178,539.3	60.8
Grants from CG	-	-	-	-	-	115,210.7	39.2
Total Revenues of LG	44,535.4	71,155.3	1231.3	21,229.9	40,387.4	293,750.0	100.0
CG Net Revenue	1,250,000.0	1,250,000.0	1,250,000.0	1,250,000.0	1,250,000.0	1,250,000.0	
%	3.6	5.7	0.1	1.7	3.2	23.5	

Note: LG - Local Governments; CG - Central Government; TAO - Tambol Administration Organization; PAO - Provincial Administration Organization; BMA - Bangkok Metropolitan Administration.

Source: Fiscal Policy Office

NOTES

1   This study is part of the UNDP project on 'Securing Fiscal Space for the Millennium Development Goals', organized by the Poverty Group of the Bureau for Development Policy, UNDP, New York. We are grateful to Rathin Roy and Antoine Heuty for their useful comments on an earlier draft.

2   In the case of Thailand, aid has played only a modest part. Total net ODA disbursements from all sources amounted to 1.4 per cent of GDP in 1960/61, decreased to 1.1 per cent in 1982/83 (OECD, 1985), and has since then fallen to negligible levels. We do not deal with aid in this chapter.

3   The growth over the last period is strongly depressed by the very deep fall in 1998. The average growth rate over the post-crisis years, 1999 to 2003, was 4.8 per cent per year. Thailand has not yet returned to the strong performance it showed before the crisis.

4   Over the years the poverty line has been adjusted making it difficult to compare the poverty rates of consecutive years. Still, the rapid decline in poverty reflected in Table 9.2 is a real phenomenon.

5   In this chapter we do not analyse the off-budget funds. In 2006 there were 91 funds controlled by the central government. The main ones are the Oil Fund, used to stabilize the local oil prices, and social security funds for public sector employees. The funds are financially independent; they have their own resources and the government cannot claim their surpluses or assets. Most of the funds are very small and their economic significance is not great. That is why we decided not to cover them. The current government policy is to normalize the situation by reducing the number of funds and regulating their operation.

6   The average expenditure ratio of advanced countries has increased from 10.7 per cent around 1870 to 22.8 per cent in 1937, 27.9 per cent in 1960 and 45.6 per cent in 1996 (Tanzi and Schuknecht, 2000). Table I.1 of Tanzi and Schuknecht (2000) includes data for 17 industrialized countries; in all of them the ratio increased substantially over the long run.

7   Zee's data are based on a sample of 25 OECD countries, 18 African countries, 15 Asian countries, 8 countries from the Middle East and 15 countries from Latin America.

8   Tanzi and Zee (2000) give a table with tax ratios, as a percentage of GDP, for developing countries. Compared to other developing countries and compared to developing countries in Asia, the ratios of personal and corporate income tax to GDP are relatively low, while that of indirect taxes is higher. The ratio of taxes on international trade to GDP is comparable to those of other countries.

9   With the financial crisis the share rebounded as the modern sector suffered the brunt of the crisis. In the years 2000 to 2003 the share stays at around 28 per cent.

10   About 17 million workers are classified as own account workers or unpaid family members.

11   World Bank (1986) shows that in the period 1980 to 1984 about 3.5 million persons filed a personal income tax return. At that time the labour force consisted of 26 million workers, of which about 6.5 million were in formal employment. It would thus appear that personal income tax coverage has not kept pace with the rapid growth in the number of formal sector workers.

12   It is not unlikely that the revolving village loans and the debt moratorium will lead to, possibly considerable, default. Many villages may have assumed that the Bt1 million was a grant rather than a loan and farmers believe that the moratorium was a debt forgiven rather than a debt suspended.

13   The scatter between the natural logarithms of real balances and real GDP is almost a straight line with a correlation coefficient of 0.99. The correlation between the revenue from the inflation tax and the rate of inflation is 0.53.

14   Agenor and Montiel (1996, p113) present a table that shows that the average revenue from the inflation tax is 1.2 per cent of GDP per year for Asian countries during the 1980s. Thailand's revenue in that period is only 0.6 per cent of GDP, the lowest of the Asian countries recorded in the table.

15   In absolute numbers the total outstanding government debt fell from Bt413 billion in 1986 to Bt174 billion in 1996.

16   If the Government expenditure to GDP ratio is at 18 per cent, this rule implies that the fiscal deficit has to be less than 3.6 per cent of GDP. Figure 9.5 shows that this limit was occasionally exceeded, but never systematically.

17   Whether the debt/GDP ratio rises or falls depends on the relative size of the primary deficit, the growth rate and the interest rate. If the primary deficit is zero, any growth rate in excess of the interest rate will imply a falling debt ratio. If there is a small primary deficit, the growth rate has to exceed the interest rate to have sustainable debt. If the primary deficit is large, say 3 per cent of GDP, then, for reasonable levels of the interest rate, the growth rate would have to be unrealistically large to maintain debt sustainability.

18   Or the cost of oil imports had increased from 4.6 per cent of GDP in 1978 to 8.6 per cent in 1986.

19   The third LOI (February 1998) projected that, due to the weak economy and the sharp depreciation, the fiscal balance would turn out at a deficit of 2 per cent of GDP rather than the target of a surplus of 1 per cent. This time, the IMF accepted that the shortfall of the fiscal balance target need not be fully offset, but still insisted on measures that would contain the deficit at 1.5 per cent rather than the projected 2 per cent of GDP. Only the fourth LOI (May 1998) moved to a more expansionary fiscal policy. By that time a substantial current account surplus had emerged and this created the room for an adjustment of the fiscal target. In particular, expenditure on social safety nets increased.

20   In 2001 Bt57 billion was spent on the programmes (which would be equivalent to about 1 per cent of GDP) and for 2002 an expenditure of Bt92 billion was foreseen (*The Nation*, 3 July 2002).

21   The correlation coefficient between current inflation and the budget balance lagged one year is indeed negative, but only -0.07.

22   Jansen (1995) built a small macroeconometric model in which private investments are explained by an output gap variable, public investment, FDI inflows, the real exchange rate and the external debt burden. Public investment has a significant positive impact. Jitsuchon and Sussangkarn (1993) constructed a three gap model and found a positive relationship between public and private investment.

REFERENCES

Agenor, P-R. and Montiel, P. J. (1996) *Development Macroeconomics*, Princeton University Press, Princeton, NJ

Bank of Thailand (1985) *Annual Economic Report, 1985*, Bank of Thailand, Bangkok

Bank of Thailand (2004) *Annual Economic Report 2004*, Bank of Thailand, Bangkok

Brown, A. (1997) 'Locating working-class power', in K. Hewison (ed) *Political Change in Thailand, Democracy and Participation*, Routledge, London, pp163–178

Brun, J-F., Chambas, G., Combes, J-L., Dulbecco, P., Gastambide, A., Guérineau, S., Guillaumont, S. and Gaziosi Rota, G. (2006) 'Evaluation of fiscal space in developing countries', Concept Paper, CERDI – University d'Auvergne, Clermont-Ferrand, France, www.undp.org/poverty/docs/prm/ESPACEFISCALCERDIENGLISHFINALJune1st06.doc

Campos, J. E. and Root, H. L. (1996) *The Key to the Asian Miracle, Making Shared Growth Credible*, The Brookings Institution, Washington DC

Dixon, C. (1999) *The Thai Economy, Uneven Development and Internationalization*, Routledge, London

Easterly, W. (1999) 'When is fiscal adjustment an illusion?', *Economic Policy*, vol 14, no 28, pp55–86

Fan, S. and Rao, N. (2003) 'Public spending in developing countries, trends, determination and impact', EPTD Discussion Paper 99, International Food Policy Research Institute (IFPRI), Washington DC

Fiscal Policy Research Institute (FPRI) (2003) *Thailand's Fiscal Stance Analysis*, Fiscal Policy Office, Ministry of Finance, Bangkok

IMF (2002) *Thailand: Selected Issues and Statistical Appendix*, IMF, Washington DC

IMF (2003) 'Public debt in emerging markets: is it too high?', in *World Economic Outlook 2003*, IMF, Washington DC, Chapter 3

Ingram, J. (1971) *Economic Change in Thailand, 1950–1970*, Stanford University Press, Stanford, CA

Jansen, K. (1995) 'The macroeconomic effects of direct foreign investment: The case of Thailand', *World Development*, vol 23, no 2, pp193–210

Jansen, K. (1997) *External Finance in Thailand's Development, an Interpretation of Thailand's Growth Boom*, Macmillan, London

Jansen, K. (2000) 'Thailand in crisis, two crises compared', *Chulalongkorn Journal of Economics*, vol 12, no 3, September, pp1–25

Jansen, K. (2001) 'Thailand, the making of a miracle?', *Development and Change*, vol 32, no 2, pp343–370

Jansen, K. (2004) 'The scope for fiscal policy: A case study of Thailand', *Development Policy Review*, vol 22, no 2, pp207–228

Jitsuchon, S. and Sussangkarn, C. (1993) 'Thailand', in L. Taylor (ed) *The Rocky Road to Reform*, MIT Press, Cambridge, MA, pp149–170

Krongkaew, M. (1993) 'Poverty and income distribution', in P. Warr (ed) *The Thai Economy in Transition*, Cambridge University Press, Cambridge, pp 401–437

Maddison, A. (2001) *The World Economy, a Millennial Perspective*, OECD, Paris

Manarungsan, S. (1989) '*Economic development in Thailand, 1850-1950: Responses to the challenge of the world economy*', unpublished PhD thesis, University of Groningen, Groningen, The Netherlands

NESDB/UN (2004) *Thailand Millennium Development Goals Report 2004*, Office of the National Economic and Social Development Board, United Nations Country Team in Thailand, Bangkok

OECD (1985) *Twenty-five Years of Development Cooperation, a Review*, OECD, Paris

Phongpaichit, P. and Baker, C. (1998) *Thailand's Boom and Bust*, Silkworm Books, Chiang Mai

Root, H. (1998) 'Distinctive institutions in the rise of industrial Asia', in H. S. Rowen (ed) *Behind East Asian Growth, the Political and Social Foundations of Prosperity*, Routledge, London, pp60–77

Sahasakul, C. (1993) 'Fiscal policy', in P. Warr (ed) *The Thai Economy in Transition*, Cambridge University Press, Cambridge, Chapter 6

Sawitree, A., Chensavasdijai, V., Manvichachai, B. and Meeyam, V. (2002) 'Fiscal sustainability, inflation targets and the appropriate policy mix', Paper presented at the Bank of Thailand Symposium, 21–22 August 2002

Sturm, J. E. (2001) 'Determinants of public capital spending in less-developed countries', CCSO Working Paper, CCSO Centre for Economic Research, University of Groningen, Groningen, The Netherlands

Tanzi, V. and Schuknecht, L. (2000) *Public Spending in the 20th Century, A Global Perspective*, Cambridge University Press, Cambridge

Tanzi, V. and Zee, H. (2000) 'Tax policy for emerging markets: Developing countries', IMF Working Paper WP/00/35, IMF, Washington DC

Unger, D. (1998) *Building Social Capital in Thailand: Fibers, Finance and Infrastructure*, Cambridge University Press, Cambridge

Warr, P. and Nidhiprabha, B. (1996) *Thailand's Macroeconomic Miracle, Stable Adjustment and Sustained Growth*, World Bank, Washington DC

Warr, P. and Sarntisart, I. (2004) *Poverty Targeting in Thailand*, Asian Development Bank Institute, Tokyo

World Bank (1986) *Thailand: Growth with Stability, a Challenge for the Sixth Plan Period: a Country Economic Report*, World Bank, Washington DC

World Bank (1993) *The East Asian Miracle, Economic Growth and Public Policy*, Oxford University Press, Oxford

World Bank (2000) *Thailand, Public Finance in Transition*, World Bank Report, World Bank, Washington DC

World Bank (2005) *Thailand Economic Monitor, November 2005*, World Bank Thailand Office, Bangkok

World Bank (2006) *Thailand Economic Monitor, April 2006*, World Bank Thailand Office, Bangkok

Zee, H. H. (1996) 'Empirics of cross-country tax revenue comparisons', *World Development*, vol 24, no 10, pp1659–1671

10

Plenty of Room? Fiscal Space in a Resource-Abundant Economy: The Case of Venezuela

María Antonia Moreno and Francisco Rodríguez[1]

INTRODUCTION

It may seem odd to write about fiscal space in an oil-abundant economy. It could certainly be argued that resource-rich economies have, if anything, an embarrassment of resources at their disposal to use in the fight to achieve poverty reduction. The typical problems faced by developing economies in financing the fight against poverty should, at the very least, be severely attenuated in mineral-rich economies. The problem for these economies, a sceptic may assert, is not finding more resources but using them more efficiently.

The Venezuelan case may seem an even stranger place to start. This oil-rich South American nation is not exactly experiencing a shortfall of resource availability. Buoyed by the seven-fold increase in oil prices experienced since the late 1990s, the Venezuelan government has embarked on a set of spending initiatives that have increased real per capita government spending by 84.7 per cent since 1998. This has included an allotment of $4.1 billion (Bs8.1 trillion) to the administration's hallmark social programmes (the Misiones, or Missions) (República Bolivariana de Venezuela, 2006), and a pledge of at least $3.0 billion in 2005 to aid neighbouring countries (*New York Times*, 2006). Venezuelan fiscal policy is not, currently, showing signs of operating under fiscal duress.

Despite these characteristics of oil abundant economies in general, and of the present Venezuelan situation in particular, we believe that there is much to learn from analysing the set of issues raised by the fiscal space debate in this economy. We will argue that oil-abundant countries are no less prone to facing shortfalls of revenues to direct in the fight against poverty than non-resource abundant economies. Indeed, they commonly experience high poverty rates despite their high levels of income. Many oil-abundant economies have also had significant experiences of increases in their fiscal space that have not shown up as improvements in poverty or well-being. These examples can be used to understand what are the pitfalls and possible mistakes that countries can face when they attempt to direct increases in available resources towards poverty reduction.

SETTING THE SCENE: RICH IN OIL BUT...

We start by looking at the prevalence of fiscal difficulties in oil-abundant countries. Figure 10.1 illustrates the relationship between budget surpluses and oil dependence for 112 countries as a function of their dependence on fuel exports. The figure displays a residual scatter plot of budget surpluses on a measure of oil export dependence (fuel exports as a percentage of GDP) after controlling for an initial level of income and a set of continent dummies. Both measures are taken from the World Development Indicators Database (World Bank, 2006) and correspond to averages for the period 1990 to 2003. As the figure shows, oil-abundant countries are not likely to have higher budget surpluses. Indeed, a few highly resource-dependent countries, such as Kuwait, Oman and the Republic of Congo, have substantially higher deficits than would be expected, given their level of income and their geographic location. Therefore, it is apparent that oil abundant countries, on average, face fiscal difficulties that are as significant as those faced by non-oil-abundant economies.[2]

Figure 10.2 illustrates the fact that oil-abundant countries do not necessarily do better in the fight against poverty than non-oil-abundant countries. Similarly to the previous exercise, Figure 10.2 displays the partial scatter plot of poverty headcount ratio (the percentage of the population below a set income level) against oil export dependence, after controlling for the log of per capita GDP and a set of continent dummies. Here again we see that oil exporting countries do not do a better job of fighting poverty than other economies. On average, a majority of oil-abundant countries have poverty headcount ratios that are as high as those of other countries, given their initial GDP and geographic location. Among these countries, it is interesting to see that Venezuela (along with Algeria and Nigeria) have positive residuals, indicating a lower than average efficiency at fighting poverty, given their available oil resources.

Figures 10.3 and 10.4 explore these facts in greater detail for Venezuela. As Figure 10.3 shows, budget deficits are not a rare phenomenon in Venezuela. Despite deriving

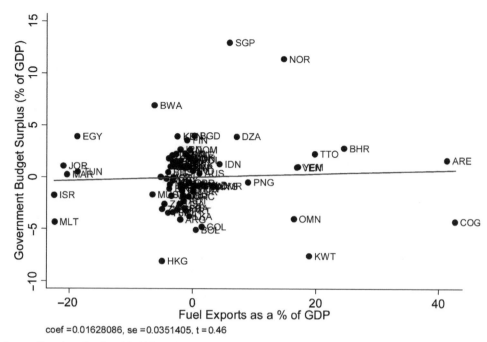

coef =0.01628086, se =0.0351405, t =0.46

Source: Based on data from World Bank (2006)

Figure 10.1 *Budget surpluses and oil dependence*

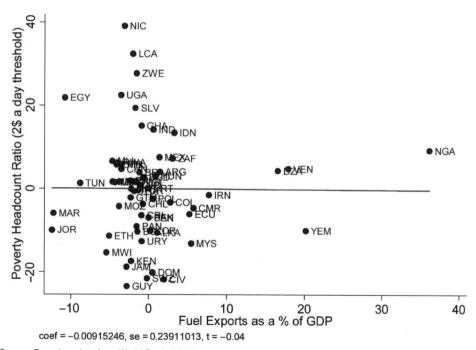

coef = −0.00915246, se = 0.23911013, t = −0.04

Source: Based on data from World Bank (2006)

Figure 10.2 *Poverty and oil dependence*

85.9 per cent of its merchandise export revenue from fuel exports during the period 1972 to 2003 and occupying the position of richest nation in the region for a good part of this period, Venezuela experienced fiscal deficits on 16 of the 31 years covered by this period, including 10 of the last 12 years. Indeed, according to the IMF statistics, as late as 2003 Venezuela did not show any improvement in its fiscal position as a result of the recent upturn in oil prices. In Venezuela's case, an abundance of oil revenues has not led to erasing concerns over fiscal sustainability.

Figure 10.4 displays the recent evolution of poverty in Venezuela, measured as the proportion of persons below the national poverty and extreme poverty lines. Table 10.1 presents a set of alternative poverty measures, based on the 1 and 2 PPP adjusted dollar-a-day World Bank thresholds. As these numbers show, there is little sign of a substantial improvement in poverty trends of the magnitude that would be necessary to meet the MDG of reducing extreme poverty to one-half of its 1990 level. Although the period is marked by a huge increase in 2002 associated with the February 2002 devaluation and the April 2002 and December 2002 general strikes, followed by a subsequent decline, there is no evident long-term trend. There has been some decrease in the total incidence of poverty between 1999 and 2005, from 42.8 per cent of the population to 37.9 per cent for total poverty, and from 16.6 per cent to 15.3 per cent for extreme poverty. This is indeed what one might expect given that per capita income increased by 10.9 per cent over the time period covered by Figure 10.4. The income elasticities implicit in these reductions (1.05 and 0.71) are not remarkably high. What is surprising about this behaviour is that it has occurred during a period of growing oil revenues. As Figure 10.5 shows, fiscal oil revenues per capita multiplied fourfold between 1998 and 2005. The lack of a significant response in the poverty rate to this huge increase in oil revenues underlines the need for systematic thinking about the mechanisms and strategies that must be implemented to ensure that greater oil wealth reaches the poor.

Whether Venezuela is likely to achieve the first MDG of reducing extreme poverty to half its 1990 value is a matter of dispute, in part because there is little certainty as to what the 1990 poverty level was. It was only in 1994 that the Venezuelan Households Survey started collecting data on all components of income, so that a precise estimate of the incidence of poverty in 1990 is hard to obtain. The data reported by World Bank (2006), based on labour income, show substantial increases in all poverty rates between 1989 and 1995, suggesting that the first MDG would be extremely difficult to attain given the post-1995 evolution observed in Figure 10.4. Similar calculations have been used recently by ECLAC (2005), which reports Venezuela and Argentina as the only two countries that have lost ground in the fight against extreme poverty. According to ECLAC's estimates, the 1990 poverty rate was 14.6 per cent, making the MDG 7.3 per cent, while extreme poverty in Venezuela in 2004 stood at 22.7 per cent. The Venezuelan National Institute of Statistics (INE) has claimed that the 1990 poverty rate was 24 per cent, making the goal of halving it to 12 per cent attainable, but the source of this estimate is unclear (Agencia Bolivariana de Noticias, 2005). A more sensible

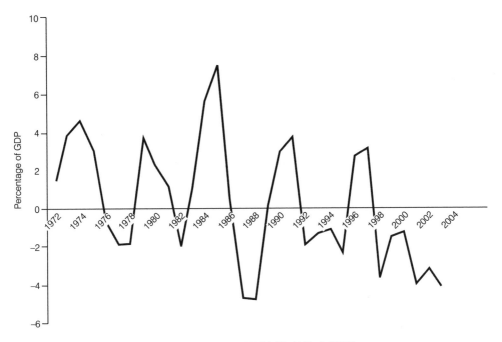

Source: Based on International Monetary Fund (2006a, 2006b); World Bank (2006)

Figure 10.3 *Consolidated central government surplus, Venezuela, 1972–2003 (% of GDP)*

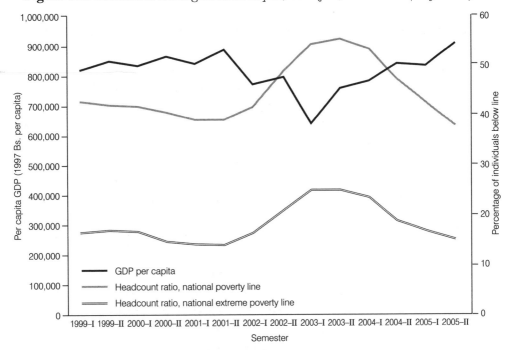

Source: Based on Instituto Nacional de Estadística (2006); Banco Central de Venezuela (2006)

Figure 10.4 *Poverty and per capita GDP, official estimates, Venezuela 1998–2005*

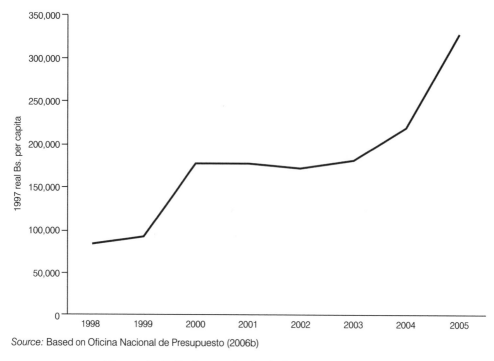

Source: Based on Oficina Nacional de Presupuesto (2006b)

Figure 10.5 *Real per capita fiscal oil revenues, 1998–2005*

approach may be to take 50 per cent of the 1995 value as a reasonable approximation of the objective, given that it is unlikely that the 1995 poverty level was significantly lower than that of 1990 and that we can adequately compare with the post-1994 series.[3] As shown in the last column of Table 10.1, barring exceptional progress in the next decade, Venezuela seems unlikely to reach this target.

In sum, studying fiscal space in a resource-abundant economy such as Venezuela is useful for two reasons. First, it allows us to understand the mechanisms through which even governments that have the economic possibilities for devoting substantial resources to poverty reduction fail to do so. Second, it allows us to identify specific reforms that can help to reallocate resources towards the fight against poverty in this type of economy. For these reasons, the focus will not be just on understanding Venezuela per se, but rather on drawing lessons that can be relevant for other economies, both resource abundant and non-resource abundant.

The source of Venezuela's failure to devote resources to poverty reduction, we will argue, is deeply rooted in its economic history. As oil revenues grew during the 20th century, Venezuela developed as an inherently weak state with restricted capacity to tax the internal economy. Our starting point is thus a brief history of the development of Venezuelan taxation institutions, which we undertake in the next section. Then we present a comparative analysis of the characteristics of the Venezuelan tax system and indicate the possible reforms that could allow resource mobilization for pro-poor

Table 10.1 $1 and $2 a day poverty indicators, 1995–2004, CPI based

	1995		1996		1997		1998		1999		2000		2001		2002		2003		2004		2005		50% of 1995 Rate
	-I	-II	-I	-II	-I	-II	-I	-II	-I	-II	-I	-II	-I	-II	-I	-II	-I	-II	-I	-II	-I	-II	
Households																							
$2 a day threshold																							
Headcount	0.3486	0.3549	0.4445	0.4781	0.4143	0.3537	0.3721	0.3259	0.3603	0.3832	0.4038	0.3889	0.3639	0.3478	0.3764	0.4149	0.4869	0.4640	0.4531	0.3975	0.3726	0.3237	0.1759
Poverty gap	0.1412	0.1474	0.1964	0.2094	0.1815	0.1431	0.1567	0.1355	0.1447	0.1635	0.1789	0.1571	0.1481	0.1431	0.1610	0.1858	0.2271	0.2139	0.1995	0.1677	0.1648	0.1493	0.0721
Poverty severity	0.0794	0.0820	0.1159	0.1261	0.1061	0.0804	0.0893	0.0771	0.0821	0.0959	0.1079	0.0896	0.0837	0.0806	0.0943	0.1105	0.1387	0.1283	0.1182	0.0965	0.1003	0.0942	0.0403
$1 a day threshold																							
Headcount	0.1212	0.1253	0.1808	0.2116	0.1684	0.1261	0.1369	0.1160	0.1321	0.1454	0.1638	0.1390	0.1283	0.1211	0.1485	0.1665	0.2200	0.1956	0.1868	0.1491	0.1486	0.1324	0.0616
Poverty gap	0.0464	0.0463	0.0731	0.0822	0.0660	0.0470	0.0529	0.0461	0.0487	0.0601	0.0700	0.0536	0.0495	0.0472	0.0585	0.0700	0.0910	0.0816	0.0746	0.0587	0.0661	0.0661	0.0232
Poverty severity	0.0270	0.0252	0.0428	0.0476	0.0377	0.0286	0.0310	0.0273	0.0291	0.0365	0.0447	0.0319	0.0286	0.0276	0.0355	0.0422	0.0547	0.0482	0.0441	0.0346	0.0451	0.0451	0.0131
Individuals																							
$2 a day threshold																							
Headcount	0.4051	0.4138	0.5029	0.5284	0.4662	0.4076	0.4260	0.3795	0.4196	0.4433	0.4679	0.4457	0.4214	0.4067	0.4364	0.4794	0.5548	0.5328	0.5198	0.4619	0.4303	0.3754	0.2047
Poverty gap	0.1678	0.1728	0.2274	0.2380	0.2076	0.1694	0.1806	0.1586	0.1695	0.1911	0.2072	0.1848	0.1747	0.1684	0.1897	0.2178	0.2658	0.2509	0.2360	0.1992	0.1907	0.1712	0.0852
Poverty severity	0.0943	0.0958	0.1347	0.1440	0.1215	0.0961	0.1021	0.0897	0.0951	0.1111	0.1237	0.1053	0.0987	0.0944	0.1107	0.1296	0.1639	0.1513	0.1408	0.1149	0.1138	0.1061	0.0475
$1 a day threshold																							
Headcount	0.1485	0.1511	0.2168	0.2408	0.1965	0.1546	0.1607	0.1382	0.1570	0.1722	0.1918	0.1680	0.1563	0.1469	0.1789	0.2008	0.2652	0.2386	0.2269	0.1823	0.1750	0.1519	0.0749
Poverty gap	0.0545	0.0535	0.0850	0.0944	0.0752	0.0564	0.0592	0.0525	0.0552	0.0680	0.0789	0.0623	0.0579	0.0544	0.0676	0.0819	0.1087	0.0970	0.0894	0.0696	0.0723	0.0723	0.0270
Poverty severity	0.0302	0.0280	0.0481	0.0536	0.0418	0.0312	0.0331	0.0299	0.0309	0.0399	0.0485	0.0354	0.0320	0.0303	0.0391	0.0476	0.0638	0.0555	0.0512	0.0392	0.0448	0.0477	0.0145

Note: Poverty thresholds use 1993 PPP-adjusted World Bank threshold of $1.08 and $2.16, adjusted for domestic inflation using CPI from Banco Central de Venezuela (2007).

Source: Own calculations using Instituto Nacional de Estadística (various years).

policies. In the subsequent section we discuss the political economy of the Venezuelan budget process and its interaction with existing fiscal rules. We argue that this interaction leads to weak incentives for coherent inter temporal planning and substantially affects the quality of public resource allocation. We also suggest avenues for the reform of the budget planning process that could lead to a freeing up of resources that could be devoted to the achievement of the MDGs. We then discuss a glaring inefficiency of the Venezuelan fiscal system. Despite the Venezuelan state's net creditor position vis-à-vis the financial sector, its poor deposit and credit management policies lead to a transfer of more than 2 per cent of GDP in net interest payments to private banks. The subsequent two sections turn to the analysis of the expenditure side. The first of these discusses Venezuela's systematic policy of cutting back infrastructure investments to pay for fiscal adjustments since the mid-1980s, while the second deals with recent attempts to devote more resources to the fight against poverty through the government's landmark Misiones social programmes and discusses their effectiveness. The final section provides some tentative concluding comments.

A SHORT HISTORY OF VENEZUELAN FISCAL POLICY (OR HOW NOT TO BUILD A TAX SYSTEM)

We are a budgetivorous people. And how not to be so if the only economically sound foundation that we have is the budget? The budget determines among us political booms and crises... meanwhile, our economy becomes deformed and every day more subordinate to the contingent solution of oil. Oil inflates the budget, is what the body is to the shadow. We live leaning on a shadow. (Valmore Rodríguez, Panorama, 24 June 1940, cited by Sosa Abascal, 1995, p17)

Venezuela's 19th century was remarkably unstable, even by Latin American standards.[4] One observer chronicled 39 national revolutions and 127 uprisings of different sorts between Independence in 1830 and 1903. Another calculated that Venezuela has enjoyed barely 16 years of peace while suffering 66 years of civil war and insurrection since Independence (Caballero, 1993). This situation began to be reversed through the gradual process of centralizing economic and political power, which started during the regime of Antonio Guzmán Blanco (1870–1888) and continued through the Andean Hegemony period (1899–1908). Understanding this centralization is the key to understanding how Venezuela developed its present-day budgetary institutions.

Antonio Guzmán Blanco was the first Venezuelan president to considerably curtail and subordinate the interests of regional *caudillos* (leaders) to those of the central government. He was able to do this by constructing a complex alliance between business groups and loyal *caudillos*, which worked because it was able to generate a marked increase in tariff revenues, which accounted for more than 90 per cent of government fiscal revenues at the time. Guzmán's ingenious plan for coalition building started with the virtual privatization of customs collection. Shortly after taking power in April 1870, he created the Compañía de Crédito, a privately owned firm with minority government participation whose main purpose was to pay off outstanding government debts. The control of the Compañía de Crédito was firmly in the hands of representatives of established trading houses. The revenues of the company, in turn, came from its entitlement to directly receive 85 per cent of customs revenues. This system worked well because the Venezuelan government's main source of credit came from these same trading houses.[5]

In order to convince local *caudillos* to buy into the deal, Guzmán had to ensure that they could receive a continuous stream of rents once they had given up control of customs houses. In order to do so, Guzmán created a set of singular institutions. Perhaps the most important one, which survives to this day, was the Situado Constitucional, a rule for the allocation of a fixed fraction of government revenues among regional governments. Guzmán also started a massive public works programme directed through the Juntas de Fomento, boards that directly administered public investment projects and on which local caudillos and financiers were given seats (Pino Iturrieta, 1997).

Guzmán's reforms were just the first step in the construction of a centralized state apparatus that would characterize Venezuela during the 20th century. In order for economic centralization to become an effective counterweight to the anarchic forces of the *caudillos*, it would have to be accompanied by an effective process of political consolidation. This would take place with the creation of professional armed forces, buttressed by a patronage-based system for the satisfaction of individual demands by the political apparatus of the state. Such a process would occur during the dictatorship of Juan Vicente Gómez (1908–1935). By the time of his death in 1935, Venezuela had solidly established a politically centralized state, reinforced by armed forces whose institutional design was particularly propitious for stability, and with abundant economic resources that could be directed toward sustaining power.

Such a state was a formidable opponent for the dictatorship's adversaries in their attempts to promote the adoption of democratic institutions. The innovation of the emerging political leaders was the creation of political parties with broad memberships that could defeat the patronage-based structure of the state by reproducing it. The success of Acción Democrática (AD) and Comité de Organización Política Electoral Independiente (COPEI), the two dominant political parties in the post-1958 20th century, came from being able to substitute the patronage-based web constructed and strengthened by the governments of the Andean hegemony with an eerily similar system of loyalties and favours articulated through populist political discourse and practices.

Unlike many other populist parties in the region, the Peruvian Alianza Popular Revolucionária Americana, the Argentinian Justicialistas or the Brazilian Workers' Party, AD and COPEI became the dominant institutionalized actors within a stable political system. They arrived in government with a broad membership base that was ready to occupy the positions of power that had been left in place by the post-gomecista (after Gómez) system, taking middle and lower positions in public administration that formed the basis of the system of rewards of the post-gomecista political structure. According to the Venezuelan historian, Germán Carrera Damas, when modern political parties like AD and COPEI emerge:

> *They do it in an atmosphere not at all propitious for the adoption of clearly institution-alized forms. One could not expect less than their mediation by practices traditionally rooted in Venezuelan society. And perhaps when we speak of the parties of the 1940s, we should think fundamentally of a civil caudillo surrounded by a group of close collaborators who attempt to counteract the inheritance of social atomization, the inheritance of basic patronage obligations.* (Carrera Damas, 1975, pD-2)

The control of the Venezuelan political process by populist parties with broad member-ships and internal patronage networks was obviously made possible to a great extent by the huge amount of oil resources that the Venezuelan economy had at its disposal start-ing in the 1920s. By 1948 just the value added of the petroleum industry is 2.37 times as large as the 1920 GDP, and 1.73 times as large as what GDP would have been if Venezuela had grown at the same rates as the rest of Latin America. By the early 1950s more than one-third of GDP came directly from oil production, and much of the rest was generated or made possible by the existence of large oil-derived foreign exchange earnings. This phenomenon is the main reason why AD and COPEI were to attain the level of dominance that similar populist parties in the region were unable to. Venezuela had the resources to pay for a huge expansion of public employment that enabled these parties to reward their members and set the basis for a stable governance system.

The mechanisms through which the Venezuelan political system consolidated its institutional stability, and the form in which these mechanisms depended on the use of fiscal resources has been studied in depth by various Venezuelan political scientists, among them Rey (1987), Urbaneja (1992) and Stambouli (2002). As these authors emphasize, Venezuelan politics would be considerably affected by two formative experi-ences for the main political parties. The first was the short period in power of AD from 1945 to 1948 (the Trienio), where the inability to forge alliances with opponents led to a military coup followed by a ten-year dictatorship. The second was the need to fight against a Cuban-financed guerrilla movement as well as various threats of right wing coups in the early 1960s. The principal political actors after 1958 directed their energies towards one fundamental objective, preserving the stability of the regime (Rey, 1987).

The emphasis on regime preservation would engineer the two basic principles that would orient public decisions during the democratic era: an obsession with consensus and an aversion to conflict (Urbaneja, 1992). The first principle embodies continuous attempts to ensure that no sector of society feels its interests are repeatedly and enduringly ignored, while the second implied a willingness to pay high costs to avoid relevant sectors of society from becoming adversaries of the system. What emerged is what Venezuelan political scientists have called the Social System of Negotiation, the key function of which was to channel the distinct social demands and interests, following 'the golden rule of political stability: to avoid too many people getting angry on the same day' (Urbaneja, 1992, p228).

By the mid-20th century, Venezuela had a state that reflected the historical influences just described. It displayed three vital characteristics that would have a profound effect on its capacity to manage public finances. In the first place, it was a highly centralized state in which state and municipal governments played minor and even decorative roles. Second, state expenditures were significantly biased towards public employment and away from public investment. Third, the state was highly dependent on oil revenues and had failed to impose significant tax rates on domestic firms or individuals, effectively redistributing oil rents towards the private sector in the form of lower tax rates.

The acute centralization of the Venezuelan state can be observed in the high degree of vertical fiscal imbalances between the central government and sub-national governments. As shown in Figure 10.6, the Venezuelan states receive 83 per cent of their revenues from the central government – the third highest level in the region and considerably higher than both the Latin American and OECD means (52 per cent and 42 per

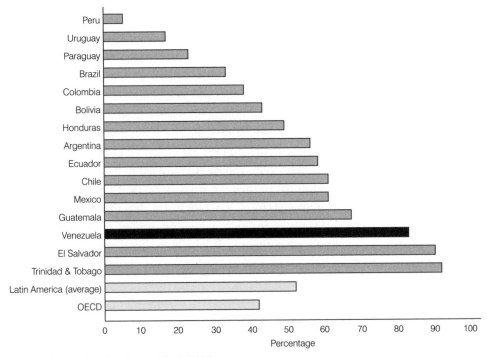

Source: Inter-American Development Bank (1997)

Figure 10.6 *Transfers as a percentage of sub-national government revenues*

Table 10.2 *Source of revenues for Venezuelan entidades federales (%)*

Year	Constitutional Situado	Intergovernmental Decentralization Fund (FIDES)	Law of Special Economic Assignments	Assignments to Cover Transferred Responsibilities	Total Transfers	Own Incomes	Other Sources
1989	98	0	0	0	98	1	1
1990	96.3	0	0	0	96.3	0.5	3.2
1991	94.7	0	0	0	94.7	4.3	1
1992	94.8	0	0	0	94.8	3	2.2
1993	92.8	n.a	0	0	n.a	4.8	n.a
1994	81.6	n.a	0	1.6	n.a	9.1	n.a
1995	83.9	n.a	0	6.9	n.a	3.2	n.a
1996	71.8	4.6	0	9.1	85.5	1.3	13.2
1997	58.6	5.8	2.3	11.3	78	1.5	20.5
1998	52.7	8.5	8.8	11.5	81.5	0.7	17.8
1999	65.3	9.1	11.5	11.9	97.8	1.2	1
Average 1989–1999	80.95	3.50	2.05	4.75	90.83	2.78	7.49

Note: Between 1993 and 1995 the Venezuelan government did not separately report FIDES allocations.

Source: Based on Barrios (2000); Oficina Nacional de Presupuesto (various years(a))

cent, respectively). Table 10.2 shows that this phenomenon is particularly acute for Venezuelan states (*entidades federales*), which commonly receive up to 98 per cent of their revenues from government transfers. Table 10.2 also illustrates the historical permanence of the Situado, which, until 1989, supplied almost all the *entidades'* revenues, and still supplies approximately two thirds of it. Guzmán Blanco's invention may well turn out to have been the longest lasting fiscal institution of Venezuelan history.

The flip side of these significant vertical imbalances is a political equilibrium in which sub-national governments depend on, and continuously lobby the central government for, increases in transfers, and the central government has no interest in giving up the power it gains from this dependence. The one attempt to modify this equilibrium, the set of political decentralization reforms initiated in 1989 by the Carlos Andrés Pérez administration (1989–1992), appears to have led to a significant collapse in the power base of the traditional parties (Penfold-Becerra, 1999). It is not then surprising that the current administration has blocked a decentralization project, approved by the National Assembly in 2001, which attempted to devolve greater taxation capacity to sub-national governments.[6] While this political equilibrium persists, regional governments have little interest in strengthening tax collection. We return to this point later.

The bias towards public employment is illustrated in Figure 10.7, which shows that Venezuela has the third largest share of public employment in the region. This is despite a significant decline in the public employment share from the 1980s, when it reached highs of more than 22 per cent.[7] According to census figures, Venezuelan employment growth was precipitous, with the public sector's share of employment going from 3.37 per cent in 1941 to 18.69 per cent in 1971, and to 25.77 per cent by 1981 (Banco Central

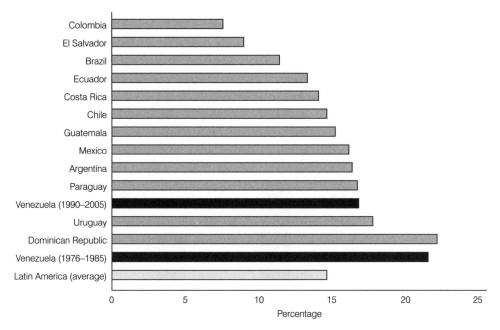

Note: Comparison covers Latin American countries with populations of more 3 million persons.
Source: Based on International Labour Organization (2006); Instituto Nacional de Estadística (2006)

Figure 10.7 *Fraction of employees in public sector employment, Latin America, 1990–2005*

de Venezuela, 1989). These trends were also reflected in other state action, such as the creation of decentralized quasi-autonomous entities within the public sector. Between 1916 and 1957, 31 of these institutes were created, or just under 1 a year. From 1957 to 1970, 102 new institutes were created, at a rate of almost 8 per year. Between 1970 and 1980, the number increased to 240, or 24 per year, with a staggering 90 new institutes created in 1980 alone (Kornblith and Maignón, 1985).

This bias is not only reflected in the aggregate employment figures. Venezuelan public employment legislation also became heavily slanted towards the protection of employment. The 1975 Law of Administrative Career guaranteed job stability to all public employees except in the case of gross and repeated violations of codes of conduct, and prohibited any type of wage cuts except those implemented by consensus between the employer and employee. The end result was a remarkable downward rigidity in public employment and wages that would make future fiscal adjustments rely on cutbacks in the provision of non-labour intensive public goods.

Venezuela's low levels of public infrastructure investment, shown in Figure 10.8, perhaps best exemplify just how lopsided the composition of public expenditures became. We have used data for the period 1981 to 1985, the earliest available, in order to avoid distorting the comparison by the effect of fiscal adjustments in Venezuela and the region during the late 1980s and 1990s. What the figure shows is striking. Despite an overabundance of oil revenues, Venezuela was significantly under-investing in public

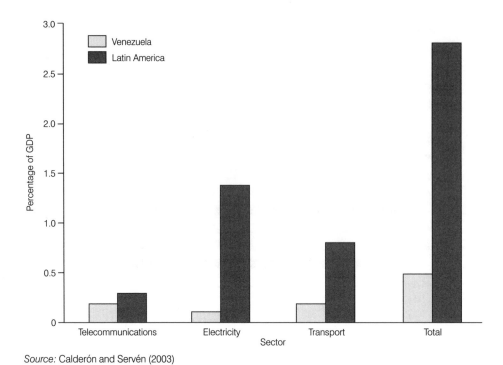

Source: Calderón and Servén (2003)

Figure 10.8 *Public infrastructure investment in Venezuela and Latin America, 1981–1985*

infrastructure in the early 1980s, while at the same time it was experiencing a vertiginous increase in public employment.

Figure 10.9 illustrates one consequence of oil dependence. At first sight, this figure, which represents central government expenditures as a percentage of GDP, appears unremarkable. Venezuela's average expenditure share for the 1990s of 18.5 per cent is nearly identical to the region average of 18.7 per cent (which is low in comparison to the rest of the world). The comparison starts to become interesting once we realize that approximately half of these expenditures are paid for from the profits of the state-owned oil company (Figure 10.10). In other words, Venezuela appears to have chosen to spend all its oil revenues in sustaining lower than average levels of internal taxation compared with other Latin American countries, instead of devoting it to higher levels of spending.

How did this striking policy choice come about? In his 1957 book, Rómulo Betancourt, the founding leader of AD who would occupy the presidency during the periods 1945 to 1948 and 1959 to 1964, sets out to explain the 1945 decision to reduce taxes on the domestic economy as a response to the greater availability of oil revenues:

> *This fiscal policy responded to a well-defined orientation and was the necessary touch-stone to demonstrate how we wanted to realize social justice and increase national capitalization at the same time. If the taxes imposed on the most profitable economic*

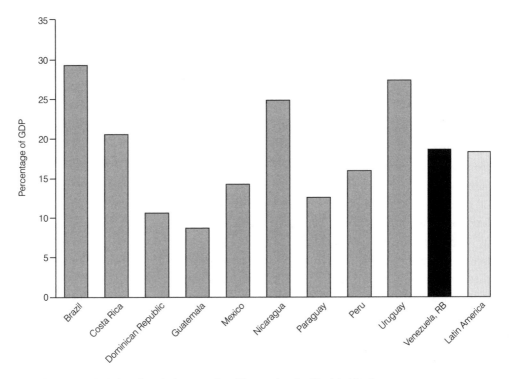

Note: Comparison includes oil producing countries with more than 3 million inhabitants.

Source: World Bank (2006)

Figure 10.9 *Central government expenditures, 1990–1999 (% of GDP)*

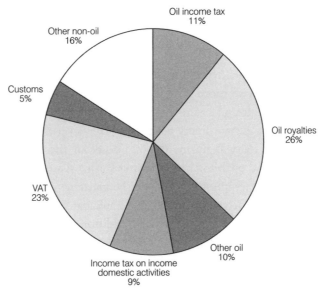

Source: Oficina Nacional de Presupuesto (2006b)

Figure 10.10 *Composition of central government revenue, 1996–2004*

activities [oil] could cover a large per cent of public expenditures, it was of national convenience that direct taxes on the wages of employees, of small and medium businesses, of the most humble members, in sum, of the Venezuelan economy, be reduced. This measure was complemented by the elimination of an appreciable number of indirect taxes. (Betancourt, 1957, pp261–262)

This way of thinking about domestic taxation was not confined to tax policies during the Betancourt years. According to Obregón and Rodríguez (2001), the design is visible from when the nation first introduced an income tax law in 1942. According to these authors, the design of the 1942 law was predominantly oriented toward the taxation of oil rents, with all other sources of income playing a secondary role. The share of oil revenues in income tax collection hovered around 70 per cent from the law's inception in 1943 until the 1970s (Vallenilla, 1973). The 1942 law was characterized by a large number of exemptions, deductions and exonerations. An important characteristic of these is that contributors could benefit from them cumulatively, and losses from one type of activity could be deducted from taxes owed on other activities. This provision was typically regressive, favouring agents involved in more than one economic activity. The 1942 law contemplated exemptions for non-profit activities, savings accounts, labour indemnities and donations. The first reform to the law added an exemption on dividends. It also established the right of the executive to concede exonerations 'when it is judged convenient for the development of the nation'. Armed with this power, the executive approved exonerations on mortgage interest, the profits of agricultural and livestock concerns, as well as those of industries which produced articles of primary necessity or transformed nationally produced primary products. The first five years of rents on new urban constructions as well as profits of savings and credit institutions and cooperatives were also added to the list of exonerated activities.

The bias against taxation of domestic activities did not just make itself felt in the initial design of the tax code. According to Obregón and Rodríguez (2001), Venezuelan tax laws were routinely made more flexible with positive petroleum shocks. The earliest example of this can be found in the 1945 reforms described by Betancourt (1957), which accompanied the extraordinary tax on the 'excess profits' of the oil companies. The tendency reached its peak during the oil booms of the 1970s. Using the power granted to it by a special enabling law,[8] the first Carlos Andrés Pérez administration (1973–1979) expanded exemptions to include the construction industry (Decree 346), tourism (Decree 377), exports (Decree 378) and bank loans destined to expand production activities (Decree 343). It also granted additional rebates of 20 per cent on investments (Decree 330), electricity and transport (Decree 379), and agriculture, livestock and fishing (Decree 377).

Another manner in which Venezuela weakened its capacity for the generation of internal incomes was through the decision to maintain low prices on fuel and derivatives sold in the domestic market. Barely a month and a half after assuming power, the 1945

AD government drastically reduced the price of gasoline and other products and sub-products of petroleum. Once again, the clearest statement of the motivation for this policy can be found in Betancourt's work:

> *We had been interpreters of the demand for a national re-vindication when we sustained over our years in the opposition the need for drastically reducing the sale price of petroleum derivatives. It was outrageous that the first petroleum exporting nation of the world imposed such high prices on gasoline and other mineral oil derivatives.*
> (Betancourt, 1957, p293)

Armed with this justification, the 1945 government virtually eliminated the gasoline tax, and lowered the sales price to 11.30 US cents a litre, less than half the US price.[9] This measure led the government to sacrifice revenues equivalent to 4 per cent of the national budget, which were more than compensated for by higher taxes on oil company profits. According to a communiqué published by Creole Petroleum that year, as a consequence of these measures, 'Venezuela sells gasoline at the lowest price in the world' (Betancourt, 1957, p294). This statement is still true to this day (see Table 10.9).

In sum, this historical evolution led Venezuelan fiscal institutions to develop built-in biases that tend to hinder attempts to mobilize greater resources in the fight against poverty. Despite having at its disposal oil profits, which account for more than 10 per cent of GDP, the Venezuelan state does not devote more resources to expenditures than the average Latin American country. Indeed, as we will show below, in some key categories, it spends considerably less. Mobilizing resources for additional expenditures would thus seem to imply greater domestic tax collection. But while this requirement is easy to identify, it can be hard to implement. Venezuela has a deeply centralized state structure in which sub-national governments have little interest in collaborating in raising tax collection (and the national government has little interest in making them less dependent on transfers). It also has a highly distorted allocation of expenditures that is severely biased against public investment and towards public employment. Reforming these state structures, which have deep historical and institutional roots, is a formidable task.

In what follows we attempt to pinpoint specific reforms that can serve to enhance fiscal space within the context of high oil dependence and a centralized and distorted system of expenditure allocations. We first turn to an analysis of the overall features of the tax system in order to attempt to identify the classes of revenues that could be increased by legislative and policy reforms. In later sections we look at the budget planning and execution stages, as well as at the composition of expenditures.

THE VENEZUELAN TAX SYSTEM: A CLOSER LOOK

We now take a closer look at the Venezuelan tax system, with a view to identifying possible sources of fiscal space that could be targeted in reform efforts. Our data will cover statistics for the central government from 1962 to 2004 and for the consolidated public sector (CPS) from 1970 to 2003. Unless otherwise stated, data have been obtained directly from the Ministry of Finance. International comparisons are based on the March 2006 edition of Government Finance Statistics Database (IMF, 2006a). We start by providing an overall evaluation of Venezuelan public finances as well as their interrelationship with oil revenues. We then turn to studying the main components of domestic taxation, focusing on the largest sources of revenues. We close by discussing the financing of social security and the fiscal relationship with states and municipalities.

Venezuela's public finances: An overview

The real fiscal stance

Evaluating fiscal sustainability in the Venezuelan case is a complex issue. The high dependence of fiscal revenues on the price of oil means that different assumptions about the long-term trend of oil prices will have significant implications for the long-run perspective of public finances. The jury is still out on whether oil prices are stationary or non-stationary, although there appears to be agreement on the fact that a random walk provides a reasonable approximation to their behaviour over the short and medium term (Chinn et al, 2001; Hamilton, 2006). Furthermore, any evaluation of fiscal sustainability requires an assumption about future per capita growth, and it is unclear what a reasonable approximation of that would be for Venezuela, given that over the past 25 years it has experienced significant negative growth in per capita GDP (Hausmann and Rodríguez, 2006).

Despite these complexities, it is clear that Venezuela's fiscal performance has not been a good one. Figure 10.11 shows the fiscal deficit for the central government and CPS since 1962. Both the central government and CPS[10] have tended to display deficits consistently since the 1970s. In contrast to the central government, the CPS position has tended to improve over the last 15 years. Indeed, CPS deficits were higher than those of the central government before 1989, but, after that year, have become consistently lower. To a great extent this has been a result of the privatization of three key state owned enterprises: CANTV (the national telephone company) and VIASA (the national airline) in 1991, and SIDOR (the steel producing company) in 1997. As Figure 10.12 shows, transfers to public enterprises are currently negligible, making it doubtful that additional fiscal space can be obtained through further privatization.

There are methodological differences between the Ministry of Finance numbers and those of the IMF shown in Figure 10.3 above. One of them is the fact that the Ministry of Finance figures report exchange gains as revenues while the IMF does not.

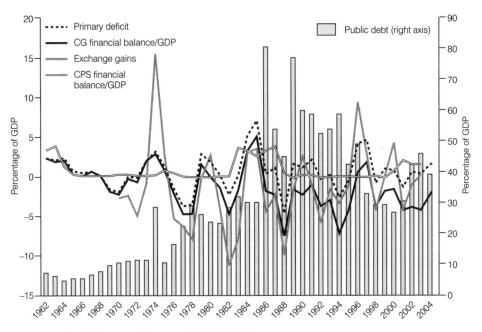

Source: Ministerio de Finanzas (various years); IMF (2006a)

Figure 10.11 *Central government and consolidated public sector debt, exchange gains and public debt, 1962–2004*

Source: Ministerio de Finanzas (various years)

Figure 10.12 *Transfers to public enterprises, 1984–2004*

Table 10.3 Indicators of fiscal performance

	1962–1973 (%)	1974–1982 (%)	1983–1988 (%)	1989–1998 (%)	1999–2004 (%)
CG Financial Balance/GDP	0.3	−1.6	−0.9	−2.5	−3.1
CG Primary Balance/GDP	0.5	−0.4	1.6	0.9	0.3
CPS Financial Balance/GDP	−2.7	−1.6	−3.0	−0.4	−0.1
CPS Primary Balance/GDP	−2.2	0.6	1.7	4.0	3.9
Public Debt/GDP (right axis)	8.3	23.3	45.3	51.5	35.1
GDP Growth Rate	5.8	2.5	1.9	1.9	−3.1
Non-oil GDP Growth Rate	8.8	7.0	2.6	0.9	−2.3
Primary Deficit/GDP	0.5	−0.4	1.6	0.9	0.3
Exchange Gains/GDP	0.8	0.2	2.7	0.0	1.2

Note: CG = central government; CPS = consolidated public sector
Source: Ministerio de Finanzas (various years); Banco Central de Venezuela (various years(c))

As Table 10.3 shows, exchange gains are significant sources of revenue for almost every period (except 1989 to 1998). After netting out these gains, the primary surplus of the central government disappears, though not that of the CPS. The existence of a primary surplus in the CPS has led policymakers to attempt to raise taxes on the state owned oil company. We discuss this strategy below. For now, it is relevant to note that the heavy weight of debt service implies that significant CPS primary surpluses are necessary for debt not to spiral out of control.

Overall public revenues
In Venezuela, from 1970 to 2003, the annual average of CPS revenues as a fraction of GDP was 30.9 per cent (see Table 10.4). Almost 60 per cent of these (18.6 per cent of GDP) came from oil sources that include exchange gains, while 15.9 per cent came from domestic taxes (4.9 per cent of GDP), and 3.2 per cent from social security contributions (1 per cent of GDP). A further 3.8 per cent came from net surpluses of non-financial public enterprises (NFPE) (1.2 per cent of GDP), 2 per cent came from resources collected by sub-national governments (0.6 per cent of GDP), and the rest came from other revenues (fees, interest and dividends, exploitation of mines, among others). The share of CPS in GDP looks large in comparison to other Latin American countries because of the large weight of the oil company, but the central government share does not (see Figure 10.9). However, if central government revenues are expressed as a proportion of non-oil GDP, this share increases to 32.9 per cent, which is large by Latin American standards. From the point of view of assessing the relevance of the government in the economy, the former may be the more relevant comparison. If one believes that public goods are normal goods, their provision should naturally go up with increases of income, whether they come from oil or from any other source.

The evolution of total public revenues is clearly associated with that of oil income (see Figure 10.13); in fact, the correlation between the shares in GDP of total and oil

Table 10.4 *Composition of central government and consolidated public sector public revenues, 1970–2003*

	Average (%)	% of GDP Standard Deviation	% of Total	Average (%)	% of Non-oil GDP Standard Deviation	% of Total
Consolidated Public Sector	30.9	5.3	100	44.6	13.3	100
Oil Revenues	18.6	5.6	60.2	27.3	12.1	61.1
Taxes	13.6	6.3	43.8	20.2	12.9	45.4
Dividends of PDVSA	0.5	1.1	1.7	0.7	1.4	1.6
Exchange Gains	0.7	1.2	2.4	1.0	1.5	2.2
Other PDVSA (Net)	3.8	3.0	12.3	5.4	4.5	12.0
Non-oil Revenues	12.3	2.3	39.8	17.3	3.3	38.9
Domestic Taxes	4.9	1.7	15.9	6.9	2.2	15.4
Social Security Contributions	1.0	0.3	3.2	1.4	0.6	3.2
Net Results NFPE	1.2	0.9	3.8	1.6	1.1	3.6
Sub-national Governments	0.6	0.2	2.0	0.9	0.4	2.0
Other	4.6	1.5	14.8	0.0	0.0	0.0
Central Government	22.6	5.1	100	32.9	12.5	100
Oil Revenues	14.6	5.9	64.8	21.7	12.3	65.9
Non-oil Revenues	8.0	2.1	35.2	11.2	2.8	34.1

Note: PDVSA started operations in 1976 and began paying dividends in 1996; oil revenues include exchange gains.

Source: Ministerio de Finanzas (various years), Banco Central de Venezuela (various years(c))

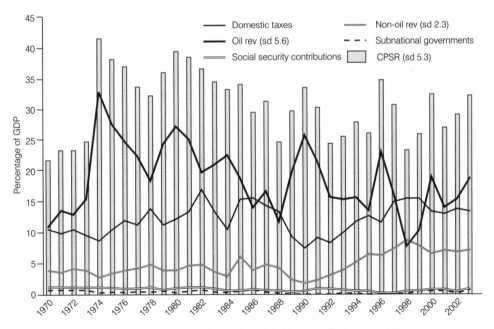

Source: Ministerio de Finanzas (various years), Banco Central de Venezuela (various years(c))

Figure 10.13 *Revenue composition and consolidated public sector revenue results (% of GDP)*

Table 10.5 *Cross correlations among revenue types*

	Consolidated public sector revenue	Non-oil revenues	Oil revenues
Consolidated public sector revenue	1.000	0.057	0.911
Non-oil revenues	0.057	1.000	-0.361
Oil revenues	0.911	-0.361	1.000

revenues is 0.9 (see Table 10.5). They are characterized by cycles of falls and recoveries, but a declining trend since the 1970s is clear. Non-oil revenues have increased during times of falling oil revenues, but the rise has not been sufficient to counteract the decline in oil revenues. Although negative, the correlation between both variables is low (-0.36).

The volatility of total public revenues is also remarkably high, as their standard deviation of 5.3 per cent of GDP shows. That volatility and the low negative correlation between oil and non-oil revenues implies that total public sector revenues also exhibit a high degree of volatility (also 5.3 per cent of GDP). Oil revenues are generally the dominant force, as is revealed by the fact that only in 4 of the 33 years covered in Figure 10.13 have domestic revenues exceeded oil revenues.

Oil revenues: Important but volatile

It is true that the share of central government revenues to GDP in Venezuela is similar to that of other countries, but few countries in the region have a comparable source of state finance that is as important. As Table 10.6 shows, non-oil revenues are extremely low in comparison to GDP. One way to understand the contribution of oil to Venezuela's public finances is to separate the fiscal accounts into their oil and non-oil balances. If we carry out that calculation (Table 10.7), we find that the non-oil fiscal gap is, on average, equivalent to nearly half the annual average of the central government budget (see Table 10.6).[11]

Table 10.6 *Central government revenues, 1990–2003 (% of GDP)*

Country	Oil	Non-oil	Total
Venezuela	10.8	9.4	20.2
Argentina			13.7
Bolivia			19.0
Brazil			23.8
Chile			21.2
Colombia			18.0
Mexico			14.7
Paraguay			14.9
Peru			15.9
Uruguay			27.6
Latin America			18.8
OECD			34.4

Source: IMF (2006a)

Table 10.7 *Central government financial results (% of GDP)*

	1962–1970	1971–1981	1982–1986	1987–1998	1999–2004
Oil balance	13.0	19.3	15.7	9.4	8.4
Non-oil Balance	−12.7	−20.0	−15.7	−12.3	−11.5
Budget	20.8	28.9	23.0	23.0	28.3

Source: Based on Banco Central de Venezuela (2000); IMF (2006a)

Oil fiscal revenues have registered strong swings during these periods. The annual real average of oil fiscal revenues for the period 1999 to 2004 have declined by 32 per cent from the 1970s and early 1980s (1970 to 1985) and by more than 50 per cent in real per capita terms, even after taking into account the recent upsurge. As Figure 10.14 shows, this has coincided with a decline of the government's average proportion of profits. It is evident from a comparison of the magnitudes in Figures 10.13 and 10.14 that the greatest contributing factor to this decline is not the decrease in taxation. One may well deduce that one strategy to increase fiscal space may be to reinstate taxes on petroleum production back to their levels of the 1980s. This strategy was behind the formulation of the 2001 Hydrocarbons Law Reform, which significantly altered the tax regime on PDVSA and its private associates. Royalty payments on production were raised from 16.67 per cent to 30 per cent, an increase that more than offset the reduction in the income tax rate (from 67.7 per cent to 50 per cent). Other recent legal changes included the elimination of Strategic Associations and Operational Contracts that had been used to bring in participation of transnational firms, and substituted for them Mixed Capital Contracts, with a required government participation of 51 per cent.

   Is increasing the tax rate on oil production a feasible way to generate fiscal space? Manzano (2006) has argued that the current tax take constitutes a significant hindrance to investment. High government takes imply fewer funds are left over for investment. Indeed, investment has generally declined when the government take has increased (see Figure 10.15). Although PDVSA can finance investment with debt, its debt is commonly viewed as a substitute for national government debt in international markets, so that it has a high cost. While current oil prices imply that some additional resources can be raised by increasing taxes on foreign companies, such a renegotiation would imply incurring significant credibility costs that may become relevant if oil prices decline.[12]

   If increasing taxes on oil production is unlikely to bring about enhanced fiscal space, how about increasing oil revenues? Maximizing oil revenues has been a cornerstone of Venezuelan fiscal policy since the 1940s, and is the obvious motivation for the country's participation in OPEC. As Figure 10.16 shows, this has implied a significant loss in world market share. Whether there have been price benefits depends on whether one thinks OPEC has effective market power, which is subject to considerable debate (Smith, 2005). If OPEC has no market power, then obviously Venezuela would be better off by leaving OPEC. If OPEC has market power, then the issue becomes more

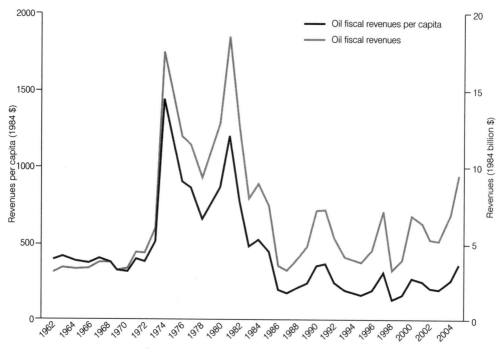

Source: Based on Ministerio de Finanzas (various years); Banco Central de Venezuela (various years(c))

Figure 10.14 *Oil fiscal revenues*

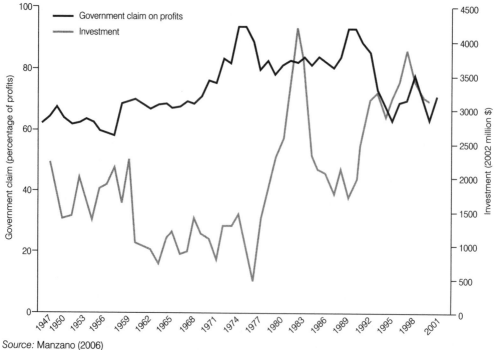

Source: Manzano (2006)

Figure 10.15 *Petroleum taxes and investments, 1947–2003*

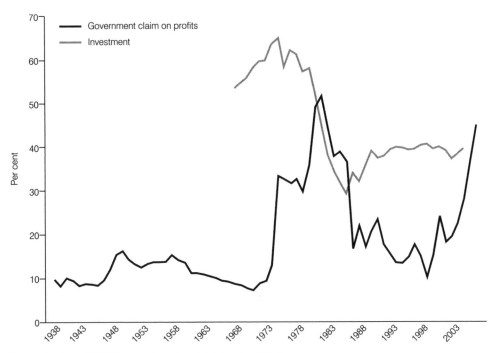

Source: Adelman (1995);Energy Information Administration (2006)

Figure 10.16 *OPEC world market share and Venezuelan oil price, 1938–2004*

complicated. Venezuela could obviously play the strategy of defecting and expect other members to not defect from the cartel. This was the policy played by Ecuador when it left OPEC in 1992. If the strategy touches off no retaliation, it is optimal. If it generates retaliation, then it is not evident that Venezuela is best poised to win a price war against OPEC. As Table 10.8 shows, Venezuela's proven reserves are approximately one quarter those of Saudi Arabia.

A less dramatic way to increase fiscal oil revenues could be by increasing domestic prices of gasoline. There are two channels through which this could impact fiscal revenues: the gasoline tax and the profits of PDVSA. Before the 2001 Hydrocarbons Law, the gasoline tax took the form of a specific tax expressed in bolívares per litre. Under the 2001 law it became an *ad valorem* tax on prices (30 per cent). The change actually involved a significant reduction in the average fiscal burden (more than 50 per cent). Since Venezuela has quite possibly the lowest price of gasoline in the world (see Table 10.9), collection on this tax is a small fraction of what it could be. As Figure 10.17 shows, this tax has constituted up to 0.9 per cent of GDP on several occasions, giving a measure of the possible increase in revenues that could be generated by a rate increase.

Table 10.10 displays a more comprehensive exercise simulating the effect of alternative scenarios of the price of gasoline on the 2004 budget. Column 2 shows the historical 2004 scenario. In it, gasoline tax collection is 0.08 per cent of GDP and

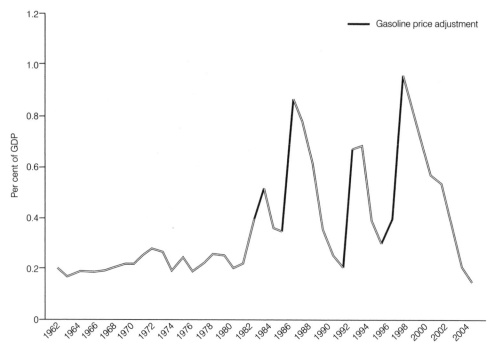

Source: Oficina Nacional de Presupuesto (2006b)

Figure 10.17 *Tax collection on domestic consumption of gasoline and oil products, 1962–2004 (% of GDP)*

Table 10.8 *World proven reserves of oil and natural gas, year end 2004, for selected countries*

Country/Region	Reserves (billion barrels)	Percentage of World Total
Saudi Arabia	262,730	22.11
Iran	132,460	11.15
Iraq	115,000	9.68
Kuwait	99,000	8.33
United Arab Emirates	97,800	8.23
Venezuela	77,226	6.50
Russia	72,277	6.08
Kazakhstan	39,620	3.33
Libya	39,126	3.29
Nigeria	35,255	2.97
US	29,299	2.47
China	17,070	1.44
Canada	16,802	1.41
Qatar	15,207	1.28
Mexico	14,803	1.25
Algeria	11,800	0.99
Brazil	11,243	0.95
Norway	9673	0.81
Other countries	92,114	7.75
World Total	1,188,505	100.00

Source: Energy Information Administration (2006)

Table 10.9 *Retail motor gasoline prices in selected countries, 1990–2004 (US$ per litre)*

Regular Unleaded

Year	Australia	Canada	China	Germany	Japan	Mexico	South Korea	Taiwan	United States	Venezuela[2]
1990	n.a.	0.494	n.a.	0.700	0.835	0.264	0.541	0.658	0.306	0.068
1991	0.518	0.507	n.a.	0.766	0.914	0.343	0.658	0.631	0.301	0.075
1992	0.499	0.457	n.a.	0.864	0.948	0.396	0.700	0.639	0.298	0.066
1993	0.457	0.415	n.a.	0.811	1.062	0.412	0.761	0.600	0.293	0.050
1994	0.486	0.383	0.254	0.930	1.160	0.391	0.758	0.565	0.293	0.032
1995	0.515	0.404	0.272	1.046	1.170	0.296	0.777	0.589	0.304	0.024
1996	0.560	0.425	0.283	1.041	0.964	0.333	0.840	0.568	0.325	0.088
1997	0.541	0.428	0.251	0.932	0.864	0.388	0.882	0.589	0.325	0.119
1998	0.431	0.365	0.251	0.882	0.747	0.396	0.803	0.491	0.280	0.120
1999	0.454	0.401	0.280	0.903	0.864	0.475	1.004	0.491	0.309	0.104
2000	0.512	0.491	n.a.	0.911	0.964	0.534	1.104	0.568	0.399	0.097
2001	0.452	0.454	n.a.	0.898	0.864	0.584	0.993	0.534	0.386	0.089
2002	0.465	0.449	n.a.	0.969	0.832	0.594	1.014	0.510	0.359	0.054
2003	0.581	0.526	n.a.	1.212	0.917	0.552	1.088	0.571	0.420	0.047
2004	0.718	0.626	n.a.	1.384	1.038	n.a.	1.191	0.650	0.497	0.039

Premium Unleaded[1]

Year	France	Italy	South Africa	Spain	Thailand	United Kingdom	United States	Venezuela[3]
1990	0.959	1.212	n.a.	n.a.	n.a.	0.745	0.357	
1991	0.911	1.189	n.a.	n.a.	n.a.	0.795	0.349	
1992	0.943	1.197	n.a.	0.924	0.357	0.808	0.349	
1993	0.901	0.972	n.a.	0.795	0.333	0.750	0.343	
1994	0.948	0.977	n.a.	0.790	0.320	0.790	0.346	
1995	1.125	1.057	n.a.	0.856	0.333	0.848	0.354	
1996	1.165	1.160	n.a.	0.877	0.394	0.882	0.372	
1997	1.057	1.075	0.454	0.795	0.335	1.012	0.375	
1998	1.022	1.014	0.399	0.740	0.288	1.072	0.330	
1999	1.017	1.022	0.409	0.745	0.322	1.133	0.359	0.150
2000	1.004	0.996	0.470	0.755	0.365	1.210	0.446	0.139
2001	0.927	0.943	0.420	0.724	0.351	1.094	0.438	0.127
2002	0.956	0.988	0.372	0.766	0.357	1.099	0.412	0.069
2003	1.149	1.197	0.504	0.924	0.401	1.241	0.470	0.061
2004	1.318	1.400	0.681	1.080		1.471	0.547	0.051

Note: 1 Research Octane Number (RON) of 95 for Energy Information Administration (2007) data. 2 There have been changes in Venezuela's RON: from 1990 to 1993 RON of 83; from 1994 to 2001 RON of 87 and 91; from 2002 to 2004 RON of 91. 3 From 1999 to 2004 RON of 97.
Notes on data presented by the EIA: Prices are those actually paid, i.e. net of rebates, and include transport costs and taxes that are not refundable. Prices in national currencies are converted to US dollars using exchange rates published by the EIA. Comparisons between prices and price trends in different countries require care. They are of limited validity because of fluctuations in exchange rates, differences in product quality, marketing practices, market structures and the extent to which the standard categories of sales are representative of total national sales for a given period. n.a. = not available.

Source: Energy Information Administration (2007) for all countries except Venezuela; Ministerio de Energía y Minas (various years)

PDVSA losses from selling gasoline at below cost are 0.62 per cent of GDP. That year the government spent 0.02 per cent of GDP on subsidizing public transportation. Scenario 2004a assumes that Venezuela sets a price of gasoline necessary for PDVSA to break even on the domestic market. This would imply an increase from 2.1 US cents a litre to 5.5 cents. The net gain from this move would be an increase of 0.71 per cent of GDP, even after assuming that the public transportation subsidy increases proportionately with the price increase. A second, more ambitious scenario, Scenario 2004b, would increase the price to that of Niger, which is 7 cents a litre. The resulting net gain is 1.04 per cent of GDP. Scenario 2004c simulates increasing the price to Saudi Arabia's price of 17.5 cents per litre. The net gain would be 3.25 points of GDP. This is 2.66 times the yearly average that the government has spent on its hallmark social programmes, the Misiones, between 2003 and 2005. These gains do not take into account the social benefits from reducing resource misallocation – overuse of roads and highways, high maintenance costs and losses associated with heavy traffic, noise and pollution.[13]

Despite the huge potential fiscal gains, Venezuelan governments have been hesitant to increase the price of gasoline ever since the rate increases of February 1989 set off massive riots. Adjustments have mainly taken place during times of extreme fiscal distress, and even then they have faced strong opposition. The Chávez administration has refused to alter the nominal price of gasoline, which has remained constant since 1999. Although the social and political impact of gas price increases should not be

Table 10.10 *Taxation of gasoline consumption (simulation)*

	Units	2001	2004	2004a	2004b	2004c
Consumption	Litre	13,079	11,535	11,535	11,535	11,535
Price	VEB/litre	39	47	121	154	384
Tariff	VEB/litre 2001; 30% on price 2004	35	14	36	46	115
Sales	Million VEB	515,313	543,321	1,393,068	1,771,849	4,429,623
Margin Rate Distributors	%	10	10	10	10	10
Total Margin Distributors	Million VEB	51,531	54,332	139,307	177,185	442,962
Tax Collection	Million VEB	457,765	162,996	417,921	531,555	1,328,887
Tax Collection	% of GDP	0.50	0.08	0.20	0.26	0.64
Cost ($1 L-1)	VEB/litre	41	121	121	121	121
Total Cost	Million VEB	536,773	1,393,068	1,393,068	1,393,068	1,393,068
PDVSA's Surplus or Deficit	Million VEB	−21,460	−849,747	0	378,781	3,036,555
PDVSA's Surplus or Deficit/GDP	%	−0.02	−0.62	0	0.28	2.21
Subsidy to Public Transportation	25% of tax collection	114,441	40,749	104,480	132,889	332,222
Subsidy to Public Transportation/GDP	%	0.13	0.02	0.05	0.06	0.16

Note: VEB = Venezuelan bolívar. Data in shaded cells are parameters used in the 2001 and 2004 Budget Law estimates of taxes on gasoline. The margin rate is assumed; cost per litre is proxied by the US dollar cost of production and refining per barrel as published by the Ministry of Energy. In scenario 2004a price is equal to cost; in 2004b Niger's price is used; in 2004c Saudi Arabia's price is used.

Source: Budget Laws 2001 and 2004; Based on Ministerio de Energía y Minas (various years)

underestimated, it is difficult to believe that the present Venezuelan pricing policy is optimal from any viewpoint.[14]

Domestic taxation

We now turn to the analysis of non-oil taxation. Potential sources of enhanced fiscal revenue are easier to find in the domestic tax space. As we have discussed above, the non-oil tax rate is extremely low by international standards. In this section we attempt to identify the specific areas of domestic taxation in which specific reforms could lead to an enhancement of fiscal space.

The Venezuelan domestic tax system relies on both direct and indirect taxes. Among the former are the corporate and individual income tax, and the tax on inheritance and donations. A tax on corporate assets existed between 1993 and 2004. Indirect taxes include VAT, customs, excises (on liquors, cigars and matches), real estate registration rights, a tax on gambling and lotteries, and a telecommunications tax. Payroll taxes, usually reported separately by the collecting entities, include social security (retirement, medical assistance and unemployment insurance) as well as specific taxes with revenues earmarked to cover work training, recreational services, housing, assistance to the elderly and day care. There are also various municipal and state taxes. Table 10.11 shows their real collection levels and their share of total domestic taxation. Although some analyses have emphasized the need for a reform in excise and other minor taxes that should report higher yields, we will concentrate on areas with the largest potential impact on revenues, namely VAT, income tax, trade, payroll and state and municipality taxes.

The entries of Table 10.11 display two remarkable facts about the Venezuelan tax system. One is the declining share of direct taxes, not only in total revenue but also as a share of GDP. The other is the negligible role played by social security taxes. These features have been systematically pointed out by previous studies on the Venezuelan tax system, including those commissioned by different administrations.[15]

Table 10.12 compares Venezuelan tax collection to that of the rest of the region. We exclude royalties and dividends from oil and present Venezuelan tax collection as a percentage both of GDP and of non-oil GDP.[16] Arguably, the correct standard is the latter for an evaluation of the tax burden. As is evident from Table 10.12, the indirect tax burden in Venezuela is similar to that in the rest of the region (8.7 per cent versus 8.6 per cent). However, the direct tax burden appears to be much lower (3.3 per cent versus 5.9 per cent). This suggests that the Venezuelan tax system may be considerably more regressive than that of the rest of the region. Indeed, Venezuela shares with Bolivia the second lowest position (after Peru) in a comparison of the share of direct taxes in the total (26.2 per cent).

Table 10.11 *Non-oil sources of domestic taxation*

% of GDP	1962–1973	1974–1983	1984–1988	1989–1998	1999–2004
Total	**6.659**	**6.356**	**5.861**	**6.374**	**7.960**
Direct	**4.303**	**4.288**	**3.826**	**2.478**	**2.502**
On Domestic Income	2.877	2.993	2.839	1.747	1.891
Inheritance and Gifts	0.071	0.073	0.070	0.024	0.027
Social Security	1.356	1.223	0.918	0.707	0.584
Indirect	**2.356**	**2.068**	**2.035**	**3.896**	**5.458**
VAT	0.000	0.000	0.000	1.917	3.728
Customs	1.185	1.208	1.075	1.312	1.066
Liquors	0.651	0.377	0.456	0.247	0.152
Cigarettes	0.505	0.361	0.385	0.237	0.280
Matches	0.009	0.004	0.000	0.000	0.001
Real Estate Rights	0.005	0.117	0.112	0.135	0.082
Gambling and Lottery	0.000	0.000	0.000	0.000	0.007
Telecommunications	0.000	0.001	0.000	0.027	0.142
Others	0.000	0.001	0.006	0.021	0.000

% Share in Total

	1962–1973	1974–1983	1984–1988	1989–1998	1999–2004
Total	**100.0%**	**100.0%**	**100.0%**	**100.0%**	**100.0%**
Direct	**64.6%**	**67.5%**	**65.3%**	**38.9%**	**31.4%**
On Domestic Income	43.2%	47.1%	48.4%	27.4%	23.8%
Inheritance and Gifts	1.1%	1.1%	1.2%	0.4%	0.3%
Social Security	20.4%	19.2%	15.7%	11.1%	7.3%
Indirect	**35.4%**	**32.5%**	**34.7%**	**61.1%**	**68.6%**
VAT	0.0%	0.0%	0.0%	30.1%	46.8%
Customs	17.8%	19.0%	18.3%	20.6%	13.4%
Liquors	9.8%	5.9%	7.8%	3.9%	1.9%
Cigarettes	7.6%	5.7%	6.6%	3.7%	3.5%
Matches	0.1%	0.1%	0.0%	0.0%	0.0%
Real Estate Rights	0.1%	1.8%	1.9%	2.1%	1.0%
Gambling and Lottery	0.0%	0.0%	0.0%	0.0%	0.1%
Telecommunications	0.0%	0.0%	0.0%	0.4%	1.8%
Others	0.0%	0.0%	0.1%	0.3%	0.0%

Source: Oficina Nacional de Presupuesto (2006b)

VAT

VAT, which is presently the most important source of ordinary[17] domestic fiscal revenues (60 per cent in 2004), was introduced into the Venezuelan tax system in 1993. This represented a significant delay in its adoption in comparison to other countries. Indeed, adoption of VAT had been recommended by the 1958 Shoup Commission as well as by the Commission for the Study of Fiscal Reform constituted in 1980. The section 'The Misiones: Is oil wealth finally reaching the poor?' below discusses the incidence of political economy factors in its adoption. It has also been reformed numerous times, including two name changes and continuous modifications to the list of exempt taxes. Since its introduction, VAT collection has averaged 4.5 per cent of GDP,[18] representing an efficiency (tax collection divided by the nominal tax rate) of 0.30. Tax collection, as a percentage of non-oil GDP, is similar to the average of Latin

Table 10.12 *Total taxes, 1990–2003 (% of GDP)*

	Indirect	Direct	Total	Direct/total (%)
Venezuela	7.1	2.2	9.6	26.2
% of Non-oil GDP	8.7	3.3	12.0	27.5
Argentina	7.6	3.7	11.3	32.7
Bolivia	10.3	3.7	13.9	26.2
Brazil	5.8	11.7	17.5	67.1
Chile	11.8	5.8	17.7	33.1
Colombia	7.3	5.8	13.2	44.1
Mexico	9.2	6.7	15.9	42.2
Paraguay	8.0	2.7	10.8	25.2
Peru	10.5	4.2	14.7	28.5
Uruguay	14.1	10.3	24.4	42.1
Latin America	8.6	5.9	14.6	40.6
OECD	10.9	19.1	30.0	63.6

Source: IMF (2006a)

America, but considerably lower than that of the best performers in the region (Bolivia, Chile, Mexico, Peru and Uruguay) (see Table 10.13).

The existence of differential tariffs, an extended list of exemptions and a high threshold for determining when firms are to contribute are among the factors that result in low collection levels. Since 1998, the authorities have chosen to reduce the VAT rate, which is now at 14.0 per cent (down from 16.5 per cent during the period 1996 to 1998 as indicated in Table 10.14). Casanegra et al (1996) argue that the establishment of additional rates on certain goods and imports in the 1994 reform appears to have increased the complexity of the system with a marginal contribution to tax collection. They also calculated that the implicit subsidy that accrued to the 25 per cent lowest income houses from exonerations and exemptions (16 per cent) was considerably lower than that received by the 25 per cent highest income houses (41 per cent).

Table 10.13 *Taxes on goods and services, 1990–2003 (% of GDP)*

Country	% of Non-oil GDP	Total
Venezuela	5.8	4.3
Argentina		3.9
Bolivia		7.5
Brazil		4.0
Chile		10.4
Colombia		5.4
Mexico		8.1
Paraguay		5.0
Peru		8.0
Uruguay		9.7
Latin America		6.3
OECD		10.2

Source: IMF (2006a) and authors' calculations

Table 10.14 *Chronology of VAT tax rates*

	1993	1994 (b)	1995	1996	1997	1998	1999	2000	2001	2002¹ (b)	2003	2004	2005
VAT/GDP (%)	0.6	2.0	3.3	3.6	4.3	5.4	4.8	4.0	4.1	4.1	4.7	6.4	7.1
Basic Rate (%)	10.0	10.0	12.5	16.5	16.5	16.5	15.5	14.5	14.5	14.5	14.5	15.0	14.0
Valid From	1/10/93		1/1/95	1/8/96			1/6/99	1/8/00		1/8/02	1/9/02		1/10/05
To	1/1/95		1/8/96	1/6/99			1/8/00	1/9/02		1/9/02			1/10/05
Basic Rate										16.0%			
Valid From										1/9/02			
To										1/9/04			
Additional Rate²		15.0%								10.0%			
Valid From		1/1/94								1/8/02			
To		1/8/94								1/9/02			
Additional Rate²		20.0%								8.0%			
Valid From		1/8/94								1/9/02			
To		1/1/95								1/9/04			
Free Zone Rate							8.0%						
Valid From							1/6/99						
To							1/8/00						

Note: 1 Two reforms in the same year; 2 Rates on luxury goods.

Source: Budget Laws; VAT Laws; Ministerio de Finanzas (various years)

Table 10.15 shows the result of the calculations of potential tax collection based on the Venezuelan Central Bank's 1997–98 Consumption and Expenditure Survey. Our estimates indicate projected evasion rates of 30 to 40 per cent. Fortunately, these have been declining over time. Not reflected in the calculations is a recent administrative reform of 2003, which imposed a payment of 75 per cent of estimated taxes before the start of the exercise. Conversations with National Integrated Customs and Revenue Service (Servicio Nacional Integrado de Administración Aduanera y Tributaria, or SENIAT) staff suggest that this simple reform has been particularly effective in improving collection rates.

Income tax
The stylized facts of the Venezuelan income tax suggest that some reforms might bring about permanent additional resources here as well. Some of the salient features of this tax are as follows: a declining share over time in revenues; a low ratio to GDP compared to other Latin American countries; a reduced tax base determined by an indiscriminate and generous system of exemptions, exonerations and discounts; a bias against labour income; and a complex system of tariffs. Several reforms have been implemented but they still limit collection of the tax.[19]

The tax was introduced in 1942 in response to falling fiscal revenues brought about by the interruptions in international trade caused by the Second World War. The design of the tax followed the 'cedular' approach, which taxes income according to the sources

Table 10.15 *VAT simulations*

% of GDP	1997	1998	1999	2000	2001	2002
Estimated Tax Base	43.6	48.3	47.5	42.9	46.1	39.8
Potential Tax Collection	7.2	8.0	7.4	6.2	6.7	5.8
Effective Tax Collection	4.3	5.4	4.8	4.0	4.1	4.1
Difference	2.9	2.6	2.6	2.2	2.6	1.7
Estimated Evasion	40.3	32.6	35.1	36.2	38.9	29.4

Source: Based on Banco Central de Venezuela (various years (b)); Oficina Nacional de Presupuesto (various years (a))

of the revenues (different taxes on manufacturing, labour, hydrocarbons and mines, retail and so on), with rates that oscillated between 1.5 per cent and 3 per cent. The cedular approach also involved a complementary tax with 20 sections of income and rates that went from 2 per cent for the lowest to 9.5 per cent for the highest sections. As discussed in the section 'A short history of Venezuelan fiscal policy (or how not to build a tax system', the law allowed for a broad set of exemptions in each case and allowed the government to establish discretionary exonerations.

The new law brought additional revenues to the treasury that amounted to less than 1 per cent of GDP. The brief democratic administration of the period 1945 to 1948 introduced three reforms grounded on the financing needs of the new political project. One of them established an extraordinary contribution on high-income sectors (1945), while the other two mainly affected oil activities – an increase in the complementary tax rate (1946) and an increase in the fiscal share in oil corporate profits to 50 per cent (1948). Taking into account a raise in the rate on fortuitous gains in 1955, the annual average revenues achieved through tax collection increased to 1 per cent of GDP until 1958.

The democratic regimes that started in 1958 showed an initial disposition towards the improvement of the non-oil public finance structure by commissioning a study of

Table 10.16 *Tax on income, 1990–2003 (% of GDP)*

Country	% of Non-oil GDP	Total
Venezuela	2.4	1.8
Argentina		0.9
Bolivia		1.5
Brazil		4.1
Chile		4.4
Colombia		5.8
Mexico		4.8
Paraguay		1.8
Peru		2.8
Uruguay		2.9
Latin America		3.6
OECD		8.6

Source: IMF (2006a)

the domestic tax system to 'Mission Shoup'[20] in 1958. This Mission recommended a radical reform that would have implied the substitution of the cedular system by a global one, but their recommendations were ignored. The reforms that took place in 1958 and 1961 were, instead, directed at raising the contributions of high-income sectors, starting with increases in the marginal rates of the complementary tax and the introduction of a pay-as-you-go system to finance social security. These changes brought about additional tax revenues that achieved an annual average tax collection that amounted to 2.5 per cent up to 1966[21] when a new income tax law was approved.

Faced with declining oil prices (see Figure 10.16), the Leoni administration finally adopted some of the Shoup Mission's suggestions in 1966, particularly in reference to the principles of global taxation of individual and corporate income. The new law, however, maintained a vast system of exemptions and exonerations. Revenues increased by 0.5 per cent of GDP, on average, during the next decade.

The efforts of future administrations to improve income tax collection would, basically, be devoted to introducing new dispositions on oil income tax. That was the case of the reforms to the 1966 law, applied in 1970, 1974, 1975 and 1976, which progressively increased the tax rate on oil activities from 52 per cent to 72 per cent. This burden was reduced to 67.7 per cent in a new law approved in 1978, two years after the nationalization of the oil industry. That law also established a higher burden on personal and corporate income through an increase in the intermediate marginal rates. A simplification of the tariff system on corporate tax, a reduction of five brackets to three, was approved in 1986 but appears to have had little effect on tax collection.

The 1989 Washington Consensus Package of Reforms contemplated an aggressive reform of income tax law. Its proposal was to considerably simplify the rate structure, introducing an inflation adjustment, increasing the threshold level on individual income tax, eliminating double taxation on dividends, and eliminating many of the differential tax rates and other sources of presumed distortion. The reform was approved in 1991. The reform did not have the intended effects. The collection of income tax declined to around 2 per cent of GDP, a loss of one percentage point of GDP with respect to the average reached before 1989. In 2001, a new law was approved to incorporate the principle of world rent (the taxing of Venezuelan citizens' income derived from foreign sources), with little discernible effect on collection.

Trade taxes
Until 1939, tax on international trade represented the main indirect tax in Venezuela. Despite Venezuela's reliance on an import substitution industrialization (ISI) strategy until 1989, effective tariff rates were actually quite low for a large part of the period. Although non-tariff barriers (NTBs), particularly a rigid exchange control, were prevalent in the period 1983 to 1989, they were marginal for the rest of the period of study. Indeed, a free trade treaty with the US made Venezuela a particularly open economy until 1972 (when the treaty was repealed).

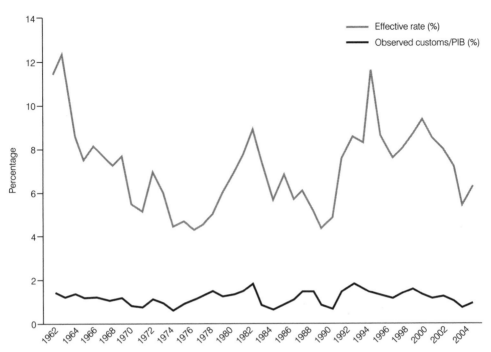

Source: Oficina Nacional de Presupuesto (various years, 2006 (b))

Figure 10.18 *Tariff revenue and effective rate (collection/imports)*

Curiously, the strategy of trade liberalization adopted in 1989 appeared to increase tariff revenues after 1989 (see Figure 10.18). Nominal tariff rates were cut from 40 per cent to 7.5 per cent while the number of different rates dropped from more than 40 to just 4 *ad-valorem* rates. Most NTBs had been eliminated by early 1992. Tax credit incentives were also gradually reduced until their total elimination in 1991 and substituted by a system of duty drawbacks. A 10 per cent export credit for some agricultural products was, however, retained. Venezuela joined the WTO in 1990. After the reform, the customs yield averaged 1.7 per cent per year and followed a pattern closer to that of imports. Improvements in the administration of the tax were reflected in the continuous increase of the effective rate between 1989 and 1994. Indeed, trade tax collection compares favourably with that of other Latin American countries (see Table 10.17).

Since 1999 the Chávez administration has reversed the openness strategy. The 1999 reform to the Organic Custom Law allowed discretionary government protection of domestic activities. This is obviously limited by Venezuela's membership in WTO. However, Venezuela has decided to renounce its membership in the Andean Community and the G-3 (a free trade area comprising Mexico, Colombia and Venezuela), as well as imposing exchange controls and significant restrictions on cross-border trade with Colombia.[22] Trends in integration are far from clear, however, as Venezuela has signalled its willingness to join Mercosur. The strong appreciation of the

Table 10.17 *Taxes on international trade, 1990–2003 (% of GDP)*

Country	% of Non-oil GDP	Total
Venezuela	2.1	1.6
Argentina		2.1
Bolivia		0.8
Brazil		0.5
Chile		0.6
Colombia		1.1
Mexico		0.8
Paraguay		2.0
Peru		1.6
Uruguay		1.3
Latin America		1.6
OECD		0.3

Source: IMF (2006a)

bolívar in recent years has also led to an increase in imports. However, in general, Figure 10.18 does show a declining trend in trade tax revenues in recent years.

Social security

Venezuelan payroll taxes include social security taxes as well as labour taxes earmarked to finance vocational training, a housing fund, unemployment insurance and day care expenditures. Their annual average share in GDP amount to 1.3 per cent for the whole period 1970 to 2003. A comparison with other countries shows that social security taxes are a very small source of revenue in Venezuela (see Table 10.18). Many government workers have their own social security programmes, but information on contributions is very dispersed and not fully reported in the public finance statistics.[23]

The present social security system consists of a pay-as-you-go mechanism under which taxes collected from current workers are used to pay current retirees. Active

Table 10.18 *Social security contributions, 1990–2003 (% of GDP)*

Country	% of Non-oil GDP	Total
Venezuela	0.9	0.7
Argentina		2.8
Bolivia		2.2
Brazil		7.6
Chile		1.5
Colombia		0.1
Mexico		1.9
Paraguay		0.9
Peru		1.4
Uruguay		7.4
Latin America		2.3
OECD		10.5

Source: IMF (2006a)

Table 10.19 *Social security taxes and contributions*

Contributions	Employer	Employee	Total	Employee's share
Social Security	13.8	3.2	17.5	
Pensions	5.4	0.8	6.8	0.1
Medical Assistance	4.7	1.6	6.3	0.3
Unemployment	2.0	0.5	2.5	
Other	1.8	0.3	2.0	
Work Training	0.3	0.1	0.3	
Housing	2.0	1.0	3.0	
Total	16.1	4.2	20.3	

Source: República Bolivariana de Venezuela (2006)

workers finance contingencies covered by the system with monthly contributions. The average tax rate on payroll income is close to 20 per cent, of which the employee's share is about a fifth (see Table 10.19). International comparisons tend to rank Venezuela as one of the countries with most regulation-imposed labour market rigidities in Latin America (Bermúdez, 2004).

One of the reasons for the declining share of social security taxes in GDP has been the dramatic increase in the size of the informal sector. From 1990 to 2001, Venezuela underwent the greatest increase in the size of the informal sector in the region (see Figure 10.20). The dependency ratio (number of workers/number of retirees) has fallen dramatically since the 1970s (from 48 in 1974 to 7 in 1999), and the relationship of the number of contributors to total number employed has fallen by almost a half (from 40 per cent in 1995 to 23 per cent in 1999). Tax evasion has also affected the collection of the tax, according to reports of the Venezuelan Social Security Institute (IVSS). The rate of non-fulfilment is 50 per cent of formal sector workers (which is about half the labour force).

The Venezuelan social security system was created in 1944 with the Mandatory Social Security Law. The reach of that law was limited to occupational illness and industrial accidents. Social security was given constitutional rank in 1961 (Article 94, Constitution of Venezuela, 1961) and referred to the contingencies of occupational accidents, diseases, disability, retirement, death, unemployment and any other work-related conditions. The development of these aspects was not immediate, though. The 1967 law included pensions (retiree and surviving worker relatives) and disability insurance. The payments for these new concepts only started in 1972. In 1975 pensions were extended to cover all workers.

The 1997 IMF/World Bank adjustment programme contemplated the adoption of measures oriented toward the reduction of labour costs. One of them was a reform of the social security system. This materialized with the approval of a new law in 1997. New laws were approved in 1998 covering pensions, health and unemployment insurance.

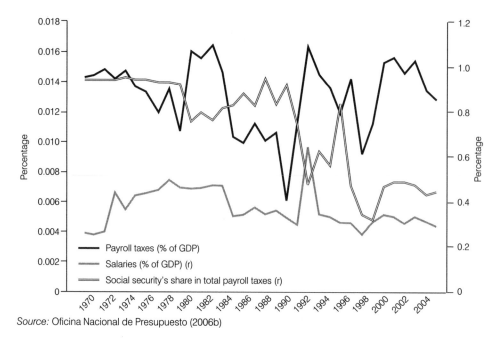

Source: Oficina Nacional de Presupuesto (2006b)

Figure 10.19 *Payroll taxes and salaries (% of GDP) and social security (% of payroll taxes), 1970–2003*

With the exception of the unemployment insurance law, the 1998 laws were suspended in 1999 by the Chávez administration. The new Constitution approved that year gave social security a wider scope, including provision for a minimum pension equal to the urban minimum wage for all workers (including rural workers). The full budget impact of the new system has been estimated at 8 per cent of GDP (Oficina de Asesoría Económica y Financiera de la Asamblea Nacional, 2001). The complexity of the new system and its large budget impact has delayed its total implementation. The new Organic Law of Social Security was only approved in 2002, but a transition period of five years was legally established before it would be fully operative. In 2003, the average pension was $167 (see Table 10.20).

Although social security would appear to be a fertile area for the application of reforms that could generate increased revenues, those revenues would be earmarked for the social security system and therefore it would be difficult to direct them towards fulfilling the MDG goals. That said, a solid social security system could be a significant

Table 10.20 *Social security pension rates*

	Bolívares per month	US dollars per month
1980	899	209
2003	321,235	167

Source: Ministerio del Trabajo (various years)

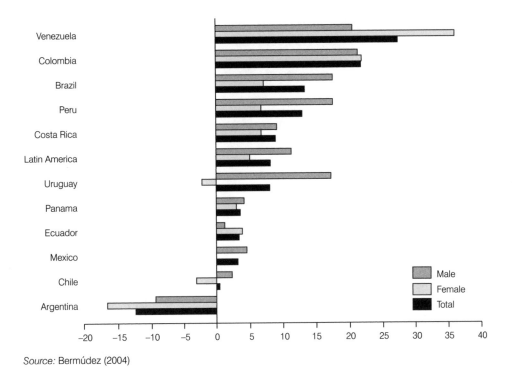

Source: Bermúdez (2004)

Figure 10.20 *Growth rate of the informal sector, 1990–2001*

contributor, in and of itself, towards achieving the MDGs. Furthermore, ensuring that the central government will not have to cover a set of contingent liabilities arising from the social security system could also free up a significant amount of resources.

State and municipal taxes

We have referred at length to issues of fiscal decentralization in the section 'A short history of Venezuelan fiscal policy (or how not to build a tax system)' above. This section makes some additional comments with reference to the imbalance between spending and taxation responsibilities.

The approval of the 1989 reforms that allowed for direct elections of governors and mayors was originally designed to occur simultaneously with greater fiscal decentralization. The idea was that the central government would progressively transfer competences in public service provision to states and municipalities, while at the same time giving them the capacity to generate the resources to cover them. In practice, what occurred was a transfer of competences accompanied by a transfer of resources derived from national tax collection. Spending by states and municipalities thus rose from 2.7 per cent to 6.8 per cent of GDP between 1990 and 2002 (see Table 10.21). However, they are still as dependent on central government transfers as at the beginning of the 1990s (see Table 10.22).

Table 10.21 *General government spending*

	1990 Revenues % of GDP	Share % of total	2002 Revenues % of GDP	Share % of total	1990 Expenses % of GDP	Share % of total	2002 Expenses % of GDP	Share % of total
Total	26.7	100	28.6	100	27.6	100	31.9	100
Central Government	22.6	84.7	21.6	75.4	25.0	90.4	25.0	78.6
States	3.32	12.5	4.8	16.9	2.2	7.9	4.6	14.5
Municipalities	76	2.9	2.2	7.7	0.5	1.7	2.2	6.9

Sources: Ministerio de Finanzas (various years); Banco Central de Venezuela (various years (b))

This strongly centralized system entails not using one of the most valuable resources that the state has at its disposal for increasing tax collection, the legitimacy and capacity of local governments. A more decentralized system could create a situation in which state and local governments make efforts to convince their constituents of the need to collect taxes in order to finance particular projects. Perhaps the most important effect of such a move would not be in that it would help resolve free rider problems in garnering support for higher marginal taxes, but in that it would allow clear communication to voters of the idea that there is a link between taxation and spending. That idea, which appears commonsensical to anyone in a developed country, is far from clear in a country where spending has typically been paid from natural resource rents.

Some tentative conclusions

How can Venezuela generate more resources for the fight against poverty? First, raise the price of gasoline to that currently charged in Niger, whose per capita GDP is 4.4 per

Table 10.22 *Revenues of states and municipalities (% of GDP)*

% of GDP	1994	1995	1996	1997	1998	1999	2000	2001	2002	2003
Transfers from										
Central Government	3.7	3.7	4.3	6.6	5.6	5.2	6.0	5.9	5.6	5.7
Constitutional Grants	3.3	3.2	3.1	4.1	3.0	3.0	3.6	3.5	3.5	3.5
AEE				0.2	0.5	0.4	0.8	0.6	0.8	0.8
FIDES			0.2	0.4	0.5	0.5	0.4	0.4	0.3	0.4
Special transfers	0.4	0.5	1.0	2.0	1.6	1.4	1.1	1.4	1.0	1.0
Own revenues	0.4	0.1	0.1	0.1		0.1	0.1	0.1	0.2	0.4
Other resources									0.7	0.4
Total	4.0	3.8	4.4	6.8	5.6	5.3	6.1	6.0	6.5	6.5
Transfers from										
Central Government	90.9	96.8	98.7	98.4	100.0	98.6	98.1	97.8	86.2	88.5
Constitutional Grants	81.6	83.9	71.8	60.7	53.2	55.8	59.0	57.7	53.8	54.5
AEE	0.0	0.0	0.0	2.4	8.8	8.2	13.7	10.7	12.0	12.3
FIDES	0.0	0.0	4.6	6.0	8.5	8.5	7.1	6.5	4.3	5.7
Special transfers	9.3	12.9	22.2	29.3	29.5	26.1	18.3	22.9	16.1	16.0
Own revenues	9.1	3.2	1.3	1.6	0.0	1.4	1.9	2.2	2.5	5.5
Other resources									11.2	6.0

Source: Oficina Nacional de Presupuesto (various years (b))

cent of that of Venezuela. This would still be only 14 per cent of the retail price in the US. Even an inept politician should be able to explain that this is not an outrageous price to pay. This will provide 1.04 per cent of GDP. Second, reform the income tax system. Randomly copying any Latin American country, except Argentina, would generate 0.9 per cent of GDP in expected value. Third, raise VAT back to 16.5 per cent, the level it was at in 1989. This will generate 0.75 per cent of GDP. Fourth, create a state sales tax surcharge that can be levied by state governors and make transfers to governors dependant on tax collection in their states and municipalities. If the average surcharge is 1 per cent, that will generate 0.3 per cent of GDP and eliminate a few headaches.

This set of simple reforms would increase tax revenues by 2.99 per cent of GDP, or 40.2 per cent of the 2004 extreme poverty gap measured by the $1 a day criterion. Raising resources for poverty reduction is not difficult in Venezuela. In the arena of tax policy, Venezuela does have plenty of room.

BUDGET MANAGEMENT AND FISCAL SPACE

In the previous section we looked at ways in which the Venezuelan state could increase its tax revenues. But resources may well be wasted at the stage of budget planning and management. If that is the case, it may be possible to reorient resources towards poverty reduction without necessarily increasing the tax burden. This section looks at this type of reform. In particular, we look at two instances in the design and implementation phase with significant implications for the efficiency of pubic resource allocation, the budget planning stage and the management of government financial assets.

Fiscal space in the budget planning process

After the budget has been approved by the legislature, the Venezuelan government has a limited number of mechanisms through which it can modify the budget. Additional budget appropriations are approved whenever unexpected increases in revenues are realized. Cancellations (*insubsistencias* in Spanish) and reductions are legal figures that allow for the elimination of budget credits that will not be used for the ends for which they were allocated. Once they are not used, they can be deducted from the total budget or they can be reallocated to expenditures. Finally, there is the '*traspaso*', which consists of reallocating resources between items. This is a limited practice that is only allowed under relatively strict restrictions. However, cancellations and reductions are in effect a perfect substitute for the *traspasos*, so that the legal restrictions on the *traspasos* end up being of little relevance.

In principle, one should expect the value of additional appropriations to be compensated for by those of the cancellations and reductions. In other words, one would expect the government to underestimate the budget on occasions (generating

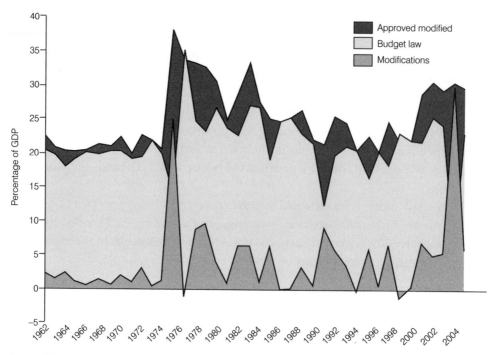

Source: Oficina Nacional de Presupuesto (various years (b))

Figure 10.21 *Budget law and approved changes*

additional appropriations) and to overestimate it on other occasions (generating budget reductions). In practice, budgets have never been reduced by a significant amount. Rather, cancellations and reductions are used to reallocate resources between expenditures. As Table 10.23 shows, additional appropriations have averaged 4.4 per cent of GDP a year. Net transfers between budget items due to cancellations and reductions average 0.9 per cent a year. In other words, Venezuelan budgets are routinely underestimated.

There are two rationales for budget underestimation. One is that additional appropriations are legally defined as extraordinary revenues and thus are not subject to earmarking rules that apply to ordinary revenues. The second is that the executive has greater bargaining power vis-à-vis parliament with additional appropriations. While the legislature has the capacity to alter the composition of the budget, it can simply vote an additional appropriation up or down.[24] As the legislature is unlikely to turn down additional appropriations, this gives the executive complete power to decide on additional appropriations. The same is true for reallocations of expenditures financed with cancellations and reductions. Budget underestimation commonly takes the form of underestimating the price of oil.

Particularly striking is the high variation in cancellations and reductions over time. While high values of additional appropriations can be understood as being the effect of

Table 10.23 *Changes to the budget during the fiscal year*
(% of GDP)

Year	Cancellations & Reductions	Additional Credits
1962	0.3	2.4
1963	0.0	1.3
1964	0.1	2.4
1965	0.0	0.9
1966	0.0	0.4
1967	0.0	1.4
1968	0.0	0.7
1969	0.2	2.2
1970	0.1	0.9
1971	0.0	3.1
1972	0.2	0.3
1973	0.0	1.4
1974	0.0	24.9
1975	5.3	3.8
1976	0.3	8.8
1977	2.9	12.5
1978	1.5	5.5
1979	1.9	4.0
1980	1.1	7.3
1981	0.3	6.7
1982	2.8	2.7
1983	0.2	1.1
1984	0.5	6.7
1985	1.1	3.2
1986	0.0	0.2
1987	1.6	10.6
1988	0.0	0.2
1989	1.6	10.6
1990	0.1	5.9
1991	0.7	3.6
1992	1.8	5.2
1993	0.8	0.7
1994	1.2	7.1
1995	1.3	1.5
1996	0.1	8.0
1997	0.2	6.8
1998	2.4	2.2
1999	1.9	3.3
2000	1.9	8.8
2001	0.5	5.8
2002	1.6	6.3
2003	3.6	0.0
Average	0.9	4.4
Standard deviation	1.2	4.5

Source: Oficina Nacional de Presupuesto (various years (b))

positive revenue (primarily oil) shocks, it is hard to think of any shock that could generate spending projections that would be off by more than 5 per cent of GDP given the level of revenues. One combined effect of the high reliance on additional appropriations, cancellations and reductions is that the budget bargaining stage does not just occur at the moment of budget formulation, but rather takes place continuously over the year. Government institutions are routinely told to wait for an additional appropriation if their requests were not included in the budget. Likewise, those who fall out of favour know that their budget can be cut indiscriminately. Such a possibility generates a scramble to overestimate budget proposals on the part of government institutions that feel that they have to protect themselves from possible future cuts.

What would a sensible reform of this system look like? It could start by limiting the role of budget modifications to a maximum percentage that could be specified, such as 1 per cent of GDP. It could also allow the assembly to reallocate resources from additional credits to other budget lines and to end the distinction between ordinary and extraordinary revenues for the effect of earmarking rules. Since the latter would, *ceteris paribus*, generate an increase in nondiscretionary spending, the percentage allocations could be proportionately reduced to keep average transfers constant. These reforms would end the incentives for revenue underestimation and limit the scramble for resources on the part of government institutions.

Limiting the use of additional appropriations requires devising a rule for the use of non-budgeted increases in oil revenues, as these will often exceed the 1 per cent threshold. This can be done through the design of a macroeconomic stabilization fund for the savings of oil revenues. Indeed, such a fund was constituted in Venezuela and operated from 1998. Despite its constitutional status, the fund has been all but dismantled by the present administration.

Closing rules matter

A second source of inefficiencies in the budget execution stage has to do with the rules for budget closure. These refer to the rules for determining the resources that a government institution has used up by year's end. These can be related either to committed expenditures or to caused expenditures. Expenditures are committed when a good or service is ordered, while they are caused when the good is received or the service is performed. Until 1976, budget closure was based on caused expenditures. This meant that budgeted expenditures that had not been used, in the sense of receiving the goods or services, would go back to the Treasury. In 1976 a new Budgetary Regime Law shifted to the committed expenditure rule. Although the 1999 law reverted to the caused expenditure rule, this provision has not been enforced by the Ministry of Finance, which has kept on applying the committed expenditures rule.[25]

The basic problem is that it is much easier to commit expenditures than to cause them. Government institutions routinely scramble to commit resources at year-end, by signing contracts which they do not always intend to satisfy. In this way, they protect

Table 10.24 *Overlapping budgets*

National Treasury	1989	1990	1991	1992	1993	1994	1995	1996	1997	1998	1999	2000	2001	2002	2003	2004	Annual average	Standard deviation
Initial Balance	1.9	7.5	18.0	14.8	10.1	6.5	4.5	1.4	2.7	3.4	0.6	0.5	0.5	0.1	0.1	0.9	4.6	5.5
Fiscal Revenues	21.7	24.8	26.3	20.5	19.5	19.3	17.9	22.0	23.8	18.1	20.9	24.9	25.5	24.0	28.0	30.0	22.9	3.5
Ordinary	19.5	22.5	22.9	17.5	16.6	16.3	15.9	18.0	20.4	13.2	15.8	17.7	18.0	17.5	19.7	21.8	18.3	2.7
Extraordinary	2.2	2.3	3.4	3.0	2.8	3.0	1.7	3.5	1.1	4.9	4.7	7.1	7.5	5.7	8.0	2.7	4.0	2.1
Financial Sources	0.0	0.0	0.0	0.0	0.0	0.0	0.0	0.0	0.0	0.0	0.0	0.0	0.0	0.0	0.0	5.4	0.3	1.3
Revenues from Previous Budget	0.0	0.0	0.0	0.0	0.0	0.0	0.3	0.5	0.0	0.0	0.4	0.1	0.0	0.8	0.0	0.0	0.2	0.3
Short–Term Treasury Bonds	7.5	15.5	0.0	0.0	0.0	0.0	0.0	0.0	0.0	0.5	0.4	0.3	0.5	0.3	0.7	0.1	1.6	4.1
Placements	0.0	0.0	0.0	0.0	0.0	0.0	0.0	0.0	0.0	1.0	-0.3	1.5	2.1	3.7	5.3	2.9	1.2	1.7
Rescue	0.0	0.0	0.0	0.0	0.0	0.0	0.0	0.0	0.0	0.5	2.6	1.2	1.6	3.4	4.6	2.8	1.1	1.5
Expenditures	19.9	23.7	24.2	21.9	19.2	18.7	19.3	19.5	22.4	21.3	20.5	25.2	26.3	24.2	27.4	27.3	22.6	3.0
Year Budget	18.8	22.3	22.2	19.3	16.4	17.5	16.9	18.2	20.5	18.9	18.7	22.6	21.7	22.0	26.0	25.9	20.5	2.9
Last Year Budget	1.1	1.3	2.0	2.6	2.8	1.3	2.4	1.3	1.9	2.4	1.8	2.6	4.6	2.3	1.5	1.4	2.1	0.9
Final Balance	11.2	24.0	20.1	13.4	10.4	7.1	3.2	4.0	4.1	0.7	0.7	0.5	0.2	0.1	1.4	3.7	6.6	7.4
Fund for Investment and Macroeconomic Stabilisation (FIEM)	0.0	0.0	0.0	0.0	0.0	0.0	0.0	0.0	0.0	0.0	0.0	1.7	0.0	0.0	0.0	0.0	0.1	0.4
Change of Reserves	9.3	16.6	2.1	-1.4	0.2	0.6	-1.3	2.5	1.4	-2.7	0.1	0.0	-0.2	0.0	1.3	2.8	2.0	4.7
Pending credits	2.4	3.0	4.2	4.9	3.8	4.1	2.7	2.8	2.8	2.2	4.6	5.1	2.8	1.8	2.1	1.7	3.2	1.1
Budget Balance from Previous Year 6–12	-1.1	-1.3	-2.0	-2.6	-2.8	-1.3	-2.1	-0.7	-1.9	-2.4	-1.4	-2.6	-4.6	-1.5	-1.1	-1.4	-1.9	0.9
Budget Expenditures Approved + Mod	21.2	25.3	26.4	24.3	20.2	22.3	20.5	21.9	24.6	21.5	22.2	28.6	30.4	29.0	30.3	29.1	24.9	3.7
% of Budget Execution 18/11	88.8	88.3	84.1	79.7	81.3	78.1	82.3	83.4	83.3	87.9	84.3	79.0	71.5	75.7	85.8	88.9	82.7	5.0

Source: Oficina Nacional de Presupuesto (2006a)

themselves from future cuts. The fact that the committed expenditures often go unspent is revealed in Table 10.24. There are two key items here, pending credits (line 16) and budget balance from the previous year (line 17). Pending credits refers to committed expenditures that are not paid on a cash basis. Budget balance from the previous year refers to expenditures that are paid for from last year's budget. That is, line 16 refers to the resources set aside to pay for committed expenditures, while line 17 refers to those that were effectively used to pay the same expenditures. The conclusion is straightforward: the government sets aside, on average, 3.2 per cent of GDP to pay for pending credits, but ends up paying only for 1.9 per cent of them. Due to poor planning, 1.3 per cent of GDP is over-budgeted.

Obviously, this does not mean that the government can increase yearly spending by 1.3 per cent of GDP, as unspent resources ultimately devolve to the Treasury. What it does mean is that at any moment in time there are 1.3 points of GDP expenditures that are not being used.

Where's the money? Management of government deposits

The previous discussion logically raises the question, 'Where is this 1.3 per cent of GDP?'. A little reflection reveals that if this represents resources that have been disbursed to government agencies, but which have not been spent, then they must be deposited in banks. This fact illustrates a broader problem that is one of the most alarming features of Venezuelan public finance management, the accrual of a large government deposits in non- or low interest bearing accounts.

At the close of 2004, the Venezuelan government held deposits in private banks equal to 4.7 per cent of GDP (see Figure 10.22). These deposits, predominantly placed in current accounts, yielded revenues of no more than 0.2 per cent of GDP,[26] a negligible amount. At the same time, outstanding government debt totalled 4.6 per cent of GDP, of which 4.1 per cent of GDP was held by private agents.[27] Interest payments on that debt amounted to 2.1 per cent of GDP, of which we estimate 1.9 per cent of GDP went to private agents.[28] Using these conservative estimates, we conclude that, *despite being a net creditor to the Venezuelan private sector*, the Venezuelan state transfers at least 1.7

Table 10.25 *Credits and deposits, Venezuelan banking sector (December 2005)*

	Universal & Commercial Banks	Treasury Bank
Credit (Bs million)	63,158,457	148,629
Public sector component (Bs million)	10,067,319	n.a.
Proportion of credit (%)	15.9	
Central Bank (Bs million)	10,431,926	128,596
Proportion of credit (%)	16.5	86.5
Deposits (Bs million)	66,429,406	121,799
Public Sector component (Bs million)	13,388,073	n.a.
Proportion of deposits (%)	20.2	

Source: Banco Central de Venezuela (various years (c))

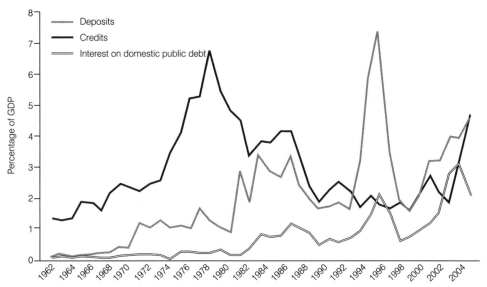

Source: Banco Central de Venezuela (various years (b))

Figure 10.22 *Public sector deposits and credits with the private financial system (% of GDP)*

per cent of GDP a year to this sector through net interest payments on its government debt.[29]

While some part of that transfer may adequately compensate for the service of financial intermediation between government agencies, it is difficult to conceive that the public sector could not perform this at a lower cost. Indeed, in August 2005, the executive created the Treasury Bank in order to centrally manage all government accounts.[30] By the end of 2005, the Treasury Bank's balance of credits and deposits amounted to 0.2 per cent of the total reported by Universal and Commercial Banks; 86.5 per cent of credits were placed in the Central Bank (see Table 10.25). Although the creation of the Treasury Bank seems a promising reform on paper, in practice it has yet to show any significant results.

In principle, similar economies could be achieved not by the unification of public financial resources but from a modernization of the methods and processes of public finance. This would involve the centralization of information on public funds by the National Treasury, the requirement that banks and collecting agencies report to the Treasury, and the effective enforcement of the National Treasury's authority and responsibility with regard to the management of public funds. These considerations, in fact, accounted for the creation in the late 1990s of the Integrated System of Financial Management and Control of Public Finance (SIGECOF). The SIGECOF was meant to provide accurate, real-time information on the management of human, financial and non-financial public resources that would help decision-makers in budgetary decision-making. This would be accomplished through four stages, legal and policy reforms, organizational and bureaucratic culture changes, modernization of methods and procedures of each management function, and the development of related information systems and complementary tools. The reform was expected to allow the integration of the financial administration systems with the internal controls and the evaluation of public expenditures (Ministerio de Finanzas, 2005). Although the Ministry of Finance has claimed that this reform is still in process,[31] there is little evidence that it has helped improve the management of public deposits.

Even more room?

Our analysis of the budget process has shown that concrete improvements in budget planning, execution and management could lead to significant improvements in resource availability. At first sight, these reforms look comparatively easier to carry out than those regarding taxation, as they would appear to have no political or social cost. However, if we think more carefully, we will find that these reforms may, if anything, be more difficult to carry out than those discussed in the section 'The Venezuelan tax system: A closer look' above. A transfer of 1.7 per cent of GDP to the banking sector does not occur without generating significant vested interests in its maintenance. Anecdotally, during our tenure in the Economic and Financial Advisory Office to the National Assembly between 2000 and 2004, we had the chance to interact with five Ministers of Finance,[32] all of whom made reference to the management of government deposits as a way to generate resources. None of them were able to alter the trend of growing deposits shown in Figure 10.21. This fact suggests that altering the distribution of government deposits between the private and public sectors' financial institutions is far from trivial, and may well be politically more difficult than raising the price of gasoline.

THE COMPOSITION OF PUBLIC EXPENDITURES: THE INFRASTRUCTURE EXAMPLE

In the section 'A short history of Venezuelan fiscal policy' above, we argued that the composition of Venezuelan public expenditures was heavily distorted by the historical influence of patronage-based politics and the strong bias towards public employment by Venezuelan political parties. Further signs of this distortion can be glimpsed by looking at the composition of public expenditures in Venezuela in comparison to other Latin American countries. This comparison is displayed in Table 10.26, which shows the breakdown of government spending by function for 12 Latin American countries, including Venezuela.

A few interesting facts are evident from this table. In the first place, Venezuela's share of spending on general public services (43.33 per cent) is the highest in the region and far above the Latin American average (24.68 per cent). This fact coincides with the assumption that Venezuela's government bureaucracy may be excessive. It is interesting

Table 10.26 *Composition of central government spending in Latin America (%)*

	Argentina	Bolivia	Brazil	Chile	Costa Rica	Dominican Republic	El Salvador	Mexico	Nicaragua	Panama	Trinidad and Tobago	Venezuela, Rep. Bol.	Latin American Average
General public services	23.20	21.13	34.58	7.12	21.88	16.50	13.34	35.83	22.53	22.39	34.30	43.33	24.68
Public debt transactions	13.57	7.70	20.54	3.15	16.83	5.81	8.00	16.92	11.12	13.92	19.24	14.74	12.63
Transfers of a general character between different levels of government		2.78		0.08									1.43
Defence	4.83	8.39	3.59	8.35	0.00	4.84	4.78	3.46	7.45	0.00	1.73	5.12	4.38
Public order and safety	3.67	7.23	2.67	5.57	6.63	4.16	13.28	1.84	8.75	7.90	6.88	3.08	5.97
Economic affairs	7.40	15.67	5.33	13.07	10.49	27.81	15.26	12.49	13.36	6.79	11.26	5.84	12.06
Agriculture, forestry, fishing and hunting	0.86	1.92	2.59		2.58	8.70	2.59	3.67	3.62	1.96	4.35	0.66	3.04
Fuel and energy	1.62	1.00	0.45		0.14	3.81	0.02	1.35	0.68	0.01	0.30	0.53	0.90
Mining, manufacturing and construction	0.42	0.40	0.12		0.20	3.74	0.07	0.48	0.00	0.20	0.31	1.74	0.70
Transport	3.48	8.94	1.29		5.55	6.76	9.00	3.77	7.86	2.82	3.60	1.84	4.99
Communication					0.00	0.05							0.02
Environment protection	0.00	0.00	0.00	0.00	0.00	0.23	0.00	0.00	0.00	0.00	0.00	0.00	0.02
Housing and community amenities	2.10	1.23	0.58	4.66	0.23	9.84	9.79	4.76	2.44	4.36	8.30	4.91	4.43
Health	2.21	6.23	6.67	12.05	21.73	11.39	10.80	3.87	13.33	19.02	8.04	6.90	10.19
Outpatient services	0.00	0.52	5.89				3.92			0.10	0.52	0.10	1.58
Hospital services	0.26	0.90	0.00				5.11			18.84	5.20	1.97	4.61
Public health services										0.00			0.00
Recreation, culture and religion	0.31	0.36	0.08	0.00	0.80	0.93	1.70	0.63	1.15	0.85	0.86	1.02	0.72
Education	5.92	19.13	4.99	16.42	20.20	14.15	15.35	24.39	15.26	17.57	13.35	19.64	15.53
Secondary education	0.38	3.19	2.78				12.70			9.91	10.50	6.58	6.58
Tertiary education	0.45	5.23	2.00				1.85			4.53	1.97	2.67	2.67
Social protection	50.63	20.63	42.78	34.98	21.03	8.48	22.86	20.04	15.68	21.13	15.28	23.64	23.64
Adjustment to total outlays	-0.27	0.00	-1.25	-2.21	-2.99	1.66	-7.15	-7.31	0.04	0.00	0.00	0.00	-1.62
Other	0.00	0.00	0.00	0.00	0.00	0.23	0.00	0.00	0.00	0.00	0.00	0.00	0.02
Total outlays	100.00	100.00	100.00	100.00	100.00	100.23	100.00	100.00	100.00	100.00	100.00	100.00	100.02

Source: IMF (2006a)

Table 10.27 *Gross enrolment rates by level, 1998–2002*

Country Name	Preschool	Primary	Secondary	Tertiary
Argentina	58.82	119.58	94.74	50.82
Aruba	98.89	112.64	100.00	28.67
Barbados	83.81	107.96	103.13	36.15
Belize	28.17	118.54	70.94	1.99
Bolivia	45.78	113.94	79.69	35.99
Brazil	60.14	151.23	104.41	15.80
Chile	69.16	102.23	83.94	37.81
Colombia	36.28	111.36	69.49	23.05
Costa Rica	67.76	108.09	54.86	18.04
Cuba	108.06	101.85	85.54	25.01
Dominica	67.63	95.51	98.25	
Dominican Republic	35.45	122.36	60.16	34.46
Ecuador	69.34	115.45	57.87	
El Salvador	44.20	111.76	54.11	17.55
Grenada	67.89	94.60		
Guatemala	43.26	100.95	36.43	9.33
Guyana	116.76	121.07	87.36	6.09
Honduras	21.35	105.82		14.45
Jamaica	85.06	98.61	83.64	15.97
Mexico	74.92	110.55	72.52	19.96
Netherlands Antilles	91.96	108.75	71.54	14.82
Nicaragua	26.33	104.22	54.51	18.35
Panama	45.75	109.39	68.26	43.78
Paraguay	28.01	111.89	57.81	16.30
Peru	57.70	121.63	85.58	31.79
St Kitts and Nevis	141.62	117.29		
St Lucia	68.82	112.24	84.36	1.43
St Vincent and the Grenadines		103.08	68.80	
Suriname	94.05	126.23	72.96	12.24
Trinidad and Tobago	62.47	100.47	81.28	6.92
Uruguay	60.09	110.63	99.75	35.40
Venezuela, RB	48.45	103.54	64.81	34.00
Latin American Average	64.77	111.05	76.09	22.45

Source: World Bank (2006)

in this respect that the country that allocates the lowest fraction of spending to general public services is Chile (7.12 per cent), which also tends to score very high in most international government efficiency and institutional quality comparisons. A second interesting fact is that Venezuela has the second lowest level of spending in the region on social protection (10.13 per cent, as opposed to a regional average of 23.64 per cent). This is primarily due to the lack of development of an adequate social security system, as was discussed in the section 'The Venezuelan tax system: A closer look'.

A closer analysis brings out additional facts. Venezuela's spending on economic affairs (5.84 per cent) is the second lowest in the region, at approximately one-half of the regional average (12.06 per cent). Particularly striking is the general trend of under-investment in transport infrastructure (1.84 per cent), less than two-fifths of the

Source: Hausmann and Rodríguez (2006)

Figure 10.23 *Per capita fiscal oil revenues in constant US$, 1943–2001*

regional average (4.99 per cent). This fact is consistent with the low levels of public investment in infrastructure also highlighted in the section 'A short history of Venezuelan fiscal policy' above. In contrast, Venezuelan investment in education (19.64 per cent) is relatively high in relation to that of the rest of the region (15.53 per cent). Table 10.A1, page 472, based on the Ministry of Finance classification, tells a similar story, with a decline in spending on productive sectors from 29.0 per cent in 1977 to 7.8 per cent in 2004. Although Venezuela does not provide a breakdown of its education budget by level of education, the fact that it has higher enrolment rates than the regional average in tertiary education, but not in primary, secondary or higher education, is a clear indicator of the fact that educational policies have not been oriented towards the neediest sectors (see Table 10.27).

Perhaps even more important than a static comparison of Venezuelan spending vis-à-vis that of other Latin American countries is the analysis of its changes over time. Similar to many other Latin American countries, Venezuela carried out a set of fiscal adjustments in the 1980s and 1990s in order to deal with the onset of the debt crisis. In contrast to other Latin American countries, however, in the mid-1980s Venezuela had to contend not only with the effects on its fiscal accounts of a drastic increase in American interest rates but also with a significant decline in oil revenues. As we show in Figure 10.23, after reaching their peak in the 1970s, per capita fiscal oil revenues fell by approximately two-thirds during the 1980s, requiring a drastic adjustment of expenditures.

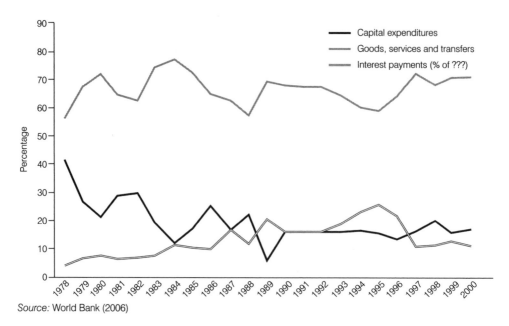

Source: World Bank (2006)

Figure 10.24 *Composition of public spending, 1978–2000*

Figure 10.24 and Table 10.28 show two key characteristics of the nature of this adjustment. The first is that it was significantly biased against government investment.
Spending on the purchases of goods, services and transfers actually increased its participation in the government budget, while the share of capital expenditures fell
dramatically from 41.4 per cent in 1978 (the year of peak non-oil GDP) to 17.3 per cent
in 2000. Venezuelan Ministry of Finance data, based on a somewhat different classification, provide direct estimates of central government gross fixed capital formation. This
goes from a peak of 4.8 per cent of GDP in 1969 to 0.4 per cent of GDP in 2004 (see
Table 10.A2, page 474). The need to make room for the increase in interest payments
was thus accommodated exclusively by a decrease in investment. The second is that a
significant cost within this adjustment was paid by infrastructure expenditures. On
average, the decline in Venezuelan public infrastructure spending was similar to that of
the rest of the region in its proportion. However, the fact that Venezuela was starting
from a much lower level of infrastructure spending, a fact discussed in the section 'A

Table 10.28 *Changes in infrastructure investment, Venezuela and Latin America*

	Venezuela			Latin America		
	1981– 1985	1996– 2000	% Change	1981– 1985	1996– 2000	% Change
Telecommunications	0.19	0.01	−94.74	0.29	0.19	−34.48
Electricity	0.11	0.03	−72.73	1.38	0.2	−85.51
Transport	0.19	0.06	−69.42	0.81	0.15	−81.48
Total	0.49	0.1	−79.59	2.81	0.56	−80.07

Source: Calderón and Servén (2003)

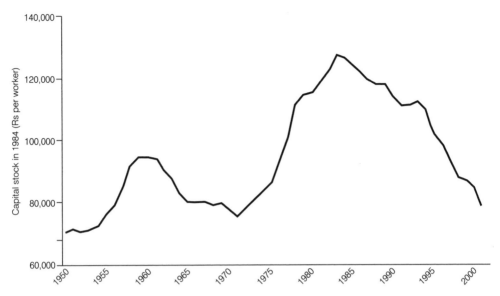

Source: Authors' estimate based on Banco Central de Venezuela (2000); Banco Central de Venezuela (various years(a)); Baptista (1997); Ministerio de Energía y Minas (various years)

Figure 10.25 *Public capital stock per worker, 1950–2001*

short history of Venezuelan fiscal policy', meant that there was much less room to cut back. Thus Venezuelan infrastructure investment shares fell to dramatically low levels. These levels of public investment were inappropriate and failed to compensate for the effects of depreciation and population growth. The end result of this process was a precipitous decline in the public capital stock, which by 2001 had fallen back to the same levels as the 1950s (see Figure 10.25).

The distorted adjustment phenomenon is not only relevant to the case of infrastructure. Table 10.29 and Figure 10.26 illustrate that a similar phenomenon took place in the arena of public education. In particular, enrolment rates continued growing while the quality of education declined significantly (Pritchett and Ortega, 2006).[33] This phenomenon is symptomatic of a process of adjustment whereby labour intensive expenditures are protected but capital intensive ones are not. Since labour laws and political arrangements make it very difficult to fire workers, public employment becomes relatively protected during fiscal adjustments. Quantity measures of perform-

Table 10.29 *Enrolment rates by level*

	1990	2002
Preschool	40.78	52.67
Primary	95.70	103.86
Secondary	34.68	68.89
Tertiary	29.17	40.25

Source: World Bank (2006)

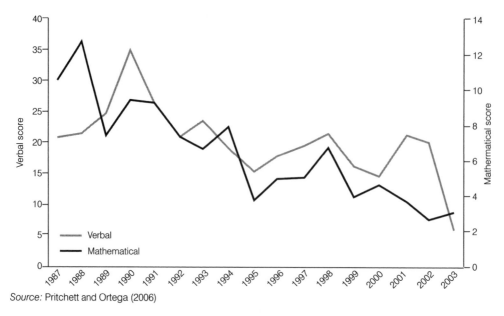

Source: Pritchett and Ortega (2006)

Figure 10.26 *Test scores for scholastic aptitude tests in Venezuela, 1987–2003*

ance that are proportional to the number of employees, such as enrolment rates, need not decline. The decline in the provision of materials, training and incentives is felt in the acute deterioration of quality indicators, such as that presented in Figure 10.26. This phenomenon of distorted adjustment appears to characterize other dimensions of public spending (see Puente, 2004).

Asymmetric adjustments that privilege current expenditures vis-à-vis capital expenditures raise a set of interesting issues from the perspective of fiscal space. If these adjustments have significant negative effects on productivity, what is their long-run effect on a nation's fiscal space? Easterly (1999) and Easterly and Servén (2002) raise a concern about the possibility of 'illusory fiscal adjustments' – fiscal adjustments that bring about long-run costs because they are financed by a reduction in capital expenditures and thus shift inwards the state's inter-temporal budget constraint. Is it possible that the quality of fiscal adjustments is an important determinant of a nation's fiscal space? Over what horizon would the effects of an asymmetric adjustment on fiscal space become manifest? Would it make sense for a country to protect public investment as a way of salvaging its fiscal space?

Another related question concerns the capacity of the state to create fiscal space in the short run for the protection of public investment. Given the existence of legal and political rigidities, which make it nearly impossible to reduce employment in the context of a fiscal adjustment, is there a set of policies that governments can adopt in order to ensure the availability of resources for public investment?

The answer to any of these questions will depend on the strength of the causal link between public investment and productivity. The existence of such a link is far from established in the empirical literature. Although there are good theoretical reasons to expect public capital to have an effect on productivity (Arrow and Kurz, 1970; Ogura and Yohe, 1977), empirical results are mixed (Aschauer, 1989; Munnell, 1990; Hulten and Schwab, 1991; Easterly and Rebelo, 1993; Esfanhani and Ramírez, 2003).[34] These studies are all confronted by a daunting empirical problem. Precisely because of the political forces in action to determine the allocation of investment projects, spending on infrastructure is likely to be an endogenous variable, making identification of its effect on productivity growth difficult. If governments are more likely to invest in prosperous and economically developed regions, then there will be a spurious positive correlation between investment in infrastructure and productivity growth. While if policymakers try to use public investment to compensate for the backwardness of existing regions or to help out regions in crisis, there will be a contrasting downward bias in estimates of the effect of infrastructure investment on productivity growth. It will be extremely difficult to find valid instruments that can address this issue.

In the rest of this section, we address these issues by looking in detail at a unique policy experiment carried out in the mid-1990s in Venezuela: the creation of a set of budget pre-allocations designed to be specifically targeted towards public investment. This example will allow us to illustrate: (1) the magnitude of the effects of public investment on productivity; (2) the time horizon over which these productivity effects have a significant effect on resource availability; and (3) the way in which mechanisms to raise fiscal space for spending on infrastructure can be designed.

The FIDES experience

In June of 1993, the Venezuelan historian and intellectual, Ramón J. Velásquez, reached an agreement with the nation's key political parties (AD and COPEI) to head a caretaker administration after Carlos Andrés Pérez's (1989–1992) impeachment by the Venezuelan Supreme Court on corruption allegations. Velásquez was among the few persons in Venezuela who had sufficient prestige so as not to generate an outcry in a period of deep discontent with the role of traditional parties. Velásquez's condition for assuming the presidency was that AD and COPEI give him special powers to allow him to adopt what he viewed as necessary immediate economic reforms.

Velásquez's concerns were not unfounded. Oil prices were winding back down after the resolution of the Persian Gulf War and the only way in which the Pérez administration had been able to get the budget deficit down to 1.8 per cent of GDP in 1992 was through the use of the proceeds of $2.03 billion (3.4 per cent of GDP) from the privatization of the state-owned telephone company (CANTV) and airline (VIASA) (Bekaert and Harvey, 2004). Pérez's proposal for VAT had been sidetracked by AD and COPEI deputies in the Venezuelan congress, who saw little benefit from its approval. Velásquez wanted the power to enact this and other reforms to make sure that he could adequately manage the economy for his year in office.

As part of the political deal that was hammered out to give Velásquez the power to adopt VAT was a commitment from the administration to design a mechanism that would ensure that a fraction of the proceeds from VAT collection would be transferred to regional governments. Regional leaders had started to become an important political force in Venezuela after the political reforms of 1989, which allowed for the direct election of mayors and governors. After this, many congressional deputies felt that their chances of political survival were linked to the prospects of these regional leaders instead of to the national parties that had lost significant levels of legitimacy (Penfold-Becerra, 1999).

Velásquez's team came up with the idea of the Intergovernmental Decentralization Fund, which we will refer to by its Spanish acronym FIDES. FIDES set apart a fraction of VAT revenues to be transferred to state and municipal governments. This fraction would start at 4 per cent and increase proportionally every year. In 1996 the law was reformed and the portion was fixed at 15 per cent, a level at which it has stayed since. Given that the Situado already ensured a 20 per cent share for regional governments, the FIDES reform effectively implied that sub-national governments would perceive 35 per cent of the additional revenues from the adoption of VAT. There was, however, a caveat. Velásquez's team insisted that these revenues not be allocated to current expenditures, since they viewed the central government as the ultimate guarantor of such expenditures. Therefore, they built into the law the proviso that the FIDES share should be allocated to public investment. In order to ensure that this would occur, they set up a formal directory of FIDES, which would have representation in the regional governments but majority control was retained by the representatives of the national executive, and which would be in charge of approving the list of investment projects. Funds would only be disbursed after approval and subject to the co-participation of the state or local government in the funding of the project.

The FIDES law contemplated a broad definition of areas in which the fund could finance public investment projects. The list included 'Projects of productive investment that promote the sustainable development of the community, states and municipalities', and 'works of infrastructure and activities within the framework of national development plans' (FIDES, 2005, Article 22). Although these provisions allow for broad definitions of the types of investment projects, the law does specifically state that these resources must only be used for 'programas y proyectos' (programmes and projects), a term that in Venezuelan legislation is formally equivalent to capital expenditures. Projects that are typically financed include construction of schools, repairs to roads and acquisition of vehicles for use by the local police force.

FIDES provides us with a fascinating natural experiment to evaluate the effect of infrastructure spending on productivity. Since the FIDES rule was held constant over time, it generated variations in transfers to regions that depended on the interaction between the parameters of the rule and national VAT collection, both of which can be taken to be exogenous at the state level. This exogenous source of variation allowed

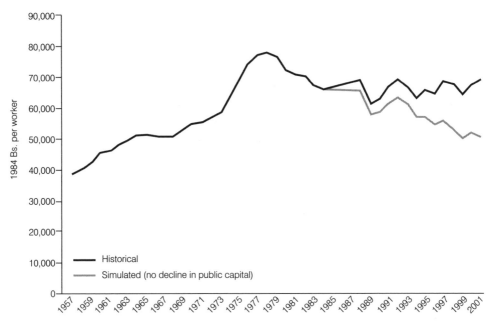

Source: Pineda and Rodríguez (2006)

Figure 10.27 *Historical and simulated per worker GDP: Scenario of no decline in infrastructure investment*

Pineda and Rodríguez (2006) to estimate the effect of state infrastructure investments on firm level productivity growth in the Venezuelan manufacturing industry using state-level data from the Venezuelan Encuesta Industrial. Pineda and Rodríguez's (2006) results indicate a strong effect of FIDES investment on productivity, with an elasticity of 0.32 to 0.4. Curiously, these estimates are remarkably similar to John Fernald's (1999) estimate of an elasticity of 0.38 with respect to public infrastructure provision in the US manufacturing industry.

The empirical estimates are economically very significant. Given a ratio of the stock of public capital to GDP of 0.615 (its 2001 value), the estimated effects imply a short-run rate of return to infrastructure investment of 0.52 to 0.65, and a long-run rate of return (that is, the partial derivative of steady state income to changes in infrastructure spending) of 0.80. Figure 10.27, taken from Pineda and Rodríguez (2006), shows these authors' estimates of the path of Venezuelan non-oil GDP that can be derived from these estimates if the public capital stock had stayed constant at its 1983 value. According to these calculations, per capita GDP would be 37 per cent higher than its present value under that scenario. It appears that the shift in the composition of government spending is an important part of the story behind Venezuela's growth collapse.

Does infrastructure pay for itself?

These high rates of return may lead to the thought that 'infrastructure pays for itself', and that concerns over fiscal space to pay for infrastructure investments should, at most, be concentrated on finding short-term financing. However, this belief would be exaggerated. Even with these high rates of return, it is unlikely that the state will be able to capture more than a fraction of the derived productivity gains. To see why this is the case, consider a stylized model where the government public sector balance, D, is the difference between expenditures, E, and revenues, R, with R being the product of a proportional tax rate, τ, and a GDP, Y. We consider expenditures to be the sum of the change in investment in public capital, ΔP ($= P_t - P_{t-1}$) in the time period t–1 to t and current expenditures, C. Thus the budget constraint is:

$$D = E\text{-}R = P_t - P_{t-1} + C - \tau^*Y \qquad (1)$$

Suppose that GDP depends on the public capital stock (with elasticity β) and on other factors of production that we label K and L, then:

$$Y = P^\beta F(K,L) \qquad (2)$$

And substituting (2) in (1) gives:

$$D_t = E_t - R_t = P_t - P_{t-1} + C_t - \tau^* P^\beta F(K,L) \qquad (3)$$

We are interested in calculating the effect of an increase of one unit of Pt on the budget deficit. In order to do this, we distinguish analytically between three moments at which this effect can be evaluated: (1) a fiscal period in which the initial infrastructure investment is made and productivity gains on existing capital are realized (the short term); (2) a period in which the government has to pay for operations and maintenance expenditures, but in which the capital stock is assumed not to vary (the medium term); and (3) a period in which the government continues paying for operations and maintenance expenditures, but in which the capital stock has gone because of a positive investment response to the increase in productivity (the long-term or steady state):[35]

$$dD_t/dP_t = 1 - \tau\beta P_t^{\beta-1}F(K_t,L_t) = 1 - \tau\beta(Y_t/P_t) \qquad (4)$$

We can derive the short-term rate of return by using the Pineda and Rodríguez estimate of β = 0.32 and the Venezuelan P/Y ratio of 0.615. If we use the non-oil average tax rate of 0.13 as our indicator of τ, this gives:

$$dD_t/dP_t = 0.933 \qquad (5)$$

So that in the immediate period in which the investment is carried out, assuming productivity gains are realized that year, the fiscal situation still worsens by 0.933 cents for every dollar of investment.

What happens after the initial period? The new infrastructure investment requires operations and maintenance (O&M) investment (so that $dC_{t+n}/dP_t > 0$). The United Nations Centre for Human Settlements (1993) estimates annual average O&M costs for public infrastructure at 7.8 per cent of the yearly public asset value. Using this figure would give:

$$dD_m/dP_t = 0.0108 \qquad (6)$$

So that, approximately, the returns from infrastructure investment pay for O&M costs in the medium term. In the long term, the capital stock should react to the higher rate of return, raising the level of the capital stock and thus $F(K,L)$. Under a Cobb-Douglas specification, the capital stock would react with an elasticity of $1/(1-\alpha)$, with α being the capital share. In other words, steady state income would be:

$$Y_{ss} = P^\beta K^\alpha L^{1-\alpha} = P\beta(K_0 P^\beta)^{\alpha/(1-\alpha)}L^{1-\alpha} = P^{\beta(1+\alpha/(1-\alpha))}G(K,L) \qquad (7)$$

Using the conventional $\alpha = 1/3$, this increases the steady state effect of infrastructure investment on tax collection by a factor of 1.5 $(= 1 + (1/3)/(2/3))$, giving a steady state change in the budget deficit of:

$$dD_{ss}/dP_t = -0.0234 \qquad (8)$$

Thus, in the steady state, infrastructure investment leads to an improvement in the fiscal position.

The bottom line is that even though in the very long term infrastructure spending can reduce deficits, this is unlikely to happen in the short term. The reason is that, given existing tax rates, the government reaps only a small fraction of the private return to public investment.

Let us think, in turn, about what can occur to the fiscal position if the government were able to recapture a greater part of the productivity gains from public investment. We can model this by assuming that the government can collect a greater marginal tax rate, τ, on productivity improvements derived from increased infrastructure provision. Suppose, for example, that $\tau = 0.4$ on the marginal increments to productivity. Then the above calculations would be modified as follows:

$$dD_t/dP_t = 0.7919 \qquad (9)$$

$$dD_m/dP_t = -0.13013 \qquad (10)$$

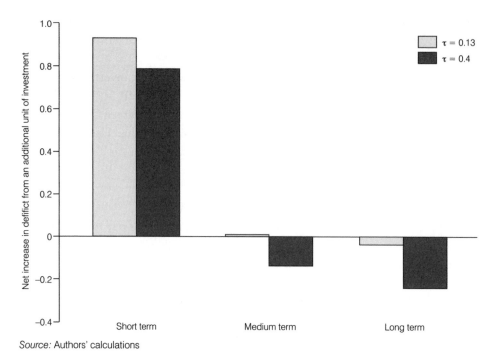

Source: Authors' calculations

Figure 10.28 *Simulated effect of infrastructure investment on budget deficit*

$$dD_{ss}/dP_t = -0.2342 \qquad\qquad (11)$$

After the initial period, the rate of return turns strongly positive and is high enough to cover any reasonable cost of financing. In the steady state, the improvement is significant and considerably enhances the public sector's resource availability. To illustrate the significance of this magnitude, suppose that Venezuela increased public infrastructure investment to its 1981 to 1985 levels, that is, from 0.1 to 0.49 per cent of GDP. Equation (11) implies that such a change would be associated with a long-term improvement of 0.09 per cent of GDP in the fiscal position. Figure 10.28 summarizes these calculations.

In sum, with tax rates similar to those currently in place in Venezuela, infrastructure does not pay for itself. Even in the very long term, the improvement in public finances is low and insufficient to pay for the cost of financing the initial investment. With higher tax rates, however, the long-term return is more than adequate and investing in infrastructure can actually generate additional fiscal space in the medium and long terms.

The key to understanding the policy relevance of this result lies in realizing that, if adequate policies are in place, the relevant tax rate need not be the economy-wide tax rate but rather the marginal tax rate on productivity improvements charged to beneficiaries. Cost recovery policies and laws that target beneficiary sectors can easily raise revenues to the levels necessary to ensure long-term, or even medium-term, fiscal viability. These policies can include targeted taxes, user fees, private/public partnerships and road funds (Gwilliam and Kumar, 2003). In order to make such policies feasible, however, much more work is needed to identify the beneficiaries of infrastructure investments.[36]

Finding room for infrastructure: Lessons from the FIDES example

The above discussion paints a very positive view of the FIDES experience. Through a skilful political deal, the Velásquez administration ensured the approval of a much needed tax reform. It also created a mechanism that helped direct much needed resources to public investment. The estimates, discussed above, point to a significant positive effect of FIDES-financed infrastructure investment on productivity. The FIDES reform is thus an interesting example that is worth studying in depth by countries thinking about mechanisms to generate fiscal space for infrastructure investments.

However, the use of earmarking rules, such as FIDES, is generally viewed negatively by economists and international financial institutions (IFIs). The generalized perception among these circles is that earmarking leads to misallocation of resources, hampers effective budgetary control, infringes on the powers and discretion of the legislature and introduces inflexibility into budgets (McCleary, 1991). It is quite probable that if Venezuela had been on an IMF or World Bank structural adjustment programme in 1993 these institutions would have taken a negative view of the FIDES law.

In the Venezuelan case, however, budget earmarking of VAT revenues through the creation of FIDES was necessary to garner approval for the adoption of VAT law. It makes little sense to criticize revenue earmarking on the grounds that it creates inflexibilities in the management of resources that would not exist if the earmarking rule were not there. Rather, the FIDES experience appears to confirm the intuitions behind some of the early public choice literature on earmarking (Buchanan, 1963; Goetz, 1968), which emphasized the political endogeneity of earmarking rules.

However, the FIDES experience does not provide us with a blanket endorsement of generalized earmarking. On the contrary, FIDES meets a set of peculiar characteristics that may or may not be reproducible in other instances. In the first place, it provides an example of a case in which earmarking was necessary to garner political support for a broader reform which generated additional tax revenues, the bulk of which were not earmarked. In the second place, the FIDES earmarking rule came together with the creation of a technical FIDES board that was required to approve investment projects for the disbursement of funds to take place. States were required to co-participate by covering 20 per cent of the investment cost, which implied that local policymakers had to believe in the benefits of the proposed project. Remarkably, the FIDES board appears to have applied technical, and not political, criteria in the approval of projects, even in the context of significant political polarization. As Table 10.30 shows, the opposition-controlled state governments had, if anything, greater execution percentages, implying that they did not find it more difficult to get approval of projects and the disbursement of funds from the FIDES board. The greater execution percentages for this group of governorships is also present in 1998 (before President Chávez was elected), implying that they, most likely, reflect structural characteristics, such as the greater technical capacity of the administrations of these states.[37] Further investigation is necessary in order to uncover the characteristics that made the FIDES board relatively insulated from political pressure. Without understanding these well it may be adventurous to try to extrapolate these lessons to other settings.

Table 10.30 *FIDES execution percentages, 1998 and 2002*

State (entidad federal)	1998	2002	2002 Government/Opposition
Amazonas	0.62	1.20	Government
Anzoátegui	0.19	0.44	Opposition
Apure		0.72	Government
Aragua	0.11	0.67	Government
Barinas	0.11	0.91	Government
Bolivar	0.24	1.04	Opposition
Carabobo	0.58	1.17	Opposition
Cojedes		0.99	Government
Delta Amacuro	0.54	0.84	Government
Distrito Capital	0.42	0.87	Opposition
Falcón	0.24	1.05	Government
Guárico	0.13	0.97	Government
Lara	0.07	0.72	Government
Mérida	0.31	0.65	Government
Miranda	0.19	1.05	Opposition
Monogas	0.48	1.48	Opposition
Nueva Esparta	0.29	0.72	Government
Portuguesa	0.02	0.96	Government
Sucre	0.41	0.99	Government
Táchira	0.29	0.90	Government
Trujillo	0.48	0.80	Government
Yaracuy	0.23	0.73	Opposition
Zulia	0.64	0.69	Opposition
Average opposition group	0.37	0.93	
Average government group	0.24	0.87	

Source: FIDES (2005)

THE MISIONES: IS OIL WEALTH FINALLY REACHING THE POOR?

On July 1 2003, President Hugo Chávez created by decree the Simón Rodríguez Extraordinary Literacy Plan, better known as the Misión Robinson. The programme's objective was to reduce Venezuela's illiteracy rate, which stood at 6.99 per cent at the close of 1998. The programme was based on the 'Yo Sí Puedo' ('Yes, I Can') method designed by Cuban educator Leonela Reys in 2001, which consisted of 65 video classes and practical exercises supervised by trained instructors (*El Impulso*, 2006).

Misión Robinson was part of an ambitious and high-profile drive by the Chávez administration to launch a set of aggressive social programmes directed at the most vulnerable groups in Venezuelan society. Over the next 3 years, the government announced the creation of 13 additional misiones. These included two additional adult education programmes (Misión Ribas and Misión Sucre), two healthcare programmes (Misión Barrio Adentro and Misión Milagro), a retraining programme for unemployed workers (Misión Vuelvan Caras) and a programme to sell subsidized food staples to low-income consumers (Misión Mercal). Between 2003 and 2005, the Venezuelan government assigned Bs8.15 trillion (equivalent to $4.14 billion) to these programmes (Oficina Nacional de Presupuesto, 2006b). Total expenditure on the misiones thus averaged 1.22 per cent of GDP over these three years.

In several respects, the misiones were a tremendous success. Opinion surveys indicate that up to 40 per cent of Venezuelans claim to have received direct benefits from some of the misiones, and approval ratings for the misiones are typically above 70 per cent (*El Nacional*, 2006). The misiones are widely viewed, at least, as part of the explanation for the turnaround in President Chávez's popularity ratings that helped him win the 2004 referendum (Alfredo Keller y Asociados, 2005).

Nevertheless, analytical studies of the impact of the misiones are lacking. A few existing analyses of their impact on poverty and well-being are based on 'back-of-an-envelope' calculations or on survey data. For example, Weisbrot et al (2006) estimated that access to free health care provided to Misión Barrio Adentro diminished Venezuelan poverty by 2.1 percentage points. Their calculations are based on the assumption that Venezuelans would have spent 5 per cent of their income on health care services that were otherwise provided by Barrio Adentro. This calculation is limited by the lack of statistics regarding the number of people who received free medical assistance before Barrio Adentro and by the assumption that Barrio Adentro covers all medical services required by the poor. However survey data can be notoriously unreliable for uncovering programme participation, as revealed by a recent experiment carried out by the Venezuelan polling firm Datanálisis (2006). In 2006, the firm conducted a survey in which they asked respondents about participation in several misiones. The designers of the survey introduced a non-existent misión, which they called Misión Patria and 20 per cent of respondents alleged being beneficiaries of that programme (*El Nacional*, 2006).

Understanding whether the misiones have been successful or not is a fundamental part of the discussion about fiscal space in Venezuela. As we argued in the introduction to this chapter, oil-abundant nations have typically not been able to make greater progress than non-oil abundant nations in the fight against poverty. This lack of success would appear to reinforce the view that the problem is not one of resource availability, but rather one of the efficiency of existing expenditures. However, if one can establish that the misiones have indeed had a significant effect on poverty reduction, then the case for mobilizing resources for financing this type of programme would be bolstered, and other countries may be well advised to carefully analyse the Venezuelan experience.

A comprehensive evaluation of the misiones is hampered by the lack of detailed disaggregated data on the amount of resources devoted to the programmes or on programme participation. Furthermore, there are few publicly available regionally disaggregated indicators in Venezuela that could allow us to track the effect of the misiones on health indicators. As Weisbrot et al (2006) accurately point out, the fact that the misiones primarily rely on cash transfers implies that there is little about their effect that can be derived from looking at the households' survey, which only captures cash income.[38]

In the rest of this section, we look in detail at two of the misiones for which sufficient data are available to help us make a preliminary evaluation. These are Misión Robinson (the literacy programme) and Misión Mercal (the food distribution programme).

Misión Robinson[39]

On 28 October 2005, President Chávez presided over a highly publicized symbolic event. Venezuela was being declared a 'Territory Freed from Illiteracy'. According to the government's claims, 1.48 million adults had learned to write between 2003 and 2005 using the Yo Sí Puedo programme. Thus Venezuela's illiteracy rate, which had stood at 9.05 per cent of the adult population in 1998, had been brought down to less than 2 per cent. During the event, the United Nations Educational, Scientific and Cultural Organization's (UNESCO) special envoy María Luisa Jáuregui stated that, 'Venezuela is the first and only country to meet the commitments adopted by the region's governments, in 2002 in Havana, to drastically reduce illiteracy'.[40]

Almost eradicating illiteracy in such a short period would be a stunning achievement. However, although the government has publicly presented figures for the number of people who were taught how to read and write, it is unclear how they have arrived at these figures. There is, however, a simple way to verify the government's story. The household survey, or Encuesta de Hogares (Instituto Nacional de Estadística, various years), regularly asks respondents about their literacy status. At the time of writing, we had at our disposal the Encuestas up to the second semester of 2005, allowing us to capture the full period of operation of Misión Robinson.[41]

Is there any discernible effect? Figure 10.29 plots the historical evolution of the Venezuelan illiteracy rate for persons 15 years and older as derived from the Encuesta de Hogares. As the figure shows, there is a long-run declining trend in illiteracy rates. At best, there appears to be a minor change in that trend after 2003. The illiteracy rate falls from 8.25 per cent to 6.94 per cent between the first semester of 2003 (before Misión Robinson) and the second semester of 2005 (after the programme's comple-

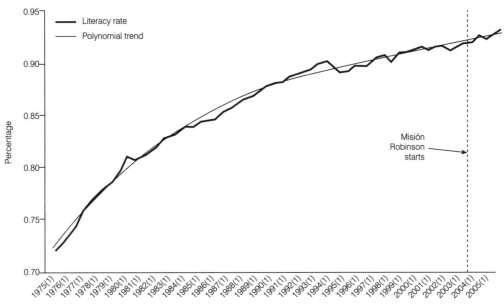

Source: Authors' calculation using Instituto Nacional de Estadística (various years)

Figure 10.29 *Venezuelan adult literacy rate, 1975–2004*

tion). The net decrease in the number of non-literate Venezuelans is 90,246 persons, a far cry from the government's claim (Table 10.31). Figure 10.29 also plots a polynomial trend.[42] As one can observe, at the first semester of 2004, Venezuelan literacy was only 0.21 percentage points higher than would be predicted by the long-run trend. This corresponds to an increase in the number of literate Venezuelans of 27,774 persons.

Obviously, there is no way to reconcile these numbers with the official claims of having taught 1.48 million persons how to read and write. Indeed, according to the Encuesta, there were only 1.004 million Venezuelans who were non-literate at the start of Misión Robinson. One possibility is that the official figure was derived from staff reports. These reports may, in themselves, include a bias towards over reporting success rates. It may also be the case that beneficiaries derived, or expected to derive, significant incentives from joining the programme and falsely claimed to be illiterate in order to gain access.[43]

Misión Mercal

Misión Mercal, launched on 24 August 2003, is a system of government-owned and franchised grocery stores that sell goods at discounts of between 20 and 40 per cent of the price at which they are sold in private establishments. Mercal currently has more than 13,359 branches in operation and covers 47 per cent of Venezuelan food distribution (Eickhacker, 2006; Datanálisis, 2006).

Table 10.31 *Literacy rates and number of non-literate persons aged 25 years or more, 1975–2004*

	1975(1)	1975(2)	1976(1)	1976(2)	1977(1)	1977(2)	1978(1)	1978(2)
Literacy Rate	0.720043	0.727494	0.735795	0.743514	0.759312	0.767130	0.775365	0.780776
Non-literate persons	1,175,733	1,153,797	1,259,396	1,248,489	1,201,517	1,185,805	1,171,475	1,165,823

	1979(1)	1979(2)	1980(1)	1980(2)	1981(1)	1981(2)	1982(1)	1982(2)
Literacy Rate	0.786667	0.797029	0.811038	0.806700	0.810747	0.814654	0.820504	0.827217
Non-literate persons	1,162,267	1,127,750	1,073,608	1,118,449	1,118,726	1,114,005	1,102,497	1,080,319

	1983(1)	1983(2)	1984(1)	1984(2)	1985(1)	1986(1)	1986(2)	1987(1)
Literacy Rate	0.830192	0.834578	0.838095	0.838711	0.843246	0.846413758	0.852489	0.855755
Non-literate persons	1,083,074	1,072,759	1,071,949	1,086,404	1,076,620	1,094,879	1,069,506	1,067,742

	1987(2)	1988(1)	1988(2)	1989(1)	1989(2)	1990(1)	1990(2)	1991(1)
Literacy Rate	0.860173	0.864833	0.867623	0.872534	0.876629	0.879255	0.880092	0.886856
Non-literate persons	1,052,653	1,037,895	1,034,307	1,014,707	999,042	986,119	995,193	954,675

	1991(2)	1992(1)	1992(2)	1993(1)	1993(2)	1994(2)	1995(1)	1995(2)
Literacy Rate	0.888916	0.891032	0.893257	0.897932	0.900422	0.890650	0.891331	0.896764
Non-literate persons	954,233	951,199	948,520	922,065	914,281	1,028,171	1,043,834	1,006,384

	1996(1)	1997(1)	1997(2)	1998(1)	1998(2)	1999(1)	1999(2)	2000(1)
Literacy Rate	0.89652	0.905053	0.907504	0.900541	0.909596	0.909732	0.912479	0.914734
Non-literate persons	1,023,632	947,171	956,141	822,558	961,471	974,107	958,041	946,750

	2000(2)	2001(1)	2001(2)	2002(1)	2003(1)	2003(2)	2004(1)	2004(2)
Literacy Rate	0.911733	0.914729	0.915486	0.911514	0.917532	0.918445	0.924815	0.922738
Non-literate persons	995,199	976,640	983,234	1,045,331	1,004,094	1,003,821	947,302	944,735

	2005(1)	2005(2)
Literacy Rate	0.927325	0.930556
Non-literate persons	943,519	913,848

Source: Authors' calculations based on Instituto Nacional de Estadística (various years)

Its distribution network includes six types of branches. Type I Mercales are supervised directly by the state and conform to two standard sizes – basic (154 square meters) and amplified (274 square meters) – selling a standard selection of products. Type II Mercales are private franchised institutions that vary according to the choices made by the owners. Supermercales are substantially larger and sell a greater variety of products. They are owned by the state and by cooperatives. There are three other types of smaller or more mobile mercales, called Bodegas Mercal, Bodegas Móviles and Megamercados al Cielo Abierto.

Mercal's website has published information on the number of Type I, Type II and Supermercales by state. This information would allow for a tentative evaluation of the impact of the Mercal programme if we had state-level nutrition or health indicators. We have been unable to find those indicators. The Encuesta de Hogares, however, does provide a mechanism to evaluate Misión Mercal through a more indirect route. The Encuesta has information on consumption of a set of durables, among which are some that we would expect to be particularly sensitive to changes in the real incomes of the poor. If Mercal raises the incomes of the poor significantly, one would expect part of that increase to be devoted to increasing the quality of dwellings (replacing earthen floors and/or upgrading zinc ceilings).

In order to test the hypothesis that Mercal leads to an increase in the real incomes of poor individuals, we test whether there is a change in three indicators of the quality of

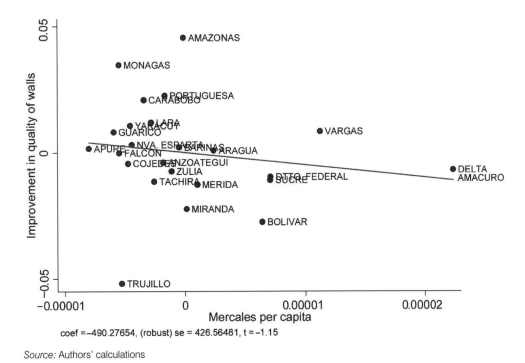

Source: Authors' calculations

Figure 10.30 *Mercal intensity and change in quality of walls*

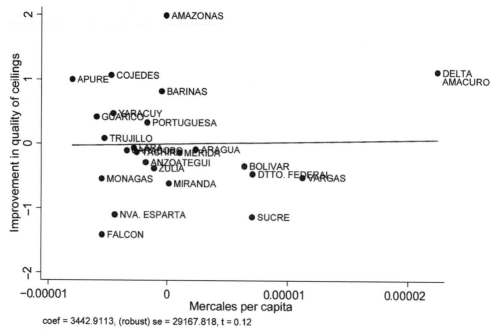

coef = 3442.9113, (robust) se = 29167.818, t = 0.12

Source: Authors' calculations

Figure 10.31 *Mercal intensity and change in quality of ceilings*

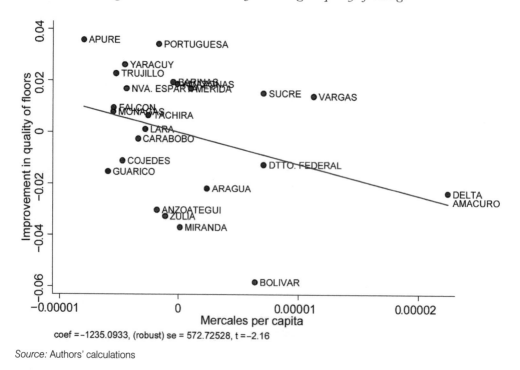

coef = −1235.0933, (robust) se = 572.72528, t = −2.16

Source: Authors' calculations

Figure 10.32 *Mercal intensity and change in quality of floors*

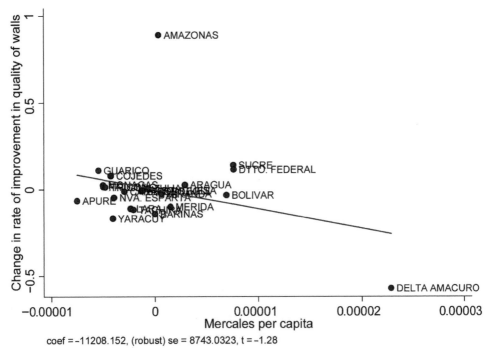

coef = -11208.152, (robust) se = 8743.0323, t = -1.28

Source: Authors' calculations

Figure 10.33 *Mercal intensity and change in rate of improvement of quality of walls*

dwelling in states with greater Mercal intensities. Our three indicators capture the quality of floors, walls and ceilings. In order to measure the quality of floors, we build an indicator that captures whether the dwelling had earthen floors (low quality) or cement, brick, granite and similar materials (high quality). Our measure of the quality of walls captures whether these are made with bricks, concrete or wood (high quality) or adobe or similar materials (low quality). Our measure of the quality of ceilings captures whether these are made of tiles or cement (high quality) or of zinc, asbestos or palms (low quality).

Figures 10.30, 10.31 and 10.32 plot the relationships between the intensity of Mercal (measured by the number of Mercal establishments per capita) and the average change in the quality of walls, ceilings and floors between the first semester of 2002 and the second semester of 2005. Only one of the three relationships (ceilings) is positive, and far from significantly so (t-statistic: 0.12). The other two point estimates are negative, implying a deterioration in average dwelling quality in states with greater Mercal intensity. Indeed, Mercal intensity is negatively and significantly related to the change in the quality of floors (t-statistic: -2.16).

It is possible that the lack of relationships in Figures 10.30, 10.31 and 10.32 is a consequence of the Chávez administration's targeting of states that were experiencing more adverse economic conditions in this period. One way to evaluate whether this is

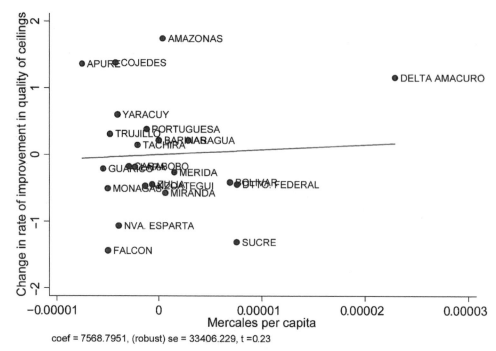

coef = 7568.7951, (robust) se = 33406.229, t =0.23

Source: Authors' calculations

Figure 10.34 *Mercal intensity and change in trend of quality of ceilings*

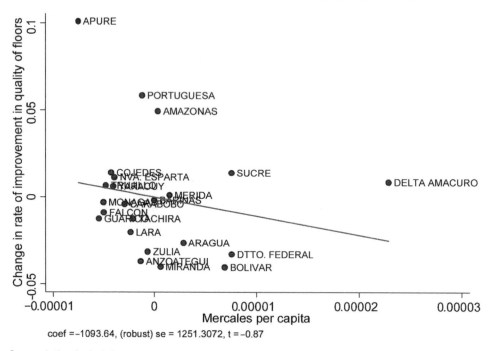

coef =−1093.64, (robust) se = 1251.3072, t =−0.87

Source: Authors' calculations

Figure 10.35 *Mercal intensity and change in trend of quality of floors*

contaminating our estimates is to look for evidence of changes in the growth rate trends in dwelling quality. In other words, we can measure not whether Mercal intensity is associated with more improvements in dwelling quality, but whether it is associated with a change in the rate of improvement (or deterioration) of dwelling quality. Figures 10.33, 10.34 and 10.35 show the scatter plots of the number of mercals per capita against the change in the growth rate in the periods 2000 to 2002 and 2002 to 2005. These scatter plots only increase the paradox. The changes in the trends of wall quality and floor quality are still negatively and not significantly related to Mercal. The coefficient estimate on quality of ceilings does turn positive but not significantly so (t-statistic = 0.23).

The analysis presented in this section does not support the claim that the Chávez administration's misiones are raising the living standards of the Venezuelan poor. Indeed, our analysis of Misión Robinson has found serious inconsistencies between the administrations claim to have taught 1.4 million people how to read and write and the fact that the absolute number of illiterate individuals has held roughly constant at 1 million throughout the implementation of the government's literacy campaign.

These conclusions should serve as a reminder that building fiscal space is only one part of the answer to poverty reduction. The second and most important part has to do with channelling those resources effectively. The four-fold increase in per capita oil revenues that occurred since 1998 has served as an exogenous increase in Venezuelan fiscal space, allowing it to target a substantial amount of resources towards poverty reduction. The evidence surveyed in this section suggests that there is still a considerable way to go before these resources are actually converted into initiatives that improve the well-being of the poorest.

CONCLUSION

We started this chapter by stating that studying fiscal space in Venezuela could leave one open to serious objections. The reader who has read this far would by now be justified in requesting an answer to the following questions. What can Venezuela teach us about fiscal space? How can non-resource-abundant developing economies gain from the analysis of this experience? Can Venezuela effectively be said to have a fiscal space problem? Or is studying fiscal space in Venezuela akin to studying overpopulation in Wyoming?

We suggest that it is useful to think about fiscal space in progressive levels of breadth as distinct from those emphasized by Heller (2005) and Brun et al (2005). We refer to objective fiscal space as the amount of resources that an economy could mobilize towards a desired purpose, without prejudice to its fiscal sustainability, if it carried out all the necessary reforms to its expenditure, taxation and budgetary policies, including necessary changes in institutional and political arrangements. Effective fiscal space, in contrast, is the amount of resources that an economy can mobilize for that same purpose, subject to the constraints that are imposed by its structural, political and institutional conditions. The notion of effective fiscal space implies that there are reforms that cannot be realized because there are significant impediments to them arising from a country's structure, politics and inherited institutions.[44] Realized fiscal space is the amount of resources that an economy is currently mobilizing for these aims.

In this sense, Venezuela's realized fiscal space is no different from that of other Latin American countries. Its share of central government spending in GDP is similar to that of most of its neighbours. Indeed, as we have argued, the central government's spending and tax regimes are particularly distorted against the poor in relation to the rest of the region, suggesting that its realized fiscal space for the goal of poverty reduction may even be more reduced than that of its natural comparison group. In this sense, Venezuela has a fiscal space problem.

Venezuela's objective fiscal space, in turn, is huge. Given its level of income, Venezuela should have internal tax levels similar to those of the most advanced economies in the region, which would have the potential to raise tax revenues by approximately 6 points of GDP. As we have shown, it can also raise revenues by between 2 and 3 per cent of GDP by making sensible changes to its pricing of gasoline in the domestic sector. On the expenditure side, moving government deposits to the Treasury Bank would allow it to save 1.7 per cent of GDP, and other administrative reforms could allow it to have at least a one time gain of more than 1 per cent of GDP, generated by eliminating asynchronies in the budget execution and completion stages. A re-composition of budget expenditures towards investment and non-labour intensive public goods could add a few decimals more and have much larger effects on long-term GDP growth. Summing all of these components, Venezuela's objective fiscal space can be expanded by more than 10 per cent of GDP in excess of current spending levels. This extraordinary level is in essence a simple reflection of Venezuela's oil abundance, since Venezuela's oil accounts produce a surplus of 10 points of GDP. Then balancing its non-oil fiscal account (that is, doing what everyone else does) should logically lead to the country having 10 points of GDP more to spend.

The real task of policymakers, in our view, is to identify a country's effective fiscal space. That is, one must recognize potential reforms, their expected payoffs and the feasibility of overcoming the political, institutional and structural impediments to carrying them out, given initial conditions. In Venezuela, such an exercise implies asking about the feasibility of overcoming widespread resistance to high gasoline prices, imposing a personal income tax on income brackets that have never paid it, and weakening the arrangements between politicians and those financial institutions that follow rent-seeking strategies. One must propose strategies that can enhance resource availability, are politically feasible, are compatible with an economy's institutions, and can reasonably be implemented by the existing public service.

Venezuela's effective fiscal space could be broader than that of other countries, though that is by no means a foregone conclusion. On the one hand, we have suggested a set of simple reforms, some of which can apparently be carried out at a reasonable political cost, which would generate a significant enhancement in fiscal resources. On the other hand, Venezuela's history of oil dependence may make it particularly difficult to reform some of the institutions that may be vital to enhancing resource availability, as our discussion of centralization has highlighted.

We believe that some of the lessons drawn from the analysis that we have conducted of Venezuela can be appealed to when looking at other countries, provided sufficient attention is paid to relevant structural and historical specificities. Studying the history of centralization and the link between patronage based, political systems and public employment is likely to be fruitful in many countries that escaped anarchy in the 19th or 20th centuries through processes of political and economic centralization. Analysing the specificities of particular taxes and studying the causes of their underperformance is a second route that should be valuable more generally. Each country is likely to have distinct characteristics in its budget planning and execution strategy, but analysing the institutional sources of a 'scramble for resources' by budget management institutions can reveal the existence of relevant binding constraints. Looking for asymmetries in past adjustments can help in understanding the links between lack of fiscal space and economic underperformance.

Our analysis also closes with a few words of necessary caution. Fiscal space is important but it is not everything. In order to reduce poverty, resources generated by fiscal space enhancement must be spent wisely. Our analysis of the current Venezuelan administration's hallmark social programmes, the misiones, has produced disappointing results, revealing wide gaps between government claims and outcomes as captured by official statistics. Hopefully, Venezuela is still in time to correct the problems in its social strategy and to take advantage of the extraordinary opportunities that the recent oil boom has given it to achieve significant advances in the war against poverty, thus allowing other countries to learn from its successes instead of from its failures.

Table 10.A1 *Composition of Spending by Sectors, Ministry of Finance*

Sector	1962	1963	1964	1965	1966	1967	1968	1969	1970	1971	1972	1973	1974	1975	1976	1977	1978	1979	1980
Social sectors	16.9	17.2	18.0	20.0	21.6	22.0	30.3	31.3	33.4	29.7	32.1	33.3	18.1	22.2	25.8	30.4	34.3	34.6	35.9
Education	9.9	10.4	10.9	12.0	12.9	13.5	14.6	14.8	17.2	16.0	17.8	20.2	10.5	14.0	14.7	16.4	17.1	19.2	15.4
Housing and related services	0.0	0.0	0.0	0.0	0.0	0.0	2.8	2.8	2.8	2.0	2.1	1.8	1.5	1.1	2.9	1.3	1.6	3.1	8.6
Health	7.0	6.8	7.1	8.0	8.7	8.5	12.9	13.7	13.3	11.7	12.2	11.3	6.1	7.1	8.2	12.7	15.5	6.2	5.7
Social development	0.0	0.0	0.0	0.0	0.0	0.0	0.0	0.0	0.0	0.0	0.0	0.0	0.0	0.0	0.0	0.0	0.0	6.1	6.2
Social security	0.0	0.0	0.0	0.0	0.0	0.0	0.0	0.0	0.0	0.0	0.0	0.0	0.0	0.0	0.0	0.0	0.0	0.0	0.0
Culture and social communication	0.0	0.0	0.0	0.0	0.0	0.0	0.0	0.0	0.0	0.0	0.0	0.0	0.0	0.0	0.0	0.0	0.0	0.0	0.0
Science and technology	0.0	0.0	0.0	0.0	0.0	0.0	0.0	0.0	0.0	0.0	0.0	0.0	0.0	0.0	0.0	0.0	0.0	0.0	0.0
Productive sectors	8.4	7.9	9.3	10.1	10.1	10.3	28.1	30.1	25.8	28.1	25.7	24.4	23.3	28.1	26.5	29.0	24.6	19.2	25.0
Agriculture	8.4	7.9	9.3	10.1	10.1	10.3	9.3	8.5	9.1	9.1	8.5	9.3	10.5	12.7	11.6	9.9	7.3	7.2	7.1
Transportation and communication	0.0	0.0	0.0	0.0	0.0	0.0	12.8	16.6	12.1	12.3	12.2	10.4	6.1	6.0	6.0	10.8	12.6	6.5	5.5
Industry and commerce	0.0	0.0	0.0	0.0	0.0	0.0	3.8	2.8	2.2	1.9	2.0	2.0	4.3	5.9	3.4	7.4	3.9	2.7	11.6
Energy, mines and oil	0.0	0.0	0.0	0.0	0.0	0.0	1.9	1.9	2.0	4.4	2.6	2.1	2.0	3.1	5.0	0.4	0.3	2.4	0.2
Tourism and recreation	0.0	0.0	0.0	0.0	0.0	0.0	0.3	0.3	0.3	0.4	0.4	0.5	0.2	0.4	0.6	0.5	0.5	0.3	0.5
General services	10.8	12.4	11.9	12.6	12.7	12.9	20.2	18.2	19.3	18.0	17.9	19.8	9.9	9.9	10.7	12.3	13.5	13.8	10.6
Security and defense	10.8	12.4	11.9	12.6	12.7	12.9	12.0	11.0	11.3	11.9	11.2	11.4	5.9	5.8	5.7	7.0	7.0	7.9	6.8
Superior direction	0.0	0.0	0.0	0.0	0.0	0.0	8.2	7.2	8.0	6.1	6.7	8.4	4.0	4.2	5.0	5.2	6.5	5.9	3.9
Other sectors	34.4	37.5	36.3	37.3	36.2	36.2	0.0	0.0	0.0	0.0	0.0	0.0	0.0	0.0	0.0	0.0	0.0	0.0	0.0
Non classified expenditures	29.5	25.0	24.6	20.0	19.4	18.6	21.5	20.4	21.5	24.2	24.2	22.6	48.7	39.8	37.0	28.3	27.7	32.4	28.5
Total	100	100	100	100	100	100	100	100	100	100	100	100	100	100	100	100	100	100	100

Source: Budget National Office

1981	1982	1983	1984	1985	1986	1987	1988	1989	1990	1991	1992	1993	1994	1995	1996	1997	1998	1999	2000	2001	2002	2003	2004
31.6	32.0	33.8	27.4	32.1	31.1	31.9	36.1	32.5	29.9	35.8	40.1	40.0	33.7	36.9	32.3	38.6	34.7	38.5	37.3	38.8	37.7	39.0	41.4
16.3	17.3	18.1	15.2	15.8	14.6	15.6	16.9	15.1	12.0	12.6	15.4	17.0	15.9	16.0	9.7	14.1	14.3	16.6	15.3	15.5	16.2	15.0	16.8
6.6	5.9	4.4	2.8	5.9	5.8	6.3	6.7	3.5	4.8	7.7	7.2	5.3	2.6	3.3	4.7	5.8	4.1	3.2	5.6	3.2	2.8	3.4	2.1
5.2	5.3	6.1	4.9	6.1	6.8	6.4	7.6	6.1	5.8	5.9	7.8	6.7	5.3	4.7	3.5	5.8	5.8	5.9	4.6	4.9	5.6	4.9	5.5
3.4	3.5	1.7	1.2	0.9	0.7	0.8	1.0	3.9	3.9	5.5	4.8	6.0	4.6	6.9	8.4	5.5	3.4	3.6	2.7	2.9	2.8	3.4	4.2
0.0	0.0	2.3	2.4	2.6	2.5	2.3	3.0	2.9	2.6	3.1	3.5	3.7	4.3	4.8	5.0	6.0	5.9	8.1	7.5	11.0	9.5	10.9	10.9
0.0	0.0	1.0	0.7	0.6	0.5	0.4	0.6	0.5	0.5	0.7	0.8	1.0	0.7	0.8	0.5	0.9	0.8	0.5	0.7	0.5	0.3	0.9	0.9
0.0	0.0	0.3	0.2	0.2	0.2	0.2	0.3	0.5	0.3	0.3	0.7	0.3	0.3	0.6	0.5	0.6	0.5	0.6	0.8	0.8	0.5	0.4	1.1
31.9	16.7	12.5	11.0	11.2	13.5	15.3	13.8	7.0	8.7	10.6	11.0	7.3	6.4	6.2	4.4	6.9	4.6	3.4	4.3	3.9	3.7	6.2	7.8
10.6	7.5	5.5	5.1	5.2	6.3	7.8	6.9	3.5	3.3	4.2	6.1	3.9	2.4	2.3	1.5	2.9	1.8	1.0	1.4	1.4	0.5	0.9	1.3
6.7	5.0	5.4	5.1	5.0	5.9	6.0	5.7	2.4	3.3	4.0	4.3	2.9	2.9	3.0	2.3	3.0	2.2	2.0	2.1	1.7	1.3	3.2	4.1
13.9	3.7	1.3	0.5	0.6	0.9	0.7	0.8	0.6	1.6	1.3	0.3	0.2	0.5	0.5	0.4	0.8	0.3	0.3	0.5	0.6	0.5	1.6	1.7
0.2	0.2	0.2	0.2	0.2	0.2	0.6	0.2	0.1	0.1	1.0	0.1	0.1	0.5	0.2	0.1	0.1	0.1	0.1	0.2	0.1	1.4	0.5	0.7
0.5	0.3	0.2	0.1	0.2	0.3	0.2	0.2	0.4	0.3	0.2	0.2	0.2	0.2	0.2	0.2	0.2	0.1	0.1	0.2	0.1	0.0	0.1	0.1
10.3	12.0	11.7	9.8	10.9	12.0	9.3	11.7	10.5	9.4	10.0	11.6	13.0	12.3	12.3	11.3	10.5	14.6	14.3	17.1	18.5	8.4	8.3	10.6
7.7	9.5	7.9	6.5	7.1	7.0	6.5	8.1	7.3	6.3	6.5	7.5	9.3	7.8	8.1	5.2	7.1	7.7	8.7	7.1	7.1	6.1	5.3	6.3
2.6	2.5	3.8	3.3	3.8	5.0	2.8	3.6	3.2	3.0	3.5	4.0	3.7	4.5	4.2	6.1	3.5	6.9	5.6	10.0	11.4	2.4	3.0	4.4
0.0	0.0	0.0	0.0	0.0	0.0	0.0	0.0	0.0	0.0	0.0	0.0	0.0	0.0	0.0	0.0	0.0	0.0	0.0	0.0	0.0	0.0	0.0	0.0
26.2	39.2	41.9	51.8	45.8	43.4	43.6	38.4	50.0	52.1	43.6	37.3	39.7	47.6	44.6	52.0	44.0	46.1	43.7	41.3	38.8	50.2	46.5	40.1
100	100	100	100	100	100	100	100	100	100	100	100	100	100	100	100	100	100	100	100	100	100	100	100

Table 10.A2 *Composition of spending by economic classification, Ministry of Finance*

Approved Modified Budget Expenditures	1962	1963	1964	1965	1966	1967	1968	1969	1970	1971	1972	1973	1974	1975	1976	1977	1978	1979	1980
Current	11.2	11.4	10.9	11.4	11.9	12.3	12.2	13.3	13.5	13.5	13.9	13.0	13.3	15.9	16.0	16.9	16.4	16.1	16.0
Consumption	7.5	7.5	7.0	7.2	7.4	7.8	7.6	7.8	7.7	7.6	7.7	7.3	6.6	7.3	7.6	7.9	7.8	7.3	7.4
Salaries	6.3	6.4	5.9	6.0	6.3	6.5	6.4	6.4	6.4	6.3	6.5	6.2	5.5	6.2	6.4	6.5	6.6	6.2	6.5
Other goods and services	1.2	1.1	1.1	1.2	1.2	1.3	1.2	1.3	1.2	1.3	1.1	1.1	1.1	1.2	1.2	1.4	1.3	1.1	0.9
Property rent	0.2	0.3	0.2	0.2	0.1	0.1	0.1	0.2	0.6	0.7	0.7	0.7	0.4	0.4	0.7	1.1	1.6	1.6	2.1
Interest	0.2	0.3	0.2	0.2	0.1	0.1	0.1	0.2	0.6	0.7	0.7	0.7	0.4	0.4	0.7	1.1	1.6	1.6	2.1
Land leasing	0.0	0.0	0.0	0.0	0.0	0.0	0.0	0.0	0.0	0.0	0.0	0.0	0.0	0.0	0.0	0.0	0.0	0.0	0.0
Transfers	3.6	3.7	3.7	4.0	4.3	4.4	4.5	5.4	5.2	5.2	5.5	5.0	6.2	8.1	7.7	7.9	7.0	7.2	6.5
Private sector	0.0	0.0	0.0	0.0	0.0	0.0	0.5	0.5	0.5	0.5	0.5	0.5	0.5	0.8	0.6	0.8	0.8	0.8	0.6
Public sector	3.5	3.6	3.6	3.9	4.3	4.4	4.0	4.9	4.6	4.7	5.0	4.5	5.5	7.2	6.7	6.9	6.1	6.1	5.8
External sector	0.0	0.0	0.1	0.0	0.0	0.1	0.0	0.0	0.0	0.0	0.0	0.0	0.2	0.1	0.3	0.3	0.1	0.3	0.1
Capital	6.9	6.6	7.0	7.3	7.3	7.4	7.6	7.5	5.1	6.3	6.3	6.2	7.9	7.2	6.2	10.2	9.8	4.8	6.6
Direct investment	3.2	3.6	3.4	3.5	3.4	3.3	3.5	4.8	2.9	3.7	3.5	3.2	3.1	3.0	3.1	3.7	3.8	1.7	1.7
Gross formation of fixed capital	3.2	3.6	3.4	3.5	3.4	3.3	3.5	4.8	2.9	3.7	3.5	3.2	3.1	3.0	3.1	3.7	3.8	1.7	1.7
Land and other fixed assets	0.0	0.0	0.0	0.0	0.0	0.0	0.0	0.0	0.0	0.0	0.0	0.0	0.0	0.0	0.0	0.0	0.0	0.0	0.0
Intangible assets	0.0	0.0	0.0	0.0	0.0	0.0	0.0	0.0	0.0	0.0	0.0	0.0	0.0	0.0	0.0	0.0	0.0	0.0	0.0
Transfers	3.6	3.1	3.6	3.8	3.9	4.1	4.1	2.7	2.2	2.6	2.9	3.0	4.8	4.3	3.1	6.5	5.9	3.0	4.9
Private sector	0.0	0.0	0.0	0.0	0.0	0.0	0.0	0.0	0.0	0.0	0.0	0.0	0.0	0.0	0.0	0.0	0.0	0.0	0.0
Public sector	3.6	3.1	3.6	3.8	3.9	4.1	4.1	2.7	2.2	2.6	2.9	3.0	4.8	4.3	3.1	6.5	5.9	3.0	4.9
External sector	0.0	0.0	0.0	0.0	0.0	0.0	0.0	0.0	0.0	0.0	0.0	0.0	0.0	0.0	0.0	0.0	0.0	0.0	0.0
Financial transactions	4.1	2.6	2.3	1.3	1.1	1.3	1.0	1.2	1.2	2.5	1.7	1.1	16.7	10.6	10.8	5.4	4.1	3.7	6.1
Assets	0.7	0.4	0.4	0.4	0.3	0.5	0.4	0.8	0.7	0.9	0.6	0.1	13.3	9.6	5.6	1.2	1.0	0.9	3.5
Stock and capital share	0.7	0.4	0.4	0.4	0.3	0.5	0.4	0.8	0.7	0.9	0.6	0.1	13.3	9.6	5.6	1.2	1.0	0.9	3.5
Loans	0.0	0.0	0.0	0.0	0.0	0.0	0.0	0.0	0.0	0.0	0.0	0.0	0.0	0.0	0.0	0.0	0.0	0.0	0.0
Liabilities	3.5	2.1	1.9	0.9	0.8	0.8	0.6	0.4	0.5	1.6	1.1	1.0	3.4	1.1	5.2	4.2	3.1	2.8	2.6
Short-term debt amortization	0.1	0.1	0.1	0.1	0.1	0.0	0.0	0.0	0.1	0.1	0.1	0.0	2.0	0.1	0.1	0.1	0.1	0.2	0.1
Long-term debt amortization	3.4	2.0	1.9	0.9	0.7	0.7	0.5	0.3	0.5	1.6	1.1	0.9	1.4	1.0	5.1	4.1	3.0	2.6	2.5
Total	22.2	20.6	20.2	20.0	20.3	21.0	20.7	22.0	19.8	22.3	21.9	20.3	37.9	33.8	33.0	32.6	30.3	24.5	28.7

Source: Budget National Office

1981	1982	1983	1984	1985	1986	1987	1988	1989	1990	1991	1992	1993	1994	1995	1996	1997	1998	1999	2000	2001	2002	2003	2004
19.3	19.0	18.9	16.9	15.3	14.5	16.1	14.3	15.3	17.6	16.2	16.8	15.4	16.6	14.4	14.8	17.6	16.0	16.9	17.9	20.3	19.0	19.8	20.4
7.8	7.4	7.6	5.6	5.6	5.9	5.5	5.5	4.9	5.0	5.4	5.6	5.0	5.1	4.5	3.4	4.4	4.5	4.3	4.9	6.0	5.8	5.5	5.9
6.7	6.5	6.7	4.9	4.7	5.2	4.7	4.6	4.0	4.1	4.5	4.7	4.1	4.3	3.8	2.8	3.6	3.5	3.5	3.9	4.9	4.7	4.6	4.7
1.1	1.0	1.0	0.7	0.8	0.7	0.8	0.8	1.0	0.9	0.9	0.9	0.9	0.8	0.8	0.6	0.8	1.1	0.8	1.0	1.1	1.0	0.9	1.2
2.4	3.5	4.3	5.7	4.7	3.5	4.4	2.8	3.6	4.5	3.7	4.2	3.5	4.5	3.1	3.7	3.1	2.5	2.8	2.6	2.9	4.6	4.6	3.8
2.4	3.5	4.3	5.7	4.7	3.5	4.4	2.8	3.6	4.5	3.7	4.2	3.5	4.5	3.1	3.7	3.1	2.5	2.8	2.6	2.9	4.6	4.6	3.8
0.0	0.0	0.0	0.0	0.0	0.0	0.0	0.0	0.0	0.0	0.0	0.0	0.0	0.0	0.0	0.0	0.0	0.0	0.0	0.0	0.0	0.0	0.0	0.0
9.1	8.0	7.0	5.6	5.1	5.1	6.2	6.0	6.8	8.1	7.1	7.1	6.8	6.9	6.8	7.7	10.1	9.0	9.8	10.5	11.4	8.7	9.7	10.7
0.7	0.7	1.2	0.9	0.6	0.6	0.9	1.0	1.3	1.6	1.9	2.0	1.8	1.4	1.3	1.2	1.1	1.4	1.0	0.8	0.9	0.9	1.4	1.1
8.4	7.2	5.7	4.7	4.4	4.5	5.3	4.9	5.5	6.5	5.1	5.1	5.0	5.5	5.4	6.5	9.0	7.6	8.8	9.7	10.4	7.7	8.3	9.6
0.0	0.0	0.0	0.1	0.0	0.0	0.0	0.1	0.1	0.1	0.1	0.0	0.0	0.1	0.0	0.0	0.0	0.0	0.0	0.0	0.0	0.0	0.0	0.0
6.6	5.5	4.8	3.3	4.8	5.6	4.9	4.9	2.3	4.0	6.2	5.6	3.4	3.4	3.7	3.2	4.7	4.2	3.5	7.1	4.4	4.6	5.8	5.9
2.4	2.2	1.4	1.1	1.6	2.5	2.2	2.1	0.7	1.1	1.8	1.8	1.2	0.6	0.8	0.7	0.8	0.6	0.2	0.7	0.8	0.3	0.2	0.5
2.4	2.2	1.4	1.1	1.6	2.5	2.1	2.1	0.7	1.1	1.8	1.7	1.1	0.5	0.8	0.6	0.7	0.6	0.2	0.6	0.7	0.2	0.2	0.4
0.0	0.0	0.0	0.0	0.0	0.0	0.0	0.0	0.0	0.0	0.0	0.0	0.0	0.0	0.0	0.0	0.0	0.0	0.0	0.0	0.0	0.1	0.0	0.0
0.0	0.0	0.0	0.0	0.0	0.0	0.0	0.0	0.0	0.0	0.0	0.0	0.0	0.0	0.0	0.0	0.1	0.0	0.0	0.0	0.0	0.0	0.0	0.0
4.2	3.3	3.4	2.2	3.2	3.2	2.8	2.8	1.6	3.0	4.4	3.8	2.3	2.8	2.9	2.6	4.0	3.5	3.3	6.4	3.6	4.3	5.6	5.5
0.0	0.0	0.0	0.0	0.0	0.0	0.0	0.0	0.0	0.0	0.0	0.0	0.0	0.0	0.0	0.0	0.0	0.0	0.0	0.0	0.0	0.0	0.0	0.0
4.2	3.3	3.4	2.2	3.2	3.2	2.8	2.8	1.6	2.9	4.4	3.8	2.3	2.8	2.9	2.6	3.9	3.5	3.2	6.4	3.6	4.3	5.6	5.5
0.0	0.0	0.0	0.0	0.0	0.0	0.0	0.0	0.0	0.0	0.0	0.0	0.0	0.0	0.0	0.0	0.0	0.0	0.0	0.0	0.0	0.0	0.0	0.0
7.2	5.4	3.6	4.4	4.3	5.2	5.1	2.6	3.5	3.7	4.0	1.8	1.4	2.4	2.4	3.8	2.3	2.5	0.4	3.6	5.8	5.0	4.6	2.8
5.1	1.4	1.3	1.2	2.2	1.9	2.0	1.2	1.3	2.5	1.7	1.0	0.5	0.6	0.2	0.3	0.3	0.2	0.2	0.3	2.8	0.1	0.3	0.1
5.1	1.4	1.3	1.2	2.2	1.4	2.0	1.1	1.2	2.4	1.6	0.8	0.4	0.6	0.2	0.3	0.3	0.2	0.1	0.3	0.2	0.1	0.3	0.1
0.0	0.0	0.0	0.0	0.0	0.5	0.1	0.1	0.1	0.1	0.0	0.1	0.1	0.0	0.0	0.0	0.0	0.0	0.0	0.0	2.6	0.0	0.0	0.0
2.1	4.0	2.3	3.2	2.1	3.3	3.1	1.4	2.2	1.2	2.3	0.9	0.9	1.8	2.2	3.6	2.0	2.3	0.3	3.3	3.0	4.9	4.3	2.7
0.2	1.6	0.1	0.1	0.1	0.0	0.1	0.1	0.1	0.1	0.1	0.0	0.1	0.1	0.1	0.7	0.2	0.0	0.3	0.2	0.4	0.3	0.1	0.4
1.9	2.4	2.3	3.1	2.0	3.2	2.9	1.4	2.1	1.1	2.2	0.8	0.8	1.6	2.2	2.9	1.8	2.3	0.0	3.0	2.6	4.6	4.2	2.2
33.1	29.8	27.3	24.6	24.4	25.4	26.1	21.8	21.2	25.3	26.4	24.3	20.2	22.4	20.5	21.9	24.6	22.7	20.8	28.6	30.5	28.6	30.3	29.1

NOTES

1   This chapter was prepared for the UNDP Bureau for Development Policy's research programme on Fiscal Space. The authors are indebted to Rathin Roy, Antoine Heuty, and the participants at the Conference 'Pro-poor Domestic Resource Mobilization: Securing Fiscal Space for the MDGs' held in Dakar, Senegal on 28–29 November 2005, for their comments and suggestions. All errors remain our responsibility.

2   This fact was originally pointed out by Tornell and Lane (1998), who showed that oil booms could generate a 'voracity effect', whereby consumption increased more than revenues, generating increases in current account and budget deficits.

3   Per capita GDP was 3.8 per cent higher in 1995 than in 1990.

4   The discussion of the Guzmán and Andean Hegemony reforms in this section borrows heavily from Rodríguez and Gomolin (2006).

5   For an in-depth discussion of the Compañía de Crédito, see Floyd (1988).

6   See Oficina de Asesoría Económica y Financiera de la Asamblea Nacional (2001). An initial project was first approved in discussions by the National Assembly in 2001, but the commission studying it was disbanded the following year. A second project was approved in 2002, but was vetoed by the president.

7   Figure 10.7 also displays the 1976 to 1985 public employment share for Venezuela, which we have calculated directly from the household surveys. Regrettably, we have been unable to find comparable data for the same time period for other Latin American countries. Nevertheless, the comparison is suggestive, as it shows that public employment in Venezuela was considerably higher than that of any other country in the region, with the exception of the Dominican Republic.

8   Venezuelan enabling laws allow direct legislation by the executive with special authorization by congress, which is typically granted for the space of a year.

9   In a way so as to not modify the law that established taxes, the tax on gasoline was lowered at least one bolívar cent per litre by executive decree (Betancourt, 1957).

10 As defined by the Central Bank of Venezuela, the CPS includes the central government, a sample of 30 non-financial public enterprises, social security institutions, some funds (investment, deposit insurance and others) and PDVSA, plus sub-national governments.

11 For analytical purposes, the period grouping of data has been selected to match the classification of the oil periods used in this work.

12 Indeed, private participation in Venezuelan oil production is relatively recent. This is a by-product of the Apertura Petrolera (Oil Opening) policy initiated in the 1980s. It began with the internationalization of the industry in 1985 (that is, the establishment of joint ventures with European and US enterprises, such as Veba Oel and Rhur Oel in Germany, Nynas Petroleum in Sweden and Citgo in the US) and continued with the process of opening the domestic industry to foreign capital in 1996 to 1997. During these years, PDVSA gained autonomy and independence from the executive and managed to reduce its fiscal contribution. Between 1993 and 1995 it procured from the authorities the progressive elimination of the export fiscal value, a device that allowed governments *ex ante* to set the price that would determine tax contributions irrespective of market conditions. PDVSA also proposed the elimination of royalties at different times, but this was not approved (Espinasa, 1999). In exchange, PDVSA would begin paying dividends to the central government.

13 Alternative massive transportation systems, such as railroads, might be more efficient but their costs are artificially raised due to the policy of a low price of gasoline. The absence of railroads forces the transportation of goods by trucks. Thus, raising the price of gasoline implies an important increase in inflation.

14 Some research has indicated that subsidizing the price of gasoline is indeed regressive (Rigobón, 1993), although the regressivity of reducing the subsidy is inextricably linked to the marginal increases in spending/reduction in taxation that would occur as a result.

15   Among the most prominent are the Misión Shoup, contracted by the Venezuelan government in 1960, and the Study and Fiscal Reform Commission created in 1980 by the administration of President Luis Herrera Campins.

16   The IMF Government Finance Statistics data do not allow us to distinguish between oil and non-oil corporate income tax, so that Venezuela's direct tax burden in Table 10.12 does include this source of oil revenue. This fact and the inclusion of gasoline taxes in Table 10.12, as well as some minor methodological differences between the National Budget Office and IMF methodology, account for the differences between this series and that reported in Table 10.11.

17   In the Venezuelan public finance terminology, 'ordinary' resources are those received for more than three years in a row (Organic Law of the Public Sector Financial Administration).

18   This average does not include the 1993–1994 figures. In 1993, the collection of the tax began in October of that year; while in 1994, the VAT law was revoked and the tax was substituted by one on Retail Sales and Luxurious Consumption whose collection started in April.

19   The Income Tax Law of 1942 was reformed twice and derogated in 1948. The law of 1955 substituted the one approved in 1958 and was reformed in 1958. This year a new law was approved and reformed in 1961. The 1966 law was reformed four times and substituted by another one in 1978. This law has been reformed seven times until a new one was approved in 2001. Between 1942 and 1966, most of the reforms focused on the modification of tariffs and in an increase of the burden on oil activities. The law of 1966 adopted the global system, but most of its reform concentrated on the tax regulations of oil activities. The adjustment for inflation and the issue of double taxation were introduced in the 1991 reform and the world rent principle in the 2001 law.

20   The mission was named after Carl Shoup, a Columbia University Economics Professor who advised several countries on tax system reform. In recognition of his contribution to Japanese reforms, he was twice decorated with the Order of the Sacred Treasure by Emperor Hirohito.

21   The average refers to the period 1958 to 1966.

22   See Gutiérrez (2002) for a discussion of the effect of restrictions on cross-border transport with Colombia in 1999.

23   Social security programmes for public workers include those of the Ministry of Education, Health and Defence, and of other decentralized entities (PDVSA and universities, among others). The costs supported by public entities are estimated as approximately 1 per cent of GDP.

24   It can alter the composition of the appropriation but cannot transfer funds to goals distinct from those for which the appropriation proposal was intended.

25   The law's Regulation 1 (Article 116), approved by the Ministry of Finance, contrary to what is ordered by the Organic Law, authorizes the automatic imputation of committed expenditures to the credit of the next budget.

26   Central government interest revenue has been less than 0.01 per cent of GDP since 1998. The interest revenues of autonomous public entities have averaged 0.1 per cent of GDP from 1998 to 2003, with a maximum of 0.2 per cent of GDP in 2002. Thus we estimate an upper bound of 0.2 per cent of GDP for CPS interest and dividends.

27   The bulk (3.6 per cent of GDP) was held by private banks, with the rest managed by private individuals and private non-financial institutions.

28   Since we do not have information on interest payments by recipient, we have assumed in our calculation that all holders of public debt (public and private) received the same return on it.

29   Our calculation may entail an underestimation for at least two reasons. The first is that government agencies are likely to be receiving a lower return on domestic debt than private banks, both because they may have less bargaining power vis-à-vis the central government than the private sector and because their financial management practices may be less efficient. The second reason is that we have put together our estimate of public sector interest revenues from those reported by the central government and those reported by autonomous entities. If part of the latter comes from its holdings of public debt, net revenues would be correspondingly reduced.

In any case, the upper bound on the opportunity cost is given by total government interest payments (2.1 per cent of GDP).

30   The Treasury Bank, which replaced the Banco Hipotecario Latinoamericano, is an agency of the Ministry of Finance.

31   By the end of 2005, a presentation of the Ministry of Finance reported that the integration of the basic systems, budget, public debt, treasury and accounting contemplated in the SIGECOF project had not yet been accomplished (Carreño, 2005).

32   José Rojas, Nelson Merentes, Francisco Usón, Jesús Bermúdez and Tobías Nóbrega.

33   Pritchett and Ortega (2006) present other measures of schooling quality, such as those derived from teacher dummies in Mincer regressions, all of which tell a similar story.

34   See Rodríguez (2005) for a survey of this literature.

35   In a growth framework, each period after the initial one would be a combination of what we have termed the medium term and the long term, with convergence occurring to the latter at an exponential rate. For purposes of exposition, we abstract from these dynamics in the text.

36   Pineda and Rodríguez (2006) find that these beneficiaries are actually concentrated among firms that do not have foreign participation and sell exclusively to the domestic sector. The interpretation the authors give to this result is that it is precisely these firms that tend to be liquidity constrained and have greater coordination problems and thus tend to be unable to resolve basic infrastructure investments through their own investments.

37   In 2002, the opposition controlled states with greater per capita income, such as Miranda, Carabobo and Zulia.

38   Weisbrot et al's (2006) argument is, however, incorrect with respect to Mercal, since the National Institute of Statistics currently uses a price indicator that is designed to cover Mercal establishments.

39   This section borrows significantly from current research with Daniel Ortega, Chiang-Tai Hsieh and Edward Miguel.

40   Interpress News Agency (2005) 'Venezuela Declares Itself Illiteracy-Free', 28 October 2005, www.ipsnews.net/news.asp?idnews=30823 (accessed 9 June 2005).

41   Misión Robinson started in the second semester of 2003 and was completed in the first semester of 2005, when the government declared its complete success in eradicating illiteracy.

42   The trend includes quadratic and cubic terms. All terms were highly significant. A pure quadratic trend generated the counterintuitive prediction of a decline in literacy around 2004.

43   These incentives could include the provision of meals during classes, the prospect of participating in other government programmes with tangible economic benefits (such as Vuelvan Caras, the job training programme whose participants received a cash transfer), and the possibility of obtaining free eyeglasses.

44   However, some institutions can be reformed and political and structural constraints can be modified. When we speak about the constraints imposed by initial conditions, we recognize the possibility of altering constraints but emphasize that our institutional, political and structural choice sets are path-dependent in that they are constrained by our historically determined starting points (North, 1993, 2005).

REFERENCES

Adelman, M. (1995) *The Genie Out of the Bottle: World Oil Since 1970*, MIT Press, Cambridge, MA

Agencia Bolivariana de Noticias (2005) 'Venezuela alcanzará otra Meta del Milenio, según INE', www.aporrea.org/dameverbo.php?docid=65830, accessed 12 September 2007

Alfredo Keller y Asociados (2005) 'Estudio de la opinión pública nacional, 2do trimestre de 2005', electronic document, Alfredo Keller y Asociados, Caracas

Arrow, K. and Kurz, M. (1970) *Public Investment, the Rate of Return and Optimal Fiscal Policy*, Johns Hopkins University Press, Baltimore, MD

Aschauer, D. A. (1989) 'Does public capital crowd out private capital?', *Journal of Monetary Economics*, vol 24, no 2, pp171–188

Banco Central de Venezuela (1991) *Estadísticas Socio-Laborales de Venezuela, Series Históricas 1936–1990, Colección Cincuentenaria*, BCV, Caracas

Banco Central de Venezuela (2000) *Series Estadísticas de Venezuela (Serie 1950–1998)*, BCV, Caracas

Banco Central de Venezuela (2006) *Serie de Producto Interno Bruto Base 1997*, electronic file, BCV, Caracas, www.bcv.org.ve

Banco Central de Venezuela (2007) *Índice de Precios al Consumidor para el Área Metropolitana de Caracas*, electronic file, BCV, Caracas, www.bcv.org.ve

Banco Central de Venezuela (various years (a)) *Anuario de Cuentas Nacionales*, electronic file, BCV, Caracas

Banco Central de Venezuela (various years (b)) *Informe Anual*, BCV, Caracas

Banco Central de Venezuela (various years (c)) *Boletín Mensual*, BCV, Caracas

Baptista, A. (1997) *Bases Cuantitativas de la Economía Venezolana, 1830–95*, Fundación Polar, Caracas

Barrios, A.J. (2000) 'El financiamiento de la descentralización en Venezuela', *Cuadernos del Cendes*, vol 17, no 45, pp51–66

Bekaert, G. and Harvey, C. (2004) 'Chronology of economic, political and financial events in emerging markets: Venezuela', www.duke.edu/~charvey/Country_risk/chronology/venezuela.htm, accessed 12 June 2006

Bermúdez, A. (2004) 'La legislación laboral en Venezuela y sus impactos sobre el mercado laboral', in *El desempleo en Venezuela: Causas, efectos e implicaciones de política*, Oficina de Asesoría Económica de la Asamblea Nacional, Caracas

Betancourt, R. (1957) *Venezuela, Política y Petróleo*, Monte Ávila Editores Latinoamericana, Caracas

Brun, J-F., Chambas, G., Combes, J-L., Dulbecco, P., Gastambide, A., Guérineau, S., Guillaumont, S. and Rota Graziosi, G. (2005) *Assessing and Enhancing Fiscal Space in Developing Countries*, United Nations Development Programme, New York

Buchanan, J. M. (1963) 'The Economics of Earmarked Taxes', *Journal of Political Economy*, vol 71, pp457–469

Caballero, M. (1993) *Gómez, el Tirano Liberal*, Monte Ávila Editores, Caracas

Calderón, C. and Servén, L. (2003) *Macroeconomic Dimensions of Infrastructure in Latin America*, Central Bank of Chile, Santiago

Carreño, I. (2005) *Compilación 2005*, National Public Accounting Office, Caracas

Carrera Damas, G. (1975) 'Entrevista con Eloy Porras', *Diario El Nacional*, Caracas, 29 March 1975, pD-2

Casanegra, M., Pellechio, A., Chua, D., Ossowski, R. and Castro, P. (1996) *Fortalecimiento de los Ingresos Tributarios no Petroleros*, IMF Public Finance Division, Washington DC

Chinn, M., LeBlanc, M. and Coibion, O. (2001) *The Predictive Characteristics of Energy Futures: Recent Evidence for Crude Oil, Natural Gas, Gasoline and Heating Oil*, University of California at Santa Cruz, Santa Cruz, CA

Datanálisis (2006) 'Mercal: lugar más visitado para comprar alimentos', www.datanalisis.com/detalle.asp?id=265&plantilla=1, accessed 12 June 2006

Easterly, W. (1999) 'When is Fiscal Adjustment an Illusion?', *Economic Policy*, April, pp55–86

Easterly, W. and Rebelo, S. (1993) 'Fiscal policy and economic growth: An empirical investigation', *Journal of Monetary Economics*, no 32, pp417–58

Easterly, W. and Servén, L. (2003) *The Limits of Stabilization: Infrastructure, Public Deficits and Growth in Latin America*, The World Bank, Washington DC

ECLAC (Economic Commission for Latin America and the Caribbean) (2005) *Objetivos de Desarrollo del Milenio: Una Mirada Desde América Latina y el Caribe*, ECLAC, Santiago

Eickhacker, N. (2006) *The Socio-economic Impact of Misión Mercal in Venezuela from 2002 through 2004: A Differences of Differences Regression Analysis*, Wesleyan University, Middletown, CT

El Impulso (2006) 'Misión Robinson: un híbrido cubano en Venezuela', *El Impulso*, 13 May

El Nacional (2006) 'Entrevista a John Magdalena', *El Nacional*, 26 February, pA-4

Energy Information Administration (2005) *International Petroleum Monthly*, December, EIA, Washington DC

Energy Information Administration (2006) 'World proved reserves of oil and natural gas, most recent estimates', EIA, Washington DC, www.eia.doe.gov/emeu/international/reserves.html, accessed 5 June 2006

Energy Information Administration (2007) 'Retail Motor Gasoline and On-Highway Diesel Fuel Prices, 1949-2006', EIA, Washington DC, www.eia.doe.gov/emeu/aer/txt/ptb0524.html, accessed 22 November 2007

Esfahani, H. S. and Ramírez, M. T. (2003) 'Institutions, infrastructure and economic growth', *Journal of Development Economics*, no 70, pp443–477

Fernald, J. G. (1999) 'Roads to prosperity? Assessing the link between public capital and productivity', *American Economic Review*, vol 89, no 3, pp619–638

FIDES (2005) 'Ley que crea el fondo intergubernamental para la descentralización', www.fides.gov.ve/, 24 accessed October 2005

Floyd, M. (1988) *Guzmán Blanco: la Dinámica de la Política del Septenio*, Instituto Autónomo Biblioteca Nacional, Caracas

Gwilliam, K. and Kumar, A. (2003) 'How effective are second-generation road funds? A preliminary appraisal', *The World Bank Research Observer*, vol 18, no 1, pp113–128

Goetz, C. J. (1968) 'Earmarked taxes and the majority rule budget process', *American Economic Review*, vol 58, March, pp128–136

Gutiérrez, A. (2002) 'Las trabas no arancelarias en el comercio bilateral agroalimentario entre Venezuela y Colombia', Documentos de Trabajo 35, Inter-American Development Bank, Washington DC

Hamilton, J. (2006) 'Oil at $15-30 a barrel?', Econbrowser weblog, February 22, www.econbrowser.com/archives/2006/02/oilat1530ab.html, accessed 12 September 2007

Hausmann, R. and Rodríguez, F. (2006) 'Why did Venezuelan growth collapse?', paper presented at the Second Conference on Venezuelan Economic Growth 1970–2005, Harvard University Centre for International Development, 28–29 April, www.cid.harvard.edu/events/papers/0604caf/Hausmann_Rodriguez.pdf, accessed 12 September 2007

Heller, M. S. (2005) 'Understanding Fiscal Space', IMF Policy Discussion Paper PDP/05/4, IMF, Washington DC

Hulten, C. and Schwab, R. A. (1991) *Is There Too Little Public Capital? Infrastructure and Economic Growth*, American Enterprise Institute, Washington DC

IMF (2006a) *Government Finance Statistics Database* (CD-ROM), International Monetary Fund, Washington DC

IMF (2006b) *International Finance Statistics Database* (CD-ROM) IMF, Washington DC

Instituto Nacional de Estadística (various years) 'Encuesta de hogares por muestreo', Electronic Database, Instituto Nacional de Estadística, Caracas

Instituto Nacional de Estadística (2006), *La Pobreza como un Fenómeno Multidimensional*, Instituto Nacional de Estadística, Caracas

Inter-American Development Bank (1997) *Informe de Progreso Económico y Social 1997: América Latina tras una Década de Reformas*, IADB, Washington DC

Kornblith, M. and Maingón, T. (1985) *Estado y Gasto Público en Venezuela, 1936–1980*, Universidad Central de Venezuela, Caracas

Manzano, O. (2006) 'Venezuela after a century of oil exploitation', paper presented at the Second Conference on Venezuelan Economic Growth 1970–2005, Harvard University Centre for International Development, 28–29 April, www.cid.harvard.edu/events/papers/0604caf/Monzano.pdf, accessed 12 September 2007

McCleary, W. (1991) 'The earmarking of government revenue: A review of some World Bank experience', *The World Bank Research Observer*, vol 6, no 1, pp81–104

Ministerio de Energía y Minas (various years) *Petróleo y Otros Datos Estadísticos*, Ministerio de Energía y Minas, Caracas

Ministerio de Finanzas (2005) *La Contabilidad en la Administración Financiera del Estado*, November, Ministerio de Finanzas, Caracas

Ministerio de Finanzas (various years) *Memoria Anual*, Ministerio de Finanzas, Caracas

Ministerio del Trabajo (various years) *Memoria Anual*, Ministerio del Trabajo, Caracas

Munnell, A. H. (1990) 'Why has productivity growth declined? Productivity and public investment', *New England Economic Review*, Jan/Feb, pp3–22

New York Times (2006) 'Chávez uses aid to win support in the Americas', *New York Times*, 4 April, pA6

North, D. C. (1990) *Institutions, Institutional Change and Economic Performance*, Cambridge University Press, Cambridge

North, D. C. (2005) *Understanding the Process of Economic Change*, Princeton University Press, Princeton

Obregón, C. L. and Rodríguez, F. (2001) 'La política fiscal Venezolana 1943–2001', Reporte de Coyuntura Anual 2001, Oficina de Asesoría Económica y Financiera de la Asamblea Nacional, Caracas

Oficina de Asesoría Económica y Financiera de la Asamblea Nacional (2001) 'La nueva descentralización', Electronic File Presentation, Oficina de Asesoría Económica y Financiera de la Asamblea Nacional Caracas

Oficina Nacional de Presupuesto (2006a) *Serie Gasto Fiscal Acordado*, Oficina Nacional de Presupuesto, Ministerio de Finanzas, Caracas

Oficina Nacional de Presupuesto (2006b) *Serie de Ingresos Fiscales*, Oficina Nacional de Presupuesto, Ministerio de Finanzas, Caracas

Oficina Nacional de Presupuesto (various years (a)) *Resumen de la Ley de Presupuesto*, Oficina Nacional de Presupuesto, Ministerio de Finanzas, Caracas

Oficina Nacional de Presupuesto (various years (b)) *Oficina Nacional de Presupuesto Exposición de Motivos de la Ley de Presupuesto* ONAPRE, Caracas

Oficina Nacional de Presupuesto (various years(c)) *Presupuesto Consolidado del Sector Público*, Oficina Nacional de Presupuesto, Ministerio de Finanzas, Caracas

Ogura, S. and Yohe, G. (1977) 'The complementarity of public and private capital and the optimal rate of return', *The Quarterly Journal of Economics*, vol 91, no 4, pp651–662

Penfold-Becerra, M. (1999) 'Institutional electoral incentives and decentralization outcomes: State reform in Venezuela', Dissertation, Columbia University, New York

Penfold-Becerra, M. (2005) *Social Funds, Clientelism and Redistribution: Chávez's 'Misiones' Programs in Comparative Perspective*, IESA, Caracas

Pineda, J. and Rodríguez, F. (2006) 'Public investment in infrastructure and productivity growth: Evidence from the Venezuelan manufacturing sector', Wesleyan Economics Working Paper No. 2006-010, Wesleyan University, Middletown, CT

Pino Iturrieta, E. (1997) 'Guzmán Blanco, Antonio, gobiernos de', in *Diccionario de Historia de Venezuela*, 4 vols, Fundación Polar, Caracas

Pritchett, L. and Ortega, D. (2006) 'Much higher schooling, much lower wages: Human capital and economic collapse in Venezuela', paper presented at the Second Conference on Venezuelan Economic Growth 1970–2005, Harvard University Centre for International Development, 28–29 April, www.cid.harvard.edu/events/papers/0604caf/Pritchett.doc, accessed 12 September 2007

República Bolivariana de Venezuela (2006) 'Recursos asignados a las misiones hasta el 2005 y su correspondiente ejecución', electronic file, Ministerio de Finanzas, Caracas

Rey, J. C. (1987) 'El futuro de la democracia en Venezuela', in J. Silva Michelena (ed) *Venezuela Hacia el Año 2000*, Nueva Sociedad, Caracas

Rigobón, R. (1993) 'Subsidio indirecto a la gasolina' in G. Márquez (ed) *Gasto Público y Distribución del Ingreso en Venezuela*, Edic. IESA, Caracas

Rodríguez, F. and Gomolin, A. J. (2006) *Anarchy, State, and Dystopia: Venezuelan Economic Institutions before the Advent of Oil*, Wesleyan Economics Working Paper No. 2006-018, Wesleyan University, Middletown, CT

Shoup, C. (1969) *Informe sobre el Sistema Fiscal de Venezuela*, Aldine Publishing Company, Chicago, IL

Smith, J. (2005) 'Inscrutable OPEC? Behavioral tests of the Cartel Hypothesis', *Energy Journal*, vol 26, no 1, pp51–82

Sosa Abascal, A. (1995) *Rómulo Betancourt y el Partido del Pueblo*, Editorial Fundación Rómulo Betancourt, Caracas

Stambouli, A. (2002) *La Política Extraviada: Una Historia de Medina a Chávez*, Fundación para la Cultura Urbana, Caracas

Tornell, A. and Lane, P. R. (1998) 'Are windfalls a curse? A non-representative agent model of the current account', *Journal of International Economics*, vol 44, no 1, pp83–112

United Nations Centre for Human Settlements (1993) *The Maintenance of Infrastructure and its Financing and Cost Recovery*, UNCHS, Nairobi

Urbaneja, D. B. (1992) *Pueblo y Petróleo en la Política Venezolana del Siglo XX*, Centro de Formación y Adiestramiento de Petróleos de Venezuela y sus Filiales, Caracas

Vallenilla, L. (1973) *Auge, Declinación y Porvenir del Petróleo Venezolano*, Editorial Tiempo Nuevo, Caracas.

Weisbrot, M., Sandoval, L. and Rosnick, D. (2006) 'Poverty rates in Venezuela: Getting the numbers right', Centre for Economic Policy and Research, London, upsidedownworld.org/main/index.php?option=com_content&task=view&id=302&Itemid=0, accessed 12 September 2007

World Bank (2006) *World Development Indicators Database*, CD-ROM, World Bank, Washington DC

Selected Economic Indicators (2006) for Morocco, Senegal, Thailand and Venezuela

---

Morocco	
GDP per capita, PPP (constant 2005 international $)	3794
Population	30,496,553
Urban population (% of total)	59
Manufacturing, value added (% of GDP)	16
Agriculture, value added (% of GDP)	16
Industry, value added (% of GDP)	28
Services, etc., value added (% of GDP)	57

Source: World Bank's World Development Indicators database, 2007

Senegal	
GDP per capita, PPP (constant 2005 international $)	1537
Population	12,072,479
Urban population (% of total)	42
Manufacturing, value added (% of GDP)	14
Agriculture, value added (% of GDP)	16
Industry, value added (% of GDP)	23
Services, etc., value added (% of GDP)	61

Source: World Bank's World Development Indicators database, 2007

Thailand	
GDP per capita, PPP (constant 2005 international $)	7364
Population	63,443,950
Urban population (% of total)	33
Manufacturing, value added (% of GDP)	35
Agriculture, value added (% of GDP)	11
Industry, value added (% of GDP)	45
Services, etc., value added (% of GDP)	45

Source: World Bank's World Development Indicators database, 2007

Venezuela	
Per capita GDP (constant 2000 PPP-adjusted US $)	6485
Population	27,020,920
Urban Population (% of total)	94
Agriculture and mining, excluding petroleum (% of GDP)	5.12
Manufacturing, excluding petroleum refining (% of GDP)	23.4
Services (% of GDP)	46.2
Petroleum, production and refining (% of GDP)	25.4

Source: Per capita GDP and population data: World Bank's World Development Indicators database, 2007.
Shares of GDP: Banco Central de Venezuela (2007) Sistema de Cuentas Nacionales Serie 2002–2004

Index

Note: **Bold** page numbers indicate figures and tables; *italic* page numbers indicate text boxes; numbers in brackets preceded by *n* refer to notes.